ISBN 978-1-330-78384-9
PIBN 10104944

1 MONTH OF
FREE
READING

at

www.ForgottenBooks.com

By purchasing this book you are eligible for one month membership to ForgottenBooks.com, giving you unlimited access to our entire collection of over 1,000,000 titles via our web site and mobile apps.

To claim your free month visit:

www.forgottenbooks.com/free104944

English
Français
Deutsche
Italiano
Español
Português

www.forgottenbooks.com

Mythology Photography **Fiction**
Fishing Christianity **Art** Cooking
Essays Buddhism Freemasonry
Medicine **Biology** Music **Ancient
Egypt** Evolution Carpentry Physics
Dance Geology **Mathematics** Fitness
Shakespeare **Folklore** Yoga Marketing
Confidence Immortality Biographies
Poetry **Psychology** Witchcraft
Electronics Chemistry History **Law**
Accounting **Philosophy** Anthropology
Alchemy Drama Quantum Mechanics
Atheism Sexual Health **Ancient History**
Entrepreneurship Languages Sport
Paleontology Needlework Islam
Metaphysics Investment Archaeology
Parenting Statistics Criminology
Motivational

POETRY

Its Origin, Nature, and History.

ERRATA.

Page 50 line 8 for *choose* . . read *chose.*

,, 108 ,, 25 ,, *were* . . . ,, *where.*

,, 321 ,, 2 ,, *feel can.* , ,, *can feel.*

,, 457 ,, 17 ,, *maids rest* ,, *maid rests.*

,, 562 ,, 19 ,, *and* . . . . ,, *not.*

,, 625 ,, 19 ,, *Thomas* , ,, *Tobias.*

OF THE WORKS OF THE POETS OF ALL TIMES AND COUNTRIES, W

EXPLANATORY NOTES, SYNOPTICAL TABLES,

A CHRONOLOGICAL DIGEST

AND A

COPIOUS INDEX.

BY

FREDERICK A. HOFFMANN.

LONDON :—

THURGATE & SONS, PADDINGTON, W.

—

1884.

PREFACE.

In presenting to the public these volumes, I feel that I am contributing to literature both a treasure and a curiosity; for I may safely assert that among the various works of this character extant, there is not one, which, in the same number of pages, embraces more information, and traces the progress of poetry through a longer period.

It will be seen by the division of this work that my object has been, not merely to give a collection of elegant extracts, but to show, by a series of notes, the growth and development of poetry up to the middle of this century. At the same time, it has no pretensions to the title of a complete history of poetry; but, in seeking, though at so humble a distance, to follow the admirable models presented by many celebrated critics—in connecting literary investigations by an historical thread—I may throw a certain interest over a subject often dry and tedious in itself, and yet of great importance in the records of the human mind. This plan whether good or not, has necessarily involved the admission of a few specimens from the productions of writers, who, although deservedly enjoying much reputation, are not reckoned amongst the classics of their own country. Where very long quotations occur it has been done to afford to those who have not had the means of being made cognisant of their works, a pleasant half hour amongst their choicest effusions.

Mention has been made of more than 5,000 poets, and particu-
lars given of all those who have in any way influenced poetry, or
deserve a place in the long *role* of poets. The space devoted to
the greater poets—as in the case of Homer, Dante, Shakespeare,
Milton, Southey, and others—will serve to impress the reader with
a vivid idea of their merits and beauties. Fuller details might
have been given of Petrarch, Goethe, Voltaire, Tasso, &c, but of
late years so many new sources of information and critical opinions
relative to these great minds have been laid open to the public,
that it would seem presumptuous to treat largely of them in a work
of this description.

I have confined the specimens more exclusively to English
poetry, it being my intention, should this work meet with any
degree of favour, shortly to follow it by another which, together
with select specimens of English poetry will comprehend choice
examples of the most distinguished European poets. The style
adopted in the body of the work is for the purpose of making
it more suitable for the advanced classes in English academies,
and to serve as a text-book for those lectures on English literature
which are now given in so many institutions for young and work-
ing men. From its pages an accurate teacher may easily form
a series of such lectures, little else being necessary than to add to
the examples.

From the necessity of limiting myself to a convenient compass,
I have been obliged, in dealing with the minor poets, both to
make my extracts shorter, perhaps, than I should have wished, and,
generally speaking, to illustrate each author by only one quotation.
It would have been undoubtebly more desirable to multiply speci-
mens from Cowley, Addison, Churchill, Joanna Baillie, Leigh
Hunt, Elliot, Hood, Hemans, and others; but this was impossible ;
and the passages I have selected will, I think, suffice to give a
complete and correct idea of the style of the various writers.

The notes in the " Compendium," are designed to supplement in
detail the notices prefixed to most of the extracts; they might have

been multiplied ten-fold, and are only confined to such elucidations as were deemed strictly indispensable. After some hesitation I resolved upon leaving out altogether our own contemporaries, save in the " Chronological Digest."

The " Chronological Digest " will be found useful as a *résumé* of the whole work. It is very probable that discrepancies may be discovered with regard to the dates, but this arises from the more or less perfect information of the authorities employed, although I have adopted the dates from the most trustworthy sources. The dates assigned to Roman, Greek, and early Eastern poets must always be received with a certain amount of diffidence and uncertainty as regards their accuracy, since the most esteemed authorities differ from each other considerably, and occasionally to a remarkable extent. When we remember the uncertainties which prevail in modern works treating of the lives of comparatively recent authors, we naturally cannot be surprised to find them existing as to those of the period before Christ. In cases of extreme doubt, however, I have signified it by an interrogation mark. The Digest, as it will be seen, gives nominal mention of many poets not spoken of in the body of the work. This has been done to render it more complete, but in each case it is distinguished by an asterisk (†).

Whatever defects and omissions are to be found in this work, it is at least the result of a long and intimate acquaintance with English and Foreign literature, and of a conscientious study of the texts of the best-known poets of ancient and modern times. Whenever secondary sources have been consulted they are carefully cited, whether historians or critics. The extracts have been made from the most correct editions I have been able to procure from the many sources at my command ; and, being the only compilation of its kind, it has necessarily been the result of considerable labour. The extensive study requisite for the production of a work like the present, has but little opportunity of displaying itself otherwise than in the judicious remarks and general mastery

somewhere designated as the pioneers of literature; and it will afford me much satisfaction if the following pages should clear the road, or lessen the toil of any student of literature.

F. A. H.

CONTENTS.

The beauty of his rhythm, with examples from the Ode "To the Progress of Poesy," etc.—His imitations of Norse and Welsh poetry—Important extracts.

His popularity as a religious poet—Observations on religious literature in England, France, and Germany at his time—The character of Cowper's poetry, and its influence on the people—His style compared to that of Milton—His nationality as a poet, and the extreme insularity of tone in his writings—Remarks on his various poems—The superiority of the "Task" to his other works—Its great success, and to what attributed—Observations by Ross and others respecting it—His deficiency in imaginative genius—The same contrasted with Collins—Exemplified by extracts—His deficiency of metaphorical language—The charms of his diction compared with Thomson and others—Various extracts—The *Hymns*—Notes upon them, with numerous extracts—Miscellaneous quotations.

His claim to popularity—Various opinions as to his genius—The faithfulness of his pictures compared with those of Hogarth, Churchill, etc.—His paintings of humble life scenes, contrasted with Burns and Bloomfield—His resemblance to Johnson, Mackintosh, and other great men—The beautiful descriptions of the *Sea* given in his works—Examples of the same—The truthfulness and reality in his writings—His similitude to Cowper and Goldsmith in this respect—His want of imagination accounted for—Extracts from his "Life" relating to the same—Imitation of Pope in the "Village" and "Library"—Extracts from the former—Various remarks upon the "Borough" and "Parish Register," with extracts.

His entire peculiarity as a poet—His religious love of nature, and truthful delineation of character—Remarks on his character and genius—His attachment to common subjects, and truthful representation of the same—The difference shown between a poet and a verse-maker—Exemplified in Burns, Bloomfield and Wordsworth—Several extracts in illustration of the latter—The religious opinions manifested in his works—Examples from his *Odes* and blank verse—Miscellaneous extracts—The "Excursion" noticed, with various quotations.

A critical opinion of his works—The power of his poetry upon the mind—Illustrated in his "Songs of the Pixies," etc.—His similarity to Wordsworth—His language contrasted with that of Southey—The peculiarity of his writings—An example from the Ode "To the Departing year"—His originality of thought;

The character of 'Venus' as given in the "Siege of Troy,"
—The same as compared with Chaucer, and illustrated by
quotations from the "Life of our Lady." JAMES I.—His
position and merit as a poet—Remarks upon the "King's
Quair," with particulars of the circumstances under which it was
written—Its superiority in language etc, to any earlier works—
The profusion of allegorical images in it—" Christ's Kirk on the
Green," and "Pebles to the Play," critically noticed—Various
extracts. OCCLEVE.—His merit as a poet—The translation
of Egidius' "De Regnum Principium"—Extract from the
same of a passage written to the memory of Chaucer—An
account of the Scotch poets of this date. HENRYSON.—
Particulars of his principal productions—His *Fables* in verse
noticed, with extracts. DUNBAR.—A general observation of
his works—Eulogium upon his genius—Remarks upon the
"Dance"—His resemblance to Dante in the latter—Extracts,
with notes. DOUGLAS.—The "Palace of Honour," "King
Hart," etc. commented upon—His translation of Virgil noticed,
with an explanatory extract. MONTGOMERY.—His reputation
at this period as a Scotch poet—Remarks upon the "Cherrie
and the Sloe,"—Quotations from his smaller poems. BLIND
HARRY.—His narrative of the "Exploits and deeds of William
Wallace"—Picturesque passages descriptive of the *Seasons*
quoted—Other extracts from the same poem. SKELTON.—His
comic and satirical poems—Against whom the latter were
directed—The peculiar doggrel measure of these poems, with
other remarks upon their metre, etc.—The genius with which
he exhibits allegorical images—Example given in his painting
of *Disdain*. MORE.—Remarks on the "Utopia," his miscella-
neous verses, etc.—Choice extracts from the latter, with notes.
HAWES.—His important position as a poet of this date—The
further importance which attaches to him as a poet—Remarks
upon his predecessors—The "Pastime of Pleasure,"—Many
striking extracts given. LYNDSAY.—Considered as a humourist
and satirical writer—The beauty of his descriptive passages—
Elegant extracts of the latter from the "Monarchy." BARCLAY.
—His translation from the German of the "Ship of Fools,"—
General remarks upon it, with examples. WYATT.—Noticed
as an imitator of Petrarch—His position as an English satirist
—His chief defects—Several elegant extracts from his lyric
poetry. SURREY.—His style, rhythm, etc.—Position as an
English classical poet—The superiority of his genius to that
of Wyatt—His representation of rural imagery—Specimen of
the latter. VAUX.—A general observation upon his works,
with specimens of his poetry. TUSSER.—His merit as a didactic
poet—Remarks upon his poem "A Hundred good points of
Husbandry"—Warton's opinion of the same—Quotation from
the above mentioned. EDWARDES.—His rank as a dramatist
—The "Paradise of Dainty Devises"—A specimen of his style.

other arts.. It does more than either sounds or colours can accomplish, though it is closely allied to both. Philustratus says "as the poets introduce the gods and heroes, and all those things which are either majestical, honest, or delightful ; in like manner the painters, by the virtue of their outlines, colours, lights, and shadows represent the same persons and things in their pictures."

Yet, notwithstanding the close affinity between these arts, the poet stands certainly first, for all the treasures of the painter and sculptor have sprung from the imagination of the poet. Both are imitative arts, yet poetry is the least so; for "*language* cannot in any way directly copy from nature, unless it be in imitation of *sound* ; and music, although said to imitate motion, in reality does little more than imitate the sounds which accompany motion. In comparison with music, poetry has a vast and acknowledged superiority, both as to the distinctness and variety of the impressions it conveys." *

Poetry is from the imagination ; it exists only in the brain of the writer, until cast forth in the shape of verse. The *senses* of the poet are really affected in the ideal world in which he lives; this it is that is peculiar to the poet. Without it, no mastery of talent or metaphysical aid shall avail him. It is a mystery of our nature that whatever internal feelings violently haunt us, we feel relieved by communicating and gaining sympathy for them. When these

* Specimens of the earlier English Poets.—S. W. Simpson.

A

feelings are of a poetical character, and are thus communicated in an adequate language, the fruit, I believe, never fails to be true poetry. Those feelings are generally produced by the created presentiments of a visionary mind. Lord Byron for example, has even carried it to a high degree of superstition.

Poets are usually tempted by the very emotions which spring from their genius, to take an opposite course. They feel so intensely all that is peculiar to themselves; they are so conscious of their own divine faculty, and so sensible to the slights which they receive from those whom they despise, that they are eager to vent feelings, almost too big for utterance in their poetry. And this is that by which a true poet may be read: they are their own biographers. The external events in their lives, as well as the movements of their feelings are often manifested in their works. We know nothing of the life, character, or actions of Homer, yet we know he must have felt the soft touches of kindred and love, and brooded over the fond recollections of early home. He must have lived happily, or he would have been an egotist. Had he been wretched he would have informed us of such in his works. He was no doubt contented with his lot, happy in the sunshine of his own mind. Milton, too, exhibits through his works, the details of his life. We can conceive how happy he was under his great affliction: he was occupied with his own glorious fancies and dwelt in a fairer creation than this material world. Shakespeare has thrown himself into a thousand characters, instead of philosophising or describing his own; he lives and breathes in the works of his own creation; and seems to exist in an immense variety of persons rather than in one. Noble sentiments and heart-stirring speeches—symbols of his own character—are thickly strown, but they come from the mouths of his heroes, and not from his own, with dramatic propriety and force! He was too much delighted with the visions and joys which poesy opened before him—for ever new and fresh—to think of the shell in which his genius had taken up its dwelling.

I never yet saw nor have I read, any full and authentic account of any one of great literary genius, who had not intense sensibility, or who was entire master of himself. Enthusiasm is an indispensable ingredient ; and the spirit will sometimes take possession of persons so gifted. The philosopher founds his work on reason, builds it up of facts and experiments; but the work of the poet is from the imagination, stimulated and increased in beauty, by passion. The poet must *live* in his world of fancy, his moveable nerves are reality; he sees, he hears, he feels by each. "Just as the idea of a thing will make us shudder, and only imagination often produce a real pain, so it is with the poet." * This state of mind has even a reality for the generality of persons ; in a theatre tears are often seen in the eyes of the spectators, who before they have time to recollect that the whole is fictitious, have been surprised for a moment by a strong conception of a present and existing scene. He therefore who can accommodate himself to the petty manners of the world, gives a proof that he is not a great genius. He may assume the tone of deep pathos in his writings; but it is factitious. The great proof of littleness is servility, courting the fashionable, and living with the gay ! I always admired Smollett's *Ode to Independence.* It was a burst of genius !

> " Thy spirit, *Independence,* let me share,
> Lord of the lion-heart and eagle eye !" &c.,

Gray, who was honourably proud, as well as fastidious, would never expose himself to the insolence of rank.

It is the business of the poet to carry us into a visionary and more beautiful world—according with our desires, rather than with our experience. This is the *inventive* quality necessary to a poet, although so many modern writers of poetry fall short of it. In the major part of our popular poetry ; we find no great and affecting truths embodied and set forth in interesting and natural fiction ; no noble and unaffected characters in conflict upon the tempestuous sea of life ! We find instead, a glittering simile, or tinsel metaphor ; a puling, sickly sentiment, or a passionate and burning tear, all brought out in the most polished forms of fashionable slang—golden goods no doubt, and of great demand in the market— *but soon forgotten.* Poetry, then, is not a progressive art, like the improvements of social life. It does not depend on external circumstances, it does not follow in the train of knowledge, nor have any connection with the progressions of time; its origin is the heart, its stimulant the imagination: nature is the poet's teacher, his school the universe. It is the art of employing words in such a manner as to produce an illusion on the imagination. Thus Shakespeare has described it :—

> "As imagination bodies forth
> The forms of things unknown, the poet's pen
> Turns them to shapes, and gives to airy nothing,
> A local habitation and a name,"

It may be said that these wild flights of genius, have as little solidity, and are as little serviceable to the practical duties of life : nay, that they withdraw, exhaust and derange the mind. On the contrary, they encourage the mightier enterprises of grand spirits : and they sometimes rouse even the sluggish and the dull.

There is nothing unnatural in the most brilliant, most extraordinary and most visionary flights of Shakespeare ; they may not in all cases be such as reason and experience admit, but they are such as an excited imagination give credence to—even in the very *Fairy* scenes of the *Midsummer Night's Dream*, which are all founded on popular superstitions ! Great genius therefore is always in earnest : it knows nothing of technical creations ; of a poetical world different from a real world ; of feelings assumed for poetry, yet inconsistent with life; of sentiments, delicacies and refinements, unlike what the author himself, or any one less has ever felt, yet set up as proper for poetical representation.

It is these high flights of imagination ; these delineations of a more beautiful world, which the poet creates for himself; a state of feeling not congenial to the coarse habits of common life. In others it is not natural either in society or in solitude : we no more feel or believe it when alone, than in the bustle of company; without poetical genius it is a mere pretence. which no more represents what has actual dominion over the mind and heart, than gold-leaf represents the solid golden ore. We may "hope, though hope be lost," and believe against reason ; but we must not put forth, not only what reason rejects, but what *unforced* imagination never suggests ; what the imagination as little confides in as the reason. It is the poet's business to embody all the more magnificent and more affecting phenomena of our intellectual nature : but it is as false in poetry as in science, to *invent* and *miscolour* phænomena. Delusive affectations bring poetry into contempt, and sink it down to the rank of an art calculated only to mislead. The true poet paints what hard experience will seldom justify ; but he paints what a passionate and noble mind, in a state of high intellectual emotion, expects and believes ; he describes things, not perhaps as they are, but as they appear to him under the temperament to which he has been raised. Artificial writers are cold-blooded, cold-hearted men, who substitute mechanism for inspiration ; and who, therefore, always mistake extravagance for grandeur or beauty. It is as much the business of the poet to be true to nature and actual existences, as it is of the philosopher :—

"Awake and faithful to its wonted fires."

Those sickly pretensions to sentiment of which I speak, which are only fit for dealers in false and simulated refinement, are worse than the mere hard fruits of the head, untouched by the heart. It is this artificial and affected invention that fatigues in ordinary poets. They represent a set of sickly sentiments and images, which are not only different from life, but more insipid than life—states of mind which neither themselves, nor any one else ever experienced. What they write is no part of their character, a tone merely assumed ; nothing but a piece of dull and laboured mechanism, fineer work, and flowers of coloured paper, and gold-leaf ! Pope could see the distinction when he spoke of Cowley.

"Forgot his Epic, nay his Lyric ART
Yet still we love the language of the HEART."

Nothing can be more true than the lines from Horace :—

"————— —————Mediocribus esse poetis,
Non Dii, non homines, non concessere columnæ."

"Poetry is a *creation*." The *materials* of poetry are in nature, but not poetry itself. The etymology of the word poet is from the

Greek word (ποιητης _-poiétes) whence *poeta* and *poet* is literally,
maker ; and *maker* it is well known was once the current term for
poet in our language ; and to write verses was to make. Sir Philip
Sydney, speaking of the Greek word, says, "wherein I know not
whether by luck or wisdom, we Englishmen have *met* with the
Greeks in calling him *maker*."*

So Spenser renders it in his "Shepherds Calender."—

> "The god of Shepherds, *Tityrus*, is dead
> Who taught me homely, as I can, *to make*," †

This however means, without doubt, *makers* of verse according
to measure, not creators of ideal objects. It is not simply verse
that is essential to poetry, but the true and impartial represent-
ing of virtue and vice, so as to instruct mankind in matter of
great importance. Verse is only the shape by which it is bounded,
"its adjunct, not its living principle." Abilities are common ; genius
is rare. We meet every day with those who apprehend with
quickness and apply with judgment. Knowledge, experience,
wisdom, must unite with a rich imagination, and a familiarity with
all the deeper and finer movements of the heart. It is by imagination
that the poet fashions out of existing materials, new conceptions
and ideas, which become intelligible to the reader through his
sympathies and sensibility, though not always justifiable by the
rules of logic and reason. This is the property of the imagination,
and thus of the poet. "Its province is to select qualifications and
circumstances from a variety of different objects ; and by combining
and disposing these, to form a new creation of its own. In this
appropriated sense of the word, it coincides with what some authors
have called *Creative or Poetical Imagination*." ‡ Hobbes says,
"The brain, or spirit therein, having been stirred by divers objects,
composeth an imagination of divers conceptions, that appeared
single to the sense. As, for example, the sense showeth at one
time the figure of *a mountain,* and at another time the colour of
gold ; but the imagination afterwards hath them both at once in a
"golden mountain." ‖ Imagination is a complex power, not a simple
faculty. It implies *Conception,* to represent those scenes in nature

---

* Defence of Poesy.   ‡ Outlines of Moral Philosophy,—D. Stewart.

with them in his memory; and *Judgment* to direct their combination It multiplies and divides and remodels. Emerson defines the imagination to be, "the use which reason makes of the material world." "By a few strokes," he says, "the poet delineates, as on the air, the sun, the mountain, the camp, the city, the hero, the maiden; not different from what we know them, but only lifted from the ground and afloat before the eye. He unfixes the land and the sea, makes them revolve around the axis of his primary thought, and disposes them anew. Possessed himself by a heroic passion, he uses matters as symbols of it. The sensual man conforms thoughts to things ; the poet conforms things to his thoughts. The one esteems nature as rooted and fast ; the other, as fluid, and impresses his being thereon. To him, the refractory world is ductile and flexible ; he invests dust and stones with humanity, and makes them the words of Reason." *

Macaulay says, " perhaps no person can be a poet or even enjoy poetry, without a certain unsoundness of mind, if anything which gives so much pleasure ought to be called unsoundness." The works of the poet, he calls, "the fruits of a fine frenzy." " Truth indeed is essential to poetry ; but it is the truth of madness. The reasonings are just, but the premises are false. After the first suppositions have been made, everything ought to be consistent; but those first suppositions require a deal of credulity which almost amounts to a partial and temporary derangement of the intellect. Hence of all people children are the most imaginative. They abandon themselves without reserve to every illusion. Every image which is strongly presented to their mental eye, produces on them the effect of reality. No man, whatever his sensibility may be, is ever affected by Hamlet or Lear, as a little girl is affected by the story of Red Riding Hood. She knows that it is all false, that wolves cannot speak, that there are no wolves in England. Yet in spite of her knowledge, she believes; she weeps; she trembles; she dares not go into a dark room, lest she should feel the teeth of the

* Emerson's Essays.—Vol. 2,

monster at her throat.   Such is the despotism of the imagination
over uncultivated minds.

This imagination, notwithstanding, is different in different people
In Shakespeare it is bright and rapid as the lightning, in Milton
awful as collected thunder.   Shakespeare possesses it beyond all
poets.   He uses nature to embody any caprice or thought that is
uppermost in his mind.   The remotest things in nature are brought
together, and all objects shrink and expand to serve the passions
of the poet.   "The freshness of youth and love dazzles him with
its resemblance to morning.

> "Take those lips away
> Which so sweetly were foresworn :
> And those eyes, the break of day,
> Lights that do mislead the morn."

What depths of fancy also is contained in the well known line,

> How sweet *the moonlight sleeps* upon this bank."

or when *Jocund day*

> " Stands tiptoe on the misty mountain tops."

How *one* thought sets his imagination soaring till he loses himself
in his new-born fancy!   If I were to attempt to quote the manifold
passages of this kind in the poet's work, I should fill pages.

A poet then, must be endued with imagination, and with a genius
to express the signs of their passions whom he represents; and
make the dumb as it were to speak.   He must mould into shape
the most abstract ideas and indefinite objects.   It is the province
of the poet to delineate the qualities and passions of men, more
than their actions.   That which is animate he must imbue with
life; the night must be "clothed in a starry train," the sun must
be as "a giant rejoicing in its strength."   He is not to describe
his subjects in common place language or delineate his cha-
racters as in prose.   It must be the anger of an Achilles, the
piety of an Æneas ; but Anger and Piety are his subjects, not
Achilles and Æneas.   And this idiosyncracy the poet must bear
upon throughout his work ; piety must be the predominant
characteristic of Æneas to the end, and revenge that of Achilles.
Had the latter been less passionate than he was, Virgil well foresaw

Yet, although the word poet has always in its strictest sense applied to a writer of verse, or one whose language has been formed into regular numbers, it cannot be considered as wholly peculiar to him. A poet, in its highest sense, is one whose imagination and shaping power can and does embody the forms of things unknown, and can create realities out of airy nothings. And I shall not be wandering from the general interpretation of the Greek word *maker*, when I say, that this energy which is the highest heaven of invention, is not entirely peculiar to a writer of verses. It may exist as vitally and essentially in prose; rhythm and metre are to this power as two wings to a soul, investing it with the robes and resemblances of a seraphim. Was not the wise man of Israel a poet, when he burst forth, "Thou art beautiful, O my love, as Tirzah; *comely as Jerusalem, terrible as an army with banners*?" Was not Jeremy Taylor a poet when he prayed for humility? "And yet I know thou resistest the proud, and did'st cast the morning stars, the angels from heaven into chains of darkness, *when they grew giddy and proud, walking upon the battlements of Heaven, beholding the glorious regions which were about them*?" This power is the essence of all rightful poetry, or in other words it is that without which poetry is not.

Rhythm then, is necessary to poetry; it is its principal feature, but it does not apply *wholly* to verse. From the Greek word (rhuthmos) a measured motion, it *especially* applies to poetry, but as the Greeks taught in a somewhat altered form, no less, as I have said, to excellent prose. Listen to a fine speaker or preacher, to Lord Beaconsfield, or Spurgeon, and you will imagine that he is speak-

B

ing in ten-syllabic verse. Take Dickens' famous description of
the Battle of Hastings, or as it should be called *Sangue lac or Sen
lac* (for it was not Hastings) ending with "and the three lions
kept watch o'er the field;" or take his *Little Nell*, "they laid
her down upon her little bed," and you will find the rhythmic beat
and pause so clear and distinct, that unless you are dull, you will
insensibly mark out the Iambic measure. In poetry, perfect rhythm
forms an important part; it must accompany poetical imagina-
tion. In verse the trochaic rhythm is perhaps the most common;
Shakespeare and Coleridge are abundant in every kind of skilfully
used rhythm, whereas Byron very commonly fails, as Coleridge's
fine ear at once detected. Read the "Ancient Mariner," and
"Christabel," of Coleridge, and revel delightfully in the rolling music
of the verse. Byron is a poet by force of his genius, not by force
of his art. It is only when his soul is moved that his cadence and
rhythm are really fine and pure. But in the best parts of " Childe
Harold," and his songs "Maid of Athens," and "The Isles of Greece,"
there may be found plenty of rhythm.

We arrive now, as to what is the object of poetry. We have
analysed its nature, it is necessary now to ascertain its property.

The *primary* aim of the poet is to please and move, without
touching the sensual, or using loose expressions, or in any-way
conveying to the mind immoral suggestions. It is this that has
partly destroyed the imaginative beauty of Byron. We do not find
it in Homer or Virgil. The only passage which comes near to it
at all, is the adventure of the cave, where Dido and Æneas were
driven by the storm ; yet even there the poet pretends a marriage
before the consummation, and Juno herself was present at it.
Dryden speaking of it, says,"There is not an expression in it which
a Roman matron might not read without a blush. Besides, the poet
passes it over as hastily as if he were afraid of staying in the cave
with two lovers, and of being a witness to their actions.

To imitate nature well is the perfection of poetry; it is the most
important property of that art to find out what is most beautiful in
nature. That poem which comes nearest to the resemblance of

nature is the best; it does not follow however that that which pleases most is the best. It is easy to put together extravagant and improbable combinations; but to pursue the course of nature in her grand and affecting features is quite a different task! To depend, not on surprise, but on force, is that for which few are qualified. Dryden says, "Our depraved appetites and ignorance of the arts often mislead our judgments, and cause us to take that for true imitation of nature, which has no resemblance of nature. To inform our judgments and to reform our tastes, rules were invented, that by them we might discern when nature was imitated, and how nearly. The imitation of nature is therefore constituted as the general rule of poetry."* And it is only in men of genius that we can get a true representation of these things, for by the mystery of his genius the poet lives and moves in that which he represents. It is this that constitutes the real enthusiasm by which we discover a true poet. They themselves cannot perceive it when under its influence, as the eye which sees all things cannot view itself. "From an enchanted man," remarks D'Israeli, "we must not expect a narrative of his enchantment; for if he could speak to us reasonably like one of ourselves, in that case he would be a man in a state of disenchantment, and then would perhaps yield us no better account than we may trace by our own observations."† Milton, languishing amidst the freshness of nature in Eden, felt all the delights of those elements which he was creating. The fierce and wild Dante, amidst the abysses of his Inferno, must often have been startled by its horrors.

That which cannot be read and approved by the soundest and strongest understanding is not genuine: if it cannot be read in our most sober moments, in those when we are seeking wisdom, it is not genuine. And with respect to this, let me speak of one author, one of our eminent poets, whose works are a great study WORDSWORTH. All the faculties of the mind are exercised in the production of his principal pieces. Intensity and originality of thought characterize him; and the reason as well as the imagination is instructed by the perusal of his compositions. They have

" · · · slation of Du Fresno.' Works.

the grand ingredient of earnestness, the actual visions of a retired, peculiar, and deeply-meditating imagination : the associations which the poet paints require a long discipline, a studied bent; but they are conformable to its nature, and such as perpetual musing can produce in one of high gifts, high morals, and high attainments. Such emanations from a seer, who has spent his days on the bosom of lakes, amid the inspiring sounds of solitary woods, and high mountains, are like a new spring of living water from the rock, throwing forth freshness and verdure, where all before was trodden and barren.

The poet has also to observe *uniformity* in the general structure of his work. A venerable pile of Gothic architecture, viewed at a distance or after the sober hand of time has stripped it of the false glare of meretricious ornament, communicates a sensation, which the same object under a close inspection in its highest degree of perfection was incapable of producing ; when the attention solicited by a thousand *minutiæ* with which the hand of caprice and super-stition had crowded its objects, was unavoidably diverted from the contemplation of the main design. The poet has to use propriety in the ornament with which he gilds his poem, as the overcrowding of the inferior component parts must be evident to the most superficial observer. Originality of sentiment, vivacity of thought, and loftiness of language may conduct the reader to the end of a work, though awkwardly designed and injudiciously constructed ; whilst the incessant adherence to poetic rule would be found insufficient to compensate for meanness of thought or vulgarity of expression. Nothing can be more directly adverse to the spirit of poetry, considered under one of its definitions as an universal lan-guage, than whatever confines it to the comprehension of a single people or a particular period of time. Dryden is strongly tinctured with the taste of the times; and those Delilahs of the Town, to use his own expression, are plentifully scattered throughout his works, esteemed in the present age for those passages only in which he ventured to oppose his own taste to that of his readers, and which have already passed the ordeal of unmerited censure.

èxigencies to postpone the powers of his own taste, and submit his judgment to the arbitrary dominion of a prevailing mode. In Dryden we meet with expressions and allusions drawn from the meanest mechanical employments, which would be unintelligible to a foreigner, who was unacquainted only with the learned parts of our language.

The poetry of ruder ages is seldom distinguished for elegance of diction or variety of imagery ; yet there are advantages so strongly peculiar to it as must raise it high in the esteem of all admirers of nature, while yet simple and unsophisticated. The state of the arts as yet rude, rendered it impossible to deviate from simplicity. The state of the arts being then but faintly delineated, no idea of superiority could be obtained but what arose from personal qualifications, and poetic praise unprostituted to power and wealth, was then the genuine tribute of gratitude and admiration. That property was in a very unsettled state in the days of Homer, may be gathered from numberless passages in his writings: among the calamities which awaited an aged father.on the death of his only son, the plunder of his possession is mentioned ; and Achilles laments, that life. unlike every other human possession, was not to be obtained by theft. Accordingly, in the epithets which accompany the name of each hero, through the Iliad and Odyssey, we see no allusions to the adventitious circumstances of wealth and power, if we except the title of *lord of rich Mycenæ*, sometimes though rarely bestowed on Agamemnon; while the subtlety of Ulysses, the swiftness of Achilles, the courage and strength of Diomed, are mentioned as often as the names of these heroes occur.

I have said the primary *object* of poetry is to please, but this is not the *sole* object of the art. In Aristotle's view, this was the great end of the art, and of all its branches: the aim however is also to instruct, although Aristotle does not anywhere give any idea that utility and instruction are the end of poetry. It may, however, in any case be rendered useful, improving, and instructive—it *ought,* to be made the latter; for though the poet addresses himself to the imaginations and passions, he may through them, lead to instruction and information. True poetry has in it that kind of utility which good men find in their Bibles. It enobles the sentiments, enlarges the affections, kindles the imagination, and gives to us an enjoyment of a life in the past and in the future, as well as in the present. Vaughan says, "the poet and the Christian, have alike a hidden life: worship in the vital element of each." And Schiller has truly said. "Poetry can be to the man, what love is to the hero. It can neither counsel him, nor smite with him, nor perform any labour for him, but it can bring him up to be a hero, can summon him to deeds, and arm him with strength for all that he ought to be." As I have said in the chapter on the Greek poets, Homer wrote his Iliad on purpose to teach mankind the mischief of discord among chiefs, and his Odyssey to prove to them the advantages of staying at home to take care of their families; Piccolomini in particular. In the case of didactic poetry the principal aim is instruction, although verse is the medium which the poet employs. The war songs of the ancients were written to stimulate the soldiers; the bitter but wholesome Iambic was wont to make villainy blush; the satire was to invite men to laugh at folly; the comedian chastised the common errors of life; and the tragedian made kings afraid to be tyrants and tyrants to be their own tormenters.

The great poet does not spend life in executing microscopic copies of the small parts of nature. He makes the universe the scaffold for his ideal. He fills the world with thoughts on pilgrimage to build shrines of his own, as well as to visit those which time has consecrated. It is his office not merely to show to the mind its workings, to hold up to the reader a reflection of his own feelings but also to display before him things that by no other means could be revealed—wonders of that of which he would never have dreamed.

No man is so senseless of natural impressions as not to be affected with the pastorals of the ancients, when, under the stories of wolves and sheep, they describe the misery of people under hard masters and their happiness under good.

To conclude this chapter— a glowing morality of bosom and conscience; an emulation of the magnificent desires, and profound regrets that alternately rule the loftier endowments of our nature; a habit of forming into shape, and putting into action, the possibility of grand and propitious or tremendously afflicting circumstances of some extraordinary fate are the fountains of poetry. As Emerson has it "the poet is the man without impediment, who sees and handles that which others dream of, traverses the whole scale of experience, and is representative of man, in virtue of being the largest power to receive and impart."

Poetry makes man *wiser* by causing truth to speak to him in a language that appeals to his own nature, not merely to a part of it, and which reaches the heart as well as the intellect. It makes him *better* by revealing as none else can do, the native loveliness of generosity and patriotism, affection and self-sacrifice.

CHAPTER II.

THE PROGRESS OF POETRY IN THE MIDDLE AGES.

It was after the conquest of Greece that the arts and sciences first began to be cherished and cultivated with assiduity, and that the military genius of the Romans first became tempered by something of a literary spirit. It is from this period that we date the era of poetry, and the works of Virgil, Lucretius and Horace. But little literary advance was made, till after the death of the tyrant Domitian, and the subsequent reign of Adrian. Even then, though Adrian was himself learned, learning was slow in its progress. He was jealous of the literary fame of others ; that it is said, he preferred Ennius to Virgil, and even the names of Homer and Plato excited his disgust. With his predecessor Trajan it was different. Bred from his earliest youth to the profession of arms, he had little time to acquire learning ; but unlike Adrian, he had both judgment to distinguish, and munificence to reward, those who possessed it.

This age, however, formed the most brilliant era of poetry, for we date from it Virgil, Tibullus, Horace and Ovid, Propertius and Livy. It was not until death had consigned the poets of the Augustan age to the grave, that the decline of poetry commenced. Then came the period when human nature was at its lowest ebb, and had relapsed into the barbarism from which the superior wisdom of the first race of man had raised it.

Berington says, "This period was distinguished by four epic poets, Lucan, Valerius Flaccus, Statius and Silius Italicus, on whose merits various judgments have been pronounced. Lucan died when in his twenty-seventh year, and in the reign of Nero. He had imprudently contended with the tyrant himself for the poetic crown, and more imprudently engaged in a conspiracy against his life. The premature age of the poet, readily accounts for the imperfections of his work ; and he might have approached nearer the excellence of Virgil, had he not aspired to eclipse his fame.* The eloquent Quintilian describes him, as, ardent and

---

* Berington's Literary History

ture ; and under the commonwealth the advances in the arts were slow and difficult. The Romans were too deeply engaged in their foreign and domestic wars, and the trumpet drowned the notes of the lyre. It was the age of conquest and patriotism, and the genius most suitable to the age, shone with distinguished lustre. The military merit was the only certain road to the dignities of the republic.

When Rome was subjected to Cæsar, her empire extended over the then known world. The Grecian elegance had softened her rougher genius ; and science had polished the ferocity of her manners. The laurel of conquest faded before the olive of peace ; and literary merit became the object of attention. Augustus only established that, of which others had laid the foundation: Ennius, Terence, Lucretius, Catullus, and Sallust were prior to him ; and the Roman eloquence, which was born, and which died with Cicero, sunk under the malignity of his influence. Certainly the Augustan age produced the best poets; yet eloquence fled, and after the death of Cicero, degenerated. " Poetry flourished only for a few years, and probably owed its temporary vigour to the mean prostitution of its talents ; in flattering the enslaver of his country and the tyrant of the world."

Greece, however, unlike Rome, produced a series of learned men ; she did not have to struggle against the jealousy of surrounding

* Instit. l. x. c. l.

states. Her internal dissensions were her only enemies, and these rather promoted than impeded the powers of her genius.

The early attempts of the poets in Greece have not reached us, probably on account of the great commotion which took place. in that country after the Trojan war.   In less than a century after, while Tisamenus the son of Orestes reigned in Mycaenæ, the Dorians invaded the Peloponnesus.   The civilization which was just beginning to increase was then destroyed.   Many of the old inhabitants were driven into ·exile, and passed over into Asia, where they occupied considerable regions along the shores.   Some of the poems which were admired in their time might probably have been taken with them in their banishment.   By degrees, however, the Peloponnesus recovered from the effects of their invasion, and the Greeks returned to their country in order to seek refuge from the Persian arms.

When civilization had again advanced in Greece, much curiosity was excited respecting the poets who had flourished before their exile, and the want of authentic history relating to them was filled by the aid of fiction, while the obscure traditions remaining of early bards, were modelled so as to gratify the national pride. Very little credit however is to be given to the details of Grecian history where the poets are concerned, before the era of the Olympians.   If so little was known of Homer, how can we give very implicit belief to the tales respecting Linus, Orpheus, Musæus, Eumolpus, and others who lived at a much recent period, the date of Linus being fixed by Archbishop Usher, 1280 years before the Christian Era.

To the Peloponnesian war we owe the history of Thucydides, the funeral orations of Pericles and Plato, and to the treachery of· Philip, the sublime invectives of Demosthenes : but when the conquering eagle of Rome enslaved the country under the pretence of protecting it, from that moment her genius withered ; and the only writers she afterwards produced, Polybius in particular, instead of recording the glories of their native country, celebrated the exploits of Rome.   Rome, therefore, now the uncontrolled mistress

acquisition of learning certainly dates from Cicero, from the time when he poured forth his feelings in eloquent oratory. It was then that men, " swallowed so thirstily that delicious beverage from the magical cup of literature." This illustrious orator carried his favorite pursuit to that pitch of eloquence which was never surpassed in any age.

Nothing important in the way of advance in literature and poetry occurred until the eleventh century, although they still found admirers and were studied. But about this period, says Berington, "poets, or rather versifiers were numerous in every convent, whilst no subject appeared to be intractable for their poetical versatility."

At the commencement of the thirteenth century when the modern languages were first introduced, we find springing up in France the Trouvers and Troubadours, and in Britain the Minstrels or bards. The Troubadours were a race of minstrels in the South of France, composers of erotic or sentimental poems; and the romancers called *Trouveurs* or finders, in the North of France, culled and compiled their domestic tales on Fabliaux, Dits, Conte, or Lais. Ellis says, " They were a romantic race of ambulatory poets; military and religous subjects their favorite themes ; yet bold and satirical on princes, and even on priests: severe moralisers, though libertines in their verse ; so refined and chaste in their manners that few husbands were alarmed at the enthusiastic language they addressed to their wives. The most romantic incidents are told of their loves. But love and its grosser passion were clearly dis-tinguished from each other in their singular intercourse with their

"Dames." The objects of their mind were separated from the object
of their senses ; the virtuous lady to whom they vowed their hearts,
was in their language styled *"la dame de ses pênsees,"* a very distinct
being from their other mistress. Such was the Platonic Chimera
that charmed in the age of chivalry, the Laura of Petrarch might
have been no other than 'the lady of his thoughts.'* These
Trouveurs, however, were certainly the most eminent narrative
poets. No people had a better right to be the founders of chiv-
alric poems than the Normans. They were the most ener-
getic generation of modern men. "By the conquest of England,
chivalry rose to its full growth as an institution, by the circumstance
of martial zeal being enlisted under the banners of superstition."
And these constituted a source of description to the Romancers or
Trouveurs, to which no exact counterpart is to be found in the
heroic poetry of antiquity.

Menetrier, menestral, or *minstrel* was he " who accompanied his
song by a musical instrument, both the words and the melody being
occasionally furnished by himself, and occasionally by others." †
These bards we know were reverenced from the earliest ages, by
all the inhabitants of Europe, whether of Celtic, or Gothic race.
We are told by ancient and modern writers, how that their skill
was considered as something divine; that kings solicited their at-
tendance, and loaded them with honours and rewards. The word
minstrel though not used in England before the Norman Conquest,
had long before that time been adopted in France. So early as
the eighth century " Menestral" we are told, was a title given to
the *Maestro di Capella* of Pepin, the father of Charlemagne.

Although Minstrelsy was probably never extinct, for a long time
after the conquest, it may be supposed to have sunk to the lowest
ebb. Campbell, in his Bssay on English Poetry, says, " No human
pursuit is more sensible than poetry, to national pride or mortifi-
cation; and a race of peasants like the Saxons, struggling for bare
subsistence, under all the dependence and without the protection
of the feudal system, were in a state the most ungenial to feelings
of poetical enthusiasm." The harp was no doubt the instrument

---

* Specimens of the Early English Metrical Romances.

might be inferred from the very word itself, which is of genuine Gothic origin, and was current among every branch of that people, viz., Anglo-Saxon *hearps* and *hearpa* ; Iceland *harpa* and *heurpa* Danes and Beltic *harpe* ; German, *harpffe* Galic *harpe* ; Spanish *harpa* ; Italian *arpa*. In the Erse its name is *crwth*. That it was also the favorite musical instrument of the Britons and other nothern nations in the middle ages, is evident from their laws, and various passages in their history. By the laws of Wales, a harp was one of the three things that were necessary to constitute a gentleman, or a free-man. A gentleman's harp was not liable to be seized for debt.*

Minstrelsy continued as far as the reign of Elizabeth, towards the end of the sixteenth century, but the honour that attached to the earlier bards wore off; they lost the protection of the wealthy, and had dwindled into mere singers of ballads. We are told that they lost all credit and sunk so low in the public opinion, that in 1597, the thirty-ninth year of the reign of Elizabeth, a statute was passed by which "minstrels wandering abroad" were included among "rogues vagabonds and sturdy beggars." This act seems to have put an end to the profession. Few of the rhymes of these minstrels have reached us. Percy says, in his "Essay on the Ancient Minstrels," that "so long as the minstrels subsisted they seem never to have designed their rhymes for literary publication, and probably never committed them to writing themselves. The copies which are preserved were doubtless taken down from their mouths."‡ We are told by Campbell that, " The minstrels or those who wrote for them, translated or imitated Norman romances ; and in so doing enriched the language with many new words which they borrowed from the originals, either from want of corresponding terms in their own vocabulary, or from the words appearing to be more agreeable." We learn also that after the conquest, popular ballads of the English in praise of their heroes, were sung about the street, and William of Malmsbury in the twelfth century, continues to make mention of them. As

* Chappell "On Popular Music." p. 57.
‡ Percy's Reliques of Ancient English Poetry.

these minstrels gradually wore out a new kind óf ballad writers succeeded "an inferior sort of minor poets, who wröte narrative songs merely for the press."

This is not the first we hear of this kind of Minstrels. They flourished in Greece from the earliest periods. Their name rhàpsodists, compounded from ραπτειν ωδην, *to join together or compose verses,* signified their occupation and character. They answered in many respects to the Celtic bards. They chanted, sung, or recited poems, chiefly,(at least in the earliest times)of their own composition, at the tables of princes, and in public assemblies, and they were held in high esteem and veneration. There were few arts at that time, distinctly marked out as cultivated· by peculiar classes, the bard had a profession of his own, which was regarded as more venerable than any other. His art was probably the parent of the poetry of Greece.

About the year 1125 first appeared the fabulous history of Britain, written in Latin by Geoffrey of Monmouth, or rather translated by him into that language from the British or Armorica, which excited a very general curiosity ; though it could only be read by scholars. It was therefore as soon as might be, translated into French by Robert Wace, a native of Jersey, and about thirty years later, that is about 1185, a Saxon version was made by Layamon, a priest. Berington says, "both versions are metrical, and the Saxon was taken or imitated not from the Latin, but from the French translation." The original copy was brought into England by Gualtier, Archdeacon of Oxford, and committed to the care of Geoffrey. The translation is allowed to have been executed by him with a certain purity, but with little fidelity, as many variations and additions sufficiently prove. *

In the thirteenth century, the number of writers increased, and the transition from the Saxon into the English language was complete, but no improvement is seen in the *vein* of poetry. The description of the land of Cokaine, a translation also, probably, from the French, presents us with a satire on the monastic orders, of which, notwithstanding the vivacity of the subject, there is

* History of Eng. Poet.—Dissert. i.

Of flesh, of fish, and a rich meat,
The like fullest that man may eat,
Flouren-cakes beth the shingles all
Of Churchy cloister, bowers and hall,
The pinnes (pinnacles) beth fat puddings,
Rich meat to princes and kings,
All is common to young and old,
To stout and stern, meek and bold.

The Germans had also been improving their language, chiefly by the means of the poets, called *Minnesingers*; their poetry differed little from that of England or France; they were principally subjects of chivalry. Latin poetry, however, claimed the first place. The harsh, and rugged dialects of the more modern times were ·not so fit to be adapted to the harmony which verse requires, and thus it was that at this period there sprung up so many imitators of its style, especially in Italy. The *Alexandreid*, a poem founded on the history of Quintus Curtius, in ten books, attained great popularity about this time.* Joseph of Exeter lived . in this century. He was the author of two heroic poems, one on the *Trojan War*, which Berington says, "is imitated rather than translated from the Greek of Dorus Phrygius;" the other on the *War of Antioch* or the third Crusade under Richard. Alexander Neckham and Peter de Blois were also poetical writers in this century. It was in the thirteenth century that rhymes were first introduced into *Latin* verse. The language had ceased to be generally read ; and the ear, which was vitiated by the rugged sounds of the modern dialects, had lost all relish for the harmonious simplicity of its prosody. Rhythm was then found necessary, without which no verse could be distinguished, and as this might

* History of Eng. Poet.—Dissert ii.

not always be deemed sufficient to mark the measure of a line, recourse was had to *rhyme,* that is, the termination of verses by a similar sound. It was then used in modern tongues without bounds. This is the most reasonable manner in which to account for the origin of rhyming at the termination of lines and verses, though it has been differently attributed by various authors.

The Norman Muse must certainly be regarded as the earliest preceptress of English poetry, and the use of rhyme and versification. Turner, however says, that "the Anglo Saxon versification possessed occasional rhyme," although we have no specimens of ryhme in our language before the conquest. An amusing anecdote is related by Goujet, as to the origin of *Bouts-rimes,* or "Rhyming Ends," "One Dulot a foolish poet, when sonnets were in demand, had a singular custom of preparing the rhymes of these poems to be filled up at his leisure. Having been robbed of his papers, he was regretting most the lost of three hundred sonnets : and his friends were astonished that he had written so many which they had never heard. They were *blank sonnets* he replied ; and explained the mystery by describing his *bout-rimes.* The idea appeared ridiculously amusing ; and it soon became fashionable to collect the most difficult rhymes and fill up the lines." *

We pass now into the fourteenth century; to Dante the greatest of our Italian poets, and Francis Petrarca his contemporary. The taste of poetry in this century, for which the public mind had been prepared by the writings of Dante ascended to a pitch of enthusiastic admiration. It was Francis Petrarca who rescued his country's name from obscurity, and rendered it the admiration of Europe. The envied excellence to which he raised the poetry of Italy—while the best specimens of the art in the other countries had a rude and barbarous appearance constitute the basis of the highest praise. "To Petrarca, was principally due the restoration of letters to Italy, and through Italy to the other realms of Europe." The name of the classical writers had almost died out, and the various accounts of them were miserably confounded, until Petrarca restored it by his diligent and laborious collection of the works of the Ancients.

Goujet s Bib. fr. xvi. p. 181.

which first sprung up in France under William de Lorris, and was afterwards taken up by Chaucer. The simple old narrative romance had become too familiar at this time to invite him to its beaten track. It was a class of poetry that we might say was too light for so strong a genius, and it must be owned that his allegorical poetry is often almost puerile. Yet we never lose entirely that peculiar grace which distinguishes him, and no one who has read his *House of Fame*, and the *Flower and Leaf*, will regret that he sported for a season in the field of allegory, Campbell says, "In this new species of romance, we perceive the youthful Muse of the language in love with mystical meanings, and forms of fancy; more remote, if possible from reality, than those of the chivalrous fable itself; and we could sometimes wish her back from her emblematic castles, to the more solid ones of the elder fables; but still she moves in pursuit of those shadows with an impulse of novelty, and an exuberance of spirit, that is not wholly without its attraction and delight. Chaucer was happily afterwards drawn to the more natural style of Boccaccio.

· When the fifteenth century opened, almost all the countries, especially Italy, were engaged in giving fresh life to the arts; books were everywhere sought, public libraries formed; the literary treasures of Greece were developed; the names of Plato and Aristotle, Demosthenes and Homer, rendered familiar to the

D

public ear and every man of learning became acquainted with their language. This period also was an important one in Greek poetry. Numerous academies were formed ; literary disputations arose ; the affluent and the great eagerly contended for the honour of being esteemed the patrons of genius and erudition. The elegant arts, painting, sculpture, and architecture, rose at the same time into life ; and to crown the felicity of the period, the **art of** printing was discovered in Germany.

CHAPTER III.

THE EARLY POETS OF GREECE.

In my last chapter, I have traced the gradual progress of poetry up to the fifteenth century. The era which this period comprised is without doubt the greatest in the poetical world, and I propose in the two following chapters commenting briefly upon the poets of that age.

LINUS– The earliest Greek poet of which we know anything at all is Linus. He was a native of Chalcis, and to him are ascribed a poem on the exploits of Bacchus in India ; a treatise on mythology, and the invention of melody and rhythm. Suidas calls him the lyric poet. A few fragments under his name are to be found in Stobœus. He is the first of that chain of bards to whom the blind reverence of Greece was directed. Eusebius speaks of him as having flourished before Moses. Diodorus Siculus represents him as being the inventor of music and poetry, or at least as having first introduced them into Greece. The Thebans distinguished between an earlier and later Linus. The latter, which is no doubt the Greek poet, is said to have instructed Hercules in music, but to have been killed by that hero. According to Diogenes Laertius, however, he was killed by Apollo because he had presumed upon a musical contest with that deity. It is a matter of doubt whether the name designates one individual or several, therefore it is difficult to im- agine whether the various incidents apply to the poet or not.

ORPHEUS—Next in the order of Greek poets stands Orpheus

held most sacred in Greece: to have taught civilization and founded religious rites; to have gently beguiled men from the savage to the social state : and to have harmonized at once the language and the morals of the people among. whom he sung." Cicero asserts that no such person ever existed, and Herodotus seems to imply that no poets existed before Homer and Hesiod; but Plato and isocrates speak of him as a real and historical person, and not a fabulous hero. No doubt, however, such a poet did exist in the earlier times of Greece, though the tales respecting him are not to be relied on. Linus is said to have been his master in poetry and music. There is scarcely an art or accomplishment that had any existence in rude times, which the Greeks do not attribute to Orpheus. Plutarch tells us, that he was the author of all music, except a few notes for the flute, which existed before him. The invention of hexameter verse and the introduction of letters to Greece have been ascribed to him.

Many accounts have been given as to the manner of his death; and the principal account,though supernatural like the rest is related in a manner which has given occasion to some of the most beautiful encomiums on the musical and poetical arts. We are told that Eurydice, flying from the attempts of Aristeus on her chastity was bitten by a serpent and died. Her lover, disconsolate, determined to follow her to the abodes of Hades, the regions of the dead. He

entered Pluto's kingdom, where the charms of his lyre suspended
the torments of the damned, and melted by its strains, those whom
human entreaties had never moved before. All hell was ravished
by his melodies ; the shades came flocking round him; the wheel
of Ixion stood still; and he won back his wife from the most inex-
orable of all deities. His prayer, however was only granted upon
one condition, that he should not look back upon his restored wife till
he had arrived again in the regions of the living. He willingly prom-
ised to perform the condition ; but, at the very moment when they
were about to pass the fatal bounds, the poet, unable to restrain
the eagerness of love, looked back—and saw Eurydice melt away
from him, never more to be granted to his prayers. Racked with
a deeper sorrow, he returned to the upper world, and found consola-
tion only in wandering with his lyre amidst the caves and desolate
places, and calling on her whom he had lost for ever. In vain the
Thracian women tried to engage his affections ; his grief for the
loss of Eurydice made him treat them with contempt. Enraged
at his coldness, they in revenge tore him to pieces under the excite-
ment of their Bacchanalian orgies, and threw his head into the
Hebrus, down which it rolled to the sea, and was borne across to
Lesbos, still calling on Eurydice. His lyre also was said to have been
carried to Lesbos, which expresses the historical fact that Lesbos
was then the great seat of music. The meaning of the allegory,
Tzetzes asserts, is that Orpheus by his great skill in physic snatched
his wife from the grave when her life was in extreme danger; while
the latter part of the account is only again showing the power of
his music as even capable of moving hell itself.

As to the works of Orpheus there are still subsisting poems which
have been ascribed to him. Many, said to have been his, were
current in the flourishing period of Greek literature, but no doubt
the extant poems bearing the names of Orpheus are forgeries of
Christian grammarians and philosophers of the Alexandrian
school ; though among the fragments are some genuine remains of
Orpheus known to the early Greek writers. The hymns have the
air of the highest antiquity of all the Orphic poems. They are

Orpheus, although Virgil gives him a very high rank amongst the poets. It is asserted by Pausanias that the Museum at Athens was so called from his having been accustomed to retire there for contemplation and poetical musing. His principal work was a poetical account of the creation, and he is also said to have sung the wars of the Titans. But nothing of his works remain now. Even in the time of Pausanias ; we are informed that a hymn to Ceres was his only genuine composition then in existence.

Next to Musæus, we turn with pleasure to him whose name has been celebrated in every age in which poetry has been held in reverence—HOMER. The sublime conceptions, vivid figures, interesting narratives, and more than all the exquisite style, and perfect common sense of the Mæonian bird, are beyond any praise which they can receive in these pages from my feeble efforts. His work is a prodigy :—we must either suppose that he was proceeded by other writers, who had brought poetry to the perfection, in which we find it in his writings ; or that he himself created the poetry of his own immortal works. With respect to the former supposition, it has been given out by many that Homer did steal from the anterior poets whatever was most remarkable in the Iliad and Odyssey, and it was argued as improbable that in a dark age, one man should have produced works which no time has equalled. But the genius which the Iliad exhibits is no proof that it is not the production of a single mind in a barbarous age. Poetry, as I have tried to show in the earlier chapters of this work, is not a progressive art; it has no connection with the progression of time and depends on no external circumstances.

Homer was generally regarded by the ancients as the author of the Iliad and Odyssey, and such continued to be the unwavering

complete poems, but small and separate epic songs celebrating single exploits of the heroes; and that these lays were for the first time written down and united by Pisistratus, the tyrant of Athens, or his son. This opinion gave rise to long controversy which was never settled and probably never will be. It was maintained about the close of the seventeenth century by two French writers, Hedlin and Perrault, but only received with derision. The honour was given by many to Pisistratus or his son. Amongst others, Cicero when he asks," Quis doctior iisdem temporibus aut cujus eloquentia literis instructior quam Pisistrati? Qui primus Homeri libros, confusos Antea, sic disposuisse dicitur ut nunc habemus."*

It must be allowed however that this expression of Cicero, that Pisistratus "primus Homeri *Coufusos antea* dispossuisse," will not prove much; for it does not follow because Homer's works were confused or disarranged in the time of their first editor, that they had never been composed in a regular series. They are supposed to have been transmitted through the medium of the rhapsodists, a class of minstrel who flourished from the earliest periods. It was from the songs recited by these men—songs which from their merit and interest, were popular among them—that Homers works were compiled at Athens.

Herodotus was of the opposite opinion to Cicero. His words are "As for the gods, whence each of them was descended, or whether they were always in being, or under what shape or form they existed, the Greeks knew nothing till very lately. Hesiod and Homer, were I believe, about 400 years older than myself, and no more and these are the men who *made a theogony* for the Greeks ; who gave the Gods their appellations, defined their qualities, appointed their honours and described their forms. As for the poets who are said to have lived before these men, I am of opinion they came after them."

But the early existence of Homer's works cannot be doubted; and

* Cic. de Orat, l. iii.

contempt of danger and death, and romantic friendships on the other; were to be seen in their utmost extremes of awful or of placid grandeur. Life was then full of adventure. *The feuds of rival chieftains afforded a perpetual succession of incidents to all, as well as a stimulus to the deepest emotions of their partizans. Friendship was cemented by the participation of hardships and of peril, and proved stronger than fortune; lasting as existence. In the breathing times of concord, a wild and generous hospitality filled up the pause, and was rendered graceful by the aid of song. The poet then found in every region the materials of his art ; passion was energy whether of the most tremendous or exalted kind ; tradition filled up the place of history, and gave ample ground for his song, while it left him verge enough for the exercise of his invention. The new religion, which was beginning to afford, even to the common people, a feeling of the grace of form and the harmony of the universe, had its altars on every shore; with its solemn rites and mysteries and trivial fond records. Surely there needed not to render this age poetical, the perfection of scholastic subtlety, the nice control of the police, or the common-place comforts and luxuries of modern times. The poet had all 'the world' of genius 'before him where to chose.' What education did he need?

What formal introduction to the muses? His infancy might have
been delighted with wondrous tales of heroes and demi-gods ; his
youth passed by the shores of the ocean, amidst the chaste scenery
of Greece ; and his manhood occupied in wandering from country
to country, admiring all that was beautiful, revering all that was
grand, and rejoicing in all that was romantic. What had he to do
with books, or with worldly knowledge : his school was the
universe. The mountains, the streams, and the ocean, were his
teachers. The wild traditions of his age afforded him the threads
from which he was to weave a glorious composition, whose colours
should be ever fresh as nature shall endure. We have no hesitation
in believing, that the ploughman of Scotland —he who "walked
in glory and in joy, beside his plough upon the mountain side,"
breathed forth the tenderest notes of poetry without the aid of
external culture. We hesitate not to think that a youth of sixteen
once fabricated an artful deception with wonderful industry and
skill, and poured forth effusions worthy of the best age of English
genius. Why then should we think it incredible that Homer
should shine as the day-star of Grecian literature, in an age when
the common incidents of life abounded with materials of song ?"

Vaughan, also, in his Poetical Essay very finely observes,
"Let it be granted that of the times and events of which Homer
sung, historically we know nothing. They are all gone—dead—
passed away ; their vacant chronicles may be silent as the tombs
in which their bones are buried. Yet there remains still to
us in Homer's verse, materials, richer perhaps than exist for any
period of the ancient world—a picture, not of the times of which
he sung but of the men among whom he lived. How they acted
how they thought, talked and felt ; what they made of this earth
and of their place in it ; we have it all delineated in the marvellous
verse of a poet who, be he what he may, was in this respect the
greatest which the earth has ever seen."

Homer is the heart of the age in which he lived. What matter
is it what his name was, or where he lived, while we have himself
and the originals from which he drew? And perhaps the parts

between us, there is no difference between their children and ours.

The little Ulysses climbing on the knees of his father's guest, coaxing for a taste of the red wine, and spilling it as he starts at the unusual taste ; or that other most beautiful picture of him running at the side of Laertes in the garden at Ithaca, the father teaching the boy the names of the fruit-trees, and making presents to him of this tree and that tree for his very own, to help him to remember what they were called; the partition wall of three thousand years melts away as we look back at scenes like these. Then, as now, the children loved to sport on the shore and watch the inrolling waves ;—then, as now, the boy architect would pile the moist sand into mimic town or castle, and when the work was finished, sweep it away again in wanton humour with foot and hand ;—then, as now, the little tired maiden would cling to her mother's skirt, and trotting painfully along beside her, look up wistfully and plead with moist eyes to be carried in her arms.

With such evidence of identity among us all, it is worth while in reading it to look closer at the old Greeks, to try and find in Homer something beyond fine poetry, or exciting adventures, or battle scenes, or materials for scholarship ; to look in him for the story of real living men—set to pilgrimage in the old way on the same old earth— men, such as we are, children of one family with the same work to do, to live the best life they could—with the same trials, the same passions, the same difficulties; if with weaker means of meeting them.

The poetry of Homer has handed down to posterity an exact picture of the customs and manners of a very distant age. By its aid we can trace through successive years the variations which gradually take place in warfare and in letters, in habits and in customs ; we can gaze with reverence upon the superstitions which have become extinct, and smile, upon comparing the nascent follies of the age of Demi-gods, with the full-blown follies of the age of men. Just as Homer stands pre-eminent among the ancient bards in all else, so he is equally in this. Almost as much as we admire the felicity of his imagination, the grandeur of his story, and the excellency of the moral precepts which are interspersed through-out it, so do we value him for the faithful representation which he has given us of the manners of his heroes.

And, in this, the Odyssey, which describes the travels and sufferings of an individual, has of course, more numerous sketches of private life than the Iliad, and the actors seem as it were to be upon a public stage. We cannot help wondering at the manner in which the poet has interwoven in his most gorgeous descriptions, allusions to the art and commerce of his countrymen. We may observe that the besiegers of Ilium were ignorant of coined money.

> " Ευδεν αρ οινιξουτο καρηκομοωντες Αχαιοι
> Αλλοι μεν χαλκω, αλλοι δ'αιθωνι οισηρω
> Αλλυς δε ρινοις, αλλοι δ'αυτοισι Βυεσσιν,
> Αλλοι δ'αυδ͵ αποδεσσι."

Each in exchange, proportioned treasure gave ;
Some brass or iron, some an ox or slave.

Not a word of the bargain of pound, shillings, and pence. And yet these ancient Greeks obtained that great proficiency in the arts without its use. From Homer's description they had in a great measure our idea of policy, our customs, and superstitions. Although living in so remote a period, they enjoyed many of our luxuries, and although corrupted and debased by the grossest of religious codes, they entertained many of our notions of morality ! The modern lustres of the drawing room sink into insignificance by the side of the candelabras of Alcinous :—

> Refulgent pedestals the walls surround,
> Which boys of gold with flaming torches crown'd ;
> The polished ore, reflecting every ray,
> Blazed on the banquets with a double day.

Many ladies would be amazed at learning in Homer the numbers and duties of the housemaids :—

> " Πευτηκουτα δε οι δμωαι κατα δωμα γυυαικες " κ.τ.λ.
>
> Full fifty handmaids form the household train ;
> Some turn the mill, or sift the golden grain ;
> Some ply the loom ; their busy fingers move
> Like poplar-trees when Zephyr fans the grove,

The greatest characteristic in the Iliad is the reality and air of truth which it bears throughout. We seem as though we are listening to a circumstantial tale, so vivid is the poet's pencil, and so minute the details. Wherever we meet with his heroes we sympathize with them as with old friends. The domestic parts of the tale not only relieve the heroic scenes but prepare us to enjoy them. We see the chief buckling on his armour in the morning, snatching a hasty repast. and taking a hurried leave of his comrades ; we follow him with breathless interest through the adventures of the field ; and we feel the deepest tragic interest when he falls in the pride and glory of his manhood.

The variety and number of characters and incidents introduced in the Iliad is astonishing. Images are poured forth from the mind of the poet as though he were unable to restrain them, and yet they have all the vividness and perfection which might have been expected from the most anxious thought, and laborious finishing.

The character of the two poems, the Iliad and the Odyssey are widely different. In turning from one to the other, we breathe under a fresh atmosphere. Pope says, " The Odyssey is the reverse of the Iliad, in moral, subject, manner, and style ; to which it has no sort of relation, but as the story happens to follow in order of time, and as some of the same persons are actors in it." And Longinus, "In my judgment it proceeds that as the Iliad was written while his spirit was in the greatest vigour, the whole strueture of that work is dramatic and full of action; whereas the greater part of the Odyssey is employed in narration which is the taste of old age : so that in this latter piece we may compare him to the setting sun, which has still the same greatness but not the same ardour or force."

The poems of Homer formed the basis of Greek literature. Every Greek who had received a moderate education was well acquainted with them, but nobody states anything about their author. The date and place of his birth were matters of dispute. Seven cities claim him as their countryman, " Smyrna, Rhodus, Colophon, Salamis, Chios, Argos, Athænæ." Most of these have but very slender evidence to support their claim, but the claims of Smyrna and Chios are the most plausible. The best modern writers place his date about 850 B.C. Herodotus, the most reliable authority, represents him as 400 years before his time, 846 B.C. as he himself flourished about 444 B.C. An account of his birth and life, which may be considered as the most correct, is given by Herodotus. The substance of it is as follows :—

The name of Homer's mother was Crytheis, who proving unlawfully with child, was driven away from Cumæ by her uncle, with Ismenias, and found refuge in Smyrna. As she was celebrating a festival near this city, she was delivered of the poet Homer. Crytheis supported herself by her labour, till Phemius, a schoolmaster at Smyrna, fell in love with her, and married her. When he died, Homer succeeded him in his school, and was renowned for his wisdom. Attracted by his fame, Mentes, the commander of a Leucadian ship, visited him and induced him to leave his occupation and travel. In his company he went to Italy and Spain ; but was at length left at Ithaca, in consequence of a defluxion in his eyes. While there he was entertained by a man of fortune named Menitor, who told him those circumstances upon which he afterwards framed the Odyssey. Soon after, he became totally blind, and on this misfortune returned to Smyrna, his native place ; but his hopes of support were disappointed by the apathy with which his productions were regarded by his countrymen.

Although this is the only circumstantial account which has reached us of Homer's adventures and condition, it is little to be relied on. It agrees in two respects with the other accounts concerning him—that he had been a great traveller, and that he was afflicted with blindness. The particulars of the latter however are mere conjectures. The character of his compositions seem rather to suppose him all eye, than destitute of sight; and if they were even framed during his blindness, they form a glorious proof of the vivid power of the imagination, more than supplying the want of the bodily organs; and not merely throwing a variety of its own tints over the objects of nature, but presenting them to the mind in a clearer light than could be shed on them by one whose powers of immediate vision were perfectiy free from blemishes. He therefore removed to Cumæ where he received great applause but no reward, the people alleging that they could not think of maintaining all the "Ομηροι, blind men," and from this repulse he obtained the name of Homer. Baffled again, he travelled to Phocæa, where Thestorides, a schoolmaster, promised to support him, on condition of being allowed to transcribe his poems; which being granted, this new friend took them away to Chios, and gained universal applause by producing them. Hearing of this, however, he resolved to lay claim to his own compositions, and, for that purpose set out for Chios, but before he met with Thestorides, he was found by Glaucus, a shepherd and introduced by him to his master at Balissus, who employed him in the education of his children. As his fame increased while he remained in this situation, his piratical foe took flight, and left him in possession of the field. On this he left his employment and went to Chios, where he acquired considerable wealth by his poems; married, and had two daughters, one of whom died young, and the other was married to the person in whose family he had recently been a teacher. He determined however to proceed to Athens; but the vessel was detained during

prosecute his voyage, but was seized with sickness, died, and was buried on the sea-shore.

The similes of Homer are another proof of the copiousness of his genius. They frequently contain the most beautiful pictures of noble objects. Even when most prolix they show the intensity of his feeling, which would not allow him to touch on anything, incidentally, or anything grand or lovely, without waiting to revel in its charms. Occasionally too, they relieve the heart by diverting an interest which becomes oppressive, and by pouring delight on the fancy, takes away the sting from a tragical catastrophe; while they render our pity gentler, and our sympathy of a gentler description. We see Sarpedon struck through the thigh, borne off the field, the long spear trailing from the wound, and there is too much haste to draw it out. Hector flies past him and has no time to speak; all is dust, hurry, and confusion. Even Hector can only pause for a moment; but in three lines, he lays the wounded hero under a tree; he brings a dear friend to his side, and we refresh ourselves in a beautiful scene when the lance is taken out and Sarpedon faints, and comes slowly back to life with the cool air fanning him Thus Pope has beautifully translated it :—

> " He said: both javelins at an instant flew ;
> Both struck, both wounded ; but Sarpedon's slew:
> Full in the boasters neck the weapon stood,
> Transfix'd his throat, and drank the vital blood;
> The soul disdainful seeks the caves of night,
> And his scal'd eyes for ever lose the light.
>   Yet not in vain, Hepolemus, was thrown
> Thy angry lance ; which piercing to the bone
> Sarpedon's thigh, had robb'd the chief of breath;
> But Jove was present, and forbade the death.
> Borne from the conflict by his Lycian throng,
> The wounded hero dragg'd the lance along.
> (His friends, each busied in his several part,
> Through haste, or danger, had not drawn the dart.)
> The Greeks with slain Hipolemus retir'd ;
> Whose fall Ulysses view'd, with fury fir'd;
> Doubtful if Jove's great son he should pursue,
> Or pour his vengeance on the Lycian crew,
> But heaven and fate the first design withstand
> Nor this great death must grace Ulysses' hand.
> Minerva drives him on the Lycian train,
> Alastor, Cromius, Halius, strew'd the plain,

Alexander, Prytanis, Noemon fell:
And numbers more his sword had sent to hell,
But Hector saw ; and furious at the sight,
Rush'd terrible amidst the ranks of fight,
With joy Sarpedon view'd the wish'd relief,
And faint, lamenting, thus implored the chief :
    Oh suffer not the foe to bear away
My helpless corpse, an unassisted prey ;
If I, unblessed, must see my son no more,
My much-loved consort, and my native shore
Yet let me die in Ilion's sacred wall ;
Troy, in whose cause I fell, shall mourn my fall
    He said ; nor Hector to the chief replies,
But shakes his plume, and fierce to combat flies ;
Swift as a whirlwind, drives the scattering foes,
And dies the ground with purple as he goes.
    Beneath a beech, Jove's consecrated shade,
His mournful friends divine Sarpedon laid :
Brave Pelagon, his fav'rite chief was nigh,
Who wrenched the javelin from his sinewy thigh.
The fainting soul stood ready wing'd for flight,
And o'er his eye-balls swam the shades of night
But Boreas rising fresh, with gentle breath,
Recall'd his spirit from the gates of death."

                              (ILIAD Book V. 1 814.)

Again in that fearful death wrestle at the Grecian wall, when gates and battlements are sprinkled over with blood, and neither Greeks nor Trojans can force their way against the other, we have first an image of the fight itself, two men in the field, with measuring rods, disputing over a land boundary ; and for the equipoise of the two armies, the softest of all home scenes, a poor working woman weighing out her wool before weaving it, to earn a scanty subsistence for herself and children. Pope's translation of this passage may be read amongst the illustrations at the end of the book. The same astonishing similes are to be found in other places. In the magnificent scene, where Achilles weary with slaughter, pauses on the bank of the Scamander, and the angry river God, whose cause is checked by the bodies of the slain, swells up to revenge them, the natural and the supernatural are marvellously blended.

Again in the eighteenth Iliad, the poet describes two cities, embodying in their condition two ideas—Peace and War. In one the terrors of a siege ; the hostile armies glitter under the walls ; the women and children press into the defence and crowd to the battlements. In the first city a quarrel rises, and wrong is made right, not by violence and fresh wrong, but by the majesty .of law and order. Under the walls of the other an ambush lies, like a wild beast on the watch for its prey. The unsuspecting herdsmen pass on with their flocks to the waterside,. the spoilers spring from their hiding places and all is strife, and death, and horror, and confusion.

There is a touchingly beautiful passage in the seventeenth Odyssey, describing the return of Ulysses—where his old dog Argus acknow-edges his master, after an absence of twenty years, and dies with joy.

> " Thus, near the gate conferring as they drew,
> Argus, the dog, his ancient master knew ;
> He, not unconscious of the voice and tread,
> Lifts to the sound his ear and rears his head ;
> Bred by Ulysses, nourish'd at his board,
> But, ah ! not fated long to please his lord !
> To him his swiftness and his strength were vain ;
> The voice of glory call'd him o'er the main.
> Till then in every sylvan chase renown'd,
> With Argus, Argus rung the woods around ;
> With him the youth pursued the goat or fawn,
> Or trac'd the mazy leveret o'er the lawn.
> Now left to man's ingratitude he lay.
> Unhous'd, neglected in the public way ;
> And where on heaps the rich manure was spread,
> Obscene with reptiles, took his sordid bed
>   He knew his lord ; he knew, and strove to meet ;
> In vain he strove. to crawl, and kiss his feet,
> Yet (all he could) his tail, his ears, his eyes,
> Salute his master and confess his joys.
> Soft pity touch'd the mighty master's soul ;
> Adown his cheek a tear unbidden stole.
> Stole unperceiv'd ; he turn'd his head and dry'd
> The drop humane : then thus impassion'd cry'd
>   What noble beast in this abandon'd state
> Lies here all helpless at Ulysses' gate ?
> His bulk and beauty speak no vulgar praise :
> If, as he seem, he was in better days,
> Some care his age deserves ; or was he priz'd
> For worthless beauty ? therefore now despis'd ;
> Such dogs and men there are, mere things of state

And always cherish'd by their friends the great.
  Not Argus so, (Eumæus thus rejoined,)
But serv'd a master of a nobler kind,
Who never, never shall behold him more !
Long, long since perish'd on a distant shore !
Oh, had you seen him, vigorous, bold, and young,
Swift as a stag, and as a lion strong :
Him no fell savage on the plain withstood,
None scap'd him bosom'd in the gloomy wood ;
His eye how piercing, and his scent how true,
To wind the vapour in the tainted dew ?
Such when Ulysses left his natal coast,
Now years unnerve him, and his lord is lost !
The women keep the generous creature bare,
A sleek and idle race is all their care :
The master gone, the servants what restrains ?
Or dwells humanity where riot reigns ?
Jove fix'd it certain, that whatever day
Makes man a slave, takes half his worth away.
This said, the honest herdsman strode before ;
The musing monarch pauses at the door :
The dog, whom Fate had granted to behold
His lord, when twenty tedious years had roll'd,
Takes a last look, and, having seen him, dies ;
So clos'd for ever faithful Argus' eyes !

We might quote many more of these poetical masterpieces—the description of the chiefs by Helen, the single combat of Paris and Menelaus, and of Ajax and Hector—the loves of Paris and Helen—the meeting of Glacius and Diomed between the armies, and the renewal of their old friendship—the journey of Prian to recover the body of his best beloved son, which is admirably conceived and touchingly described—the brilliant description of the death of Hector ; the pathetic lamentation of Helen over the body of Hector, in which she declares that while others have reviled her, he had never given her one unkind word or upbraiding—and perhaps superior to all the rest, the battle in which the immortals join, superior to any battle ever depicted in verse, in grandeur, and richness of colouring.

HESIOD.—The next great poet after Homer, whose works have reached us, is Hesiod. Fortunately, Hesiod has given an account of his own life in his *Work and Days*, and from that we learn that he was born in Ascra, a village in Bæotia, at the foot of Mount

Helicon. From this he derived the name of Ascræus, by which he
is often called in the classical writers. He is the representative of
the Bæotian school of poetry, as Homer is of the Ionic, but the
two, except in respect to the dialect, are entirely different. Homer
takes for his subjects the restless activity of the heroic age, while
Hesiod turns his attention to the quiet pursuits of ordinary life,
rural occupation, and the gods and heroes. The two principal
works of Hesiod, which have come down to us, are his *Works and
Days*, containing ethical, political, and economical precepts ; and
a *Theogony* or a generation of the Gods, giving an account of the
generation of the world. The great excellence of Hesiod, consists
in his natural and simple style ; though in his delineations he
displays a daring and ardent conception, which is not afraid to
grasp the mightiest things. Take, for instance, the following
passage, translated by Broome :—

> "Then Jove omnipotent display'd the God,
> And all Olympus trembled as he trod :
> He grasps ten thousand thunders in his hand,
> Bares his red arm, and wields the forky brand ;
> Then aims the bolts, and bids his lightnings play ;
> They flash, and rend through heaven their flaming way :
> Redoubling blow on blow, in wrath he moves ;
> The sing'd earth groans, and burns with all her groves ;
> The floods, the billows, boiling hiss with fires,
> And bickering flame, and smouldering smoke aspires :
> A night of clouds blots out the golden day ;
> Full in their eyes the writhen lightnings play :
> Ev'n chaos burns : again earth groans, heaven roars,
> As tumbling downward with its shining towers ;
> Or burst this earth, torn from her central place,
> With dire disruption from her deepest base :
> Nor slept the wind : the wind new horror forms,
> Clouds rush on clouds before th' outrageous storms,
> While, tearing up the sands, in drifts they rise,
> And half the desert mount th' encumber'd skies :
> At once the tempest bellows, lightnings fly,
> The thunders roar, and clouds involve the sky :
> Stupendous were the deeds of heavenly might ;
> What less, when Gods conflicting cope in fight."

The *Theogony* is also a valuable history of the Pagan mythology ;
it is no doubt the most accurate account of the deities of Greece.
It has been imitated by Milton, in his *Battle of the Angels*, but

certainly not exceeded. Though Hesiod, however, will be always interesting to lovers of antiquity, as exhibiting an accurate picture of simple manners, and will be admired by the lover of poetry for a few passages of rugged sublimity ; he possesses none of those charms of story or of character, which can render a translation of his works, however extended, popular amongst the unlearned. A further extract from the *Theogony* will be found among the " Select Translations."

ALCÆUS.—The next poet of whom we have any authentic information, was Alcæus, the first of the Æolian lyric poets and inventor of the well-known Alcaic metre. Our knowledge of his character is chiefly to be derived from the excellent imitations of his poems bequeathed to us by Horace ; while our estimation of his genius may be gathered from the extant fragments of his poems. Those which have received the highest praise are his warlike odes, in which he endeavoured to raise the spirits of the nobles, the *Alcæi minaces Carminæ* of Horace. Alcæus is said to have paid his addresses to Sappho, another great leader of the Æolian school.

SAPPHO.—Our knowledge of Sappho is gathered principally from the ancient writers, all of whom agree in expressing the most unbounded admiration for her poetry. She was the second of the two great leaders of the Æolian school. Her lyrics formed nine books, but of these only fragments have come down to us. The most important is a splendid ode to Aphrodite (Venus), a translation of which will be found at the end of the book.

ANACREON.—The next poet of importance that we know anything of is the Greek lyric poet Anacreon. It is generally admitted that he was born at Teos, an Ionian city, in Asia Minor. Only a few of his poems have come down to us, in all of which he celebrates the praises of love and wine. Many of them are singularly beautiful and elegant, and have obtained great popularity in modern times ; perhaps, however, this is indebted to the admirable English translations that have been made, of which Moore's is the most elegant. Several are reserved for quotation later on.

PINDAR.—Pindar, a famous lyric poet of Thebes, is celebrated chiefly for his Odes, of which there are four books extant. They are entitled the *Epinicia*—triumphal odes—and are called respectively Olympian, Pythean, Nemean, and Isthmian. His other works, of which there are a few extant, are enmumerated in our "Compendium." Pindar studied music and poetry under Myrtis and Corinna, and is said to have first gained fame by winning a prize over the former poet; but the beauty of Corinna is said to have proved so attractive to the judges that she gained the prize five times successively. · Pindar, however, speedily became famous, and acted as poet-laureate to the states throughout Greece.

ÆSCHYLUS.—This brings us to Æschylus, one of the most famous tragic Grecian poets. His mind very easily received an impulse from the poetry of Homer, to which he was enthusiastically devoted. He improved the stage, which was then in a very rude state ; he elevated the language of tragedy, and exchanged recitation for dialogue. Force, grandeur, and sublimity are the characteristics of his works, and for energy of style and sentiment, he may vie with the greatest dramatic writers of any age.

The later Greek poets, whose works are more or less known, but who are too numerous to be detailed at length in this stage of our work, we reserve for mention in the "Compendium." In most cases their works, or some material traces of them have reach us, and in all such cases they will be found carefully cited in Notes systematically arranged for the better accommodation of space. Some will be found among these of whom little or no particulars are given, as no really reliable information is to be gathered of them, while in cases such as those of Agatho, said to be contemporary with Socrates, Carcinus, to whom a few trifling lines are attributed, Dicæogenes, mentioned by Suidas, Nichocharis (or Michochares) a comic poet said to be comtemporary with Aristophanes, Phormis, Polyides, Zenarchus, Sosistratus, Pauson, &c., beyond this nominal mention, we omit altogether, although many such might be gathered from the writings of Diodorus Siculus, Aristotle, Quintilian, Victorius, and later, Dacier, Bayle, &c.

CHAPTER IV.

THE EARLY ROMAN POETS.

PLAUTUS.—Plautus, although not the earliest, was the first Latin cômic poet of any importance. The first in point of chronology was Livius Andronicius a writer of several *Tragedies* and *Comedies*, but which were, however, obsolete in Cicero's time. The *Plays* of Plautùs, which are twenty in number, were adaptations from the Greek, and became very popular, and they are even now admired. They were represented with great applause on the Roman stage for about five hundred years.

TERENCE.—Terence, the next inportant poet, was chiefly celebrated for his *Comedies*, which are mostly adaptations of the Greek poet Menander. He is said to have written as many as a hundred and eight, though of these only six remain. The style of the latter is very elegant, and the sentiments delicate; Quintilian pronounced him the most elegant and refined of all the Latin writers. His first play *Andrea* got referred to Caecilius, at that time one of the most popular play-writers in Rome. Unknown, and meanly clad, Terence began reading from a low stool his opening scene. A few verses showed the elder poet that no ordinary writer stood before him, and the young aspirant, then in his twenty-seventh year, was invited to share the couch and supper of his judge. The *Andrea*, which was perfo rmed two years later, was successful, and, aided by the accomplishments and good addresses of Terence himself, was the means of introducing him to the *élité* of Rome.

ENNIUS.—Ennius is represented as the father of Latin poetry, and is thus characterized by Ovid:

" Ennius ingenio maximus, arte rudis."

but, except for a few fragments, all his works are lost. He wrote *Tragedies, Comedies, Epigrams* and *Satiers*; but his most important work was an epic poem in dactylic hexameters, called *Annates*, being a history of Rome from the earliest times to his own day. We learn that he was patronized by Scipio Africanus and other

Romans of distinction, and that he maintained himself by teach·ing the youths of the Roman nobles. His style was necessarily rough, from the period in which he lived, but he is warmly commended by Quintilian, and Virgil has incorporated many of his lines without change.

LUCRETIUS.—The next Latin poet and philosopher was Lucretius. His celebrated poem *De Rerum Natura* was written during the intervals of reason, which alleviated an insanity to which he was subject. It is in heroic hexameters, and is divided into six books. It forms the first account of the Epicurean philosophy, and the atheistical doctrine of atoms or materialism, and gives a striking example of the great freedom with which opinions contradictory to the established religion were at that time maintained. No writer has more pointedly controverted the popular notions of heathenism. The *De Rerum Natura* has been admitted by all modern critics to be the greatest of didactic poems. Though the language and versification partake of the rudeness of an early period of literature, yet no poet has exhibited in his works greater sublimity, or more elevated sentiment. The most abstruse speculations are clearly explained in majestic verse.

CATULLUS.—The compositions of this poet consist chiefly of *Epigrams*, which though elegant are tinctured with licentiousness, and disfigured by indelicacies. He satirized Cæsar, whose only revenge was to entertain him sumptuously. He was intimate with the great men of his age, and was the first to imitate with success the Greek writers, and introduce their rhythms.

MARTIAL.—This poet was also highly distinguished as an epigrammatist about the same period. He was a native of Spain, though of Roman descent. In his twenty-first year he went to Rome to study the law, but he afterwards appears to have neglected his profession to cultivate his talent for poetry, through which he secured the favour of the Flavian Emperors, Domitian in particular. His fourteen books of *Epigrams* sparkle with witticisms, and display great power of imagination but many of them are debased with coarseness and impurity of thought and expression.

Contemporary with him, we may mention Valerius Flaccus, author of an unfinished heroic poem in eight books, on the subject of the argonautic expedition. It is highly spoken of by Quintilian. The eighth book was completed by an Italian named Pius.

POLLIO.—This Roman poet was also contemporary with Virgil, The fourth and eighth *Eclogues* of Virgil are addressed to him. He was a patron of Virgil, Horace, and other great poets, and it is said he was the first person to establish a public library at Rome. Unfortunately, all his works have perished in the lapse of ages, but there can be no doubt as to the merit of them, as his name has been classed with the greatest poets of his age, His works were *Tragedies*, *Orations*, and a *History*. Virgil and Horace speak in high terms of his *Tragedies*, though no subsequent writer has mentioned them.

HORACE.—This brings us to Horace, the most celebrated of the Roman lyric poets. His poems are distinguished from all other writers of his time for their sweetness of rhythm and elegance of diction. They consist of four books of *Odes*, one of *Epodes*, two of *Epistles*, two of *Satires*, a *Carmen Seculare*, and an *Ars Poetica*. In his *Odes* he has successfully imitated Pindar and Anacreon ; his *Satires* and *Epistles*--full of wit and satirical humour, but with little poetry, and of a simple unadorned style--differ little from prose ; and his *Art of Poetry* displays much taste and judgment and neatly expresses, in Latin hexameters, the precepts delivered in the Greek prose of Aristotle. The Epicurian system of philosophy forms the theme of nearly all his poems, but not luxurious revelry, so much as a homely fare and refined enjoyment.

A book of verses underneath the bough,
A jug of wine, a loaf of bread—and thou
Beside me singing in the wilderness—
Oh, wilderness were Paradise enow !

These are the delights of which Horace loved to sing, and of which nearly all his poems are characteristic no less than for their intrinsic beauty and grace. He describes the banquet, but he loves the farm ; and while others seek costly wines which can transmute "life's leaden metal into gold," the cheap vintage of Samnium is for the poet a "sovereign alchemist." Wealth, anxiously sought, and avariciously kept or profligately squandered, he dispised ; he saw that contentment was the secret of happiness and peace. We may select the ode *To Dellius* as a happy illustration of the original and of our modern version ; the lines will be familar to many.

> " Let not the frowns of fate
>   Disquiet thee, my friend,
> Nor when she smiles on thee, do thou, elate
>   With vaunting thoughts, ascend
> Beyond the limits of becoming mirth,
> For, Dellius, thou must die, become a clod of earth !
>
> Whether thy days go down
>   In gloom, and dull regrets,
> Or, shunning life's vain struggle for renown,
>   Its fevers and its frets,
> Stretched on the grass, with old Falernian wine,
> Thou giv'st the thoughtless hours a rapture all divine.
>
> Where the tall spreading pine
>   And white-leaved poplar grow,
> And mingling their broad boughs in leafy twine,
>   A grateful shadow throw,
> Where down its broken bed the wimpling stream.
> Writhes on its envious way with many a quivering-gleam.
>
> There wine, there perfumes bring,
>   Bring garlands of the rose,
> Fair and too short-lived daughter of the spring,
>   While youth's bright current flows
> Within thy veins,—ere yet hath come the hour
> When the dread sisters three shall clutch thee in their power.
>
> Thy woods, thy treasured pride,
>   Thy mansion's pleasant seat,
> Thy lawns, washed by the Tiber's yellow tide,
>   Each favourite retreat,
> Thou must leave all—all, and thine heir shall run
> In riot through the wealth thy years of toil have won.
>
> It seeks not whether thou
>   Be opulent, and trace
> Thy birth from Kings, or bear upon thy brow
>   Stamp of a beggar's race ;
> In rags or splendour, death at thee alike,
> That no compassion hath for aught of earth, will strike.
>
> One road, and to one bourne
>   We all are goaded. Late
> Or soon will issue from the urn
>   Of unrelenting Fate;
> The lot that in yon bark exiles us all
> To undiscovered shores, from which is no recall."

playful skill. His preceptive piece, the "Epistle to the Pisos" or "Art of Poetry" though desultory and immethodical, displays much good sense and taste. It has been agreed that it was not intended for a complete theory of the poetic art, but has been conjectured that it was intended to dissuade one of the younger Pisos from devoting himself to poetry for which he had little genius; or at least to suggest the difficulties of attaining to perfection. Crusius says, "Horace is peculiarly the poet for apt and elegant quotations; even the variety of his humour and unfixedness of his philosophy tend to increase his attraction in this respect, by allowing him to occasionally moralise in the lofty manner of the Stoics ; and at other times to indulge in the lighter strain of the Epicurean school, to which his genius and practice were probably more naturally conformable." *

In sentiment and thought, there is nothing more extraordinary or excellent than in his contemporaries ; but his language is inimitable, and I doubt whether the most learned critic of the Augustan age, allowing him the best taste as well as judgment, could have mended a single expression in any of the Odes, or even have changed one word for a better. This is what Petronius calls the *curiosa felicitas* of Horace, which two words are as happily joined together as *simplex munditus,* and these four words are perhaps

* Crusius' Lives of Rom. Poet s.

G

sufficent to characterize the poet, and express the beauty of his style in his own manner. It is almost impossible to read the first stanza in the *Carmen Seculare* without falling into a fit of devotion. Likewise those beautiful odes *Donec gratus eram* &c., and *Quem tu, Melpomene* &c., of which Scaliger once said he would rather be the author than the King of *Arragon*.

It is impossible in translations to see the great beauty of the Odes of Horace. They are beautiful beyond description. Even where he has imitated Pindar in the beginning of that Ode,

Quem virum aut Heroa, &c.,

he has evidently excelled him; but they never were, nor never can be translated so as to display the beauties of the original, which wholly consist in the language and expression. Still, Cowper's and other translations may be read with pleasure by those who are unacquainted with the Latin language. For example,—

> SEEST thou yon mountain laden with deep snow,
> The groves beneath their fleecy burden bow,
>   The streams, congeal'd, forget to flow,
> Come, thaw the cold, and lay a cheerful pile
>   Of fuel on the hearth;
> Broach the best cask, and make old winter smile
>   With seasonable mirth.
>
> This be our part,—let Heaven dispose the rest
>   If Jove command, the winds shall sleep,
>   That now wage war upon the foamy deep,
> And gentle gales spring from the balmy west.
>   E'en let us shift to-morrow as we may,
>   When to-morrow's pass'd away,
>   We at least shall have to say,
>   We have lived another day,
> Your auburn locks will soon be silver'd o'er,
> Old age is at our heels, and youth returns no more.
>   Book 1. Ode IX.

> AND is this all! Can Reason do no more
> Than bid me shun the deep, and dread the shore!
> Sweet moralist! afloat on life's rough sea,
> The Christian has an art unknown to thee:
> He holds no parley with unmanly fears;
> Where Duty bids he confidently steers,
> Faces a thousand dangers at her call,
> And, trusting in his God, surmounts them all.
>   Book 2. Ode XVI.

Augustus and Maecenas had conceived for him. Among other short stories he has left us two which are not more diverting than they are instructive, the *Ibam forte via sacra*, and the account of *Philippus* and the Crier.*

The Epistle to Augustus commences with great art and elegance of expression. The public character which he has drawn of that prince in four or five short sentences, a modern dedicator would easily spin out in forty or fifty pages ; while the praises given to the Emperor at the end of this epistle are equally as elegant and refined.

> *Cum tot sustineas, et tanta negotia solus,*
> *Res Italas bello tuteris, moribus ornes,*
> *Legibus emendes :* in publica commoda peccem,
> Si longo sermone morer tua tempora CÆSAR.

PROPERTIUS.—Propertius is the next Roman poet after Tibullus, of whom we hear anything. He was very intimate with Tibullus and with Ovid, with whom he was contemporary. He began to write poetry at a very early age, and the merit of his productions attracted the atention, and obtained the patronage of Maecenas and Gallus. He is one of the principal of the elegiac poets. Though inferior to Tibullus in tenderness, and to Ovid in variety, his works exhibit more learning. He certainly gave the first specimen of

* Epist. 7. B. I

the poetical epistle, which Ovid is said to have afterwards claimed as his own invention.

OVID.—This renowned Roman poet was born in the year B.C. 43. He was destined for the law, but his love for poetry led him to desert that profession. After living for many years at Rome and enjoying the favour of Augustus, he was suddenly banished by the Emperor to Tomi a town on the Euxine, near the mouth of the Danube. The general conjecture of his banishment was his licentious poem on the Art of Love (_Ars Amatoria_) which had been published nearly ten years previously, but the true cause of his exile is unknown. It is supposed by some that he had been guilty of an intrigue with the younger Julia, the grand-daughter of the Emperor Augustus, who was banished in the same year with Ovid. The poet seems in the following lines to plainly intimate that it was owing to something which he had inadvertently seen, and not to any crime :—

> " _Cur aliquid vidi ? Cur noxia lumina feci ?_
> _Cur imprudenti cognita culpa mihi ?_
> _Juscius Actæon vidit sine veste Dianam ;_
> _Præda fuit canibus non minus ille suis_
> _Scilicet in superis etiam_ fortuna luenda est _:_
> _Nec veniam læso numine casus habet._"

Ovid draws an affecting picture of the miseries to which he was exposed in his place of exile. He sought some relief in the exercise of his poetical talents, and wrote many of his poems during his exile.

In the earlier period of his life, Ovid was one in a circle of the best and most learned poets of the Augustan age. He is loved and admired for the elegance of his wit, and the sweetness of his manners. Even his imperfections are pleasing, and we can excuse all his faults on account of his many excellencies, particularly in his descriptions, which have never been equalled. As much as I reverence Virgil, and admire Horace, as Roman poets; so I love Ovid. The Georgics of Virgil is perhaps the most finished poem of all that are now extant in any language ; but neither of these great poets knew how to move the passions like Ovid. Take for example, his Metamorphoses, particularly the history of _Ceyx_ and

poet of the Augustan age. The fault generally imputed to him is, that his fancy is too luxuriant. This he would probably have corrected if he had had the liberty of reviewing his Metamorphoses.

"Emendaturus, si licuisset, erat."

The Metamorphoses consists of such legends or fables as involved a transformation, from the Creation to the time of Julius Cæsar, the last being that Emperor's change into a star.

The *Fasti*, which is a sort of poetical calendar, is undoubtedly one of the most important works which have come down to us. It contains in the comparatively short space of some five thousand verses, a summary of the religion, the history, and civil institutions of Rome, from its foundation to the death of Augustus. It is no doubt incomplete, for Ovid says in his *Tristia* that he threw on the fire when going into exile, his Metamorphoses *and other writings*, ('sicut bene multa meorum'); that as they still exist, he supposes several copies of them must have been taken; but that they are confusedly imperfect:--

"Nec tamen illa legi poterunt patienter ab ullo,
Nesciet his summam si quis abesse manum,
Ablatum mediis opus est incudibus istud,
Defuit et scriptus ultima lima meis."

The *Fasti* may be regarded as a repertory of the Italian traditions, many of which modern philology has enabled us to distinguish from or compare with the Greek in a more perfect manner, and with greater certainty than either the author himself or the contemporary Romans could do. In spite of the hackneyed assertion that Roman literature is nothing but a bad copy of the Greek, it may safely be maintained that there is a very large admixture of genuine Italian sentiments, and yet more of genuine Italian mythology in the Roman poets, which is often indeed disguised, but seldom wholly obscured by Greek imagery. This is especially

true of Ovid and Virgil. In the literature of every nation ther
must of necessity be much which is strictly original ; for ever
nation has a history and heroes of its own, even when neither it
laws nor its religious observances are peculiar to it. The Roman
borrowed or rather adapted from the Greeks because it was th
fashion of the age. They were not so much dependent on them fo
intellectual resources, as willing to accept an excellence they coul
not hope to surpass. It would be as unfair to argue that nothing trul
Italian remained to the Romans, as it would be to infer from cer
tain French manners and habits imported from Normandy, tha
the old Celtic and Anglo-Saxon traditions had perished fron
England. And it is to these national customs and traditions tha
Ovid carries us back—to the primitive pastoral worship, and th
simple life of the wild mountaineers of Italy. It will of course b
urged that the legends recorded by Ovid are either pure inventions
or totally devoid of authority as traditions. But it is very easy t
carry our distrust of traditions too far. Tradition does not alway
lie, even in very minute matters. A thoughtful person will hav
little difficulty in making out some plausible truth, even from th
wildest and most ancient legends. For instance ; who would doub
that the fall of a meteoric stone is the origin of the strange stor
of the *Ancile III.* 873 ? Or that *Delos* 'the appearing island,' fa
bled to have once floated, and to have been fixed by Apollo, ros
from the bed of the ocean ? Yet the immense antiquity of th
event is unquestionable. The island existed in Homer's time
These, however, are matters of little importance; not so the earl
history of Rome. And for this we owe much to the *Fasti* of Ovid
There is reason to believe that he took much pains with it as i
national work. He calls himself "Latinorum dierum vate
operosus"* and in the *Tristia* he appears to allude to the *Fasti* ii
these lines :—

attire ; we impress the Palatine bay and oak on our coins, (*Lib IV.* 943); we place afflicted persons in abodes named after the 'Asylum' of Romulus ; and we call our money after the temple of Juno Moneta. We still keep the ancient feast of the *Floralia* in our May-day revelries ; the *Ambarvalia* in 'beating the Parish bounds;' and we still retain orders of knight-hood, borrowed from the Equites of the old Republic.

Here then without doubt lies the immense importance of the Latin language and Roman literature, and of such works as the *Fasti*.

I have prefixed to this chapter a few of the choicest translations from Dryden and Cowper, for the interest of those who are unacquainted with the Latin tongue, which may be read with interest:

PYTHAGOREAN PHILOSOPHY.

For I will sing of mighty mysteries,
Of truths conceal'd before from human eyes ;
Dark oracles unveil, and open all the skies.
Pleas'd as I am to walk along the sphere,
Of shining stars, and travel with the year ;
To leave the heavy earth, and scale the height
Of Atlas, who supports the heav'nly weight ;
To look from upper light, and thence survey
Mistaken mortals wand'ring from the way,
And wanting wisdom, fearful for the state
Of future things, and trembling at their fate.
                                        DRYDEN.

CEYX AND ALCYONE.

But ah ! be warn'd to shun the wat'ry way,
The face is frightful of the stormy sea,
Too late I saw adrift disjointed planks,
And empty tombs erected on the banks.
Nor let false hopes to trust betray thy mind,
Because my sire in caves constrains the wind,
Can with a breath a clam'rous rage appease,
They fear his whistle, and forsake the seas ;
Not so, for once indulg'd, they sweep the main :
Deaf to the call, or hearing, hear in vain ;
But bent on mischief bear the waves before,
And not content with seas, insult the shore ;
When ocean, air, and earth, at once engage,
And rooted forests fly before their rage ;
At once the clashing clouds to battle move,
And lightnings run across the fields above :
I know them well, and mark'd their rude comport,
While yet a child, within my father's court
In times of tempest they command alone,
And he but sits precarious on the throne.

DRYDEN.

METAMORPHOSES.

In this confusion while their work they ply,
The winds augment the winter of the sky,
And wage intestine wars, the suff'ring seas
Are toss'd, and mingled as their tyrants please.
The master would command, but, in despair
Of safety, stands amaz'd with stupid care,
Nor what to bid, or what forbid, he knows,
Th' ungovern'd tempest to such fury grows ;
Vain is his force, and vainer is his skill ;
With such a concourse comes the flood of ill ;
The cries of men are mix'd with rattling shrouds,
Seas dash on seas, and clouds encounter clouds ;
At once from east to west, from pole to pole,
The forky lightenings flash, the roaring thunders roll.

DRYDEN.

While smoothly wafted on a calmer sea.
But can a wretch like Ovid pant for fame?
No, rather let the world forget my name."

COWPER.

BAUCIS AND PHILEMON.

The fire thus form'd, she sets the kettle on,
(Like burnish'd gold the seether shone,)
Next took the coleworts which her husband got
From his own ground (a small well-water'd spot,)
She stripp'd the stalks of all their leaves; the best
She cull'd, and then with handy care she dress'd.
High o'er the hearth a chine of bacon hung ;
Good old Philemon seiz'd it with a prong,
And from the sooty rafter drew it down,
Then cut a slice, but scarce enough for one :
Yet a large portion of a little store,
Which for their sakes alone he wish'd were more.
This in the pot he plung'd without delay,
To tame the flesh, and drain the salt away.
The time between, before the fire they sat.
And shorten'd the delay by plea   chat.

LUCAN.—The poet Lucan was born at Corduba in Spain, in the
year B.C .37. His father was a brother of Seneca the philosopher
The *Pharasalia*, (an unfinished poem in ten books) has occa-
sional faults of harshness, and extraordinary description, yet it will
ever rank among the leading productions of the Latin muse, by its
moral sublimity, and noble spirit of freedom.   The narrative of the
tenth book, which is imperfect, breaks off abruptly in the middle of
the Alexandrian war.   The *Pharasalia* relates the struggle in the

H

civil war between Cæsar and Pompey. Lucan gave proof of his poetical talents at a very early age, and thereby excited the jealousy of Nero, whose passion it was, to be regarded as the first poet of the age. He was afterwards treated by the angry emperor with so much indignity, that he took part in the conspiracy of Piso against that execrable tyrant. On the discovery of the plot he was arrested with the. other conspirators, and condemned to die. Being allowed to make choice as to the manner of his death, he choose that which terminated the life of his uncle Seneca. His veins were accordingly opened in a hot bath, and when he found himself growing faint and cold with the loss of blood, he repeated some of his own verses, describing a wounded soldier sinking in a similar manner.

VIRGIL—We now turn with pleasure from these more obscure poets to Virgil, the greatest of the Roman poets. This poet's writings prove that he received a learned education; and traces of Epicurean opinions are apparent in them. After completing his education, Virgil appears to have retired to his father's farm at Andes, and here he may have written some of the small pieces which are attributed to him. In the division of land among the soldiers after the battle of Philippi (42) Virgil was deprived of his property; but it was afterwards restored at the command of Octavian. It is supposed that Virgil wrote the Eclogue which stands first in our editions to commemorate his gratitude to Octavian. Soon after this, Virgil probably became acquainted with Maecenas as he is not mentioned in the Eclogues. The *Georgica*, his most finished work, was undertaken at the suggestion of Maecenas (*Georg : III.* 41.) The *Æneid* was probably long contemplated by the poet. While Augustus was in Spain (27), he wrote to Virgil expressing a wish to have some monument of his poetical talent, and this appears to have been the time when he commenced the Æneid. Virgil had the friendship of all the most accomplished

that venality and corruption by which the first Cæsar overturned the liberties of his country, and fixed his usurpation. There are two passages, one in the sixth and the other in the eighth book of the Æneid, which sufficiently show this :—

"*Venditi hic auro patriam, dominumque potentem Imposuit.*"

Virgil probably in this passage alludes to Curio, who sold Rome to Julius Cæsar, and was the principal cause of the ruin of the commonwealth. But whether he alludes to Curio or not, he certainly avows his own principles by placing in the most horrible regions of his poetical hell, the man who sells his country and erects it into a tyranny. The other passage is in the eighth book :—

"*Secretosque pios: his dantem jura Catonem.*"

It is a noble encomium on Cato, for the poet does not only assign to Cato the first seat in the happy abodes, but he places him at the head of all the other blessed spirits as their guide and director. He certainly designed this for a republican and patriotic spirit, for one who had been a constant and steady friend to virtue and his country.

If not possessed of the mighty inventive genius of Homer or Æschylus, Virgil was beyond all others in the true perception of elegance, in the unaffected love of his subject, and in the exquisite finish and sublimity of his episodes. In the delineation of character, Virgil certainly does not anywhere approach Homer. All Homer's characters are human, and therefore interest by their successes and misfortunes. And in this Virgil fails. With the exception of Dido and perhaps of Turnus in his latest hour, he has scarcely introduced into the Æneid a person who either imposes by the grand, or interests by the amiable features of his character. Æneas is worse than insipid—he disgusts by his fears, his shiverings, and his human sacrifices; and in his interview with Helen while Troy was on fire, he is below contempt. *Amata*, however, is Virgil's crime ; he had invested Dido with grandeur, he might have made her lovely; and as he had excited our admiration for the Tyrian queen, he might have drawn our tears for the daughter of Latinus. Certainly Homer's women are preferable to Virgil's.

The magic of exquisite poetry is perhaps nowhere more conspicuous than in the description of Dido's silent and indignant scorn of Æneas in the Stygian regions, and her return to Sichæus. Stripped of the charm, with which it is invested by the poet, the scene is ludicrous, but as Virgil relates it, it rises to sublimity. If the whole adventure on the Tyrian shore had been told by an ordinary poet, the widower and the widow would always have been in view and been comic. Yet there is no part of Homer, which we read with more pleasure than we read the second, fourth, and fifth books of Virgil. The story of Nisus and Euryalus is exquisite, nor is it exceeded by the night adventure of Ulysses and Diomedes in which we hear every step and feel every breath.

Homer's language is uniformly idiomatic; Virgil's occasionally too highly polished. The poem of *Lucretius*, and the hexameter of Catullus, and the epistles of *Horace* have more of the true raciness of the Latin soil than Virgil. But Virgil is the true example of epic poetry. The love, despair, and death of Dido, and the parting scene between old Evander and his son, which are sublime in their descriptions, may be found amongst the illustrations at the end of the book.

The similes of Virgil are mostly obvious, such as would have occurred to the reader without the poet's aid. The murmuring crowd, like the murmuring gusts ; the struggling armies, like the struggling winds ; warriors like wild animals or monsters; one man against a host, like a rock against waves ; and so forth. In all these cases it is not the selection of the simile that can be admired in Virgil, as in the expression and workmanship, and the beauty of the language. In Virgil the details are worked out independently, to relieve the epic narrative, and form a picture by itself ; but the comparison is usually limited to a single point, and that common-place.

The modern use of the simile is quite different. There are indeed many passages in the modern poets where the simile is worked out after the Virgilian method, but then these are cases of imitation. If however we open Shelley, we read,

> "The golden gates of sleep unbar
> When strength and beauty, met together,
> Kindle their image *like a star*
> *In a sea of glassy weather.*"

Here there is nothing obvious in the comparison : we should never have thought, without the aid of the poet's superb imagination of comparing the union of love, to a star mirrored in the smooth sea : Or again,

> "Life, *like a dome of many coloured glass*
> *Stains the white radiance of Eternity,*
> Until Death tramples it to fragments."

Here again the comparison is not at all obvious ; it is fetched from far by the poet's deeper insight and quicker sensibility : and it is splendidly illustrative all through : the bright colours compar-ed with the pure white light, resemble the chequered shifting, imperfect beauties of life; compared with the changeless perfection of eternity : the narrow limited dome, and the endless vault of heaven giving another equally deep contrast : and lastly, the per-ishable glass contrasted with the eternal spaces of the universe.

Virgil aims at something widely different in his similes to this : for in order to appreciate his true poetry, it is necessary to under-stand his object and so avoid the mistake of judging him by an erroneous standard. Virgil is a poet of the artificial kind. His aim was not to express his thoughts in the simplest and most direct way—on the contrary. He employs "an elaboration of language which disdains or is unable to say, a plain thing in a plain way," but his works are full of melody, dignity, imagin-

ation, and skill. Prefixed to this chapter as illustrations, **are a few**
of the choicest passages form Dryden's translations of this Poet.

VIRGIL—EIGHTH PASTORAL.

"I know thee, Love ; in deserts thou wert bred,
And at the dugs of savage tigers fed :
Alien of birth, usurper of the plains ;
Begin with me, my flute, the sweet Mœnalian strains.

Relentless love the cruel mother led
The blood of her unhappy babes to shed ;
Love lent the sword ; the mother struck the blow ;
Inhuman she ; but more inhuman thou."

GEORGICS.

"Ye swains, invoke the pow'rs who rule the sky,
For a moist summer, and a winter dry :
For winter drought rewards the peasant's pain,
And broods indulgent on the buried grain.
When first the soil receives the fruitful seed.
Make no delay, but cover it with speed :
So fenc'd from cold, the pliant furrows break,
Before the surly clod resists the rake :
And call the floods from high, to rush amain
With pregnant streams, to swell the teeming grain.
Then when the fiery suns too fiercely play,
And shrivell'd herbs on with'ring stems decay,
The wary ploughman, on the mountain's brow,
Undams his wat'ry stores, huge torrents flow,
And, rattling down the rocks, large moisture yield.
Temp'ring the thirsty fever of the field."

"Ev'n when the farmer, now secure of fear,
Sends in the swains to spoil the finish'd year ;
Ev'n while the reaper fills his greedy hands,
And binds the golden sheaves in brittle bands :
Oft have I seen a sudden storm arise,
From all the warring winds that sweep the skies ;
The heavy harvest from the root is torn,
And whirl'd aloft the lighter stubble borne ;
With such a force the flying rock is driv'n
And such a winter wears the face of heav'n.
And oft old sheets descend of sluicy rain,
Suck'd by the spongy clouds from off the main ;
The lofty skies at once come pouring down,
The promis'd crop and golden labours drown,
The dykes are fill'd and with a roaring sound
The rising rivers float the nether ground;
And rocks the bellowing voice of rising seas abound,

At length her fury fell, her foaming ceas'd,
And, ebbing in her soul, the god decreas'd.
Then thus the chief: No terror to my view,
No frightful face of danger can be new;
Inur'd to suffer, and resolv'd to dare.
The fates, without my pow'r, shall be without my care,

Thus having said, she sinks beneath the ground
With furious haste, and shoots the Stygian sound,
To rouse Alecto from th' infernal seat
Of her dire sisters, and their dark retreat.
This fury, fit for her intent, she choose;
One who delights in wars and human woes.
Ev'n Plato hates his own misshapen race:
Her sister furies fly her hideous face:
So frightful are the forms the monster takes,
So fierce the hissings of her speckled snakes.

Grim Cerberus, who soon began to rear,
His crested snakes, and arm'd his bristling hair.
The prudent sibyl had before prepar'd
A sop, in honey steep'd, to charm the guard.
Which, mix'd with pow'rful drugs, she cast before
His greedy, grinning jaws, just op'd to roar:
With three enormous mouths he gapes, and straight,
With hunger press'd, devours the pleasing bait.
Long draughts of sleep his monstrous limbs enslave;
He reels, and falling fills the spacious cave.
The keeper charm'd, the chief without delay
Pass'd on, and took th' irremeable way.

She wrench'd the jav'lin with her dying hands :
But wedg'd within her breast the weapon stands ;
The wood she draws, the steely point remains,
She staggers in her seat, with agonizing pains ;
A gath'ring mist o'er clouds her cheerful eyes,
And from her cheeks, the rosy colour flies.
Then turns to her, whom, of her female train,
She trusted most, and thus she speaks with pain.
Acca, 'tis past, he swims before my sight
Inexorable death, and claims his right.

Bear my last words to Turnus, fly with speed,
And bid him timely to my charge succeed, .
Repel the Trojans, and the town relieve ;
Farewell ; and in this kiss my parting breath receive
She said, and sliding, sunk upon the plain ;
Dying, her open'd hand forsakes the rein ;
Short, and more short, she pants ; by slow degrees
Her mind the passage from her body frees.
She drops her sword, she nods her pluming crest
Her drooping head declining on her breast ;
In the last sigh her struggling soul expires,
And murm'ring with disdain, to Stygian sounds retires,

Weak as I am, can I, alas ! contend
In arms with that inexorable fiend ?
Now, now, I quit the field ! forbear to fight
My tender soul, ye baleful birds of night !
The lashing of your wings I know too well :
The sounding flight, and fun'ral screams of hell !
These are the gifts you bring from haughty Jove,
The worthy recompence of ravish'd love !
Did he for this exempt my life from fate ?
O hard conditions of immortal state !
Though born to death, nor priveleg'd to die,
But forc'd to bear impos'd eternity !
Take back your envious bribes, and let me go,
Companion to my brot
The joys are vanish'd : nothing now remains
Of life immortal, but immortal pains.
What earth will open her devouring womb,
To rest a weary goddess in the tomb !

CHAPTER V.

DANTE.

DANTE.--The cities of Italy contend as eagerly for the honour
of this great poet's work, as those of Greece once did for that of
Homer's nativity. His great poem the *Divina Commedia,* contains

Dante may be thought to his great prototype, it is with
· pleasure we peruse the following lines, which show that the
Mantua after the long lapse of ages of tasteless ignorance,
nd a reader who could admire and rival his beauties. Art
·gil? he asks, on his first presenting himself to his view :—

> "Oh degli altri poeti onore e lume
> Vagliami 'l lungo studio, e'l grande amore,
> Che m'han fatto cercar lo tuo volume.
> Tu se 'lo mio maestro, e'l mio autore ;
> Tu se solo colui, du cu' io tolsi
> Lo bello stile, che m'ha fatto onore."

> "Glory and light of all the tuneful train !
> May it avail me, that I long with zeal
> Have sought thy volume, and with love immense
> Have conn'd it o'er. My master thou, and guide !
> Thou he from whom alone I have derived
> That style, which for its beauty into fame
> Exalts me."

ais matters little, Milton might have originally sought the
hint of his great work from a similar source. In the words
e himself,

> "Poca favilla gran fiamma seconda."
> *Il Paradiso. Can* 1.

> "————From a small spark
> Great flame hath risen."—CARY.

want the true origin of Dante's sublime work, we may find
own words—" I found the ORIGINAL OF MY HELL in the
which we inhabit." And this principle seems illustrated in
;reat poets : we find that every great genius is influenced
bjects and the feelings which occupy his own times, only

ıe, pathetic, and animated; and passages of the most exquisite
ness. The genius of man never produced a more pathetic
than that contained in the 33rd canto of this work, the
ɔf Count Ugolino and his children.

has displayed in this story more true poetry than in the best
fictions. The poet wandering through the depths of hell,
ʍo of the damned knawing the skulls of each other, which
heir daily food. He inquires the meaning of this dreadful

.

> " O tu che mostri per si bestial segno
> Odio sovra colui che tu ti mangi;
> Dimmi 'l perche, diss'is per tal convegno:
>   Che se tu a ragion di lui ti piangi,
> Sappiendo chi voi siete e la sua pecca,
> Nel mondò suso ancor io te ne cangi;
> Se quella, con ch'io parlo, non si secca.";
>
> " O thou ! who show'st so beastly sign of hate
> 'Gainst him thou prey'st on, let me hear," said I
>   "The cause, on such condition, that if right
> Warrant my grievance, knowing who ye are,
> And what the colour of his sinning was,
> I may repay thee in the world above,
> If that, wherewith I speak, be moist so long."

ɔlino, quitting his companion's half-devoured skull, begins his
ɔ this effect. "We are Ugolino, count of Pisa, and archbishop
.eri. Trusting in the perfidious counsels of Ruggieri, I was
ht to a miserable death. I was committed with four of my
en to the dungeon of hunger. The time came when we

suddenly up, exclaimed. " O father, our grief would be less if you would eat us !"

> " Ambo le mani per dolor mi morsi :
> E quei pensando ch'io 'l fessi per voglia.
> Di manicar di subito levorsi
> E disser, *Padre, assai ci fia men doglia.*
> Se tu mangi di noi !——"

" I restrained myself that I might not make them more miserable. We were all silent, that day and the following. Ah, cruel earth, why did'st thou not swallow us up at once ?"

> " Quel di, et l'altro, stemmo tutti muti,
> Ahi ! dura terra, perche non l' apristi ? "

" The fourth day being come, Gaddo falling all along at my feet, cried out, ' *My father, why do you not help me,*' and died. The other three expired one after the other, between the fifth and sixth days, famished as you see me now. And I, being seized with blindness began to crawl over them *sovra ciascuno,* on hands and feet ; and for three days after they were dead, continued calling them by their names. At length, famine finished my torments." Having said this the poet adds, 'with distorted eyes he again fixes his teeth on the mangled skull.' Cary has beautifully translated this passage in the following language :—

> " His jaws uplifting from their fell repast,
> That sinner wiped them on the hairs o'the head,
> Which he behind had mangled then began :
> "Thy will obeying, I call up afresh
> Sorrow past cure ; which, but to think of, wrings
> My heart, or ere I tell on't. But if words,
> That I may utter, shall prove seed to bear
> Fruit of eternal infamy to him,
> The traitor whom I gnaw at, thou at once
> Shall see me speak and weep. Who thou mayst be

I know not. nor how here below art come:
But Florentine thou seemest of a truth,
When I do hear thee. Know, I was on earth
Count Ugolino, and the Archbishop he
Ruggieri. Why I neighbour him so close,
Now list. That through effect of his ill thoughts
In him my trust reposing, I was ta'en
And after murder'd, need is not I tell.
What therefore thou canst not have heard, that is,
How cruel was the murder, shalt thou hear,
And know if he have wrong'd me. A small grate
Within that mew, which for my sake the name
Of famine bears, where others yet must pine,
Already through its opening several moons
Had shown me, when I slept the evil sleep
That from the future tore the curtain off.
This one, methought, as master of the sport,
Rode forth to chase the gaunt wolf, and his whelps,
Unto the mountain which forbids the sight
Of Lucca to the Pisan. With lean brachs
Inquisitive and keen, before him ranged
Lanfranchi with Sismondi and Gualandi.
After short course the father and the sons
Seem'd tired and lagging, and methought I saw
The sharp tusks gore their sides. When I awoke,
Before the dawn, amid their sleep I heard
My sons (for they were with me) weep and ask
For bread. Right cruel art thou. if no pang
Thou feel at thinking what my heart foretold ;
And if not now, why use thy tears to flow?
Now had they waken'd ; and the hour drew near
When they were wont to bring us food ; the mind
Of each misgave him through his dream, and I
Heard, at its outlet underneath lock'd up
The horrible tower: whence, uttering not a word
I look'd upon the visage of my sons.
I wept not : so all stone I felt within.
They wept : and one, my little Anselm, cried,
'Thou looke~t so ! Father, what ails thee ?' Yet
I shed no tear, nor answer'd all that day
Nor the next night, until another sun
Came out upon the world. When a faint beam
Had to our doleful prison made its way,
And in four countenances I descried
The image of my own, on either hand
Through agony I bit ; And they, who thought
I did it through desire of feeding, rose
O' the sudden, and cried, 'Father, we should grieve
'Far less, if thou wouldst eat of us: thou gavest
'These weeds of miserable flesh we wear ;
'And do you strip them off from us again.'

Whence I betook me, now grown blind, to grope
Over them all, and for three days aloud
Call'd on them who were dead. Then, fasting got
The mastery of grief." Thus having spoke,
Once more upon the wretched skull his teeth
He fasten'd like a mastiff's 'gainst the bone,
Firm and unyielding. Oh, thou Pisa ! shame
Of all the people, who their dwelling make
In that fair region, where the Italian voice
Is heard ; since that thy neighbours are so slack
To punish, from their deep foundations rise
Capraia and Gorgona, and dam up
The mouth of Arno ; that each soul in thee
May perish in the waters. What if fame
Reported that thy castles were betray'd
By Ugolino, yet no right hadst thou
To stretch his children on the rack. For them,
Brigata, Uguccione, and the pair
Of gentle ones, of whom my song hath told.
Their tender years, thou modern Thebes, did make
Uncapable of guilt."

The conception of the *Divina Commedia* is framed on a scale
of magnificence, and the parts so wonderfully developed, that
Dante ranks among the few minds to whom the power to a great
creative faculty can fairly be ascribed. The Divine Comedy is
a personal narrative, Dante is the eye-witness and ear-witness
of that which he relates. He is the very man who has heard
the tormented spirits crying out for the second death, who has
read the dusky characters on the portals within which there is
no hope. As Macaulay finely remarks, "His own hands have
grasped the shaggy sides of Lucifer, his own feet have climbed
the mountains of expiation; his own brow has been marked by
the purifying angel. The distinguishing character of Dante is his
intensity of feeling. The melancholy of Dante was no fastidious
caprice, it was not the effect of external circumstances, it was

from within. It turned every consolation and every pleasure into its own nature. His mind was, in the noble language of the Hebrew poet, 'a land of darkness, as darkness itself, and where the light was as darkness.' The gloom of his character discolours all the passages of men, and all the face of nature, and tinges with its own livid hue, the flowers of Paradise and the glories of the eternal throne."* At the commencement of this work Dante is bewildered in an unfrequented forest ; he attempts to climb a mountain, whose summit is illuminated by the rising sun.

> "In the midway of this our mortal life,
> I found me in a gloomy wood, astray,
> Gone from the path direct: and e'en to tell,
> It were no easy task, how savage wild
> That forest, how robust and rough its growth,
> Which to remember only, my dismay
> Renews, in bitterness not far from death.
> Yet, to discourse of what there good befel,
> All else will I relate discovered there.
> How first I enter'd it I scarce can say,
> Such sleepy dulness in that instant weigh'd
> My senses down, when the true path I left ;
> But when a mountain's foot I reach'd, where closed
> The valley that had pierced my heart with dread,
> I look'd aloft, and saw his shoulders broad
> Already vested with that planet's beam,
> Who leads all wanderers safe through every way."

A furious leopard, pressed by hunger, and a lion at whose appearance, the *air is affrighted*, accompanied by a she-wolf oppose his progress; and force him to fly precipitately into the profundities of a pathless valley, where the *sun was silent*. ("Mi ripingeva la dove'l Sol tace.")

> "The hour was morning's prime, and on his way
> Aloft the sun ascended with those stars,
> That with him rose, when Love divine first moved
> Those its fair works: so that with joyous hope
> All things conspired to fill me, the gay skin
> Of that swift animal, the matin dawn,
> And the sweet season. Soon that joy was chased,
> And by new dread succeeded, when in view
> A lion came, 'gainst me as it appear'd,
> With his head held aloft and hunger-mad,
> That e'en the air was fear-struck. A she-wolf

---

* Macaulay's Essays.

Dinanzi agli occhi mi si fu offerto
Chi per lungo silenzio parea fioco.
   Quand' i' vidi costui nel gran diserto:
Miserere di me, gridai a lui,
Qual che tu sii od ombra, od uomo certo."

   "While to the lower space with backward step
I fell, my ken discern'd the form of one.
Whose voice seemed faint through long disuse of speech
When him in that great desert I espied,
"Have mercy on me." cried I out aloud
"Spirit ! or living man ! whate'er thou be."

The spectre hastens to his cries: it was the shade of Virgil whom
Beatrice, Dante's mistress had sent, to give him courage, and to
guide him into the legends of hell. Virgil begins a long discourse
with Dante: and expostulates with him for choosing to wander
through the rough obscurities of a barren and dreary vale, when
the top of a neighbouring mountain afforded every delight.

   Ma tu, perche ritorni a tanta noia ?
Perche non sali il dilettoso monte,
Ch 'e principio e cagion di tutta gioa ?

   " But thou. say wherefore to such perils past
Return'st thou ? wherefore not this pleasant mount
Ascendest, cause and source of all delight ? "

The conversation of Virgil and the name of Beatrice, by degrees
dissipate the fears of the poet, who explains his situation. He
returns to himself, and compares this revival of his strength and
spirits to a flower smitten by the frost of night, which again lifts its
shrinking head, and expands its vivid colours, at the first gleam-
ings of the morning sun.

> "Quale i foretti dal notturno gielo
> Chinatie chiusi, poi che'l Sol gl' imbianca,
> Li drizzan tutti aperti in loro stelo;
> Tal mi fcc'io di mia virtude stanca."

> "As florets, by the frosty air of night
> Bent down and closed, when day had blanch'd their leaves
> Rise all unfolded on their spiry stems;
> So was my fainting vigour new restored,—"

This poem abounds in comparisons of this kind. In *Canto XXIV* of the *Inferno*, in the passage where Virgil is angry with Dante, but is soon reconciled; the poet compares himself to a cottager in the early part of a promising spring, who looks out in the morning from his humble shed, and sees the fields covered with a severe and unexpected frost. But the sun soon melts the ground, and he drives his goats afield.

> "In the year's early nonage, when the sun
> Tempers his tresses in Aquarius' urn,
> And now towards equal day the nights recede;
> When as the rime upon the earth puts on
> Her dazzling sister's image, but not long
> Her milder sway endures; then riseth up
> The village hind, whom fails his wintry store,
> And looking out beholds the plain around
> All whiten'd; whence impatiently he smites
> His thighs, and to his hut returning in,
> There paces to and fro, wailing his lot,
> As a discomfited and helpless man;
> Then comes he forth again, and feels new hope
> Spring in his bosom, finding e'en thus soon
> The world had changed its countenance, grasps his crook
> And forth to pasture drives his little flock:
> So me my guide dishearten'd, when I saw
> His troubled forehead; and so speedily
> That ill was cured; for at the fallen bridge
> Arriving, towards me with a look as sweet,
> He turn'd him back, as that I first beheld
> At the steep mountain's foot."

Dante, therefore, under the conduct of Virgil penetrates hell. He describes his hell to be a prodigious and almost bottomless abyss, which from its aperture to its lowest depth preserves a rotund shape: or rather an immense perpendicular cavern, which opening as it descends into different circles, forms so many distinct subterranean regions. We are struck with horror at the commencement of this dreadful adventure.

> "Through me you pass into the city of woe :
> Through me you pass into eternal pain :
> Through me among the people lost for aye.
> Justice the founder of my fabric moved :
> To rear me was the task of power divine,
> Supremest wisdom, and primval love.
> Before me things create were none, save things
> Eternal, and eternal I endure.
> All hope abandon, ye who enter here. "

Milton evidently remembered this passage of Dante, and the exclusion of hope from hell in the passage where he describes,

> " Regions of sorrow, doleful shades, where peace
> And rest can never dwell, *Hope never comes*
> *That comes to all.*" (*Par. L.*, *I.* 65,)

Then follows numerous, dialogues and adventures with spirits, which he meets in the course of his infernal journey; wherein the reader may see much of the politics and facts of the times at which Dante lived.

The short comparison by Virgil of the souls lingering on the banks of Lethe, to the numerous leaves falling from the trees in autumn, Dante has beautifully enlarged.

K

" Come d' Autumno si levan le foglie
L'un appresso del' altra, infin che'l ramo
Vede a la terre tutte le sue, spoglie ;
Similmente, il mal seme d' Adamo
Gette si di quel lits ad una ad una
Per cenni, com 'augel per suo richiamo."

" As fall off the light autumnal leaves,
One still another following, till the bough
Strews all its honours on the earth beneath ;
E'en in like manner Adam's evil brood
Cast themselves, one by one, down from the shore,
Each at a beck, as falcon at his call."

Milton also employs this comparison in his Paradise Lost.

"Thick as autumnal leaves, that strew the brooks
In Vallombrosa, where th' Etrurian shades,
High over-arched in bower." (*Book I.* 304.)

Among many other of his friends, Dante sees **Francisca**, the daughter of Guido di Polento ; and Paulo one of the sons of Malatesta Lord of Rimini. This lady fell in love with Paulo ; the passion was mutual, and she was betrothed to him in marriage : but her family chose rather that she should be married to Lanciotto, Paulo's eldest brother. This match had the most fatal consequences. The injured lovers could not dissemble or stifle their affection: they were surprised, and both assassinated by Lanciotto. Dante finds the shades of these distinguished victims of an unfortunate attachment at a distance from the rest, in a region of his *Inferno* desolated by the most violent tempests.

"Into a place I came
Where light was silent all. Bellowing there **groan'd**
A noise, as of a sea in tempest torn
By warring winds. The stormy blast of hell
With restless fury drives the spirits on,
Whirl'd round and dash'd amain with sore annoy
When they arrive before the ruinous sweep,
There shrieks are heard, their lamentations **moans**,
And blasphemies 'gainst the good Power in heaven.
I understood, that to this torment sad
The carnal sinners are condemn'd, in whom
Reason by lust is sway'd. As in large troops
And multitudinous, when winter reigns,
The starlings on their wings are borne abroad ;
So bears the tryannous gust those evil souls.
On this side and on that, above, below,

It drives them : hope of rest to solace them
Is none, nor e'en of milder pang. As cranes,
Chanting their dolorous notes, traverse the sky,
Stretch'd out in long array ; so I beheld
Spirits, who came loud wailing, hurried on
By their dire doom."

Dante accosts them both, and Frascisca relates their history. Yet the ·conversation is carried on with some difficulty, on account of the impetuosity of the storm which was perpetually raging.

" Of whatsoe'er to hear or to discourse
It pleases thee, that will we hear, of that
Freely with thee discourse, while e'er the wind,
As now is mute."

Dante, who from many circumstances of his own amours, appeared to have possessed the most refined sensibilities, about the delicacies of love, enquires in what manner when in the other world they first communicated their passion to each other.

" Francesca ! your sad fate
Even to tears my grief and pity moves.
But tell me; in the time of your sweet sighs,
By what, and how Love granted, that ye knew
Your yet uncertain wishes?"

Francesca answers, that they were one day sitting together, and reading the romance of *Lancelot* ; where two lovers are represented in the same critical situation with themselves. Their changes of colour and countenance, while they were reading, often tacitly betrayed their yet undiscovered feelings.

'Noi leggevamo un giorno per diletto
'Di *Lancilotto*, comme amor lo strinse;
Soli eravamo, et senza alcun sospetto.
Per piu fiate gli occhi ci sospinse
Quella lettura et scolorocci il viso :"

"One day,
For our delight we read of Lancelot,
How him love thrall'd. Alone we were, and no
Suspicion near us. Oft-times by that reading
Our eyes were drawn, together, and the hue
Fled from our alter'd cheek."

When they came to that passage in the Romance, where the lovers after many tender aproaches, are gradually drawn by one uniform reciprocation of involuntary attraction to kiss each other, the book dropped from their hands.

> "Ma solo un punto fu quel che ci vinse.
>   Quando leggemmo il disiato riso
> Esser baciato da cotanto amante,
> Questi, che mai da me non fia diviso,
>   La bocca mi bacio tremante:
> Galeotto fu il libro e chi lo scrisse:
> Quel giorno piu non vi leggemmo avante, "

>   "But at one point,
> Alone we fell.   When of that smile we read,
> The wished smile, so rupturously kiss'd
> By one so deep in love, then he, who ne'er
> From me shall separate, at once my lips
> All trembling kiss'd.   The book and writer both
> Were love's purveyors.   In its leaves that day
> We read no more."

While they are wandering along the banks of Phlegethon, as the twilight of evening approaches, Dante suddenly hears the sound of a horn more loud than thunder.

> "Noi demmo 'l dosso al misero vallone
> Su per la ripa, che'l cinge dintorno,
> Attraversando senza alcun sermone.
>   Quivi era men che notte emen che gioino,
> Si che'l viso m'andava innanzi poco:
> Ma io senti' sonare un alto corno
>   Tanto, che avrebbe ogni tuon fatto fioco."

> "Turning our back upon the vale of woe,
> We cross'd the encircled mound in silence.   There
> Was less than day and less than night, that far
> Mine eye advanced not : but I heard a horn
> Sounded so loud, the peal it rang had made
> The thunder feeble.   Following its course
> The adverse way, my strained eyes were bent
> On that spot.   So terrible a blast
> Orlando blew not, when that dismal rout
> O'erthrew the host of Charlemain, and quench'd
> His saintly warfare."

Dante descries through the gloom, what he thinks to be many high and vast towers, (*molte alte torri.*) These are the giants who warred against heaven, standing in a row, half concealed within and half visible out of an immense abyss or pit.

> "Poco portai in la volta la testa,
> Che mi parve veder molte alte torri ;
> Ond 'io : Maestro di,' che terra e questa ?

"Yet know," said he, "ere farther we advance,
That it less strange may seem, these are not towers,
But giants. In the pit they stand immersed,
Each from his navel downward, round the bank."

One of them cries out to Dante with a horrible voice.

"Comincio a gridar la fiera bocca,
Cui non si convenien pui dolce salmi."

"So shouted his fierce lips, which sweeter hymns
Became not :"

Another is clothed in iron and covered with huge chains.

"Facemmo adunque piu lungo viaggio,
Volti a sinistra : ed al trar d'un balestro
Trovammo l'altro, assai pui fiero e maggio.
A cinger lui, qual che fosse il maestro,
Non so io dir : ma ci tenea succinto
Dinanzi l'altro, e dietro 'l braccio destra,
D'una catena che'l tenea avvinto
Dal collo in giu si che'n su lo scoperto
Si ravvolgeva infino al giro quinto.".

"Then to the leftward turning sped we forth,
And at a sling's throw found another shade
Far fiercer and more huge. I cannot say
What master hand had girt him ; but he held
Behind the right arm fetter'd, and before,

> The other, with a chain, that fasten'd him
> From the neck down ; and five times round his form
> Apparent met the wreathed links."

Dante wishes to see Briareus, he is answered that he is in an inner cavern biting his chains.

> "S'esser puote, i 'vorrei
> Che dello smisurato Briareo
> Esperienza avesser gli occhi miei.
> Ond'ei rispose : Tu vedrai Anteo
> Presso di que, cha parla, ed e disciolto;
> Che ne porra nel fondo d'ogni reo.
> Quel, che tu vuoi veder, piu la e molto ;
> Ed e legato, e fatto come questo ;
> Salvo che piu feroce par nel volto."

> "Fain would I, if 'twere possible, mine eyes,
> Of Briareus immeasurable, gain'd
> Experience next." He answer'd : "Thou shalt see
> Not far from hence Antæus, who both speaks
> And is unfetter'd, who shall place us there
> Where guilt is at its depth. Far onward stands
> Whom thou wouldst fain behold, in chains, and made
> Like to this spirit, save that in his looks
> More fell he seems."

Immediately Ephialtes arose from another cavern, and shook himself like an earthquake.

> "Non tu tremnoto mai tanto rubesto,
> Che scotesse una torre cosi forte,
> Come Fialte a scuotersi fu presto."

> "By violent earthquake rock'd
> Ne'er shook a tower, so reeling to its base,
> As Ephialtes."

Dante then views the horn which had sounded so vehemently, hanging by a leather thong from the neck of one of the giants. Antaeus, whose body stands ten ells high from the pit, is commanded by Virgil to advance.

> "Noi procedemmo piu avanti alotta,
> E venimmo ad Anteo, che ben cinqu alle,
> Senza la testa, uscia fuor della grotta."

> "————————We, straightway journeying on
> Came to Antæus, who, five ells complete
> Without the head, forth issued from the cave."

They both mount on his shoulders and are thus carried about Cocytus.

One of the torments of the damned in Dante's *Inferno*, is the punishment of being eternally confined in lakes of ice. The ice is described to be like that of the Danube or Tanais. This species of infernal torment, which is neither directly warranted by scripture nor suggested in the systems of the Platonic fabulists has its origin in the legendary hell of the monks. Both Shakespeare and Milton have adopted it. Warton says, "the hint seems to have been taken from the Book of Job dilated by St. Jerome and the early commentators. *"Drought and heat consume the snow waters: so doth the grave those which have sinned."* The torments of hell, in which the punishment by cold is painted at large had formed a visionary romance, under the name of St. Patrick's Purgatory or Cave, long before Dante wrote."

"Per ch 'io mi volsi, e vidimi davante
E sotto i piedi un lago, che per gielo
Avea di vetro, e non d'acqua, sembiante.
Non fece al corso suo si grosso velo
Di verno la Danoia in Austericch,

Ne il Tanai la sotto lo freddo cielo.
  Com 'era qufvi : che se Tabernicch
Vi fosse su caduto, o Pietrapana,
Non avria piu dall 'orlo fatto cricch.
  E come a gracidar si sta la rana
Col muse fuor dell 'acqua, quando sogna
Di spigolar sovente la villana,
  Livide insin la dove appar vergogna; .
Eran l'ombre dolenti nella ghiaccia,
Mettendo i denti in nota di cicogna.
  Ognuna in giu tenea volta la faccia :
Da bocca 'l freddo, e dagli occhi 'l cuor triato
Tra lor testimonianza si procaccia."

          "Thereupon I turn'd,
And saw beneath and underneath my feet
A lake, whose frozen surface liker seem'd
To glass than water.   Not so thick a veil
In water e'er hath Austrian Danube spread
O'er his still course, nor Tanais far remote
Under the chilling sky.   Roll'd o'er that mass
Had Tabernich or Pietrapana fallen
Not e'en its rim had creak'd.   As peeps the frog
Croaking above the wave, what time in dreams
The village gleaner oft pursues her toil,
So, to where modest shame appears, thus low
Blue pinch'd and shrined in ice the spirits stood,
Moving their teeth in shrill note like the stork.
His face each downward held ; their mouth the cold
Their eyes express'd the dolour of their heart."

In some passages the guilty are made objects of contempt by a transformation into beastly or ridiculous shapes.   In others, the human figure is rendered ridiculous by distortion.

    "   Io era gia disposto tutto quanto
A risguardar nello scoverto fondo,
Che si bagnava d'angoscioso pianto :
    E vidi gente per lo vallon tondo
Venir. tacendo e lagrimando, al passo
Che fanno le letane in questo mondo."

          "Earnest I look'd
Into the depth, that open'd to my view,
Moisten'd with tears of anguish, and beheld
A tribe, that came along the hollow vale.
In silence weeping : such their step as walk
Quires, chanting solemn litanies, on earth."

  *   *   *   *
    "Mira c'ha fatto petto delle spalle :
Perche volle veder troppo davante,
Dirietro guarda, e fa ritroso calle."

Perche'l veder dinanzi era lor tolto.
　　Forse per forza gia di parlasia
Si travolse cosi alcun del tutto ;
Ma io nol vidi, ne credo che sia."

"As on them more direct mine eye descends,
Each wonderously seem'd to be reversed
At the neck-bone, so that the countenance
Was from the reins averted , and because
None might before him look, they were compell'd
To advance with backward gait. Thus one perhaps
Hath been by force of palsy clean transposed,
But I ne'er saw it nor believe it so. "

Dante's *Purgatory* is not on the whole less fantastic than his
Hell. As his hell was a vast perpendicular cavity in the earth, he
supposes Purgatory to be a cylindric mass elevated to a prodigious
height.   At intervals are recesses projecting from the outside of the
cylinder. In these recesses, some higher and some lower, the wick-
ed expiate their crimes, according to the proportion of their guilt.
From one department they pass to another by steps of stone ex-
ceedingly steep.   On the top of the whole, or the summit of
Purgatory, is a platform adorned with trees and vegetables of every
kind.

"Come la scala tutta sotto noi
Fu corsa, e fummo in su 'l grado superno,
In me ficco Virgilio gli occhi suoi,
　　E disse: Il temporal fuoco e l'eterno
Veduto hai, figlio ; e se' venuto in parte,
Ov'io per me piu oltre non discerno.
　　Tratto t'ho qui con ingegno e con arte :
Lo tuo piacare omai prendi per duce :
Fuor se' dell' erte vie, fuor se' dell' arte.

Vedi il Sol, che in la fronte ti riluce ;
Vedi l' erbetta, i fiori e gli arboscelli,
Che quella terra sol da se produce.
　Mentre che vegnon lieti gli occhi belli
Che lagrimando a te venir mi fenno,
Seder ti puoi, e puoi andar tra elli.
　Non aspettar mio dir piu, ne mio cenno:
Libero, dritto, sano e lo tuo arbitrio ;
E fallo fora non fare a suo senno:
　Per ch' io te sopra te corono e mitrio."

"　　　　　　　　When we had run
O'er all the ladder to its topmost round,
As there we stood, on me the Mantuam fix'd
His eyes, and thus he spake : "Both fires, my son,
The temporal and eternal, thou hast seen ;
And art arrived, where of itself my ken
No further reaches. I, with skill and art,
Thus far have drawn thee. Now thy pleasure take
For guide. Thou hast o'ercome the steeper way,
O'ercome the straiter. Lo ! the sun, that darts
His beam upon thy forehead : lo ! the herb,
The arborets and flowers, which of itself
This land pours forth profuse. Till those bright
With gladness come, which, weeping, made me haste
To succour thee, thou mayst or seat thee down,
Or wander where thou wilt. Expect no more
Sanction or warning voice or sign from me,
Free of thy own arbitrement to chuse,
Discreet, judicious. To distrust thy sense
Were henceforth error. I invest thee then
With crown and mitre, sovereign o'er thyself."

The first canto contains an agreeable description of the first region which he traverses after leaving Hell. The heavens are tinged with sapphire, and the star of love, or the sun, makes all the orient laugh.

"Dolce colord 'oriental zaffiro,
Che s' accoglieva nel sereno aspetto
Dell'aer puro, infino al primo giro,
　Agli occhi miei ricomincio diletto,
Tosto ch'io fuori usci 'dell' aura morta,
Che m'avea contristato gli occhi e'l petto.
　Lo bel pianeta, ch'ad amar conforta,
Faceva tutto rider l'oriente.
Velando i Pesci ch'erano in sua scorta."

"Sweet hue of eastern sapphire, that was spread
O'er the serene aspect of the pure air,
High up as the first circle, to mine eyes

Unwonted joy renew'd, soon as I scap'd
Forth from the atmosphere of deadly gloom,
That had mine eyes and bosom fill'd with grief.
The radiant planet, that to love invites,
Made all the orient laugh, and veil'd beneath
The Pisces' light, that in his escort came."

He sees a venerable sage approach.   This is, Cato of Utica, who
astonished to see a living man in the mansion of ghosts, questions
Dante and Virgil about the vision which brought them hither.

"As from this view I had desisted, straight
Turning a little towards the other pole,
There from whence now the wain had disappear'd,
I saw an old man standing by my side
Alone, so worthy of reverence in his look,
That ne'er from son to father more was owed.
Low down his beard, and mix'd with hoary white
Descended, like his locks, which, parting, fell
Upon his breast in double fold.   The beams
Of those four luminaries on his face
So brightly shone, and with such radiance clear
Deck'd it, that I beheld him as the sun.
"Say who are ye, that stemming the blind stream,
Forth from the eternal prison-house have fled?"
He spoke and moved those venerable plumes.
"Who hath conducted, or with lantern sure
Lights you emerging from the depth of night,
That makes the infernal valley ever black?
Are the firm statutes of the dread abyss
Broken, or in high heaven new laws ordain'd,
That thus, condemn'd, ye to my caves approach?"

Virgil answers : and Cato advises Virgil to wash Dante's face,
which was soiled with the smoke of Hell, and to cover his head
with one of the reeds which grew on the borders of the neighbour-
ing river.

"Not of myself I come ; a Dame from heaven
Descending, him besought me in my charge
To bring.   But since thy will implies, that more
Our true condition I unfold at large,
Mine is not to deny thee thy request.
This mortal ne'er hath seen the farthest gloom,
But erring by his folly had approach'd
So near, that little space was left to turn.
Then as before I told, I was despatch'd
To work his rescue ; and no way remain'd.
Save this which I have ta'en.   I have display'd
Before him all the regions of the bad ;

And purpose now those spirits to display,
That under thy command are purged from sin.
How I have brought him would be long to say.
From high descends the virtue, by whose aid
I to thy sight and hearing him have led.
Now may our coming please thee. In the search
Of liberty he journeys : that how dear,
They know who for her sake have life refus'd."

　　*　　*　　*　　*　　*　　*

"Then by her love we implore thee, let us pass
Through thy seven regions ; for which, best thanks
I for thy favour will to her return,
If mention there below thou not disdain."

　　*　　*　　*　　*　　*　　*

"Go therefore now : and with a slender reed
See that thou duly gird him, and his face
Lave, till all sordid stain thou wipe from thence.
For not with eye, by any cloud obscured,
Would it be seemly before him to come,
Who stands the foremost minister in heaven.
This islet all around, there far beneath,
Where the wave beats it, on the oozy bed
Produces store of reeds.   No other plant,
Cover'd with leaves, or harden'd in its stalk,
There lives, not bending to the water's sway,
After, this way return not; but the sun
Will show you, that now rises, where to take
The mountain in its easiest ascent."

Virgil takes his advice ; and having gathered one reed, sees
another spring up in its place. This is the golden bough of Virgil's
Æneid, *uno avulso non deficit alter.*

"When we had come, where yet the tender dew
Strove with the sun, and in a place where fresh
The wind breathed o'er it, while it slowly dried :
Both hands extended on the watery grass
My master placed, in graceful act and kind.
Whence I of his intent before apprized,
Stretch'd out to him my cheeks suffused with tears.
There to my visage he anew restored
That hue which the dun shades of hell conceal'd.
　Then on the solitary shore arrived,
That never sailing on its waters saw
Man that could after measure back his course,
He girt me in such manner as had pleased
Him who instructed ; and O strange to tell !
As he selected every humble plant,
Wherever one was pluck'd, another there
Resembling, straighway in its place arose,"

deliverance of a soul from Purgatory.   This is the soul of the poet
Stalius.

> "The natural thirst, ne'e r quench'd but from the well
> Whereof the woman of Samaria craved,
> Excited ; haste, along the cumber'd path,
> After my guide, impell'd ; and pity moved
> My bosom for the 'vengeful doom though just,
> When lo l even so Luke relates, that Christ
> Appear'd unto the two upon their way,
> New-risen from his vaulted grave ; to us
> A shade appear'd, and after us approach'd,
> Contemplating the crowd beneath its feet. "

Although a very improper companion for Virgil, Stalins imme-
diately joins our adventures, and accompanies them in their
progress.   It is difficult to discover what pagan or christian idea
regulates Dante's dispensation of rewards and punishments.
Stalius passes from Purgatory to Paradise, Cato remains in the
place of expiation, and Virgil is condemned to eternal torments.
In the twenty-third Canto, Dante meets with his old acquaintance
Forese, a debauchee of Florence.   On finishing the conversation,
Forese asks Dante when he shall again behold him.   This question
in Purgatory is diverting enough.

> "And as a man,
> Tired with the motion of a trotting steed,
> Slacks pace, and stays behind his company,
> Till his o'erbreathed lungs keep temperate time ;
> E'en so Forese let that holy crew
> Proceed, behind them lingering at my side,
> And saying : 'When shall I again behold thee l'"

·Dante answers with much serious gravity, " I know not the time
of death : but it cannot be too near.   Look back on the troubles
in which my country is involved."

> "How long my life may last," said I, "I know not:
> This know, how soon soever I return,
> My wishes will before me have arrived :

Sithence the place, where I am set to live,
Is, day by day, more scoop'd of all its good ;
And dismal ruin seems to threaten it. ''

Here again we see the force of Dante's Poem, as a satirical his-
tory of his own times. But these pages will not allow me more
quotations from this work than the few examples I have given.

The Paradise of Dante, the third part of this Poem, resembles
his Purgatory. Its fictions and allegories, which would only suffer
by being translated and explained are all conceived in the same
chimerical spirit. The poet successively views the glory of the
saints, of angels, of the holy Virgin, and at last of God himself.
The poet's vision ends with the Deity, and we know not by what
miraculous assistance he returned. The close of the poem is
beautifully translated by Cary, as follows :—

"As one, who from a dream awaken'd, straight,
All he hath seen forgets ; yet still retains
Impression of the feeling in his dream ;
E'en such am I : for all the vision dies,
As 't were, away ; and yet the sense of sweet,
That sprang from it, still trickles in my heart.
Thus in the sun-thaw is the snow unseal'd ;
Thus in the winds on flitting leaves was lost
The Sibyl's sentence. O eternal beam !
(Whose height what reach of mortal thought may soar?)
Yield me again some little particle
Of what thou then appearedst ; give my tongue
Power, but to leave one sparkle of thy glory,
Unto the race to come, that shall not lose
Thy triumph wholly, if thou waken aught
Of memory in me, and endure to hear
The record sound in this unequal strain.
Such keenness from the living ray I met,
That, if mine eyes had turn'd away, methinks
I had been lost ; but, so embolden'd, on
I pass'd, as I remember, till my view
Hover'd the brink of dread infinitude.
O grace, unenvying of thy boon ! that gavest
Boldness to fix so earnestly my ken
On the everlasting splendour, that I look'd,
While sight was unconsumed ; and, in that depth,
Saw in one volume clasp'd of love, whate'er
The universe unfolds ; all properties
Of substance and of accident, beheld,
Compounded, yet one individual light
The whole. And of such bond methinks I saw

The universal form ; for that whene'er
I do but speak of it, my soul dilates
Beyond her proper self : and, till I speak,
One moment seems a longer lethargy,
Than five-and-twenty ages had appear'd
To that emprize, that first made Neptune wonder
At Argo's shadow darkening on his flood.
  With fixed heed, suspense and motionless,
Wondering I gazed ; and admiration still
Was kindled as I gazed. It may not be,
That one, who looks upon that light, can turn
To other object, willingly, his view.
For all the good, that will may covet, there
Is summ'd ; and all, elsewhere defective found,
Complete. My tongue shall utter now, no more
E'en what remembrance keeps, than could the babe's
That yet is moisten'd at his mother's breast.
Not that the semblance of the living light
Was changed (that ever as at first remain'd)
But that my vision quickening, in that sole
Appearance, still new miracles descried,
And toil'd me with the change. In that abyss
Of radiance, clear and lofty, seem'd, methought,
Three orbs of triple hue, clipt in one bound :
And, from another, one reflected seem'd,
As rainbow is from rainbow : and the third
Seem'd fire, breathed equally from both. O speech !
How feeble and how faint art thou to give
Conception birth. Yet this to what I saw
Is less than little. O eternal light !
Sole in thyself that dwell'st; and of thyself
Sole understood, past, present, or to come ;
Thou smiledst, on that circling, which in thee
Seem'd as reflected splendour, while I mused ;
For I therein, methought, in its own hue
Beheld our image painted : stedfastly
I therefore pored upon the view. As one,
Who versed in geometric lore would fain
Measure the circle ; and, though pondering long
And deeply, that beginning, which he needs,
Finds not : e'en such was I, intent to scan
The novel wonder, and trace out the form.
How to the circle fitted, and therein
How placed : but the flight was not for my wing.
Had not a flash darted athwart my mind.
And, in the spleen, unfolded what it sought.
  Here vigour fail'd the towering fantasy :
But yet the will roll'd onward, like a wheel
In even motion, by the love impell'd,
That moves the sun in heaven and all the stars.'

Scarcely had this poem, we are told, seen the light, than the public mind was seen as if by a charm. Copies were multiplied, and comments written within the course of a few years. "Even chairs," we read, "with honourable stipends, were founded in Florence, Bologne, Pisa, Venice, and Piacenza; whence able professors delivered lectures on the *Divina Commedia* to an admiring audience."

We admire Dante the more when we consider what the Italian poetry was before him—merely an assemblage of rhymed phrases on love or some moral topic, without being animated by a single spark of genius. "Inspired by him whom he calls his master (Virgil), he rose to the heights of real poesy; spoke of things not within the reach of human minds; poured life into inanimate nature; and all this in a strain of language to which as yet no ear had listened." Dante laid the ground work of a better taste in poetry, and diffused throughout Italy, a spirit of rivalry. He furnishes throughout his works, examples of the age in which he lived, and which are scarcely credible in an age like ours, in which nothing retains sufficient novelty to make a strong impression.

Dante invested all the arts and literature of the age with a rich colouring; he has augmented the interest of his work by bringing forward the well-known characters of the time in which he lived, and telling their good and bad deeds without reserve.

This poet's work is entirely Gothic; nothing of classical antiquity resembles it; it is a picture of his times alone, of his own ideas and of the people about him. The terrors which Dante employs were without doubt used as the most effective means of touching upon the religion of his age. According to Ugo Foscolo, "Religion in Italy was overgrown with heresies, and schisms, which often produced the most sanguinary conflicts. Saint Francis founded his order about the beginning of the thirteenth century; and preached the faith, according to the doctrines of the church of Rome, in opposition to the sects which the Italian chronicles of that age call Valdesi, Albigesi,

Cattari, and Paterini, but more commonly by the latter name. These four sects were all in the main Manicheans. At the same time, St. Dominick arrived from Spain, carrying fire and sword wherever his opinions were disputed. It was he who founded the Inquisition ; and was himself the first *magister sacri palati*, an office always held at Rome, even in our own time, by a Dominician, who examines new books, and decides upon their publication. Before the institution of those two orders, the monks were almost all of the different rules of St. Benedict, reformed by St. Bernard and other abbots. But, being occupied in tilling the land, or in perusing manuscripts of ancient authors,—in fine, never going beyond their convents, unless to become the ministers of kingdoms, where they sometimes exercised kingly power,—their wealth, education, and even pride, rendered them unfit for the business of running from place to place, and employing hypocrisy, impudence, and cruelty, in the service of the Popes. St. Bernard, by his eloquence and rare talents, exercised great influence over kings and pontiffs. He succeeded in firing Europe to undertake the crusade ; but, to give durability to the opinions he produced, there was still wanting the pertinacity and roguery of the mendicant friars, to exhibit to the people spectacles of humility and privation, and of *auto-da-fe.* They had their convents in towns, and spread themselves over the country : whilst the Benedictines were living like the great feudal lords in their castles."

The Similes which Dante has conjured up by his genius throughout his work, though nearly always obvious to the reader are sublime in conception. We have a fine example in the first canto of the *Inferno.*

> " *E come quei che con lena affannata,*
> *Uscito fuor del pelago alla riva,*
> *Si volge all' acqua perigliosa, e guata,*"

which Cary has translated.

> "And as a man with difficult short breath
> Forespent with toiling, 'scaped from sea to shore
> Turns to the perilous wide waste, and stands
> At gaze——— ——— ——— ———————"

In this simile we are left at once in full possession of the image conjured up by the poet. The words "fuor del pelago," present to us the man, having despaired of escape, and at the very last gasp vomited up by the ocean ; and the concluding verse places him in that sort of stupor which is felt upon passing at once to safety from despair, without any intervention of hope. He looks back upon perdition with a stare, unconcious how he had escaped it. The word "guata" which ends the stanza and the sentence, presents all this to the imagination as if by magic.

Dante condenses all his thoughts and feelings in the facts he relates ; he does not stop to fill up the design with minute touches, but passes hastily on in his subject without pausing to heighten the effect. " A single word," Macauley says, "flung in apparently without design often gives its whole light and character to the picture." A passage in the third canto of the Purgatoria gives a delightful example of this—in the passage where the poet gazes with fixed eyes upon the shades as they move over the mountain. One stands still and addresses him.

> "*E un di loro incomincio: chiunque*
> *Tu se,' cosi andando volgi 'l viso,*
> *Pon mente, se di la mi vedesti unque,*
> *Io mi volsi ver lui, e guardail fiso,*
> *Bionda era, e bello, e di gentile aspetto ;*
> *Ma l'un de'cigli un colpo avea diviso*
> *Quando mi fui umilmente disdetto*
> *D'averlo visti mai, el disse: Or vedi ;*
> *E mostrommi una piaga a sommo il petto*
> *Poi* sorridendo *disse: Io son Manfredi.*"

> Then of them one began—" Who'er thou art
> Who journeyest thus this way, thy visage turn.
> Think if me elsewhere thou hast ever seen."
> I towards him turn'd, and with fix'd eyes beheld,
> Comely and fair and gentle of aspéct.
> He seem'd : but on one brow a gash was mark'd ;
> When humbly I disclaim'd to have beheld
> Him ever. "Now behold," he said ; and show'd,
> High on his breast, a wound ; then smiling, spake,
> "I am Manfredi."

Manfredi was the most powerful prince in Italy ; and fell on the field of battle in the flower of his age. It is easy to imagine what

discovering in that *smile,* his contempt of the vindictive fury of his enemies.

Dánte greatly improved the lyric poetry of Italy, though he was not the inventor of it. He mentions himself in his prose works, that "lyric composition had been introduced above a century before by Sicilian poets, into Italy ;" from which time it was gradually cultivated down to Guido Cavalcanti, the finest before Dante. The verses which celebrate Beatrice are enchanting. It is out of my powers to comment further on this great poet's works : unwearied reading, and a profound knowledge of the Italian language and of the rise and progress of Italian civilization, are requisite for illustrating the genius and the works of Dante.

It is a peculiar trait in the character of the earlier poets that they continually reveal to us in their writings their inmost feelings and dispositions of their souls. They say as it were to the reader :—

> *Tibi nunc, hortant Camœna,*
> *Executienda damus prœcordia.*

And this trait is particularly seen in many passages of Dante's works. We may see his pride and haughtiness of demeanour—for we read he was naturally proud—in the following passage in which he compares himself to his contemporaries and exhibits his feelings and superiority.

> *Sotto l'usbergo del sentirsi puro.*

> "Conscience makes me firm ;
> The boon companion, *who her strong breastplate*
> *Buckles on him that feels no quilt within*
> And bids him on, and fear not."

Yet earlier on we find this pride melt again into the softest deference and docility, when he meets with those who have claims

upon his gratitude and respect.   In conversing with the shade of
Brunetti Latini, who was damned for a shameful crime, he still
attends his master with his head bent down :—

> Il capo chino
> Tenea, com' uom che riverente vada—
> Held my head
> Bent down as one who walks in reverent guise.

The nobleness of Dante's character, is beautifully shown, and
sweetly expressed, in the passage of his entrance into Purgatory,
where he meets his friend Casella, a celebrated musician, who had
died a short time before, and whom he deeply lamented.

> "Then one I saw, darting before the rest
> With such fond ardour to embrace me, I
> To do the like was moved : O shadows vain,
> Except in outward semblance! "Thrice my hands
> I clasped behind it ; they as oft returned
> Empty into my breast again : Surprise
> I need must think, was painted in my looks,
> For that the shadow smiled and backward drew.
> To follow it I hastened, but with voice
> Of sweetness it enjoined me to desist :
> Then who it was I knew, and pray'd of it
> To talk with me it would a little pause,
> It answered, "Thee as in my mortal frame
> I loved, so loosed from it I love thee still,
> And therefore pause; but why walkest thou here."

Like Shakespeare, Dante must have desired fame.   There is
a curious passage in the Purgatorio, where describing the transi-
tory nature of literary fame, and the variableness of human opinion,
the poet alludes with confidence to his future greatness. Of two
Authors of the name of Guido, one having eclipsed the other, the
poet writes :—

> " Cose ha tolto l'mo all'altro Guido,
> La gloria della lingua; e forse e nato,
> Chi l'mo e l'altro caccera di nodo."

Dante is perhaps the poet most spoken of, and least read. He
has marvellously exhibited his feelings in his works, which so
nearly correspond with his life, and the events of the age in which
he lived, that we, as it were, have before us a narrative account

of his life and actions. We have revealed to us, his inmost feelings, but in order to obtain just views of them, his works must be read through and through. And yet the poet seems to be living away from us and our world, and we feel unable to find any correspondence in our emotions and his. Poggius relates of Dante, that "he indulged his meditations more strongly than any man he knew; whenever he read he was only alive to what was passing in his mind; to all human concerns, he was as if they had not been." The following anecdote, illustrative of the poet's meditative disposition, is related amongst D'Israeli's Literary Curiosities, "Dante went one day to a great public procession; he entered the shop of a bookseller, to be a spectator of the passing show. He found a book which greatly interested him; he devoured it in silence, and plunged into an abyss of thought. On his return, he declared that he had neither seen nor heard the slightest occurrence of the public exhibition which passed before him." This is the enthusiasm which we can see in reading this great poet's works, and which seemed to have rendered every thing which surrounded him as if an immense interval separated him from the scenes.

CHAPTER VI.

CHAUCER.

CHAUCER.—The most illustrious ornament of the reign of Edward III. and of his successor Richard II., was Chaucer; a poet with whom the history of our poetry is by many supposed to have commenced.* Johnson has pronounced him to be "the first English versifier who wrote poetically." Chaucer it is said, studied at Oxford, and that he completed his studies in the Inns of Court, and saw the reigns of Edward III., Richard II and the beginning of that of Henry IV., being born in 1328, and dying in 1400, aged 72, years. He was much in favour with Edward III., from whom he received many tokens of regard. During this reign Chaucer went to France, where he was entrusted with a mission of delicacy and importance.

* Warton's History of Eng. Poetry.

While there he obtained a great reputation by his literary exercises, and deeply impressed on his mind, the wit, the beauties, and elegancies of that highly-polished tongue. In consequence of this, we learn that he afterwards made translations from foreign languages,by which his knowledge of them became correct and as he transfused their beauties, he added to the polish of his own vernacular idiom. * He certainly entertained a mean opinion of his native language, in which he was likely to be more confirmed by his skill in French, and still more in Italian ; and from this circumstance it is doubted whether he deemed himself sufficiently qualified to undertake an original composition before his sixtieth year. From French or Latin originals, Chaucer imitated or translated his *Knights Tale*, and the *Romaunt of the Rose*.

Chaucer's poetry is essentially dramatic and picturesque—he only describes external objects as connected with character—as the symbols of internal passions. This applies in the same way to his description of natural scenery—he describes inanimate objects from the effect which they have on the mind of the spectator and as they have a reference to the interest of the story.

Richard II. reign was not so favourable to the fortunes of Chaucer ; but had he lived to see Richard IV, the son of his constant benefactor, firmly seated on the throne, he would probably have experienced the richest returns of royal favour. Leland says of Chaucer that "he was an acute dialectician, an orator full of sweetness, a pleasant poet, a deep philosopher, an ingenious mathematician, and a holy divine." And yet Chaucer is read, not as a *poet* who delights by the richness of his imagery, or the harmony of his numbers—but as a *writer*, who has portrayed with truth, the manners, customs and habits of the age in which he lived. We are told that his sole design in writing was to improve his native tongue, and attempt something for his country. Chaucer may take the first rank among our English poets, if we consider

beauty shrouded in her bowery and listening in the morning of the year to the singing of the nightingale, while her joy rises with the rising song, and gushes out afresh at every pause, and is borne along with the full tide of pleasure, and still increases and repeats and prolongs itself and knows no end. The coolness of the arbour —its retirement—the early time of the day—the sudden starting up of the birds in the neighbouring bushes—the eager delight with which they devour and rend the opening buds and flowers, are expressed with a truth of feeling which makes the whole seem like the recollection of an actual scene. Dryden has thus translated it :—

> "When Chanticleer the second watch had sung,
> Scorning the scorner sleep, from bed I sprung ;
> And dressing, by the moon. in loose array,
> Pass'd out in open air, preventing day,
> And sought a goodly grove, as fancy led my way.
> Of oaks unshorn a venerable wood :
> Fresh was the grass beneath, and ev'ry tree,
> At distance planted in a due degree,
> Their branching arms in air with equal space
> Stretch'd to their neighbours with a long embrace :
> And the new leaves on ev'ry bough were seen
> Some ruddy colour'd, some of lighter green.

The painted birds, companions of the spring,
Hopping from spray to spray, were heard to sing,
Both eyes and ears receiv'd a like delight,
Enchanting music, and a charming sight,
On Philomel I fixed my whole desire ;
And listen'd for the queen of all the choir ;
Fain would I hear her heav'nly voice to sing ;
And wanted yet an omen to the spring.

   *   *   *   *   *   *

  Thus as I mus'd, I cast aside my eye,
And saw a medlar-tree was planted nigh.
The spreading branches made a goodly show,
And full of op'ning blooms was every bough :
A goldfinch there I saw with gaudy pride
Of painted plumes, that hopp'd from side to side,
Still pecking as she pass'd : and still she drew
The sweets from ev'ry flow'r, and suck'd the dew :
Suffic'd at length, she warbled in her throat,
And tun'd her voice to many a merry note,
But indistinct, and neither sweet nor clear,
Yet such as sooth'd my soul and pleas'd my ear ;
  Her short performance was no sooner tried,
When she I sought, the nightingale, replied :
So sweet, so shrill, so variously she sung.
That the grove echo'd, and the valleys rung :
And so I ravish'd with her heav'nly note,
I stood entranc'd, and had no room for thought.
But all o'erpower'd with ecstacy of bliss,
Was in a pleasing dream of paradise ;
At length I wak'd, and looking round the bow'r,
Search'd ev'ry tree, and pried on ev'ry flow'r,
If any where by chance I might espy
The rural poet of the melody :
For still me thought she sung not far away :
At last I found her on a laurel spray,
Close by my side she sat, and fair in sight,
Full in a line, against her opposite ;
Where stood with eglantine the laurel twin'd ;
And both their native sweets were well conjoin'd."

The allegorical strangeness of this poem is exceedingly beautiful, where it contains mysterious allusions to the virtues or beauties of the vegetable world and of the flowers and plants. A great deal of morality is couched under the symbols which Chaucer employs in this poem. The Flower denotes indolence and pleasure ; the Leaf signifies perseverence and virtue. Some of the knights **and** ladies do obeisance to the leaf, and some to the flower. **And there**

are many other symbols, clothed in beautiful rural descriptions.
These fancies seem to have taken their rise from the *Floral Games*
instituted in France in the year 1324, which filled the French
poetry with images of this sort. They were founded by Clem-
entina Isaure, Countess of Thoulouse, and annually celebrated
in the month of May. She published an edict which assem-
bled all the poets of France in artificial arbours dressed
with flowers : and he that produced the best poem, was rewarded
with a violet of gold. There were likewise inferior prizes of flowers
made in silver. This account agrees exactly with Chaucer's
Flower and Leaf. We see the poet placed in a delicious arbour,
interwoven with eglantine.

> "Twas bench'd with turf, and goodly to be seen,
> The thick young grass arose in fresher green :
> The mound was newly made, no sight could pass
> Betwixt the nice partitions of the grass ;
> The well-united sods so closely lay ;
> And all around the shades defended it from day,
> For sycamores with eglantine were spread,
> A hedge about the sides, a cov'ring overhead.
> And so the fragrant brier was wove between,
> The sycamore and flow'rs were mix'd with green,
> That nature seem'd to vary the delight,
> And satisfied at once the smell and sight."

Imaginary troops of knights and ladies advance : some of the
ladies are crowned with flowers, and others with chaplets of *agnus
castus*, and these are respectively subject to a *Lady of the Flower*,
and a *Lady of the Leaf.*

> " Thus while I sat intent to see and hear,
> And drew perfumes of more than vital air,
> All suddenly I heard th'approaching sound
> Of vocal music on th'enchanted ground :
> A host of saints it seem'd, so full the choir ;
> As if the bless'd above did all conspire
> To join their voices, and neglect the lyre.
> At length there issu'd from the grove behind
> A fair assembly of the female kind :
> A train less fair, as ancient fathers tell,
> Seduc'd the sons of heaven to rebel.
> I pass their form, and ev'ry charming grace,
> Less than an angel would their worth debase :
> But their attire, like liv'ries of a kind
> All rich and rare, is fresh within my mind."

any of the knights are distinguished in much the same man-
but others are crowned with leaves of oak, and of other trees:
rs carrying branches of oak, laurel, hawthorne and wood-bine.
des this profusion of vernal ornaments, the whole procession
ers with gold, pearls, rubies, and other costly decorations.

> "The ladies dress'd in rich symars were seen,
> Of florence satin, flow'r'd with white and green,
> And for a shade betwixt, the gloomy gridelin.
> The border of their petticoats below
> Where guarded thick with rubies on a row;
> And ev'ry damsel wore upon her head
> Of flow'rs a garland blended white and red.
> Attir'd in mantles all the knights were seen,
> That gratified the view with cheerful green:
> The chaplets of their ladies' colours were,
> Compos'd of white and red, to shade their shining hair."

:y are preceded by minstrels clothed in green, and crowned
ı flowers.

> "Before the merry troop the minstrels play'd;
> All in their master's liv'ries were array'd,
> And clad in green, and on their temples wore
> Their chaplets white and red their ladies bore.
> Their instruments were various in their kind,
> Some for the bow, and some for breathing wind:
> The psalt'ry, pipe, and hautboy's noisy band,
> And the soft lute trembling beneath the touching hand."

e of the ladies then sings a bargaret or pastoral in praise of the
sy.

> "A tuft of daisies on a flow'ry lay
> They saw, and thitherward they bent their way;

" Amid the plain a spreading laurel stood,
The grace and ornament of all the wood :
That pleasing shade they sought, a soft retreat
From sudden April showers, a shelter from the heat;
Her leafy arms with such extent were spread,
So near the clouds was her aspiring head,
That hosts of birds, that wing the liquid air,
Perch'd in the boughs, had nightly lodging there :
And flocks of sheep beneath the shade from far
Might hear the rattling hail, and wintry war ;
From heav'n's inclemency here found retreat,
Enjoy'd the cool, and shunn'd the scorching heat :
A hundred knights might here at ease abide ;
And ev'ry knight a lady by his side ;
The trunk itself such odours did bequeath,
That a Moluccan breeze to these was common breath."

Some of the knights and ladies do obeisance to the leaf, and
some to the flower of the daisy. Others are represented as wor-
shipping a bed of flowers. The lady of the leaf invites the lady
of the flower to a banquet.

" The lady of the leaf ordain'd a feast,
And made the lady of the flow'r her guest :
When lo, a bow'r ascended on the plain,
With sudden seats ordain'd, and large for either train.
This bow'r was near my pleasant arbour plac'd,
That I could hear and see whatever pass'd ;
The ladies sat with each a knight between,
Distinguish'd by their colours, white and green :
The vanquish'd party with the victors join'd,
Nor wanted sweet discourse, the banquet of the mind,
Meantime the minstrels play'd on either side,
Vain of their art, and for the mast'ry vied ;
The sweet contention lasted for an hour,
And reach'd my secret arbour from the bow'r."

Among those who are crowned with the leaf, are the knights of
King Arthur's table, and Charlemagne's Twelve Peers : together
with the knights of the order of the Garter, now just established
by Edward III.

Chaucer's works abound in allegories, and it is remarkable that
the early poets of Greece and Rome were fond of these creations.
Warton gives an admirable analysis of this fact. He says, "Homer
has given us *Strife, Contention, Fear, Terror, Tumults, Desire,
Persuasion* and *Benevolence.* We have in Hesiod, *Darkness,* and

figure of *Superstition* ('Que caput e cœli regionibus ostendebat')
He also mentions in a beautiful procession of the Seasons, *Calo
Aridus, Hyems* and *Algus*. And introduces *Medicine*, 'muttering
with silent fear' in the midst of the deadly pestilence at Athens.
Euripides gives the person of *Death* in his Alcestis, from which
Milton took his noble but romantic allegory of *Sin and Death*."
Though Chaucer is but an imitator of these immortal poets,
the allegories he has employed are grand in the extreme. As
knowledge and learning increased, poetry began to deal less in
imagination ; and these fantastic beings gave way to real manners
and lively characters.

Chaucer appears to have been a great reader, and his learning is
sometimes mistaken for genius. We are surprised to find in a
poet of such antiquity numbers so nervous and flowing. The
Knight's Tale abounds in unexpected and striking incidents,
opening in sublime description, and interesting by pathetic situa-
tions. There is a beautiful description of the morning which
vies both in sentiment and expression with the most finished
modern poetical landscapes, and finely displays the poet's talent
in delineating the beauties of nature.

> "The.merry lark, messenger of the day,
> Saluteth in her song the morrow gray ;
> The firy Phœbus riseth up so bright,
> That all the horison laugheth at the sight.
> And with his streams drieth in the greves †
> The silver drops left hanging in the leaves.

Pathetic description is also one of Chaucer's peculiar excellencies.
Nothing can be more ingeniously contrived than the occasion on
which the *Canterbury Tales* are supposed to be recited. A com-
pany of pilgrims on their journey to visit the shrine of Thomas a

† Groves.

Beckett at Canterbury lodge at the Taborde-inn at Southwark. Although strangers to each other, they are assembled in one room at supper, as was then the custom ; and agree, not only to travel together the next morning, but to relieve the fatigue of the journey by each telling a story.   This is without doubt, an imitation of the Decameron of Boccaccio. The pathos of this poem which is exquisite, consists in the invention of incidents and the contrivance of the story.   In the *Miller's Tale*, and also in other parts of Chaucer's writings, the levity of the story frequently amounts to indelicacy.   But this obscurity of Chaucer's may be in a great measure imputed to his age.   "We are apt" says Warton, "to form romantic and exaggerated notions about the moral innocence of our ancestors.   Ages of ignorance and simplicity are thought to be ages of purity. The direct contrary, I believe, is the case.   Rude periods have that grossness of manners which is not less friendly to virtue than luxury itself.   In the middle ages, not only the most flagrant violations of modesty were frequently practised and permitted, but the most infamous vices.   Men are less ashamed as they are less polished.   Great refinement multiplies criminal pleasures, but at the same time prevents the actual commission of many enormities ; at least it preserves public decency, and suppresses public licentiousness."[*] In Chaucer's characters we get an exact picture of the ancient manners, of the customs and diversions of our ancestors, represented with truth and spirit, as no contemporary nation has transmitted to posterity. We see in Chaucer the lustre and dignity of a true poet, in an age which compelled him to struggle with a barbarous language, and a natural want of taste ; and when, to write verses at all was regarded as a singular qualification.

CHAPTER VIII.

THE ELIZABETHAN ERA OF POETRY.

With Chaucer in reality commenced the great era of English poetry, but there followed a relapse, caused by almost a century

---

[*] Warton's History of Eng. Poetry.

of conspiracies, proscriptions and bloodshed. This chasm extended to Spenser, in the reign of Elizabeth. Certainly, a feeble attempt was made in the reign of Henry VIII. but Campbell says, "highest genius seems to have come forth, but half assured that her day of emancipation was at hand." Poetry was not firmly established until towards the end of the sixteenth century. Many minor poets intervened, but of little note, if we except Sir Thomas Moore, who sprung up towards the end of the fifteenth century. Warton says, "I consider Chaucer as a genial day in an English spring. A brilliant sun enlivens the face of nature with an unusual lustre; the sudden appearance of cloudless skies, and the unexpected warmth of a tepid atmosphere, after the gloom and inclemencies of a tedious winter, fill our hearts with the visionary prospect of a speedy summer : and we fondly anticipate a long continuance of gentle gales and vernal serenity. But winter returns with redoubled horrors: the clouds condense more formidably than before : and those tender buds, and early blossoms, which were called forth by the transient gleam of a temporary sunshine, are nipped by frosts, and torn by tempests." This simile represents the period that succeeded Chaucer, in which most of the poets seemed rather to have relapsed into barbarism.

Lydgate attained some eminence in the reign of Henry VI. He possessed a lively genius and numerous accomplishments, he was not only a poet and a rhetorician, but a geometrician and astronomer and a theologist. Warton says of him, "I am of opinion that Lydgate made considerable additions to the amplications of our language, in which Chaucer, Gower, and Occleve led the way: and that he is the first of our writers whose style is clothed with that perspicuity in which the English phraseology appears at this day to an English reader." Two other poets also appeared in this reign, Hugh Campeden and Thomas Chester, but they obtained no great celebrity.

The only poets of Edward the Fourth's reign were Harding, John Norton, and John Ripley, of whom Warton gives a detailed account in his History of English poetry.

The subsequent reign of Richard III., Edward V. and Henry VII. abounded in obscure versifiers, the only one of which who deserved the name of a poet, being Stephen Hawes. He flourished about the close of the fifteenth century, and was patronised by Henry VII,

We hear of John Skelton as having lived during the reign of Henry VIII. and feel he deserves notice amongst all others of this era, as having lived at a time when literature and poetry was at its worst stage.

Little or nothing of a poetical description has descended to us from the reigns of Edward II. and Mary. The latter was too unpropitious and turbulent, for the exercise of genius ; a spiritual warfare polluted every part of England with murders more atrocious than the slaughters of the most bloody civil contest on record.

But the splendid era of our literature, commonly called the Elizabethan Period, may be said to have begun with Spenser. From this great poet we heard the first notes of :—

"Those melodious bursts that fill
The spacious times of great Elizabeth
With sounds that echo still."

Spenser is the foremost chronology of those great spirits who towards the end of the sixteenth century, lifted up their immortal voices, and spoke words to be heard and heeded for all time. This period produced us Shakspeare, Spenser, Sidney, Bacon, Jonson, Beaumont and Fletcher, men who by their works have become ornaments of human nature and patterns to all mankind. To these may be added others, not less learned and great, but whose names have sunk into "mere oblivion," and whose only record may be found in their works. Webster, Decker, Marston, Marlowe, Chapman, Heywood, Middleton, and Rowley, though the friends and fellow labourers of Shakspeare are little noticed. As Hazlitt finely observes. " They went out one by one unnoticed, like evening lights." The genious of Great Britain never shone out greater or brigher than at this period. There is a natural love and fondness for whatever was done in this age ; we look upon the reign of Queen Elizabeth, as the golden age ; and the great men who lived in it, as our chief heroes of virtue; and greatest examples of wisdom, courage, integrity and learning. There never was anywhere, anything like the sixty or seventy years that elapsed from the middle of Elizabeth's reign to the period of the Restoration. In point of real force and originality of genius, neither the age of Pericles, nor the age of Augustus, nor the times of Leo X., nor of Louis the XIV., can come at all into comparison. No writers of tragedy and dramatic poetry of any age, can be compared to the great men of the age of Shakspeare, and immediately after. Hazlitt says, "They are a mighty phalanx of kindred spirits closing him round, moving in the same orbit, impelled by the sane causes in their whirling and eccentric career. They had the same faults and the same excellencies; the same strength and depth of richness; the same truth of character, passion, imagination, thought, and language, thrown, heaped, massed together, without careful polishing or exact method, but poured out in unconcerned profusion from the lap of Nature and Genius in boundless and unrivalled magnificence. The sweetness of Decker, the thought of Marston, the gravity of Chapman, the grace of Fletcher and his young-eyed wit, Jonson's learned rock, the flowing vein of Middleton, Heywood's ease, the pathos of Webster, and Marlowe's deep designs, add a double lustre to the sweetness, thought, gravity, grace, wit, artless nature, copiousness, ease, and sublime conceptions of Shakspeare's Muse. Our admiration of them, does not lessen our relish for him. They are the true scale by which we ascend to the true knowledge and love of him."

One of the great sources of the poetry of this period, was the numerous translations of Italian tales into English. They gave rise to innumerable plays and poems, which would not otherwise have existed; and turned the thoughts of our writers to new inventions of the same kind. It was from these that our dramatic poets borrowed the ideas of a legitimate plot. In proportion as knowledge increased, genius had wanted subjects and materials. These pieces usurped the places of legends and chronicles. And although the

and the cauldron of incantation. But the productions of this age were not too violent for common sense : the point had been reached, when the national credulity became chastened by reason. In this age, every man indulged his own capriciouness of invention. There was an insatiable desire of the mind to beget its own image, and to construct out of itself. The poet's appeal was chiefly to his own voluntary feeling, his own immediate and peculiar mode of conception. Sentiments and images were not absolutely determined by the canons of composition. And this freedom of thought was often expressed in an undisguised frankness of diction, which afterwards degenerated into dissonance and asperity. Warton, in speaking of this circumstance, says of Shakespeare, "we behold him breaking the barriers of imaginary method. In the same scene he descends from the meridian of the noblest tragic sublimity, to puns and quibbles, to the meanest merriments of a plebeian farce. In the midst of his dignity, he resembles his own Richard II, the *skipping king*, who sometimes discarding the state of a monarch,

"Mingled his royalty with carping fools,"
Henry iv. Act iii. Scene ii.

He seems not to have seen any impropriety, in the most abrupt transitions, from dukes to buffoons, from senators to sailors, from

* Warton's History of Eng. Poetry.

O

which was engrafted on the national genius;" in a word there
was a natural genius in this age, as there had never been be-
fore, and this was fed by the circumstances of the times that
preceded it.

CHAPTER IX.

THE EARLY ELIZABETHAN POETS.

SACKVILLE.—The date of this poet is placed under the year
1530. His eminent accomplishments and abilities having acquired
the confidence and esteem of Queen Elizabeth, the poet was soon
lost in the statesman, and negociations and embassies extinguished
the milder ambitions of the ingenious Muse. His principal work
is a poem entitled the *Induction*. In the plan of it, all the illus-
trions but unfortunate characters of English history, from the
conquest to the end of the fourteenth century, pass in review
before the poet, who descends like Dante into the infernal regions,
and is conducted by *Sorrow*. The shadowy inhabitants of Hell,
are conceived by the poet with the vigour of a creative imagination,
and described with great force of expression and are delineated
with that fulness of proportion, that invention of picturesque
attributes, distinctness, animation, and amplitude of which Spen-
ser is commonly supposed to have given the first specimens in
our language, and which are characteristic of his poetry. We
may venture to pronounce that Spenser, at least, caught his
manner of designing allegorical personages from this model,

Beholding dark, oppressing day so near ;
The sudden sight reduced to my mind
The sundry changes that in earth we find."

The *Gorboduc* of Sackville is perhaps the first specimen in our language of an heroic tale written in blank verse, divided into acts and scenes, and clothed in all the formalities of a regular tragedy.   There are many of the same defects in this tragedy, as may be seen in Shakespeare, although he has cloaked them in the magic of his exquisite poetry—the unities of time and place are visibly violated.

The most beautiful part of it is the fourth Act, in which Prince Porrex is murdered by his brother Viden.   King Gorboduc is lamenting the death of his eldest son Ferrex, whom Porrex the younger has slain, when Marcella a court lady enters and relates the miserable end of Porrex.

Gorboduc.—"What cruel destiny
What froward fate hath sorted us this chance ?
That ev'n in those where we should comfort find,
Where our delight now in our aged days
Should rest and be, even there our only grief
And deepest sorrows to abridge our life,
Most pining cares and deadly thoughts do grave.
Arostus.—Your grace should now, in these grave years of yours,
Have found ere this the price of mortal joys,
How full of change, how brittle our estate,

How short they be, how fading here in earth,
Of nothing sure, save only of the death,
To whom both man and all the world doth owe
Their end at last ; neither should nature's power
In other sort against your heart prevail,
Than as the naked hand whose stroke assays
The armed breast where force doth light in vain.

Gorboduc.—Many can yield right grave and sage advice
Of patient sprite to others wrapt in woe,
And can in speech both rule and conquer kind,
Who, if by proof they might feel nature's force,
Would show themselves men as they are indeed,
Which now will needs be gods : but what doth mean
The sorry cheer of her that here doth come ?

MARCELLA, enters.

Marcella.—Oh where is ruth? or where is pity now?
Whither is gentle heart and mercy fled?
Are they exiled out of our stony breasts,
Never to make return? is all the world
Drowned in blood, and sunk in cruelty?
If not in women mercy may be found,
If not, alas ! within the mothers breast
To her own child, to her own flesh and blood;
If ruth be banish'd thence, if pity there
May have no place, if there no gentle heart
Do live and dwell, were should we seek it then?

Gorboduc.—Madam, alas ! what means your woful tale?

Marcella.—O silly woman I, why to this hour
Have kind and fortune thus deferr'd my breath,
That I should live to see this doleful day?
Will ever wight believe that such hard heart
Could rest within the cruel mother's breast,
With her own hand to slay her only son?
But out, alas ! these eyes beheld the same,
They saw the dreary sight, and arebecome
Most ruthful records of the bloody fact.
Porrex, alas! is by his mother slain,
And with her hand, a woful thing to tell,
While slumbering on his careful bed he rests,
His heart stabb'd in with knife is reft of life.

Gorboduc.—O Eubulus, O draw this sword of ours,
And pierce this heart with speed. O hateful light,
O loathsome life, O sweet and welcome death.
Dear Eubulus, work this we thee beseech.

Eubulus.—Patient, your grace, perhaps he liveth yet,
With wound received but not of certain death.

Garboduc.—O let us then repair unto the place,
And see if Porrex live, or thus be slain.

Marcella.—Alas ! he liveth not, it is too true,
That with these eyes, of him a peerless prince,
Son to a king, and in the flower of youth,
Even with a twink * a senseless stock I saw.

Arostus.—O damned deed !

Marcella.—But hear his ruthful end.

    The noble prince, pierced with the sudden wounds,
    Out of his wretched slumber hastily start, *
    Whose strength now failing, straight he overthrew,
    When in the fall his eyes ev'n now unclosed,
    Beheld the queen, and cried to her for help ;
    We then, alas ! the ladies which that time
    Did there attend, seeing that heinous deed,
    And hearing him oft call the wretched name
    Of mother, and to cry to her for aid,
    Whose direful hand gave him the mortal wound,
    Pitying, alas ! (for nought else could we do)
    His rueful end, ran to the woful bed,
    Dispoiled straight his breast, and all we might
    Wiped in vain with napkins next at hand
    The sudden streams of blood, that flushed fast
    Out of the gaping wound : O what a look,
    O what a ruthful stedfast eye methought
    He fix'd upon my face, which to my death
    Will never part from me, —wherewith abraid
    A deep-fetch'd sigh he gave, and there withal
    Clasping his hands, to heaven he cast his sight ;
    And straight, pale death pressing within his face,
    The flying ghost his mortal corpse forsook.

Arostus.—Never did age bring forth so vile a fact.

Marcella.—O hard and cruel hap that thus assign'd
    Unto so worthy wight so wretched end :
    But most hard cruel heart that could consent,
    To lend the hateful destinies that hand,
    By which, alas ! so heinous crime was wrought,—
    O queen of adamant, O marble breast,
    If not the favour of his comely face,
    If not his princely cheer and countenance,
    His valiant active arms, his manly breast,
    If not his fair and seemly personage ;
    His noble limbs, in such proportion cast,
    As would have rapt a silly woman's thought ;
    If this might not have moved the bloody heart,
    And that most cruel hand the wretched weapon
    Ev'n to let fall, and kiss'd him in the face,
    With tears, for ruth to reave such one by death ;
    Should nature yet consent to slay her son ?
    O mother, thou to murder thus thy child !
    Ev'n Jove with justice must with lightning flames
    From heaven send down some strange revenge on thee.
    Ah noble prince, how oft have I beheld
    Thee mounted on thy fierce and trampling steed,
    Shining in armour bright before the tilt,
    And with thy mistress' sleeve tied on thy helm,
    There charge thy staff, to please thy lady's eye,

---

      * Started.

Which never now these eyes may see again !
Arostus.—Madam, alas ! in vain these plaints are shed.
Rather with me depart; and help assuage
The thoughtful griefs, that in the aged king
Must needs by nature grow, by death of this
His only son, whom he did hold so dear.
Marcella.—What wight is that which saw that I did see,
And could refrain to wail with plaint and tears ?
Not I, alas ! that heart is not in me ;
But let us go, for I am grieved anew,
To call to mind the wretched father's woe.

CHORUS OF AGED MEN.

When greedy lust in royal seat to reign
Hath reft all care of gods and eke of men ;
And cruel heart, wrath, treason, and disdain,
Within the ambitious breast are lodged, then
Behold how mischief wide herself displays,
And with the brother's hand the brother slays.
    When blood thus shed doth stain this heaven's face,
Crying to Jove for vengeance of the deed,
The mighty God ev'n moveth from his place,
With wrath to wreak ; then sends he forth with speed
The dreadful Furies, daughters of the night,
With serpents girt, carrying the whip of ire,
With hair of stinging snakes, and shining bright
With flames and blood, and with a brand of fire :
These, for revenge of wretched murder done,
Doth cause the mother kill her only son.
    Blood asketh blood, and death must death requite.
Jove by his just and everlasting doom
Justly hath ever so requited it.
This times record and times to come,
Shall find it true, and as doth present proof
Present before our eyes for our behoof.
    O happy wight that suffers not the snare
Of murderous mind to tangle him in blood :
And happy he that can in time beware
By others' harms, and turn it to his good :
But woe to him that fearing not to offend,
Doth serve his lust, and will not see the end."

MARSTON.—This poet was almost the next in importance at this period. He seems to have been a bitter satirist against the vices and follies of the men of his age. Throughout all his works, he has not exhibited any tender or soft emotions ; nothing but impatient scorn and indignation. His greatest satire is the " Scourge of Villany"

in which he ridicules the people and things of his time with great
vigour of expression. Amongst other things, he appears to have
been a violent enemy to the Puritans.

> "————But thou, rank Puritan,
> I'll make an ape as good a christian :
> I'll force him chatter, turning up his eye,
> Look sad, so grave, Demure civility
> Shall scorn to say, *good brother, sister dear !*
> As for the rest, to snort in belly cheer,
> To bite, to knaw, and boldly intermell
> With holy things in which thou dost excel,
> Unforc'd he'll do. O take compassion
> Even on your souls : make not Religion
> A bawd to lewdness. Civil Socrates,
> Clip not the youth of Alcibiades
> With unchaste arms. Disguised Messaline,
> I'll tear thy mask, and bare thee to the eye."

Most of Marston's satires are vitiated with impure expressions.
" His stream of poetry, if sometimes bright and unpolluted, almost
always betrays a muddy bottom. "

His principal tragedy is Antonio's Revenge and is written with
considerable force and pathos. The prologue is full of passionate
earnestness, and as Lamb says," for the tragic note of preparation
which it sounds, it might have preceded one of those old tales of
Thebes, or Pelop's line, which Milton has so highly commended.
It is as solemn a preparative as the ' warning voice which he who
saw the Apocalypse, heard cry. "

> "The rawish dank of clumsy winter ramps
> The fluent summer's vein : and drizzling sleet
> Chilleth the wan bleak cheek of the numb'd earth,
> Whilst snarling guests nibble the juiceless leaves
> From the naked shuddering branch, and pills the skin
> From off the soft and delicate aspects.
> O, now methinks a sullen tragic scene,
> Would suit the time with pleasing congruence !
> May we be happy in our weak devoir,
> And all part pleased in most wish'd content.
> But sweat of Hercules can ne'er beget
> So blest an issue. Therefore we proclaim,
> If any spirit breathes within this round.
> Uncapable of weighty passion,
> (As from his birth being hugged in the arms
> And nuzled 'twixt the breasts of Happiness)
> Who winks and shuts his apprehension up

om common sense of what men were, and are ;
ho would not know what men must be : let such
irry amain from our black-visaged shows ;
e shall affright their eyes.   But if a breast,
iil'd to the earth with grief ; if any heart,
erced through with anguish, pant within this ring ;
there be any blood, whose heat is choked
id stifled with true sense of misery :
aught of these strains fill this consort up,
iey arrive most welcome.   O, that our power
iuld lacky or keep wing with our desires ;
iat with unused poise of style and sense,
e might weigh massy in judicious scale !
it here's the prop that doth support our hopes :
hen our scenes falter, or invention halts,
iur favour will give crutches to our faults."

ige in which Maria describes the death of Mellida her

law, is evry beautiful :—

eing laid upon her bed she grasp'd my hand,
nd kissing it spake thus :   Thou very poor,
'hy dost not weep ? the jewel of thy brow,
ie rich adornment that enchased thy breast,
  lost ; thy son, my love, is lost, is dead.
nd have I lived to see his virtues blurr'd
'ith guiltless blots ? O world, thou art too subtle
or honest natures to converse withal :
nerefore I'll leave thee : farewell, mart of woe ;
fly to clip my love Antonio.—
'ith that, her head sunk down upon her breast ;
er cheek changed earth, her senses slept in rest :
ntil my fool, that crept unto the bed,
ireech'd out so loud that he brought back her soul,
all'd her again, that her bright eyes 'gan ope
nd stared upon him : he audacious fool
ared kiss her hand, wish'd her *soft rest, loved bride* ;
ie fumbled out, *thanks, good* ; and so she died."

alcontent the interest of the plot is perpetually broken,

tinual changes that occur,   In the part where the

describes himself, there is much to admire.

cannot sleep, my eyes 'ill-neighbouring lids
'ill hold no fellowship, O thou pale sober night.
hou that in sluggish fumes all sense dost steep ;
hou that givest all the world full leave to play,
nbend'st at the feebled veins of sweaty labour
he gally-slave, that all the toilsome day
ugs at the oar against the stubborn wave,
training his rugged veins, snores fast ;

"This study fits a mercenary drudge,
Who aims at nothing but eternal trash,
Too servile and illiberal for me.
When all is done, Divinity is best.
Jerome's bible, Faustus: view it well,
Stipendium peccati mors est : ha ! *Stipendium &c,*
The reward of sin is death : that's hard.
Si pecasse negamus, fallimur, et nulla est in nobis veritas,   [in us.
If we say that we have no sin, we deceive ourselves and there is no truth
Why then belike we must sin, and so consequently die
Ay, we must die an everlasting death.
What doctrine call you this ? *Che, sera, sera* :
What will be shall be.   Divinity adieu.
These Metaphysics of Magicians,
And necromatic books, are heavenly.
Lines, Circles, Letters, Characters :
Ay, these are those that Faustus most desires.
O what a world of profit and delight,
Of power, of honour, and omnipotence,
Is promised to the studious artizan !
All things that move between the quiet poles.
Shall be at my command, Emperors and kings,
Are but obeyed in their several provinces ;
But his dominion that exceeds in this,
Stretcheth as far as doth the mind of man :
A sound magician is a Demigod,
Here tire my brains to gain a deity."

P

death of Doctor Faustus. It is a proof of the credulous ignorance which still prevailed, and a specimen of the subjects which then were thought not improper for tragedy. The characters of Faustus are finely conceived. He is hurried away, tormented with a desire to enlarge his knowledge to the utmost bounds of nature and art, and to extend his power with his knowledge. He is desirous of solving the most subtle speculations of abstract reason : and for this purpose leagues himself with demoniacal power.

> "Till swoln with cunning and a self-conceit,
> His waxen wings did mount above his reach,
> And melting, heavens conspired his overthrow :
> For falling to a devilish exercise,
> And glutted now with Learning's golden gifts,
> He surfeits on the cursed necromancy.
> Nothing so sweet as magic is to him,
> Which he prefers before his chiefest bliss."

In his impatience to fulfil all the immediate desires and conceptions of his soul ; he is willing to give in exchange, his soul and body to the great enemy of mankind. By this means whatever he fancies becomes present to his sense, and whatever he commands shall be done. He calls back time past, and anticipates the future ; all the delights of fortune and pleasure, ambition, and learning are centred in his person ; and from a short-lived dream of supreme felicity and drunken power, he sinks into an abyss of darkness and perdition This is the alternative to which he submits ; the bond which he signs with his blood. At the commencement of the play, he opens his mind in the following manner :—

> "How am I glutted with conceit of this !
> Shall I make Spirits fetch me what I please?
> Resolve me of all ambiguities ?
> Perform what desperate enterprises I will?
> I 'll have them fly to India for gold,
> Ransack the ocean for orient pearl,
> And search all corners of the new-found world
> For pleasant fruits and princely delicates.
> I 'll have them read me strange philosphy ;
> And tell the secrets of all foreign Kings.
> I'll have them wall all Germany with brass,
> And with swift Rhine circle all Wertemburg :

I'll have them fill the public schools with skill,
Wherewith the students shall be bravely clad :
I'll levy soldiers with the coin they bring ,
And chase the Prince of Parma from your land ;
And reign sole king of all the provinces :
Yea, stranger engines for the brunt of war
Than was the fiery keel at Antwerp bridge,
I'll make my servile spirits to invent.
Come, German Valdes, and Cornelius,
And make me wise with your sage conference."

One of the most beautiful passages in the whole play, is the interest taken by the three scholars in the fate of their master, and their unavailing attempts to dissuade him from his relentless career.

First Sch.—"Come, gentleman, let us go visit Faustus
For such a dreadful night' was never seen
Since first the world's creation did begin !
Such fearful shrieks and cries were never heard.
Pray heaven the Doctor have escaped the danger !
Second Sch.—O help us heaven, see here are Faustus' limbs
All torn asunder by the hand of death.
Third Sch.—The devil whom Faustus served hath torn him thus
For twixt the hours of twelve and one, methought,
I heard him shriek and call aloud for help ;
At which same time the house seem'd all on fire
With dreadful horror of these damned fiends.
Second Sch.—Well, gentleman, though Faustus' end be such
As every Christian heart laments to think on ;
Yet, for he was a scholar once admired
For wondrous knowledge in our German schools,
We'll give his mangled limbs due burial ;
And all the scholars, clothed in mourning black,
Shall wait upon his heavy funeral.
Chorus.—Cut is the branch that might have grown full straight
And burned is Apollo's laurel bough
That sometime grew within this learned man :
Faustus is gone. Regard his hellish fall,
Whose fiendful fortune may exhort the wise
Only to wonder at unlawful things :
Whose deepness doth entice such forward wits,
To practise more than heavenly power permits."

Strikingly touching also are his own conflicts of mind and agoniz-ing doubts on the subject before him, struggling with the extremity of his fate. In the following passage for instance, where he exclaims to his friend :—

"But Faustus' offence can ne'er be pardoned. The serpent that tempted Eve may be saved, but not Faustus. O, gentlemen, hear me with patience, and tremble not at my speeches ; though my heart pant and quiver to remember that I have been a student here these thirty years. O would I had ne'er seen Wirtemburg, never read book ! and what wonders I have done, all Germany can witness, yea all the world : for which Faustus hath lost both Germany and the world, yea, heaven itself, heaven the seat of God, the throne of the blessed, the kingdom of joy, and must remain in hell for ever. Hell, O hell, for ever. Sweet friends, what shall become of Faustus being in hell for ever ?"

The ending of this play is terrible : the horror of the scene is thrown up in vivid and passionate language ; and his last exclamation betrays an anguish of mind, not to be contemplated without shuddering :—

FAUSTUS *alone. The clock strikes eleven.*
Faust.—"O Faustus.
　　Now hast thou but one bare hour to' live
　　And then thou must be damn'd perpetually.
　　Stand still, you ever-moving spheres of heaven,
　　That time may cease and midnight never come.
　　Fair nature's eye, rise, rise again, and make
　　Perpetual day : or let this hour be but
　　A year, a month, a week, a natural day,
　　That Faustus may repent and save his soul.
　　O lente, lente currite noctis equi.
　　The stars move still, time runs, the clock will strike
　　The devil will come, and Faustus must be damn'd.
　　O, I will leap to heaven : who pulls me down ?
　　See where Christ's blood streams in the firmament :
　　One drop of blood will save me : O, my Christ,
　　Rend not my heart for naming of my Christ,
　　Yet will I call on him : O spare me, Lucifer."

The growing horrors of Faustus' last scene are awfully marked by the hours and half hours as they expire and bring him nearer to the exactment of his dire compact.

　　"Where is it now ? 'tis gone ;
　　And see. a threatening arm, and angry brow.
　　Mountains and hills, come, come, and fall on me,
　　And hide me from the heavy wrath of heaven.
　　No ? then will I headlong run into the earth :
　　Gape earth. O no, it will not harbour me,
　　You stars that reign'd at my nativity,
　　Whose influence have alloted death and hell,
　　Now draw up Faustus like a foggy mist
　　Into the entrails of yon labouring cloud ;
　　That when you vomit forth into the air,

My limbs may issue from your smoky mouths,
But let my soul mount and ascend to heaven.
        The watch strikes.
O half the hour is past ; 'twill all be past anon.
O if my soul must suffer for my sin,
Impose some end to my incessant pain,
Let Faustus live in hell a thousand years,
A hundred thousand, and at last be saved :
No end is limited to damned souls.
Why wert thou not a creature wanting soul?
Or why is this immortal that thou hast?
O Pythagoras' Metempshchosis! were that true,
That soul should fly from me and I be changed,
Into some brutish beast.
All beasts are happy, for when they die,
Their souls are soon dissolved in elements :
But mine must live still to be plagued in hell.
Curst be the parents that engender'd me :
No, Faustus curse thyself, curse Lucifer,
That hath deprived thee of the joys of heaven.
        The clock strikes twelve.
It strikes, it strikes, now, body, turn to air,
Or Lucifer will bear thee quick to hell.
O soul, be changed into small water drops,
And fall into the ocean ; ne'er be found.
        Thunder, and enter the devils.
O mercy, Heaven! look not so fierce on me.
Adders and serpents, let me breathe awhile :
Ugly hell gape not ; come not Lucifer :
I'll burn my books : O, Mephostophilis."

And see what's past and learn what is to come.
If thou lay claim to Strength, armies shall quake
To see thee frown : as kings at mine do lie
So shall thy feet trample on empery.
Make Health thine object, thou shalt be strong **proof**,
'Gainst the deep searching darts of surfeiting,
Be ever merry, ever revelling.
Wish but for Beauty, and within thine eyes
Two naked Cupids amorously shall swim,
And on thy cheeks I'll mix such white and red.
That Jove shall turn away young Ganymede,
And with immortal arms shall circle thee.
Are thy desires Long Life ? thy vital thread
Shall be stretch'd out ; thou shalt behold the change
Of monarchies, and see those children die
Whose great great grandsires now in cradles lie.
If through Gold's sacred hunger thou dost pine ;
Those gilded wantons which in swarms do run
To warm their slender bodies in the sun,
Shall stand for number of those golden piles
Which in rich pride shall swell before thy feet ;
As those are, so shall these be infinite.
Fortunatus.—O, whither am I wrapt beyond myself ?
More violent conflicts fight in every thought,
Than his whose fatal choice Troy's downfall **wrought**.
Shall I contract myself to Wisdom's love ?
Then I lose Riches : and a wise man poor
Is like a sacred book that's never read ;
To himself he lives and to all else seems dead.
This age thinks better of a gilded fool,
Than of a threadbare saint in Wisdom's school.
I will be Strong : then I refuse Long Life ;
And though mine arm should conquer twenty **worlds**
There's a lean fellow beats all conquerors:
The greatest strength expires with loss of breath,
The mightiest in one minute stoop to death.
Then take Long Life, or Health ; should I do so,
I might grow ugly, and that tedious scroll
Of months and years much misery may enroll :
Therefore I'll beg for Beauty, yet I will not:
The fairest cheek hath oftentimes a soul
Leprous as sin itself, than hell more foul.
The Wisdom of this world is idiotism ;
Strength a weak reed ; Health, Sickness' enemy,
And it at length will have the victory.
Beauty is but a painting ; and Long Life
Is a long journey in December gone,
Tedious and full of tribulation.
Therefore, dread sacred empress, make me rich :
My choice is Store of Gold; the rich are wise:

her profession, poor humanity struggling with destiny.

> "Like an ill husband, though I knew the same
> To be my undoing, followed I that game,
> O, when the work of lust had earn'd my bread,
> To taste it how I trembled, lest each bit
> Ere it went down should choke me chewing it.
> My bed seem'd like a cabin hung in hell,
> The bawd hell's porter, and the lickorish wine
> The pander fetch'd was like an easy fine
> For which methought I leas'd away my soul ;
> And oftentimes even in my quaffing-bowl
> Thus said I to myself :   I am a whore,
> And have drunk down thus much confusion more."

And then follow the lines where she contrasts the different regard
shown to the modest or the abandoned of her sex :—

> "——————When in the street
> A fair young modest damsel I did meet,
> She seem'd to all a dove, when I pass'd by
> And I to all a raven : every eye
> That followed her went with a bashful glance ;
> At me each bold and jeering countenance
> Darted forth scorn : to her as if she had been
> Some tower unvanquished would they vail ;
> 'Gainst me swoln rumour hoisted every sail :
> She crown'd with reverend praises pass'd by them,
> I though with face mask'd could not scape the hem ;
> For, as if Heaven had set strange marks on whores
> Because they should be pointing stocks to man,
> Drest up in civilest shape a courtezan,
> Let her walk saint-like noteless and unknown,
> Yet she's betrayed by some trick of her own."

The definition which is contained in this work of *The Happy Man,*
is also finely written : —

> "He that makes gold his wife, but not his whore,
> He that at noonday walks by a prison door,
> He that in the sun is neither beam nor moat,
> He that's not mad after a petticoat.
> He for whom poor men's curses dig no grave,
> He that is neither lord's nor lawyer's slave,
> He that makes This his sea and That his shore,
> He that in's coffin is richer than before,
> He that counts Youth his sword and Age his staff,
> He whose right hand carves his own epitaph,
> He that upon his death-bed is a swan,
> And dead, no crow : he is a Happy Man."

HEYWOOD.—Lamb says of this poet, that he is a sort of *prose*
Shakespeare.   His scenes are to the full as natural and affecting:
But we miss *the poet,* that which in Shakespeare always appears
out and above the surface of *the nature.*   There is nothing
startling in Heywood's works.   He exhibits the passions in the
simplest circumstances of every day life.   His style is natural
and constrained : and the dialogue such as might be uttered in
ordinary conversation.   Heywood's are characters of what we see
in life, truly and strikingly written.

There is an admirable passage in the play *A woman killed with
kindness,* where Mr. Frankford discovers his wife's unfaithfulness
to him, beautifully and tenderly written :—

> "————————Woman, hear thy judgment ;
> Go make thee ready in thy best attire;
> Take thee with all thy gowns, all thy apparel :
> Leave nothing that did ever call thee mistress,
> Or by whose sight, being left here in the house,
> I may remember such a woman was.
> Choose thee a bed and hangings from thy chamber ;
> Take with thee everything which hath thy mark,
> And get thee to my manor seven miles off ;
> Where live ; tis thine, I freely give it thee :
> My tenants by shall furnish thee with wains
> To carry all thy stuff within two hours ;
> No longer will I limit thee my sight.
> Choose which of all my servants thou likest best,
> And they are thine to attend thee.
> *Mrs. Fra.*—A mild sentence.
> But as thou hopest for heaven, as thou believest

Nic.—Here's her lute flung in a corner.

Fran.—Her lute? O God! upon this instrument
    Her fingers have ran quick division,
    Swifter than that which now divides our hearts,
    These frets have made me pleasant, that have now
    Frets of my heart strings made. O master Cranwell,
    Oft hath she made this melancholy wood.
    (Now mute and dumb for her disastrous chance)
    Speak sweetly many a note, sound many a strain
    To her own ravishing voice which being well strung
    What pleasant strange airs have they jointly rung!
    Post with it after her; now nothing's left;
    Of her and her's I am at once bereft."

And then again in the following passage, where Mrs. Frankford is overtaken on her journey by Nicholas with the lute, nothing can be more affecting :—

Mrs. Fra.—" I know the lute; oft have I sung to thee:
    We both are out of tune, both out of time.

Nic.—My master commends him unto ye;
    There's all he can find that was ever yours,
    He prays you to forget him, and so he bids you farewell.

Mrs. Fra.—I thank him, he is kind, and ever was.
    All you that have true feeling of my grief,
    That know my loss, and have relenting hearts,

Q

Gird me about ; and help me with your tears,
To wash my spotted sins: my lute shall groan ;
It cannot weep, but shall lament my moan.
If you return unto your master, say,
(Though not from me, for I am unworthy
To blast his name so with a strumpet's tongue.)
That you have seen me weep, wish myself dead.
Nay you may say too, (for my vow is past)
Last night you saw me eat and drink my last.
This to your master you may say and swear :
For it is writ in heaven and decreed here.
Go break this lute on my coach's wheel,
As the last music that I e'er shall make ;
Not as my husbands' gift, but my farewell
To all earth's joy ; and so your master tell.
Nic.—I'll do your commendations.
Mrs. Fra.—O no :
I dare not so presume ; nor to my children :
I am disclaim'd in both, alas ! I am.
O never teach them, when they come to speak,
To name the name of mother ; chide their tongue.
If they by chance light on that hated word,
Tell them 'tis naught, for when that word they name
(Poor pretty souls!) they harp on their own shame.
So, now unto my coach, then to my home,
So to my death-bed ; for from this sad hour,
I never will eat, nor drink, nor taste,
Of any cates that may preserve my life :
I never will nor smile, nor sleep, nor rest.
But when my tears have wash'd my black soul white,
Sweet Saviour, to thy hands I yield my sprite."

CHAPMAN.—This poet belonged also to the class of dramatic writers of this age. He does not seem to have mingled in the dissipations and indiscretions which then marked his profession. Wood says, that "he was a person of the most reverent aspect, religious and temperate." Chapman, however, is best known as a translator of Homer, than as a dramatist. His best tragedy is *Bussy d'Amboise*, but this is written more in the form of a dialogue than a poem or tragedy. Chapman aims at the highest things in poetry, but his work is utterly destitute of imagination and passion. Dryden says, that "this play pleased only in its representation, like a star which glitters only while it shoots." The following are one or two specimens of his writings :—

Which, with heroic forms without o'erspread,
Within are naught, but mortar, flint, and lead."

VIRTUE.—POLICY.

"——As great seamen using all their wealth
And skills in Neptune's deep invisible paths,
In tall ships richly built and ribb'd with brass,
To put a girdle round about the world ;
When they have done it, coming near the haven,
Are fain to give a warning piece, and call
A poor staid fisherman that never pass'd
His country sight, to waft and guide them in ;
So when we wander furthest through the waves
Of glassy glory, and the gulps of state.
Topp'd with all titles, spreading all our reaches,
As if each private arm would sphere the earth,
We must to Virtue for her guide resort,
Or we shall shipwreck in our safest port."

NICK OF TIME.

"There is a deep nick in Time's restless wheel
For each man's good, when which nick comes, it strikes;
As rhetoric yet works not persuasion,
But only is a mean to make it work ;
So no man riseth by his real merit,
But when it cries clink in his Raiser's spirit."

MIDDLETON.—This poet has no particular style of his own, his works appear to be made up of the faults and excellencies equally, of his contemporaries. There is a great deal of real life drawn in his characters particularly in that of Livia the "good neighbour." Middleton's *Witches* are fine creations, and contain equally fine poetry.

Hecate.—" Now I go, now fly,
Malkin my sweet Spirit and I

O, what a dainty pleasure 'tis
To ride in the air
When the moon shines fair,
And sing, and dance, and toy, and kiss ?
Over woods, high rocks, and mountains,
Over seas (our mistress' fountains),
Over steep towers and turrets,
We fly by night 'mongst troops of Spirits.
No ring of hells to our ear sounds,
No howl of wolves, no yelp of hounds ;
No, not the noise of waters breach,
Or cannon's throat, our height can reach."

WEBSTER.—The works of this poet, are overflowing with wild
and terrible imaginings, carried sometimes almost to an excess.
His characters are to a degree, unnatural ; and his sentiments are
all adorned with some tender or awful beauty. Yet nothing can
be finer than the general conception of his works. Lamb says,
" To move a horror skilfully, to touch a soul to the quick, to lay
upon fear as much as it can bear, to wean and weary a life till it
is ready to drop, and then step in with mortal instruments to take
its last forfeit : this only a Webster can do. Inferior genuises may
upon horror's head, horror's accumulate; but they cannot do this.
They mistake quantity for quality ; they 'terrify babes with painted
devils,' but they know not how a soul is to be moved. Their
terrors want dignity, their affrights are without decorum." This
extraordinary power is seen particularly in the death of the *Duchess
of Malfy* :—

DIRGE.

"Hark, now every thing is still;
This screech-owl, and the whistler shrill,
Call upon our dame aloud,
And bid her quickly d'on her shroud.
Much you had of land and rent :
Your length in clay's now competent.
A long war disturb'd your mind ;
Here your perfect peace is sign'd.
Of what is't fools make such vain keeping ?
Sin, their conception ; their birth, weeping :
Their life, a general mist of error ;
Their death, a hideous storm of terror.
Strew your hair with powder sweet,
D'on clean linen. bathe your feet :

And (the foul fiend more to check).
A crucifix let bless your neck.
'Tis now full tide 'tween night and day:
End your groan, and come away.
Cariola.—Hence, villians, tyrants, murderers : alas !
What will you do with my lady ? Call for help.
Duch.—To whom ; to our next neighbours? They are mad folks
Farewell, Cariola.
I pray thee look thou givest my little boy
Some syrup for his cold ; and let the girl
Say her prayers ere she sleep.—Now what you please;
What death ?
Bos.—Strangling.   Here are your executioners.
Duch.—I forgive them.
The apoplexy, catarrh, or cough of the lungs,
Would do as much as they do.
Bos.—Doth not death fright you ?
Duch.—Who would be afraid on't,
Knowing to meet such excellent company
In the other world ?
Bos.—Yet methinks,
The manner of your death should much afflict you ;
This cord should terrify you.
Duch.—Not a whit.
What would it pleasure me to have my throat cut
With diamonds ? or to be smother'd
With cassia ? or to be shot to death with pearls ?
I know, death hath ten thousand several doors
For men to take their exits : and 'tis found
They go on such strange geometrical hinges,
You may open them both ways; any way: (for heavens sake)
So I were out of your whispering : tell my brothers,
That I perceive, death (now I'm well awake)
Best gift is, they can give or I can take.
I would fain put off my last woman's fault,
I'd not be tedious to you.
Pull and pull strongly, for your able strength
Must pull down heaven upon me.
Yet stay, heaven gates are not so highly arch'd
As princes' palaces ; they that enter there
Must go upon their knees.   Come violent death:
Serve for Mandragora to make me sleep.
Go tell my brothers ; when I am laid out,
They then may feed in quiet.*(They strangle her, kneeling)*
                    FERDINAND *enters*
Ferdinand.—Is she dead ?
Bos.—She is what you would have her.
Fix your eye here.
Ferd.—Constantly.
Bos.—Do you not weep ?

Others sins only speak ; murder shrieks out.
The element of water moistens the earth,
But blood flies upward and bedews the heavens.
Ferd.—Cover her face : mine eyes dazzle ; she died young
Bos.—I think not so : her infelicity
Seem'd to have years too many.
Ferd.—She and I were twins.
And should I die this instant, I had lived
Her time to a minute."

*　　*　　*　　.*　　*　　*

SINGLE LIFE.

"O fie upon this single life ! forego it.
We read how Daphne, for her peevish flight,
Became a fruitless bay-tree : Syrinx turn'd
To the pale empty reed : Anaxarate
Was frozen into marble : whereas those
Which married, or proved kind unto their friends
Were, by a gracious influence, trans-shaped.
Into the olive, pomegranate, mulberry ;
Became flowers, precious stones, or eminent stars."

The funeral dirge in *The White Devil* is also magnificent in its
intensity of feeling :—

Funeral Dirge for ᴍARCELLO.

"Call for the robin-redbreast, and the wren,
Since o'er shady groves they hover,
And with leaves and flowers do cover.
The friendless bodies of unburied men.
Call unto his funeral dole
The ant, the field-mouse, and the mole,
To raise him hillocks that shall keep him warm,
And (when gay tombs are robb'd) sustain no harm ;
But keep the wolf far thence, that's foe to men,
For with his nails he'll dig them up again."

These are what Hazlit terms the *horrible graces* of Webster, a
faculty which we see in no other dramatist of his time except
Shakespeare. Let me quote as a last illustration the description
by Fracisco of the grief of Cornelia at Marcello's funeral :—

"Your reverend mother
Is grown a very old woman in two hours.
I found them winding of Marcello's corpse :
And there is such a solemn melody,
'Tween doleful songs, tears, and sad elegies ;
Such as old grandames, watching by the dead. ;

BEAUMONT.—In point of variety and effect, Beaumont stands below the other dramatists of his time. His style is widely different from theirs, and we may say that he was the first who deviated from the tragic style of that age. He is not a follower of nature like his contemporaries : the character of his writings seem rather to *anticipate* nature and reason. His poetry leaves a want; and the mind after reading seems to be unsatisfied. There is nothing in his writings at all masculine. Shakespeare's tone is manly and bracing—Beaumont's weak and meretricious.

FLETCHER.—This poet is a writer of the same caste. There is that same mixture of effeminacy of character, and weakness, as in Beaumont. They both had immense control over fancy and passion; but they dealt too much in common-place extravagancies and theatrical trick. Hazlitt says, "they were the first who laid the foundation of the artificial diction and tinselled pomp of the next generation of poets, by aiming at a profusion of ambitious ornaments, and by translating the commonest circumstances into the language of metaphor and passion." There are however many prodigious merits in their works, and many passages worthy of the highest admiration.

In *The Maid's Tragedy*, though it is one of the poorest of their works, the passage where Evadne implores forgiveness of Amintor for marrying him while she was the King's mistress; and Amintor's speech when she makes confession of her unlooked-for remorse, we see a fine specimen of poetical writing :—

> *Evadne.*—"O my lord.
> *Amintor.*—How now!
> *Evad.*—My much abused lord!
> *Amin.*—This cannot be.
> *Evad.*—I do not kneel to live, I dare not hope it:
>   The wrongs I did are greater; look upon me,
>   Though I appear with all my faults.
> *Amin.*—Stand up.
>   This is no new way to beget more sorrow:
>   Heaven knows I have too many ; do not mock me ;

Though I am tame and bred up with my wrongs,
Which are my foster-brothers, I may leap
Like a hand-wolf into my natural wilderness,
And do an outrage: pray thee, do not mock me.
Evad.—My whole life is so leprous, it infects
All my repentance, I would buy your pardon
Though at the highest set, even with my life.
That slight contrition, that's no sacrifice
For what I have committed.
Amin.—Sure I dazzle:
There cannot be a faith in that foul woman,
That knows no god more mighty than her mischiefs.
Thou dost still worse, still number on thy faults,
To press my poor heart thus.   Can I believe
There's any seed of virtue in that woman
Left to shoot up, that dares go on in sin
Known, and so known as thine is? O Evadne!
Would there were any safety in thy sex,
That I might put a thousand sorrows off,
And credit thy repentance: but I must not;
Thou hast brought me to the dull calamity,
To that strange misbelief of all the world,
And all things that are in it, that I fear
I shall fall like a tree, and find my grave,
Only remembering that I grieve.
Evad.—My lord,
Give me your griefs: you are an innocent.
A soul as white as heaven; let not my sins
Perish your noble youth: I do not fall here
To shadow my dissembling with my tears,
As all say women can, or to make less
What my hot will hath done, which Heaven and you
Knows to be tougher than the hand of time
Can cut from man's remembrance; no, I do not;
I do appear the same, the same Evadne,
Dress'd in the shames I lived in, the same monster.
But these are names of honour, to what I am;
I do present myself the foulest creature,
Most poisonous, dangerous, and despised of men,
Lerna e'er bred, or Nilus; I am hell,
Till you, my dear lord, shoot your light into me,
The beams of your forgiveness: I am soul-sick,
And wither with the fear of one condemn'd,
Till I have got your pardon.
Amin.—Rise, Evadne.
Those heavenly powers that put this good into thee,
Grant a continuance of it: I forgive thee;
Make thyself worthy of it, and take heed,
Take heed, Evadne, this be serious;
Mock not the powers above, that can and dare

Reach constantly at something that is near it ;
I will redeem one minute of my age,
Or like another Niobe I'll weep.
Till I am water.
Amin.—I am now dissolved :
My frozen soul melts : may each sin thou hast,
Find a new mercy : rise, I am at peace :
Hadst thou been thus, thus excellently good,
Before that devil king tempted thy frailty,
Sure thou hadst made a star : give me thy hand ;
From this time I will know thee, and as far
As honour gives me leave, be thy Amintor :
When we meet next, I will salute thee fairly,
And pray the gods to give thee happy days :
My charity shall go along with thee,
Though my embraces must be far from thee.—
    Men's Natures more hard and subtile than Women's
How stubbornly this fellow answer'd me !
There is a vile dishonest trick in man,
More than in woman : all the men I meet
Appear thus to me, are harsh and rude,
And have a subtility in everything,
Which love could never know ; but we fond women
Harbour the easiest and smoothest thoughts
And think all shall go so : it is unjust
That men and women should be match'd together."

MASSINGER.—As a poet and dramatist, Massinger ranks **far** below his contemporaries. He rarely touches the heart, or kindles the fancy. There is something in his characters vulgar **and** unnatural, and they are read with little sympathy or enthusiasm.

The Italian comedy which had so much influence on our early dramatic poets, is seen clearly in this poet's writings, **and** several passages in his works have a striking resemblance to Moliere. He certainly was a follower of the Italian theatre, which then consisted of nothing else but these burlesque comedies. His Comedy *The City Madam* which is a satire against the city women for aping the fashions of the Court ladies, is worth quoting as an example of his productions:—

> *Luke.*—" Save you, sister.
> I now dare style you so. You were before
> Too glorious to be look'd on : now you appear
> Like a city matron, and my pretty nieces
> Such things
> As they were born and bred there. Why should you ape
> The fashions of court ladies, whose high titles
> And pedigrees of long descent give warrant
> For their superfluous bravery ? 'twas monstrous.
> Till now you ne'er looked lovely.
> *Lady.*—Is this spoken?
> In scorn
> *Luke.*—Fie, no ; with judgment. I make good
> My promise, and now show you like yourselves,
> In your own natural shapes.
> *Lady.*—We acknowledge
> We have deserved ill from you, yet despair not,
> Though we'er at your disposure, you'll maintain us
> Like your brother's wife and daughters.
> *Luke.*—'Tis my purpose.
> *Lady.*—And not make us ridiculous.
> *Luke.*—Admired rather,
> As fair examples for our proud city dames
> And their proud blood to imitate. Hear
> Gently, and in gentle phrase I'll reprehend
> Your late disguised deformity.
> Your father was
> An honest country farmer, Goodman Humble,
> By his neighbours ne'er called master. Did your pride
> Descend from him? but let that pass. Your fortune,
> Or rather your husband's industry, advanced you
> To the rank of merchant's wife. He made a knight,
> And your sweet mistress-ship ladyfied, you wore
> Satin on solemn days, a chain of gold,
> A velvet hood, rich borders, and sometimes
> A dainty miniver cap, a silver pin
> Headed with a pearl worth threepence : and thus far
> You were privileged, and no man envied it ;
> It being for the city's honour that
> There should be distinction between
> The wife of a patrician and a plebeian,—
> But when the height

No English workman then could please your fancy;
The French and Tuscan dress, your whole discourse;
This bawd to prodigality entertain'd,
To buz into your ears, what shape this countess
Appear'd in, the last mask; and how it drew
The young lord's eyes upon her: and this usher
Succeeded in the eldest 'prentice's place,
To walk before you. Then, as I said,
(The reverend hood cast off) your borrow'd hair,
Powder'd and curl'd, was by your dresser's art
Form'd like a coronet, hang'd with diamonds,
And the richest orient pearls; your carkanets,
That did adorn your neck, of equal value;
Your Hungerland bands, and Spanish Quellio ruffs:
Great lords and ladies feasted, to survey
Embroider'd petticoats; and sickness feign'd,
That your nightrails of forty pounds a-piece
Might be seen with envy of the visitants:
Rich pantables in ostentation shown,
And roses worth a family. You were served
In plate;
Stirr'd not a foot within a coach; and going
To church, not for devotion, but to show
Your pomp, you were tickled when the beggars cried
Heaven save your honour! This idolatry
Paid to a painted room. And, when you lay
In childbed, at the christening of this minx,
I well remember it, as you had been
An absolute princess (since they have no more),
Three several chambers hung; the first with arras,
And that for waters; the second, crimson satin,
For the meaner sort of guests; the third of scarlet
Of the rich Tyrian dye: a canopy
To cover the brat's cradle; you in state,
Like Pompey's Julia.
Lady.—No more, I pray you.
Luke.— Of this be sure you will not. I'll cut off
Whatever is exorbitant in you,
Or in your daughters; and reduce you to
Your natural forms and habits; not in revenge
Of your base usage of me; but to fright
Others by your example."

FORD.—We may class Ford as one of the first order of poets.

His works exhibit a grandeur of soul, and sublimity of conception. As Lamb truly says " He sought for sublimity, not by parcels, in metaphors or visible images, but directly where she has her full residence in the heart of man : in the actions and sufferings of the greatest minds." Nothing can be grander than the solemn address at the Altar by Calantha to the dead body of her husband, contained in the last scene of *The Broken Heart* :—

> "Of my contracted lord : bear witness all,
> I put my mother's wedding-ring upon
> His finger ; 'twas my father's last bequest.
> Thus I new marry him, whose wife I am ;
> Death shall not separate us.   O my lords,
> I but deceived your eyes with antick gesture,
> When one news straight came huddling on another
> Of death, and death, and death ; still I danced forward ;
> But it struck home, and here, and in an instant.
> Be such mere women, who with shrieks and outcries
> Can vow a present end to all their sorrows ;
> Yet live to vow new pleasures, and outlive them.
> They are the silent griefs which cut the heart-strings.
> Let me die smiling."

For another example of Ford's writings, *The Lover's Melancholy* is almost incomparable :—

> "Passing from Italy to Greece, the tales
> Which poets of an elder time had feign'd,
> To glorify their Tempe, bred in me
> Desire of visiting that paradise,
> To Thessaly I came, and living private,
> Without acquaintance of more sweet companions
> Than the old inmates to my love, my thoughts,
> I day by day frequented silent groves
> And solitary walks.. One morning early
> This accident encounter'd me : I heard
> The sweetest and most ravishing contention
> That art or nature ever were at strife in.
> A sound of music touch'd mine ears, or rather
> Indeed entranced my soul : as I stole nearer,
> Invited by the melody, I saw
> This youth, this fair-faced youth, upon his lute
> With strains of strange variety and harmony
> Proclaiming (as it seem'd) so bold a challenge
> To the clear quiristers of the woods, the birds,
> That as they flock'd about him, all stood silent,
> Wondering at what they heard.   I wonder'd too.
> A nightingale,
> Nature's best skill'd musician, undertakes

Meeting in one full centre of delight.
The bird (ordain'd to be
Music's first martyr) strove to imitate
These several sounds : which when her warbling throat
Fail'd in, for grief down dropt she on his lute
And brake her heart. It was the quaintest sadness,
To see the conqueror upon her hearse
To weep a funeral elegy of tears.
He looks upon the trophies of his art.
Then sigh'd, then wiped his eyes, then sigh'd, and cried
"Alas! poor creature, I will soon revenge
This cruelty upon the author of it.
Henceforth this lute, guilty of innocent blood,
Shall never more betray a harmless peace
To an untimely end :" and in that sorrow,
As he was pashing it against a tree,
I suddenly stept in."

BEN JONSON. —The works of Jonson appear to be the result of severe and continual labour. The subjects of his plays are generally wearisome, and his greatest fault is that he holds too long on to one idea. Fuller says of him. "His parts were not so ready to *run of themselves,* as able to answer the spur, so that it may be truly said of him, that he had an *elaborate wit,* wrought out of his own industry. He would *sit silent* in learned company, and suck in (*besides wine*) their several humours into his observation. What was *ore* in others, he was able to *refine* himself." * His works manifest great depth of knowledge, both classical and general, but they strike one as being too strained. It has been said of him, that "his plays were works. while others works, were

* Fuller's "Worthies of England."

plays." He has described with unflinching truth, the vices and
passions of his time, and has delineated human nature with extra-
ordinary keenness and power.

Jonson stands without doubt the first comedy writer of that age
and his comedies will endure reading, in spite of their occasional
vulgarities, so long as there are men of learning to read and admire
them. He was not a favourite with his brother writers, perhaps
from the fact that he possessed a great amount of arrogance and was
desirous of ruling the realms of Parnassus with a despotic sceptre.
It appears also that his plays were frequently unsuccessful.
D'Israeli in his Literary Curiosities has given three Satiric odes,
written by Jonson, upon the failure of his *" New-Inn* or *The Light
Heart,"* the title of which was printed in the following manner :—
" New-Inn or *The Light Heart*; a Comedy never acted, but
most negligently played by some, the King's servants ; and more
squeamishly beheld and censured by others, the King's subjects,
1629. Now at last set at liberty to the readers, his Majesty's
servants and subjects, to be judged, 1631." At the end of this
play he published the following ode, in which he threatens to
quit the stage for ever ; and turn at once a Horace, an Anacreon,
and a Pindar.

> "Come, leave the loathed stage,
>   And the more loathsome age ;
> Where pride and impudence (in fashion knit)
>   Usurp the chair of wit.
> Inditing and arraigning every day
>   Something they call a play.
>   Let their fastidious, vaine
>   Commission of braine
> Run on, and rage, sweat, censure, and condemn ;
> They were not made for thee,—less thou for them.
>
>   Say that thou pour'st them wheat,
>   And they will acorns eat ;
> 'Twere simply fury, still, thyself to waste
>   On such as have no taste !
> To offer them a surfeit of pure bread,
>   Whose appetites are dead !
>   No, give them graines their fill,
>   Husko, Draff, to drink and swill.

If they love less, and leave the lusty wine,
Envy them not their palate with the swine.

    No doubt some mouldy tale
    Like PERICLES, and stale
As the shrieve's crusts, and nasty as the fish,
    Scraps, out of every dish
Thrown forth, and rak'd into the common tub,
    May keep up the play-club:
    There sweepings do as well
    As the best-ordered meale.
For who the relish of these guests will fit,
Needs set them but the almes-basket of wit.

    And much good do't you then,
    Brave plush and velvet men
Can feed on orts, and safe in your stage-clothes,
    Dare quit, upon your oathes,
The stagers, and the stage-wrights too (your peers).
    Of larding your large ears
    With their foul comic socks,
    Wrought upon twenty blocks:
Which, if they're torn, and turn'd, and patch'd enough,
The gamesters share your guilt, and you their stuff.

    Leave things so prostitute.
    · And take the Alcæich lute,
Or thine own Horace or Anacreon's lyre;
    Warm thee by Pindar's fire;
And, tho' thy nerves be shrunk, and blood be cold,
    Ere years have made thee old,
    Strike that disdainful heat
    Throughout, to their defeat;
As curious fools, and envious of thy strain,
May, blushing, swear no palsy's in thy brain.

    But when they hear thee sing
    The glorious of thy king,
His zeal to God, and his just awe o'er men;
    They may blood-shaken then,
Feel such a flesh-quake to possess the powers,
    As they shall cry like ours,
    In sound of peace, or wars,
    No harp ere hit the stars,
In turning forth the acts of his sweet raign,
And raising Charles his chariot 'bove his wain. "

pedantical use of his learning." In it Jonson has revived the
whole court of Augustus by a learned spell, and we are admitted
to the society of the illustrious dead. It is a very fine passage
where Ovid bewails his hard condition in being banished from
the Court, and the society of the princess Julia :—

> " Banish'd the Court? let me be banish'd life,
> Since the chief end of life is there concluded.
> Within the court is all the kingdom bounded ;
> And as her sacred sphere doth comprehend
> Ten thousand times so much, as so much place
> In any part of all the empire else,
> So every body, moving in her sphere,
> Contains ten thousand times as much in him
> As any other her choice orb excludes,
> As in a circle a magician, then,
> Is safe against the spirit he excites,
> But out of it is subject to his rage,
> And loseth all the virtue of his art ;
> So I, exiled the circle of the court,
> Lose all the good gifts that in it I joy'd.
> No virtue current is, but with her stamp ;
> And no vice vicious, blanch'd with her white hand.
> The court's the abstract of all Rome's desert,
> And my dear Julia the abstract of the court.
> Methinks, now I come near her, I respire
> Some air of that late comfort I received :
> And while the evening with her modest veil.
> Gives leave to such poor shadows as myself
> To steal abroad, I, like a heartless ghost,
> Without the living body of my love,
> Will here walk, and attend her.   For I know
> Not far from hence she is imprisoned,
> And hopes of her strict guardian to bribe
> So much admittance, as to speak to me,
> And cheer my fainting spirits with her breath.
>   JULIA *appears above at her chamber window.*
> *Julia.*—Ovid! my love !
> *Ovid.*—Here, heavenly Julia.
> *Julia.*— Here! and not here! O, how that word doth play
> With both our fortunes, different, like ourselves;
> But one, and yet divided, as opposed ;
> I high, thou low ! O, this our plight of place
> Doubly presents the two lets of our love,
> Local and ceromonial height and lowness ;
> Both ways, I am too high, and thou too low.
> Our minds are even, yet : O, why should our bodies
> That are their slaves, be so without their rule?

I'll cast myself down to thee ; if I die,
I'll ever live with thee: no height of birth
Of place, of duty, or of cruel power,
Shall keep me from thee; should my father lock
This body up within a tomb of brass, ·
Yet I'll be with thee.   If the forms, I hold
Now in my soul, be made one substance with it ;
That soul immortal ; and the same 'tis now;
Death cannot raze the effects she now retaineth :
And then may she be anywhere she will.
The souls of parents rule not children's souls ;
When death sets both in their dissolved estates,
Then is no child nor father : then eternity
Frees all from any temporal respect.
I come, my Ovid ; take me in thine arms;
And let me breathe my soul into thy breast.
Ovid.—O stay, my love ; the hopes thou dost conceive
Of thy quick death, and of thy future life,
Are not authentical.   Thou choosest death,
So thou might'st joy thy love in the other life.
But know, my princely love, when thou art dead,
Thou only must survive in perfect soul ;
And in the soul are no affections :
We pour out our affections with our blood ;
And with our blood's affection fade our loves.
No life hath love in such sweet state as this ;
No essence is so dear to moody sense,
As flesh and blood, whose quintessence is sense.
Beauty, composed of blood and flesh, moves more,
And is more plausible to blood and flesh,
Than spiritual beauty can be to the spirit.
Such apprehension as we have in dreams
(When sleep, the bond of senses, locks them up),
Such shall we have when death destroys them quite.
If love be then thy object, change not life ;
Live high and happy still ; I still below,
Close with my fortunes, in thy height shall joy."

* * * *

Ovid.— "Ay me ! there is no stay
In amorous pleasures.   If both stay, both die.
I hear thy father.   Hence, my deity,
Fear forgeth sounds in my deluded ears ;
I did not hear him : I am mad with love.
There is no spirit, under heaven, that works
With such illusion : yet, such witchcraft kill me,
Ere a sound mind, without it, save my life.
Here on my knees I worship the blest place,
That held my goddess ; and the loving air,
That closed her body in his silken arms ;

> Vain Ovid! kneel not to the place, nor air,
> She's in thy heart, rise then, and worship there."

The comparison of the mind to a temple contained in the *New-Inn* is also very fine, and there are some striking passages in the *Conspiracy of Cataline.* For instance, on the morning of the conspiracy :—

> *Lentulus.*—"It is methinks a morning full of fate :
> It riseth slowly, as her sullen car
> Had all the weights of sleep and death hung at it.
> She is not rosy-finger'd, but swoln black.
> Her face is like a water turn'd to blood,
> And her sick head is bound about with clouds,
> As if she threaten'd night ere noon of day.
> It does not look as it would have a hail
> Or health wish'd in it, as on other morns."

In the Comedy *The Case is altered,* the passage of Jacques worshipping his gold is excellently written :—

> "'Tis not to be told
> What servile villanies men will do for gold.
> O, it began to have a huge strong smell,
> With lying so long together in a place:
> I'll give it vent, it shall have shift enough ;
> And if the devil, that envies all goodness,
> Have told them of my gold, and where I kept it,
> I'll set his burning nose once more at work
> To smell where I removed it.   Here it is ;
> I'll hide and cover it with this horse-dung.
> Who will suppose that such a precious nest
> Is crown'd with such a dung-hill excrement ?
> In, my dear life, sleep sweetly, my dear child,
> Scarce lawfully begotten, but yet gotten,
> And that's enough.   Rot all hands that come near thee
> Except mine own.   Burn out all eyes that see thee,
> Except mine own.   All thoughts of thee be poison
> To their enamour'd hearts, except mine own.
> I'll take no leave, sweet prince, great emperor,
> But see thee every minute : king of kings,
> I'll not be rude to thee, and turn my back
> In going from thee, but go backward out,
> With my face toward thee, with humble courtesies."

Shirley, Lord Brooks and a few others, claim a place amongst the worthies of this era, but these pages will not allow of comment upon them. Warton has given an admirable account of these more obscure poets, in his History of English Poetry.

CHAPTER XII.

SPENSER.

SPENSER.—The name of Spenser, is a name justly revered by all Englishmen. If Chaucer be called the day-star, Spenser may certainly be pronounced, the sunrise of our poetry. Yet their geniuses were eminently different, that of Chaucer was of the active type ; Spenser's of the contemplative : Chaucer was dramatic, Spenser philosophical: Chaucer objective, Spenser subjective. The epitaph on Spenser's tomb is strangely characteristic of this.

> "Here nigh to Chaucer, Spenser lies ; to whom
> In genius next he was, as now in tomb."

> "Here nigh to Chaucer, Spenser, stands thy hearse.
> Still nearer standst thou to him in thy verse ;
> Whilst thou didst live, lived English poetry,
> Now thou art dead, it fears that it shall die."

Spenser, however antiquated his style, is certainly the earliest of our modern English poets. The great thing which seems to have prevented him from reaching the pinnacle of poetic excellence, seems to be the excessive wildness of the machinery which he has adopted from the Italian School—from Ariosto and Tasso.

The *Fairy Queen,* with all its faults of structure, is still the wonder of a third century, and the fountain from which our great poets of the last age imbibed their inspiration most deeply. We cannot with its few defects, be blind to the beauty of its many passages. The sublime description of "*Him who with the night durst ride,*" the "*House of Riches,*" the "*Canto of Jealousy,*" the "*Mask of Cupid,*" are splendid specimens of genius. Schlegel says, " The *Fairy Queen* conveys to us a good idea of the romantic spirit manifest in England under Elizabeth, the virgin Queen, whose vanity was flattered by allusions delicately veiled in mythological and poetic guise." Spenser is rich and picturesque; his lyrics breathe an idyalic tenderness, and his muse is altogether redolent of the old Troubadours.

There is a richness in the allegorical fictions of Spenser, which almost vies with the splendour of the ancient mythology, although inconsistent to an excess. In reading his works, we live among ideal beings ; he is the painter of abstracts, and he is picturesque solely from his intense love of beauty : but his delineations are not guided by truth—rather by the movements of an inexhaustible imagination. His strength assumes the character of vastness and sublimity, seen through the same visionary and preternatural medium. Take, as an example, his *Cave of Mammon,* of which I will quote a few verses :—

"At last he came unto a gloomy glade,
Cover'd with boughs and shrubs from heaven's light,
Whereas he sitting found in secret shade
An uncouth, savage, and uncivil wight,
Of griesly hue and foul ill favour'd sight ;
His face with smoke was tann'd, and eyes were blear'd,
His head and beard with soot were ill bedight,
His coal black hands did seem to have been sear'd,
In smith's fire-spitting forge, and nails like claws appear'd.

His iron coat, all overgrown with rust,
Was underneath enveloped with gold,
Whose glist'ning gloss, darkened with filthy dust,
Well yet appeared to have been of old
A work of rich entail and curious mould,
Woven with antics and wild imagery ;
And in his lap a mass of coin he told,
And turned upside down, to feed his eye
And covetous desire with his huge treasury.

And round about him lay on every side
Great heaps of gold that never could be spent ;
Of which some were rude ore, not purified,
Of Mulciber's devouring element ;
Some others were new driven and distent
Into great ingots and to wedges square ;
Some in round plates without a moniment ;
But most were stamp'd, and in their metal bare
The antique shapes of kings and kesars strange and rare.

Soon as he Guyon saw, in great affright
And haste he rose for to move aside
Those precious hills from stranger's envious sight,
And down them poured through an hole full wide
Into the hollow earth, them there to hide,
But Guyon, lightly to him leaping, stay'd
His hand that trembled as one terrified ;
And though himself were at the sight dismayed,
Yet him perforce restrain'd, and to him doubtful said;

What art thou man, (if man at all thou art)
That here in desert hast thine habitance,
And these rich hills of wealth dost hide apart
From the world's eye, and from her right usance? *
Thereat, with staring eyes fixed askance,
In great disdain he answer'd : 'Hardy Elf,
That darest view my direful countenance,
I read thee rash and heedless of thyself,
To trouble my still seat, and heaps of precious pelf.

God of the world and worldlings I me call,
Great Mammon, greatest god below the sky,
That of my plenty pour out unto all,
And unto none my graces do envy :
Riches, renown, and principality,
Honour, estate, and all this world's good,
For which men toil and sweat incessantly,
From me do flow into an ample flood,
And in the hollow earth have their eternal brood.

    *   *   *   *

At length they came into a larger space,
That stretch'd itself into an ample plain ;
Through which a beaten broad highway did trace
That straight did lead to Pluto's griesly reign.
By that wayside there sat internal Pain,
And fast beside him sat tumultuous strife :
The one in hand an iron whip did strain ;
The other brandished a bloody knife ;
And both did gnash their teeth, and both did threaten life.

On the other side in one consort there sate
Cruel Revenge, and rancorous Despite,
Disloyal Treason, and heart-burning Hate ;
But gnawing Jealousy, out of their sight
Sitting alone, his bitter lips did bite,
And trembling Fear still to and fro did fly,
And found no place where safe he shroud him might :
Lamenting Sorrow did in darkness lie,
And Shame his ugly face did hide from living eye.

And over them sad horror with grim hue
Did always sore, beating his iron wings ;
And after him owls and night-ravens flew,
The hateful messengers of heavy things,
Of death and dolor telling sad tidings ;
While sad Celeno, sitting on a cliff,
A song of bale and bitter sorrow sings,
That heart of flint asunder could have rift ;
Which having ended after him she flieth swift.

All these before the gates of Pluto lay,
By whom they passing spake unto them nought,

* Usage.

But th' elfin knight with wonder all the way,
Did feed his eyes, and filled his inner thought.
At last him to a little door he brought.
That to the gate of hell, which gaped wide,
Was next adjoining, nor them parted ought :
Betwixt them both was but a little stride,
That did the house of Riches from hell's mouth divide.

     *   *   *   *

In all that room was nothing to be seen
But huge great iron chests, and coffers strong,
All barred with double bends that none could ween,
Them to efforce by violence or wrong :
On every side they placed were along ;
But all the ground with skulls were scattered,
And dead men's bones, which round about were flung,
Whose lives, it seemed, whilome there were shed,
And their vile carcases now left unburied.

They forward pass ; nor Guyon yet spoke word,
Till that they came unto an iron door.
Which to them opened of his own accord,
And showed of riches such exceeding store,
As eye of man did never see before,
Nor ever could within one place be found,
Though all the wealth which is, or was of yore,
Could gathered be through all the world around,
And that above were added to that underground.

The charge thereof unto a covetous Sprite
Commanded was, who thereby did attend,
And warily awaited day and night,
From other covetous fiends it to defend,
Who it to rob and ransack did intend,
Then Mammon, turning to that warrior, said ;
Lo ! here the world's bliss : lo ! here the end,
To which all men do aim, rich to be made,
Such grace now to be happy is before thee laid.

'Certes,' (said he) I'll not thine offer'd grace,
Nor to be made so happy do intend :
Another bliss before mine eyes I place,
Another happiness, another end.
To them that list these base regards I lend ;
But I in arms, and in achievement brave,
Do rather choose my flitting hours to spend,
And to be Lord of those that riches have,
Than them to have myself and be their servile slaves.

Thereat the fiend his gnashing teeth did grate,
And griev'd so long to lack his greedy prey ;
For well he weened that so glorious bait,
Would tempt his guest to take thereof assay :

Had he so done, he had him snatched away,
More light than Culver in the falcon's fist.
Eternal God thee save from such decay!
But, when as Mammon saw his purpose miss'ed,
Him to entrap unwares another way he wist.

Thence forward he him led, and shortly brought
Unto another room, whose door forthright
To him did open, as it had been taught,
Therein a hundred ranges there were pight,
And hundred furnaces all burning bright:
Deformed creatures, horrible in sight,
And every end his busy pains applied
To melt the golden metal ready to be tried.

One with great bellows gathered filling air,
And with forc'd wind the fuel did inflame,
Another did the dying brands repair,
With iron tongs, and sprinkled oft the same,
With liquid waves, fierce Vulcans rage to tame,
Who, mast'ring them, renewed his former heat:
Some secured the dross that from the metal came,
Some stirred the molten ore with ladles great:
And every one did toil, and every one did sweat.

But, when an earthly wight they present saw,
Glistening in arms and battailous array,
From their hot work they did themselves withdraw,
To wonder at the sight; for till that day
They never creatures saw that came that way:
Their staring eyes sparkling with fervent fire,
And ugly shapes did nigh the man dismay,
That, were it not for shame, he would retire ;
Till that him thus bespake their sovereign Lord and sire."

The description of Cellas in the Cave of Despair is also exquisitely drawn. In the *Fairy Queen* the three first books are very superior to the others. Macaulay says, "The story of the Fairy Queen is more like a succession of triumphal arches than a regular building : we pass on with admiration and delight, and yet both are occasionally cooled by the labrynthical irregularity of the design. We miss that regular subserviency of minor events and characters to those which are great and important, which constitute the charm of a perfect story, whether we call it epic or by any other appellation." Spenser's personification, notwithstanding, is excessively inconsistent. Superlative heroes and peerless beauties are crowded upon us in such numbers, that we lose sight of them in the blaze of each other.

Many of Spenser's allegories contain allusions to living historical personages of that time. *Gloriana* is an emblem of Queen Elizabeth ; *Envy* a type of the unfortunate Mary, Queen of Scots, and the *Knight* in dangerous distress, is Henry IV of France.

Two of the finest examples of this poet's writings are the passages where Una is followed by the lion in *Canto III.* of the first Book ; and when Belphæbe finds Smais wounded, and conveys him to her dwelling. (*Book III Canto V.*)

"Nought is there under heaven's wild hollowness,
That moves more dear compassion of mind,
Than beauty brought t'unworthy wretchedness
Through envy's snares, or fortune's freaks unkind.
I, whether lately through her brightness blind,
Or through all allegiance, and fast fealty,
Which I do owe unto all womankind,
Feel my heart press'd with so great agony,
When such I see, that all for pity I could die.

And now it is impassioned so deep,
For fairest Una's sake, of whom I sing,
That my frail eyes these lines with tears do steep,
To think how she through guileful handling,
Though true as touch, though daughter of a king,
Though fair as ever living wight was fair,
Though nor in word nor deed ill meriting,
Is from her knight divorced in de
And her due loves deriv'd to that vile witches share.

Yet she, most faithful lady all this while
Forsaken, woful, solitary maid,
Far from all people's press, as in exile,
In wilderness and wasteful deserts stray'd,
To seek her knight ; who, subtily betray'd
Through that late vision which th' enchanter wrought,
Had her abandon'd. She of nought afraid,
Through woods and waste wide him daily sought ;
Yet wished tidings none of him unto her brought.

One day, nigh weary of the irksome way,
From her unhasty beast she did alight ;
And on the grass her dainty limbs did lay,
In secret shadow, far from all men's sight.
From her fair head her fillet she undid,
And laid her stole aside. Her angel's face,
As the great eye of heaven, shined bright,
And made a sunshine in the shady place ;
Did never mortal eye behold such heavenly grace.

It fortuned, out of the thickest wood,
A ramping lion rushed suddenly,
Hunting full greedy after savage blood.
Soon as the royal virgin he did spy,
With gaping mouth at her ran greedily,
To have at once devoured her tender corse;
But to the prey when as he drew more nigh,
His bloody rage assuaged with remorse,
And, with the sight amazed, forgat his furious force.

Instead thereof, he kiss'd her weary feet,
And lick'd her lily hands with fawning tongue,
As he her wronged innocence did weet;
O, how can beauty master the most strong,
And simple truth subdue avenging wrong!
Whose yielded pride and proud submission,
Still dreading death, when she had marked long,
Her heart gan melt in great compassion
And drizzling tears did shed for pure affection.

'The Lion, lord of every beast in field,'
Quoth she, 'his princely puissance doth abate,
And mighty proud to humble weak does yield,
Forgetful of the hungry rage, which late
Him prick'd, in pity of my sad estate:
But he, my Lion, and my noble Lord,
How does he find in cruel heart to hate
Her, that him lov'd and ever most ador'd,
As the God of my life? why hath he me abhorr'd.'

Redounding tears did choke th' end of her plaint,
Which softly echoed from the neighbouring wood;
And, sad to see her sorrowful constraint,
The kingly beast upon her gazing stood:
With pity calmed down fell his angry mood;
At last in close heart shutting up her pain,
Arose the virgin, born of heavenly brood
And to her snowy palfrey got again,
To seek her stray'd champion if she might attain.

The Lion would not leave her desolate,
But with her went along, as a strong guard.
Of her chaste person, and a faithful mate
Of her sad troubles and misfortunes hard:
Still, when she slept he kept both watch and ward;
And, when she wak'd, he waited diligent,
With humble service to her will prepared:
From her fair eyes he took commandment,
And ever by her looks conceived her intent.

Long she thus travelled through deserts wide,
By which she thought her wand'ring knight should pass,
Yet never show of living wight espied

T

Till that at length she found the trodden grass,
In which the tract of people's footing was,
Under the steep foot of a mountain hore:
The same she follows, till at last she has
A damsel spied, slow looting her before,
That on her shoulders sad a pot of water bore.

To whom approaching she to her gan call,
To wit if dwelling place were nigh at hand,
But the rude wench her answered nought at all,
She could not hear, not speak, nor understand;
Till, seeing by her side the lion stand,
With sudden fear her pitcher down she threw,
And fled away: for never in that land
Face of fair Lady she before did view,
And that dread lion's look her cast in deadly hue.

Full fast she fled, nor ever looked behind,
As if her life upon the wager lay;
And home she came, whereas her mother blind,
Sate in eternal night, nought could she say;
But, sudden catching hold, did her dismay
With quaking hands, and other signs of fear:
Who, full of ghastly fright and cold affray,
Gan shut the door. By this arrived there
Dame Una, weary Dame, and entrance did require.

Which when none yielded, her unruly page,
With his rude claws the wicket open rent,
And let her in; where, of his cruel rage
Nigh dead with fear, and faint astonishment,
She found them both in darksome corner pent,
Where that old woman day and night did pray
Upon her beads, devoutly penitent:
Nine hundred *Pater Nosters* every day,
And thrice nine hundred *Aves* she was wont to say.

And to augment her painful penance more,
Thrice every week in ashes she did sit,
And next her wrinkled skin rough sackcloth wore.
And thrice three times did fast for any bit;
But now, for fear her beads she did forget:
Whose needless dread for to remove away,
Fair Una framed words and count'nance fit;
Which hardly done, at length she gan them pray,
That in their cottage small that night she rest her may.

The day is spent; and cometh drowsy night,
When every creature shrouded is in sleep.
Sad Una down her lays in weary plight,
And at her feet the lion watch doth keep:
Instead of rest she does lament and weep,
For the late loss of her dear loved knight,

members by right of birth. The defects of her personal character were scarcely discernible in the blaze of ideal splendour that surrounded her throne, while her nobler qualities had full scope and instant recognition. In this poem we see reflected and interpreted the history of this great era of the English nation, the era which succeeded the defeat of the Spanish Armada. By this event "domestic treason," had been crushed, and Englishmen were fulfilling and transcending the aspirations of chivalry. With the Elizabethan worthies, it was an instinct to uphold, each in his own person, and in the performance of the task assigned him, the honour of the English names, and to heed no cost, sacrifice, or danger where that was concerned. And these are the facts that we see so correctly and strikingly exemplified in this great poet's work.

Spenser's life is wrapt in an obscurity similar to that of his great contemporary, Shakespeare. The birth year of each poet is determined by inference. The only sure information we have is, that they were both men of the greatest learning—that they both died in the close vicinity of Westminster Abbey, and lie buried near each other in that splendid cemetery.

We may see much of Spenser's life in various parts of his works, even to his birth; for in his *Prothalamium* he sings of certain swans whom in a vision he saw floating down the river "Themmes," that,

"At length they all to merry London came,
To merry London, my most kindly nurse,
That to me gave this life's first native source,
Though from another place I take my name,
An house of ancient fame."

In the same way we learn that his mother's name was Elizabeth. This appears from *Sonnet* seventy-four where he apostrophizes those

For heat of heedless lust me so did sting,
That I of doubted danger had no fear :
    I went the wasteful woods and forest wide,
    Without a dread from wolves to be espied.

I wont to range, amid the mazy thicket,
And gather nuts to make me Christmas game,
And joyed oft to chase the trembling pricket,
Or hunt the artless hare till she were tame.
    What recked I of wintry ages waste?—
    Tho' deemed I my spring would ever last.

How often have I scaled the craggy Oke,
All to dislodge the raven of her nest?
How have I wearied with many a stroke
The stately walnut-tree, the while the rest
    Under the tree fell all for nuts at strife?
    For like to me was liberty and life.

And for I was the same in loser years,
(Whether the Muse so wrought me from my birth,
Or I too much believed my shepherd peers,)
Somewhat inclin'd to song and music's mirth,
    A good old shepherd, Wrenock was his name,
    Made me by art more cunning in the same.

From thence I durst in daring-deeds compare
With shepherd swain that ever fed in field;

CHAPTER XI.

SHAKESPEARE.

SHÁKESPEARE.—Campbell says, "Shakespeare is the poet of the world. The magnitude of his genius puts it beyond all private opinion to set defined limits to the admiration which is due to it. We dread the interference of criticism with a fascination so often inexplicable by critical laws, and justly apprehend that any man in standing between us and Shakespeare, may show for pretended spots upon his disk, only the shadows of his own opacity."

In this work, I have only aimed at expressing a passing thought, and quoted a few of what have not only appeared to me, but are generally acknowledged as the finest inspirations of this immortal bard. And even this has in it somewhat of a difficulty ; for the passages which we most admire are those which appeal nearest to our feelings ; and it is possible that those which I admire the most, may not accord with the admiration of my readers. Emerson observes, "Shakespeare is the only biographer of Shakespeare; and even he can tell nothing, except to the Shakespeare in us ; that is, to our most apprehensive and sympathetic hour." We have his recorded convictions on those questions which knock for answer at every heart—on life and death, on love and wealth, and poetry, on the prizes of life, and the ways whereby we come at them ; on the characters of men, and the influences, occult and open, which affect their fortunes ; and on those mysterious and demoniacal powers which defy our science, and which yet intervene their malice and their gift in our brightest hours.

The works of Shakespeare have become to a large part of the world, one of the necessities of life. In no other man's books probably, is there to be found, so much truth, wisdom, and beauty as in his. Great to all men, he is great to the greatest, and the homage of the highest intellects in the world is silently or with eloquent speech yielded to him. Among the many terms which have been applied to him, the following are some of the phrases in which other great men have striven to express their sense of his superiority : he has been called, the "myriad-minded man," the "greatest intellect who in one recorded world has left record of himself in the way of literature," the "poet of the human race," the "melodious priest of a *true* Catholicism." Ben Jonson, Milton, Dryden, Pope, and in our own day Coleridge, De Quincey, Carlyle, and Emerson, have led the chorus of his praise. In Germany, Lessing, Herder, Tieck, Wieland, Schlegel and Goethe, have contributed to establish his supremacy.

Pope says, "If ever any author deserved the name of an *original,* it was Shakespeare. Homer himself drew not his art so immediately from the fountains of nature : it proceeded through Egyptian strainers and channels, and came to him not without some tincture of the learning, or some cast of the models of those before him. The poetry of Shakespeare was inspiration : indeed, he is not so much an imitator, as an instrument of nature; and it is not so just to say that he speaks from her, as that she speaks through him. His *characters* are so much nature herself, that it is a sort of injury to call them by so distant a name as copies of her. Those of other poets have a constant resemblance, which shows that they received them from one another, and were but multipliers of the same image: each picture, like a mock-rainbow, is but a reflection of a reflection. But every single character in Shakespeare is as much an individual as those in life itself, it is as impossible to find any two alike; and such as from their relation or affinity in any respect appear most to be twins, will upon comparison be found remarkably distinct. To this life and variety of character we must add the wonderful preservation of it; which is such throughout his plays, that had all the speeches

been printed without the very names of the persons, I believe one
might have applied them with certainty to every speaker."

And this power, as Pope has truly said, "Shakespeare alone
possessed. He is the only one who has put into the mouth of an
actor, a speech which the person whom that actor was intended to
represent, might have spoken on the occasion to which it was as-
signed." In the well-known dialogue between Brutus and Antony,
it seems to us they must have uttered the same words. We per-
ceive the same reality, and exact representation of characters
in many other places. Hamlet might have pronounced the very
soliloquy, Macbeth and his Lady might have held the same dialogue,
and Falstaff and the merry Wives of Windsor, might have had
the same conversations as Shakespeare has ascribed to them.

It is observed by Schlegel of Shakespeare. "Profound sympathy
with Nature is diffused throughout his works, constituting, as it
were, their very soul : and it is this which animates his muse with
a fascinating grace of rich transparent beauty. This peculiar
element of Shakespeare's poetry, still remains a characteristic of
modern art, and will yet obtain a fuller development, when a
higher poetry shall no longer represent the superficial aspects of
every day life, but the secret life of the soul, in man as well as in
Nature. In this point of view, his profound insight into Nature's
secret workings, transports Shakespeare beyond the limits of
dramatic verse." *

This poet has attained a height and depth of dramatic represen-
tation which completely throws into the shade the most elaborate
efforts of educated and artistic bards : his works are a mirror of
actual life, inspired with glorious poetry, arousing in men all the
deeper, and hidden feelings of humanity. Fuller says, " He was an
eminent instance of the truth of that rule, *poeta non fit, sed nas-
citur* ; one is not made but born a poet. Indeed his *learning* was
but very little; so that as Cornish diamonds are not polished by any
lapidary, but are polished and smoothed even as they are taken
out of the earth, so *Nature* itself was all the art which was used
upon him."† It seems difficult to say anything of Shakespeare

---

* Schlegel's History of Literature.

that has not been said before. Whoever has read the volume of the Sonnets without finding that the poet had there revealed under masks, that are no marks to the intelligent, the core of friendship and of love, the confusion of sentiments in the most susceptible, and at the same time the most intellectual of men. Almost every trait in his private life, we can see delineated and exemplified in his dramas. In his numerous pictures of the gentleman and the king, we may see what forms and humanities pleased him; his delight in troops of friends, in large hospitality and cheerful giving. Let Simon, let Warwick, let Antonio the merchant, answer for his great heart. Little as we seem to know of Shakespeare, he is the one person in all modern history best known to us.

As a dramatist Shakespeare ranks first in the world, nor can there be found a single poet, ancient or modern, worthy to be compared with him: by his fancy he raises before us, as it were, the veil of an invisible world.

Shakespeare's youth fell at a time when the English were importunate for dramatic entertainments; every convenient place was made into a theatre. The best proof of its validity is the crowd of writers which suddenly broke into the field; most of which I have already spoken in the earlier chapters of this work. Thus it was that those who had to supply its demands, laid their hands upon everything within their reach, they were not particular as to the scenes, as long as they gained their ends. And Shakespeare in common with the rest worked upon popular tradition. We read, "The poet owes to his legend, what sculpture owed to the temple." Sculpture in Egypt and in Greece, grew up in subordination to architecture. It was the ornament of the temple wall: at first a rude relief carved on pediments, then the relief became bolder, and a head or arm was projected from the wall, the groups being still arranged with reference to the building, which serves also as a frame to hold the figures; and when, at last the greatest freedom of style and treatment was reached, the prevailing genius of architecture still enforced a certain calmness and continence in the statue. As soon as the statue was begun for itself, and with no reference to the temple or palace, the art began to decline: freak extravagance and exhibition took the place of the old temperance. This balance-wheel which the sculptor found in architecture, the perilous irritability of poetic talent found in the accumulated dramatic materials to which the people were already wonted, and which had a certain excellence which no single genius, however extraordinary, could hope to create." Shakespeare knew that tradition supplies a better fable than invention can. The demand for originality was not so much then as it is now. There was no literature for the million. The cheap press was unknown. Shakespeare accordingly attached himself to the drama, but even in his rudest efforts, he has introduced elements of gigantic grandeur and horror; even the representations of human degradation, which passed for merry jests with the vulgar, were in his reflecting spirit, joined with feelings of contempt or sorrowful sympathy. It is remarked, "Shakespeare has no peculiarity,—no importunate topic; but all is duly given, the great he tells greatly; the small, subordinately. He is wise without emphasis or assertion; he is strong as nature is strong, who lifts the land into mountain slopes without effort, by the same rule as she floats a bubble in the air, and like as well to do the one as the other."

There is no doubt that Shakespeare borrowed from all directions and used whatever he found. But he used them well. It was part of his genius; he

Exhausted world, and then imagined new;

although in reality the new world could only be made up of the elements supported by the old.

Shakespeare represents the world as it stood before him; he refleets in his writings what he felt and saw, though all separate from himself. To again quote Schlegel's words, "Others have sought to transport us for a moment, to an ideal condition of humanity: he presents us with a picture of man, in the depths of his fall and moral disorganization, with all his doings and sufferings, his thoughts and desires, with a painful minuteness." The youthful fervour of love in his Romeo is a mere inspiration of death:—

"O, she doth teach the torches to burn bright !
Her beauty hangs upon the cheek of night
Like a rich jewel in an Ethiop's ear :
Beauty too rich for use, for earth too dear !
So shows a snowy dove trooping with crows,
As yonder lady o'er her fellows show,
The measure done, I'll watch her place of stand,
And, touching hers, make happy my rude hand,
Did my heart love till know ? foreswear it, sight !
For I ne'er saw true beauty till this night."

*　　　*　　　*　　　*

'Tis torture, and not mercy : heaven is here,
Where Juliet lives ; and every cat, and dog,
And little mouse, every unworthy thing,
Live here in heaven, and may look on her,
But Romeo may not.—More validity,
More honourable state, more courtship lives
In carrion flies, than Romeo : they may seize
On the white wonder of dear Juliet's hand,
And steal immortal blessing from her lips ;
Who, even in pure and vestal modesty,
Still blush, as thinking their own kisses sin ;
But Romeo may not ; he is banished.
Flies may do this, when I from this must fly,
They are free men, but I am banished ?
And say'st thou yet, that exile is not death ?
Hadst thou no poison mix'd, no sharp-ground knife,
No sudden mean of death, though ne'er so mean,
But—banished—to kill me ; banished ?
O friar, the damned use that word in hell ;
Howlings attend it : How hast thou the heart,
Being a divine, a ghostly confessor,
A sin-absolver, and my friend profess'd,
To mangle me, with that word—banishment."

Again in his character of Lear he has wonderfully depicted pain
and grief, to a climax of rage and madness. For an example, the
passage in which the storm is raging on the heath :—

"Blow, wind, and crack your cheeks ! rage ! blow !
You cataracts, and hurricanes, spout,
Till you have drench'd our steeples, drown'd the cocks !
You sulphurous and thought-executing fires,　　.
Vaunt-couriers to oak-cleaving thunder bolts.
Singe my white head ! and thou, all-shaking thunder,
Strike flat the thick rotundity o'er the world !
Crack nature's moulds, all germens spill at once,
That make ungrateful men."

*　　　*　　　"　　　*

"Rumble thy belly full ! Spit, fire ! spout rain ;
Nor rain, wind, thunder, fire. are my daughters :
I tax not you, you elements, with unkindness,
I never gave you kingdom, call'd you children.
Yet owe me no subscription ; why then let fall
Your horrible pleasure ; here I stand, your slave,
A poor, infirm, weak, and despised old man :—
But yet I call you servile ministers,
That have with two pernicious daughters join'd
Your high-engender'd battles 'gainst a head
So old and white as this. O ! O ! 'tis foul."

Then again, where Hamlet's sceptical views of life, invest him
with a strange mysteriousness, we see the poet's own feelings, and
nobility of soul, brought forth in sublime philanthrophy and en-
thusiasm :—

" To be, or not to be, that is the question :—
Whether 'tis nobler in the mind, to suffer
The stings and arrows of outrageous fortune ;
Or to take arms against a sea of troubles,
And, by opposing, end them ?—To die,—to sleep,
No more ;—and, by a sleep, to say we end
The heart-ache, and the thousand natural shocks,
That flesh is heir to,—'tis a consummation.
Devoutly to be wish'd. To die ;—to sleep ;—
To sleep ! perchance to dream ;—ay, there's the rub
For in that sleep of death what dreams may come,
When we have shuffled off this mortal coil,
Must give us pause : There's the respect,
That makes calamity of so long life :
For who would bear the whips and scorns of time.
The oppressor's wrong, the proud man's contumely,
The pangs of despis'd love, the law's delay,
The insolence of office, and the spurns
That patient merit of the unworthy takes,
When he himself might his quietus make
With a bare bodkin ? who would fardels bear,
To grunt and sweat under a weary life ;
But that the dread of something after death,—
The undiscover'd country, from whose bourne
No traveller returns,—puzzles the will ;
And makes us rather bear those ills we have,
Than fly to others that we know not of :
Thus conscience does make cowards of us all
And thus the native hue of resolution
As sicklied o'er with the pale cast of thought ;
And enterprises of great pith and moment,
With this regard, their current turn away.
And lose the name of action."

Who's there?

Macbeth.—A friend.

Banquo.—What, sir, not yet at rest? The king's a-bed
He hath been in unusual pleasure, and
Sent forth great largess to your officers ;
This diamond he greets your wife withal,
By the name of most kind hostess ; and shut up
In measureless content.

Macbeth.—Being unprepared,
Our will became the servant to defect ;
Which else should free have wrought.

Banquo.—All's well.
I dreamt last night of the three weird sisters :
To you they have shew'd some truth.

Macbeth.—I think not of them :
Yet, when we can entreat an hour to serve,
Would spend it in some words upon that business,
If you would grant the time.

Banquo.—At your kind'st leisure.

Macbeth.—If you shall cleave to my consent,—when 'tis,
It shall make honour for you.

Banquo.—So I lose none.
In seeking to augment it, but still keep
My bosom franchised, and allegiance clear,
I shall be counsell'd.

Macbeth.—Good repose the while !

Banquo.—Thanks, sir ; the like to you !

To feeling, as to sight ? or art thou but
A dagger of the mind ; a false creation,
Proceeding from the heat-oppressed brain ?
I see thee yet, in form as palpable
As this which now I draw.
Thou marshal'st me the way that I was going :
And such an instrument I was to use.
Mine eyes are made the fools o' the other senses,
Or else worth all the rest.   I see thee still ;
And on thy blade, and dudgeon, gouts of blood,
Which was not so before.—There's no such thing :
It is the bloody business, which informs
Thus to mine eyes,—Now o'er the one half world.
Nature seems dead, and wicked dreams abuse
The curtain'd sleep; now witchcraft celebrates
Pale Hecate's offerings ; and wither'd murder,
Alarum'd, by his sentinel, the wolf,
Whose howl's his watch, thus with his stealthy pace,
With Tarquin's ravishing strides, towards his design
Moves like a ghost.—Thou sure and firm set earth,
Hear not my steps, which way they walk, for fear
The very stones prate of my whereabout,
And take the present horror from the time,
Which now suits with it.—Whiles I threat he lives ;
Words to the heat of deeds too cold breath gives.
I go, and it is done ; the bell invites me.
Hear it not, Duncan ; for it is a knell,
That summons thee to heaven or to hell. "

Shakespeare has explained all his characters, too, with terrible
vividness.   Take for example, the incantations of the witches in
Macbeth ; though they are in a great measure grotesque, yet the
effect upon is both serious and appalling, and we almost feel spell-
bound as was Macbeth.   We cannot laugh in their presence.   As
Lamb says, "we might as well laugh under a consciousness of the
principle of evil himself being truly and really present with us."

There is the same perfection and beauty in his descriptions.
Who but Shakespeare could have given the description of Dover
Cliff in " Lear."
" Come on sir; here's the place —stand still—How fearful,
And dizzy 'tis, to cast one eyes so low !

> The crows and choughs, that wing the midway air.
> Shew scarce so gross as beetles: half way down,
> Hangs one that gathers samphire,—dreadful trade!
> Methinks, he seems no bigger than his head:
> The fishermen, that walk upon the beach,
> Appear like mice; and yon tall anchoring bark,
> Diminish'd to her cock; her cock a buoy,
> Almost too small for sight: the murmuring surge,
> That on the unnumber'd idle pebbles chafes
> Cannot be heard so high:—I'll look no more:
> Lest my brain turn, and the deficient sight
> Topple down headlong."

Shakespeare has also beautifully described and represented the melody of music and sweet sounds in *The Merchant of Venice*:—

> "How sweet the moonlight sleeps upon the bank!
> Here will we sit, and let the sounds of music
> Creep in our ears, soft stillness, and the night,
> Become the touches of sweet harmony.
> Sit. Jessica: Look, how the floor of heaven
> Is thick inlaid with patines of bright gold:
> There's not the smallest orb, which thou behold'st,
> But in his motion like an angel sings,
> Still quiring to the young-ey'd cherubims:
> Such harmony is in immortal souls;
> But, whilst this muddy vesture of decay
> Doth grossly close it in, we cannot hear it.—
> Come, ho, and wake Diana with a hymn;
> With sweetest touches pierce your mistress' ear.
> *Jessica.*—I am never merry, when I hear sweet music.
> *Lor.*—The reason is, your spirits are attentive:
> For do but note a wild and wanton herd,
> Or race of youthful and unhandled colts,
> Fetching mad bounds, bellowing, and neighing loud,
> Which is the hot condition of their blood;
> If they but hear perchance a trumpet sound,
> Or any ear of music touch their ears,
> You shall perceive them make a mutual stand,
> Their savage eyes turn'd to a modest gaze,
> By the sweet power of music: Therefore the poet
> Did feign that Orpheus drew trees, stones, and floods;
> Since nought so stockish, hard, and full of rage,
> But music for the time doth change his nature:
> The man that hath no music in himself.
> Nor is not mov'd with concord of sweet sounds,
> Is fit for treasons, stratagems, and spoils;
> The motions of his spirit are dull as night,
> And his affections dark as Erebus:
> Let no such man be trusted.—Mark the music.

*   *   *   *

beautiful than the poet's description of *Sleep*, in the soliloquy of Henry IV? In it the immortal poet has shown the restlessness which often hangs round the thorny pillow of royalty, and prevents the wearied eye of greatness from tasting that sweet and comfortable repose, which relieves the unambitious toil of humble industry:—

> "How many thousand of my poorest subjects
> Are at this hour asleep!—Sleep, gentle sleep,
> Nature's soft nurse, how have I frighted thee,
> That thou no more will weigh my eyelids down,
> And sleep my senses in forgetfulness?
> Why rather, sleep, liest thou in smoky cribs
> Upon uneasy pallets stretching thee,
> And hush'd with buzzing night-flies to thy slumbers,
> Than in the perfumed chamber of the great,
> Under the canopies of costly state,
> And lull'd with sounds of sweetest melody?
> O thou dull god, why liest thou with the vile
> In loathsome beds: and leav'st the kingly couch,
> A watch-case, or a common 'larum bell?
> Wilt thou upon the high and giddy mast
> Seal up the ship-boy's eyes, and rock his brains
> In cradle of the rude imperious surge,

　　　　And in the visitations of the winds,
　　　　Who take the ruffian billows by the top,
　　　　Curling their monstrous heads, and hanging them.
　　　　With deaf'ning clamours in the slippery clouds.
　　　　That with the hurly, death itself awakes?
　　　　Can'st thou. O, partial sleep! give thy repose
　　　　To the wet sea-boy in an hour so rude:
　　　　And, in the calmest and most stillest night;
　　　　With all appliances and means to boot,
　　　　Deny it to a king? Then, happy low, lie down;
　　　　Uneasy lies the head that wears a crown."

Or again in his description of flowers in the *Winter's Tale*.

　　Per.—"Give me those flowers there, Dorcas.—Reverend Sirs,
　　　　For you there's rosemary, and rue; these keep
　　　　Seeming, and savour, all the winter long:
　　　　Grace, and remembrance, be to you both,
　　　　And welcome to our shearing!
　　Pol.—Shepherdess,
　　　　(A fair one are you,) well you fit our ages.
　　　　With flower of winter.
　　Per.—Sir, the year growing ancient,—
　　　　Nor yet on summer's death, nor on the birth
　　　　Of trembling winter,—the fairest flowers o' the season
　　　　Are our carnations, and streak'd gilly—flowers,
　　　　Which some call nature's bastards: of that kind
　　　　Our rustic garden's barren; and I care not,
　　　　To get slips of them.

　　　　　　*　　　　　　*

　　　　I'll not put
　　　　The dibble in earth to set one slip of them:
　　　　No more than, were I painted, I would wish
　　　　This youth should say, 'twere well; and only therefore
　　　　Desire to breed by me.—Here's flowers for you
　　　　Hot lavender, mints savory, marjoram;
　　　　The marigold, that goes to bed with the sun,
　　　　And with him rises weeping, these are flowers
　　　　Of middle summer, and, I think, they are given
　　　　To men of middle age: You are very welcome.
　　Cam.—I should leave grazing, were I of your flock,
　　　　And only live by grazing.
　　Per.—Our, alas!
　　　　You'd be as lean, that blasts of Jannary
　　　　Would blow you through and through—Now, **my fairey**
　　　　I would, I had some flowers and the spring that might
　　　　Become your time of day; and yours, and yours;
　　　　That wear upon your virgin branches yet
　　　　Your maidenheads growing:—O Proserpina
　　　　For the flowers now, that, freighted, thou let'st fall
　　　　From Dis' waggon! daffodils,

"To-day, my lord of Amiens, and myself,
Did steal behind him, as he lay along
Under an oak, whose antique root peeps out
Upon the brook that brawls along this wood :
To the which place a poor sequester'd stag,
That from the hunter's aim had ta'en a hurt,
Did come to languish ; and, indeed, my lord,
The wretched animal heaved forth such groans,
That their discharge did stretch his leathern coat.
Almost to bursting ; and the big round tears
Coursed one another down his innocent nose
In piteous chase ; and thus the hairy fool,
Much marked which the melancholy Jaques,
Stood on the extremest verge of the swift brook.
Augmenting it with tears.''

Or again in the mountain scene in *Cymbeline*.

Belarius.—"A goodly day not to keep house, with such
Whose roof's as low as ours ! Stoop, boys : This gate
Instructs you how to adore the heavens ; and bows you
To morning's holy office : The gates of monarchs
Are arch'd so high, that giants may jet through
And keep their impious turbands on, without
Good morrow to the sun.—Hail, thou fair heaven !
We house i' the rock, yet use thee not so hardly
As prouder livers do.

Guiderius.—Hail, heaven !

Arviragus.—Hail, heaven !

Belarius.—Now, for our mountain sport : Up to yon hill,
Your legs are young ; I'll tread these flats.   Consider,
When you above perceive me like a crow,
That it is place which lessens, and sets off
And you may then revolve what tales I have told you

Of courts, of princes, of the tricks in war
This service is not service, so being done,
But being so allow'd : To apprehend thus,
Draws us a profit from all things we see :
And often, to our comfort, shall we find
This sharded beetle in a safer hold
Than is the full wing'd eagle. O this life
Is nobler, than attending for a cheek ;
Is richer than doing nothing for a babe ;
Prouder, than rustling in unpaid-for silk :
Such gain the cap of him, that makes them fine,
Yet keeps his book uncross'd : No life to our.

*　　　*　　　*　　　*

Ar.—What should we speak of,
When we are old as you ? when we shall hear
The rain and wind beat dark December, how,
In this our pinching cave, shall we discourse
The freezing hours away? We have seen nothing :
We are beastly ; subtile as a fox, for prey ;
Like warlike as the wolf, for what we eat :
Our valour is, to chase what flies ; our cage.
We make a quire, as doth the prison bird,
And sing our bondage freely.

*　　　*　　　*　　　*　　　*

————This twenty years,
This rock; and these demcones have been my world;
Where I have liv'd at honest freedom ; paid
More pious debts to heaven, than in all
The fore-end of my time.—But, up to the mountains ;
This is not hunters' language :—He, that strikes
The venison first, shall be the lord o'the feast ;
To him the other two shall minister ;
And we will fear no poison, which attends—
In place of greater state. I'll meet you in the valleys. "

Even in his description of treason and midnight murder, he
brings in a sweet and rural image.

"This guest of summer,
To temple haunting martlett does approve
By his loved masonry, that heaven's breath
Smells wooing by here. No jutting frieze,
Buttress, nor coigne of vantage but this bird
Has made his pendent bed and procreant cradle. "

The same splendid descriptions of natural imagery may be found
in many other parts of this immortal poet's works. There is the
same taste exhibited in that proud boast of the bloody Richard;—

again to bear upon stern and repulsive passions, in the cynic rebukes of Apemantus to Simion.

> "—————————— Will these moss'd reds
> That have outlived the eagle page thy heels,
> And skip, when thou point'st out? Will the cold brow
> Candied with ice, candle thy morning taste,
> To cure thy o'ernight's surfeit?"

Again in the passionate exaltation of the beauty of Imogen, from one who is even not a lover.

> "—————————— 'Tis her breathing that
> Perfumes the chamber thus. The flame o'the taper
> Bows towards her and would under peep her lids,
> To see the enclosed lights now canopied
> Under those windows,—white and azure,
> Laced with blue of heaven's own trick . . . .
> . . . . On her left breast
> A mole unique—spotted, like the crimson drops
> I'the bottom of a cowslip. , . . , . .

The beauties of Shakespeare are not of that type as to be only understood by the learned; his finest passages are those which please all classes of readers. Shakespeare was more full of wisdom, ridicule, and profundity than all the moralists and satirists that ever lived. He wrote out of himself, a faculty that no other writer, perhaps, ever possessed. He developed the characters of men, but never intruded himself among them. He is more pathetic and fantastic in his works than any poet in all ages of the world: yet he is so temperate, that no one can accuse him of want of reason, in his characters and descriptions; but his characters are described with a truth and force that no other poet has ever shown. We have in his Richard III, a picture of cruelty, and envy; ambitious by nature, fearful to lose his high estate, trusting none, generous for a purpose and hardy to revenge, that tyrant's real character is faithfully and marvellously drawn; while in Henry IV, we see in contrast, his gentle, mild nature, easily persuaded .

and ready to forgive, careless for wealth, suspecting none and merciful to all.

The *Tempest* is one of the most original and perfect of Shakespeare's productions. It is purely romantic, not relying upon any historical circumstances or events ; it is entirely a birth of the imagination, and addresses itself entirely to that faculty. The character of Ariel has in it everywhere the airy tint from which it is named, and it is admirable that the poet has never brought Miranda in direct comparison with Ariel, lest the natural and human of the one, and the supernatural of the other should tend to neutralize each other. Caliban on the other hand is all earth, all condensed, and grows in feelings and images. Coleridge observes, "he has the dawnings of understanding, without reason or the moral sense ; and in him, as in some brute animals, this advance to the intellectual faculties without the moral sense, is marked by the appearance of vice ; for it is in the primacy of the moral being only, that man is truly human." Lamb says, "The character of Caliban is justly thought to be one of the author's masterpieces. . . . . It is one of the wildest and most abstracted of all Shakespeare's characters, whose deformity whether of body or mind is redeemed by the power and truth of the imagination displayed in it. It is the essence of grossness, but there is not a particle of vulgarity in it. . . . . . . It is 'of the earth, earthy.' It seems almost to have been dug out of the ground, with a soul instinctively superadded to it answering to its wants and origin." Schlegel remarks in speaking of Caliban, " He never falls into the prosaic and low familiarity of his drunken associates, for he is, in his way a poetical being: he always speaks in verse. " The passage in the *Tempest* where Caliban is first introduced may be read as a fine example of this :—

> *Cal.*—"As wicked dew as e'er my mother brush'd
> With raven's feather from unwholesome fen,
> Drop on you both ! a south-west blow on ye,
> And blister you all o'er !
> *Pros.*—For this, be sure, to-night thou shalt have cramps,
> Side-stitches that shall pen thy breath up ; urchins

Shall, for that vast of night that they may work,
All exercise on thee : thou shalt be pinch'd
As thick as honey-combs, each pinch more stinging
Than bees that made them.

Cal.—I must eat my dinner.
This island's mine, by Sycorax my mother,
Which thou tak'st from me.   When thou camest first,
Thou strokedst me; and madest much of me, would'st give me
Water with berries in't ; and teach me how
To name the bigger light, and how the less,
That burn by day and night : and then I loved thee,
And shew'd thee all the qualities o'er the isle,
The fresh springs, brine-pits, barren place, and fertile ;
Cursed be I that did so !—All the charms
Of Sycorax, toads, beetles, bats, light on you!
For I am all the subjects that you have,
Which first was mine own king : and here you sty me
In this hard rock, whiles you do keep from me
The rest of the island."

And for a magnificent specimen of the contrast shown by the poet between the material and the spiritual, the following melodious songs, which Shakespeare has represented as sounding in the air: of which Hazlitt says, "without conveying any distinct images, they seem to recall all the feelings connected with them, like snatches of half-forgotten music, heard distinctly and at intervals :—

ARIEL'S *song*.
"Come unto these yellow sands,
    And then take hands :
Court'sied when you have, and kiss'd,—
    (The wild waves whist,)
Foot it featly here and there ;
And, sweet sprites, the burden bear.
    Hark, Hark !
        Bow, wow.
    The watch dogs-bark :
        Bow, wow.
Hark, hark ! I hear
The strains of strutting chanticleer,
    Cry, Cock-a-doodle-do."

Fer.—"Where should this music be ? 'i'the air or the earth?
It sounds no more : and, sure, it waits upon
Some god of the island.   Sitting on a bank,
Weeping again the king my father's wreck,
This music crept by me upon the waters;
Allaying both their fury, and my passion,
With it's sweet air : thence I have follow'd it,

Or it hath drawn me rather :—But 'tis gone.
No, it begins again. "

ARIEL *sings.*
"Full fathom five my father lies ;
    Of his bones are coral made ;
Those are pearls that were his eyes :
    Nothing of him that doth fade,
But doth suffer a sea-change
Into something rich and strange,
Sea-nymphs hourly ring his knell :
Hark! now I hear them,—Ding-Dong, Bell."

I cannot pass over the *Tempest* without quoting the two beauti-
full passages, the first where the vision conjured up by Prospero
disappears, and he resolves to bury fathoms deep his rod and books
of power. In this we see Shakespeare's times again before us, when
first the interest of the New World began so powerfully to arouse the
imagination and the energies of the English people : and as the
Old World associations resumed their sway, the spell which en-
tranced them was broken, and as we read in the "Tempest," the
receding island is left lonely and disenchanted.

"You do look, my son, in a mov'd sort,
As if you were dismay'd : be cheerful, Sir :
Our revels now are ended : these our actors,
As I foretold you, were all spirits, and
Are melted into air, into thin air :
And, like the baseless fabric of this vision,
The cloud-capp'd towers, the gorgeous palaces,
The solemn temples, the great globe itself,
Yea, all which it inherits, shall dissolve ;
And, like this insubstantial pageant faded,
Leave not a wreck behind : We are such stuff
As dreams are made of, and our little life
Is rounded with a sleep."

The other, is the address Prospero makes in abjuring his art :—

"Ye elves of hills, brooks, standing lakes, and groves ; ·
And ye, that on the sands with printless foot
Do chase the ebbing Neptune, and do fly him,
When he comes back ; you demi-puppets, that
By moon-shine do the green-sour ringlets make,
Whereof the ewe not bites ; and you, whose pastime
Is to make midnight-mushrooms ; that rejoice
To hear the solemn curfew : by whose aid
(Weak masters though you be,) I have bedimm'd
The noon-tide sun, call'd forth the mutinous winds,

As 'twixt the green sea and the azur'd vault
Set roaring war : to the dread rattling thunder
Have I given fire, and rifted Jove's stout oak
With his own bolt : the strong-bas'd promontory
Have I made shake ; and by the spurs pluck'd up
The pine, and cedars : graves at my command,
Have waked their sleepers ; oped, and let them forth
By my so potent art : But this rough magic
I here abjure : and, when I have required
Some heavenly music, (which even now I do,)
To work my end upon their senses, that
This airy charm is for, I'll break my staff,
Bury it certain fathoms in the earth,
And, deeper than did ever plummet sound,
I'll drown my book."   *Solemn music.*

There is the same mysterious beauty, and extraordinary powers of imagination to be seen in the *Midsummer Night's Dream*, yet we see the same profound view of the inward life of Nature and her mysterious springs. Puck, in a different type, is the "Ariel" of the Tempest. The scene between Puck and the Fairy, where he gives an account of himself and his employments, and Titania's dispute with Oberon about the Indian boy, I may quote it as beautiful examples of this play :—

Puck.—"How now, spirit, whither wander you ?
Fairy.—Over hill, over dale,
        Thorough bush, thorough brier,
     Over park, over pale,
        Thorough flood, thorough fire,
     I do wander every where.
     Swifter than the moones sphere ;
        And I serve the fairy queen,
        To dew her orbs upon the green :
        The cowslips tall her pensioners be ;
        In their gold coats; spots you see
        Those be rubies fairy favours,
        In those freckles live their savours :
     I must go seek some dew-drops here,
     And hang a pearl in every cowslip's ear.
     Farewell, thou lob of spirits, I'll be gone ;
     Our queen and all our elves come here anon.
Puck.—The king doth keep his revels here to-night,
     Take heed, the queen come not within his sight.
     For Oberon is passing fell and wrath
     Because that she, as her attendant, hath
     A lovely boy stolen from an Indian king ;
     She never had so sweet a changeling:

And jealous Oberon would have the child
Knight of his train, to trace the forests wild:
But she, perforce, withholds the lovely boy,
Crowns him with flowers, and makes him all her joy:
And now they never meet in grove, or green,
By fountain clear, or spangled starlight sheen,
But they do square ; that all their elves, for fear,
Creep into acorn cups, and hide them there.
Fairy.—Either I mistake your shape and making quite,
Or else you are that shrewd and knavish sprite,
Call'd Robin Goodfellow : are you not he,
That fright the maidens of the villagery ;
Skim milk ; and sometimes labour in the quern,
And bootless make the breathless house wife churn ;
And sometimes make the drink to bear no barm ;
Mislead night-wanderers, laughing at their harm!
Those that Hobgoblin call you, and sweet Puck.
You do their work, and they shall have good luck .
Are not you he?
Puck.—Thou speak'st aright :
I am that merry wanderer of the night.
I jest to Oberon, and make him smile,
When I a fat and bean-fed horse beguile,
Neighing in likeness of a filly foal :
And sometime lurk I in a gossip's bowl,
In very likeness of a roasted crab ;
And, when she drinks, against her lips I bob,
And on her wither'd dew-lap pour the ale.
The wisest aunt, telling the saddest tale,
Sometimes for three-foot stool mistaketh me ;
Then slip I from her bum, down topples she,
And *tailor* cries, and falls into a cough ;
And then the whole quire hold their hips, and loffe :
And waxen in their mirth, and neeze, and swear
A merrier hour was never wasted there,—
But room, Fairy, here comes Oberon.
Fairy.—And here my mistress.—Would that he were gone!"

The character of *Lear* is another of Shakespeare's marvellous conceptions. Never was the passions of man represented with such power and force. I could not quote a better authority than Hazlitt, when he says," the mind of Lear staggering between the weight of attachment, and the hurried movements of passion, is like a tall ship driven about by the winds, buffeted by the furious winds, but that still rides above the storm, having its anchor fixed in the bottom of the sea ; or it is like the sharp rock circled by the eddying whirlpool, that foams and beats against it, or like the solid prom-

⸹ youngest daughter :—

   Lear.—"Peace, Kent!
      Come not between the dragon and his wrath :
      I lov'd her most, and thought to set my rest
      On her kind nursery.—Hence, and avoid my sight ! —
      So be my grave my peace, as here I give
      Her father's heart from her !—Call France;—Who stirs?
      Call Burgundy.—Cornwall, and Albany,
      With my two daughters' dowers digest this third :
      Let pride, which she calls plainness, marry her.
      I do invest you jointly with my power,
      Pre-eminence, and all the large effects
      That troop with majesty.—Ourself, by monthly course,
      With reservation of a hundred knights,
      By you to be sustain'd, shall our abode
      Make with you by due turns.   Only we still retain
      The name, and all the additions to a king ;
      The sway,
      Revenue, execution of the rest,
      Beloved sons, be yours : which to confirm.
      This coronet part between you.
   Kent.—Royal Lear,
      Whom I have ever honour'd as my king,
      Lov'd as my father, as my master follow'd,
      As my great patron thought on in my prayers,—
   Lear.—The bow is bent and drawn, make from the shaft.
   Kent.—Let it fall rather, though the fork invade
      The region of my heart : be Kent unmannerly,
      When Lear is mad.   What wouldst thou do, old man ?
      Think'st thou, that duty shall have dread to speak,
      When power to flattery bows? To plainness honour's bound,
      When majesty stoops to folly.   Reverse thy doom ;
      And, in thy best consideration, check
      This hideous rashness : answer my life, my judgment,
      Thy youngest daughter does not love thee least ;
      Nor are those empty-hearted, whose low sound
      Reverbs no hollowness.
   Lear.—Kent, on thy life, no more.
   Kent.—My life I never held but as a pawn
      To wage against thine enemies ; nor fear to lose it,
      Thy safety being the motive.
   Lear.—Out of my sight !
   Kent.—See better, Lear ; and let me still remain
      The true blank of thine eye.
   Lear.—Now, by Apollo,—

                                         W

Kent.—Now, by Apollo, king,
    Thou swear'st thy gods in vain.
Lear.—O, vassal ! miscreant ! (*Laying his hand on his sword.*)
Alb. and Corn.—Dear Sir, forbear.
Kent.—Do ;
    Kill thy physician, and the fee bestow
    Upon the foul disease.   Revoke thy gift ;
    Or, whilst I can vent clamour from my throat,
    I'll tell thee, thou dost evil.
Lear.—Hear me, recreant !
    On thine allegiance hear me !—
    Since thou hast sought to make us break our vow,
    (Which we durst never yet,) and, with strain'd pride,
    To come betwixt our sentence and our power ;
    (Which nor our nature nor our place can bear,)
    Our potency make good, take thy reward,
    Five days we do allot thee, for provision
    To shield thee from diseases of the world ;
    And, on the sixth, to turn thy hated back
    Upon our kingdom : if, on the tenth day following,
    Thy banish'd trunk be found in our dominions,
    The moment is thy death :   Away ! by Jupiter,
    This shall not be revok'd.
Kent.—Fare thee well, king : since thus thou wilt appear,
    Freedom lives hence, and banishment is here.—
    The gods to their dear shelter take thee, maid,
    That justly think'st, and hast most rightly said !—
    And your large speeches may your deeds approve,
    That good effects may spring from words of love.—
    Thus Kent, O princes, bids you all adieu ;
    He'll shape his old course in a country new."

Othello is another striking instance of this astonishing exempli-
fication of passion—its pauses and feverish starts, and then its
accumulating force.   We see the impetuous passions, and nnsus-
pecting frankness of the Moor exasperated by the artful dexterity
of Iago, until we are filled with almost terror and pity.   For instance,
when Iago first begins to practise upon Othello's unsuspecting
friendship, he replies :—

        "Why ? why is this ?
        Think'st thou. I'd make a life of jealousy,
        To follow still the changes of the moon
        With fresh suspicions ? No : to be once in doubt,
        Is--once to be resolv'd : Exchange me for a goat,
        When I shall turn the business of my soul
        To such exsufflicate and blown surmises,
        Matching thy inference. 'Tis not to make me jealous,
        To say my wife is fair, feeds well, loves company.

Is free of speech, sings, plays, and dances well ;
Where virtue is, there are more virtuous :
Nor from mine own weak merits will I draw
The smallest fear, or doubt, of her revolt ;
For she had eyes, and chose me : No, Iago ;
I'll see, before I doubt ; when I doubt, prove ;
And, on the proof, there is no more but this,
Away at once with love, or jealousy.

     *   *   *

Never, Iago. Like to the Pontic sea,
Whose icy current and compulsive course
Ne'er feels retiring ebb, but keeps due on
To the Propontic, and the Hellespont ;
Even so my bloody thoughts, with violent pace,
Shall ne'er look back, ne'er ebb to humble love,
Till that a capable and wide revenge
Swallow them up.—Now, by yond marble heaven,
In the due reverence of a sacred vow
I here engage my words.
Iago.—Do not rise yet.—
Witness, you ever-burning lights above !
You elements that clip us round about !
Witness, that here Iago doth give up
The execution of his wit, hands, heart,
To wrong'd Othello's service ! let him command,
And to obey shall be in me remorse,
What bloody work soever.
Othello.—I greet thy love,
Not with vain thanks, but with acceptance bounteous,
And will upon the instant put thee to 't :
Within these three days let me hear thee say,
That Cassio's not alive.
Iago.—My friend is dead ; 'tis done, at your request :
But let her live.
Othello. —Damn her, lewd minx ! O, damn her !
Come, go with me apart ; I will withdraw,
To furnish me with some swift means of death
For the fair devil. Now art thou my lieutenant.
Iago.—I am, your own for ever."

And again in Othello's exclamation in the fourth act during his
terview with Desdemona, his noble spirit is thrown up in the
ost vivid language :—

"Had it pleas'd heaven
To try me with affliction ; had he rain'd
All kinds of sores, and shames, on my bare head ;
Steep'd me in poverty to the very lips ;
Given to captivity me and my utmost hopes ;
I should have found in some part of my soul

A drop of patience : but (alas !) to make me
A fixed figure, for the time of scorn
To point his slow unmoving finger at,—
O ! O !
Yet could I bear that too ; well, very well
But there, where I have garner'd up my heart ;
Where either I must live, or bear no life ;
The fountain from the which my current runs,
Or else dries up ; to be discarded thence !
Or keep it as a cistern, for foul toads
To knot and gender in !—turn thy complexion there !
Patience, thou young and rose-lipp'd cherubim ;
Ay, there, look grim as hell !"

In these passages we see the frankness and generosity of Othello's
nature, which moves us to sympathy and compassion for his fate.
We can see his noble and generous character gradually goaded on
by passion, till his love and confidence turn into the madness of
hatred ; and we see his revenge increasing in strength day by day,
under the malicious suggestions of Iago. And at last his remorse
is shown to us as dreadful as his revenge had been; particularly in
his farewell speech before he kills himself :—

"Soft you ; a word or two, before you go.
I have done the state some service, and they know it ;
No more of that :—I pray you, in your letters,
When you shall these unlucky deeds relate,
Speak of me as I am ; nothing extenuate,
Nor set down aught in malice : then must speak
Of one, that lov'd not wisely, but too well ;
Of one, not easily jealous, but, being wrought,
Perplex'd in the extreme ; of one, whose hand,
Like the base Júdean, threw a pearl away,
Richer than all his tribe; of one, whose subdu'd eyes,
Albeit unused to the melting mood,
Drop tears as fast as the Arabian trees
Their medicinal gum : Set you down this :
And say, besides,—that in Aleppo once,
Where a malignant and a turban'd Turk
Beat a Venetian, and traduc'd the state,
I took by the throat the circumcised dog,
And smote him—thus. " (*Stabs himself.*)

Shakespeare's play of *Macbeth*, like Othello and Lear, is charac-
teristic throughout of the inner feelings, and just as Lear stands
first for the profundity of his passion, and Othello for an intensity

of vindictiveness, so Macbeth for the excessive wildness of his imagination and impulsiveness of action. It is by this we see the overpowering genius of Shakespeare to that of his contemporaries. All his representations of the passions, either good or evil, are brought home to us as a part of our experience. He exhibits the same means of supernatural agency, over human passion ; and we see Macbeth hurried on with daring impatience to verify the prediction of the *Witches*, anxious with impious and bloody hand to tear aside the veil which hides the uncertainty of the future. He rushes blindly forward, bent only on the objects of his ambition and revenge ; sometimes cowed and overpowered by his conscience, and abashed with his success ; then encouraged by the firmness of his wife, who holds determinedly to her object, until we shudder at her wickedness. We see her goading him on with wily taunts, to the accomplishment of her great end, till Macbeth is at last overpowered by her commanding presence of mind and inexorable self-will :—

> "———Art thou afear'd
> To be the same in thine own act and valour
> As thou art in desire ? Wouldst thou have that
> Which thou esteem'st the ornament of life,
> And live a coward in thy own esteem ;
> Letting *I dare not* wait upon *I would,*
> Like the poor cat i' the adage."

And in his reply we behold a mixture of manly thought and feeling, which in spite of his crimes lead our minds to a pitch of admiration.

> "Pr'ythee, peace :
> *I dare do all that may become a man ;*
> *Who dares do more, is none.*"

And then we have again the same grand and striking picture of remorse, after the murder has been perpetrated, thrown up in the poet's same vivid and unsurpassed language.

> *Macbeth.*—"There's one did laugh in his sleep, and one cried, *Murder !*
> That they did wake each other ; I stood and heard them :
> But they did say their prayers, and address'd them
> Again to sleep.
> *Lady M.*—There are two lodg'd together.
> *Mac.*—One cried, *God bless us !* and *Amen,* the other ;
> As they had seen me with these hangman's hands.

Glamis hath murder'd sleep, and therefore Cawdor
Shall sleep no more, Macbeth shall sleep no more."

There is the same extraordinary and powerful delineation of the evil passions of man, in *Richard III.* only as distinct in character from *Othello* and *Macbeth* as it is possible to conceive. Richard's character is naturally cruel ; from his birth he is deformed in mind and body. His crimes are the result of violent temper, and love of mischief ; he revels and rejoices in his evil deeds; and we see him, as a hardened tyrant, serving only his own ends, working only to secure them, and making the periods of bloodshed, his holidays. We have no sympathy for him; even in his very last extremity we think of him only as a "wild beast taken in his toils." The courtship scene with Lady Anne exhibits finely Richard's smooth and smiling villany, as like the first Tempter he craftily approaches his prey :—

Gloster.—" ————But, gentle lady Anne,—
    To leave this keen encounter of our wits,
    And fall somewhat into a slower method;—
    Is not the causer of the timeless deaths
    Of these Plantagenets, Henry and Edward,
    As blameful as the executioner ?
Anne.—Thou wast the cause, and most accurs'd effect.
Glo.—Your beauty was the cause of that effect;
    Your beauty, which did haunt me in my sleep,
    To undertake the death of all the world,
    So I might live one hour in your sweet bosom.
Anne.—If I thought that, I tell thee, homicide,
    These nails should rend that beauty from my cheeks.

Glo.—These eyes could not endure that beauty's wreck,
    You should not blemish it, if I stood by:
    As all the world is cheered by the sun,
    So I by that; it is my day, my life.
Anne.—Black night o'ershade thy day, and death thy life!
Glo.—Curse not thyself, fair creature; thou art both.
Anne.—I would I were, to be reveng'd on thee.
Glo.—It is a quarrel most unnatural,
    To be reveng'd on him that loveth thee.
Anne.—It is a quarrel just and reasonable,
    To be reveng'd on him that kill'd my husband.
Glo.—He that bereft thee, lady, of thy husband,
    Did it to help thee to a better husband.
Anne.—His better doth not breathe upon the earth.
Glo.—He lives, that loves you better than he could.
Anne.—Name him.
Glo.—Plantagenet.
Anne.—Why, that was he.
Glo.—The self-same name, but one of better nature.
Anne.—Where is he?
Glo.—Here: (*she spits at him*) Why dost thou spit at me?
Anne.—'Would it were mortal poison, for thy sake!
Glo.—Never came poison from so sweet a place.
Anne.—Never hung poison on a fouler toad.
    Out of my sight! thou dost infect mine eyes.
Glo.—Thine eyes, sweet lady, have infected mine.
Anne.—'Would they were basilisks, to strike thee dead!
Glo.—I would they were, that I might die at once;
    For now they kill me with a living death.
    Those eyes of thine from mine have drawn salt tears,
    Shamed their aspécts with store of childish drops:
    These eyes, which never shed remorseful tear,—
    Not, when my father York and Edward wept,
    To hear the piteous moan that Rutland made,
    When black-fac'd Clifford shook his sword at him:
    Nor when thy warlike father, like a child,
    Told the sad story of my father's death;
    And twenty times made pause, to sob, and weep,
    That all the standers-by had wet their cheeks,
    Like trees bedash'd with rain: in that sad time,
    My manly eyes did scorn an humble tear;
    And what these sorrows could not thence exhale,
    Thy beauty hath, and made them blind with weeping.
    I never su'd to friend, nor enemy;
    My tongue could never learn sweet soothing word;
    But now thy beauty is proposed my fee,
    My proud heart sues, and prompts my tongue to speak.
                    (*She looks scornfully at him*)
    Teach not thy lip such scorn; for it was made
    For kissing, lady, not for such contempt.

If thy revengeful heart cannot forgive,
Lo! here I lend thee this sharp-pointed sword
Which if thou please to hide in this true breast,
And let the soul forth that adoreth thee,
I lay it naked to the deadly stroke,
And humbly beg the death upon my knee.
(He lays his breast open; she offers at it with his sword.)
Nay, do not pause; for I did kill king Henry;—
But 'twas thy beauty that provoked me.
Nay, now despatch; 'twas I that stabb'd young Edward;—
     (She again offers at his breast.)
But 'twas thy heavenly face that set me on.
     (She lets fall the sword.)
 Take up the sword again, or take up me.
Anne.—Arise, dissembler: though I wish thy death,
I will not be thy executioner.
Glo.—Then bid me kill myself, and I will do it.
Anne.—I have already.
Glo.—That was in a rage:
Speak it again, and, even with the word,
This hand, which, for thy love, did kill thy love,
Shall, for thy love, kill a far truer love;
To both their deaths shalt thou be accessory.
Anne.—I would, I knew thy heart.
Glo.—'Tis figured in my tongue.
Anne.—I fear me, both are false.
Glo.—Then man was never true.
Anne.—Well, well, put up your sword.
Glo.—Say then, my peace is made.
Anne.—That shall you know hereafter.
Glo.—But shall I live in hope?
Anne.—All men, I hope, live so.
Glo.—Vouchsafe to wear this ring.
Anne.—To take, is not to give.
     (She puts on the ring.)
Glo.—Look, how this ring encompasseth thy finger,
Even so thy breast encloseth my poor heart;
Wear both of them, for both of them are thine.
And if thy poor devoted servant may
But beg one favour at thy gracious hand.
Thou dost confirm his happiness for ever.
Anne.—What is it?
Glo.—That it may please you, leave these sad designs
To him that hath more causes to be a mourner,
And presently repair to Crosby-place;
Where —after I have solemnly interr'd,
At Chertsey monast'ry, this noble king,
And wet his grave with my repentant tears,—
I will with all expedient duty see you:

Brak.—"Why looks your grace so heavily to-day ?
Clar.—O, I have pass'd a miserable night,
    So full of fearful dreams, of ugly sights,
    That, as I am a Christian faithful man,
    I would not spend another such a night,
    Though 'twere to buy a world of happy days ;
    So full of dismal terror was the time.
Brak.—What was your dream, my lord ? I pray you, tell me
Clar.—Methought, that I had broken from the Tower,
    And was embark'd to cross to Burgundy ;
    And, in my company, my brother Gloster :
    Who from my cabin tempted me to walk
    Upon the hatches ; thence we look'd toward England,
    And cited up a thousand heavy times,
    During the wars of York and Lancaster
    That had befall'n us.   As we pac'd along
    Upon the giddy footing of the hatches,
    Methought that Gloster stumbled ; and, in falling,
    Struck me, that thought to stay him, over-board,
    Into the tumbling billows of the main.
    O Lord ! methought, what pain it was to drown !
    What dreadful noise of water in mine ears !
    What sights of ugly death within mine eyes !
    Methought, I saw a thousand fearful wrecks ;
    A thousand men that fishes gnaw'd upon ;
    Wedges of gold, great anchors, heaps of pearl,
    Inestimable stones, unvalued jewels,
    All scattered in the bottom of the sea.
    Some lay in dead men's skulls ; and, in those holes
    Where eyes did once inhabit, there were crept
    (As 'twere in scorn of eyes,) reflecting gems,
    That woo'd the slimy bottom of the deep,
    And mock'd the dead bones that lay scatter'd by.
Brak.—Had you such leisure in the time of death

To gaze upon these secrets of the deep?
Clar.—Methought I had; and often did I strive
   To yield the ghost: but still the envious flood
   Kept in my soul, and would not let it forth
   To seek the empty, vast, and wand'ring air;
   But smother'd it within my panting bulk,
   Which almost burst to belch it in the sea.
Brak. —Awak'd you not with this sore agony?
Clar.—O, no, my dream was lengthen'd after life;
   O, then began the tempest to my soul!
   I pass'd, methought, the melancholy flood,
   With that grim ferryman which poets write of,
   Unto the kingdom of perpetual night.
   The first that there did greet my stranger soul,
   Was my great father-in-law, renowned Warwick,
   Who cried aloud,—*What scourge for perjury*
   Can this dark monarchy afford false Clarence?
   And so he vanish'd: Then came wand'ring by
   A shadow like an angel, with bright hair
   Dabbled in blood; and he shriek'd out aloud,—
   Clarence is come,—false, fleeting, perjur'd Clarence,--
   That stabb'd me in a field by Tewksbury:—
   Seize on him, furies, take him to your torments!
   With that, methought, a legion of foul fiends
   Environ'd me, and howled in mine ears
   Such hideous cries, that, with the very noise,
   I trembling wak'd, and, for a season after,
   Could not believe but that I was in hell;
   Such terrible impression made my dream."

The other is Tyrell's account of the children's death, in the
Tower:—

   "The tyrannous and bloody act is done;
   The most arch deed of piteous massacre,
   That ever yet this land was guilty of.
   Dighton, and Forrest, whom I did suborn
   To do this piece of ruthless butchery,
   Albeit they were flesh'd villains, bloody dogs,
   Melting with tenderness and mild compassion,
   Wept like two children, in their death's sad story.
   O thus, quoth Dighton, *lay the gentle babes,—*
   Thus, thus, quoth Forrest, *girdling one another*
   Within their alabaster innocent arms:
   Their lips were four red roses on a stalk,
   Which, in their summer beauty, kiss'd each other.
   A book of prayers on their pillow lay:
   Which once, quoth Forrest, *almost chang'd my mind*;
   But, O, the devil—there the villian stopp'd;
   When Dighton thus told on,—*we smothered*
   The most replenished sweet work of nature,

The play of Hamlet is entirely different in style to those of *Othello, Lear, Macbeth,* and *Richard III.* Of Shakespeare's plays, it is one of the most popular and most thought of. It is the most naturally written and original. The passages are not exhibited as in his other plays; they were not written for the motive of the play, but are suggested by the other scenes as they occur ; the characters speak as they would if they were left entirely to themselves, they are not forced or strained. I would not attempt to pass a comment upon this play, so I will pass on, by merely quoting what appears to me the finest passage; it is that in which Hamlet attempts to reason with his own weakness:—

"How all occasions do inform against me,
And spur my dull revenge! What is a man,
If his chief good, and market of his time
Be but to sleep and feed? a beast, no more.
Sure, he, that made us with such large discourse,
Looking before, and after, gave us not
That capability and godlike reason
To fust in us unus'd. Now, whether it be
Bestial oblivion, or some craven scruple
Of thinking too precisely on the event,—
A thought, which, quarter'd, hath but one part wisdom,
And, ever, three parts coward,—I do not know
Why yet I live to say, *This thing's to do;*
Since I have cause, and will, and strength, and means
To do't. Examples, gross as earth, exhort me :
Witness, this army of such mass, and charge,
Led by a delicate and tender prince ;
Whose spirit with divine ambition puff'd,
Makes mouths at the invisible event ;
Exposing what is mortal, and unsure,
To all that fortune, death, and danger, dare,
Even for an egg-shell. Rightly to be great,
Is, not to stir without great argument ;
But greatly to find quarrel in a straw,
When honour's at the stake. How stand I then,
That have a father kill'd, a mother stain'd,
Excitements of my reason and my blood,
And let all sleep? while, to my shame, I see
The imminent death of twenty thousand men,
That, for a fantasy, and trick of fame,

> Go to their graves like beds : fight for a plot
> Whereon the numbers cannot try the cause,
> Which is not tomb enough, and continent,
> To hide the slain ? O, from this time forth
> My thoughts be bloody, or be nothing worth !"

In reading *Richard II.* our passions are little moved : we can only sympathise with the king's want of resolution, and pity his weakness. His character from first to last shows him falling under the superior weight of Bolingbroke's genius ; meeting stroke after stroke of ill fortune, and goaded with insults which he has neither courage nor principle to withstand. Finely as this character is exhibited throughout the whole play, *Richard II.* does not come near in beauty to any of those already mentioned. Perhaps the finest passage in it, is that in which Mowbray complains of his banishment. The language is overflowing with beauty :—

> "A heavy sentence, my most sovereign liege,
> And all unlook'd for from your highness' mouth :
> A dearer merit, not so deep a maim
> As to be cast forth in the common air,
> Have I deserved at your highness' hand.
> The language I have learn'd these forty years,
> My native English, now I must forego : .
> And now my tongue's use is to me no more
> Than an unstringed viol or a harp ;
> Or like a cunning instrument cas'd up,
> Or, being open, put into his hands
> That knows no touch to tune the harmony :
> Within my mouth you have engaol'd my tongue,
> Doubly portcullis'd, with my teeth and lips ;
> And dull, unfeeling, barren ignorance
> Is made my gaoler to attend on me.
> I am too old to fawn upon a nurse,
> Too far in years to be a pupil now ;
> What is thy sentence then, but speechless death,
> Which robs my tongue from breathing native breath ? "

Of the admired love story of *Romeo and Juliet,* I need not speak ; every one is acquainted with it. It is full of romantic feeling, and poetical tenderness, without being sickly or sentimental. Their love is a passion, not a sickness ; and the whole is thrown out in the language of a Shakespeare only. It is like the rest of his plays, a picture of purely human life. In it we have shown to us, all the novelty and rapture of youthful passion, when the heart is first

Juliet.—"Gallop apace, you fiery-footed steeds,
　　Towards Phœbus' mansion; such a waggoner,
　　As Phæton would whip you to the west,
　　And bring in cloudy night immediately.—
　　Spread thy close curtain, love-performing night!
　　That run-away's eyes may wink; and Romeo
　　Leap to these arms, untalk'd of, and unseen!—
　　Lovers can see to do their amorous rites
　　By their own beauties: or, if love be blind,
　　It best agrees with night.—Come, civil night,
　　Thou sober-suited matron, all in black,
　　And learn me how to lose a winning match,
　　Play'd for a pair of stainless maidenhoods:
　　Hood my unmann'd blood bating in my cheeks.
　　With thy black mantle; till strange love, grown bold,
　　Think true love acted, simple modesty.
　　Come, night!—Come, Romeo! come, thou day in night
　　For thou wilt lie upon the wings of night
　　Whiter than new snow on a raven's back.—
　　Come, gentle night; come, loving, black-brow'd night,
　　Give me my Romeo: and, when he shall die,
　　Take him and cut him out in little stars,
　　And he will make the face of heaven so fine,
　　That all the world will be in love with night,
　　And pay no worship to the garish sun.—
　　O, I have bought the mansion of a love,
　　But not possess'd it; and, though I am sold,
　　Not yet enjoy'd: So tedious is this day,
　　As is the night before some festival
　　To an impatient child, that hath new robes,
　　And may not wear them."

Or the still more beautiful passage of the parting between **Romeo**

* " Shakespeare's Characters."

and Juliet in the Third Act :—

> *Juliet.*—" Wilt thou be gone ? it is not yet near day:
> It was the nightingale, and not the lark,
> That pierc'd the fearful hollow of thine ear ;
> Nightly she sings on yon pomegranate-tree :
> Believe me, love, it was the nightingale.
> *Romeo.*—It was the lark, the herald of the morn,
> No nightingale: look, love, what envious streaks
> Do lace the severing clouds in yonder east :
> Night's candles are burnt out, and jocund day
> Stands tiptoe on the misty mountain-tops;
> I must be gone and live, or stay and die.
> *Juliet.*—Yon light is not daylight, I know it, I :
> It is some meteor that the sun exhales,
> To be to thee this night a torch-bearer,
> And light thee on thy way to Mantua :
> Therefore stay yet, thou need'st not to be gone.
> *Romeo.*—Let me be ta'en, let me be put to death;
> I am content, as thou wilt have it so,
> I'll say, yon grey is not the morning's eye,
> 'Tis but the pale reflex of Cynthia's brow ;
> Nor that is not the lark, whose notes do beat,
> The vaulty heaven so high above our heads :
> I have more care to stay, than will to go ;—
> Come, death, and welcome! Juliet wills it so.—
> How is't, my soul ? let's talk, it is not day.
> *Juliet.*—It is, it is, hie hence, be gone, away ;
> It is the lark that sings so out of tune,
> Straining harsh discords, and unpleasing sharps.
> Some say, the lark makes sweet division ;
> This doth not so, for she divideth us :
> Some say, the lark and loathed toad change eyes ;
> O, now I would they had chang'd voices too !
> Since arm from arm that voice doth us affray,
> Hunting thee hence with hunts-up to the day.
> O, now be gone ; more light and light it grows,
> *Romeo .*—More light and light ?—more dark and dark our woes."

There is the same intensity of feeling manifested in Shakespeare's *Timon of Athens*—the same reality and earnestness, with that glowing depth of passion peculiar only to this great man. In the transition of Timon from pomp and splendour to the most abject state of life, cut off from all social intercourse, we seem to realize his painful position; but our admiration for him is none the less. Indeed we admire him the more, when we see him exposed like a wild animal in the forest, digging roots from the earth for bare existence :—

Timandra.—"That nature, being sick of man's unkindness
    Should yet be hungry!—Common mother, thou,
    Whose womb unmeasurable, and infinite breast,
    Teems, and feeds all; whose self-same mettle,
    Whereof thy proud child, arrogant man, is puff'd,
    Engenders the black toad, and adder blue,
    The gilded newt, and eyeless venom'd worm,
    With all the abhorred births below crisp heaven
    Whereon Hyperion's quickening fire doth shine,
    Yield him. who all human sons doth hate,
    From forth thy plenteous bosom one poor root!
    Ensear thy fertile and conceptious womb,
    Let it no more bring out ingrateful man!
    Go great with tigers, dragons, wolves, and bears;
    Teem with new monsters, whom thy upward face,
    Hath to the marbled mansion all above
    Never presented!—O, a root,—Dear thanks!
    Dry up thy marrows, vines, and plough-torn leas;
    Whereof ingrateful man, with liquorish draughts,
    And morsels unctuous, greases his pure mind,
    That from it all consideration slips!"

It is Timon's scorn of the world and self-denial that rouses our
feeling towards him, and we see him with terror, admiration, and
pity. The contrast is vividly and marvellously drawn, and the
language vies with almost any of Shakespeare's plays. Timon's
most fearful imprecation is that on leaving Athens:—

    "Let me look back upon thee, O thou wall,
    That girdlest in those wolves! Dive in the earth,
    And fence not Athens! Matrons, turn incontinent!
    Obedience fail in children! slaves, and fools,
    Pluck the grave wrinkled senate from the bench,
    And minister in their steads! to general filths
    Convert o'the instant green virginity!
    Do't in your parent's eyes! bankrupts, hold fast,
    Rather than render back, out with your knives,
    And cut your trusters' throats! bound servants, steal!
    Large handed robbers your grave masters are,
    And pill by law! maid, to thy master's bed;
    Thy mistress is o'the brothel? son of sixteen,
    Pluck the lined crutch from the old limping sire,
    With it beat out his brains! piety, and fear,
    Religion to the gods, peace, justice. truth,
    Domestic awe, night-rest, and neighbourhood,
    Instruction, manners, mysteries, and trades,
    Degrees, observances, customs, and laws,
    Decline to your confounding contraries,
    And yet confusion!—Plagues, incident to men,

Your potent and infectious fevours heap
On Athens, ripe for stroke! thou cold sciatica,
Cripple our senators, that their limbs may halt
As lamely as their manners! lust and liberty
Creep in the minds and marrows of our youth;
That 'gainst the stream of virtue they may strive,
And drown themselves in riot! itches, blains,
Sow all the Athenian bosoms; and their crop
Be general leprosy! breath infect breath;
That their society, as their friendship, may
Be merely poison! Nothing I'll bear from thee,
But nakedness, thou detestable town!
Take thou that too, with multiplying banns!
Timon will to the woods; where he shall find
The unkindest beast more kinder than mankind.
The gods confound (hear me, ye good gods all,)
The Athenians both within and out that wall!
And grant, as Timon grows, his hate may grow
To the whole race of mankind, high and low!
Amen."

The passage is also beautiful which contains Timon's last words—

"Come not to me again, but say to Athens,
Timon hath made his everlasting mansion
Upon the beached verge of the salt flood;
Which once a day with his embossed froth
The turbulent serge shall cover, thither come,
And let my grave-stone be your oracle,—
Lips, let sour words go by, and language end:
What is amiss, plague and infection mend!
Graves only be men's works; and death, their gain!
Sun, hide thy beams! Timon hath done his reign."

Although there is equal merit and beauty in the remainder of
Shakespeare's plays, I have only remarked upon the most popular,
and even in those, I have preferred to my feeble language in giving
the more fitting and admirable words of Hazlitt. It seems insolence
to open Shakespeare with an attempt to criticize, we can only
regard it with admiration and revel in its beauties, and then close
it with reverence and awe.

CHAPTER XII.

MILTON.

The effect of Milton's poetry is not so much in what it expresses,
as by what it suggests. As Macauley says, "He electrifies the

mind through conductors. Unlike Homer, who sets the images in such a light that it is impossible to be blind to them; Milton cannot be comprehended or enjoyed, unless the mind of the reader co-operates with that of the writer. He does not paint a finished picture, or play for a mere passive listener. He sketches, and leaves others to fill up the outline : he strikes the key-note, and expects his hearers to make out the melody. The merit of his poetry lies less in its obvious meaning, than in its excellent power. There would seem at first sight to be no more in his words than in other words ; but they are words of enchantment. No sooner are they pronounced, than the past is present, and the distant near : new forms of beauty start at once into existence, and all the burial places of the memory give up their dead. Change the structure of the sentence, substitute one synonyme for another, and the whole effect is destroyed. The spell loses its power ; and he who should then hope to conjure with it, would find himself as much mistaken as Cassim in the Arabian Tale, when he stood crying, ' Open Wheat,' 'Open Barley,' to the door which obeyed no sound but 'Open Sesame.'"

The subject of Milton in some points, resembled that of Dante, although he has treated it in a widely different manner. The images which Dante employs speak for themselves, they stand simply for what they are. Those of Milton have a signification which is often discernible only to the initiated. However strange and grotesque, Dante never shrinks from describing any appearance or character. His similes are not introduced for the sake of any ornament which they may impart to the poem, but to make the meaning of the writer as close to the reader as it is to himself.

Campbell says, "Milton's genius had too great a supremacy to belong to any school. Though he acknowledged a filial reverence for Spenser as a poet, he left no Gothic irregular tracery in the design of his own great work, but gave a classical harmony of parts to its stupendous pile. It thus resembles a dome, the vastness of which is at first sight concealed by its symmetry, but

which expands more and more to the eye while it is contemplat-
ed." His immense reading extended over the whole field of
literature, and in every direction ; and it required all his learning
collected by painful study during the best years of his life, to build
up his immortal poem. Let us consider that the materials were
a few verses in Genesis, and that the rest is created by his im-
agination, supported by industrious and solid reading. There
is something that overawes the mind in conceiving his long
deliberated selection of that theme ; his attempting it when his
eyes were shut upon the face of nature ; his dependence, we might
almost say, on supernatural inspiration; and in the calm air of
strength with which he opens this poem, beginning a mighty per-
formance without the appearance of an effort. Taking the subject
all in all, his powers could nowhere else have enjoyed the same
scope. It was only from the height of this great argument that he
could look back upon eternity past, and forward upon eternity to
come; that he could "survey the abyss of infernal darkness, open
visions of Paradise, or ascend to heaven, and breathe empyreal air."

In the loss of his sight, Milton's *minds' eye* opened, and afforded
him ample compensation for the loss of the corporeal organ. Light
and life flowed into his mind through surrounding darkness, bless-
ing it with the enjoyment of higher thoughts and visions. This
reminds us of his beautiful and affecting lines in "*The Address to
Light.*"

> "   .   .   .   Thee I revisit safe
> And feel thy sovran vital lamp; but thou
> Revisit'st not these eyes, that roll in vain
> To find thy piercing ray, and find no dawn :
> So thick a drop serene hath quench'd their orbs,
> Or dim suffusion veil'd. Yet not the more
> Cease I to wander where the muses haunt,
> Clear spring or shady grove, or sunny hills,
> Smit with the love of sacred song.   .   ."

What an attestation to the medicinal value of intellectual labour,
that it has often cheered, even such desolation as his ! How strong
must be the natural love of knowledge in the human mind, that
even in the midst of such impediments to its gratification, it has in

so many instances so eagerly sought, and so largely attained its end. "Invention," 'says Dr. Johnson,' " is almost the only literary labour which blindness cannot obstruct; and therefore Milton naturally solaced his solitude by the indulgence of his fancy, and the melody of his numbers."

I will not detail the various portions of the *Paradise Lost,* nor attempt to analyse its beauties or discrepancies : the extent of this work will only give me scope to show as near as I can the main idea of this great poem, and its bearing upon the time at which Milton lived.

Obedience, and obedience of a negative kind is set forth as the tenure by which man held his original happiness.

> " Of man's first disobedience and the fruit,
> Of that forbidden tree, whose mortal taste
> Brought Death into the world, and all our woe,
> With loss of Eden———————"

The tone of this poem, is distinctively Puritan; we see in the presentation of the solitary pair as the type of human society, the working of the spirit, which, aiming at a noble simplicity has achieved barren nakedness, and which induced Milton to disparage all human hearts and wisdom as vain and corrupt. The Puritan preaching is seen again in the emphasis in which the past is laid in the future world ; the existing state of things being regarded as the insignificant "point between two eternities." It differs from the *Inferno* of Dante, in that Milton gives the action in the far away past and refers to the far-away future; while Dante in his Hell, Purgatory, and Paradise, describes three phrases of existence, as present and real as the life in Florence streets; and the revelation of men is made in the most matter-of-fact tone, by one who had himself performed the awful journey. In Milton, we could not expect any such proclamation of a present order and kingdom of a reigning God, as we find in Dante, who resembled him in his stern, firm belief in his own inspiration.

It is certainly no disparagement to Milton's genius to admit that both in the scheme and in the details of his great work, he attempted

"O Son, in whom my soul hath chief delight,
Son of my bosom, Son who art alone
My word, my wisdom, and effectual might,
All hast thou spok'n as my thoughts are, all
As my eternal purpose hath decreed:
Man shall not quite be lost, but sav'd who will;
Yet not of will in him, but grace in me.
Freely vouchsafed; once more I will renew
His lapsed powers, though forfeit and enthrall'd
By sin to foul exorbitant desires:
Upheld by me, yet once more he shall stand
On even ground against his mortal foe;
By me upheld, that he may know how frail
His fall'n condition is, and to me owe
All his deliv'rance, and to none but me."

   * * * * * *

"O thou in Heaven and Earth the only peace
Found out for mankind under wrath! O thou
My sole complacence? well thou know'st how dear
To me are all my works, nor man the least
Though last created: that for him I spare
Thee from my bosom and right hand, to save,
By losing thee awhile, the whole race lost.
Thou, therefore, whom thou only canst redeem,
Their nature also to thy nature join;
And be thyself Man among men on earth,
Made flesh, when time shall be, of virgin seed,
By wondrous birth: be thou in Adam's room
The head of all mankind, thou Adam's son,
As in him perish all men, so in thee,
As from a second root, shall be restor'd
As many as are restored, without thee none."

"————————Now storming fury rose,
And clamour such as heard in Heav'n till now
Was never, arms on armour clashing bray'd
Horrible discord, and the madding wheels
Of brazen chariots rag'd ; dire was the noise
Of conflict ; overhead the dismal hiss
Of fiery darts in flaming vollies flew,
And flying vaulted either host with fire.
So under fiery cope together rush'd
Both battles main, with ruinous assault,
And inextinguishable rage ; all Heav'n
Resounded, and had earth been then, all earth
Had to her centre shook.   What wonder? when
Millions of fierce encount'ring angels fought
On either side, the least of whom could wield
These elements, and arm him with the force
Of all their regions : how much more of power,
Army against army numberless to raise
Dreadful combustion warring, and disturb,
Though not destroy, their happy native seat ,
Had not th' Eternal King omnipotent
From his strong hold of Heav'n high o'er-rul'd
And limited their might ; though number'd such
As each divided legion might have seem'd
A numerous host, in strength each armed hand
A legion ; led in fight, yet leader seem'd
Each warrior single as in chief, expert
When to advance, or stand, or turn the sway
Of battle; open when, and when to close
The ridges of grim war; no thought of flight,
None of retreat, no unbecoming deed
That argu'd fear; each on himself relied
As only in his arm the moment lay
Of victory ; deeds of eternal fame
Were done, but infinite : for wide was spread
That war and various ; sometimes on firm ground

> A standing fight, then soaring on main wing
> Tormented all the air ; all air seem'd then
> Conflicting fire : long time in even scale
> The battle hung, till Satan, who that day
> Prodigious power had shewn, and met in arms
> No equal, ranging through the dire attack
> Of fighting seraphim confus'd, at length
> Saw where the sword of Michael smote, and fell'd
> Squadrons at once ; with huge two-handed sway
> Brandish'd aloft the horrid edge came down
> Wide wasting ; such destruction to withstand
> He hasted, and oppos'd the rocky orb
> Of tenfold adamant, his ample shield,
> A vast circumference."

In the *Paradise Regained* we have the triumph of obedience. This obedience is no longer a mere passive submission, or observance of a prohibitive command, but an active seeking after the indications of a Higher Will and an energetic concurrence in his purposes.

> "I who erewhile the happy garden sung,
> By one man's disobedience lost, now sing
> Recover'd Paradise to all mankind,
> By one man's firm obedience fully tried
> Through all temptation, and the Tempter foil'd
> In all his wiles, defeated and repuls'd,
> And Eden rais'd in the waste wilderness."

In selecting the Temptation rather than the Crucifixion as the climax of the self-surrender of Him who became obedient unto death, the poet was partly influenced by the antithesis between the scene, the circumstances and the event of this, and of the primeval assault of the Enemy of man. And in this, particularly, we may see a reference to the times at which Milton lived. The down-trodden Puritans brooded over the disappointment of their darling hopes, 'and as the days increased, increased their doubt.' It was surely natural that their poet should turn to contemplate the circumstances in which the Kingdom of Heaven did come with power, and seek to realize rather the victory of the Son of Man over the perplexities of life and the suggestions of evil, than the final triumph of his death.

In this poem Milton claims the highest sanction for the Puritan opinion, of the sole sufficiency of Scripture for all purposes of life. In its assertion, he exalts Holy Writ as the triumphant rival of all

nspired poetry of Homer, we are not called on to participate
n his Paganism. In reading over Dante, our pleasure is not di-
ninish'ed by the firm Romanism of his Creed.

In *"Paradise Lost,"* the doctrine is certainly Trinitarian,

"That glorious form, that light insufferable,
And that far beaming blaze of majesty,
Wherewith he wont at Heaven's high council-table
To sit the midst of *Trinal Unity,*
He laid aside."

although in later years Milton must have adopted Arian opin-
ons, as are clearly seen by his work on *"Christian Doctrine."*
'God by his decree begot his only Son before the foundations
of the world, who was thus the first of all creatures, and by him
all things in heaven and earth were made." In *"Paradise Re-
gained,"* there is also a singular passage in which his opinions are
certainly Arian or Socinian, where God the Father is introduced
as saying :—

"That all the angels and ethereal powers,
They now, and men hereafter may discern,
From what consummate virtue I have chose
This perfect man, by merit call'd my son,
To earn salvation for the sons of men."

In the Creation also, as described in *"Paradise Lost,"* it may be observed that Milton does not ascribe to God the creation of matter. On the contrary, the angels who attend the Deity to his creative work.—

> "Viewed the vast immeasurable abyss,
> Outrageous as a sea, dark, wasteful, wild,
> Up from the bottom turned by furious winds,
> And surging waves as mountains, to assault
> Heaven's height, and with the centre mix the pole."

That is, they beheld matter already, not only created, but in action. And this is further confirmed in his later theological work. Butler in his *Reminiscences* says, " The general doctrine, however, contained in the Paradise Regained comprises the doctrines of the old divines, *viz*, that the *immediate* consequence of Christ's victory over the temptation in the wilderness, was the diminution of the spiritual power, and the previously allowed dominion on the earth."

Milton is supposed to have been in the fifty-fourth year of his age, when he commenced the composition of his immortal Epic, although the high theme had doubtless for some time before occupied his thoughts. At this period of his life he was quite blind, and he uttered his harmonious numbers in darkness, as he himself expresses it,

> " in darkness and with danger compass'd round."

He lost his sight, which had early begun to decay, through the intensity of his studies, during the composition of his famous "Defence of the people of England," in answer to Salmasius ; and though he felt the calamity that was coming upon him, he did not relax in his work. We find him afterwards in one of his majestic strains consoling himself under the loss of his sight by the thought of the cause in which he had sacrificed it :—

> "What supports me, dost thou ask ?
> The conscience friend, to have lost them overplied
> In liberty's defence, my noble task,
> Whereof all Europe rings from side to side."

Paradise Lost, was probably only the work of three or four years; but this poem, as is well known, was not the only fruit of the noble intellect of Milton. Besides a mass of political and other tracts,

delightful, and perhaps the finest parts of the poem :—

"No war, or battle's sound
Was heard the world around:
   The idle spear and shield were high up hung;
The hooked chariot stood
Unstain'd with hostile blood,
  . The trumpet spake not to the armed throng;
And kings sate still with awful eye,
As if they surely knew their sovran Lord was by.

But peaceful was the night
Wherein the Prince of light
   His reign of peace upon the earth began :
The winds with wonder whist
Smoothly the waters kist,
   Whispering new joys to the mild Ocean,
Who now hath quite forgot to rave,
While birds of calm sit brooding on the charmed wave.

The stars with deep amaze
Stand fixt in stedfast gaze,
   Bending one way their precious influence;
And will not take their flight,
For all the morning light,
   Or Lucifer that often warn'd them thence;
But in their glimmering orbs did glow,
Until their Lord himself bespake, and bid them go.

And though the shady gloom
Had given day her room,
   The sun himself withheld his wonted speed;
And hid his head for shame,
As his inferior flame
   The new-enlighten'd world no more should need;

He saw a greater Sun appear
Than his bright throne, or burning axle-tree could bear."

Milton then gives us a splendid contrast in the *Passion,* written
in language that impresses us at once with the awfulness and sig-
nificance of the details. The following are some of the most
beautiful of the stanzas :—

"Erewhile of music, and ethereal mirth,
Wherewith the stage of air and earth did ring,
And joyous news of Heav'nly Infant's birth,
My muse with angels did divide to sing ;
But headlong joy is ever on the wing ;
In wintry solstic like the short'nd light,
Soon swallow'd up in dark and long out-living night.

For now to sorrow must I tune my song,
And set my harp to notes of saddest woe,
Which on our dearest Lord did seize ere long ;
Dangers, and snares, and wrongs, and worse than so,
Which he for us did freely undergo.
Most perfect hero, tried in heaviest plight
Of labours huge and hard, too hard for human wight !

*   *   *   *

Befriend me Night, best patroness of grief,
Over the pole thy thickest mantle throw,
And work my flatter'd fancy to belief
That Heav'n and Earth are colour'd with my woe ;
My sorrows are too dark for day to know :
The leaves should all be black whereon I write,
And letters where my tears have wash'd a wannish white,

*   *   *   *

Mine eye hath found that sad sepulchral rock
That was the casket of Heav'ns richest store ;
And here though grief my feeble hands up lock,
Yet on the soft'ned quarry would I score
My plaining verse as lively as before :
For sure so well instructed are my tears,
That they would fitly fall in order'd characters.

Or should I thence hurried on viewless wing,
Take up a weeping on the mountains wild,
The gentle neighbourhood of grove and spring
Would soon unbosom all their echoes mild ;
And I (for grief is easily beguiled)
Might think th' infection of my sorrows loud
Had got a race of mourners on some pregnant cloud.'

In the Odes on *Time,* and *At a Solemn Music,* there is expressed
the ideal of a passive celestial felicity, in an expansion and exag-

"Fly envious Time, till thou run out thy race,
Call on the lazy leaden-stepping hours,
Whose speed is but the heavy plummet's pace;
And glut thyself with what thy womb devours,
Which is no more than what is false and vain,
And merely mortal dross;
So little is our loss,
So little is thy gain.
For when as each thing bad thou hast entomb'd,
And last of all, thy greedy self-consum'd;
Then long Eternity shall greet our bliss
With an individual kiss;
And joy shall overtake us as a flood;
When every thing that is sincerely good
And perfectly divine,
With Truth, and Peace, and Love shall ever shine
About the supreme throne
Of him, t' whose happy-making sight alone,
When once our heav'nly-guided soul shall climb,
Then all this earthy grossness quit,
Attir'd with stars, we shall for ever sit,
Triumphing over Death, and Chance, and thee O Time."

The other, *At a Solemn Music*, has in it all that expressive melody
for which much of Milton's poetry is admired.

"Blest pair of Sirens, pledges of Heavens joy,
Sphere-born harmonius sisters, Voice and Verse,
Wed your divine sounds; and mixt power employ
Dead things with inbreath'd sense able to pierce;
And to our high rais'd phantasy present
That undisturbed song of pure content,
Aye sung before the sapphire-colour'd throne
To him that sits thereon
With saintly shout, and solemn jubilee;
Where the bright seraphim in burning row
Their loud up-lifted angel trumpets blow,
And the cherubic host in thousand quires
Touch their immortal harps of golden wires,
With those just spirits that wear victorious palms,
Hymns devout and holy psalms
Singing everlastingly:
That we on Earth with undiscording voice
May rightly answer that melodious noise;
As once we did, till disproportion'd sin
Jarr'd against nature's chime, and with harsh din
Broke the fair music that all creatures made

To their great Lord ; whose love their motion **sway'd**
In perfect diapason, whilst they stood
In first obedience, and their state of good.
O may we soon again renew that song,
And keep in tune with Heav'n, till God ere long
To his celestial consort us unite,
To live with him, and sing in endless morn of light."

The *Samson Agonistes* may be considered as one of the noblest dramas in our language, although the plot is not skilfully arranged, and the lyrical measures are totally destitute of any intelligible rhythm ; but its pathetic feeling, its rich and select language, its wise and weighty thoughts, give elevation to the whole poem.

The *Comus* was unacknowledged by the author when it first appeared, and *Lycidas* appeared at first only with his initials. The former is, with the exception of a few passages, one of the most finished poems in our language. It has all the sweetness of Fletcher, with a richer structure of versification, more foreign idioms and a higher reach of fancy. It is full of sublime sentiment, picturesque description, and ornamental experiments. The numbers in some parts of this poem, are often as melodious as the verse of Shakespeare himself. The following speech of Comus is one amongst many examples that might be given :—

" I know each lane, and every alley green,
Dingle, or bushy dell of this wild wood.
And every bosky bourn from side to side,
My daily walks and ancient neighbourhood
And if your stray attendance be yet lodg'd,
Or shroud within these limits, I shall know,
Ere morrow wake, or the low roosted lark,
From her thatch'd pallet rouse ; if otherwise
I can conduct you, lady to a low
But loyal cottage, where you may be safe,
Till further quest."

For clearness of design, beauty of form, and precision of language, this allegory is unrivalled. The epilogue by which it is closed, shadows forth in its mythical characters, the sluggishness and sadness of mere earthly passion, and the superior worth and dignity of the love which may have its beginning therein, but must await its developement and joyful consummation in a higher and holier

"To the ocean now I fly,
And those happy climes that lie
Where day never shuts his eye,
Up in the broad fields of the sky :
There I suck the liquid air
All amidst the gardens fair
Of Hesperus, and his daughters three
That sing about the golden tree:
Along the crisped shades and bowers
Revels the spruce and jocund Spring ;
The Graces, and the rosy-bosom'd Hours,
Thither all their bounties bring,
That their eternal summer dwells ;
And west winds, with musky wing
About the cedarn alleys fling
Naid, and Cassia's balmy smells.
Iris there with humid bow.
Waters the odorous banks that blow
Flowers of more mingled hue
Than her purfl'd scarf can show ;
And drenches with Elysian dew
(List mortals, if your ears be true)
Beds of hyacinth and roses,
Where young Adonis oft reposes,
Waxing well of his deep wound
In slumber soft ; and on the ground
Sadly sits th' Assyrian queen :
But far above in spangled sheen
Celestial Cupid her fam'd son advanc'd,
Holds his dear Psyche sweet entranc'd,
After her wand'ring labours long ;
Till free consent the gods among
Make her his eternal bride ;
And from her fair unspotted side
Two blissful twins are to be born,
Youth and Joy; so Jove hath sworn.
    But now my task is smoothly done,
I can fly, or I can run
Quickly to the green earth's end,
Where the bow'd welkin slow doth bend ;
And from thence can soar as soon
To the corners of the moon.
    Mortals that would follow me,
Love virtue ; she alone is free :
She can teach thee how to climb
Higher than the sphery chime ;
Or if virtue feeble were,
Heav'n itself would stoop to her,"

There was a pause between the *Comus* and the *Lycidas*. At the conclusion of the former poem, Milton was prepared to rest, until his life's "mellowing year," should bring to him the inward ripeness he had so long watched for. "Long choosing and beginning late" his lofty theme, he was anxious not to forestall the season due of his laurels, by strains which to his purged ears would be "harsh and crude," though to others they might seem the resounding grace of Heaven's harmony. But though thus self-contained, he shrank from no obligation that human kindness might lay upon him. His friend's memory claimed and received the meed of a melodious tear. In *Lycidas* the event which gave occasion for the poem has the first place, and the various changes of theme are subordinate. As he recalls his life at Cambridge with his friends, and all the rich promises that Death had blighted,

> "For we were nurs'd upon the self-same hill,
> Fed the same flock, by fountain, shade, and rill.
> Together both, ere the high lawns appear'd
> Under the opening eyelids of the Morn,
> We drove afield; and both together heard
> What time the gray-fly winds her sultry horn,
> Batt'ning our flocks with the fresh dews of night,
> Oft till the star that rose at ev'ning, bright,
> Towards Heav'ns descent had slop'd his westering wheel.
> Meanwhile the rural ditties were not mute,
> Temper'd to the oaten flute ;
> Rough Satyrs danc'd, and Fauns with clov'n heel
> From the glad sound would not be absent long,
> And old Damœtus lov'd to hear our song.
> But O the heavy change, now thou art gone,
> Now thou art gone, and never must return !
> Thee shepherd, thee the woods, and desert caves,
> With wild thyme and the gadding vine o'er grown,
> And all their echoes mourn.
> The willows, and the hazel copses green,
> Shall now no more be seen,
> Fanning their joyous leaves to thy soft lays :
> As killing as the canker to the rose,
> Or taint-worm to the weanling herds that graze,
> Or frost to flowers, that their gay wardrobe wear,
> When first the white-thorn blows ;
> Such, Lycidas, thy loss to shepherd's ear."

The thought presses on him, that even for one, for whom uni-

His gory visage down the stream was sent,
Down the swift Hebrus to the Lesbian shore?
Alas! what boots it with incessant care
To tend the homely slighted shepherd's trade.
And strictly meditate the thankless Muse?
Were it not better done as others use,
To sport with Amaryllis in the shade,
Or with the tangles of Neœra's hair?
Fame is the spur that the clear spirit doth raise,
(That last infirmity of noble minds)
To scorn delights, and live laborious days;
But the fair guerdon when we hope to find,
And think to burst out into sudden blaze,
Comes the blind Fury with th' abhorred shears,
And slits the thin spun life. 'But not the praise,
Phœbus repli'd, and touch'd my trembling ears;
'Fame is no plant that grows on mortal soil,
Nor in the glistering foil
Set off to th' world, nor in broad rumour lies
But lives and spreads aloft by those pure eyes,
And perfect witness of all-judging Jove;
As he pronounces lastly on each deed,
Of so much fame in Heav'n expect thy meed.'"

After this outburst on Fame, that strain is said to be of a higher
mood, and the pastoral pipe proceeds. Then the stern denuncia-
tion of "the pilot of the Galilean lake" scares away the lighter
mythologic fancies, till they are wooed back by the melodious
invocation to the Sicilian Muse, with its echoes of Perdita's cata-
logue of flowers.

"————————return Sicilian Muse,
And call the vales, and bid them hither cast,
Their bells, and flow'rets of a thousand hues.
Ye valleys low, where the mild whispers use
Of shades and wanton winds, and gushing brooks,
On whose fresh lap the swart star sparely looks,
Throw hither all your quaint enamell'd eyes,
That on the green turf suck the honied show'rs,
And purple all the ground with vernal flow'rs.
Bring the rathe primrose that forsaken dies,
The tufted crow-toe, and pale jessamine,
The white pink, and the pansy freak'd with jet,

The glowing violet,
The musk-rose, and the well attir'd woodbine ;
With cowslips wan that hang the pensive head,
And every flower that sad embroidery wears :
Bid Amaranthus all his beauty shed,
And daffadillies fill their cups with tears,
To strew the laureat hearse where Lycid lies. "

The following melodious passage concludes this poem, which as
a pastoral poem ranks first in our language : —

" Weep no more, woful shepherds, weep no more ;
For Lycidas your sorrow is not dead,
Sunk though he be beneath the wat'ry floor ;
So sinks the day-star in the ocean bed ;
And yet anon repairs his drooping head,
And tricks his beams, and with new-spangled ore
Flames in the forehead of the morning sky :
So Lycidas sunk low, but mounted high,
Through the dear might of him that walk'd the waves ;
Where other groves and other streams along,
With nectar pure his oozy locks he laves,
And hears the unexpressive nuptial song,
In the blest kingdoms meek of joy and love.
There entertain him all the saints above,
In solemn troops, and sweet societies,
That sing, and singing in their glory move,
And wipe the tears for ever from his eyes.
Now, Lycidas, the shepherds weep no more ;
Henceforth thou art the genius of the shore,
In thy large recompense ; and shall be good
To all that wander in that perilous flood."

Of the picturesque imagery, the musical versification and brilliant
language of the Allegro and Penseroso, praise too high cannot be
heard. They have all the pastoral beauties and sweet descriptions
of our elder poets, embellished by a richer style and more refined
combination. They are described by Macauley, as "collections of
hints, from each of which the reader is to make out a poem for
himself. Every epithet is a text for a stanza." They do not possess
those soul-moving passages and lines, glowing with a fiery intensity,
which abound in the Paradise Lost ; but they are rich with beau-
tiful touches, and exemplify the sweetness of Milton's verse.

In the L' Allegro, Milton's mirth is sportive and innocent. The
delight in the common country sights and sounds, recalls the for-
esters of Arden, and the carol of Amiens. His " woodnotes wild"

Where brooding Darkness spreads his jealous wings,
And the night-raven sings;
There under ebon shades, and low-brow'd rocks
As ragged as thy locks,
   In dark Cimmerian desert ever dwell.

*   *   *

   Haste thee, nymph, and bring with thee.
Jest and youthful Jollity,
Quips, and cranks, and wanton wiles,
Nods and becks, and wreathed smiles,
Such as hangs on Hebe's cheek.
And long to live in dimple sleek:
Sport that wrinkled Care derides,
And laughter holding both his sides.
Come, and trip it as you go
On the light fantastic toe ;
And in thy right hand lead with thee,
The mountain nymph, sweet Liberty ;
And if I give thee honour due,
Mirth, admit me of thy crew,
To live with her, and live with thee,
In unreproved pleasures free,
To hear the lark begin his flight,
And singing startle the dull Night,
From his watch tower in the skies,
Till the dappled dawn doth rise ;
Then to come in spite of Sorrow,
And at my window bid good-morrow,

I A.

Through the sweet-briar, or the vine,
Or the twisted eglantine:
While the cock with lively din
Scatters the rear of Darkness thin,
And to the stack, or the barn-door
Stoutly struts his dames before:
Oft list'ning how the hounds and horn
Cheerly rouse the slumb'ring Morn,
From the side of some hoar hill,
Through the high wood echoing shrill.
   Sometime walking not unseen
By hedge-row elms, or hillocks green,
Right against the eastern gate,
Where the great Sun begins his state,
Roh'd in flames, and amber light,
While the ploughman near at hand
Whistles o'er the furrow'd land,
And the milk-maid singeth blithe,
And the mower whets his scythe,
And every shepherd tells his tale
Under the hawthorn in the dale.
   Straight mine eye hath caught new pleasures,
Whilst the landscape round it measures:
Russet lawns, and fallows gray,
Where the nibbling flocks do stray,
Mountains on whose barren breast
The lab'ring clouds do often rest;
Meadows trim with daisies pied ;
Shallow brooks and rivers wide :
Towers and battlements it sees
Bosom'd high in tufted trees,
Where perhaps some beauty lies,
The Cynosure of neighb'ring eyes."

In the *Penseroso* the past and the foreign are present and familiar.
It is a striking contrast to the homely simplicity of the L'Allegro.
The one is the daughter of Zephyr and Aurora, born of the breeze
and the moaning in the prime of May, when the spring time stirs
the youthful blood and buoyant fancy.

"————————heart-easing Mirth,
Whom lovely Venus, at a birth,
With two sister Graces more
To ivy crown'd Bacchus bore ;
Or whether (as some sages sing)
The frolic wind that breathes the springs,
Zephyr, with Aurora playing,
As he met her once a-Maying ;

"Hence vain deluding joys,
The brood of Folly without father bred,
How little you bested,
    Or fill the fixed mind with all your toys ;
Dwell in some idle brain ;
    And fancies fond with gaudy shapes possess,
As thick and numberless
As the gay motes that people the sun-beams,
Or likest hovering dreams,
    The fickle pensioners of Morpheus' train.
But hail thou Goddess, sage and holy,
Hail divinest Melancholy—

    *   *   *   *   *

Come pensive Nun, devout and pure,
Sober, stedfast, and demure,
All in a robe of darkest grain,
Flowing with majestic train,
And sable stole of cipres lawn,
Over the decent shoulders drawn.
Come, but keep thy wonted state,
With ev'n step, and musing gait,
And looks commercing with the skies,
Thy rapt soul sitting in thine eyes :
There held in holy passion still,
Forget thyself to marble, till
With a sad leaden downward cast,
Thou fix them on the earth as fast.
And join with the calm Peace, and Quiet,
Spare Fast, that oft with gods doth diet,
And hears the Muses in a ring,
Aye round about Jove's altar sing.
And add to these retired Leisure,
That in trim gardens takes his pleasure ;
But first, and chiefest, with thee bring,
Him that soars on golden wing,
Guiding the fiery-wheeled throne,
The cherub Contemplation,

And the mute Silence hist along,
'Less Philomel will design a song,
In her sweetest, saddest plight,
Smoothing the rugged brow of Night,
While Cynthia checks her dragon yoke,
Gently o'er th' accustom'd oak :
Sweet bird that shunn'st the noise of folly,
Most musical, most melancholy !
Thee chauntress oft the woods among,
I woo to hear thy even-song ;
And missing thee, I walk unseen,
On the dry smooth shaven green,
To behold the wandering Moon,
Riding near her highest noon,
Like one that had been led astray
Through the Heav'ns wide pathless way ;
And oft, as if her head she bow'd,
Stooping through a fleecy cloud.
Oft on a plat of rising ground,
I hear the far-off curfew sound,
Over some wide-water'd shore,
Swinging slow with sullen roar ;
Or if the air will not permit,
Some still removed place will fit,
Where glowing embers through the room
Teach light to counterfeit a gloom,
Far from all resort of mirth,
Save the cricket on the hearth,
Or the bellman's drowsy charm,
To bless the doors from nightly harm :
Or let my lamp at midnight hour
Be seen in some high lonely tow'r,
Where I may oft out-watch the Bear,
With thrice-great Hermes ; or umsphere
The spirit of Plato to unfold
What worlds, or what vast regions hold
The immortal mind that hath forsook
Her mansion in this fleshy nook;
And of those demons that are found
In fire, air, flood, or under ground,
Whose power hath a true consent
With planet, or with element,
Sometime let gorgeous Tragedy
In scepter'd pall come sweeping by,
Presenting Thebes, or Pelop's line,
Or the tale of Troy divine,
Or what (though rare) of later age,
Ennobled hath the buskin'd stage."

*   *   *

> But let my due feet never fail
> To walk the studious cloister's pale.
> And love the high embowed roof,
> With antique pillars massy proof,
> And storied windows richly dight,
> Casting a dim religious light.
> There the peeling organ blow
> To the full voic'd quire below
> In service high, and anthems clear,
> As may with sweetness, through mine ear,
> Dissolve me into ecstasies,
> And bring all Heav'n before mine eyes.
>   'And may at last my weary age
> Find out the peaceful hermitage,
> The hairy gown and mossy cell,
> Where I may sit, and rightly spell
> Of every star, that Heav'n doth show,
> And every herb that sips the dew ;
> Till old experience do attain
> To something like prophetic strain.
>   These pleasures Melancholy give,
> And I with thee will choose to live."

Milton is the most sublime of all poets. To write with sublimity is to chose the greatest, the most splendid or the most awful, existing or imaginable objects and to express or display them with a corresponding propriety, force and majesty of expression. His greatness is established by the testimony which every mind alive to the beautiful and great will bear to his genius. To again use Macaulay's words, "he is the first of poets, in splendour of conception, pomp of language, and in description of prodigious things. The impression it leaves is analagous to that elevating pleasure which cartoon paintings of the first masters excite, and nothing can exceed in beauty or sublimity, those pictures of the fallen angels in their march over hell, and in their council of Pandemonium." Yet, though Milton may be considered the most sublime of poets, we could not justly call him the first of poets. The superiority is certainly with Shakespere. He is a noble example of what perseverence may accomplish in the face of the most formidable difficulties. It would seem almost as if life could scarcely continue desirable, to him whose hourly thought may be expressed in his beautiful and pathetic lamentations.

"————————————with the year
Seasons return ; but not to me returns
Day, or the sweet approach of even or morn,
Or sight of vernal bloom, or summer's rose,
Or flocks, or herds, or human face divine ;
But cloud instead, and ever-during dark
Surrounds me, from the cheerful ways of men
Cut off, and, for the book of knowledge fair,
Presented with a universal blank
Of Nature's works, to me expunged and rased."

We cannot mourn over the sightless orbs of Milton ; he could
not have done greater things than he did in his blindness :—

"————————Samson hath quit himself
Like Samson, and heroically hath finished
A life heroic.
Nothing is here for tears, nothing to wail,
Or knock the breast, no weakness, no contempt,
Dispraise or blame ; nothing but well and fair."

We may here quote that beautiful stanza which he himself wrote
on his blindness :—

"When I consider how my light is spent,
    Ere half my days, in this dark world and wide,
    And that one talent which is death to hide
    Lodg'd with me useless, though my soul more bent
To serve therewith my Maker, and present
    My true account, lest he returning chide ;
    'Doth God exact day labour, light deni'd ?'
    I fondly ask : but Patience, to prevent
That murmur, soon replies, God doth not need
    Either man's work, or his own gifts ; who best
    Bear his mild yoke, they serve him best : his state
Is kingly ; thousands at his bidding speed,
    And post o'er land and ocean without rest ;
    They also serve who only stand and wait' : "

I will conclude by quoting the beautiful lines of Tennyson,
written upon Milton :—

"O mighty mouth'd inventor of harmonies
O skill'd to sing of Time or Eternity
God-gifted organ-voice of England
MILTON, a name to resound for ages
Whose Titan angels, Gabriel, Abdiel,
Starr'd from Jehovah's gorgeous armories,
Tower, as the deep-domed Empyrean,
Rings to the roar of an angel onset—
Me rather all that bowery loneliness,

imagination, but possessed a mastery over his language which no other writer has ever attained. Yet his merits have always been indifferently acknowledged. Our zeal for the poets who preceded the civil wars, like most reactions, is become too exclusive. But we are too much inclined to confound with the period, which began with Addison and Pope, that intermediate time, from the Restoration to the end of the century, in which, though French taste had a good deal of effect, the former nature, or Italian spirit still operated, and the taste of the French themselves had not yet quite arrived at its most corrected and characterized form.

• Sir Walter Scott speaks of Dryden as the "Great High Priest of all the Nine." Gray wrote to Beattie, " Remember Dryden, and be blind to all his faults.'' and Pope's enthusiastic praise of him is familiar to us all. Dryden is our best model of language, in prose or verse. His want of popularity is partly owing to his inequalities. Much of his poetry is uninteresting, and a good deal is incorrect, over-fanciful or course ; so much of the latter that it is alone a sufficient reason, why his entire poems cannot be given to women or to young persons with a view to education. Many of his poems, too, are occasional ; and relate as a whole, to subjects no longer interesting.

Upon none of our poets have more conflicting judgments been
pronounced than upon Dryden. The unanimous verdicts of his
critics give him a high place ; but remarkable differences exist, in
determining exactly what the place is. Hazlitt places him below
Pope, and at the head of the second class of poets. Coleridge—who
will not admit him to be a poet at all—places him immeasurably
above Pope. "Cowley *was* a poet," observes Coleridge, "which
with all my unfeigned admiration of his vigorous sense, his agile
logical wit, and his high excellencies of diction and metre, is worse
than (in the *strict* sense of the word poet), I can conscientiously
say of Dryden. Only if Pope was a *poet*, as Lord Byron swears,
then Dryden, I admit, was a *very great poet*."* Out of this con-
flict of judgments comes an indestructible fame, commanding the
common assent of all. There must have been a permanent element
in his genius to produce this. What was it? In one word—power.
It was this great characteristic that raised Dryden above all his
contemporaries, and preserves him on his elevation. He was
distinguished above all things else, for strength of thought, strength
of purpose, strength of diction. He was a strong man in verse
and prose ; bold, energetic, self-reliant, and wide in his reach.
There was no weakness in Dryden ; no compromise of means or
ends. Perhaps there was not much tenderness ; yet he had a
certain manly sweetness at times, that was all the more precious
and affecting from its rarity, and because it seemed to come from
the depth of his nature. There was real physical passion, undis-
guised sensuousness ; *no love*. Robust in all things, his poetry
has an insight and an earnestness, that takes it out of the atmos-
phere of the imaginative. It is never airy, never sportive. He
made poetry the vehicle of politics and controversy not of feeling
or of fancy. There is not a single love passage throughout the
whole, such as we find in Shakespeare or in Fletcher, touching
the springs of tears in the heart, and awakening in the reader the
emotion it depicts. When he ventures in this direction; it is to
exhibit highly wrought artificial turns of gallantry. His *Lines on
the Duchess of Portsmouth*, or the luscious descriptions in *Cymon*

---

* Notes on Pepy's, *Notes and Queries*, VI. 214.

and Iphigenia, will testify to this. He treads heavily, and every foot-fall crushes the earth beneath.

There was nothing of what is termed sentiment in Dryden. He seldom produces any other emotions than those of indignation, ridicule, or surprise. He constantly makes you think, but very rarely makes you feel. There are some few lines in his plays, and occasionally a whole passage, that reaches the verge of pathos ; but you are conscious that it is not real, and that what is real in him, and paramount, is sarcasm, scorn, logic, and wit. Yet Dryden's mind is eminently poetical. He turns everything into imagination. It is like great painters, such as Titian and Rubens, representing common objects ; quite naturally, indeed, but at the same time with a warmth and richness which they do not suggest to the minds of the vulgar observers, nor derive from the pencil of inferior artists. His elegant ideas and expressions are thrown out with a real delight, and scattered with an easy profuseness, where a writer of the later school would crow over them, and make much of them, individually. When we then see the spirit of Dryden, bursting into poetry and imagination upon every subject, and particularly when, becoming more and more matured, he discards the love of ingenious conceits which he had been taught, and perhaps had taught himself, in his youth; it forms an extraordinary contrast with the very prosaic subjects, nay style, which he so frequently chooses and cultivates. But he was an eminently manly character. Poet as he was, he did not like, as Byron says, to be "all poet." Besides this, it was not a poetical age. If he did not write on poetical subjects, nobody else did.

One of the greatest merits of Dryden lies in his diction. He has avoided whatever was antiquated or pedantic in his predecessors, and in the treatment of a lower range of subjects, has observed that idiomatic purity which they exhibited in the higher walks of poetry. Pope says, " he always uses proper language : lively, natural, and fitted to the subject. It is scarcely ever too high or too low ; never perhaps, except in his plays." Dryden not only uses the right word in the right place ; but he never uses it in an ambiguous sense, and strictly confines himself to the forms and resources of his own language. Perhaps, of all English poets, Dryden is the most English. He is as emphatically Saxon, as Pope is conspicuously French. As a prose writer, the Saxon flavour of his language, is as strong as his matter is full and weighty. His style is everywhere fluent, masterly and idiomatic. The same boldness and largeness of conception marked everything he undertook. To remodel Shakespeare and turn Milton into rhyme, were not the projects of an ordinary mind ; and if he failed in the execution of these designs, there was a waste of splendour in the failure that makes its example illustrious. It has been observed, that what was said of Rome adorned by Augustus, might be applied by an easy metaphor to English poetry. He found it brick, and left it marble. His tragedies though they consist chiefly in "absurd bluster, chop-logic, and Frenchified gallanterie," have scattered about them, bursts of imagination, the more remarkable because they seem to force their way in spite of the spirit of the age, instead of harmonizing with it, as in the case of Shakespeare : gushes of simple, child-like, and tender feeling—more rarely that feeling which is expected in tragedy; grand flow of manly spirit. This may be seen more so in the *Conquest of Granada,* from which I have selected one or two passages :—

> *Benz.*—"Love, then, my Ozmyn ; I will be content
> To make you wretched by your own consent :
> Live poor, despis'd, and banish'd for my sake,
> And all the burden of my sorrows take ;
> For, as for me, in whatso'er estate,
> While I have you, I must be fortunate.
> *Ozmyn.*—Thus, then, secur'd of what we hold most dear
> (Each other's love) we'll go—I know not where.
> For where, alas, should we our flight begin ?
> The foe's without ; our parents are within.
> *Benz.*—I'll fly to you ; and you shall fly to me :
> Our flight but to each other's arms shall be.
> To Providence and chance permit the rest ;
> Let us but love enough, and we are blest."

> * * * * * *

> *Almanz*—"A hollow wind comes whistling through that door:
> And a cold shiv'ring seizes me all o'er :

My teeth, too, chatter with a sudden fright:
These are the raptures of too fierce delight,
The combat of the tyrants, hope and fear;
Which hearts, for want of field-room, cannot bear.
I grow impatient; this, or that's the room:
I'll meet her; now, methinks, I hear her come.
 Again by Heav'n I do conjure thee, speak,
What art thou, spirit? and what dost thou seek?
Ghost.—I am the ghost of her who gave thee birth;
The airy shadow of her mould'ring earth.
Love of thy father me through seas did guide;
On seas I bore thee, and on seas I died.
I died: and for my winding sheet a wave
I had; and all the ocean for my grave.
But when my soul to bliss did upward move,
I wander'd round the crystal walls above,
But found th' eternal fence so steeply high,
That, when I mounted to the middle sky,
I flagg'd, and flutter'd down, and could not fly.
Then, from the battlements of th' heav'nly tow'r
A watchman angel bid me wait this hour;
And told me I had yet a task assign'd,
To warn that little pledge I left behind;
And to divert him, ere it were too late,
From crimes unknown, and errors of his fate.
 Once more I'll see thee: then my charge is done,
Far hence, upon the Mountains of the Moon,
Is my abode; where Heav'n and nature smile,
And strew with flow'rs the secret bed of Nile.
Bless'd souls are there refin'd and made more bright;
And, in the shades of Heav'n prepar'd for light.
Almanz.—O Heav'n, how dark a riddle's thy decree,
Which bounds our wills, yet seems to leave them free.
Since thy fore-knowledge cannot be in vain,
Our choice must be what thou didst first ordain.
Thus, like a captive in an isle confin'd,
Man walks at large, a pris'ner of the mind."

The *Almanzor* in this play is decidedly a romance character,
beyond any even in Corneille: (though hardly beyond Achilles in
Homer;) one who frightens a whole army with shouting. One of
the passages spoken by Almahide runs:—

"Where should I find the heart to speak one word
Your voice, sir, is as killing as your sword
As you have left the lightning of your eye,
So would you please to lay your thunder by.

  * * * * * *

Your passion, like a fright, suspends my pain:
It meets, o'erpow'rs, and beats mine back again:
But, as when tides against the current flow,

And half unready, with their bodies come.

Those who have homes, when home they do repair,
   To a last lodging call their wandering friends :
Their short uneasy sleeps are broke with care,
   To look how near their own destruction tends.

Those who have none sit round where once it was,
   And with full eyes each wonted room require ;
Haunting the yet warm ashes of the place,
   As murdered men walk where they did expire.

Some stir up coals, and watch the vestal fire ;
   Others, in vain from sight of ruin run ;
And, while through burning labyrinths they retire,
   With loathing eyes repeat what they would shun.

The most, in fields, like herded beasts, lie down,
   To dews obnoxious, on the grassy floor ;
And while their babes in sleep their sorrows drown,
   Sad parents watch the remnants of their store.

While by the motion of the flames they guess
   What streets are burning now, and what are near ;
An infant, waking, to the paps would press,
   And meets, instead of milk, a falling tear.

No thought can ease them but their sovereign's care,
   Whose praise the afflicted as their comfort sing ;
E'en those whom want might drive to just despair,
   Think life a blessing under such a king,

Meantime he sadly suffers in their grief,
   Out-weeps an hermit, and out-prays a saint ;
All the long night he studies their relief,
   How they may be supplied, and he may want.

'O God' said he, 'thou patron of my days,
   Guide of my youth in exile and distress !
Who me, unfriended, brought'st by wondrous ways,
   The kingdom of my fathers to possess :

'Be thou my judge, with what unwearied care
   I since have laboured for my people's good ;
To bind the bruises of a civil war,
   And stop the issues of their wasting blood.' "

to this chapter, did space permit ; but the few I have given, are, certainly, some of the most beautiful examples.

Boab.—"As some fair tulip, by a storm opprest,
    Shrinks up, and folds its silken arms to rest ;
    And, bending to the blast, all pale and dead,
    Hears, from within, the wind sing round its head :
    So, shrouded up, your beauty disappears ;
    Unveil, my love, and lay aside your fears.
    The storm that caus'd your fright, is past and done,
Almah.—So flow'rs peep out too soon, and miss the sun."

"Now ask your life.
——————'Tis gone, that busy thing
The soul, is packing up, and just on wing,
Like parting swallows when they seek the spring.
Like them, at its appointed time, it goes ;
And flies to countries more unknown than those."

"As some faint pilgrim, standing on the shore,
First views the torrent he would venture o'er ;
And then his inn upon the farther ground.
Loth to wade through, and lother to go round ;
Then, dipping in his staff, does trial make,
How deep it is ; and, sighing, pulls it back :
Sometimes resolv'd to fetch his leap : and then
Runs to the bank, but there stops short again,
So I at once————
Both heav'nly faith, and human fear obey ;
And feel before me in an unknown way,
For this blest voyage I with joy prepare ;
Yet am asham'd to be a stranger there."

"Shake not his hour-glass, when his hasty sand
Is ebbing to the last :
A little longer, yet a little longer,
And nature drops him down, without your sin ;
Like mellow fruit, without a winter-storm."

"No, Pandarus ; I stalk about your doors
Like a strange soul upon the Stygian banks,

Staying for waftage : O be thou my Charon,
And give me a swift transportance to Elysium,
And fly with me to Cressida."

"Our loves, like mountains high above the clouds,
Though winds and tempests beat their aged feet,
Their peaceful heads, nor storm, nor thunder know,
But scorn the threat'ning rack that rolls below."

"My joys are gloomy, but withal are great ;
The lion, though he sees the toils are set,
Yet, pinch'd with raging hunger, scours away,
Hunts in the face of danger all the day ;
At night, with sullen pleasures, grumbles o'er his prey."

"Beauty, like ice, our footing does betray :
Who can tread sure on the smooth slippery way ?
Pleas'd with the passage, we slide swiftly on :
And see the dangers which we cannot shun."

"I will; and yet
A kind of weight hangs heavy at my heart ;
My flagging soul flies under her own pitch,
Like fowl in air too damp, and lugs along,
As if she were a body in a body,
And not a mounting substance made of fire.
My senses too are dull and stupefied,
Their edge rebated ; sure some ill approaches,
And some kind sprite knocks softly at my soul,
To tell me fate's at hand."

"As when a sudden storm of hail and rain,
Beats to the ground the yet unbearded grain,
Think not the hopes of harvest are destroy'd,
On the flat field, and on the naked void;
The light unloaded stem, from tempest freed,
Will raise the youthful honours of his head ;
And soon restor'd by native vigour, bear
The timely product of the bounteous year."

"A mighty secret labours in my soul,
And like a rushing stream breaks down the dam : ・
This day must give it vent, it rests in you
To make it end in a tempestuous night,
Or in a glorious evening."

"For what I see, or only think I see,
Is like a glimpse of moonshine, streak'd with red ;
A shuffled, sullen, and uncertain light,
That dances through the clouds, and shuts again :
Then 'ware a rising tempest on the main."

"And as the Indies were not found, before
Those rich perfumes, which, from the happy shore,
The winds upon their balmy wings convey'd,
Whose guilty sweetness first their world betray'd ;
So by your counsels we are brought to view
A rich and undiscover'd world in you."

"As, where the lightning runs along the ground,
No husbandry can heal the blasting wound ;
Nor bladed grass, nor bearded corn succeeds,
But scales of scurf and putrefaction breeds,
Such wars, such waste, such fiery tracks of dearth,
Their zeal has left, and such a teemless earth."

"True love's a miser, so tenacious grown,
He weighs to the least grain of what's his own.
More delicate than honour's nicest sense :
Neither to give nor take the least offence.
With, or without you, I can have no rest :
What shall I do? you're lodged within my breast :
Your image never never will be thence displac'd,
But there it lies, stabb'd, mangled, and defac'd,"

"Dim as the borrowed beams of moon and stars.
To lonely, weary, wand'ring travellers,
Is reason to the soul : and, as on high,
Those rolling fires discover but the sky,
Not light us here ; so reason's glimmering ray
Was lent, not to assure our doubtful way,
But guide us upward to a better day.
And as those nightly tapers disappear
When day's bright lord ascends our hemisphere ;
So pale grows reason at religion's sight ;
So dies, and so dissolves in supernat'ral light."

"As from some steep and dreadful precipice,
The frighted traveller casts down his eyes,
And sees the ocean at so great a distance,
It looks as if the skies were sunk below him,
Yet if some neighb'ring shrub (how weak soe'er)

"I feel my love to Philocles within me.
Shrink, and pull back my heart from this hard trial,
But it must be, when glory says it must.
As children wading from some river's bank,
First try the water, with their tender feet,
Then shudd'ring up with cold, step back again,
And straight a little further venture on,
  Till at last, they plunge into the deep,
  And pass at once, what they were doubting long.'

———————

"This love, that never could my youth engage,
Peeps out his coward head to dare my age.
Where hast thou been thus long, thou sleeping form,
Thou wak'st, like drowsy seamen, in a storm.
A sullen hour thou choosest for thy birth:
My love shoots up in tempests, as the earth
Is stirr'd and loosen'd in a blust'ring wind,
Whose blasts to waiting flowers her womb unbind."

———————

"As when some great and gracious monarch dies,
Soft whispers, first, and mournful murmurs rise
Among the sad attendants; then the sound
Soon gathers voice, and spreads the news around,
Through town and country, till the dreadful blast
Is blown to distant colonies at last;
Who, then, perhaps, were off'ring vows in vain,
For his long life, or for his happy reign."

CHAPTER XIV.

POPE.

POPE.—"Neither time, nor distance, nor age," Byron wrote, "can ever diminish my veneration for him, who is the great moral poet of all times, of all climes, of all feelings, and of all stages of existence. The delight of my boyhood, the study of my manhood, perhaps (if allowed to me to attain to it), he may be the consolation of my old age. His poetry is the book of life. Without canting and yet without neglecting religion, he has assembled all that a good and a great man can gather together of moral wisdom, clothed in consummate beauty."

Perhaps this avalanche of enthusiasm in Byron may be overstretched, yet it truly expresses the genius and power of Pope. He is himself a literature. He is the foremost of our classical poets, that is, if the term be correctly applied to a school which sought in

I C.

the masterpieces of ancient times, the starting-point of their own literary developement. Pope, however, was less under the influence of French and other models than Dryden, although the influence of the latter exerted itself in its turn upon him.

This poet may be considered more a critic, satirist, and fine writer than a poet. He scarcely ever touches any of the greater passions. Still, everything that Pope wrote in verse, was invariably, to use a homely term, good as far as it went. The *Pastorals*, the *Messiah*, and *Windsor Forest*, continue to give the pleasure which finished copies of verse, can never fail to afford to an educated ear. Take for instance the following passage :—

> "Hark ! a glad voice the lonely desert cheers ;
> Prepare the way ! a God, a God appears :
> A God, a God ! the vocal hills reply,
> The rocks proclaim the approaching Deity.
> Lo, earth receives him from the bending skies !
> Sink down ye mountains, and ye valleys rise,
> With heads declined, ye cedars homage pay ;
> Be smooth ye rocks, ye rapid floods give way !
> The Saviour comes ! by ancient bards foretold :
> Hear him, ye deaf, and all ye blind, behold !
> He from thick films shall purge the visual ray,
> And on the sightless eyeball pour the day :
> 'Tis he the obstructed paths of sound shall clear,
> And bid new music charm the unfolding ear :
> The dumb shall sing, the lame his crutch forego,
> And leap exulting like the bounding roe.
> No sigh, no murmur the wide world shall hear,
> From every face he wipes off every tear.
> In adamantine chains shall death be bound,
> And hell's grim tyrant feel the eternal wound."

Or for a passage immediately opposite in description and character, the following lines from *Windsor Forest* :—

> "See! from the brake the whirring pheasant springs
> And mounts exulting on triumphant wings:
> Short is his joy ; he feels the fiery wound,
> Flutters in blood, and panting beats the ground.
> Ah ! what avail his glossy, varying dyes,
> His purple crest, and scarlet-circled eyes,
> The vivid green his shining plumes unfold,
> His painted wings, and breast that flames with gold ?
> Nor yet, when moist Arcturus clouds the sky,
> The woods and fields their pleasing toils deny.
> To plains with well-breathed beagles we repair,

And trace the mazes of the circling hare :
(Beasts, urged by us, their fellow beasts pursue,
And learn of man each other to undo.)
With slaught'ring guns the unwearied fowler roves,
When frosts have whitened all the naked groves ;
Where doves in flocks the leafless trees o'ershade,
And lonely woodcocks haunt the watery glade.
He lifts the tube, and levels with his eye ;
Straight a short thunder breaks the frozen sky :
Oft, as in airy rings they skim the heath,
The clamorous lapwings feel the leaden death :
Oft, as the mounting larks their notes prepare,
They fall, and leave their little lives in air.
   In genial spring, beneath the quivering shade,
Where cooling vapours breathe along the mead,
The patient fisher takes his silent stand,
Intent, his angle trembling in his hand :
With looks unmoved, he hopes the scaly breed,
And eyes the dancing cork, and bending reed.
Our plenteous streams a various race supply,
The bright-eyed perch with fin of Tyrian's dye,
The silver eel, in shining volumes rolled,
The yellow cary, in scales bedropped with gold,
Swift trouts, diversified with crimson stains,
And pikes, the tyrants of the watery plains."

In neither the lyric, dramatic, or epic poetry of this writer, do we see marked out any original power, or species of poetical composition signally his own. The first two of these he barely attempted ; his *Ode on St. Cecilia's day* is only a feeble duplicate of Dryden. It may be found at the end of the book. For epic poetry he seems to have lacked the historic sense. It is in the didactic poety of Pope, that he is truly master. The *Essay on Criticism*, as a juvenile effort, is marvellously finished ; and succeeds in enforcing many truths in a form in which the incisiveness has rarely been surpassed. It might be read by many of the critics of the present day with considerable advantage.

"Of all the Causes which conspire to blind
Man's erring judgment, and misguide the mind,
What the weak head with strongest bias rules,
Is *Pride*, the never failing voice of fools.
Whatever nature has in worth denied,
She gives in large recruits of needful pride ;
For as in bodies, thus in souls, we find
What wants in blood and spirits, swell'd with wind :
Pride, where wit fails, steps in to our defence,

Short views we take, nor see the lengths behind
But more advanc'd, behold with strange surprise
New distant scenes of endless science rise !
So pleas'd at first the tow'ring Alps we try,
Mount o'er the vales, and seem to tread the sky,
Th' eternal snows appear already past,
And the first clouds and mountains seem the last;
But, those attain'd, we tremble to survey
The growing labours of the lengthen'd way,
Th' increasing prospects tires our wand'ring eyes,
Hills peep o'er hills, and Alps on Alps arise !
  A perfect Judge will read each work of Wit
With the same spirit that its author writ:
Survey the WHOLE nor seek slight faults to find
Where nature moves, and rapture warms the mind;
Nor lose, for that malignant dull delight,
The gen'ions pleasure to be charm'd with Wit.
But in such lays as neither ebb, nor flow,
Correctly cold, and regularly low,
That shunning faults, one quiet tenour keep ;
We cannot blame indeed—but we may sleep.
In wit, as nature, what affects our hearts
  Is not th' exactness of peculiar parts,
'Tis not a lip, or eye, we beauty call,
But the joint force and full result of all.
Thus then we view some well proportion'd dome,
(The world's just wonder, and ev'n thine, O Rome !)
No single parts unequally surprize,
All comes united to th' admiring eyes ;
No monstrous height, or breadth, or length appear ;
The Whole at once is bold, and regular.
  Whoever thinks a faultless piece to see,
Thinks what ne'ei was, nor is, nor e'er shall be.
In ev'ry work regard the writer's End,
Since none can compass more than they intend ;
And if the means be just, the conduct true,
Applause, in spite of trivial faults, is due ;
As men of breeding, sometimes men of wit,

T' avoid great errors, must the less commit :
Neglect the rules each verbal Critic lays,
For not to know some trifles is a praise.
Most Critics, fond of some subserviant art,
Still make the whole depend upon a part :
They talk of principles, but notions prize,
And all to one lov'd Folly sacrifice.

*   *   *   *

Some to *Conceit* alone their taste confine,
And glitt'ring thoughts struck out at ev'ry line ;
Pleas'd with a work where nothing's just or fit ;
One glaring Chaos and wild heap of wit.
Poets like painters, thus, unskill'd to trace
The naked nature and the living grace,
With gold and jewels cover ev'ry part,
And hide with ornaments their want of art.
True Wit is Nature to advantage dress'd,
What oft was thought, but ne'er so well express'd.
Something whose truth convinc'd at sight we find,
That gives us back the image of our mind.
As shades more sweetly recommend the light,
So modest plainness sets off sprightly wit.
For works may have more wit than does 'em good,
As bodies perish thro' excess of blood.
Others for *Language* all their care express,
And value books, as women men, for Dress :
Their praise is still,—the Style is excellent :
The Sense, they humbly take upon content.
Words are like leaves ; and where they most abound,
Much fruit of sense beneath is rarely found.
False eloquence, like the prismatic glass,
Its gaudy colours spreads on ev'ry place ;
The face of Nature we no more survey,
All glares alike, without distinction gay :
But true expression, like th' unchanging Sun,
Clears and improves whate'er it shines upon,
It gilds all objects, but it alters none.
Expression is the dress of thought, and still
Appears more decent, as more suitable ;
A vile conceit in pompous words express'd,
Is like a clown in regal purple dress'd :
For diff'rent Styles with diff'rent subjects sort,
As several garbs with country, town, and court.
Some by old words to fame have made pretence,
Ancients in phrase, mere moderns in their sense ;
Such labour'd nothings, in so strange a style,
Amaze th' unlearn'd, and make the learned smile.
Unlucky, as Fungoso in the play,
These sparks with awkward vanity display
What the fine gentleman wore yesterday ;

And but so mimic ancient wits at best,
So ape our grandsires, in their doublets drest.
In words, as fashions,the same rule will hold;
Alike fantastic, if too new, or old:
Be not the first by whom the new are try'd,
Nor yet the last to lay the old aside.
  But most by Numbers judge a Poet's song;
And smooth or rough; with them is right or wrong:
In the bright Muse though thousand charms conspire,
Her voice is all these tuneful fools admire;
Who haunt Parnassus but to please their ear,
Not mend their minds; as some to Church repair,
Not for the doctrine, but the music there.
These equal syllables alone require,
Tho' oft the ear the open vowels tire;
While expletives their feeble aid to join;
And ten low words oft creep in one dull line.
While they ring round the same unvary'd chimes,
With sure returns of still expected rhymes;
Wheree'er you find 'the cooling western breeze,'
In the next line, it 'whispers through the trees:'
If crystal streams 'with pleasing murmurs creep,'
The reader's threaten'd (not in vain) with 'sleep,'
Then, at the last and only couplet fraught
With some unmeaning thing they call a thought,
A needless Alexandrine ends the song
That, like a wounded snake, drags its slow length along
Leave such to tune their own dull rhymes, and know,
What's roundly smooth or languishly slow;
And praise the easy vigour of a line,
Where Denham's strength, and Waller's sweetness join.
True ease in writing comes from art, not chance,
As those move easiest who have learn'd to dance.
'Tis not enough no harshness gives offence,
The sound must seem an Echo to the sense:
Soft is the strain when Zephyr gently blows,
And the smooth stream in smoother numbers flows,
But when loud surges lash the sounding shore,
The hoarse, rough verse should like the torrent roar.
When Ajax strives some rock's vast weight to throw,
The line too labours, and the words move slow.
Not so, when swift Camilla scours the plain,
Flies o'er th' unbending corn, and skims along the main
Hear how Timotheus' varied lays surprize,
And bid alternate passions fall and rise!
While, at each change, the son of Libyan Jove,
Now burns with glory, and then melts with love,
Now his fierce eyes with sparkling fury glow,
Now sighs steal out, and tears begin to flow:
Persians and Greeks like turns of nature found,

And the world's victor stood subdu'd by sound !
The pow'r of Music all our hearts allow,
And what Timotheus was, is DRYDEN now.
  Avoid extremes ; and shun the fault of such,
Who still are pleas'd too little or too much.
As ev'ry trifle scorn to take offence,
That always shows great pride, or little sense ;
Those heads, as stomachs, are not sure the best,
Which nauseate all, and nothing can digest.
Yet let not each gay Turn thy rapture move ;
For Fools admire, but men of sense approve :
As things seem large which we thro' mists descry,
Dulness is ever apt to magnify.
  Some foreign writers, some our own despise,
The Ancients only, or the Moderns prize.
Thus Wit, like Faith, by each man is apply'd,
To one small sect, and all are damn'd beside.
Meanly they seek the blessing to confine,
And force that sun but on a part to shine,
Which not alone the southern wit sublimes,
But ripens spirits in cold northern climes ;
Which from the first has shone on ages past.
Enlights the present, and shall warm the last ;
Tho' each may feel increases and decays,
And see now clearer and now darker days.
Regard not then if Wit be old or new,
But blame the false, and value still the true.
  Some ne'er advance a Judgment of their own,
But catch the spreading notion of the Town ;
They reason and conclude by precedent,
And own stole nonsense which they ne'er invent.
Some judge of authors' names, not works, and then
Nor praise nor blame the writings, but the men.
Of all this servile herd the worst is he,
That in proud dulness joins with Quality.
A constant Critic at the great man's board,
To fetch and carry nonsense for my Lord.
What woful stuff this madrigal would be,
In some starv'd hackney sonneteer, or me ?
But let a Lord once own the happy lines,
How the wit brightens ! how the style refines !
Before his sacred name flies ev'ry fault,
And each exalted stanza teems with thought.

    *   *   *   *

  Be thou the first true merit to befriend ;
His praise is lost, who stays till all commend.
Short is the date, alas, of modern rhymes,
And 'tis but just to let them live betimes.
No longer now that golden age appears,
When Patriarch-wits surviv'd a thousand years :

Now length of Fame (our second life) is lost,
And bare three-score is all ev'n that can boast,
Our sons their father's failing language see,
And such as Chaucer is, shall Dryden be.
So when the faithful pencil has design'd,
Some bright Idea of the master's mind,
Where a new world leaps out at his command,
And ready nature waits upon his hand,
When the ripe colours soften and unite.
And sweetly melt into just shade and light ;
When mellowing years their full perfection gives,
And each bold figure just begins to live,
The treach'rous colours the fair art betray,
And all the bright creation fades away !"

Again in the *Essay on Man* Pope succeeds, by his mastery of
form, and in producing a string of poetic proverbs which will serve
for many a future text.   In the third Epistle we read :—

"Thus then the man the voice of nature spake—
Go, from the Creatures thy instructions take :
Learn from the birds what food the thickets yield ;
Learn from the beasts the physic of the field ;
Thy arts of building from the bee receive ;
Learn of the mole to plough, the worm to weave ;
Learn of the little Nautilus to sail,
Spread the thin oar, and catch the driving gale.
Here too all forms of social union find,
And hence let reason, late, instruct Mankind :
Here subterranean works and cities see ;
There towns aerial on the waving tree.
Learn each small people's genius, policies,
The Ant's republic, and the realm of bees ;
How those in common all their wealth bestow.
And anarchy without confusion know ;
And these for ever, though a monarch reign,
Their separate cells and properties maintain.
Mark what unwearied laws preserve each state,
Laws wise as nature, and as fixed as fate.
In vain they reason finer webs shall draw,
Entangled justice in her net of law,
And right, too rigid, harden into wrong ;
Still for the strong too weak, the weak too strong.
Yet go ! and thus o'er all the creatures sway,
Thus let the wiser make the rest obey ;
And, for those arts mere instinct could afford,
Be crowned as monarchs, or as gods adored. "

Or for another example the following passage from the Fourth
Epistle :—

"What makes all physical or moral ill?
There deviates nature, and here wanders will.
God sends not ill ; if rightly understood,
Or partial ill is universal good,
Or change admits, or nature lets it fall,
Short, and but rare, till man improved it all.
We just as wisely might of heaven complain,
That righteous Abel was destroyed by Cain,
As that the virtuous son is ill at ease,
When his lewd father gave the dire disease.
Think we, like some weak prince, the Eternal Cause
Prone for his favorites to reverse his laws?
   Shall burning Ætna, if a sage requires,
Forget to thunder, and recall her fires?
On air or sea new motions be imprest,
Oh, blameless Bethel! to relieve thy breast?
When the loose mountain trembles from on high,
Shall gravitation cease, if you go by?
Or some old temple, nodding to its fall,
For Chartres' head reserve the hanging wall?
   But still this world (so fitted for the knave)
Contents us not. A better shall we have?
A kingdom of the just then let it be :
But first consider how those just agree.
The good must merit God's peculiar care ;
But who, but God, can tell us who they are?
One thinks on Calvin Heaven's own spirit fell ;
Another deems him instrument of hell ;
If Calvin feel Heaven's blessing, or its rod,
This cries there is, and that, there is no God.
What shocks one part will edify the rest,
Nor with one system can they all be blest.
The very best will variously incline,
And what rewards your virtue, punish mine.
WHATEVER IS, IS RIGHT.—This world, 'tis true,
Was made for Cæsar—but for Titus too:
And which more blest? who chained his country, say,
Or he whose virtue sighed to lose a day?
   'But sometimes virtue starves, while vice is fed.'
What then? Is the reward of virtue-bread?
That, vice may merit, 'tis the price of toil ;
The knave deserves it, when he tills the soil,
The knave deserves it, when he tempts the main,
Where folly fights for kings, or dives for gain.
The good man may be weak, be indolent ;
Nor is his claim to plenty, but content.
But grant him riches, your demand is o'er?
'No—shall the good want health, the good want power?'
Add health, and power, and every earthly thing,
'Why bounded power? why private? why no king?'

Nay, why external for internal given ?
Why is not man a god, and earth a heaven ?
Who ask and reason thus, will scarce conceive
God gives enough, while he has more to give :
Immense the power, immense were the demand ;
Say, at what part of nature will they stand.
    What nothing earthly gives, or can destroy,
The soul's calm sunshine, and the heart-felt joy
Is virtue's prize : A better would you fix ?
Then give humility a coach and six,
Justice a conqueror's sword, or truth a gown,
Or public spirit its great cure, a crown.
Weak, foolish man ! will Heaven reward us there
With the same trash mad mortals wish for here ?
The boy and man an individual makes,
Yet sighest thou now for apples and for cakes ?
Go, like the Indian, in another life
Expect thy dog, thy bottle, and thy wife :
As well as dream such trifles are assigned,
As toys and empires, for a god-like mind.
Rewards, that either would to virtue bring
No joy, or be destructive of the thing ;
How oft by these at sixty are undone
The virtues of a saint at twenty-one !
To whom can riches give repute, or trust,
Content, or pleasure, but the good and just ?
Judges and Senators, have been bought for gold.
Esteem and love were never to be sold.
O fool ! to think God hates the worthy mind,
The lover and the love of human-kind,
Whose life is healthful, and whose conscience clear,
Because he wants a thousand pounds a year."

Pope's satirical poetry is also didactic in its aim.   It has a posi-
tive purpose ; it contrasts excellence and virtue with dulness and
vice ; and its examples are illustrations of its precepts,   And in this
again Pope is master : his ability in representing types of character
is unsurpassed.   The men and women of his Satires and Epistles,
his Atticus and Atossa, and Sapho and Sporus, are real types,
whether they be more or less faithful portraits of Addison and the
old Duchess : of Lady Mary and Lord Hervey.   Pope's creative
power in this respect surpasses that of the Roman satirists, and
leaves Dryden himself behind.

In poetic form, Pope was master.   He perfected an English
metre, the heroic couplet, which, for the purpose of didactic and
satirical poetry, has since remained the chosen vehicle of expression

in our language. To his command over this metre he had attained
rapidly, though not at once. Whether Pope could have attained
to equal mastery over other metres, seems an idle question ; for
none could have equally suited the peculiarity of his genius. The
heroic couplet and no other form of verse, was that adapted to
the genius of Pope. The clear conception of a thought was in
each case his first step ; next came the indefatigable labour of con-
densing and compressing it into the form in which its expression,
most finished in form, is at the same time most finished in memory.
Thus he, as it were, engraved ideas ; and his poems are full of
those couplets which can cleanly and without damage to themselves,
be taken out of their setting. In versification, Pope was a pupil of
Dryden, but he far surpassed his master. Dryden's verse is often
slovenly, and abounds in weak lines: in Pope there is never a sylla-
ble, hardly ever a line, too much.

As the poet of an artificial age, and an artificial life, we may be
proud of Pope, under such circumstances an artificial poet is the
truest poet attainable ; his very artificiality of matter and style is
his authentication as poet. This may sound like a paradox, yet it
is hardly more paradoxical than the statement that a gold coin is
equally gold, whether stamped with the effigy of Alexander the
Great, or of Louis Quinze ; of Cromwell or of Charles the Second ;
of Napoleon the First, or Napoleon the third. The only condition
then, on which we can have real poets in an artificial age, is that
they should also be in a measure artificial ; and the age in which
Pope lived, was to him his atmosphere, partly his nature. That
he should have been as natural as Theocritus, as terrible as
Æschylus, as austere as Lucretius, as supernatural as Dante, as
knightly as Chaucer, as noble as Milton, was simply impossible ;
nay, had it even been possible, such a result would in him have been
in some degree spurious ; for it could only have ensued from his
prepensely and pertinaciously going out of his age and of himself,
and that is not the process which makes a poet or ever did make
one. For this reason, let us then rest contentedly in the conviction
that Pope was a poet—the only sort of poet that we were likely to

get out of the reigns of Anne and George the First.

Pope may be determined the poet of the Understanding, not merely in the limited, though strictly true acceptation in which Johnson says that good sense was the fundamental principle of his intellect, but in something of the same spirit in which Kent distinguishes the Understanding, as the faculty for knowledge in man, from the Reason, as the primary, intuitional, conguitive power. The range of the author of the *Rape of the Lock*, the *Eloise to Abelard*, the *Dunciad*, and *Essay on Man*, and the Homeric translations was certainly not a narrow one, though it appears to the reader more restricted than it really is, seeing that the writer passed all his subject-matter through a somewhat uniform and in expansive mould of execution : but alike in these several excellent works, the Understanding predominates—everything is brought to the judging and comparing mind. We can all say, and say with the utmost truth, that a great creative and emotional nature has a larger share in what is highest in poesy: the riches and strength of Pope were not in that direction It was his faculty to discern, analyse, and express; and this he did with admirable force of mind and of speech ; and with amplest possession and skilfullest use of such means of poetry as were more specially germane to his time.

CHAPTER XV.

PRIOR.

PRIOR.—The works of Prior who was really the only poet of his time, consist of that rapid, picturesque narrative kind, which is mixed up with wit and naïvaté. .There is combined in his poetry, perhaps, more than any other poet, that airiness and extreme sweetness, which renders all poetry pleasing. He is a peculiarly interesting writer, from the situation which he occupies in the history of literature, coming between Dryden and Pope. Prior has the extreme of harmony.   In his *Solomon*, particularly, there are several remarkable passages.

"Tell me, ye studious, who pretend to see
Far into Nature's bosom, whence the bee
Was first inform'd her vent'rous flight to steer
Through trackless paths, and an abyss of air.
Whence she avoids the slimy marsh and knows
The fertile hills, where sweeter herbage grows,
And honey-making flow'rs their op'ning buds disclose.
How from the thicken'd mist, and setting sun
Finds she, the labour of her day is done?
Who taught her against winds and rains to strive,
To bring her burden to the certain hive,
And through the liquid fields again to pass,
Duteous, and heark'ning to the sounding brass.

*   *   *   *   *   *

This Alpha and Omega, first and last,
Who, like the potter, in a mould has cast
The world's great fame, commanding it to be
Such as the eyes of sense and reason see;
Yet if he wills, may change or spoil the whole;
May take yon beauteous, mystic, starry roll,
And burn it like a useless parchment scroll;
May from its basis in one moment pour
This melted earth———
Like liquid metal, and like burning ore;
Who, sole in pow'r, at the beginning said,
Let sea, and air, and earth, and heav'n be made,
And it was so———and when he shall ordain
In other sort, has but to speak again,
And they shall be no more: of this great theme,
This glorious, hallow'd, everlasting name,
This God, I would discourse.———"

In his earlier poem, *Henry and Emma*, these passages do not so much occur. This practice is curious when compared to Pope, who, as I have already said, pulled in exactly the opposite direction, and condensed his ideas and thoughts into a single couplet, so that they could almost be moved without injury to the general work. In the use of parenthesis, Prior is also remarkably natural and elegant.

In the later works of this poet we can see a disposition to imitate the French, of which style he ultimately became a great follower. The elegance and lightness of some of his smaller pieces no French writer can surpass. His imitation of Adrian's verses to his soul is not a little superior to that of Fontenelle :—

"Poor little, pretty, flutt'ring thing,
　Must we no longer live together?
And must thou prune thy trembling wing,
　To take thy flight, thou know'st not whither?
Thy hum'rous vein, thy pleasing folly,
　Lies all neglected, all forgot:
And pensive, wav'ring melancholy,
　Thou dread'st, and hop'st thou know'st not what."

He wrote one very elegant little stanza in French, in a company, where they sung in rotation, on the burden "Bannissons la melancholie," and when it came to his turn to sing after the performance of a young lady who sat next him.

"Mais cette voix, et ces beaux yeux.
Font Cupidon trop dangereux,
Et je sinistriste quand je crie
'Bannissons la melancholie.'"

One may see this resemblance also in the verses written on his own birth-day.

"I, my dear, was born to-day,
So all my jolly comrades say;
They bring me music, wreaths, and mirth,
And ask to celebrate my birth:
Little, alas! my comrades know,
That I was born to pain and woe;
To thy denial, to thy scorn;
Better I had ne'er been born,
I wish to die e'en whilst I say,
I, my dear, was born to-day.

I, my dear, was born to day,
Shall I salute the rising ray?
Well-spring of all my joy and woe,
Clotilda, thou alone dost know;
Shall the wreath surround my hair?
Or shall the music please my ear;

> Shall I my comrades' mirth receive,
> And bless my birth, and wish to live?
> Then let me see great Venus chase,
> Imperious anger from thy face;
> Then let me hear thee smiling say,
> Thou, my dear, was born to day."

Prior did not possess any of that elevation of mind or manliness of spirit which shows itself in Dryden. In his lighter pieces it is from Swift, rather than Pope that we have to distinguish him. I believe we may safely claim for him the originality, as between them, in point of date. As to merit, Swift is harder and more exact: Prior much more easy, natural, gentlemanlike, good-natured, and pleasant. He was familiar with the epigrams, as they are called, of the Greeks, at School: probably cultivated their taste, and translated a few of them very well. Some of his own Epigrams are very interesting :—

> "To John I owed great obligation;
> But John unhappily thought fit
> To publish it to all the nation:
> Sure John and I are more than quit."

> "Yes, every poet is a fool.
> By demonstration Ned can show it.
> Happy, could Ned's inverted rule
> Prove every fool to be a poet."

> "Thy nags, the leanest things alive,
> So very hard thou lov'st to drive,
> I heard thy anxious coachman say,
> It costs thee more in whips, than hay."

His *Henry and Emma* is beautifully and elegantly written, and contains constant bursts of true and poetical feeling. The plot, which is founded on an old English poem, *The Nut-brown Maid*, is beautifully laid down and exemplified.

I may conclude this poet, by quoting one or two passages from *Solomon* which is undoubtedly Prior's finest work :—

> "But O! ere yet original man was made,
> Ere the foundations of this earth were laid
> It was, opponent to our search, ordain'd,
> That joy, still sought, should never be attain'd.

This, sad experience cites me to reveal;
And what I dictate, is from what I feel.
. Born as I was, great David's fav'rite son,
Dear to my people, on the Hebrew throne
Sublime, my court with Ophir's treasures blest.
My name extended to the farthest east,
My body cloth'd with ev'ry outward grace,
Strength in my limbs, and beauty in my face,
My shining thought with fruitful notions crown'd,
Quick my invention, and my judgment sound,
Arise, (I commun'd with myself), arise;
Think, to be happy, to be great, be wise;
Content of spirit must from science flow,
For 'tis a godlike attribute, to know,
   I said, and sent my edict through the land:
Around my throne the letter'd rabbins stand,
Historic leaves resolve, long volumes spread,
The whole discoursing, as the younger read:
Attent I heard, propos'd my doubts, and said:
   The vegetable world, each plant and tree,
Its seed, its name, its nature, its degree,
I am allow'd, as fame reports, to know;
From the fair cedar, on the craggy brow
Of Lebanon nodding supremely tall:
Yet just, and conscious to myself, I find
A thousand doubts oppose the searching mind.
   I know not why the beech delights the glade
With boughs extended, and a rounder shade,
Whilst tow'ring firs in conic forms arise,
And with a pointed spear divide the skies:
Nor why, again, the changing oak should shed
The yearly honour of his stately head;   ·
While the distinguish'd yew is ever seen,
Unchang'd his branch, and permanent his green.
Wanting the sun, why does the caltha fade?
Why does the crypress flourish in the shade?
The fig and date, why love they to remain
In middle station, and an even plain,
While in the lower marsh the gourd is found,
And while the hill with olive-shade is crown'd?
Why does one climate and one soil, endue
The blushing poppy with a crimson hue.
Yet leave the lily pale, and tinge the violet blue?
Why does the fond carnation love to shoot
A various colour from one parent root,
While the fantastic tulip strives to break
In twofold beauty, and a parted streak?
The turning jasmine, and the blushing rose,
With lavish grace their morning scents disclose;
The smelling tub-rose and jonquil declare

The stronger impulse of an ev'ning air.
Whence has the tree (resolve me) or the flow'r
A various instinct, or a diff'rent pow'r?
Why should one earth, one clime, one stream, one breath
Raise this to strength, and sicken that to death?
    Whence does it happen, that the plant, which well
We name the *sensitive*, should move and feel?
Whence know her leaves to answer her command,
And with quick horror fly the neighb'ring hand?
    Along the sunny bank, or wat'ry mead,
Ten thousand stalks their various blossoms spread:
Peaceful and lowly in their native soil,
They neither know to spin, nor care to toil;
Yet with confess'd magnificence deride
Our vile attire, and impotence of pride.
The cowslip smiles, in brighter yellow dress'd
Than that which veils the nubile virgin's breast.
A fairer red stands blushing in the rose,
Than that which on the bridegroom's vestment flows.
Take but the humblest lily of the field,
And, if our pride will to our reason yield,
It must, by sure comparison, be shown
That on the regal seat great David's son,
Array'd, in all his robes, and types of pow'r,
Shines with less glory than that simple flow'r.
    Of fishes next, my friends, I would inquire,
How the mute race engender, or respire;
From the small fry that glide on Jordan's stream
Unmark'd, a multitude without a name,
To that Leviathan, who o'er the seas
Immense rolls onward his impetuous ways
And mocks the wind, and in the tempest plays.
How they in warlike bands march greatly forth
From freezing waters, and the colder north,
To southern climes directing their career,
Their station changing with th' inverted year.
How all with careful knowledge are endu'd,
To choose their proper bed, and wave, and food,
To guard their spawn, and educate their brood.
    Of birds, how each according to her kind
Proper materials for her nest can find;
And build a frame, which deepest thought in man
Would, or amend, or imitate in vain.
How in small flights they know to try their young,
And teach the callow child her parent's song;
Why these frequent the plain, and those the wood,
Why ev'ry land has her specific brood,
Where the tall crane, or winding swallow goes,
Fearful of gath'ring winds, and falling snows:
If into rocks or hollow trees they creep,

In temporary death confin'd to sleep ;
Or, conscious of the coming evil, fly
To milder regions, and a southern sky.
    Of beasts and creeping insects shall we trace
The wond'rous nature, and the various race ;
Or wild or tame, or friend to man or foe,
Of us what they, or what of them we know?"

CHAPTER XVI.

SWIFT.

SWIFT.—Of true poetical feeling, Swift possessed not a grain,
He not only had it not, but except in his youth, when he wrote
Pindaric odes, he professedly despised it, avoided every appearance
of it, and sometimes directly attacked it by parodies &c. We must
think of the verses of Butler to judge by him ; not of such poets as
Dryden, much less Milton or Shakespeare. It is inconceivable
how large a proportion of Swift's poems are uninteresting. The
indelicacy of many is well known. It is a strange combination, of
great purity and correctness in one sense, and of studied violation
of them in the other. But, laying aside this fault, there are many
that are still more insipid. The matter not being important, the
style tires from its very correctness of uniformity ; the merit, except
in comparatively few specimens, is chiefly negative : and the same
might be said of the ideas. They have no absurdity nor affectation;
it is impossible to find fault. If they were the casual thoughts
and language of a more careless writer, some of them might attract;
and the whole be more worth dipping into, at least. Many are
occasional ; written on a self-prescribed subject ; not produced by
the spontaneous occurrence of ideas. Very many were written
originally merely for his friends. The Poem *Written in a Lady's
Ivory Table-Book* may be read, as a fair specimen of Swift's strong
and peculiar vein of humour,

> 'Madam I die without your grace.'—
> 'Item, for half a yard of lace.'
> Who that had wit would place it here,
> For every peeping fop to jeer ?
> To think that your brains' issue is
> Exposed to th' excrement of his,
> In power of spittle and a clout,
> Whene'er he please to blot it out ;
> And then, to heighten the disgrace,
> Clap his own nonsense in the place.
> Whoe'er expects to hold his part
> In such a book, and such a heart,
> If he be wealthy, and a fool,
> Is in all points the fittest tool ;
> Of whom it may be justly said,
> He's a gold pencil tipp'd with lead."

Imagination, inventive fancy in the way of wit, and of circum-
stances to compare or heighten an entertaining idea, Swift possessed
in a great degree ; but the fancy which produces rich, pleasing, or
entertaining imagery, he hardly ever shows ; not in substance nor
in the ornaments of language: metaphors he almost wholly avoids.
In his rhymes, he is peculiarly fond of what Butler led the way
in ; odd unexpected combinations, chiefly in double endings.   In
one of his poems, the *Legion Club* is a very ingenious attempt to
give the names of the Parliament-men whom he satirises, without
printing them, by means of the rhymes to which they answer.   The
Lilliputian Ode to the Man-mountain is amusing :—

> "In amaze
> Lost I gaze !
> Can our eyes
> Reach thy size !

      May my lays
      Swell with praise,
      Worthy thee!
      Worthy me!
      Muse inspire
      All thy fire!
      Bards of old
      Of him told,
      When they said,
      Atlas' head
      Propp'd the skies;
See! and believe your eyes!
      See him stride
      Valleys wide,
      Over woods,
      Over floods!
      When he treads,
      Mountains' heads
      Groan and shake:
      Armies quake;
      Lest his spurn
      Overturn
      Man and steed:
      Troops take heed!
      Left and right,
      Speed your flight!
      Lest a host
Beneath his foot be lost!
      Turn'd aside
      From his hide,
      Safe from wound
      Darts rebound.
      From his nose
      Clouds he blow:
      When he speaks,
      Thunder breaks!
      When he eats
      Famine threats!
      When he drinks
      . Neptune shrinks!
      Nigh thy ear,
      In mid-air,
      On thy hand
      Let me stand:
      So shall I,
Lofty poet! touch the sky."

His easy finished style was acquired by considerable **pains** probably, and not very early: but when acquired he seems to have taken delight in the exercise of the faculty, and to have written

Grand Question debated," whether Hamilton's Bawn should **be** turned into a Barrack or Malt-house.

"Thus spoke to my lady the knight full of care,
'Let me have your advice in a weighty affair.
This Hamilton's bawn, while it sticks in my hand,
I lose by the house what I get by the land ;
But how to dispose of it to the best bidder,
For a barrack, or malt-house, we now must consider.
'First, let me suppose I make it a malt-house,
Here I have computed the profit will fall t' us ;
There's nine hundred pounds for labour and grain,
I increase it to twelve, so three hundred remain ;
A handsome edition for wine and good cheer,
Three dishes a-day, and three hogsheads a-year ;
With a dozen large vessels my vault shall be stor'd
No little scrub joint shall come on my board ;
And you and the Dean no more shall combine
To stint me at night to one bottle of wine ;
Nor shall I, for this humour, permit you to purloin
A stone and a quarter of beef from my sirloin.
If I make it a barrack, the crown is my tenant ;
My dear, I have ponder'd again and again on't :
In poundage and drawbacks I lose half my rent,
Whatever they give me, I must be content,
Or join with the court in every debate ;

And rather than that, I would lose my estate."
  Thus ended the Knight; thus began his meek wife
'It must, and it shall be a barrack, my life.
I'm grown a mere *mopus*; no company comes
But a rabble of tenants, and rusty dull rums.
With parsons what lady can keep herself clean?
I'm all over daub'd when I sit by the Dean.
But if you will give us a Barrack, my dear.
The Captain, I'm sure, will always come here;
I then shall not value his Deanship a straw,
For the Captain, I warrant, will keep him in awe;
Or, should he pretend to be brisk and alert,
Will tell him that chaplains should not be so pert;
That men of his coat should be minding their pray'rs
And not among ladies to give themselves airs."
  Thus argued my Lady, but argued in vain;
The Knight his opinion resolv'd to maintain.
  But Hannah, who listen'd to all that was pass'd,
And could not endure so vulgar a taste,
As soon as her Ladyship call'd to be dress'd,
Cried, 'Madam, why surely my master's possess'd.
Sir Arthur the Malster! how fine it will sound!
I'd rather the bawn were sunk underground.
But, Madam, I guess'd there would never come good,
When I saw him so often with Darby and Wood.
And now my dream's out; for I was a-dream'd.
That I saw a huge rat—O dear, how I scream'd!
And after, methought, I had lost my new shoes;
And Molly, she said, I should hear some ill-news.'
  'Dear madam, had not you but the spirit to tease,
You might have a barrack whenever you please:
And, madam, I always believ'd you so stout,
That for twenty denials you would not give out.
If I had a husband like him, I *purtest*,
Till he gave me my will, I would give him no rest;
And, rather than come in the same pair of sheets
With such a cross man, I would lie in the streets:
But, madam, I beg you, contrive and invent,
And worry him out till he gives his consent.
Dear madam, whene'er of a barrack I think,
An I were to be hang'd I cant sleep a wink:
For if a new crotchet comes into my brain,
I can't get it out, though I ne'er so fain.
I fancy already, a barrack contriv'd
At Hamilton's bawn, and the troop is arriv'd;
Of this to be sure, Sir Arthur has warning,
And waits on the Captain betimes the next morning.
  'Now see, when they meet, how their honours behave
'Noble Captain, your servant'—'Sir Arthur, your slave;'
You honour me much'—'The honour is mine.'—

At last comes the troop, by word of command,
Drawn up in our court, when the Captain cries, STAND!
Your Ladyship lifts up the sash to be seen,
For sure I had dizen'd you out like a queen.
The Captain, to show he is proud of the favour,
Looks up to your window, and cocks up his beaver:
(His beaver is cock'd; pray, madam, mark that;
For a Captain of horse never takes off his hat;
Because he has never a hand that is idle,
For the right holds the sword, and the left holds the bridle
Then flourishes thrice his sword in the air,
As a complement due to a lady so fair;
(How I tremble to think of the blood it has spilt!)
Then he low'rs down the point, and kisses the hilt,
Your Ladyship smiles, and thus you begin:
    'Pray, Captain, be pleased to alight and walk in.'
The Captain salutes you with _congé_ profound.
And your Ladyship curts'ys half way to the ground.
'Kit, run to your master and bid him come to us;
I'm sure he'll be proud of the honour you do us;
And, Captain, you'll do us the favour to stay,
And take a short dinner here with us to day:
Yon're heartily welcome; but as for good cheer,
You come in the very worst time of the year,
If I had expected so worthy a guest——'

'Lord, madam ! your Ladyship sure is in jest ;
You banter me, madam : the kingdom must grant'—
'You officers, Captain, are so complaisant.'
　　'Hist, hussey, I think I hear somebody coming.'—
'No, madam : 'tis only Sir Arthur a-humming.
To shorten my tale, (for I hate a long story,)
The Captain at dinner appears in his glory ;
The Dean and the Doctor have humbled their pride,
For the Captain's entreated to sit by your side ;
And, because he's their betters, you carve for him first ;
The parsons for envy are ready to burst.
The servants, amazed, are scarce ever able
To keep off their eyes, as they wait at the table ;
And Molly and I have thrust in our nose,
To peep at the Captain in all his fine *clo'es*.
Dear madam, be sure he's a fine spoken man,
Do but hear on the clergy how glib his tongue ran ;
And 'Madam,' says he, 'if such dinners you give,
You'll ne'er want for parsons as long as you live.
I ne'er knew a parson without a good nose ;
But the devil's as welcome wherever he goes :
————me ! they bid us reform and repent,
But,——! by their looks, they never keep Lent :
Mister Curate, for all your grave looks, I'm afraid
You cast a sheep's eye on her Ladyship's maid :
I wish she would lend you her pretty white hand,
In mending your cassock, and smoothing your band :
(For the Dean was so shabby, and look'd like a ninny,
That the Captain suppos'd he was curate to Jinny.)
'Whenev'r you see a cassock and gown,
A hundred to one but it covers a clown.
Observe how a parson comes into a room ;
————me, he hobbles as bad as my groom ;
A *scholard*, when just from his college broke loose,
Can hardly tell how to cry *bo* to a goose ;
Your *Noveds*, and *Bluturks*, and *Omurs*. and stuff,
By————, they don't signify this pinch of snuff.
To give a young gentleman right education,
The army's the only good school in the nation ;
My schoolmaster call'd me a dunce and a fool,
But at cuffs I was always the cock of the school ;
I never could take to my book for the blood o'me,
And the puppy confess'd he expected no good o'me.
He caught me one morning coquetting his wife,
But he maul'd me, I ne'er was so maul'd in my life.
So I took to the road, and, what's very odd,
The first man I robb'd was a parson, by————
Now, madam, you'll think it a strange thing to say,
But the sight of a book makes me sick to this day !
　　'Never since I was born did I hear so much wit,
And, madam, I laugh'd till I thought I should split.

But be durst not so much as once open his lips,
And the Doctor was plaguily down in the hips,'
   Thus merciless Hannah ran on in her talk,
Till she heard the Dean call. 'Will my Ladyship walk?'
Her Ladyship answers, 'I'm just coming down:'
Then, turning to Hannah, and forcing a frown,
Although it was plain in her heart she was glad,
Cried, Hussey, why surely the wench is gone mad !
How could these chimeras get into your brains!—
Come hither, and take this old gown for your pains.
But the Dean, if this secret should come to his ears,
Will never have done with his gibes and his jeers :
For your life, not a word of the matter, I charge ye ;
Give me but a barrack, a fig for the clergy."

CHAPTER XVII.

BUTLER.

BUTLER.—*Poeta nascitur non fit* is a sentence of as great truth
; antiquity ; it being most certain that all the acquired learning
1aginable is insufficient to complete a poet, without a natural
:nius and propensity to so noble and sublime an art. And this
1rase refers with remarkable truth to Butler, as any reader of his
ɔrks will immediately allow. As I have before said, without this
nate faculty, the most learned men could not be true poets, and
any have often rendered themselves obnoxious to that satirical

disdained the assistance of other arts and sciences, we are then blessed with those lasting monuments of wit and learning, which may justly claim a kind of eternity upon earth : and this author may justly claim a place among these few rare genii. Butler's celebrated poem of *Hudibras*, as a composition of natural unassumed wit and humour, may rank first in the catalogue of such works by our English poets.

Although Butler had not the opportunity of higher learning, or the happiness of an academical education ; it may be perceived throughout his whole poem, that he had read much, and was very well accomplished in the most useful parts of human learning. A great French writer speaking of the necessary qualities belonging to a poet, tells us, " he must have a genius extraordinary ; great natural gifts ; a wit just, fruitful, piercing, solid and universal ; an understanding clear and distinct ; an immagination neat and pleasant ; an elevation of soul, that depends not only on art or study, but is purely the gift of heaven ; which must be sustained by a lively sense and vivacity ; judgment to consider wisely of things and vivacity for the beautiful expression of them." This character is justly due to Butler, of which any reader of his famous poem will have seen. The reputation of this incomparable composition is so thoroughly established in the world, that it would be superfluous, if not impertinent, to endeavour any panegyric upon it. There is a passage in the Introduction to one of the editions of *Hudibras*, in which we are told "that King Charles II, whom the judicious part of mankind will readily acknowledge to be a sovereign judge of wit, was so great an admirer of it, that he would often pleasantly quote it in his conversation." Butler's description of Sir Hudibras in the opening of the poem not only overflows with humour and shows a ready knowledge of general well-known circumstances, but also exhibits considerable acquaintance with the less known parts of classical literature.

> "When civil dudgeon first grew high,
> And men fell out they knew not why ;
> When hard words, jealousies and fears,

Set folks together by the ears,
And made them fight, like mad or drunk,
For dame Religion as for punk
Whose honesty they all durst swear for,
Tho' not a man of them knew wherefore;
When gospel-trumpeter surrounded
With long-ear'd rout, to battle sounded,
And pulpit, drum ecclesiastic,
Was beat with fist instead of a stick;
Then did Sir Knight abandon dwelling,
And out he rode a colonelling.
A wight he was whose very sight would
Entitle him Mirror of Knighthood;
That never bow'd his stubborn knee
To anything but chivalry;
Nor put up blow, but that which laid
Right worshipful on shoulder-blade:
Chief of domestic knights and errant,
Either for chartel or for warrant;
Great on the bench, great in the saddle,
That could as well bind o'er as swaddle:
Mighty he was at both of these,
And styl'd of war as well as peace.
(So some rats, of amphibious nature,
Are either for the land or water.)
But here our author makes a doubt
Whether he were more wise or stout.
Some hold the one, and some the other;
But howso'er they make a pother,
The diff'rence was so small, his brain
Outweigh'd his rage but half a grain
Which made some take him for a tool
That knaves do work with, call'd a fool.
For't has been said by many, that
As Montaigne, playing with his cat,
Complains she thought him but an ass,
Much more she would Sir Hudibras
(For that's the name our valiant Knight
To all his challenges did write,)
But they're mistaken very much;
'Tis plain enough he was no such.
We grant, altho' he had much wit,
H' was very shy of using it;
As being loth to wear it out,
And therefore bore it not about;
Unless on holy-days, or so,
As men their best apparel do.
Beside, 'tis known he could speak Greek
As naturally as pigs do squeak:
That Latin was no more difficile,

Than to a blackbird 'tis to whistle
Being rich in both, he never scanted
His bounty unto such as wanted :
But much of either would afford
To many that had not one word,
For Hebrew roots, altho' they're found
To flourish most in barren ground,
He had such plenty as suffic'd
To make some think him circumcis'd.
   He was in Logic a great critick,
Profoundly skill'd in analytick,
Or could distinguish and divide
A hair 'twixt south and south-west side ;
On either which he could dispute,
Confute, change hands, and still confute.
He'd undertake to prove, by force
Of argument, a man's no horse,
He'd prove a buzzard is no fowl,
And that a lord may be an owl.
A calf an alderman, a goose a justice,
And rooks committee-men and trustees.
He'd run in debt by disputation
And pay with ratiocination
All this by syllogism, true
In mood and figure, he would do.
For Rhetoric, he could not ope
His mouth, but out there flew a trope :
And when he happen'd to break off
I' th' middle of his speech, or cough,
H' had hard words ready to shew why,
And tell what rules he did it by :
Else, when with greatest art he spoke,
You'd think he talk'd like other folk :
For all a rhetorician's rules
Teach nothing but to name his tools.
But, when he pleas'd to show't, his speech,
In loftiness of sound, was rich ;
A Babylonish dialeck,
Which learned pedants much affect.
It was a party-colour'd dress
Of patch'd and pye-ball'd languages :
'Twas English cut on Greek or Latin,
Like fustian heretofore on satin.
It had an odd promiscuous tone,
As if h' talk'd three parts in one ;
Which made some think, when he did gabble.
Th' had heard three labourers of Babel
Or Cerberus himself pronounce
A leash of languages at once.
This he as volubly would vent

As if his stock would ne'er be spent ;
And truly to support that charge,
He had supplies as vast and large :
For he could coin or counterfeit
New words, with little or no wit ;
Words, so debas'd and hard. no stone
Was hard enough to touch them on :
And when with hasty noise he spoke 'em,
The ignorant for current took 'em ;
That had the orator, who once
Did fill his mouth with pebble stones*
When he harangu'd, but known his phrase,
He would have us'd no other ways,
In Mathematics he was greater
Than Tycho Brahe or Erra Pater †
For he, by geometric scale,
Could take the size of pots of ale ;
Resolve, by signs and tangents, straight,
If bread or butter wanted weight ;
And wisely tell what hour o' th' day
The clock does strike by algebra.
Beside, he was a shrewd philosopher,
And had read ev'ry text and gloss over :
Whate'er the crabbed'st author hath,
He understood b' implicit faith :
Whatever sceptic could inquire for,
For ev'ry why he had a wherefore ;
Knew more than forty of them do,
As far as words and terms could go :
All which he understood by rote,
And, as occasion serv'd, would quote:
No matter whether right or wrong,
They might be either said or sung.
His notions fitted things so well,
That which was which he could not tell ;
But oftentimes mistook the one
For th' other, as great clerks have done.
He could reduce all things to acts,
And knew their natures by abstracts ;
Where entity and quiddita,
The ghosts of defunct bodies fly ;
Where truth in person does appear,
Like words congeal'd in northern air.
He knew what's what, and that's as high
As metaphysic wit can fly.

---

* Demosthenes, who is said to have had a defect in his pronunciation, which he cured by using to speak with little stones in his mouth.

† Tycho Brahe was an eminent Danish Mathematician.

In school-divinity as able
As he that hight Irrafragable ;*
A second Thomas,† or, at once
To name them all, another Dunce :‡
Profound in all the nominal
And real ways beyond them all ;
For he a rope of sand could twist
As tough as learned Sorbonist ;
And weave fine cobwebs, fit for skull
That's empty when the moon is full ;
Such as take lodgings in a head
That's to be let unfurnished.
He could raise scruples dark and nice,
And half solve 'em in a trice ;
As if Divinity had catch'd
The itch on purpose to be scratch'd ;
Or, like a mountebank, did wound,
And stab herself with doubts profound,
Only to show with how small pain
The sores of faith are cur'd again ;
Altho' by woful proof we find
They always leave a scar behind.
He knew the seat of Paradise,
Could tell in what degree it lies ;
And, as he was dispos'd, could prove it
Below the moon, or else above it :
What Adam dreamt of, when his bride
Came from her closet in his side :
Whether the Devil tempted her
By a High-Dutch interpreter: ||
If either of them had a navel ¶
Who first made music malleable :
Whether the serpent, at the fall,

---

* Some specific epithets were added to the title of some famous doctors, as Angelicus, Irrefragabilis, Subtilis &c, which is no doubt meant by this.

† Thomas Aquinas, a Dominican friar, was born in 1224, and studied at Cologne and Paris. He new-modelled the school divinity, and was therefore called the Angelic Doctor, and Eagle of Divines. The most illustrious persons of his time were ambitious of his friendship, and put a high value on his merits so that they offered him bishoprics, which he refused with as much ardour as others seek after them.

‡ Johannes Dunscotas was a very learned man, who lived about the end of the thirteenth and beginning of the fourteenth century. He is said to have been extraordinary learned in physics, metaphysics, mathematics and astronomy ; that his fame was so great when at Oxford, that 30,000 scholars came thither to hear his lectures : that when at Paris his arguments and authority carried it for the immaculate conception of the Blessed Virgin: so that they appointed a festival on that account, and would admit no scholars to degrees, but such as were of this mind.

|| Goropius Becanus endeavoured to prove that High-Dutch was the language that Adam and Eve spoke in Paradise.

¶ Adam and Eve, being made, and not conceived and formed in he womb, had no navels, as some learned men have supposed, because they had no need of them.

Had cloven feet, or none at all,
All this, without a gloss or comment,
He could unriddle in a moment,
In proper terms, such as men smatter,
When they throw out, and miss the matter.
For his religion, it was fit
To match his learning and his wit:
'Twas Presbyterian true blue ;
For he was of that stubborn crew
Of errant saints whom all men grant
To be the true church militant ;
Such as do build their faith upon
The holy text of pike and gun ;
Decide all controversies by
Infallible artillery ;
And prove their doctrine orthodox
By apostolic blows and knocks.
Call fire, and sword, and desolation,
A godly thorough reformation,
Which always must be carried on,
And still be doing, never done :
As if religion were intended
For nothing else but to be mended.

   *   *   *   *

His back, or rather burthen, shew'd
As if it stoop'd with its own load ;
For as Æneas bore his sire
Upon his shoulders thro' the fire.
Our knight did bear no less a pack
Of his own buttocks on his back ;
Which now had almost got the upper
Hand of his head, for want of crupper.
To poise this equally, he bore
A paunch of the same bulk before ;
Which still he had a special care
To keep well cramm'd with thrifty fare ;
As white-pot, butter-milk, and curds,
Such as a country-house affords ;
With other vittle, which anon
We farther shall dilate upon,
When of his hose we come to treat.
The cupboard where he kept his meat."

The same self-attained knowledge, with deep insight to an-
cient fables and events, may be seen in the description of the
Squire, which abounds—as does the whole of the poem—with the
keenest touches of wit and satire.

      ''A squire he had, whose name was Ralph,
      That in th' adventure went his half:

Tho' writers for more stately tune,
Do call him Ralpho ; 'tis all one ,
And when we can with metre safe,
We'll call him so; if not, plain Ralph
(For rhyme the rudder is of verses
With which like ships they steer their courses.
An equal stock of wit and valour
He had laid in ; by birth a tailor.
The mighty Tyrian queen, that gain'd
With subtle shreds a tract of land,
Did leave it with a castle fair
To his great ancestor, her heir.
From him descended cross-legg'd knights,
Fam'd for their faith, and warlike fights
Against the bloody cannibal,
Whom they destroy'd both great and small.
This sturdy Squire, he had, as well
As the bold Trojan knight, seen Hell ;
Not with a counterfeited pass
Of golden bough, but true gold-lace.
His knowledge was not far behind
The Knight's, but of another kind,
And he another way came by't :
Some call it Gifts, and some New-Light ;
A liberal art, that costs no pains
Of study, industry, or brains.
His wit was sent him for a token.
But in the carriage crack'd and broken,
Like commendation nine-pence crook'd,
With—To and from my love—It look'd.
He ne'er considered it as loth
To look a gift-horse in the mouth ;
And very wisely would lay forth
No more upon it than 'twas worth,
But as he got it freely, so
He spent it frank and freely too.
For saints themselves will sometimes be,
Of gifts that cost them nothing, free.
By means of this, with hem and cough,
Prolongers to enlighten'd stuff,
He could deep mysteries unriddle
As easily as thread a needle.

*   *   *   *

Thus Ralph became infallible
As three or four-legg'd oracle,
The ancient cup, or modern chair ;
Spoke the truth point-blank, tho' unaware.
For mystic learning, wondrous able
In magic Talisman and Cabal,

Whose primitive tradition reaches
As far as Adam's first green breeches:
Deep sighted in intelligences,
Ideas, atoms, influences;
And much of terra incognita,
Th' intelligible world could say:
A deep occult Philosopher,
As learned as the wild Irish are,
Or Sir Agrippa; for profound.
And solid lying much renown'd.
He Anthroposophus * and Floud,
And Jacob Behmen † understood:
Knew many an amulet and charm,
That would do neither good nor harm:
In Rosy-crucian lore as earned.
As he that Vere adeptus learned.
He understood the speech of birds
As well as they themselves do words;
Could tell what subtlest parrots mean,
That speak and think contrary clean:
What member 'tis of whom they talk,
When they cry Rope, and Walk, knave, walk.
He'd extract numbers out of matter,
And keep them in a glass, like water;
Of sov'reign power to make men wise;
For dropp'd in blear thick-sighted eyes,
They'd make them see in darkest night,
Like owls, tho' purblind in the light."

The *Hudibras* appears to have been written in portions, and
under somewhat peculiar circumstances; nor was it ever finished.
The first three cantos were published in 1663, and introduced to the
attention of the Court by the Earl of Dorset. In the following year,
the second part made its appearance; and we learn that such
was the general popularity of this poem and the particular favour
with which it was received by the king and courtiers, that everyone
expected some special reward would be bestowed on the ingenious
author: but, except three hundred guineas which the king is said
to have sent to him (though there is no authority whatever for this)
no trace is found of any reward or promotion whatever. Dis-

This is only a compound Greek word, which signifies a man that is wise in the knowledge
of men. It was used in Butler's time by some anonymous author, to conceal his real
name.
Two Authors of Butler's time.

couraging as this treatment was, he published the third part in
1678 which still leaves the story imperfect.

Butler is said to have made no figure in conversation,—propor-
tionate to the wit displayed in his immortal poem, and King Charles
who had a curiosity to see him, could never be brought to believe
that he wrote Hudibras. He has usually been ranked amongst the
unfortunate poets who have been neglected by their age; yet although
no proof is to be found of royal munificence having been extended
to him, there is no reason to think that he was poor in the most
unfavourable sense.

Although the persons and events introduced in *Hudibras,* are now
forgotten, or known only to historic students ; the exquisite humour
of this piece is still as keenly relished as when first presented to
the public, and much of it has long been introduced into conver-
sation as axioms of wit and sense. A writer has said, "that
concerning Hudibras, there is but one sentiment ; it is universally
allowed to be the first and last poem of its kind ; the learning, wit,
and humour, certainly stand unrivalled."

The humourous manner in which love is variously described,
deserves quoting as examples of this excellent work.

> "Such thoughts as these the Knight did keep,
> More than his bangs or fleas, from sleep.
> And as an owl, that in a barn
> Sees a mouse creeping in the corn,
> Sits still, and shuts his round blue eyes,
> As if he slept, until he spies
> The little beast within his reach,
> Then starts, and seizes on the wretch ;
> So from his couch the Knight did start
> To seize upon the widow's heart;
> Crying with hasty tone, and hoarse,
> Ralpho, despatch; to horse, to horse."

>   *   *   *   *
> ' Love is a burglarer, a felon
> That at the windore eye does steal in,
> To rob the heart, and with his prey
> Steals out again a closer way,
> Which whoever can discover,
> He's sure (as he deserves) to suffer.
> Love is a fire, that burns and sparkles
> In men as nat'rally as in charcoals,

*   *   *

For as the Pythagorean soul
Runs through all beast, and fish, and fowl,
And has a smack of ev'ry one,
So love does, and has ever done ;
And therefore though 'tis ne'er so fond,
Takes strangely to the vagabond.
'Tis but an ague that's reverst,
Whose hot fit takes the patient first
That after burns with cold as much
As ir'n in Greenland does the touch ;
Melts in the furnace of desire
Like glass, that's but the ice of fire ;
And when his heat of fancy's over,
Becomes as hard and frail a lover :
For when he's with love-powder laden,
And prim'd and cock'd by Miss or Madam,
The smallest sparkle of an eye
Gives fires to his artillery ;
And off the loud oaths go ; but, while
They're in the very act, recoil.
Hence 'tis so few dare take their chance
Without a sep'rate maintenance ;
And widow's, who have try'd one lover,
Trust none again, till th' have made over ;
Or if they do, before they marry,
The foxes weigh the geese they carry ;
And, e'er they venture o'er a stream,
Know how to size themselves and them ;
Whence wittiest ladies always choose
To undertake the heaviest goose :
For now the world is grown so wary.
That few of either sex dare marry,
But rather trust on tick t'amours,
The cross and pile for better or worse ;
A mode that is held honourable,
As well as French, and fashionable ;
For when it falls out for the best,
Where both are incommoded least

In soul and body two unite
To make up one hermaphrodite,
Still amorous, and fond, and billing,
Like Philip and Mary on a shilling.

      *   *   *

For love should, like a deodand,
Still fall to th' owner of th' land,
And where there's substance for its ground,
Cannot but be more firm and sound
Than that which has the slightest basis
Of airy virtue, wit, and graces;
Which is of such thin subtlety,
It steals and creeps in at the eye,
And, as it can't endure its stay,
Steals out again as nice a way.
  But love, that its extraction owns
From solid gold and precious stones,
Must, like its shining parents, prove
As solid, and as glorious love.
Hence 'tis you have no way t' express
Our charms and graces but by these:
For what are lips, and eyes, and teeth,
Which beauty invades and conquers with,
But rubies, pearls, and diamonds,
With which a philter love commands?
This is the way all parents prove,
In managing their children's love,
That force 'em t' intermarry and wed,
As if th' were burying of the dead ;
Cast earth to earth, as in the grave,
To join in wedlock all they have,
And, when the settlement's in force,
Take all the rest for better or worse:
For money has a power above
The stars and fate to manage love,
Whose arrows, learned poets hold,
That never miss, are tipp'd with gold."

His humourous description of Evening, and the passage **upon**
Hypocrisy are most interesting.

    "The sun grew low, and left the skies,
    Put down (some write) by ladies' eyes.
    The moon puli'd off her veil of light,
    That hides her face by day from sight
    (Mysterious veil, of brightness made,
    That's both her lustre and her shade),
    And in the lantern of the night
    With shining horns hung out her light;
    For darkness is the proper sphere,

Where all false glories use t' appear,
The twinkling stars began to muster,
And glitter with their borrow'd lustre,
While sleep the weary'd world reliev'd,
By counterfeiting death reviv'd.
His whipping penance till the morn.
Our vot ry thought it best t' adjourn,
And not to carry on a work
Of such importance in the dark,
With erring haste, but rather stay
And do't in th' open face of day;
And in the meantime go in quest
Of next retreat to take his rest."

"Why didst thou choose that cursed sin,
Hypocrisy, to set up in?
Because it is the thriving'st calling,
The only saints'-bell that rings all in;
In which all churches are concern'd,
And is the easiest to be learn'd:
For no degrees, unless they employ't,
Can ever gain much, or enjoy't:
A gift that is not only able
To domineer among the rabble,
But by the laws empower'd to rout,
And awe the greatest that stand out;
Which few hold forth against, for fear
Their hands should slip, and come too near:
For no sin else among the saints
Is taught so tenderly against."

CHAPTER XVIII.

YOUNG.

In his excellent poem the *Last Day*, one of his earliest works, he calls his Muse "*The Melancholy Maid*,"

"Whom dismal scenes delight,
Frequent at tombs, and in the realms of night."

In some of his works however, he indulges in occasional sallies of wit, of which his well-known epigram on Vollaire is a specimen:—

"Thou art so witty, profligate, and thin,
Thou seem'st a Milton with his Death and Sin."

But perhaps there was more of indignation than pleasantry in his wit, as his Satire was always pointed against indecency and religion. His Satire the *Love of Fame* is a great performance. The shafts of his wit are directed against the folly of being devoted to the fashion, and aiming to appear what we are not. It is written with smoothness of style, pointed sentences, solid sentiments, and the sharpness of resistless truth. His finest poem, the *Night Thoughts*, which is almost universally known, abounds in the most exalted flights and the utmost stretch of thought. This is the great excellency of Young's poetry. In this marvellous poem he has exhibited a very wide display of original poetry, variegated with deep reflexions, and stricking allusions, a wilderness of thought, in which the fertility of fancy scatters flowers of every hue and of every odour. What deep philosophy is contained in Young's work, and with what eloquence he has conveyed those profound speculations! They are written in such language as to be almost received by the meanest capacities. From them we are brought home to a keener knowledge of what we ourselves are ; from whence we came, and whether we must go. Like a good philosopher also, he has invincibly proved the immortality of man from the grandeur of his conceptions and the meanness and misery of his state; and thus his work forms a complete view of the power, situation, and end of man. He has taught us to meditate upon ourselves: self-reflection being the only way to valuable and true knowledge: and in doing this, has used an eloquence and force of language peculiar to himself. This poem is said to have been occasioned by a family distress—the loss of his wife and two children, who died within a short time of each other. The two latter are shown to us in the characters of Philander and Narcissa. The circumstance of his being obliged to bury *Narcissa* in a field by night, not being allowed interment in a churchyard, being a protestant, is beautifully and indelibly recorded in Night III. of this divine poem :—

"——————————O Philander!
What was thy fate? A double fate to me ;
Portent, and pain ! a menace and a blow !
Like the black raven hov'ring o'er my peace,
Not less a bud of omen than of prey.
It call'd Narcissa long before her hour ;
It call'd her tender soul, by break of bliss,
From the first blossom, from the birds of joy ;
Those few our noxious fate unblasted leaves
In this inclement clime of human life.

 Sweet harmonist ! and beautiful as sweet !
And young as beautiful ! and soft as young !
And gay as soft ! and innocent as gay !
And happy (if aught happy here) as good !
For fortune fond had built her nest on high.
Like birds quite exquisite of note and plume,
Transfix'd by fate (who loves a lofty mark).
How from the summit of the grove she fell,
And left it unharmonious ! All its charms
Extinguish'd in the wonders of her song !
Her song still vibrates in my ravish'd ear,
Still melting there, and with voluptuous pain
(O to forget her !) thrilling thro' my heart !

 Song, beauty, youth, love. virtue, joy ! this group
Of bright ideas, flow'rs of paradise,
As yet unforfeit ! in one blaze we bind,
Kneel, and present it to the skies ; us all
We guests of heav'n : and these were all her own ;
And she was mine ; and I was—was ! most blest—
Gay title of the deepest misery !

 *   *   *   *   *

 Turn, hopeless thought ! turn from her :—thought repell'd,
Resenting rallies, and wakes ev'ry woe.
Snatch'd ere thy prime ! and in thy bridal hour.
And when kind fortune, with thy lover, smil'd !
And when high-flavour'd thy fresh-op'ning joys !
And when blind man pronounc'd thy bliss complete,
And on a foreign shore ; where strangers wept !
Strangers to thee ; and, more surprising still,
Strangers to kindness, wept.   Their eyes let fall
Inhuman tears: strange tears ! that trickled down,
From marble hearts ! obdurate tenderness !

A tenderness that call'd them more severe,
In spite of nature's soft persuasion, steel'd;
While nature melted, superstition rav'd;
That mourn'd the dead; and this deny'd a grave.
    Their sighs incens'd; sighs foreign to the will;
Their will the tigers suck'd, outrag'd the storm.
For, Oh! the curst ungodliness of zeal!
While sinful flesh relented, spirit nurst,
In blind infallibility's embrace;
The fainted spirit petrify'd the breast;
Deny'd the charity of dust, to spread,
O'er dust! a charity their dogs enjoy.
What could I do? What succour? What resource?
With pious sacrilege, a grave I stole;
With impious piety, that grave I wrong'd;
Short in my duty; coward in my grief!
More like her murderer, than friend. I crept
With soft suspended step, and muffled deep.
In midnight darkness, whisper'd my last sigh.
I whisper'd what should echo thro' their realms;
Nor writ her name, whose tomb shou'd pierce the skies.
Presumptuous fear, how durst I dread her foes,
While nature's loudest dictates I obey'd:
Pardon necessity, blest shade! of grief
And indignation rival bursts I pour'd;
Half execration mingled with my pray'r;
Kindled at man, while I his God ador'd,
Sore grudg'd the savage land her sacred dust,
Stamp'd the curst soil; and with humanity
(Deny'd *Narcissa*) wish'd them all a grave."

There is scarcely a passage in this work, however sombre or gloomy, that does not paint, with the most lively fancy, the true feelings of the heart, the vanity of human things, with its fleeting honours and enjoyments, and certainly the strongest arguments in support of the immortality of the soul. The former are beautifully illustrated in the following passages

VANITY.

" O the dark days of vanity! while here
How tasteless! and how terrible, when gone!
Gone! they ne'er go, when past, they haunt us still,
The spirit wakes of ev'ry day deceas'd;
And smiles and angel, or a fury frown.
Nor death, nor life delight us. If time past;
And time possest, both pain us, what can please?
That which the Deity to please ordain'd,
Time us'd. The man who consecrates his hours

By vig'rous effort, and an honest aim,
At once he draws the sting of life and death,
He walks with nature ; and her paths are peace.

     *   *   *   *   *

    Ye well-array'd! Ye lilies of our land !
Ye lilies male ! who neither toil, nor spin,
(As sister lilies might) if not so wise
As Solomon, more sumptuous to the sight!
Ye delicate ! whom nothing can support,
Yourselves most insupportable ! for whom
The winter rose must blow, the sun put on
A brighter beam in Leo ; silky-soft
Favonius breathe still softer, or her chid ;
And other worlds send odours, sauce, and song,
And robes, and notions, fram'd in foreign looms !
O ye LORENZOS of our age! who deem
One moment unamus'd, a misery
Not made for feeble man ! who call aloud
For ev'ry bawble, drivell'd o'er by sense ;
For rattles, and conceits of ev'ry cast,
For change of follies, and relays of joy,
To drag your patient, through the tedious length
Of a short winter's day ;—say, sages! say,
Wits oracles ! say, dreamers of gay dreams !
How will you weather an eternal night,
Where such expedients fail ?"

FAME.

"Fame is the shade of immortality,
And in itself a shadow. Soon as caught,
Contemn'd, it shrinks to nothing in the grasp.
Consult th' ambitious, 'tis ambition's cure,
'And is this all ?' cry'd CÆSAR at his height
Disgusted. This third proof ambition brings
Of immortality. The first in fame,
Observe him near, your envy will abate :
Sham'd at the disproportion vast, between
The passion, and the purchase, he will sigh
At such success, and blush at his renown.
And why ? because far richer prize invites.
His heart ; far more illustrious glory calls ;
It calls in whispers, yet the deafest hear :"

AMBITION.

"————————Man must soar ;
An obstinate activity within,
An insuppressive spring, will toss him up.
In spite of fortune's load,   Not kings alone,
Each villager has his ambition too ;

No sultan prouder than his fetter'd slave:
Slaves build their little Babylons of straw,
Echo the proud Assyrian in their hearts,
And cry—'Behold the wonders of my might'!
And why? Because immortal as their Lord;
And souls immortal must for ever heave
At something great, the glitter or the gold;
The praise of mortals, or the praise of Heav'n."

LOVE OF PRAISE,

"As love of pleasure is ordain'd to guard
And feed our bodies, and extend our race.;
The love of praise is planted to protect
And propogate the glories of the mind,
What is it, but the love of praise, inspires,
Matures, refines, embellishes, exalts,
Earth's happiness? From that, the delicate,
The grand, the marvellous, of civil life.
Want and convenience, under-workers, lay,
The basis, on which love of glory builds.
Nor is thy life, O virtue! less in debt
To praise, thy secret stimulating friend:
Were men not proud, what merit should we miss!
Pride made the virtues of the Pagan world.
Praise is the salt that seasons right to man,
And whets his appetite for moral good.
Thirst of applause is virtue's second guard;
Reason her first but reason wants an aid;
Our private reason is a flatterer;
Thirst of applause calls public judgment in,
To poise our own, to keep an even scale,
And give endanger'd virtue fairer play."

AVARICE.

"To store up treasure, with incessant toil,
This is a man's province, this his highest praise.
To this great end keen instinct stings him on.
To guide that instinct, reason! is thy charge;
'Tis thine to tell us where true treasure lies:
But reason failing to discharge her trust,
Or to the deaf discharging it in vain,
A blunder follows: and blind industry,
Gall'd by the spur, but stranger to the course
(The course where stakes of more than gold are won)
The jaded spirits of the present hour,
O'erloading, with the cares of distant age, ·
Provides for an eternity below.
　"Thou shalt not covet," is a wise command:
But bounded to the wealth the sun surveys,
Look farther, the command stands quite revers'd

And av'rice is a virtue most divine,
Is faith a refuge for our happiness?
Most sure: and is it not for reason too?
Nothing this world unriddles, but the next.
Whence inextinguishable thirst of gain?
From inextinguishable life in man.
Man, if not meant, by worth, to reach the skies,
Had wanted wing to fly so far in guilt.
Sour grapes, I grant, ambition, avarice:
Yet still their root is immortality.
These its wild growths so bitter and so base,
(Pain and reproach!) religion can reclaim,
Refine, exalt, throw-down their pois'nous lee,
And make them sparkle in the bowl of bliss.''

PLEASURE.

"Since nature made us not more fond than proud
Of happiness (whence hypocrites in joy!
Makers of mirth! artificers of smiles!)
Why should the joy most poignant sense affords,
Burn us with blushes, and rebuke our pride?—
Those heav'n-born blushes tells us man descends,
Ev'n in the zenith of his earthly bliss:—
Should reason take her infidel repose,
This honest instinct speaks our lineage high;
This instinct calls on darkness to conceal
Our rapturous relation to the stalls.
Our glory covers us with noble shame,
And he that's unconfounded is unmann'd.
The man that blushes is not quite a brute.
Thus far with thee, Lorenzo! will I close:
Pleasure is good, and man for pleasure made;
But pleasure full of glory as of joy;
Pleasure, which neither blushes nor expires."

Although Young possessed an exuberance of fancy, his genius
was not always under the control of taste and judgment. Still
his works are full of passages that would do honour to any
poet. Such are some of the remarkable passages of this great poet's
works, exhibiting so minutely, and exemplifying so divinely the
mythical honours and follies of this life. There is something at
once majestic and awful in the language Young employs, exciting
in the mind feelings, which the common language of poetry could
never create. Many of this poet's fine thoughts however, are over-
cast with a gloom of melancholy, so as to have an effect rather to
be dreaded by minds of a morbid hue: such in character, though

And is there in creation, what, amidst
This tumult universal, wing'd dispatch,
And ardent energy, supinely yawns?—
Man sleeps; and man alone; and man, whose fate,
Fate irreversible, entire, extreme,
Endless, hair-hung, breeze-shaken, o'er the gulph
A moment trembles; drops! and man, for whom
All else is in alarm! man, the sole cause
Of this surrounding storm! and yet he sleeps,
As the storm rock'd to rest:—Throw years away?
Throw empires, and be blameless.   Moments seize;
Heavens on their wing.   A moment we may wish;
When worlds want wealth to buy.   Bid day stand still
Bid him drive back his car, and reimport,
The period past, regive the given hour.

*   *   *   *   *

Is death at distance? No: he has been on thee;
And given sure earnest of his final blow.
Those hours that lately smil'd, where are they now?
Pallid to thought, and ghastly! drown'd, all drown'd
In that great deep, which nothing disembogues!
And, dying, they bequeathed thee small renown.
The rest are on the wing: how fleet their flight!
Already has the fatal train took fire;
A moment, and the world's blown up to thee;
The sun is darkness and the stars are dust.

*   *   *   *   *

The Bell strikes One.   We take no note of time
But from its loss.   To give it then a tongue
Is wife in man.   As if an angel spoke,
I feel the solemn sound: If heard aright,
It is the knell of my departed hours:
Where are they?   With the years beyond the flood,
It is the signal that demands dispatch:
How much is to be done?   My hopes and fears
Start up alarm'd, and o'er life's narrow verge
Look down— On what? a fathomless abyss;
A dread eternity! how surely mine!
And can eternity belong to me,
Poor pensioner on the bounties of an hour?
    How poor, how rich, how abject, how august,
How complicate, how wonderful, is man!

who center'd in our make such strange extremes !
From diff'rent nature's marvellously mix'd,
Connexion exquisite of distant worlds !
Distinguish'd link in being's endless chain !
Midway from nothing to the Deity !
A beam ethereal, sully'd, absorpt !
Tho' sully'd, and dishonour'd, still divine !
Dim miniature of greatness absolute.
An heir of glory ! a frail child of dust !
Helpless immortal ! insect infinite !
A worm ! a god !—I tremble at myself,
And in myself am lost ! at home a stranger,
Thought wanders up and down, surpriz'd, aghast,
And wond'ring at her own : How reason reels !
O what a miracle to man is man,
Triumphantly distress'd ! what joy, what dread !
Alternately transported, and alarm'd !
What can preserve my life ! or what destroy ?
An angel's arm can't snatch me from the grave ;
Legions of angels can't confine me there.
    'Tis past conjecture : all things rise in proof :
While o'er my limbs sleep's soft dominion spread,
What tho' my soul phantastic measures trod
O'er fairy fields ; or mourn'd along the gloom,
Of pathless woods ; or down the craggy steep
Hurl'd headlong, swam with pain the mantle pool,
Or scal'd the cliff ; or danc'd on hollow winds,
With antic shapes, wild natives of the brain ?
Her ceaseless flight, tho' devious, speaks her nature
Of subtler essence than the trodden clod,
Active, aerial, tow'ring, unconfin'd,
Unfetter'd with her gross companion's fall.
Ev'n silent night proclaims my soul immortal :
Ev'n silent night proclaims eternal day.
Or human weal, heav'n husbands all events ;
Dull sleep instructs, nor sport vains dream in vain."

I have already quoted from this work, I cannot refrain
one more passage, which has always appeared to me
the choicest of the many magnificent strains in this

Religion ! thou the soul of happiness ;
And, groaning Calvary, of thee ! there shine
The noblest truth ; there strongest motives sting ;
There sacred violence assaults the soul ;

He sighs—the sigh earth's deep foundation shakes,
If in his love so terrible, what then
His wrath inflam'd ? his tenderness on fire ?
Like soft, smooth oil, outblazing other fires ?
Can pray'r, can praise avert it ?—Thou my all !
My theme ! my inspiration ! and my crown !
My strength in age ! my rise in low estate !
My soul's ambition, pleasure, wealth !—my world !
My light in darkness ! and my life in death !
My boast thro' time ! bliss through eternity !
Eternity, too short to speak thy praise !
Or fathom thy profound of love to man !
To man of men the meanest, ev'n to me !
My sacrifice ! my God !—what things are these !
   What then art Thou ? by what name shall I call thee?
Knew I the name devout archangels use,
Devout archangels should the name enjoy,
By me unrivall'd ; thousands more sublime,
None half so dear, as that, which, tho' unspoke,
Still glows at heart: O how omnipotence
Is lost in love ! thou great PHILANTHROPIST !
Father of angels ! but the friend of man.
Like Jacob, fondest of the younger born !
Thou, who didst save him, snatch the smoking brand
From out the flames, and quench it in thy blood !
How art thou pleas'd, by bounty to distress !
To make us groan beneath our gratitude,
Too big for birth ! to favour and confound ;
To challenge, and to distance, all return !
Of lavish love, stupendous heights to soar,
And leave praise panting in the distant vale !
Thy right too great defrauds thee of thy due :
And sacrilegious our sublimest song.

     *   *   *   *   *

——————Oh for warmer still !
Guilt chills my zeal, and age benumbs my pow'rs ;
Oh for an humbler heart, and prouder song !
Thou, my much-injur'd theme ! with that soft eye,
Which melted o'er doom'd Salem, deign to look
Compassion to the coldness of my breast ;
And pardon to the winter in my strain.
   Oh ye cold-hearted, frozen, formalists !
On such a theme, 'tis impious to be calm ;
Passion is reason, transport temper, here.
Shall heav'n, which gave us ardour, and has shewn
Her own for man so strongly, not disdain
What smooth emollients in theology,
Recumbent virtue's downy doctors preach,
That prose of piety, a lukewarm praise ?

Rise odours sweet from incense uninflam'd ?
Devotion, when lukewarm, is undevout :
But when it glows, its heat is struck to heav'n ;
To human hearts her golden harps are strung ;
High heav'n's orchestra chaunts Amen to man.
   Hear I, or dream I hear, their distant strain,
Sweet to the soul, and tasting strong of heav'n,
Soft wasted on celestial pity's plume,
Thro' the vast spaces of the universe,
To cheer me in this melancholy gloom?
O when will death (now stingless) like a friend,
Admit me of their choir? O when will death,
This mould'ring, old, partition-wall throw down ?
Give beings, one in nature, one abode?
Oh death divine ! that giv'st us to the skies !
Great future ! glorious patron of the past,
And present ! when shall I thy shrine adore?
From nature's continent, immensely wide,
Immensely blest, this little isle of life,
This dark, incarcerating colony,
Divides us.   Happy day ! that breaks our chain ;
That manumits ; that calls from exile home ;
That leads to nature's great metropolis,
And re-admits us, thro' the guardian hand
Of elder brothers, to our Father's throne ;
Who hears our advocate, and, thro' his wounds
Beholding man, allows the tender name.
'Tis this makes christian triumph a command :
'Tis this makes joy a duty to the wise ;
'Tis impious in a good man to be sad."

CHAPTER XIX.

AKENSIDE.

AKENSIDE.—Cooper in his Lectures on Taste, says, "For my part I am of opinion, that there is now living a poet of as genuine a genius as this kingdom ever produced, Shakespeare alone excepted. By poetical genius, I do not mean the mere talent of making verses, but that glorious enthusiasm of soul, that fine phrenzy in which the *eye rolling glances from heaven to earth, from earth to heaven,* as Shakespeare feelingly describes it.   This alone is poetry : aught else is a mechanical art of putting syllables harmoniously together.

mote the cause of public and private virtue. His works mark
once originality of genius, and sublimity of sentiment. He appe;
to the heart, disdaining to misguide the feeling by the lure
harmony, or amuse the fancy at the expense of the understandir
We read the man throughout his numerous and varied subject
from a general view of which it will appear, that he was fully in
pressed with the truth of his own remark, that, "the writer wl
held the pen without duly considering the welfare of society. shou
be considered an alien, heedless of its interests, and in everyw
unworthy its blessings." And Akenside has not only written tl
remark, but every line of his beautiful poem on *The Pleasures
Imagination* convinces his reader that he was fully satisfied wi
the truth of it. It is a poem which will bear to be compared
point of sublimity of language and harmony of arrangement, wi
the most celebrated productions of antiquity. We may also di
cover in his works, an extensive acquaintance with the ancie
literature, and his ardent attachment to the cause of civil and re'
gious liberty. His politics were thougth to incline to republicanisi
but no evidence to this point is to be deduced from his poem
His theology also was supposed to have verged towards Deisn
but in his *Ode to the Bishop of Winchester* and *To the Author
Memoirs of the House of Brandenburgh* ; he has testified his rega'
for pure christianity, and of his dislike of attempts for setting mi
free from the restraints of religion, but a solicitude to have tl
christian revelation preserved in its native purity.

For example in the last two stanzas of the latter Ode,

"O evil foresight and pernicious care !
Wilt thou indeed abide by this appeal?

Ye who made Rome victorious, Athens wise,
Ye first of mortals with the bless'd enroll'd,
Say did not horror in your bosoms rise,
When thus by impious vanity impell'd
A magistrate, a monarch, ye beheld
Affronting civil orders holiest bands?
Those bands which ye so labour'd to improve?
Those hopes and fears of justice from above,
Which tam'd the savage world to your divine commands."

From this and many other passages of Akenside's works, we may see his sincere reverence for the great and fundamental principles of religion : his veneration for the Supreme Being, his exalted sentiments of the wisdom and benevolene of the Divine Providence, and his zeal for the cause of virtue. In the Ode *To the Earl of Huntingdown*, there is an illustration of his attachment to the cause of liberty, religious and civil, expressed and displayed with considerable ardour.

"The Muse's awful art,
And the blest function of the poet's tongue,
Ne'er shalt thou blush to honour ; to assert
From all that scorned vice or slavish fear hath sung.
Nor shall the blandishment of Tuscan strings
Warbling at will in pleasure's myrtle bower ;
Nor shall the servile notes to Celtic kings
By flattering minstrels paid in evil hour,
Move thee to spurn the heavenly Muse's reign.
A different strain,
And other themes
From her prophetic shades and hallow'd streams
(Thou well canst witness) meet the purged ear :
Such, as when Greece to her immortal shell
Rejoicing listen'd, godlike sounds to hear ;
To hear the sweet instructress tell
(While men and heroes throng'd around)
How life its noblest use may find,
How well for freedom be resign'd ;
And how, by glory, virtue shall be crown'd.

Such was the Chian father's strain
To many a kind domestic train,

Whose pious hearth and genial bowl,
Had cheer'd the reverend pilgrim's soul :
When, every hospitable rite
With equal bounty to requite,
He struck his magic strings ;
And pour'd spontaneous numbers forth,
And seiz'd their ears with tales of ancient worth,
And fill'd their musing hearts with vast heroic things.

　　＊　　　＊　　　＊　　　＊　　　＊

'Tis highest heaven's command,
That guilty aims should sordid paths pursue ;
That what ensnares the heart should maim the hand.
And virtue's worthless foes be false to glory too.
But look on freedom : see, through every age,
What labours, perils, griefs, hath she disdain'd !
What arms, what regal pride, what priestly rage,
Have her dread offspring conquer'd or sustain'd !
For Albion well have conquer'd.　Let the strains
　　Of happy swains,
　　Which now resound
Where Scarsdale's cliffs the swelling pastures bound,
Bear witness.　There, oft let the farmer hail
The sacred orchard which embowers his gate,
And shew to strangers passing down the vale,
　　Where Candish, Boothe, and Osborne sate ;
　　When bursting from their country's chain,
　　Even in the midst of deadly harms,
　　Of papal snares and lawless arms,
They plann'd for freedom this her noblest reign."

Possessed with such liberal sentiments as those of **Akenside,**
it is the less to be wondered at, that at an early period of his life,
he planned and wrote his *Pleasures of Imagination;* which so long
as genius owns an admirer will ever be valued for chasteness of
design, sublimity of thought, and all that pleasing witchery which
marks the spontaneous effusions of genuine poetry.　It is said of
Akenside that "he seems to have possessed an independent mind,
disposed to free enquiry and liberal investigation, impatient of the
fetters of superstition, and desirous of avoiding those mazes of
casuistical theology, which have ever bewildered the imagination,
and engaged great and good men in endless controversies without
settling the main point in dispute."　It is this disposition which is
highly laudable in the opinion of men of comprehensive minds,
that subjected him to the censure of Johnson, who though a pro-

have studied the metaphysics of the mind, and have been accus-
tomed to investigate abstract ideas, will read with the most lively
pleasure ; but those who suppose that in perusing a poem, the mind
remains passive, and has nothing to do but to receive impressions,
will find many inferior productions much better suited to their
purpose. In a passage written by an eminent essayist, the true
merit of Akenside is truly and excellently appreciated. "If the
genius of Akenside is to be estimated from his poem, it will be found
to be lofty and elegant ; chaste, correct, and classical ; not marked
with strong traits of originality ; not ardent or exuberant. His
enthusiasm was rather of that kind which kindled by reading and
imbibing the spirit of authors, than by contemplating at first hand
the works of nature. As a versifier, Akenside is allowed to stand
amongst those who have given the most finished models in blank
verse. His periods are long but harmonious : the cadences fall
with grace, and the measure is supported with uniform dignity.
His muse possesses the *mien erect, and high commanding gait.*
We shall scarcely find a low or trivial expression introduced ; a
careless or unfinished line permitted to stand. His stateliness,

however, is somewhat allied to stiffness ;—his verse is sometimes feeble through too rich a redundancy of ornament, and sometimes laboured into a degree of obscurity from too anxious-a desire of avoiding natural and simple expressions. "

The Pleasures of Imagination is a subject the most happy that could have been chosen by a didactic poet, for every step of the disquisition must call up objects of the most attractive kind, and Fancy be made as it were to hold a mirror up to her own charms. Imagination is the very source of poetry, and nothing forced or foreign to the muse, could easily flow from such a subject. The *Pleasures of Imagination* is a noble and beautiful poem, exhibiting many bright displays of genius and fancy, and holding out sublime views of nature, providence, and morality.

There are many passages in this poem of uncommon beauty and originality, which may be taken as ample proofs of the poetic genius of Akenside. In pointing cut the natural connection of beauty with truth and good, nothing can exceed the following lines for poetry and sentiment.

> "————————Yon flowery bank
> Cloth'd in the soft magnificence of spring,
> Will not the flocks approve it? will they ask
> The reedy fen for pasture? that clear rill
> Which trickleth murmuring from the mossy rock,
> Yields it less wholesome beverage to the worn
> And thirsty traveller, than the standing pool
> With muddy weeds o'ergrown? Yon rugged vine
> Whose lean and sullen clusters mourn the rage
> Of Eurus, will the vine-press or the bowl
> Report to her, as of the swelling grape
> Which glitters through the tendrils, like a gem
> When first it meets the sun? Or what are all
> The various charms to life and sense adjoin'd?
> Are they not pledges of a state entire,
> Where native order reigns, with every part
> In health, and every function well perform'd?
>   Thus then at first was beauty sent from heaven,
> The lovely ministress of truth and good
> In this dark world. For truth and good are one ;
> And beauty dwells in them, and they in her,
> With like participation. Wherefore then,
> O sons of earth, would ye dissolve the tie?
> O ! wherefore with a rash and greedy aim
> Seek ye to rove through every flattering scene

"————————Ask the faithful youth,
Why the cold urn of her whom long he lov'd
So often fills his arms; so often draws
His lonely footsteps at the silent hour,
To pay the mournful tribute of his tears!
O! he will tell thee, that the wealth of worlds
Should ne'er seduce his bosom to forego
That sacred hour, when, stealing from the noise
Of care and envy, sweet remembrance soothes
With virtue's kindest looks his aching breast,
And turns his tears to rapture. "

His description of a shipwreck, is picturesque and affecting; it is call upon pity and cannot fail to awaken its sentiments.

"————————— Ask the crowd.
Which flies impatient from the village-walk
To climb the neigh'bouring cliffs, when far below
The cruel winds have hurl'd upon the coast
Some helpless bark; while sacred pity melts
The general eye, or terror's icy hand
Smites their distorted limbs and horrent hair;
While every mother closer to her breast
Catches her child, and pointing where the waves
Foam through the shatter'd vessel, shrieks aloud
As one poor wretch that spreads his piteous arms
For succour, swallow'd by the roaring surge,
As now another, dash'd against the rock,
Drops lifeless down."

Who journeys homeward from a summer day's
Long labour, why, forgetful of his toils
And due repose, he loiters to behold
The sunshine gleaming as through amber clouds,
O'er all the western sky ; full soon, I ween,
His rude expression and untutor'd airs,
Beyond the power of language, will unfold
The form of beauty smiling at his heart,
How lovely ! how commanding ! But though heaven
In every breast hath sown these early seeds
Of love and admiration, yet in vain,
Without fair culture's kind parental aid,
Without enlivening suns, and genial showers,
And shelter from the blast, in vain we hope
The tender plant should rear its blooming head,
Or yield the harvest promis'd in its spring.
Nor yet will every soil with equal stores
Repay the tiller's labour; or attend
His will, obsequious, whether to produce
The olive or the laurel. Different minds
Incline to different objects: one pursues
The vast alone, the wonderful, the wild ;
Another sighs for harmony, and grace,
And gentlest beauty. Hence when lightning fires
The arch of heaven, and thunders rock the ground,
When furious whirlwinds rend the howling air
And ocean, groaning from his lowest bed,
Heaves his tempestuous billows to the sky ;
Amid the mighty uproar, while below
The nations tremble, Shakespeare looks abroad
From some high cliff superior, and enjoys
The elemental war; but Waller longs,
All on the margin of some flow'ry stream
To spread his careless limbs amid the cool
    Of plantain shades, and to the list'ning deer

"——————Then listen while my tongue
The unalter'd will of heaven with faithful awe
Reveals ; what old Harmodius wont to teach
My early age ; Harmodius, who had weigh'd
Within his learned mind whate'er the schools
Of wisdom, or thy lonely-whispering voice,
O faithful nature! dictate of the laws
Which govern and support this mighty frame
Of universal being. Oft the hours
From morn to eve have stolen unmark'd away,
While mute attention hung upon his lips,
As thus the sage his awful tale began.
  'Twas in the windings of an ancient wood,
When spotless youth with solitude resigns
To sweet philosophy the studious day,
What time pale autumn shades the silent eve,
Musing I rov'd. Of good and evil much,
And much of mortal man my thought revolv'd ;
When starting full on fancy's gushing eye
The mournful image of Parthenia's fate.
That hour, O long belov'd and long deplor'd !
When blooming youth, nor gentlest wisdom's arts,
Nor Hymen's honours gather'd for thy brow,
Nor all thy lover's, all thy father's tears
Avail'd to snatch thee from the cruel grave ;
Thy agonizing looks, thy last farewell
Struck to the inmost feeling of my soul
As with the hand of death. At once the shade
More horrid nodded o'er me, and the winds
With hoarser murmuring shook the branches. Dark
As midnight storms, the scene of human things
Appear'd before me ; deserts, burning sands,
Where the parch'd adder dies ; the frozen south,
And desolation blasting all the west
With rapine and with murder : tyrant power
Here sits enthron'd with blood ; the baleful charms

Of superstition there infect the skies,
And turn the sun to horror, Gracious Heaven!
What is the life of man? Or cannot these,
Not these portents thy awful will suffice?
That, propagated thus beyond their scope,
They rise to act their cruelties anew
In my afflicted bosom, thus decreed
The universal sensitive of pain.
The wretched heir of evils not its own!
   Thus I impatient; when, at once effus'd,
A flashing torrent of celestial day
Burst thro' the shadowy void. With slow descent
A purple cloud came floating through the sky,
And pois'd at length within the circling trees,
Hung obvious to my view; till opening wide
Its lucid orb, a more than human form
Emerging lean'd majestic o'er my head,
And instant thunder shook the conscious grove.
Then melted into air the liquid cloud,
And all the shining vision stood reveal'd.
A wreath of palm his ample forehead bound
And o'er his shoulder, mantling to his knee,
Flow'd the transparent robe, around his waist
Collected with a radiant zone of gold
Etherial: there in mystic signs engrav'd,
I read his office high and sacred name,
Genius of human kind. Appall'd I gaz'd
The godlike presence; for athwart his brow
Displeasure, temper'd with a mild concern,
Look'd down reluctant on me, and his words
Like distant thunders broke the murmuring air.

     *   *   *   *   *   *

   I look'd, and lo! the former scene was chang'd;
For verdant alleys and surrounding trees,
A solitary prospect, wide and wild,
Rush'd on my senses. 'Twas an horrid pile
Of hills with many a shaggy forest mix'd,
With many a sable cliff and glittering stream.
Aloft recumbent o'er the hanging ridge,
The brown woods wav'd; while ever-trickling springs
Wash'd from the naked roots of oak and pine
The crumbling soil; and still at every fall
Down the steep windings of the channell'd rock,
Remurmuring rush'd the congregated floods
With hoaser inundation; till at last
They reach'd a grassy plain, which from the skirts
Of that high desert spread her verdant lap,
And drank the gushing moisture. where confin'd
In one smooth current, o'er the lilied vale

Clearer than glass it flow'd. Autumnal spoils
Luxuriant spreading to the rays of morn,
Blush'd o'er the cliffs, whose half-encircling mound
As in a sylvan theatre enclos'd
That flowery level. On the river brink
I spy'd a fair pavilion, which diffus'd
Its floating umbrage 'mid the silver shade
Of osiers. Now the western sun reveal'd
Between two parting cliffs his golden orb,
And pour'd across the shadows of the hills,
On rocks and floods, a yellow stream of light
That cheer'd the solemn scene. My listening powers
Were aw'd, and every thought in silence hung
And wondering expectation. Then the voice
Of that celestial power, the mystic show
Declaring, thus my deep attention call'd.

    *   *   *   *   *

——————Looking up, I view'd
A vast gigantic spectre striding on
Through murmuring thunders and a waste of clouds,
With dreadful action. Black as night his brow
Relentless frowns involv'd. His savage limbs
With sharp impatience violent he writh'd,
As through convulsive anguish ; and his hand,
Arm'd with a scorpion-lash, full oft he rais'd
In madness to his bosom ; while his eyes
Rain'd bitter tears, and bellowing loud he shook
The void with horror. Silent by his side
The virgin came. No discomposure stirr'd
Her features. From the glooms which hung around,
No stain of darkness mingled with the beam
Of her divine effulgence. Now they stoop
Upon the river bank ; and now to hail
His wonted guests, with eager steps advanc'd
The unsuspecting inmate of the shade.

    As when a famish'd wolf, that all night long
Had rang'd the Alpine snows, by chance at morn
Sees from a cliff incumbent o'er the smoke
Of some lone village, a neglected kid
That strays along the wild for herb or spring ;
Down from the winding ridge he sweeps amain,
And thinks he tears him : so with tenfold rage,
The monster sprung remorseless on his prey,
Amaz'd the stripling stood : with panting breast
Feeble he pour'd the lamentable wail
Of helpless consternation, struck at once,
And rooted to the ground. The queen beheld
His terror, and with looks of tenderest care
Advanc'd to save him. Soon the tyrant felt
Her awful power. His keen, tempestuous **arm**

Hung nerveless, nor descended where his rage
Had aim'd the deadly blow: then dumb retir'd
With sullen rancour.   Lo! the sovran maid
Folds with a mother's arms the fainting boy,
Till life rekindles in his rosy cheek;
Then grasps his hands, and cheers him with her tongue.
   O wake thee, rouse thy spirit! Shall the spite
Of yon tormenter thus appal thy heart,
While I, thy friend and guardian, am at hand
To rescue and to heal? O let thy soul
Remember, what the will of heaven ordains
Is ever good for all; and if for all,
Then good for thee."

Of his other poems little is to be said.   It is impossible to guess why he addicted himself so diligently to lyric poetry, having neither the ease or airiness of the lighter, nor the vehemence and elevation of the grander ode.   "When he lays his ill-fated hand upon his harp," says one writer, "his former powers seem to desert him; he has no longer his luxuriance of expression, nor variety of images. His thoughts are cold and his words inelegant."

In his Odes, the sentiment generally wants force or novelty; the diction is sometimes harsh and the rhymes dissonant and too distant from each other; but still there is in them a noble vein of poetry, united with manly sense, and applied and excellent purposes.   The two following Odes, entitle him justly to a place amongst the principal lyric writers of this country.

TO SLEEP.

"Thou silent power, whose welcome sway
Charms every anxious thought away;
In whose divine oblivion drown'd,
Sore pain and weary toil grow mild,
Love is with kinder looks beguil'd,
And grief forgets her fondly-cherish'd wound;
Oh whither hast thou flown, indulgent god?
God of kind shadows and of healing dews,
Whom dost thou touch with Lethan rod?
Around whose temples now thy opiate airs diffuse?

Lo, midnight from her starry reign
Looks awful down on earth and main.
The tuneful birds lie hush'd in sleep,
With all that crop the verdant food,
With all that skim the crystal flood,
Or haunt the caverns of the rocky steep.

No rushing winds disturb the tufted bowers ;
No wakeful sound the moonlight valley knows,
Save where the brook its liquid murmur pours,
And lulls the waving scene to more profound repose.

O let not me alone complain,
Alone invoke thy power in vain !
Descend, propitious, on my eyes ;
Not from the couch that bears a crown,
Not from the courtly statesman's down,
Nor where the miser and his treasure lie ;
Bring not the shapes that break the murderer's rest,
Nor those the hireling soldier loves to see,
Nor those which haunt the bigot's gloomy breast ;
Far be their guilty nights, and far their dreams from me !

Nor yet those awful forms present,
For chiefs and heroes only meant :
The figur'd brass, the choral song,
The rescued people's glad applause,
The list'ning senate, and the laws
Fix'd by the counsels of Timoleon's tongue,
Are scenes too grand for Fortune's private ways,
And tho' they shine in youth's ingenious view,
The sober-gainful arts of modern days
To such romantic thoughts have bid a long adieu.

I ask not, god of Dreams ! thy care
To banish love's presentiments fair :
Nor rosy cheek, nor radiant eye
Can arm him with such strong command,
That the young sorc'rer's fatal hand
Should round my soul his pleasing fetters tie :
Nor yet the courtier's hope, the giving smile.
(A lighter phantom and a baser chain.)
Did e'er in slumber my proud lyre beguile
To lend the pomp of thrones her ill according strain.

But, Morpheus ! on thy balmy wing
Such honourable visions bring,
As sooth'd great Milton's injur'd age,
When in prophetic dreams he saw
The race unborn with pious awe
Inhibe each virtue from his heav'nly page :
Or such as Mead's benignant fancy knows
When health's deep treasures, by his art explor'd,
Have sav'd the infant from an orphan's woes,
Or to the trembling sire his age's hope restor'd."

ON RECOVERIMG FROM A FIT OF SICKNESS.
(In the Country.)
"Thy verdant scenes, O Goulder's hill,
Once more I seek, a languid guest :

With throbbing temples and with burden'd breast
Once more I climb thy steep aerial way.
O faithful cure of oft returning ill,
   Now call thy sprightly breezes round,
   Dissolve this rigid cough profound,
And bid the springs of life with gentler movement play.

   How gladly 'mid the dews of dawn
   By weary lungs thy healing gale,
The balmy west or the fresh north, inhale !
How gladly, while my musing footsteps rove
Round the cool orchard or the sunny lawn,
   Awak'd I stop, and look to find
   What shrub perfumes the pleasant wind,
Or what wild songster charm the Dryads of the grove.

   Now, ere the morning walk is done,
   The distant voice of health I hear
Welcome as beauty's to the lover's ear.
'Droop not, nor doubt of my return,' she cries;
   ' Here will I, 'mid the radiant calm of noon,
   Meet thee beneath yon chestnut bower,
   And lenient on thy bosom pour
That indolence divine which lulls the earth and skies.'

   The goddess promis'd not in vain.
   I found her at my fav'rite time.
Nor wish'd to breathe in any softer clime,
White (half-reclin'd, half-slumbering as I lay)
She hover'd o'er me. Then, among her train
   Of nymphs and zephyrs to my view
   Thy gracious form appeared anew,
Then first, O heavenly Muse, unseen for many a day.

   In that soft pomp the tuneful maid
   Shone like the golden star of love.
I saw her hand in careless measures move ;
I heard sweet preludes dancing on her lyre,
While my whole frame the sacred sound obeyed.
   New sunshine o'er my fancy springs,
   New colours clothe external things,
And the last glooms of pain and sickly plaint retire.

   O Goulder's hill, by thee restor'd
   Once more to this enliven'd hand,
My harp, which late resounded o'er the land
The voice of glory, solemn and severe.
My Dorian harp shall now with mild accord
   To thee her joyful tribute pay,
   And send a less ambitious lay
Of friendship and of love to greet thy master's ear.

   For when within thy shady seat
   First from the sultry town he chose,
And the tir'd senate's cares, his wish'd repose,

Then wast thou mine ; to me a happy home
For social leisure : where my welcome feet,
    Estrang'd from all the entangling ways
    In which the restless vulgar strays,
Through nature's simple paths with ancient faith might roam.

    And while around his sylvan scene
    My Dyson led the white wing'd Hours.
Oft from th' Athenian Academic bow'rs
There sages came : oft' heard our ling'ring walk,
The Mantuan music warbling o'er the green ;
    And oft did Tully's rev'rend shade,
    Tho' much for liberty afraid,
With us of letter'd ease or virtuous glory talk.

    But other guests were on their way,
    And reach'd ere long this favour'd grove,
Even the celestia progeny of Jove,
Bright Venus ! with her all subduing son,
Whose golden shaft most willingly obey
    The best and wisest. As they came,
    Glad Hymen wav'd his genial flame,
And sang their happy gifts, and prais'd their spotless throne.

    I saw when thro' yon festive gate
    He led along his chosen maid,
And to my friend with smiles presenting said ;
'Receive that fairest wealth which Heav'n assign'd
To human fortune. Did thy lonely state
    One wish, one utmost hope confess ?
    Behold ! she comes t' adorn and bless :
Comes worthy of thy heart, and equal to thy mind.'"

CHAPTER XX.

LANGHORNE.

LANGHORNE.—As a poet Langhorne's compositions are distinguished by undoubted marks of genius; a fine imagination and a sensible heart. Imagery and enthusiasm, the great essentials of poetry, inspirit all his works, and place them far above the strain of vulgar compositions. The tenderness of love, and the soft language of complaint, were adapted to his genius, as well as elevation of thought, opulence of imagery, and the highest beauties of poetry. But the qualities for which he is chiefly distinguished, are imagination, pathos, and simplicity, animated sentiment,

warmth and vivacity of expression, and a melodious **versification.**
His sentimental productions are exquisitely tender and beautiful ;
his descriptive compositions show a feeling heart, and a warm
imagination ; and his lyric pieces are pregnant with the genuine
spirit of poetical enthusiasm : but his style in the midst of much
splendour and strength, is sometimes harsh and obscure, and may
be censured as deficient in ease and distinctness.   His chief faults
are redundant decoration, and an affectation of false and **unneces-**
sary ornament.   He is not always contented with that concise and
simple language, which is sufficient to express his sentiments, but is
tempted to indulge in superfluous diction, by the facinating charms
of novelty and harmony.   By giving way to the luxury of words,
and immoderate embellishment, he sometimes, though rarely, vio-
lates simplicity and becomes unavoidably inaccurate and redundant.
His sentiments, however, are always just, often new, and generally
striking.   A great deal of elegance and classical simplicity runs
through all his compositions ; and his descriptions of nature, rural
imagery, pictures of private virtue, and pastoral innocence, have a
judicious selection of circumstances, a graceful plainness of expres-
sion, and a happy mixture of pathos and sentiment which mark
the true poet.   His *Death of Adonis* is a classical and spirited
translation of one of the most beautiful pastoral poems of antiquity.
The numbers are musical and flowing, and the diction easy and
elegant.   The opening passage will amply illustrate the foregoing
remarks.

> "Adonis dead, the muse of woe shall mourn ;
> Adonis dead, the weeping loves return.
> The queen of beauty o'er his tomb shall shed
> Her flowing sorrows for Adonis dead ;
> For earth's cold lap her velvet couch forego,
> And robes of purple for the weeds of woe.
> Adonis dead, the muse of woe shall mourn ;
> Adonis dead, the weeping loves return.
>   Stretch'd on this mountain thy torn lover lies,
> Weep, queen of beauty ! for he bleeds—he dies.
> Ah ! yet behold life's last drops faintly flow,
> In streams of purple, o'er those limbs of snow !
>   From the pale cheek the perish'd roses fly,
> And death dims slow the ghastly gazing eye.

Kiss, kiss those fading lips, ere chill'd in death ;
With soothing fondness stay the fleeting breath.
'Tis vain ! —ah ! give the soothing fondness o'er!
Adonis feels the warm salute no more.
Adonis dead, the muse of woe shall mourn ;
Adonis dead, the weeping loves return.
His faithful dogs bewail their master slain :
And mourning dryads pour the plaintive strain.
  Not the fair youth alone the wound opprest,
The queen of beauty bears it in her breast,
Her feet unsandled, floating wild her hair,
Her aspect woeful, and her bosom bare,
Distrest, she wanders the wild waste forlorn,
Her sacred limbs by ruthless brambles torn,
Loud as she grieves, surrounding rocks complain,
And echo through the long vales calls her absent swain.
Adonis hears not: Life's last drops falls slow
In streams of purple, down his limbs of snow.
The weeping Cupids round their queen deplore,
And mourn her beauty and her love no more.
Each rival grace that glow'd with conscious pride,
Each charm of Venus with Adonis dy'd.
Adonis dead, the vocal hills bemoan
And hollow groves return the saddening groan.
The swelling floods with sea-born Venus weep,
And roll in mournful numbers to the deep :
In melting tears the mountain-springs comply :
The flow'rs low-drooping, blush with grief, and die.
Cythera's groves with strains of sorrow ring:
The dirge funereal her sad cities sing.

      *   *   *   *   *

  Thus Venus griev'd—the Cupids round deplore,
And mourn her beauty and her love no more.
Now flowing tears in silent grief complain,
Mix with the purple streams, and flood the plain.
Yet not in vain those sacred drops shall flow,
The purple streams in blushing roses glow ;
And catching life from ev'ry falling tear,
Their azure heads anemonies shall rear,"

The *Poem to the Memory of Handel*, may be considered as
the genuine and animated wailings of poetry, who deplores her
sister's loss in Handel, in very elegant and harmonious verse.
There is a considerable variety in the numbers, but they are excel-
lently adapted to the subject, and modulated to a judicious
correspondence with the images, and the sentiments. In the fol-
lowing passage, the pauses and cadences of the numbers are, so
sweet and mutable, that it must revive the idea of a band in the

mind of every amateur of the science of music.

> "I feel, I feel the sacred impulse, hark!
> Wak'd from according lyres the sweet strains flow
> In symphony divine; from air to air
> The trembling numbers fly : swift bursts away
> The flow of joy—now swells the flight of praise.
> Springs the shrill trump aloft ; the toiling chords
> Melodious labour through the flying maze ;
> And the deep base his strong sound rolls away,
> Majestically sweet—Yet, Handel, raise,
> Yet wake to higher strains thy sacred lyre :
> The name of ages, the supreme of things
> The great Messiah asks it ; He whose hand
> Led into form yon everlasting orbs,
> The harmony of nature—He whose hand
> Stretch'd o'er the wilds of space this beauteous hall,
> Whose spirit breathes, through all his smiling works
> Music and love—yet Handel raise the strain."

The *Ode to the River Eden*, is pretty and fanciful, and another specimen of the harmony of his numbers, especially the fourth stanza :—

> "But, Fancy, can thy mimic power
> Again those happy moments bring?
> Cans't thou restore that golden hour,
> When young Joy wav'd his laughing wing?
> When first in Eden's rosy vale,
> My full heart pour'd the lover's tale,
> The vow sincere, devoid of guile !
> While Delia in her panting breast,
> With sighs the tender thought supprest,
> And looked as angels smile."

Again in the *Hymn to Hope*, the versification and diction is smooth and elegant, while the imagery is most pleasing, and the sentiment simple and pathetic. The following are the first seven stanzas.

> "Sun of the soul ! whose cheerful ray
> Darts o'er this gloom of life a smile;
> Sweet Hope, yet further gild my way,
> Yet light my weary steps awhile,
> Till thy fair lamp dissolve in endless day.
>
> O come with such an eye and mien,
> As when by amorous shepherd seen ;
> While in the violet-breathing vale
> He meditates his evening tale !
> Nor leave behind thy fairy train,
> Repose, belief, and fancy vain ;
> That, towering on her wing sublime,

O come! and to my pensive eye
Thy far-foreseeing tube apply,
Whose kind deception steals us o'er
The gloomy waste that lies before;
Still opening to the distant sight
The sunshine of the mountains height;
Where scenes of fairer aspect rise,
Elysian groves, and azure skies.

Nor, gentle Hope, forget to bring
The family of Youth and Spring;
The Hours that glide in sprightly round,
The mountain nymphs with wild thyme crown'd;
Delight that dwells with raptur'd eye
On stream, or flower, or field or sky:
And foremost in thy train advance
The Loves and Joys in jovial dance;
Nor last be Expectation seen,
That wears a wreath of evergreen.

Attended thus by Belcau's streams,
Oft hast thou sooth'd my waking dreams,
When, prone beneath an osier shade,
At large my vacant limbs were laid;
To thee and fancy all resign'd,
What visions wander'd o'er my mind!

Illusions dear, adieu! no more
Shall I your fairy haunts explore;
For Hope withholds her golden ray, .
And fancy's colours faint away.
To Eden's shores, to Enon's groves,
Resounding once with Delia's loves,
Adieu! that name shall sound no more
O'er Enon's groves or Eden's shore;
For Hope withholds her golden ray,
And fancy's colours faint away.

Life's ocean slept—the liquid gale
Gently mov'd the waving fail.
Fallacious Hope! with flattering eye
You smil'd to see the streamers fly.
The thunder bursts, the mad wind raves
From slumber wake the frighted waves:
You saw me, fled me thus distrest.
And tore your anchor from my breast.
Yet come, fair fugitive, again!
I love thee still, though false and vain,
Forgive me, gentle Hope, and tell
Where, far from me, you deign to dwell.

> To soothe Ambition's wild desires;
> To feed the lover's eager fires;
> To swell the miser's mouldy store;
> To gild the dreaming chymist's ore;
> Are these thy cares? or more humane?
> To loose the war-worn captive's chain,
> And bring before his languid sight
> The charms of liberty and light;
> The tears of drooping grief to dry;
> And hold thy glass to Sorrow's eye."

His *Visions of Fancy*, are the effusions of a contemplative mind, sometimes plaintive and always serious, but too attentive to the glitter of the slight ornaments. The thoughts are pure, simple, and pathetic; and the lines are such as elegy requires smooth, easy, and flowing; but the same fault prevails, and the diction is often affected, while the phrase is unskilfully inverted. They are too long to be fully quoted, but the reader can fully estimate their true value, by the following, the first of the four elegies.

> "Children of Fancy whither are ye fled?
> Where have you borne those hope-enliven'd hours,
> That once with mirtle garlands bound my head,
> That once bestrew'd my vernal path with flowers?
>
> In you fair vale, where blooms the beechen grove,
> Where winds the slow wave thro' the flowery plain,
> To these fond arms you led the tyrant, Love,
> With Fear and Hope and Folly in his train.
>
> My lyre, that, left at careless distance, hung
> Light on some pale branch of the osier shade,
> To lays of amorous blandishment you strung,
> And o'er my steep the lulling music play'd.
>
> 'Rest, gentle youth! while on the quivering breeze
> Slides to thine ear this softly breathing strain;
> Sounds that move smoother than the steps of ease,
> And pour oblivion in the ear of pain.
>
> 'In this fair vale eternal spring shall smile,
> And Time unenvious crown each roseat hour;
> Eternal joy shall every care beguile,
> Breathe in each gale, and bloom in every flower.
>
> 'This silver stream, that down its crystal way
> Frequent has led thy musing steps along,
> Shall, still the same, in sunny mazes play,
> And with its murmurs melodious the song.
>
> Unfading green shall these fair groves adorn;
> Those living meads immortal flowers unfold;

'Come gentle Loves ! your myrtle garlands bring ;
The smiling bower with cluster'd roses spread ;
Come gentle Airs ! with incense dropping wing,
The breathing sweets of vernal odour shed.

'Hark as the strains of swelling music rise,
How the notes vibrate on the fav'ring gale !
Auspicious glories beam along the skies,
And powers unseen the happy moments hail !

'Ecstatic hours ! so every distant day
Like the serene on downy wings shall move ;
Rise crown'd with joys that triumph o'er decay,
The faithful joys of Fancy and of Love.'"

The *Autumnal Elegy* deserves still more, and unqualified commendation. Take for instance, the following stanzas.

"Yet, ere ye slumber, songsters of the sky,
Through the long night of winter wild and drear
O let us tune, ere love and fancy die,
One tender farewell to the fading year.

Farewell ye wild hills, scatter'd o'er with spring !
Sweet solitude, where Flora smil'd unseen !
Farewell each breeze of balmy burden'd wing !
The violet's blue bank, and the tall wood green l

Ye tuneful groves of Belvidere, adieu !
Kind shades that whisper o'er my Crauford's rest !
From courts, from senates, and from camps to you,
When fancy leads him, no inglorious guest.

Dear shades, adieu ! where late the moral muse,
Led by the Dryad, Silence, oft reclin'd,
Taught Meanness to extend her little views,
And look on Nature to enlarge her mind.

Farewell the walk along the woodland vale l
Flower-feeding rills in murmurs drawn away !
Farewell the sweet breath of the early gale,
And the dear glories of the closing day !

The nameless charms of high, poetic thought,
That Spring's green hours to Fancy's children bore ;
The words divine, imagination wrote
On Slumber's light leaf, by the murmuring shore.

All, all adieu ! from Autumn's sober power
Fly the dear dreams of Spring's delightful reign ;
Gay summer strips her rosy-mantled bower,
And rude winds waste the glorious of her train.

Yet Autumn yields her joys of humbler kind ;
Sad o'er the golden ruins as we stray,
Sweet Melancholy soothes the musing mind,
And Nature's charms, delightful in decay.

All-bounteous power, whom happy worlds adore,
With every scene some grateful change she brings—
In winter's wild snows, autumn's golden store,
In glowing summers, and in blooming springs!

O most belov'd ! the fairest and the best
Of all her works ! may still thy lover find
Fair Nature's frankness in thy gentle breast ;
Like her be various, but like her be kind.

Then, when the spring of smiling youth is o'er ;
When summer's glories yields to autumn's sway ;
When golden autumn sinks in winter's hoar ;
And life's declining yields its last weak ray ;

In thy lov'd arms my fainting age shall close,
On thee my fond eye bends its trembling light :
Remembrance sweet shall soothe my last repose,
And my soul bless thee in eternal night."

In fire and force of numbers and in the use and harmonious
flow of his versification, his *Genius and Valour,* is equal to any
poem of its kind.   In the passage where he celebrates the natives
of North Britain, who have been distinguished for their genius and
learning; the representation of the four seasons appearing to Thom-
son and claiming the palm, like the fabled competition of the rural
goddesses before the royal shepherd, is entitled to the highest
praise.   The "*Seasons*" are distinguished by a brilliancy of colour-
ing, and a distinctness and propriety of attribute, that rival, if not
surpass, what we meet with of the kind even in Thomson.

"O favour'd stream ! where thy fair current flows,
The child of nature, gentle Thomson, rose.
Young as he wander'd on thy flowery side,
With simple joy to see thy bright waves glide,

Thither, in all their native charms array'd,
From climes remote the sister Seasons stray'd.
　Long each in beauty boasted to excel,
(For jealousies in sister-bosoms dwell)
But now, delighted with the liberal boy,
Like heaven's fair rivals in the groves of Troy,
Yield to an humble swain their high debate,
And from his voice the palm of beauty wait.
　Her naked charms, like Venus, to disclose,
Spring from her bosom through the shadowing rose ;
Bar'd the pure snow that feeds the lover's fire,
The breast that thrills with exquisite desire ;
Assum'd the tender smile, the melting eye,
The breath savonian, and the yielding sigh.
One beauteous hand a wilding's blossom grac'd,
And one fell careless o'er her zoneless waist.
Majestic Summer, in gay pride adorn'd,
Her rival sister's simple beauty scorn'd.
With purple wreaths her lofty brows were bound,
With glowing flowers her rising bosom crown'd.
In her gay zone, by artful Fancy fram'd,
The bright rose blush'd, the full carnation flam'd ;
Her cheeks the glow of splendid clouds display,
And her eyes flash insufferable day.
　With milder air the gentle Autumn came,
But seem'd to languish at her sister's flame.
Yet, conscious of her boundless wealth, she bore
On high the emblems of her golden store.
Yet could she boast the plenty pouring hand,
The liberal smile, benevolent and bland ;
Nor might she fear in beauty to excel,
From whose fair head such golden tresses fell ;
Nor might she envy Summer's flowery zone,
In whose sweet eye the star of evening shone.
　Next, the pale power, that blots the golden sky,
Wreath'd her grim brows, and roll'd her stormy eye ;
'Behold,' she cried, with voice that shook the ground,
(The bard, the sisters trembled at the sound)
'Ye weak admirers of a grape, or rose,
'Behold my wild magnificence of snows !
'See my keen frost her glassy bosom bare !
'Mock the faint sun, and bind the fluid air !
'Nature to you may lend a painted hour,
'With you may sport, when I suspend my power.
'But you and nature, what that power obey,
'Shall own my beauty, or shall dread my sway.' "

The diction contains an elegant compliment to the noble poet
of the Seasons.

"————the bard, whose gentle heart ne'er gave

> One pain or trouble that he knew to save
> No favour'd nymph extols with partial lays,
> But gives to each her picture for her praise."

The poet's love of nature is seen throughout all his works. In the *Enlargement of the Mind,* he recommends the study of nature in order to enlarge our minds by a due contemplation of her works.

> "Judg'd not the old philosopher aright,
> When thus he preach'd, his pupils in his sight?
> It matters not, my friends, how low or high,
> Your little walk of transient life may lie;
> Soon will the reign of hope and fear be o'er,
> And warring passions militate no more:
> And trust me, he who, having once survey'd
> The good and fair which nature's wisdom made,
> The soonest to his former state retires,
> And feels the peace of satisfied desires,
> (Let others deem more wisely if they can)
> I look on him to be the happiest man.
> So thought the sacred sage, in whom I trust,
> Because I feel his sentiments are just.
> 'Twas not in lustrums of long counted years
> That swell'd th' alternate reign of hopes and fears;
> Not in the splendid scenes of pain and strife,
> That wisdom plac'd the dignity of life;
> To study Nature was the task design'd,
> And learn from her th' enlargement of the mind.
> Learn from her works whatever truth admires,
> And sleep in death with satisfied desires."

This poem, however, on the whole, is rather defective, though it possesses in many parts, the concise and happy expression, and the melodious versification of Pope's *Essay on Man*; which may be seen by comparing the passages already quoted from that work. In the first and second Epistles, there is more poetry than plan. The panegyric on Reason is eminently beautiful.

> " O! still censorious? art thou then possess'd
> Of Reason's power, and does she rule thy breast?
> Say what the use—had providence assign'd
> To infant years maturity of mind?
> That thy pert offspring, as their father wife,
> Might scorn thy percepts, and thy pow'r despise?
> Or mourn, with ill-match'd faculties of stife?
> Or limbs unequal to the task of life?
> To feel more sensibly the woes that wait
> On every period, as on every state;
> And flight, sad convicts of the painful truth,

The happier trifles of unthinking youth?
  Conclude we then the progress of the mind
Ordain'd by wisdom infinitely kind
No innate knowledge on the soul imprest,
No birthright instinct acting on the breast,
No natal light, no beams from heav'n display'd,
Dart through the darkness of the mental shade.
Perceptive powers we hold from heaven's decree,
Alike to knowledge as to virtue free,
In both a liberal agency we bear,
The moral here, the intellectual there;
And hence in both an equal joy is known,
The conscious pleasure of an act our own.
When first the trembling eye perceives the day,
External forms on young Perception play;
External forms affect the mind alone,
Their diff'rent powers and properties unknown.
See the pleas'd infant court the flaming brand,
Eager to grasp the glory in its hand!
The crystal wave as eager to pervade,
Stretch its fond arms to meet the smiling shade!
When Memory's call the Mimic words obey,
And wing the thought that falters on his way;
When wise Experience her slow verdict draws.
The sure effect exploring in her cause,
In Nature's rude, but not unfruitful wild,
Reflection springs, and Reason is her child,
On her fair stock the blooming scyon grows,
And brighter through revolving seasons blows.
  All beauteous flower! immortal shalt thou shine,
When dim with age yon golden orbs decline;
Thy orient bloom, unconcious of decay,
Shall spread, and flourish in eternal day.
  O! with what art, my friend, what early care,
Should wisdom cultivate a plant so fair!
How should her eye the rip'ning mind revise,
And blast the buds of folly as they rise?
How should her hand, with industry restrain,
The thriving growth of passion's fruitful train,
Aspiring weeds, whose lofty arms would tow r
With fatal shade o'er reason's tender flower."

The description of the graceful arts that flock round the throne of science, particularly *Poetry, Painting, Sculpture, and Music* is appropriate and striking, besides being elegantly and pleasingly written.

    "See favour'd first, and nearest to the throne,
    By the rapt mien of musing Silence known
    Fled from herself the pow'r of numbers plac'd.

Her wild thoughts watch'd by Harmony and Taste.
There (but at distance never ment to vie.)
The full-form'd image glancing on her eye,
See lively painting! on her various face,
Quick-gliding forms a moment find a place
She looks, she acts the character he gives,
And a new feature in each feature lives.
See attic ease in Sculpture's graceful air,
Half loose her robe, and half unbound her hair;
To life, to life, she smiling seems to call,
And down her fair hands negligently fall
Last, but not meanest, of the glorious choir,
See Music, list'ning to an angel's lyre.
Simplicity, their beauteous handmaid, drest
By Nature, bears a field-flower on her breast.
O arts divine! O magic powers that move
The springs of Truth, enlarging Truth, and Love!
Lost in their charms each mean attachment ends,
And Taste and Knowledge thus are Virtue's friend."

The Verses to the Memory of a Lady, rank with the celebrated elegiac composition of Lyttleton and Shaw, to which they are equal in poetical merit, and scarcely inferior in pathetic tenderness. They must please everybody, because there are beauties in them which affect everybody. The following lines must touch every heart,

" See the last aid of her expiring state,
See Love, e'en Love, has lent his darts to Fate!
Oh! when beneath his golden shafts I bled,
And vainly bound his trophies on my head;
When, crown'd with flowers, he led the rosy day,
Liv'd to my eye, and drew my soul away—
Could fear, could fancy at that tender hour,
See the dim grave demand the nuptial flower?

There, there his wreaths dejected Hymen strew'd;
And mourn'd their bloom unfaded as he view'd,
There each fair hope, each tenderness of life,
Each nameless charm of soft obliging strife,
Delight, love, fancy, pleasure, genius fled,
And the best passions of my soul lie dead;
All, all is there in cold oblivion laid,
But pale remembrance bending o'er a shade."

In his *Fables of Flora*, the plan is somewhat enlarged, and the province is far extended that the original narrative and moral may be accompanied with imagery, description, and sentiment. The plan is judicious, and the execution admirable. None of his compositions bear stronger marks of poetical invention and enthusiasm

"In this dim cave a druid sleeps,
Where stops the passing gale to moan;
The rock he hollow'd, o'er him weeps,
And cold drops wear the fretted stone.

In this dim cave, of different creed,
An hermit's holy ashes rest:
The school-boy finds the frequent bead,
Which many a formal matin blest.

That truant-time full well I know,
When here I brought, in stolen hour,
The druid's magic misletoe,
The holy hermit's passion-flower.

The offerings on the mystic stone
Pensive I laid, in thought profound,
When from the cave a deep'ning groan
Issued, and froze me to the ground.

I hear it still—dost thou not hear?
Does not thy haunted fancy start?
The sound still vibrates through mine ear—
The horror rushes on my heart.

Unlike to living sounds it came,
Unmix'd, unmelodized with breath;
But, grinding through some scrannel frame,
Creak'd from the bony lungs of death.

I hear it still—'Depart,' it cries:
'No tribute bear to shades unblest:
Know, here a bloody druid lies,
Who was not nurs'd at Nature's breast.

'Associate he with demons dire,
O'er human victims held the knife,
And pleas'd to see the babe expire,
Smil'd grimly o'er its quivering life.

'Behold his crimson-streaming hand
Erect!—his dark, fix'd murd'rous eye!
In the dim cave I saw him stand;
And my heart died—I felt it die.

'I see him still—Dost thou not see
The haggard eyeball's hollow glare?
And gleams of wild ferocity
Dart through the sable shade of hair?

I M.

What meagre forms behind him moves,
With eye that rues th' invading day ;
And wrinkled aspect wan, that proves
The mind to pale remorse a prey?

What wretched—Hark !—the voice replies,
'Boy, bear these idle honours hence !
For, here a guilty hermit lies
Untrue to nature, virtue, sense.

'Though nature lent him powers to aid
The moral cause, the mutual weal ;
Those powers he sunk in this dim shade,
The desperate suicide of zeal.

'Go, teach the drone of faintly haunts,
Whose cell's the sepulchre of time ;
Though many a holy hymn he chaunts,
His life in one continuous crime.

'And bear them hence, the plant, the flower;
No symbols those of systems vain !
They have the duties of their hour ;
Some bird, some insect, to sustain.'"

There is the same spirit of poetry and humanity, recommended by the charms of a flowing and elegant versification in *The Country Justice.* This poem opens with a retrospective view of the forlorn state of liberty and civil security in England, before the institution of justices of the peace in the reign of Edward III.

"The social laws from insult to protect,
To cherish peace, to cultivate respect ;
The rich from wanton cruelty restrain,
To smooth the bed of penury and pain ;
The hapless vagrant to his rest restore,
The maze of fraud, the haunts of theft explore;
The thoughtless maiden, when subdu'd by art,
To aid, and bring her rover to her heart ;
Wild riot's voice with dignity to quell,
Forbid unpeaceful passions to rebel,
Wrest from revenge the meditated harm,
For this fair justice rais'd her sacred arm,"

In the description of an ancient Justice Hall, there are some exquisite strokes of humour and pleasantry, and the moral character of a country justice, such as that of every magistrate ought to be, is admirably drawn.

"There Herbert sat—The love of human kind,
Pure light of truth, and temperance of mind,
In the free eye the featur'd soul display'd,

Honour's strong beam, and Mercy's melting shade :
Justice, that in the rigid paths of law,
Would still some drops from Pity's fountain draw,
Bend o'er her urn with many a gen'rous fear,
Ere his firm seal should force one orphan's tear ;
Fair Equity, and Reason scoring art,
And all the sober virtues of the heart—
These sat with Herbert, these shall best avail
Where statutes order, or where statutes fail.
　Be this, ye rural magistrates, your plan :
Firm be your justice, but be friends to man.
He whom the mighty master of this ball
We fondly deem, or farcically call,
To own the patriarch's truth, however loth,
Holds but a mansion crush'd before the moth.
　Frail in his genius, in his heart too frail,
Born but to err, and erring to bewail,
Shalt thou his faults with eyes severe explore,
And give to life one human weakness more ?
　Still mark if vice or nature prompts the deed ;
Still mark the strong temptation and the need :
On pressing want, on famine's powerful call,
At least more lenient let thy justice fall."

The general motives for lenity in the exercise of the justice's office, are enforced with energy and benevolence ; and in his apology for vagrants, he guards the probable misery of the widowed parent who might have borne one of those wretches, in the richest vein of fancy and pathos.

"For him, who, lost to ev'ry hope of life,
Has long with fortune held unequal strife,
Known to no human love, no human care,
The friendless, homeless object of despair ;
For the poor vagrant feel, while he complains,
Not from sad freedom send to sadder chains.
Alike if folly or misfortune brought
Those last of woes his evil days have wrought ;
Believe with social mercy and with me,
Folly's misfortune in the first degree.
　Perhaps on some inhospitable shore
The houseless wretch a widow'd parent bore ;
Who then, no more by golden prospects led,
Of the poor Indian begg'd a leafy bed.
Cold on Canadian hills, or Minden's plain,
Perhaps that parent mourn'd her soldier slain ;
Bent o'er her babe, her eye dissolv'd in dew,
The big drops mingling with the milk he drew,
Gave the sad presage of his future years,
The child of misery, baptiz'd in tears."

And his declaration against that pernicious species of vagrants, the gipsies, will be read with peculiar pleasure.

> "The gipsy-race my pity rarely move ;
> Yet their strong thirst of liberty I love.
> Not Wilkes, our freedom's holy martyr, more ;
> Nor his firm phalanx of the common shore.
>   For this in Norwood's patrimonial groves
> The tawny father with his offspring roves ;
> When summer suns lead slow the sultry day,
> In mossy caves, where welling waters play,
> Fann'd by each gale that cools the fervid sky,
> With this in ragged luxury they lie.
> Oft at the sun the dusky Elfin's strain
> The sable eye, then smuggling sleep again
> Oft as the dews of cooler evening fall,
> For their prophetic mother's mantle call.
> For other cares that wand'ring mother wait,
> The mouth, and oft the minister of fate !
> From her to hear, in ev'ning's friendly shade,
> Of future fortune, flies the village maid,
> Draws her long-boarded copper from its hold ;
> And rusty half-pence purchase hopes of gold.
>   But, ah ! ye maids, beware the gipsy's lures!
> She opens not the womb of time, but yours.
> Oft has her hands the hapless Marian wrung,
> Marian, whom Gay in sweetest strains has sung !
> The parson's maid—sore cause had she to rue
> The gipsy's tongue ; the parson's daughter too.
> Long had that anxious daughter sigh'd to know
> What Vellum's sprucy clerk, the valley's beau,
> Meant by those glances which at church he stole,
> Her father nodding to the psalm's slow drawl ;
> Long as she sigh'd : at length a prophet came,
> By many a sure prediction known to fame,
> To Marian known, and all she told, for true :
> She knew the future, for the past she knew."

His *Owen of Carron*, is a pathetic tale told with simplicity and elegance. There is something pathetically beautiful in the passage where Ellen, unconscious of her lover's fate, goes to meet him at the accustomed bower, and finds him dead.

> "When all the mountain gales were still,
> And the wave slept against the shore,
> And the sun sunk beneath the hill,
> Left his last smile on Lammermore.
>
> Sweet Ellen takes her wonted way
> Along the fairy-featur'd vale ;

Bright o'er his wave does Carron play,
And soon she'll meet her Nitbisdale.

She'll meet him soon—for at her sight,
Swift as the mountain deer he sped ;
The evening shades will sink in night,
Where art thou, loitering lover, fled ?

O ! she will chide thy trifling stay,
E'en now the soft reproach she frames :
'Can lovers brook such long delay ?
Lovers that boast of ardent flames ! '

He comes not—weary with the chase,
Soft slumber o'er his eyelids throws
Her veil—we'll steal one dear embrace,
We'll gently steal on his repose.

This is the bower—we'll softly tread—
He sleeps beneath yon poplar pale—
Lover, if e'er thy heart has bled,
Thy heart will far forego my tale !

Ellen is not in princely bower,
She's not in Moray's splendid train ;
Their mistress dear, at midnight hour,
Her weeping maidens seek in vain.

Her pillow swells not deep with down ;
For her no balms their sweets exhale :
Her limbs are on the pale turf thrown,
Press'd by her lovely cheek as pale :

On that fair cheek, that flowing hair,
The brown its yellow leaf hath shed,
And the chill mountain's early air
Blows wildly o'er her beauteous head.

As the soft star of orient day,
When clouds involve his rosy light,
Darts through the gloom a transient ray,
And leaves the world once more to night ;

Returning life illumes her eye,
And slow its languid orb unfolds—
What are those bloody arrows nigh ?
Sure, bloody arrows she beholds !

What was the form so ghastly pale,
That low beneath the poplar lay ?—
'Twas some poor youth—'Ah Nithisdale ! '
She said, and silent sunk away."

And her situation, when found by a friendly shepherd, who conveys her to his cottage, where she returns to life but not to reason, is finely described.

" 'O hide me in thy humble bower,'
Returning late to life, she said ;
'I'll bind thy crook with many a flower ;
With many a rosy wreath thy head.

'Good shepherd, haste to yonder grove,
And, if my love asleep is laid,
Oh! wake him not ; but softly move
Some pillow to that gentle head.

'Sure, thou wilt know him, gentle swain,
Thou know'st the sun rise o'er the sea—
But Oh! no lamb in all thy train
Was e'er so mild, so mild as he.

'His head is on the wood-moss laid ;
I did not wake his slumber deep—
Sweet sings the redbreast o'er the shade—
Why, gentle lady, would you weep?'

As flowers that fade in burning day,
At evening find the dew-drop dear,
But fiercer feel the noon-tide ray,
When soften'd by the nightly tear ;

Returning in the flowing tear,
This lovely flower, more sweet than they,
Found her fair soul, and wand'ring near,
The stranger, Reason, cross'd her way.

Found her fair soul —Ah! so to find
Was but more dreadful grief to know !
Ah? sure the privilege of mind
Cannot be worth the wish of woe!"

I will not quote more from Langhorne's poems. They are all
distinguished by the same tenderness of sentiment, luxuriance of
description, force of pathos, and harmony of numbers. I have
already quoted largely from this poet for two reasons. In the
first place the poems are of that character, which require more
than a general observation, and to be fully understood and admired
require to be particularised. It would be impossible to attempt a
comment upon a poet of this kind without quoting variously from
his works, which are in almost every case, opposite in subject and
character. The other reason arises from a desire to render Lang-
horne's works more popular amongst the general readers of poetry:
they have never yet obtained that place in the ranks of poetry,
which they fully and justly merit.

CHAPTER XXI.

GOLDSMITH.

GOLDSMITH.—In reading Goldsmith's. poems, we are able at
.ce to analyse the elements of his genius. They exhibit at every
int, a keen perfection and enjoyment of the surface beauties of
.ture ; an intuitive knowledge of the human heart ; and a power
instinct or common sense which supplies the lack of knowledge
ıd learning. Besides this, he possessed a fine healthy tone of
oral feeling ; an exquisite taste ; a mild but sincere enthusiasm
ıd a humour at once rich and delicate. Although not a profound,
)werful or subtle thinker, there lay in him a vein as exquisitely
ıtural and true, within its limits, as any writer ever possessed.
n imagination of the highest order—of that order, which con-
ructs great epics, swelters out deep tragedies, or soars up into
fty odes—this Goldsmith had not; but he had a fine fancy which
ımetimes, as in *The Traveller*, and portions of *The Deserted
'illage*, verges on the imaginative and produces short-lived bursts
ʿ grandeur. He had pathos too, of a very tender and touching
ınd. He opens up at times, a vein of quiet, serious reflection,
hich, if never profound is very pleasing and poetical. Best of all
a childlike simplicity, which, wherever it is found in an author,
ːrves to cover a multitude of sins, but which, in Goldsmith, co-
ːists with manly sense, acute appreciation of character, and refined
ıtive genius.

His *Traveller* is a poem in the style of Pope —less finely finished
an *his* masterpieces, but warmed by a finer poetic enthusiasm,
ıd abounding in those slight successful touches, which best exhibit
e artist's hand. He takes you with him in every step of his tour, you

"Run the great circle, and are still at home."

And the moral that he draws from the whole, if not strictly cor-
ct, is ideally beautiful. The opening of this poem is perhaps the
ost beautiful part.

"Remote, unfriended, melancholy, slow,
Or by the lazy Scheld, or wandering Po ;
Or onward, where the rude Carinthian boor

Against the houseless stranger shuts the door ;
Or where Campania's plain forsaking lies,
A weary waste expanding to the skies ;
Where'er I roam, whatever realms to see,
My heart untravell'd, fondly turns to thee   :
Still to my brother turns, with ceaseless pain,
And drags at each remove a lengthening chain.
 Eternal blessings crown my earliest friend,
And round his dwelling guardian saints attend ;
Blest be that spot, where cheerful guests retire
To pause from toil, and trim their evening fire :
Blest that abode, where want and pain repair,
And every stranger finds a ready chair :
Blest be those feasts with simple plenty crown'd,
Where all the ruddy family around
Laugh at the jests or pranks that never fail,
Or sigh with pity at some mournful tale ;
Or press the bashful stranger to his food,
And learn the luxury of doing good.
 But me, not destined such delights to share,
My prime of life in wandering spent and care :
Impell'd with steps unceasing to pursue
Some fleeting good, that mocks me with the view ;
That, like the circle bounding earth and skies,
Allures from far, yet, as I follow, flies ;
My fortune leads to traverse realms alone !
 E'en now, where Alpine solitudes ascend,
I sit me down a pensive hour to spend ;
And, placed on high above the storm's career,
Look downward where a hundred realms appear—
Lakes, forests, cities, plains extending wide,
The pomp of kings, the shepherd's humbler pride.
 When thus Creation's charms around combine,
Amidst the store should thankless pride repine ?
Say, should the philosophic mind disdain
That good which makes each humbler bosom vain ?
Let school-taught pride dissemble all it can,
These little things are great to little man ;
And wiser he, whose sympathetic mind
Exults in all the good of all mankind.
Ye glittering towns, with wealth and splendour crown d;
Ye fields, where summer spreads profusion round ;
Ye lakes, whose vessels catch the busy gale ;
Ye bending swains, that dress the flowery vale;
For me your tributary stores combine :
Creation's heir, the world, the world is mine !
 As some lone miser, visiting his store,
Bends at his treasure, counts, recounts it o'er ;
Hoards after hoards his rising raptures fill,
Yet still he sighs, for hoards are wanting still :

Thus to my breast alternate passions rise,
Pleased with each good that Heaven to man supplies:
Yet oft a sigh prevails, and sorrows fall,
To see the hoard of human bliss so small ;
And oft I wish, amidst the scene, to find
Some spot to real happiness consign'd,
Where my worn soul, each wandering hope at rest,
May gather bliss, to see my fellows blest.
  But, where to find that happiest spot below,
Who can direct, when all pretend to know ?
The shuddering tenant of the frigid zone
Baldly proclaims that happiest spot his own ;
Extols the treasures of his stormy seas,
And his long nights of revelry and ease ;
The naked negro, panting at the line,
Boasts of his golden sands and palmy wine,
Basks in the glare, or stems the tepid wave,
And thanks his gods for all the good they gave.
Such is the patriot's boast, where'er we roam,
His first, best country, ever is at home.
And yet, perhaps, if countries we compare,
And estimate the blessings which they share,
Though patriots flatter, still shall wisdom find
An equal portion dealt to all mankind ;
As different good, by Art and Nature given,
To different nations, makes their blessings even."

   *   *   *   *

"Thine, Freedom, thine the blessings pictured here,
Thine are those charms that dazzle and endear ;
Too blest, indeed, were such without alloy,
But foster'd e'en by Freedom, ills annoy ;
That independence Britons prize too high,
Keeps man from man, and breaks the social tie :
The self-dependant lordlings stand alone,
All claims that bind and sweeten life unknown.
Here, by the bonds of nature feebly held,
Minds combat minds, repelling and repell'd ;
Ferments arise, imprisoned factions roar,
Repress'd ambition struggles round her shore.
Till over-wrought, the general system feels
Its motions stop, or frenzy fire the wheels.
  Nor this the worst. As nature's ties decay,
As duty, love, and honour fail to sway,
Fictitious bonds, the bonds of wealth and law,
Still gather strength, and force unwilling awe.
Hence all obedience bows to these alone,
And talent sinks, and merit weeps unknown.
Till time may come, when, stripp'd of all her charms,
The land of scholars, and the nurse of arms,
Where noble stems transmit the patriot flame,
Where king's have toil'd, and poets wrote for fame,

One sink of level avarice shall lie,
And scholars. soldiers, kings, unhonour'd die.
　　Yet think not, thus when Freedom's ills I state,
I mean to flatter kings. or court the great.
Ye powers of truth, that bid my soul aspire,
Far from my bosom drive the low desire !
And thou, fair Freedom, taught alike to feel
The rabble's rage. and tyrant's angry steel ;
Thou transitory flower, alike undone
By proud contempt, or favour's fostering sun,
Still may thy blooms the changeful clime endure !
I only would repress them to secure ;
For just experience tells, in every soil,
That those who think must govern those that toil ;
And all that Freedom's highest aims can reach
Is but to lay proportioned loads on each.
Hence, should one order disproportioned grow,
Its double weight must ruin all below.
Oh then how blind to all that truth requires,
Who think it freedom when a part aspires l
Calm is my soul, nor apt to rise in arms,
Except when fast-approaching danger warms ;
But, when contending chiefs blockade the throne,
Contracting regal power to stretch their own.
When I behold a factious band agree
To call it freedom when themselves are free ;
Each wanton judge new penal statutes draw,
Laws grind the poor, and rich men rule the law ;
The wealth of climes, where savage nations roam,
Pillaged from slaves to purchase slaves at home ;
Fear, pity, justice, indignation start,
Tear off reserve, and bare my swelling heart ;
Till half a patriot, half a coward grown,
I fly from petty tyrants to the throne. "

In the *Deserted Village*, he chooses a less ambitious but a more
interesting field.　Like the chased hare, he flies back to his form—
his dear native village ; and the poem is just a daguerrotype of
Lishoy and its inhabitants—only so far coloured as memory colours
all the past with its own poetic lines.

"Sweet Auburn ! loveliest village of the plain,
Where health and plenty cheered the labouring swain,
Where smiling spring its earliest visit paid,
And parting summer's lingering blooms delayed :
Dear lovely bowers of innocence and ease,
Seats of my youth, when every sport could please,
How often have I loitered o'er thy green,
Where humble happiness endeared each scene !
How often have I paused on every charm,
The sheltered cot, the cultivated farm,

The never-failing brook, the busy mill,
The decent church that topt the neighbouring hill,
The hawthorn bush, with seats beneath the shade,
For talking age and whispering lovers made !
How often I have blessed the coming day,
When toil remitting lent its turn to play,
And all the village train, from labour free,
Led up their sports beneath the spreading tree,
While many a pastime circled in the shade,
The young contending as the old surveyed ;
And many a gambol frolicked o'er the ground,
And sleights of art and feats of strength went round :
And still, as each repeated pleasure tired
Succeeding sports the mirthful band inspired ;
The dancing pair that simply sought renown
By holding out to tire each other down ;
The swain mistrustless of his smutted face,
While secret laughter tittered round the place ;
The bashful virgin's sidelong looks of love,
The matron's glance that would those looks reprove.
These were thy charms, sweet village ! sports like these,
With sweet succession, taught even toil to please;
These round thy bowers their cheerful influence shed;
These were thy charms—but all these charms are fled."

Then follows the charming description of the melodies of Evening,
which as a descriptive passage of its kind is almost unsurpassed.

"Sweet was the sound, when oft, at evening's close
Up yonder hill the village murmur rose;
There as I passed with careless steps and slow,
The mingling notes came softened from below ;
The swain responsive as the milk-maid sung,
The sober herd that lowed to meet their young ;
The noisy geese that gabbled o'er the pool,
The playful children just let loose from school;
To watch-dog's voice that bay'd the whispering wind,
And the loud laugh that spoke the vacant mind ;
These all in sweet confusion sought the shade,
And filled each pause the nightingale had made.
But now the sounds of population fail,
No cheerful murmurs fluctuate in the gale,
No busy steps the grass-grown footway tread,
For all the blooming flush of life is fled.
All but yon widowed, solitary thing,
That feebly bends beside the plushy spring ;
She, wretched matron—forced in age, for bread,
To strip the brook with mantling cresses spread,
To pick her wintry fagot from the thorn,
To seek her nightly shed, and weep till morn—
She only left of all the harmless train,
The sad historian of the pensive plain !' "

He has applied the same powers of delicate, minute, and rapid painting in *Retaliation,* to living men ; and Plutarch, as a character painter, is a dauber to Goldsmith, nor has even Reynolds excelled these little sketches, where the artist not only draws the literal features, but gives at once the inner soul, and the future history of his subjects.   The characters of Garrick and Burke have never been equalled.

> "Here lies David Garrick, describe him who can,
> An abridgement of all that was pleasant in man ;
> As an actor, confess'd without rival to shine ;
> As a wit, if not first, in the very first line :
> Yet, with talents like these, of an excellent heart,
> The man had his failings—a dupe in his art.
> Like an ill-judged beauty, his colours he spread,
> And beplaster'd with rouge his own natural red.
> On the stage he was natural, simple, affecting ;
> 'Twas only that when he was off, he was acting
> With no reason on earth to go out of his way,
> He turn'd and he varied full ten times a day ;
> Though secure of our hearts, yet confoundedly sick,
> If they were not his own by finessing and trick :
> He cast off his friends, as a huntsman his pack ;
> For he knew, when he pleased, he could whistle them back.
> Of praise a mere glutton, he swallow'd what came,
> And the puff of a dunce, he mistook it for fame ;
> Till his relish grown callous, almost to disease,
> Who pepper'd the highest was surest to please,
> But let us be candid, and speak out our mind :
> If dunces applauded, he paid them in kind."

*   *   *   *

> " Here lies honest Richard, whose fate I must sigh at,
> Alas ! that such frolic should now be so quiet !
> What spirits were his ! what wit and what whim !
> Now breaking a jest, now breaking a limb !
> Now wrangling and grumbling to keep up the ball ;
> Now teasing and vexing, yet laughing at all.
> In short, so provoking a devil was Dick,
> We wish'd him full ten times a day at old Nick,
> But missing his mirth and agreeable vein,
> As often we wish'd Dick back again."

Of his plays I will say little.   In the *Good Natured Man* the comic element predominates, but in *She Stoops to Conquer,* the farcical.   They have produced more mirth than any other two plays out of Shakespeare—in the whole drama.   But they have no poetry, or pretensions to poetry in them.   The Epilogue of the atter is excellently written.

> "As puffing quacks some caitiff wretch procure
> To swear the pill, or drop, has wrought a cure
> Thus on the stage, our play-nights still depend,
> For Epilogues and Prologues on some friend,
> Who knows each art of coaxing up the town,
> And makes full many a bitter pill go down.
> Conscious of this, our bard has gone about,
> And teased each rhyming friend to help him out.
> 'An Epilogue things can't go on without it ;
> It could not fail, would you but set about it.'
> 'Young man,' cries one (A bard laid up in clover)
> Alas ! young man, my writing days are over ;
> Let boys play tricks, and kick the straw, not I ;
> Your brother Doctor there, perhaps may try.'—
> 'What, I, dear sir ?' the doctor interposes ;
> 'What, plant my thistle sir, among his roses !
> No no ; I've other contests to maintain ;
> To-night I heard our troops at Warwick Lane,
> Go, ask your manager.'—'Who, me ? your pardon ;
> Those things are not our forte at Covent Garden.'
> Our author's friends, thus placed at happy distance
> Give him good words indeed, but no assistance.
> As some unhappy wight, at some new play,
> At the pit-door stands elbowing away,
> While oft with many a smile and many a shrug,
> He eyes the centre, where his friends sit snug ;
> His simpering friends, with pleasure in their eyes,
> Sink as he sinks, and as he rises rise :
> He nods, they nod ; he cringes, they grimace ;
> But not a soul will budge to give him place.
> Since then, unhelp'd, our bard must now conform
> To 'bide the pelting of this pitiless storm ;
> Blame where you must, be candid where you can,
> And be each critic the Good-natured Man.
> Well, having stoop'd to conquer, with success,
> And gain'd a husband without aid from dress ;
> Still as a barmaid, I could wish it too,
> As I have conquer'd him, to conquer you :
> And, let me say, for all your resolution,
> That pretty barmaids have done execution.
> Our life is all a play, composed to please,
> 'We have our exits and our entrances.'
> The First Act shows the simple country maid,
> Harmless and young, of everything afraid ;
> Blushes when hired, and with unmeaning action,
> *I hopes as how to give you satisfaction.*
> Her Second Act displays a lovelier scene,—
> Th' unblushing barmaid of a country inn,
> Who whisks about the house, at market caters,

Talks loud, coquets the guests, and scolds the waiters.
Next, the scene shifts to town, and there she soars,
The chop-house toast of ogling connoisseurs.
On squires and cits she there displays her arts,
And on the gridiron broils her lover's heart—
And as she smiles, her triumphs to complete,
Even common-council men forget to eat.
The Fourth Act shows her wedded to the Squire,
And madam now begins to hold it higher,
Pretends to taste, at operas cries *Caro,*
And quits her Nancy Dawson for *Che Faro*
Doats upon dancing, and in all her pride.
Swims round the room, the *Heniel* of Cheapside :
Ogles and leers with artificial skill,
Till having lost in age the power to kill,
She sits all night at cards, and ogles at spadille.
Such, through our lives, th' eventful history—
The Fifth and Last Act still remains for me.
The barmaid now for your protection prays,
Turns female barrister, and pleads for boys. "

Goldsmith's *Hermit,* and his other small pieces are very dew-
drops of loveliness and simplicity "from the womb of the morning."
The former will ever be read with delight.

" 'Turn, gentle Hermit of the dale,
      And guide my lonely way,
   To where yon taper cheers the vale
      With hospitable ray.

'For here forlorn and lost I tread
   With fainting steps and slow;
Where wilds, immeasurably spread,
   Seem lengthening as I go,

'Forbear my son,' the Hermit cries,
   'To tempt the dangerous gloom ;
For yonder faithless phantom flies
   To lure thee to thy doom.

Here, to the houseless child of want
   My door is open still ;
And though my portion is but scant,
   I give it with good will.

'Then turn to-night, and freely share
   Whate'er my cell bestows ;
My rushy couch and frugal fare,
   My blessing and repose.

'No flocks that range the valley free
   To slaughter I condemn ;
Taught by that power that pities me,
   I learn to pity them :

'But from the mountain's grassy side
  A guiltless feast I bring,
A scrip with herbs and fruits supplied,
  And water from the spring.

'Then, pilgrim, turn, thy cares forego :
  All earth-born cares are wrong ;
Man wants but little here below,
  Nor wants that little long.'

Soft as the dew from heaven descends,
  His gentle accents fell ;
The modest stranger lowly bends,
  And follows to the cell.

Far, in a wilderness obscure
  The lonely mansion lay ;
A refuge to the neighbouring poor
  And strangers led astray.

No stores beneath its humble thatch
  Required a master's care ;
The wicket opening with a latch,
  Received the harmless pair.

And now, when busy crowds retire
  To take their evening rest,
The Hermit trimm'd his little fire
  And cheer'd his pensive guest.

And spread his vegetable store,
  And gaily press'd and smiled,
And, skill'd in legendary lore,
  The lingering hours beguiled.

Around in sympathetic mirth
  Its tricks the kitten tries ;
The cricket chirrups in the hearth :
  The crackling fagot flies.

But nothing could a charm impart,
  To soothe the stranger's woe ;
For grief was heavy at his heart,
  And tears began to flow.

His rising cares the Hermit spied,
  With answering care opprest :
And, 'Whence unhappy youth,' he cried,
  'The sorrows of thy breast ?'

'From better habitations spurn'd
  Reluctant dost thou rove ?
Or grieve for friendship unreturn'd,
  Or unregarded love ?

'Alas the joys that fortune brings
  Are trifling, and decay ;

A shade that follows wealth or fame,
   And leaves the wretch to weep ?

'And love is still an emptier sound,
   The modern fair one's jest ;
On earth unseen, or only found,
   To warm the turtle's nest.

'For shame, fond youth ! thy sorrows hush,
   And spurn the sex,' he said :
But, while he spoke, a rising blush
   His love-lorn guest betray'd:

Surpris'd he sees new beauties rise,
   Swift mantling to the view,
Like colours o'er the morning skies,
   As bright, as transient too.

The bashful look, the rising breast,
   Alternate spread alarms :
The lovely stranger stands confess'd
   A maid in all her charms.

And 'Ah ! forgive a stranger rude,
   A wretch forlorn' she cried ;
'Whose feet unhallow'd thus intrude,
   Where heaven and you reside.

'But let a maid thy pity share,
   Whom love has taught to stray ;
Who seeks for rest, but finds despair
   Companion of her way.

'My father lived beside the Tyne,
   A wealthy lord was he ;
And all his wealth was mark'd as mine,
   He had but only me.

'To win me from his tender arms
   Unnumber'd suitors came ;
Who praised me for imputed charms,
   And felt or feigned a flame.

'Each hour a mercenary crowd,
   With richest proffers strove ;
Among the rest, young Edwin bow'd,
   But never talk'd of love.

In humblest, simplest habit clad,
   No wealth nor power had he ;
Wisdom and worth were all he had,
   But these were all to me.

'And when, beside me in the dale
  He carolled lays of love:
His breath lent fragrance to the gale,
  And music to the grove.

'The blossom of opening to the day,
  The dew of heaven refined,
Could nought of purity display
  To emulate his mind.

'The dew, the blossom on the tree,
  With charms in constant shines:
Their charms were his; but woe to me,
  Their constancy was mine.

'For still I tried each fickle art,
  Importunate and vain ;
And while his passion touched my heart,
  I triumphed in his pain.

'Till quite dejected with my scorn,
  He left me to my pride ;
And sought a solitude forlorn
  In secret, where he died.

'But mine the sorrow, mine the fault,
  And well my life shall pay ;
I'll seek the solitude he sought,
  And stretch me where he lay.

  'And there forlorn, despairing, hid,
  I'll lay me down and die ;
' Twas so for me that Edwin did,
  And so for him will I.'

'Forbid it, Heaven ! ' the Hermit cried,
  And clasp'd her to his breast ;
The wondering fair one turn'd to chide—
  'Twas Edwin's self that prest !

'Turn, Angelina ever dear—
  My charmer, turn to see
Thy own, thy long-lost Edwin here ;
  Restored to love and thee.

'Thus let me hold thee to my heart,
  And every care resign ;
And shall we never, never part,
  My life—my all that's mine?

'No never; from this hour to part,
  We'll live and love so true ;
The sigh that rends thy constant heart
  Shall break thy Edwin's too.' "

ndoubtedly, Goldsmith's *Traveller* and *Deserted Village*, are
of the finest smaller poems, in the poetry of the world.

CHAPTER XXII.

COLLINS.

COLLINS.—"Genius," it is said by a writer, " is not only a mystery in itself, but equally mysterious in the manner in which it distributes its favours and scatters its fire. Truly may it be compared to that 'wind which bloweth where it listeth.' Now it rests on the coroneted brow of a peer ; and now it finds its votary at the plough. Now its wisdom dwells with prudence in the counting-house or bank; and now it serves to gild, without glorifying, the excesses and the haunts of vulgar debauchery and riot. Now it stands with a holy Herbert in the pulpit ; and now recoils from men, and mouths high heaven, with a Byron plunging into his 'Wilderness of Sin.' Now it sits serene in the blind eyes of a Milton, alone in his obscure chamber, and meditating times to come ; and now it pines away in the dull madness of a Collins, or serves to exasperate his misery, as, in a wilder mood he runs, howling like a dog, through the aisles of Chichester Cathedral. Verily it is a fearful gift ; and if all men say, 'we are fearfully and wonderfully made,' men of genius may say it with a far deeper emphasis, and often with a more melancholy meaning."*

This beautiful passage very fitly precedes a sketch of Collins' life by the same writer. There is something very pitiful in this poet's career; projecting, but never carrying into execution; perhaps through poverty, or for want of resolution and energy of character. Like Coleridge, he spent his life in elaborating gigantic prospectuses to works which were never written ; piling up portals to palaces, that were never built. Collins, instead of working in the studies of London only dreamed along its streets. He was eminently delighted with those flights of imagination which pass the bounds of nature; he loved fairies, genii, giants, and monsters, he delighted to rove through the meanders of enchantment, to gaze on the magnificence of golden palaces, to repose by the Elysian waterfalls. "While men saw him gazing, with lack-lustre eye at the streets and parks, river and St. Pauls," says another writer, "his mind was in

---

* Rev. Geo. Gilfillan.

ty straying through cities, where all the inhabitants were mag-
y stiffened into stone; chasing ghouls through the halls of Eblis;
:cting variation in Aladdin's palace, swimming the Euphrates,
oking down' with Mirza from the high hills of Bagdad ; upon
'ast tide rolling on towards the cloud-girt ocean of Eternity."
vas a dreamer in a city—and the dreams of the desert are not
:ep or so wonderful as those which insulate the imaginative in
:entre of crushing crowds.

it dreams cannot support the body, however gorgeous and
cal, and here it is that we sympathise with Collins; for he soon
1 that dreaming was a vague, a poor, and a very miserable
1ess ; and that in the strong line of Byron,

"Of such materials wretched men are made."

e are told that his immortal Odes, after many vain endeavours
.roduce them to the public, were wholly unsuccessful, and that
.infortunate author in proud humility and indigent despair,
. the unsold copies with his own hands. The blaze which
consumed these Odes, seems to us as significant as it was
ge and melancholy ; and it casts a light upon many things.
ee by its glare the "keen eyes, and brown complexion" of
1oet, suffused with pale and silent rage, and that "frown of
5e and habitual thought," which sat upon his brow, darkened
. deeper shade, as his hot and tremulous hands, are hastily
1ing into the fire the memorials of early genius and baffled
ion; a proud tear standing in his eye, and a proud sigh
ing his lips, as he says, "If they are only worthy of the
.ion they have met with, they shall not, at least, live to
.ce my memory."

s poet's genius was of that highly imaginative order, which
more with abstractions than with human forms or feelings.

"First Fear his hand, its skill to try,
    Amid the chords bewilder'd laid,
And back recoil'd, he knew not why,
    Even at the sound himself had made.
Next Anger rush'd ; his eyes on fire,
    In lightnings own'd his secret stings :
In one rude clash he struck the lyre,
    And swept with hurried hand the strings.
With woful measures wan Despair—
    Low sullen sounds his grief beguil'd ;
A solemn, strange, and mingled air ;
    'Twas sad by fits, by starts 'twas wild.
But thou, O Hope, with eyes so fair,
    What was thy delightful measure?
Still it whisper'd promised pleasure,
    And bade the lovely scenes at distance hail !
Still would her touch the strain prolong,
    And from the rocks. the woods, the vale,
She call'd on Echo still through all the song,
    And where her sweetest theme she chose
A soft responsive voice was heard at every close,
And Hope enchanted smil'd, and wav'd her golden hair.
    And longer had she sung,—but with a frown,
        Revenge impatient rose :
He threw his blood-stain'd sword in thunder down,
        And, with a withering look,
    The war-denouncing trumpet took,
And blew a blast so loud and dread,
Were ne'er prophetic sounds so full of woe !
        And ever and anon he beat
        The doubling drum with furious heat ;
    And though sometimes, each dreary pause between,
        Dejected Pity at his side,
        Her soul subduing voice applied,
    Yet still he kept his wild unalter'd mien.
While each strain'd ball of sight seem'd bursting from his h
Thy numbers, Jealousy, to nought were fix'd ;
    Sad proof of thy distressful state,
Of differing themes the veering song was mix'd;
    And now it courted Love, now raving call'd on Hate.
With eyes upraised, as one inspired,
Pale Melancholy sat retired :
And from her wild sequester'd seat,
In notes by distance made more sweet,
Pour'd through the mellow horn her pensive soul :
    And dashing soft from rocks around,
    Bubbling runnels join'd the sound ;
Through glades and glooms the mingled measure stole,

> Or, o'er some haunted stream, with fond delay,
>   Round a holy calm diffusing,
>   Love of peace, and lonely musing,
> In hollow murmurs died away.
> But O how alter'd was its sprightlier tone !
> When Cheerfulness, a nymph of healthiest hue,
>   Her bow across her shoulder flung,
>   Her buskins gemm'd with morning dew,
> Blew an inspiring air, that dale and thicket rung.
>   The hunter's call, to Faun and Dryad known !
>   The oak-crown'd sisters, and their chaste-eyed queen.
>   Satyrs and sylvan boys were seen,
>   Peeping from forth their alleys green :
> Brown Exercise rejoic'd to hear,
>   And Sport leapt up and seiz'd his beechen spear.
> Last came Joy's ecstatic trial :
> He, with viny crown advancing,
>   First to the lively pipe his hand address ;
> But soon he saw the brisk awakening viol,
> Whose sweet entrancing voice he loved the best ;
>   They would have thought, who heard the strain,
>   They saw in Tempe's vale, her native maids,
>   Amid the festal sounding shades,
> To some unwearied minstrel dancing,
>   While, as his flying fingers kiss'd the strings,
>   Love framed with Mirth a gay fantastic round :
>   Loose were her tresses seen, her zone unbound ;
>   And he, amidst his frolic play,
> As if he would the charming air repay,
> Shook thousand odours from his dewy wings. "

And yet, although he has so exquisitely described the Passions, the great want of his poetry *is* passion. His figures have in them the breath of genius, but little human interest. He excels, however, in lyrics, and the lyrical poet has little inclination to study the human heart, or to look abroad upon universality. He is wrapt in a dream of his own, and chained to his lyre. As a beautiful example of this, read the spirit and glowing dialogues of the *Gentle Shepherd.* His figures are less numerous than they are intense; he deals little in similes, but much in burning metaphor. His thought is not often subtle, but it is never shallow or common-place. His versification has in parts, a fine music, and more melodious cadence than any verse between Milton and Coleridge.

The three best compositions of Collins are the *Ode to Evening*, distinguished for its delicate personification and beautiful selection of poetical images : his *Ode to Liberty*, the most ambitious and perhaps the grandest of his strains—"dark, rugged, bold and soaring as the wing of the Eagle;" and his *Ode on the Superstitions of Scotland*—less poetical but more complete and interesting than any of his poems. For an example take the following, his *Ode to Liberty* —

> " Who shall wake the Spartan fife,
>   And call in solemn sounds to life,
>   The youths, whose locks divinely spreading,
>   Like vernal hyacinths in sullen hue,
>   At once the breath of fear, and virtue shedding,
>   Applauding Freedom lov'd of old to view?
>   What new Alcœus, fancy-blest,
>   Shall sing the sword in myrtles drest,
>   At Wisdom's shrine awhile its flame concealing,
>   (What place so fit to seal a deed renown'd?)
>   Till she her brightest lightnings round revealing,
>   It leap'd in glory forth, and dealt her prompted wound!
>   O Goddess, in that feeling hour,
>   When most its sounds would court thy ears,
>   Let not my shell's misguided power,
>   E'er draw thy sad, thy mindful tears.
> No Freedom, no, I will not tell,
> How Rome, before thy weeping face,
> With heaviest sound, a giant statue, fell,
> Push'd by a wild and artless race
> From off its wide ambitious base,
> When Time his northern sons of spoil awoke,
>   And all the blended work of strength and grace,
>   With many a rude repeated stroke,
> And many a barbarous yell, to thousand fragments broke."

There are many other very beautiful specimens of Collins' poetry, the choicest of which are perhaps the two following. The first, the *Dirge in Cymbeline*, is a tender and pathetic strain.

> "To fair Fidele's grassy tomb,
>   Soft maids and village hinds shall bring
>   Each opening sweet, of earliest bloom,
>   And rifle all the breathing Spring.
>
> No wailing ghost shall dare appear
>   To vex with shrieks this quiet grove,
>   But shepherd lads assemble here,
>   And melting virgins own their love.
>
> No wither'd witch shall here be seen,
>   No goblins lead their nightly crew ;
>   The female fays shall haunt the green,
>   And dress thy grave with pearly dew !

The redbreast oft at evening hours
   Shall kindly lend its little aid,
With hoary moss and gather'd flowers,
   To deck the ground where thou art laid.

When howling winds and beating rain,
   In tempest shake the sylvan cell ;
Or 'midst the chase on every plain,
   The tender thought on thee shall dwell.

Each lonely scene shall thee restore,
   For thee the tear be duly shed ;
Belov'd till life can charm no more,
   And mourn'd till Pity's self be dead."

The other, the *Ode to Pity* is delicate both in imagery and per-
sonification, and as interesting as any of his lyrical pieces.

"O Thou, the friend of man assign'd,
With balmy hands his wounds to bind,
   And charm his frantic woe :
When first Distress with dagger keen,
Broke forth to waste his destin'd scene,
   His wild unsated foe !

By Pella's Bard, a magic name,
By all the griefs his thought could frame,
   Receive my humble rite :
Long, Pity, let the nations view
Thy sky-worn robes of tenderest blue,
   And eyes of dewy light !

But wherefore need I wander wide
To old Ilissus' distant side,
   Deserted stream, and mute ?
Wild Arun too has heard thy strains,
And echo 'midst my native plains,
   Been sooth'd by Pity's lute.

There first the wren thy myrtles shed,
On gentlest Otway's infant head,
   To him thy cell was shown ;
And while he sung the female heart,
With Youth's soft notes unspoil'd by Art,
   Thy turtles mix'd their own.

Come, Pity, come, by Fancy's aid,
Ev'n now my thoughts, relenting maid,
   Thy temple's pride design ;
Its southern rite, its truth complete
Shall raise a wild enthusiast heat,
   In all who view the shrine.

There Picture's toil shall well relate,
How chance, or hard involving fate,
   O'er mortal bliss prevail ;

The buskin'd muse shall near her stand,
And sighing prompt her tender hand,
    With each disastrous tale.
There let me oft, retir'd by day,
In dreams of passion melt away,
    Allow'd with thee to dwell:
There waste the mournful lamp of night,
Till, Virgin, thou again delight
    To hear a British shell!"

CHAPTER XXIII.

GRAY.

GRAY.—Gray was perhaps one of the most learned men in Europe. There is seen in his works an equal acquaintance with both the elegant and profound parts of science. We learn moreover that he knew every branch of history, both natural and civil; that he had read all the original historians of England, France, and Italy; and was a great antiquarian; that criticism, metaphysics, morals and politics, made a principal part of his study, and travels of all kinds were his favorite amusements; and that he had a fine taste in painting, prints, architecture and gardening.*

Speaking of his poems, it may be said, that they all bear the stamp of true poetry. The most famous, are the *Elegy*, his *Ode on the Passions*, *The Progress of Poesy*, and *The Bard*. They are all more remarkable for art and elaboration, than for passion or genius. The *Elegy* has been perhaps the most popular poem in the English language. General Wolfe, when advancing to the brilliant action in which he fell, is said to have declared that he would rather have been the author of the Elegy than have the honour of taking Quebec. There is a 'melancholy grace,' to use his own expression, in the *Elegy*, which seems to give it greater excellence, and which no doubt resulted from its having been written shortly after the death of his friend Mr. West, upon whom also the following beautiful Sonnet was written.

* Mason's 'Life of Gray.'

ODE ON A DISTANT PROSPECT OF ETON COLLEGE.

Ye distant spires, ye antique towers,
  That crown the watery glade,
Where grateful Science still adores
  Her Henry's holy shade;
And ye, that from the stately brow
Of Windsor's heights the' expanse below
  Of grove, of lawn, of mead, survey,
Whose turf, whose shade, whose flowers among
Wanders the hoary Thames along
  His silver-winding way:
Ah, happy hills! ah pleasing shade!
  Ah fields belov'd in vain
Where once my careless childhood stray'd.
  A stranger yet to pain!
I feel the gales that from ye blow
A momentary bliss bestow,
  As waving fresh their gladsome wing,
My weary soul they seem to soothe,
And, redolent of joy and youth,
To breathe a second Spring.
Say, Father Thames (for thou hast seen
  Full many a sprightly race
Disporting on thy margent green,
  The paths of Pleasure trace),
Who foremost now delight to cleave,
With pliant arm, thy glassy wave?
  The captive linnet which enthral?

I P.

What idle progeny succeed
To chase the rolling circle's speed,
  Or urge the flying ball?
Whilst some, on earnest business bent,
  Their murmuring labours ply
'Gainst graver hours, that bring constraint
  To sweeten liberty :
Some bold adventures disdain
The limits of their little reign,
  And unknown regions dare descry :
Still as they run they look behind,
They hear a voice in every wind,
  And snatch a fearful joy.
Gay Hope is theirs, by Fancy fed,
  Less pleasing when possess'd.
The tear forgot as soon as shed,
  The sunshine of the breast :
Theirs buxom Health, of rosy hue,
Wild Wit, invention ever new,
  And lively cheer, of vigour born ;
The thoughtless day, the easy night,
The spirits pure, the slumbers light,
  That fly the' approach of morn.
Alas ! regardless of their doom,
  The little victims play ;
No sense have they of ills to come,
  No care beyond to-day :
Yet see, how all around them wait
The ministers of human fate,
  And black Misfortune's baleful train !
Ah, shew them where in ambush stand,
To seize their prey the murderous band !
  Ah ! tell them, they are men.
These shall the fury Passions tear,
  The vultures of the mind,
Disdainful Anger, Pallid Fear,
  And Shame that skulks behind ;
Of pining Love shall waste their youth,
Or Jealousy, with rankling tooth,
  That inly gnaws the secret heart;
And Envy wan, and faded Care.
Grim-visag'd comfortless Despair,
  And Sorrow's piercing dart.
Ambition this shall tempt to rise,
  Then hurl the wretch from high,
To bitter Scorn a sacrifice,
  And bitter Infamy.
The stings of Falsehood those shall try
And hard Unkindness' alter'd eye,
  That mocks the tear it forc'd to flow

And keen Remorse, with blood defiled,
And moody Madness laughing wild
   Amid severest woe.
Lo ! in the valley of years beneath,
A grisly troop are seen,
The painful family of Death,
   More hideous than their queen :
This racks the joints, this press the veins
That every labouring sinew strains:
   Those in the deeper vitals rage.
Lo ! Poverty, to fill the band,
That numbs the soul with icy hand,
   And slow--consuming Age.
To each his sufferings all are men,
   Condemn'd alike to groan ;
The tender for another's pain.
   The' unfeeling for his own.
Yet, ah ! why should they know their fate?
Since sorrow never comes too late,
   And happiness too swiftly flies?
Thought would destroy their paradise,
No more ;—where ignorance is bliss,
   'Tis folly to be wise. "

TO ADVERSITY.

"Daughter of Jove, relentless power,
   Though tamer of the human breast,
Whose iron scourge and torturing hour
   The bad affright, afflict the best !
Bound in thy adamantine chain,
The proud are taught to tasks of pain,
And purple tyrants vainly groan
With pangs unfelt before, unpitied and alone.

When first thy sire to send on earth
   Virtue, his darling child, design'd,
To thee he gave the heavenly birth,
   And bade to form her infant mind.
Stern rugged nurse ! thy rigid lore
With patience many a year she bore :
What sorrow was, thou bad'st her know,
And from her own she learn'd to melt as others' woe,

Scared at thy frown terrific, fly
   Self-pleasing Folly's idle brood,
Wild Laughter, Noise, and thoughtless Joy,
   And leave us leisure to be good.
Light they disperse, and with them go
The summer friend, the flattering foe ;
By vain Prosperity received,
To her they vow their truth, and are again believed.

Wisdom in sable garb array'd
  Immersed in rapturous thought profound,
And Melancholy, silent maid,
  With leaden eye that loves the ground,
Still on thy solemn steps attend:
Warm Charity, the general friend,
With Justice, to herself severe,
And Pity, dropping soft the sadly pleasing tear.

Oh! gently on thy suppliant's head,
  Dread goddess, lay thy chastening hand!
Not in thy Gorgon terrors clad,
  Not circled with the vengeful band,
(As by the impious thou art seen);
With thundering voice, and threatening mien,
With screaming Horror's funeral cry,
Despair, and fell Disease, and ghastly Poverty.

The form benign, oh goddess, wear,
  Thy milder influence impart,
Thy philosophic train be there
  To soften, not to wound my heart.
The generous spark extinct revive,
Teach me to love, and to forgive,
Exact my own defects to scan,
What others are to feel, and know myself a **Man**."

The *Ode on the Progress of Poesy* is very highly finished, and describes the power and influence of poetry, as well as its progress, with all the accuracy of metaphysical precision. The opening is exquisitely conceived.

"AWAKE, Æolian lyre, awake,
And give to rapture all thy trembling strings,
From Helicon's harmonies springs
  A thousand rills their mazy progress take
The laughing flowers, that round them blow,
Drink life and fragrance as they flow.
Now the rich stream of music winds along,
Deep, majestic, smooth, and strong,
Through verdant vales, and Ceres' golden reign;
Now rolling down the steep amain,
Headlong. impetuous, see it pour:
The rocks and nodding groves rebellow to the roar."

And the third stanza is a master-piece of rhythm; it charms the ear by its well-varied cadence, as much as the imagery which it contains ravishes the fancy.

" Thee the voice, the dance, obey.
Temper'd to thy warbled lay.

O'er her warm cheek, and rising bosom, move
The bloom of young Desire aud purple light of Love."

The lines which follow the words

"Glance their many twinkling feet."

ɪre sweetly introduced by the short and unequal measures which ʼrecede them. What is gone before dwells upon the ear, and insensibly harmonises with the present line.

Another splendid specimen of Gray's poems, are those fine imita-ʼions of Norse and Welsh poetry, *The descent of Odin, &c.* They ɪre executed with fire and at the same time with judgment, while ɪe has kept up through them all the wild romantic spirit of his ʼriginals. The two best are *The descent of Odin,* and *The triumph ʼf Owen.*

"Owen's praise demands my song,
Owen swift, aud Owen strong;
Fairest flower of Rhoderic's stem.
Gwyneth's shield, aud Britain's gem,
He nor heaps his brooded stores
Nor on all profusely pours ;
Lord of every regal art,
Liberal hand and open heart.
 Big with hosts of mighty name,
Squadrons three against him came ;
This the force of Eiren hiding,
Side by side as proudly riding,
On her shadow long and gay
Locklin ploughs the watery way,
There the Norman sails afar
Catch the winds and join the war
Black and huge along they sweep,
Burdens of the angry deep;
 Dauntless on his native sands

"Uprose the king of men with speed,
And saddled straight his coal black steed:
Down the yawning steep he rode,
That leads to Hela's dread abode.
Him the dog of darkness spied ;
His shaggy throat he open'd wide,
While from his jaws, with carnage filled,
Foam and human gore distill'd :
Hoarse he bays with hideous din,
Eyes that glow, and fangs that grin ;
And long pursues, with fruitless yell,
The father of the powerful spell.
Onward still his way he takes
(The groaning earth beneath him shakes),
Till full before his fearless eyes
The portals nine of hell arise.
 Right against the eastern gate,
By the moss-grown pile he sate ;
Where long of yore to sleep was laid
The dust of the prophetic maid.
Facing to the northern clime,
Thrice he traced the Runic rhyme ;
Thrice pronounced, in accents dread,
The thrilling verse that wakes the dead :
Till from out the hollow ground
Slowly breathe sullen sound."

Prophetess.—What call unknown, what charms presume
　　To break the quiet of the tomb?
　　Who thus afflicts my troubled sprite,
　　And drags me from the realms of night?
　　Long on these mould'ring bones have beat
　　The winter's snow, the summers heat,
　　The drenching dews, and driving rain!
　　Let me, let me sleep again.
　　Who is he, with voice unblest,
　　That calls me from the bed of rest?
Odin.—A traveller, to thee unknown,
　　Is he that calls, a warrior's son,
　　Thou the deeds of light shall know;
　　Tell me what is done below,
　　For whom yon glittering board is spread,
　　Drest for whom yon golden bed?
Prophetess.—Mantling in the goblet see
　　The pure bev'rage of the bee:
　　O'er it hangs the shield of gold;
　　'Tis the drink of Balder bold:
　　Balder's head to death is giv'n.
　　Pain can reach the Sons of Heav'n!
　　Unwilling I my lips unclose:
　　Leave me, leave me to repose.
Odin.—Once again my call obey,
　　Prophetess, arise, and say,
　　What dangers Odin's Child await,
　　Who the Author of his fate.
Prophetess.—In Hoder's hand the Hero's doom;
　　Brother sends him to the tomb,
　　Now my weary lips I close;
　　Leave me, leave me to repose.
Odin.—Prophetess, my spell obey,
　　. Once again arise, and say　•
　　Who the' Avenger of his guilt
　　By whom shall Hoder's blood be spilt?
Prophetess.—In the caverns of the west,
　　By Odin's fierce embrace comprest,
　　A wond'rous Boy shall Rinda bear,
　　Who ne'er shall comb his raven-hair,
　　Nor wash his visage in the stream,
　　Nor see the sun's departing beam,
　　Till he on Hoder's corpse shall smile
　　Flaming on the funeral pile.
　　Now my weary lips I close:
　　Leave me, leave me to repose.
Odin.—Yet awhile my call obey;
　　Prophetess, awake, and say,
　　What Virgins these, in speechless woe,
　　That bend to earth their solemn brow,

That their flaxen tresses tear,
And snowy veils that float in air?
Tell me whence their sorrows rose ;
Then I leave thee to repose.
Prophetess.—Ha ! no traveller art thou,
King of men, I know thee now
Mightiest of a mighty line———
Odin.—No bodin maid of skill divine
Art thou, nor prophetess of good ;
But mother of the giant brood l
Prophetess.—Hie the hence. and boast at home,
That never shall inquirer come
To break my iron sleep again,
Till Lok has burst his tenfold chain
Never, till substantial night
Has reasumed her ancient right ;
Till wrapp'd in flames, in ruin hurl'd,
Sinks the fabric of the world. "

CHAPTER XXIII.

COWPER.

COWPER.—There is perhaps no poet more securely fixed in the affections of his countrymen than Cowper. Many people who pride themselves on their indifference to poetry in general, and consider all time thus spent is time lost, make an exception in his case, and take a pleasure in reading his verse, as genuine as it is rare. Yet Cowper's poems are not of that description which affect or call for our sympathies, although we cannot hold back our admiration and respect for his works, full, as they are, of pure and grave religious sentiment. It is this for which Cowper's works have so considerable a popularity. Whatever English society in itself may be, it has a decided bias in favour of religious literature, and heartily admires those authors who are serious, moral, or pious, or who even write as if they were. It does not demand or desire mystics or transcendalists, like France or Germany, but writers of clear biblical views, strong practical convictions, and hearty in their

written more forcibly or pungently against the foibles, faults
vices of his countrymen. He denounces the slave trade, gin-
ting, fox-hunting, balls, theatres, card-playing, church-hireling,
luxurious habits of the rich, the rude vices of the poor, the
igacy of cities, the swagger, the swearing, and the drunkenness
ldiers—quite in the style of an eloquent platform-lecturer; and
eels as if the proper conclusions to his poetic perorations on
: topics was "loud applause." The religious world found in
per a powerful ally, and prized him accordingly. He had just
uch poetry, wit, humour and sentiment as fitted him to illus-
without veiling in doubtful haze the truths of christianity.
e is nothing fantastic, *outre,* or heretical about him ; all is as
)dox as a sermon. Before his day England had produced no
: poet whose piety was of a popular kind, for Milton—the only
ing instance to the contrary—was too grandly imaginative,
ichly adorned with classic learning, and too scanty in his di-
c precepts, to be sincerely appreciated by the mass. Cowper
pied a far lower level, but he was for that reason much nearer
s readers, who could understand him as easily as they did their
ymen on Sundays. Another element of attractiveness in Cow-
is the intensely *English* character of his genius. It was no mere
le of patriotic feeling that made him write the following strain.

"England, with all thy faults, I love thee still—
My country ! and, while yet a nook is left
Where English minds and manners may be found,
Shall be constrain'd to love thee. Though thy clime
Be fickle, and thy year, most part deform'd
With dripping rains, or wither'd by a frost,
I would not exchange thy sullen skies,
And fields without a flower, for warmer France
With all her vines ; nor for Ansonia's groves
Of golden fruitage, and her myrtle bowers.
To shake thy senate, and from heights sublime
Of patriot eloquence to flash down fire

Upon thy foes, was never meant my task ;
But I feel can thy fortunes, and partake
Thy joys and sorrows, with as true a heart
As any thunderer there. "

There have been many English poets who have entertained a
deeper, passionate, and more tender sentiment for their native land
than Cowper was capable of ; but there is naturally something so
broadly humane in the genius of poetry, that even where the
themes are purely local, a cosmopolitan spirit breathes out, that
makes the whole world kin, as in the songs of Robert Burns.
Cowper, however, has nothing of this ; he is exclusively national.
Except in occasional political and philanthropical allusions, he
does not seem conscious that there is a world of living beings, with
other ideas and aims than his, beyond the English Channel. One
is keenly conscious of a certain insularity of tone in his writings.
and can readily comprehend why he is not, and never will be,
much cared for on the Continent. Yet this very insularity is one
of his charms for English readers, and in those moods when we
are weary of speculation and subtle fancies, and seek for some-
thing more simple and clear, there are few finer pleasures than
listening to the quiet stream-like murmur of his muse as it passes
from object to object and from scene to scene. *The Task* reveals
unmistakably the entire nature of the poet, showing him essentially
to be a sound and vigorous thinker, playful as well as truthful,
warm in his social no less than in his religious feelings, and as
sarcastic as any city wit.

His principal poems are *The Progress of Error*, *Truth*, *Table
Talk*, *Expostulation and The Task*. They are all conceived in a
gravely religious and ethical spirit, but abound in couplets and
passages of singular felicity, where something of the strength of
Dryden is combined with more of the keenness of Pope. In them
he has censured the social and moral abuses of the time, with a
sharpness of wit, and sternness of invective hardly to be expected
from a timid recluse like Cowper. Sometimes, however, the verses
are marked by a kind of serious extravagance of sentiment, yet the

. . . . was the least successful and obtained the least
popularity at the time of its publication. The success it afterwards
received, is, in fact, accounted for less in the real merit of the poem,
than in the circumstances under which it was written, and the
condition of English poetry at that period. In a brief sketch of
Cowper's life, which is attached to one of the later editions of his
poems, the author* accounts for the success of the *Task* in the
following remarks. "Never was the muse so silent as in the last
twenty or thirty years of the eighteenth century. Pope had been
long dead, and he had left no genuine successors ; Collins and
Gray were also dead ; and though both were possessed of an
exquisitely pure genius, and may be pronounced the finest poetic
artists of their age, the subjects of their verse were not calculated
to awaken much interest in ordinary readers ; Goldsmith had
written too little, and even that little, however sweet and natural,
was not decisively enough original to constitute him a reformer ;
Robert Burns indeed was alive, but his first volume did not appear
until the following year, and even if it had been contemporary with
The Task, the dialect in which he wrote unintelligible to English-
men ; and south of the Border, in spite of his extraordinary powers,
he would have been, at the time, as uninfluential for good or
evil as the obscurest back in Grub Street ; the rest of Cowpers po-
tic contemporaries were utterly ignoble, and even their names
have for the most part passed out of human remembrance. Thus
he had the field entirely to himself. Of course this was not alto-
gether an advantage. The absence of a supply in such a case
argues the absence of a demand. Poets do not come to us by
accident ; they spring up in answer to the deep desires of a people
and if they are not found at a particular period, it is because they
are not then wanted. The temper of the age, so to speak, was
not poetical. A singular dullness had crept over the national mind

J. M. Ross.

or at least over the national sensibilities. The Church was dead
asleep, and Wesley's vehement evangelization was only a rough
attempt to rouse her from her slumbers. In the country it was the
golden age of squirearchy. The peasantry were submissive and
stupid; the country-gentlemen, kindly, homely, and honest, as
they have always been, but immersed in rural pleasures, and in
many instances nearly as illiterate as the swains themselves. The
town (*i.e.*, London) was intolerably gay, and its dissipation unre-
lieved, as at present, by the counteracting influences of a wide-
spread art and science. The French Revolution had to come
before the hearts of men could be set on fire again and poetry
deepen into a passion." This passage well sets forth the difficulties
to which Cowper was subject, and account accurately for the non-
success of this beautiful poem; his readers not being in a condition
to vividly sympathise. There is another way however in which to
interpret this, without, in the slightest manner, suggesting any
detriment in Cowper's works, which are, in their style, true and
fine specimens of his peculiar genius. His peculiarity lay in this,
that he did not make any powerful demand on the sympathies of
the public. His thoughts were neither mystical nor profound; they
were not even subtle or warmly poetical. Seldom indeed has so
genuine a poet possessed so poor an imagination. He was as far
as possible from realizing his own description of the poet :—

> "A terrible sagacity informs
> The poet's heart; he looks to distant storms;
> He hears the thunder ere the tempest lowers;
> And arm'd with strength surpassing human powers,
> Seizes events as yet unknown to man,
> And darts his soul into the dawning plan."

In point of *imaginative* genius, Collin's *Ode to the Passions*,
though small in compass, far transcends everything that Cowper
wrote. Nature, whether animate or inanimate, revealed nothing to
him that it did not reveal to the humblest of his readers. The
plainness, even the *hardness*, of his landscape and figure painting,
is astonishing. Let any one study, for instance, in the *Winter
Morning Walk*, in the Fifth Book of *The Task*, the poet's descrip-

tion of his own appearance as he moves across "the dazzling deluge" of hardened snow.

> " 'Tis morning ; and the sun, with ruddy orb
> Ascending, fires the horizon : while the clouds
> That crowd away before the driving wind,
> More ardent as the disk emerges more,
> Resemble most some city in a blaze,
> Seen through the leafless wood.   His slanting ray
> Slides ineffectual down the snowy vale,
> And, tinging all with his own rosy hue,
> From every herb and every spiry blade
> Stretches a length of shadow o'er the field.
> Mine, spindling into longitude immense,
> In spite of gravity, and sage remark
> That I myself am but a fleeting shade,
> Provokes me to a smile.   With eye askance
> I view the muscular proportion'd limb
> Transform'd to a lean shank.   The shapeless pair
> As they design'd to mock me, at my side
> Take step for step ; and as I near approach
> The cottage, walk along the plaster'd wall,
> Preposterous sight ! the legs without the man.
> The verdure of the plain lies buried deep
> Beneath the dazzling deluge."

Or again the more minute and elaborate picture of the woodman.

> "————————leaving unconcern'd
> The cheerful haunts of man ; to wield the axe
> And drive the wedge in yonder forest drear,
> From morn to eve his solitary task.
> Shaggy, and lean, and shrewd, with pointed ears
> And tail cropp'd short, half lurcher and half cur,
> His dog attends him.   Close behind his heel
> Now creeps him slow ; and now, with many a frisk
> Wide scampering, snatches up the drifted snow
> With ivory teeth, or ploughs it with his snout ;
> Then shakes his powder'd coat, and barks for joy.
> Heedless of all his pranks, the sturdy churl
> Moves right towards the mark ; nor stops for aught,
> But now and then with pressure of his thumb
> To adjust the fragrant charge of a short tube
> That fumes beneath his nose : the trailing cloud
> Streams far behind him, scenting all the air.
> Now from the roost, or from the neighbouring pale,
> Where, diligent to catch the first fair gleam
> Of smiling day, they gossip'd side by side,
> Come trooping at the housewife's well-known call
> The feather'd tribes domestic."

and he will at once admit the truth of our observation.   It must not be forgotten, however, that there may be found in his works

many descriptions of a truly artistic kind, which would **almost**
vie in conception and language with any of Dryden or Pope. **Take**
for example the following, in the sixth book :—

> "The night was winter in its roughest mood,
> The morning sharp and clear. But now at noon
> Upon the southern side of the slant hills,
> And where the woods fence off the northern blast,
> The season smiles, resigning all its rage,
> And has the warmth of May. The vault is blue
> Without a cloud, and white without a speck
> The dazzling splendour of the scene below.
> Again the harmony comes o'er the vale,
> And through the trees I view the embattled tower
> Whence all the music. I again perceive
> The soothing influence of the wafted strains,
> And settle in soft musings as I tread
> The walk still verdant, under oak and elm,
> Whose outspread branches overarch the glade.
> The roof though movable through all its length
> As the wind sways it, has yet well sufficed,
> And intercepting in their silent fall
> The frequent flakes has kept a path for me.
> No noise is here, or none that hinders thought.
> The redbreast warbles still, but is content
> With slender notes and more than half suppress'd ;
> Pleased with his solitude, and flitt'ing light
> From spray to spray, where'er he rests he shakes
> From many a twig the pendent drops of ice,
> That tinkle in the wither'd leaves below.
> Stillness, accompanied with sounds so soft,
> Charms more than silence."

Or the beautiful passages that immediately follows it, in which
we get as it were, a catalogue of flowers :—

> "——— ——It sleeps ; and the icy touch
> Of unprolific winter has impress'd
> A cold stagnation on the intestine tide.
> But let the months go round, a few short months,
> And all shall be restored. These naked shoots,
> Barren as lances, among which the wind
> Makes wintry music, sighing as it goes,
> Shall put their graceful foliage on again,
> And more aspiring, and with ampler spread,
> Shall boast new charms, and more than they have lost.
> Then, each in its peculiar honours clad,
> Shall publish, even to the distant eye,
> Its family and tribe. Laburnum rich
> In streaming gold ; syringa ivory pure ;
> The scentless and the scented rose, this red

Her blossoms ; and luxuriant above all
The jasmine, throwing wide her elegant sweets,
The deep dark green of whose unvarnish'd leaf
Makes more conspicuous, and illumines more
The bright profusion of her scatter'd stars.
These have been, and these shall be in their day ;
And all this uniform, uncolour'd scene
Shall be dismantled of its fleecy load,
And flash into variety again."

There is a total absense in this poet nevertheless, of those fine
analogies between the outer world of appearances and the inner
world of thought, the perception of which invests the former with a
most mysterious beauty, and thrills the soul with an exquisite joy.
The light that never was on sea or shore," does not once play
upon his page. Even the ordinary simile, with which every poet is
wont at intervals to decorate his verse, is wanting. But again on the
other hand, there is a quiet unaffected love of common English scen-
ry, of green fields and river's banks, of woodlands and leafy lanes
f domestic scenes and fireside joys in this poem, that every-body
could appreciate and relish without supposing himself sentimental.
For instance, what could be more truthfully and yet elegantly writ-
ten in this style than the following two or three passages : —

"O Winter ! ruler of the inverted year,
Thy scatter'd hair with sleet like ashes fill'd,

Thy breath congeal'd upon thy lips, thy cheeks
Fringed with a beard made white with other snows
Than those af age, thy forehead wrapp'd in clouds,
A leafless branch thy sceptre, and thy throne
A sliding car, indebted to no wheels,
But urged by storms along its slippery way,
I love thee, all unlovely as thou seem'st,
And dreaded as thou art. Thou hold'st the sun
A prisoner in the yet undawning east,
Shortening his journey between morn and noon,
And hurrying him, impatient of his stay,
Down to the rosy west ; but kindly still
Compensating his loss with added hours
Of social converse and instructive ease,
And gathering, at short notice, in one group
The family dispersed, and fixing thought,
Not less dispersed by daylight and its cares,
I crown thee King of intimate delight,
Fireside enjoyments, homeborn happiness,
And all the comforts that the lowly roof
Of undisturb'd retirement, and the hours
Of long uninterrupted evening know.
No rattling wheels stop short before these gates ;
No powder'd pert proficient in the art
Of sounding an alarm, assaults these doors
Till the street rings ; no stationary steeds
Cough their own knell, while, heedless of the sound,
The silent circle fan themselves, and quake :
But here the needle plies its busy task,   .
The pattern grows, the well-depicted flower,
Wrought patiently into the snowy lawn,
Unfolds its bosom ; buds, and leaves, and sprigs,
And curling tendrils, gracefully disposed,
Follow the nimble finger of the fair ;
A wreath that cannot fade, of flowers that blow
With most success when all besides decay."

        *   *   *

"I saw the woods and fields at close of day
A variegated show ; the meadows green,
Though faded ; and the lands, where lately waved
The golden harvest of a mellow brown,
Upturn'd so lately by the forceful share ;
I saw far off the weedy fallows smile
With verdure not unprofitable, grazed
By flocks, fast feeding, and selecting each
His favourite herb ; while all the leafless groves
That skirt the horizon, wore a sable hue.
Scarce noticed in the kindred dusk of eve.
To-morrow brings a change, a total change !
Which even now, though silently perform'd

"————————The spring and playtime of the year,
That calls the unwonted villager abroad
With all her little ones, a sportive train,
To gather kingcups in the yellow mead,
And prink their air with daises, or to pick
A cheap but wholesome salad from the brook,
These shades are all my own.   The timorous hare,
Grown so familiar with her frequent guest,
Scarce shuns me ; and the stockdove unalarm'd,
Sits cooing in the pine tree, nor suspends
His long love-ditty for my near approach.
Drawn from his refuge in some lonely elm,
That age or injury has hollow'd deep,
Where, on his bed of wool and matted leaves,
He has outslept the winter, ventures forth
To frisk a while, and bask in the warm sun,
The squirrel, flippant, pert, and full of play:
He sees me, and at once, swift as a bird,
Ascends the neighbouring beech, there whisks his brush,
And perks his ears, and stamps and scolds aloud,
With all the prettiness of cries alarm,
And anger insignificantly fierce. "

The diction in this poem also, is clear, picturesque and nervous
at we cannot deny its charms.   It is the complete opposite of the
nid splendour of Thomson's style.   There is also something very
:ractive in its versification.   It is perfect in originality, and pos-
sses a wonderful flexibility, pitched for the most part in a kind of
ick-changing conversational tone, but rising often into a noble
ergy, especially at the close of an animated passage, in a line of
arp rising strength, the sound of which rings long on the ear.
e are bound to admire *The Task* not only for the freshness and
althiness of Cowper's feeling for nature, his strong love of in-
or comfort and happiness, and his power of facile rhythm; but
the true religious spirit that pervades it.   Nothing can be more
nest or written with greater truth and gravity than the passage

in which he describes with simple dignity the genuine preacher, and reproves the trifler or jester in religious offices. We see in the stirring and beautiful language which he has employed, a truly grave and religious spirit.

"The pulpit, therefore (and I name it filled
With solemn awe, that bids me well beware
With what intent I touch that holy thing)—
The pulpit (when the satirist has at last,
Strutting and vapouring in an empty school,
Spent all his force, and made no proselyte)—
I say the pulpit (in the sober use
Of its legitimate, peculiar powers)
Must stand acknowledged, while the world shall stand,
The most important and effectual guard,
Support, and ornament of virtue's cause.
There stands the messenger of truth : there stands
The legate of the skies !—His theme 'divine,
His office sacred, his credentials clear.
By him the violated law speaks out
Its thunders ; and by him, in strains as sweet
As angels use, the Gospel whispers peace.
He 'stablishes the strong, restores the weak,
Reclaims the wanderer, binds the broken heart,
And, armed himself in panoply complete
Of heavenly temper, furnishes with arms
Bright as his own, and trains, by every rule
Of holy discipline, to glorious war,
The sacramental host of God's elect !
Are all such teachers ?—would to heaven all were !
But hark—the doctor's voice !—fast wedged between
Two empires he stands, and with swoll'n cheeks
Inspires the news, his trumpet. Keener far
Than all invective is his bold harangue,
While through that public organ of report
He hails the clergy ; and, defying shame,
Announces to the world his own and theirs l
He teaches those to read, whom schools dismiss'd,
And colleges, untaught ; sells accents, tone,
And emphasis in score, and gives to prayer
The adagio and andante it demands.
He grinds divinity of other days
Down into modern use ; transforms old print
To zigzag manuscript, and cheats the eyes
Of gallery critics by a thousand arts.
Are there who purchase of the doctor's ware ?
Oh. name it not in Gath !—it cannot be
That grave and learned clerks should need such aid,
He doubtless is in sport and does but droll,
Assuming thus a rank unknown before—
Grand caterer and dry nurse of the church !

Coincident, exhibit lucid proof
That he is honest in the sacred cause;
To such I render more than mere respect,
Whose actions say that they respect themselves,
But loose in morals, and in manners vain,
In conversation frivolous, in dress
Extreme, at once rapacious and profuse;
Frequent in parks with lady at his side,
Ambling and prattling scandal as he goes;
But rare at home, and never at his books,
Or with his pen, save when he scrawls a card;
Constant at routs, familiar with a round
Of ladyships—a stranger to the poor;
Ambitious of preferment for its gold,
And well prepared, by ignorance and sloth,
By infidelity and love of world,
To make God's work a sinecure; a slave
To his own pleasures and his patron's pride:
From such apostles, O ye mitred head
Preserve the church! and lay not careless hands
On skulls that cannot teach, and will not learn,
 Would I describe a preacher, such as Paul,
Were he on earth, would hear, approve, and own—
Paul should himself direct me. I would trace
His masters strokes, and draw from his design.
I would express him simple, grave, sincere;
In doctrine uncorrupt; in language plain,
And plain in manner; decent, solemn, chaste,
And natural in gesture; much impress'd
Himself, as conscious of his awful charge,
And anxious mainly that the flock he feeds
May feel it too; affectionate in look,
And tender in address, as well becomes
A messenger of grace to guilty men."

nd then he continues by lashing with satiric scorn,

 "The things that mount the rostrum with a skip,
And then skip down again; pronounce a text;
Cry—hem; and reading what they never wrote,
Just fifteen minutes, huddle up their work,
And with a well-bred whisper close the scene!
 In man or woman, but far most in man,
And most of all in man that ministers
And serves the altar, in my soul I loathe
My affectation. 'Tis my perfect scorn,
Object of my implacable disgust.
 What! will a man play tricks? will he indulge
A silly fond conceit of his fair form,
And just proportion, fashionable mien,

A pretty face, in presence of his God?
Or will he seek to dazzle me with ropes,
As with the diamond on his lily hand,
And play his brilliant parts before my eyes,
When I am hungry for the bread of life?
He mocks his maker, prostitutes and shames
His noble office, and, instead of truth,
Displaying his own beauty, starves his flock!
Therefore, avaunt all attitude, and stare,
And start theatric practised at the glass!
I seek divine simplicity in him
Who handles things divine; and all besides,
Though learned with labour, and though much admired
By curious eyes and judgments ill inform'd,
To me is odious as the nasal twang
Heard at conventicle, where worthy men,
Misled by custom, strain celestial themes
Through the press'd nostril, spectacle-bestrid.
Some, decent in demeanour while they preach,
Their task perform'd, relapse into themselves;
And, having spoken wisely, at the close
Grow wanton, and give proof to every eye,
Whoe'er was edified, themselves were not!
Forth comes the pocket mirror,—First we stroke
An eyebrow; next compose a straggling lock,
Then with an air most gracefully perform'd
Fall back into our seat, extend an arm,
And lay it at its ease with gentle care,
With hankerchief in hand depending low:
The better hand more busy gives the nose
Its bergamot, or aids the indebted eye
With opera-glass to watch the moving scene,
And recognise the slow retiring fair.
Now this is fulsome, and offends me more
Than in a Churchman slovenly neglect
And rustic coarseness would. A heavenly mind
May be indifferent to her house of clay,
And slight the hovel as beneath her care;
But how a body so fantastic, trim,
And quaint in its deportment and attire,
Can lodge a heavenly mind—demands a doubt.
  He that negotiates between God and man,
As God's ambassador, the grand concerns
Of judgment and of mercy, should beware
Of lightness in his speech. 'Tis pitiful
To court a grin, when you should woo a soul;
To break a jest, when pity would inspire
Pathetic exhortation; and to address
The skittish fancy with facetious tales,
When sent with God's commission to the heart!
So did not Paul. Direct me to a quip

"O for a lodge in some vast wilderness,
Some boundless contiguity of shade,
Where rumour of oppression and deceit,
Of unsuccessful or successful war,
Might never reach me more ! My ear is pain'd,
My soul is sick, with every day's report
Of wrong and outrage with which earth is fill'd.
There is no flesh in man's obdurate heart,
It does not feel for man ; the natural bond
Of brotherhood is sever'd as the flax
That falls asunder at the touch of fire.
He finds his fellow guilty of a skin
Not colour'd like his own ; and, having power
To enforce the wrong, for such a worthy cause
Dooms and devotes him as his lawful prey.
Lands intersected by a narrow frith
Abhor each other.   Mountains interposed
Make enemies of nations, who had else
Like kindred drops been mingled into one.
Thus man devotes his brother, and destroys :
And, worse than all, and most to be deplored,
As human nature's broadest, foulest blot,
Chains him, and tasks him, and exacts his sweat
With stripes, that Mercy, with a bleeding heart,
Weeps when she sees inflicted on a beast.
Then what is man ? And what man, seeing this,
And having human feelings, does not blush
And hang his head, to think himself a man ;
I would not have a slave to till my ground,
To carry me, to fan me while I sleep,
And tremble when I wake, for all the wealth
That sinews bought and sold have ever earn'd.
No : dear as freedom is, and in my heart's
Just estimation prized above all price.
I had much rather be myself the slave,
And wear the bonds, than fasten them on him.
We have no slaves at home :—then why abroad ?

> And they themselves, once ferried o'er the wave
> That parts us, are emancipate and loosed.
> Slaves cannot breathe in England; if their lungs
> Receive our air, that moment they are free;
> They touch our country, and their shackles fall.
> That's noble, and bespeaks a nation proud
> And jealous of the blessing. Spread it then,
> And let it circulate through every vein
> Of all your empire; that where Britain's power
> Is felt, mankind may feel her mercy too."

Cowper's Hymns—sixty-eight in number are remarkably beautiful. Some of them. "O for a closer walk with God," "Hear what God the Lord hath spoken," "Far from the world, O Lord, I flee." and his last, "God moves in a mysterious way," deservedly rank among the first in the English language:

> "God moves in a mysterious way
>   His wonders to perform;
> He plants his footsteps in the sea,
>   And rides upon the storm.
>
> Deep in unfathomable mines
>   Of never-failing skill,
> He treasures up his bright designs,
>   And works his sovereign will.
>
> Ye fearful saints, fresh courage take
>   The clouds ye so much dread
> Are big with mercy, and shall break
>   In blessings on your head.
>
> Judge not the Lord by feeble sense,
>   But trust him for his grace:
> Behind a frowning providence
>   He hides a smiling face.
>
> His purposes will ripen fast,
>   Unfolding every hour;
> The bud may have a bitter taste,
>   But sweet will be the flower.
>
> Blind unbelief is sure to err,
>   And scan his work in vain:
> God is his own interpreter,
>   And he will make it plain."

His little poem *To Mary* is a miracle of sweet, pathetic tenderness, but Cowper could only write so feelingly when his heart was strongly moved. We may see in these verses, the deep and sorrow-laden affection which swelled the poet's bosom, written while watching her life slowly settling down into night.

My Mary!

Thy spirits have a fainter flow
I see thee daily weaker grow
'Twas my distress that brought thee low,
My Mary!

Thy needles, once a shining store,
For my sake restless heretofore,
Now rust disused, and shine no more;
My Mary!

For, though thou gladly wouldst fulfil
The same kind office for me still,
Thy sight now seconds not thy will,
My Mary!

But well thou play'dst the housewife's part,
And all thy threads with magic art
Have wound themselves about this heart.
My Mary!

Thy indistinct expression seem
Like language utter'd in a dream :
Yet me they charm, whate'er the theme,
My Mary!

Thy silver locks, once auburn bright,
Are still more lovely in my sight
Than golden beams of orient light,
My Mary!

For, could I view nor them nor thee,
What sight worth seeing could I see ?
The sun would rise in vain for me,
My Mary!

Partakers of thy sad decline,
Thy hands their little force resign ;
Yet gently press'd, press gently mine,
My Mary

Such feebleness of limbs thou provest,
That now at every step thou movest
Upheld by two ; yet still thou lovest,
My Mary!

And still to love, though press'd with ill,
In wintry age to feel no chill,
With me is to be lovely still,
My Mary!

But ah ! by constant heed I know,
How oft the sadness that I show

Transforms thy smiles to looks of woe,
　　　　　　My Mary!
And should my future lot be cast
With much resemblance of the past,
Thy worn-out heart will break at last,
　　　　　　My Mary!"

The *Lines on receipt of his Mother's picture,* exhibit in the same manner as the previous poem, the force of his mind and imagination; and the beautiful exclamation with which it opens, reflects the whole beauty of the poem itself.

"O that those lips had language! Life had pass'd
With me but roughly since I heard thee last.
Those lips are thine—thy own sweet smile I see,
The same that oft in childhood solaced me ;
Voice only fails, else how distinct they say,
'Grieve not, my child, chase all thy fears away!'
The meek intelligence of those dear eyes
(Blest be the art that can imortalize,
The art that baffles Time's tyrannic claim
To quench it) here shines on me still the same,
Faithful remembrance of one so dear,
O welcome guest, though unexpected here :
Who bidst me honour with an artless song,
Affectionate, a mother lost so long.
I will obey, not willingly alone,
But gladly, as the precept were her own :
And, while that face renews my filial grief,
Fancy shall weave a charm for my relief,
Shall steep me in Elysian reverie,
A momentary dream, that thou art she.
　　My Mother! when I learn'd that thou wast dead,
Say, wast thou conscious of the tears I shed?
Hover'd thy spirit o'er thy sorrowing son,
Wretch even then, life's journey just begun?
Perhaps thou gavest me, though unfelt, a kiss ;
Perhaps a tear, if souls can weep in bliss—
Ah, that maternal smile! it answers—Yes.
I heard the bell toll'd on thy burial day,
I saw the hearse that bore thee slow away,
And turning from my nursery window, drew
A long, long sigh, and wept a last adieu!
But was it such?—It was.—Where thou art gone,
Adiens and farewells are a sound unknown.
May I but meet thee on that peaceful shore,
The parting word shall pass my lips no more!
Thy maidens, grieved themselves at my concern,
Oft gave me promise of thy quick return.
What ardently I wish'd, I long believed,
And, disappointed still, was still deceived.

"Toll for the brave !
  The brave that are no more ;
All sunk beneath the wave,
  Fast by their native shore !

Eight hundred of the brave,
  Whose courage well was tried,
Had made the vessel heel,
  And laid her on her side.

A land-breeze shook the shrouds,
  And she was over-set ;
Down went the Royal George,
  With all her crew complete.

Toll for the brave !
  Brave Kempenfelt is gone ;
His last sea-fight is fought ;
  His work of glory done.

It was not in the battle ;
  No tempest gave the shock ;
She sprang no fatal leak ;
  She ran upon no rock.

His sword was in its sheath ;
  His fingers held the pen.
When Kempenfelt went down
  With twice four hundred men.

Weigh the vessel up,
  Once dreaded by our foes !
And mingle with our cup
  The tears that England owes.

Her timbers yet are sound,
  And she may float again,
Full charged with England's thunder,
  And plough the distant main.

But Kempenfelt is gone,
  His victories are o'er ;
And he and his eight hundred
  Shall plough the wave no more."

Cowper's poems were the genuine utterance of his own heart ; and the manly thought, vigour and simplicity; their mingled humour and pathos; the variety and felicity of their descriptions of men and things; and the elevated strain of Christian sentiment by which they are pervaded, have secured their popularity while our language endures.

CHAPTER XXV.

CRABBE.

CRABBE.—Very few poets have a stronger claim to popularity than Crabbe, for all he wrote had good for its basis. No mysticism, no extravagant misleading theories, or unintelligible flights of imagination disfigure his manly verse ; it is truth clothed in sense, and uttered in an impressive style, that fixes it in the memory of the reader. He is said to be a "stern painter," but his pictures of the class that formed the objects of his writings are not such as to create antagonism between them, and other classes ; he can, as in his "Noble Peasant," draw attractive pictures of the poor, as well as sketches to claim pity for their state.*

Crabbe was a poet of great and original genius ; indeed there is no poet of ancient or modern times more original, in point of subject, language, imagery or sentiment. Created by circumstances the poet of the poor, Crabbe has given us pictures faithful as Hogarth's, without the painter's biting satire ; they are stern as Churchill's, without the poets malignant venom. His Annals of the Poor, are revealments of man's life, which author's love not to make, or readers to contemplate; they are the hard reality of too large a section of our race, for even the philanthropist to hope greatly to ameliorate. When Burns or Bloomfield seek to interest us in humble life, we have the *Cotter's Saturday Night,* or the *Fair Day,* to warm us into good and kindly feeling; but Crabbe grapples with every-day miseries, with keen want and bitter thought. "To th'e reader who would study human nature in a degraded sphere, he' is an anatomist who unshrinkingly tears away the skin and the flesh, and reveals the muscles, arteries and inward organs in all their bare repulsive truthfulness." And in this lies his power and beauty, but beyond this Crabbe is nothing. He possessed none of the high-wrought feeling or powerful imagination which creates for its possessor a world independent of that which surrounds him; he was insensible to music, he saw no attractiveness in painting or architecture, and still more strange, took no delight in beautiful scenery. "He resembled in all these deficiences," says a writer of his life, "Johnson, Mackintosh, and other great men ;" but then they were not what he was—he was essentially a poet. The only great object of nature that appeared to strike him was the SEA. There is a passage in his *Richard* which exemplifies this fact :—

> "———————————I to the ocean gave
> My mind and thoughts as restless as the wave.
> Where crowds assembled I was sure to run,
> Hear what was said, and muse on what was done.
> To me the wives of seamen loved to tell
> What storms endanger'd men esteem'd so well ;
> No ships were wreck'd upon that fatal beach
> But I could give the luckless tale of each.
> In fact, I lived for many an idle year
> In fond pursuit of agitations dear :
> For ever seeking, ever pleased to find
> The food I sought, I thought not of its kind.
> I loved to walk where none had walk'd before,
> About the rocks that ran along the shore ;
> Or far beyond the sight of men to stray,
> And take my pleasure when I lost my way :
> For then 'twas mine to trace the hilly heath,
> And all the mossy moor that lies beneath.
> Here had I favourite stations, where I stood
> And heard the murmurs of the ocean-flood,
> With not a sound beside, except when flew
> Aloft the lapwing, or the grey curlew . . ,
> When I no more my fancy could employ—
> I left in haste what I could not enjoy,
> And was my gentle mother's welcome boy."

It is the truthfulness of Crabbe's pictures that had stamped him as a man of genius, and given him an enduring fame. Yet no poetry has less ornament than his ; sometimes indeed, it is mean and prosaic, but it always maintains its influence by its truthfulness. To lovers of sense and reason in poetry, such men as Crabbe, Cowper and Goldsmith stands first. They do not plunge into wild metaphysical theories, or produce illusion that dazzle for the moment ; they deal in realities only ; and in this peculiarity stand distinctly eminent.

Crabbe's want of imagination, may perhaps be accounted for by the ungenial situation in which his early days were spent—a gloomy sombre marshy coast, with nothing but the sea to give birth to the least romantic feeling. In his *Life,* written by his son it is described as, "a poor, wretched place ; lying between a low hill or cliff, on which the church and a few better houses were then situated, and the beach of the German Ocean. It consisted of two parellel and unpaved streets, running between mean and scrambling houses, the abodes of sea-faring men, pilots and fishers. The range of houses nearest the sea had suffered so much from repeated invasions of the waves, that only a few scattered tenements remained erect among the desolation." Nor was the landscape in the vicinity of a more engaging aspect—"open commons and sterile farms, the soil poor and sandy, the herbage bare and rushy, the trees, 'few and far between,' and withered and stunted by the bleak breezes of the sea." What situation could be less likely to create or feed the imagination than this ? There can be little doubt that the prosaic part of his character, and that insensibility to nature's beauties which he always evinced, was the effect of early impressions. "The characters he met with in early life," says his son, "were unsophisticated and rough ; masculine and robust frames, rude manners, stormy passions, laborious days, and occasionally boisterous nights of merriment—among such accompaniments was born and bred the Poet of the Poor." We get a beautiful copy in *The Village* from this scene of his nativity and boyish days :—

> "———Cast by Fortune on a frowning coast,
> Which either groves nor happy valleys boast ;
> Where other cares than those the Muse relates,
> And other shepherds dwell with other mates :

By such examples taught, I paint the cot,
As Truth will paint it and as bards will not :
Nor you, ye poor, of letter'd scorn complain,
To you the smoothest song is smooth in vain ;
O'ercome by labour, and bow'd down by time,
Feel you the barren flattery of a rhyme ?
Can poets soothe you, when you pine for bread,
By winding myrtles round your ruin'd shed ?
Can their light tales your weighty griefs o'erpower,
Or glad with airy mirth the toilsome hour ?
　　Lo ! where the heath, with withering brake grown o'er
Lends the light turf that warms the neighb'ring poor;
From thence a length of burning sand appears,
Where the thin harvest waves its wither'd ears ;
Rank weeds, that every art and care defy,
Reign o'er the land and rob the blighted rye :
There thistles stretch their prickly arms afar,
And to the ragged infant threaten war ;
There poppies nodding, mock the hope of toil ;
There the blue bugloss paints the sterile soil ;
Hardy and high, above the slender sheaf,
The slimy mallow waves her silky leaf ;
O'er the young shoot the charlock throws a shade,
And clasping tares cling round the sickly blade ;
With mingled tints the rocky coasts abound
And a sad splendour vainly shines around ;
So looks the nymph whom wretched arts adorn,
Betray'd by man, then left for man to scorn ;
Whose cheek in vain assumes the mimic rose,
While her sad eyes the troubled breast disclose;
Whose outward splendour is but folly's dress,
Exposing most when most it gilds distress. "

He goes on then to describe the common people of Aldborough
with the same truth and interest.　He speaks of them as :—

"————————a wild amphibious race,
Who, far from civil arts and social fly,
And scowl at strangers with suspicious eye. "

Then follows in the same poem the beautiful passage, in which
he expresses the gloomy feelings he felt on quitting his native
place, a specimen of pure and true poetry.

"Here, wand'ring long, amid these frowning fields,
I sought the simple life that Nature yields ;
Rapine and Wrong, and Fear usurp'd her place,
And a bold, artful, surly, savage race ;
Who, only skill'd to take the finny tribe,
The yearly dinner, or septennial bride,
Wait on the shore, and, as the waves run high,

On the toss'd vessel bend their eager eye ;
Which to their coasts directs its vent'rous way,
Theii s, or the ocean's miserable prey.
    As on their neighbouring beach yon swallows stand,
And wait for favouring winds to leave the land ;
While still for flight the ready wing is spread
So waited I the favouring hour, and fled ;
Fled from these shores were guilt and famine reign,
And cried, Ah ! hapless they who still remain ;
Who still remain to hear the ocean roar,
Whose greedy waves devour the lessening shore ;
Till some fierce tide, with more imperious sway,
Sweeps the low hut and all it holds away ;
When the sad tenant weeps from door to door,
And begs a poor protection from the poor l"

Crabbe was a studier of Pope, and both *The Village* and *The Library* his earliest poems, are mainly formed on this model. Though they were his earliest however and do not exhibit that rare union of force and minuteness for which his later works are so distinguished, yet in themselves they are complete and faultless, and show frequently traces of his own extraordinary peculiarity. The description of the Parish Workhouse in *The Village* is the best example of this.

"Behold yon house that holds the parish poor,
Whose walls of mud scarce bear the broken door ;
There, where the putrid vapours, flagging, play,
And the dull wheel hums doleful through the day ;—
There children dwell who know no parents' care ;
Parents, who know no children's love, dwell there !
Heart-broken matrons on their joyless bed,
Forsaken wives, and mothers never wed ;
Dejected widows with unheeded tears,
And crippled age with more than childhood fears ;
The lame, the blind, and—far the happiest they—
The moping idiot and the madman gay !
Here, too, the sick their final doom receive,
Here brought, amid the scenes of grief to grieve,
Where the loud groans from some sad chamber flow
Mix'd with the clamours of the crowd below ;
Here sorrowing, they each kindred sorrow scan,
And the cold charities of man to man :
Whose laws indeed for ruin'd age provide,
And strong compulsion plucks the scrap from pride ;
But still that scrap is bought with many a sigh,
And pride embitters what it can't deny.
Say ye, oppress'd by some fantastic woes,

> Some jarring nerve that baffles your repose;
> Who press the downy couch, while slaves advance
> With timid eye, to read the distant glance;
> Who with sad pray'rs the weary doctor tease
> To name the nameless ever-new disease;
> Who with mock patience dire complaints endure,
> Which real pain, and that alone, can cure;
> How would you bear in real pain to lie,
> Despis'd, neglected, left alone to die?
> How would you bear to draw your latest breath
> Where all that's wretched paves the way for death?
> Such is that room which one rude beam divides,
> And naked rafters form the sloping sides;
> Where the vile bands that bind the thatch are seen,
> And lath and mud are all that lie between;
> Save one dull pane, that, coarsely patch'd, gives way
> To the rude tempest, yet excludes the day:
> Here, on a matted flock, with dust o'er spread,
> The drooping wretch reclines his languid head,
> For him no hand the cordial cup applies,
> Or wipes the tear that stagnates in his eyes;
> No friends with soft discourse his pain beguile,
> Or promise hope till sickness wears a smile."

In point of real merit, the *Parish Register* far exceeds either of the two former poems. They contain certainly a few minute and excellent descriptions, but this poem is a succession of these descriptions; it forms a chain of stories, whereas the former contains no tale whatever, "they are didactic—whereas in this, no moral influence, is directly inculcated at all." In this poem the manner of expression is as entirely his own as the singular minuteness of his delineation, and the strictness of his adherence to the literal truth of nature. Amongst the descriptive passages in this poem, the following is admirably drawn. The description of the interior of the cottage.

> "Behold the cot, where thrives th' industrious swain,
> Source of his pride, his pleasure, and his gain;
> Screen'd from the winter's wind, the sun's last ray
> Smiles on the window and prolongs the day;
> Projecting thatch the woodbine's branches stop,
> And turns their blossoms to the casement's top;
> All needs require is in that cot contain'd,
> And much that Taste, untaught and unrestrain'd,
> Surveys delighted; there she loves to trace,
> In one gay picture, all the royal race;
> Around the walls are heroes, lovers, kings;

The print that shows them and the verse that sings.
· Here the last Louis on his throne is seen,
And there he stands imprison'd, and his queen ;
To these the mother takes her child and shows
What grateful duty to his God he owes ;
Who gives to him a happy home, where he
Lives and enjoys his freedom with the free ;
When kings and queens, dethroned, insulted, tried,
Are all these blessings of the poor denied.
There is King Charles, with all his golden rules,
Who proved misfortune was the best of schools :
And there his sons, who, tried by years of pain,
Proved that misfortunes may be sent in vain.
 The magic mill that grinds the gran'nams young.
Close at the side of kind Godiva hung ;
She, of her favourite place the pride and joy,
Of charms at once most lavish and most coy,
By wanton act the poorest fame could raise,
And give the boldest deed the chastest praise.
 There stands the stoutest ox in England fed,
There fights the boldest Jew Whitechapel bred ;
And here Saint Monday's worthy votaries live,
In all the joys that ale and skittles give.
 Now, lo ! on Egypt's coast that hostile fleet,
By nations dreaded, and by Nelson beat ;
And here shall soon another triumph come,
A deed of glory in a day of gloom ;
Distressing glory ! grievous boon of fate !
The proudest conquest at the dearest rate.
 On shelf of deal beside the cuckoo clock,
Of cottage reading rests the chosen stock ;
Learning we lack, not books, but have a kind
For all our wants, a meat for every mind.
The tale for wonder and the joke for whim,
The half-sung sermon and the half-groan'd hymn.
No need of classing, each within its place,
The feeling finger in the dark can trace ;
'First from the corner, farthest from the wall ;'
Such all the rules, and they suffice for all.
There pious works for Sunday's use are found ;
Companions of that Bible newly bound ;
That Bible, bought by sixpence weekly saved,
Has choicest prints by famous hands engraved ;
Has choicest notes by many a famous head,
Such as to doubt have rustic readers led ;
Have made them stop to reason *why ?* and *how ?*
And, where they once agreed, to cavil now.
Oh ! rather give me commentators plain,
Who with no deep researches vex the brain ;
Who from the dark and doubtful love to run,
And hold their glimmering tapers to the sun ;

Who simple truth with ninefold reasons back,
And guard the point no enemies attack.
    Bunyan's famed Pilgrim rests that shelf upon ;—
A genius rare but rude was honest John ;
Not one who, early by the muse beguiled,
Drank from her well the waters undefiled ;
Not one who slowly gain'd the hill sublime,
Then often sipp'd and little at a time ;
But one who dabbled in the sacred springs,
And drank them muddy, mixed with baser things.
    Here to interpret dreams we read the rules,
Science our own, and never taught in schools,
In moles and specks we Fortune's gifts discern,
And Fate's fix'd will from Nature's wanderings learn.
    Of Hermit Quarll we read, in island rare,
Far from mankind and seeming far from care ;
Safe from all want, and sound in every limb ;
Yes ! there was he, and there was care with him.
    Unbound and heap'd, these valued works beside,
Lay humbler works, the pedlar's pack supplied ;
Yet these, long since, had all acquired a name :
The Wandering Jew had found his way to fame ;
And fame, denied to many a labour'd song,
Crowns Thumb the Great, and Hickathrift the strong.
    There too is he, by wizard power upheld,
Jack, by whose arm the giant brood were quell'd :
His shoes of swiftness on his feet he plac'd ;
His coat of darkness on his lions he brac'd,
His sword of sharpness in his hand he took,
And off the heads of doughty giants stroke :
Their glaring eyes beheld no mortal near ;
No sound of feet alarm'd the drowsy ear ;
No English blood their pagan sense could smell,
But heads dropp'd headlong, wondering why they fell.
    These are the peasant's joy, when, placed at ease,
Half his delighted offspring mount his knees. "

We have selected one tale from each part of this poem, *Baptisms,*
Marriages and *Burials,* which will sufficiently testify to the merit
it has already held.

    "Twin infants then appear, a girl, a boy,
Th' o'erflowing cup of Gerard Ablett's joy :
Seven have I nam'd, and but six years have passed
By him and Judith since I bound them fast ;
Well pleas'd, the bridegroom smil'd to hear—'a vine
Fruitful and spreading round the walls be thine,
And branch-like be thine offspring !' – Gerard then
Look'd joyful love, and softly said, ' Amen.'
Now of that vine he would no more increase,
Those playful branches now disturb his peace ;
Them he beholds around his table spread,

But finds, the more the branch, the less the bread ;
And while they run his humble walls about,
They keep the sunshine of good-humour out.
  Cease, man, to grieve ! thy master's lot survey,
Whom wife and children, thou and thine obey ;
A farmer proud. beyond a farmer's pride,
Of all around the envy or the guide ;
Who trots to market on a steed so fine,
That when I meet him, I'm asham'd of mine ;
Whose board is high up-heav'd with generous fare,
Which five stout sons and three tall daughters share:
Cease, man, to grieve, and listen to his care.
  A few years fled, and all thy boys shall be
Lords of a cot, and labourers like thee ;
Thy girls unportion'd neighbouring youths shall lead,
Brides from my church, and thenceforth thou art freed:
But then thy master shall of cares complain,   ·
Care after care, a long connected train;
His sons for farms shall ask a large supply,
For farmers' sons each gentle miss shall sigh ;
Thy mistress, reasoning well of life's decay,
Shall ask a chaise and hardly brook delay ;
The smart young cornet, who, with so much grace,
Rode in the ranks and betted at the race,
While the vex'd parent rails at deeds so rash,
Shall d—-n his luck, and stretch his hand for cash.
Sad troubles, Gerard ! now pertain to thee,
When thy rich master seems from trouble free ;
But 'tis one fate at different times assign'd.
And cares from thee departing, he must find. "

As an illustration of the next part, we have chosen the interesting
and beautiful story of Phœbe Dawson.

  "Next at our altar stood a luckless pair,
  Brought by strong passions and a warrant there ;
  By long rent cloak, hung loosely, strove the bride,
  From every eye, what all perceived, to hide.
  While the boy-bridegroom, shuffling in his pace,
  Now hid awhile and then exposed his face;
  As shame alternately with anger strove,
  The brain, confused with muddy ale, to move ;
  In haste and stammering he perform'd his part,
  And look'd the rage that rankled in his heart;
  (So will each lover inly curse his fate,
  Too soon made happy and made wise too late);
  I saw his features take a savage gloom,
  And deeply threaten for the days to come ;
  Low spake the lass and lisp'd and minced the while,
  Look'd on the lad, and faintly tried to smile ;
  With softened speech and humbled tone she strove

To stir the embers of departed love;
While he a tyrant, frowning walk'd before,
Felt the poor purse and sought the public door,
She sadly following in submission went,
And saw the final shilling foully spent;
Then to her father's hut the pair withdrew,
And bade to love and comfort long adieu!
   Ah! fly temptation, youth, refrain! refrain!
I preach for ever; but I preach in vain!
Two summers since, I saw at Lammas fair,
The sweetest flower that ever blossom'd there;
When Phœbe Dawson gaily cross'd the green,
In haste to see, and happy to be seen;
Her air, her manners, all who saw, admir'd:
Courteous though coy, and gentle though retir'd;
The joy of youth and health her eyes display'd,
And ease of heart her every look convey'd;
A native skill her simple robes express'd,
As with untutor'd elegance she dress'd;
The lads around admired so fair a sight,
And Phœbe felt, and felt she gave, delight.
Admirers soon of every age she gain'd,
Her beauty won them and her worth retain'd;
Envy itself could no contempt display,
They wish'd her well, whom yet they wish'd away,
Correct in thought, she judged a servant's place
Preserved a rustic beauty from disgrace;
But yet on Sunday eve, in freedom hour,
With secret joy she felt that beauty's power;
When some proud bliss upon the heart would steal,
That, poor or rich, a beauty still must feel.
   At length, the youth, ordain'd to move her breast,
Before the swains with bolder spirit press'd;
With looks less timid made his passion known,
And pleas'd by manners, most unlike her own;
Loud though in love, and confident though young;
Fierce in his air, and voluble of tongue;
By trade a tailor, though, in scorn of trade,
He served the squire, and brush'd the coat he made;
Yet now, would Phœbe her consent afford,
Her slave alone, again he'd mount the board;
With her should years of growing love be spent,
And growing wealth:—See sigh'd, and look'd consent.
   Now, through the lane, up hill, and cross the green,
(Seen but by few and blushing to be seen—
Dejected, thoughtful, anxious, and afraid,)
Led by the lover, walk'd the silent maid:
Slow through the meadows rov'd they, many a mile,
Toy'd by each bank and trifled at each stile;
Where, as he painted every blissful view,

And highly colour'd what he strongly drew,
The pensive damsel, prone to tender fears,
Dimm'd the false prospect with prophetic tears:
Thus pass'd the allotted hours, till lingering late,
The lover loiter'd at the master's gate ;
There he pronounc'd adieu ! and yet would stay,
Till chidden—sooth'd—entreat'd—forc'd away ;
He would of coldness, though indulged, complain,
And oft retire and oft return again ;
When, if his teasing vex'd her gentle mind,
The grief assum'd, compell'd her to be kind !
For he would proof of plighted kindness crave,
That she resented first, and then forgave ;
And to his grief and penance yielded more,
Than his presumption had required before,
Ah ! fly temptation, youth ; refrain ! refrain ! ·¾
Each yielding maid and each presuming swain,
　　Lo ! now with red rent cloak and bonnet black.
And torn green gown loose hanging at her back,
One who an infant in her arms sustains,
And seems in patience striving with her pains ;
Pinch'd are her looks, as one who pines for bread,
Whose cares are growing and whose hopes are fled ;
Pale her parch'd lips, her heavy eyes sunk low,
And tears unnoticed from their channels flow ;
Serene her manner, till some sudden pain
Frets the meek soul, and then she's calm again ;—
Her broken pitcher to the pool she takes,
And every step with cautious terror makes ;
For not alone that infant in her arms,
But nearer cause, her anxious soul alarms.
With water burthen'd, then she picks her way,
Slowly and cautious, in the clinging clay :
Till, in mid-green, she trusts a place unsound,
And deeply plunges in th' adhesive ground ;
Thence, but with pain, her slender foot she takes,
While hope the mind as strength the frame forsakes :
For when so full the cup of sorrows grows,
Add but a drop, it instantly o'erflows.
And now her path, but not her peace, she gains,
Safe from her task, but shivering with her pains ;
Her home she reaches, open leaves the door,
And placing first her infant on the floor,
She bares her bosom to the wind, and sits,
And sobbing struggles with the rising fits :
In vain, they come, she feels th' inflating grief,
That shuts the swelling bosom from relief ;
That speaks in feeble cries a soul distress'd,
Or the sad laugh that cannot be repress'd ;
The neighbour-matron leaves her wheel and flies

With all the aid her poverty supplies ;
Unfee'd, the calls of nature she obeys,
Not led by profit, nor allured by praise ;
And waiting long, till these contentions cease,
She speaks of comfort and departs in peace.
Friend of distress! the mourner feels thy aid,
She cannot pay thee, but thou wilt be paid.
   But who this child of weakness, want, and care?
'Tis Phœbe Dawson, pride of Lammas fair ;
Who took her lover for his sparkling eyes,
Expressions warm, and love-inspiring lies :
Compassion first assail'd her gentle heart,
For all his suffering, all his bosom's smart :
'And then his prayers ! they would a savage move,
And win the coldest of the sex to love :'—
But ah ! too soon his looks success declar'd,
Too late her loss the marriage-rite repair'd :
The faithless flatterer then his vows forgot.
A captious tyrant or a noisy sot :
If present, railing, till he saw her pain'd ;
If absent, spending what their labours gain'd ;
Till that fair form in want and sickness pin'd,
And hope and comfort fled that gentle mind.
   Then fly temptation, youth ; resist, refrain !
Nor let me preach for ever and in vain !"

And for the third part, the truthful and impressive description of
the "noble peasant" Isaac Ashford.

" Next to these ladies, but in nought allied,
A noble peasant, Isaac Ashford, died.
Noble he was, contemning all things mean,
His truth unquestion'd, and his soul serene :
Of no man's presence Isaac felt afraid ;
At no man's question Isaac look'd dismay'd :
Shame knew him not, he dreaded no disgrace ;
Truth, simple truth, was written in his face :
Yet while the serious thought his soul approv'd,
Cheerful he seem'd, and gentleness he loved ;
To bliss domestic he his heart resign'd,
And with the firmest had the fondest mind ;
Were others joyful, he look'd smiling on,
And gave allowance where he needed none ;
Good he refused with future ill to buy,
Nor knew a joy that caused reflection's sigh ;
A friend to virtue, his unclouded breast
No envy stung, no jealousy distress'd
(Bane of the poor ! it wounds their weaker mind,
To miss one favour which their neighbours find):
Yet far was he from stoic pride removed ;
He felt humanely, and he warmly loved :

I mark'd his action when his infant died,
And his old neighbour for offence was tried;
The still tears stealing down that furrow'd cheek,
Spoke pity, plainer than the tongue can speak.
If pride were his, 'twas not their vulgar pride,
Who, in their base contempt, the great deride ;
Nor pride in learning,—though my clerk agreed,
If fate should call him, Ashford might succeed ;
Nor pride in rustic skill, although we knew
None his superior, and his equals few :—
But if that spirit in his soul had place
It was the jealous pride that shuns disgrace ;
A pride in honest fame, by virtue gain'd,
In sturdy boys to virtuous labours train'd ;
Pride in the power that guards his country's coast,
And all that Englishmen enjoy and boast ;
Pride in a life that slanders tongue defied,—
In fact a noble passion, misnamed Pride.
    He had no party's rage, no sect'ry's whim ;
Christian and countryman was all with him :
True to his church he came; no Sunday shower
Kept him at home in that important hour ;
Nor his firm feet could one persuading sect,
By the strong glare of their new light direct :—
'On hope, in mine own sober light, I gaze,
But should be blind, and lose it, in your blaze.'
In time severe, when many a sturdy swain
Felt it his pride, his comfort to complain ;
Isaac their wants would soothe his own would hide,
And feel in *that* his comfort and his pride.
    At length he found, when seventy years were run,
His strength departed and his labour done ;
When he, save honest fame, retain'd no more,
But lost his wife, and saw his children poor :
'Twas then a spark of—say not discontent,
Struck on his mind, and thus he gave it vent :—
    'Kind are your laws ('tis not to be denied),
That in yon house for ruin'd age provide,
And they are just ;—when young we give you all,
And for assistance in our weakness call,—
Why then this proud reluctance to be fed,
To join your poor, and eat the parish bread ?
But yet I linger, loth with him to feed,
Who gains his plenty by the sons of need ;
He who, by contract, all your paupers took,
And gauges stomachs with an anxious look :
On some old master I could well depend;
See him with joy and thank him as a friend ;
But ill on him who doles the day's supply,
And counts our chances who at night may die :

Yet help me, Heav'n! and let me not complain
Of what I suffer, but my fate sustain.'
   Such were his thoughts, and so resign'd he grew;
Daily he placed the workhouse in his view!
But came not there; for sudden was his fate,
He dropp'd, expiring, at his cottage gate.
   I feel his absence in the hours of prayer,
And view his seat, and sigh for Isaac there
I see no more these white thinly spread
Round the bald polish of that honour'd head;
No more that awful glance on playful wight,
Compell'd to kneel and tremble at the sight,
To fold his fingers, all in dread the while,
Till Mister Ashford soften'd into a smile;
No more that meek and suppliant book in prayer,
Nor the pure faith (to give it force), are there:—
But he is blest, and I lament no more
A wise good man contented to be poor."

The Poem of *The Borough* possesses even still greater beauties
than its predecessor, *The Parish Register*. The incidents, char-
acters, and descriptions of the latter are truthfully and admirably
drawn; but in *The Borough*, there is that which not only pleases
the fancy, but grapples with the heart. Take for example the tale
of the condemned Highwayman. We are shown in the picture,
the virtuous young man, the happy lover, and the despairing felon,
in succession, with enough of each state to give full force to its
contrasts. It is a true and affecting picture, painted in vivid and
exact colours.

"Not so he felt, who with her was to pay,
The forfeit, life—with dread he view'd the day,
And that short space which yet for him remain'd,
Till with his limbs his faculties were chain'd:
He paced his narrow bounds some ease to find,
But found it not,—no comfort reach'd his mind:
Each sense was palsied; when he tasted food,
He sigh'd and said; 'Enough—'tis very good,
Since his dread sentence, nothing seem'd to be
As once it was—he seeing could not see,
Nor hearing, hear aright;—when first I came
Within his view, I fancied there was shame,
I judged resentment: I mistook the air,—
These fainter passions live not with despair;
Or but exist and die:—Hope, fear, and love,
Joy, doubt, and hate, may other spirits move,
But touch not his, who every waking hour,

Has one fix'd dread, and always feels its power.
　'But will not Mercy?'—No! she cannot plead
For such an outrage;—'twas a cruel deed:
He stopp'd a timid traveller;—to his breast,
With oaths and curses, was the dagger press'd:—
No! he must suffer: pity we may find
For one man's pangs, but must not wrong mankind.
Still I behold him, every thought employ'd
On one dire view!—all others are destroy'd;
This makes his features ghastly, gives the tone,
Of his few words resemblance to a groan;
He takes his tasteless food and when 'tis done,
Counts up his meals, now lessen'd by that one;
For expectation is on Time intent,
Whether he brings us joy or punishment.
　Yes! e'en in sleep the impressions all remain,
He·hears the sentence and he feels the chain;
He sees the judge and jury, when he shakes,
And loudly cries, 'Not guilty,' and awakes:
Then chilling tremblings o'er his body creep,
Till worn-out nature is compell'd to sleep.
　Now comes the dream again: it shows each scene,
With each small circumstance that comes between—
The call to suffering and the very deed—
There crowds go with him, follow, and precede;
Some heartless shout, some pity, all condemn,
While he in fancied envy looks at them:
He seems the place for that sad act to see,
And dreams the very thirst which then will be:
A priest attends—it seems, the one he knew
In his best days, beneath whose care he grew.
　At this his terrors take a sudden flight,
He sees his native village with delight;
The house, the chamber, where he once array'd
His youthful person; where he knelt and pray'd:
Then too the comforts he enjoy'd at home,
The days of joy; the joy themselves are come;—
The hours of innocence:—the timid look
Of his loved maid, when first her hand he took,
And told his hope, her trembling joy appears,
Her forced reserve and his retreating fears.
　All now is present;—'tis a moment's gleam
Of former sunshine—stay, delightful dream!
Let him within his pleasant garden walk,
Give him her arm, of blessings let them talk.
　Yes! all are with him now, and all the while
Life's early prospects and his Fanny's smile:
Then come his sister and his village friend,
And he will now the sweetest moments spend
Life has to yield;—No! never will he find

Again on earth such pleasure in his mind :
He goes through shrubby walks these friends among,
Love in their looks and honour on the tongue:
Nay, there's a charm beyond what nature shows,
The bloom is softer and more sweetly glows;
Pierced by no crime, and urged by no desire
For more than true and honest hearts require,
They feel the calm delight, and thus proceed
Through the green lane,—then linger in the mead,—
Stray o'er the heath in all its purple bloom,—
And pluck the blossom where the wild bees hum ;
Then through the broomy bound with ease they pass,
And press the sandy sheep-walk's slender grass,
Where dwarfish flowers among the gorse are spread,
And the lamb browses by the linnet's bed ;
Then 'cross the bounding brook they make their way
O'er its rough bridge—and there behold the bay !—
The ocean smiling to the fervid sun—
The waves that faintly fall and slowly run—
The ships at distance and the boats at hand
And now they walk upon the seaside sand,
Counting the number and what kind they be,
Ships softly sinking in the sleepy sea :
Now arm in arm, now parted, they behold
The glitt'ring waters on the shingles roll'd :
The timid girls, half dreading their design,
Dip the small foot in the retarded brine,
And search for crimson weeds, which spreading flow,
Or lie like pictures on the sand below ;
With all those bright red pebbles, that the sun
Through the small waves so softly shines upon ;
And those live lucid jellies which the eye
Delights to trace as they swim glittering by :
Pearl-shells and rubied star-fish they admire,
And will arrange above the parlour-fire,—
Tokens of bliss !—' Oh ! horrible ! a wave
Roars as it rises—save me, Edward ! save !'
She cries :— Alas ! the watchman on his way
Calls, and lets in—truth, terror, and the day."

The number and variety of characters employed in this poem, is astonishing the more so when we remember that they are drawn from a particular class, or order of people. In an observation upon this poem, the poet himself says, " I have chiefly, if not exclusively, taken my subjects and characters from that order of society, where the least display of vanity is generally to be found, which is placed between the humble and the great. It is in this class of mankind

" A quiet, simple man was Abel Keene,
He meant no harm, nor did he often mean ;
He kept a school of loud rebellious boys,
And growing old, grew nervous with the noise ;
When a kind merchant hired his useful pen,
And made him happiest of accompting men ;
With glee he rose to every easy day,
When half the labour brought him twice the pay.
    There were young clerks, and there the merchant's son
Choice spirits all, who wish'd him to be one ;
It must, no question, give them lively joy,   .
Hopes long indulged to combat and destroy ;
At these they levell'd all their skill and strength.—
He fell not quickly, but he fell at length :
They quoted books, to him both bold and new,
And scorn'd as fables all he held as true ;
    'Such monkish stories, and such nursery lies,'
That he was struck with terror and surprise.
    'What ! all his life had he the laws obey'd,
Which they broke through and were not once afraid?
Had he so long his evil passions check'd,
And yet at last had nothing to expect ?
While they their lives in joy and pleasure led,
And then had nothing at the end to dread ?
Was all his priest with so much zeal convey'd
A part ! a speech ! for which the man was paid !
And were his pious books, his solemn prayers,
Not worth one tale of the admired Voltaire's ?
Then was it time, while yet some years remain'd,
To drink untroubled and to think unchain'd,
And on all pleasures, which his purse could give,
Freely to seize, and while he lived, to live.'
    Much time he passed in this important strife,

The bliss or bane of his remaining life ;
For converts all are made with care and grief;
And pangs attend the birth of unbelief ;
Nor pass they soon ; —with awe and fear he took
The flowery way, and cast back many a look.
   The youths applauded much his wise design,
With weighty reasoning o'er their evening wine ;
And much in private 'twould their mirth improve,
To hear how Abel spake of life and love ;
To hear him own what grievous pains it cost,
E'er the old saint was in the sinner lost,
Ere his poor mind, with every deed alarm'd,
   By wit was settled, and by vice was charm'd.
   For Abel enter'd in his bold career,
Like boys on ice, with pleasure and with fear ;
Lingering, yet longing for the joy, he went,
Repenting now, now dreading to repent :
With awkward pace, and with himself at war,
Far gone, yet frighten'd that he went so far ;
Oft for his efforts he'd solicit praise,
And then proceed with blunders and delays :
The young more aptly passions' call pursue,
But age and weakness start at scenes so new,
And tremble, when they've done, for all they dared to do.
   At length example Abel's dread removed,
With small concern he sought the joys he loved ;
Not resting here, he claim'd his share of fame,
And first their votary, then their wit became ;
His jest was bitter and his satire bold,
When he his tales of former brethren told ;
What time with pious neighbours he discuss'd
Their boasted treasure and their boundless trust :
'Such were our dreams,' the jovial elder cried ;—
' Awake and live,' his youthful friends replied.
   Now the gay clerk a modest drab despised,
And clad him smartly, as his friends advised ;
So fine a coat upon his back he threw,
That not an alley-boy old Abel knew ;
Broad polish'd buttons blazed that coat upon,
And just beneath the watch's trinkets shone, —
A splendid watch, that pointed out the time,
To fly from business and make free with crime :
The crimson waistcoat and the silken hose
Rank'd the lean man among the Borough beaux ;
His raven hair he cropp'd with fierce disdain,
And light elastic locks encased his brain :
More pliant pupil who could hope to find,
So deck'd in person and so changed in mind ?
   When Abel walk'd the streets, with pleasant mien,
He met his friends, delighted to be seen ;

And when he rode along the public way,
No beau so gaudy, and no youth so gay.
   His pious sister, now an ancient maid,
For Abel fearing, first in secret pray'd :
Then thus in love and scorn her notions she convey'd :—
   'Alas ! my brother ! can I see thee pace
Hoodwink'd to hell, and not lament thy case,
Nor stretch my feeble hand to stop thy headlong race ?
Lo ! thou art bound, a slave in Satan's chain ;
The righteous Abel turn'd the wretched Cain ;
His brother's blood against the murderer cried,
Against thee thine, unhappy suicide.
Are all our pious nights and peaceful days,
Our evening readings and our morning praise,
Our spirits' comfort in the trials sent,
Our hearts' rejoicings in the blessings lent,
All that over grief a cheering influence shed,
Are these' for ever and for ever fled ?
   'When in the years gone by, the trying years
When faith and hope had strife with wants and fears,
Thy nerves have trembled till thou couldst not eat,
(Dress'd by this hand) thy mess of simple meat :
When grieved by fastings, gall'd by fates severe,
Slow pass'd the days of the successless year ;
Still in these gloomy hours, my brother then
Had glorious views, unseen by prosperous men :
And when thy heart has felt its wish denied,
What gracious texts hast thou to grief applied ;
Till thou hast enter'd in thine humble bed,
By lofty hopes and heavenly musings fed ;
Then I have seen thy lively looks express
The spirit's comforts in the man's distress.
   'Then didst thou cry, exulting, 'yes, 'tis fit,
'Tis meet and right, my heart ! that we submit :'
And wilt though, Abel, thy new pleasures weigh
Against such triumphs ?—Oh ! repent and pray.
   'What are thy pleasures ? with the gay to sit,
And thy poor brain torment for awkward wit ;
All thy good thoughts (thou hat'st them) to restrain,
And give a wicked pleasure to the vain ;
Thy long, lean frame by fashion to attire,
That lads may laugh and wantons may admire ;
To raise the mirth of boys, and not to see,
Unhappy maniac ! that they laugh at thee.'
   'These boyish follies, which alone the boy
Can idly act, or gracefully enjoy.
Add new approaches to thy fallen state,
And make men scorn what they would only hate.'
   'What pains, my brother, dost thou take to prove
A taste for follies which thou canst not love !

Why do thy stiffening limbs the steed bestride —
That lads may laugh to see thou canst not ride?
And why (I feel the crimson tinge my cheek)
Dost thou by night in Diamond-Alley sneak?'
    'Farewell! the parish will thy sister keep,
Where she in peace shall pray and sing and sleep,
Save when for thee she mourns, thou wicked, wandering sheep,
When youth is fallen, there's hope the young may rise.
But fallen age for ever hopeless lies;
Torn up by storms, and placed in earth once more,
The younger tree may sun and soil restore,
But when the old and sapless trunk lies low,
Nor care or soil can former life bestow;
Reserved for burning is the worthless tree —
And what, O Abel! is reserved for thee?'
    These angry words our hero deeply felt,
Though hard his heart, and indisposed to melt!
To gain relief he took a glass the more,
And then went on as careless as before;
Thenceforth, uncheck'd, amusements he partook,
And (save his ledger) saw no decent book;
Him found the merchant punctual at his task,
And that perform'd, he'd nothing more to ask;
He cared not how old Abel play'd the fool,
No master he beyond the hours of school:
Thus they proceeding had their wine and joke,
Till merchant Dixon felt a warning stroke,
And, after struggling half a gloomy week,
Left his poor clerk another friend to seek.
    Alas! the son who led the saint astray,
Forgot the man whose follies made him gay;
He cared no more for Abel in his need,
Than Abel cared about his hackney steed:
He now, alas! had all his earnings spent,
And thus was left to languish and repent;
No school nor clerkship found he in the place,
Now lost to fortune, as before to grace.
    For town relief the grieving man applied,
And begg'd with tears what some with scorn denied;
Others look'd down upon the glowing vest,
And frowning, ask'd him at what price he dress'd?
Happy for him his country's laws are mild,
They must support him, though they still revil'd;
Grieved, abject, scorn'd, insulted, and betray'd,
Of God unmindful, and of man afraid, —
No more he talk'd; 'twas pain, 'twas shame to speak,
His heart was sinking, and his frame was weak.
His sister died with such serene delight,
He once again began to think her right;
Poor like himself, the happy spinster lay,

And sweet assurance bless'd her dying day :
Poor like the spinster, he, when death was nigh,
Assured of nothing, felt afraid to die.
The cheerful clerks who sometimes pass'd the door,
Just mention'd ' Abel !' and then thought no more.
So Abel, pondering on his state forloin,
Look'd round for comfort, and was chased by scorn.
And now we saw him on the beach reclined,
Or causeless walking in the wintry wind ;
And when it raised a loud and angry sea,
He stood and gazed, in wretched reverie :
He heeded not the frost, the rain, the snow,
Close by the sea he walk'd, alone and slow :
Sometimes his frame though many an hour he spread
Upon a tombstone, moveless as the dead ;
And was there found a sad and silent place,
There would he creep with slow and measured pace ;
Then would he wander by the river's side,
And fix his eyes upon the falling tide;
The deep dry ditch, the rushes in the fen,
And mossy crag-pits were his lodgings then:
There, to his discontented thoughts a prey,
The melancholy mortal pined away."

The poet has also introduced into this poem, many descriptive passages of uncommon beauty—gems that will ever adorn his works with genuine lustre. Such in character is the following elegant passage.

"Thy walks are ever pleasant ; every scene
Is rich in beauty, lively, or serene—
Rich—is that varied view with woods around,
Seen from the seat within the shrubbery bound,
Where shines the distant lake, and where appear
From ruins bolting, unmolested deer ;
Lively—the village green, the inn, the place
Wheie the good widow schools her infant-race.
Shops, whence are heard the hammer and the saw.
And village pleasures unreproved by law :
Then how serene, when in your favourite room,
Gales from your jasmines soothe the evening gloom
When from your upland paddock you look down,
And just perceive the smoke which hides the town ;
When weary peasants at the close of day
Walk to their cots, and part upon the way ;
When cattle slowly cross the shallow brook,
And shepherd
We prune our   es,
And nothing looks untutor'd and at ease.
On the wide heath or in the flowery vale,

We scent the vapours of the sea-born gale ;
Broad-beaten paths lead on from stile to stile,
And sewers from streets the road-side banks defile ;
Our guarded fields a sense of danger show,
Where garden-crops with corn and clover grow ;
Fences are form'd of wreck, and placed around,
(With tenters tipp'd) a strong repulsive bound ;
Wide and deep ditches by the gardens run,
And there in ambush lie the trap and gun ;
Or yon broad board, which guards each tempting prize,
'Like a tall bully, lifts its head and lies.'
There stands a cottage with an open door,
Its garden undefended blooms before :
Her wheel is still, and overturn'd her stool,
While the lone widow seeks the neighb'ring pool :
This gives us hope, all views of town to shun—
No ! here are tokens of the sailor-son ;
That old blue jacket, and that skirt of check,
And silken kerchief for the seaman's neck ;
Sea-spoils and shells from many a distant shore.
And furry robe from frozen Labrador."

CHAPTER XXVI.

WORDSWORTH.

WORDSWORTH.—Wordsworth is a poet in a sense peculiar to himself; the whole of his poems from the shortest to the longest, from the most humble to the most impassioned, are composed strictly upon the principles of one grand comprehensive system.

Wordsworth is a lover of nature ; not a blind confounder of the creator with his own creation—but a genuine, pure, religious lover of the Universe, as a symbol of the immeasurable wisdom and majesty of God. Penetrated, as he himself says, to his 'heart of hearts,' with this living idea, he does not pass by in neglect or contempt any component part of this mysterious whole ; he denies not to any animate or inanimate being its due share of his love; he recognises in all, the finger and impress of a superior being; in winter and summer, in storm or sunshine; in solitudes or in crowds; in joy or affliction, he is the same ; always extracting from human contingencies their universal essence ; inspiring in return his own passionate and blended sympathies, and chastening and purifying every thought and wish, by a spirit of unutterable love. Wordsworth is the greatest of those poets who have gone to common life, to the feelings of universal nature, and to the obscure and neglected portions of society for beautiful and touching themes. " Genius is not a creator," in the sense of feigning and fancying what does not exist. Its distinction is to discern more of truth than common minds. It sees under disguises and humble forms, everlasting beauty. This is the prerogative of Wordsworth to discern and reveal, in the ordinary walks of life, and in the common human heart. He has revealed the loneliness of the primitive feelings, of the universal affectiveness of the human soul. The grand truth that pervades his poetry, is that the beautiful is not confined to the rare, the new, the distant—to scenery and modes of life open only to the few ; but that it is poured forth profusely on the common earth and sky ; that it gleams from the loneliest flower; that it lights up the humblest sphere; that the sweetest affection lodge in lowliest hearts; that there is sacredness, dignity, and loveliness in lives which few eyes rest on—that, even in the absence of all intellectual culture, the domestic relations can quietly nourish that disinterestedness which is the element of all greatness, and without which, intellectual power is a splendid deformity. Wordsworth is the poet of humanity ; he teaches reverence for our universal nature; he breaks down the factitious barriers between human hearts. "* In this beautiful observation, the writer describes those simpler, but for the popular mind, more attractive characteristics which so touchingly and so powerfully appeal to the instincts and feelings of our common humanity. From Wordsworth we learn that no natural object or incident can be too low or insignificant for poetry, nay, that in rustic life the passages are often more vigorous and decisive; and the whole system of society more genuine and unadulterated than when encumbered and concealed by forms of city ceremonial, and deadened by the depraving habitude of perpetual though unconcious deceit. Still these are only the rude

* William Ellery Channing.

"He scans the ass from limb to limb;
And Peter now uplifts his eyes;—
Steady the moon doth look and clear,
And like themselves the rocks appear,
And quiet are the skies.

Whereat, in resolute mood, once more
He stoops the ass's neck to seize—
Foul purpose, quickly put to flight!
For in the pool a startling sight
Meets him, beneath the shadowy trees.

It is the moon's distorted face?
The ghost-like image of a cloud?
It is a gallow there portrayed?
Is Peter of himself afraid?
It is a coffin,—or a shroud?

A grisly idol hewn in stone?
Or imp from witch's lap let fall?
Or a gay ring of shining fairies,
Such as pursue their brisk vagaries
In sylvan bower, or haunted hall?

It is a fiend that to a stake
Of fire his desperate self is tethering?
Or stubborn spirit doomed to yell
In solitary ward or cell,
Ten thousand miles from all his brethren.

Never did pulse so quickly throb,
And never heart so loudly panted;

I V.

> He looks. he cannot choose but look ;
> Like one intent upon a book—
> A book that is enchanted.

> Ah, well a day for Peter Bell—
> He will be turned to iron soon,
> Meet statue for the court of fear !
> His hat is up—and every hair
> Bristles—and whitens in the moon !

> He looks—he ponders—looks again :
> He sees a motion—hears a groan ;—
> His eyes will burst—his heart will break —
> He gives a loud and frightful shriek,
> And drops, a senseless weight, as if his life were flown."

Can anything, especially if read in connexion with the original poem, be more intensely terrific than this passage?—and yet what is the real cause of the terror ?   Again :—

> " And the smoke and respiration
> Rising like an exhalation
> Blend with the mist,—a morning shroud
> To form—an undissolving cloud ;
> Which, with slant ray, the merry Sun
> Takes delight to play upon.
> Never, surely, old Apollo,
>   He, or other God as old
>   Of whom in story we are told
> Who had a favorite to follow
> Through a battle or elsewhere,
> Round the object of his care,
> In a time of peril threw
> Veil of such celestial hue ;
> Interposed so bright a screen
> Him and his enemies between !"

Can anything be more natural and exquisitely beautiful than this?—and yet what is the object which has become the cause of this beauty?

Observe again, the miraculous fineness of melody and imagination displayed in the following lines :—

> "Withered leaves—one—two—and three—
> From the lofty Elder-tree !
> Through the calm and frosty air,
> Of this morning bright and fair,
> Eddying round and round they sink
> Softly, slowly : one might think
> From the motions that are made,
> Every little leaf conveyed

Sylph and Fairy hither tending, —
To this lower world descending,
Each invisible and mute,
In his wavering parachute. "

And yet inimitably beautiful as the passages of this kind are, they are as dust in the balance when brought in contact with those mighty energies of the soul, of which many of his longer odes and blank verse are composed. We can see in them one eternal master feeling—an earnest faith in the intrinsic godliness and immortality of the soul, raised upon the platonic theory of pre-existence; differing from the sordid feeling of metempsychosis, in that he believes the spark within us hath never been sullied or dimmed by mortal incarnation before, but comes, as it were, fresh and original from some unimaginable vision and enjoyment of the Deity. Hence those passionate addresses to infancy; those melancholy retrospects upon what is never to return again : for in our downward course of life we go daily further from the fountain of our existence, and become more and more 'earthy,' and forgetful of that, 'imperial palace whence we came.' Read his own intense and exalted creed in his own matchless numbers :—

"Our birth is but a sleep and a forgetting,
The soul that rises with us, our life's Star,
    Hath had elsewhere its setting,
        And cometh from afar ;
    Not in entire forgetfulness,
    And not in utter nakedness,
But trailing clouds of glory do we come
    From God who is our home :
Heaven lies about us in our infancy !
Shades of the prison-house begin to close
        Upon the growing Boy,
But he beholds the light, and whence it flows,
        He sees it in his joy ;
The youth, who daily further from the east
Must travel, still is Nature's priest,
    And by the vision splendid
    Is on his way attended ;
At length the man perceives it die away,
And fade into the light of common day. "

These "shadowy recollections" then, are the master-light of all our seeing ; they cherish us—and have power to make :—

> "Our noisy years seem moments in the being
>   Of the eternal silence."

And then for the retrospect which a meditative and imaginative mind can exercise :—

> "Hence in a season of calm weather,
>   Though inland far we be,
> Our souls have sight of that immortal sea
>   Which brought us hither ;
>   Can in a moment travel thither,—
> And see the children sport upon the shore,
> And hear the mighty waters rolling evermore."

And still one more, and perhaps the most affecting of all ; the lines from the poem on *Revisiting the Wye,* which should not be read without also *thinking.* They are—

> "———————————Nor less I trust,
> To them I may have owed another gift,
> Of aspect more sublime ; that blessed wood,
> In which the burthen of the mystery,
> In which the heavy and the weary weight
> Of all this unintelligible world
> Is lightened :—that serene and blessed mood,
> In which the affectiveness gently lead us on,—
> Until, the breath of this corporeal frame,
> And even the motion of our human blood,
> Almost suspended, we are laid asleep
> In body, and become a living soul :
> While with an eye made quiet by the power
> Of harmony, and the deep power of joy,
> We see into the life of things.
>   If this
> Be but a vain belief, yet, oh ! how oft
> In darkness, and amid the many shapes
> Of joyless daylight ; when the fretful stir
> Unprofitable, and the fever of the world,
> Have hung upon the beatings of my heart,
> How oft, in spirit, have I turn'd to thee,
> O sylvan Wye ! Thou wanderer thro' the woods,
> How often has my spirit turned to Thee !"

Such passages as the following, show Wordsworth to be a great poet, and the following are such as neither Milton nor Southey in their highest moments would have been ashamed of. First in the Address to *H. C., six years old:*—

> "O THOU ! whose fancies from afar are brought ;
> Who of thy words dost make a mock apparel,
> And fittest to unutterable thought

*   *   *   *

Through dream and vision did she sink,
Delighted all the while to think
That on those lonesome floods,
And green savannas, she should share
His board with lawful joy, and bear
His name in the wild woods.

*   *   *   *

Nor less, to feed voluptuous thought,
The beauteous forms of nature wrought,
Fair trees and lovely flowers;
The breezes their own languor lent :
The stars had feelings, which they sent
Into those gorgeous bowers."

Or in those two exquisite stanzas from "Peter Bell :"—

"At noon, when by the forest's edge,
He lay beneath the branches high,
The soft blue sky did never melt
Into his heart.—he never felt
The witchery of the soft blue sky!

On a fair prospect some have looked
And felt as I have heard them say,

> As if the moving time had been
> A thing as stedfast as the scene
> On which they gazed themselves away."

*   *   *   *   *

There is nothing comparable with some of the passages in the *Excursion*, in any ancient or modern poet. The following two or three passages will amply illustrate the entire beauty of Wordsworth's greatest poem.

> " From his sixth year, the boy of whom I speak,
> In summer, tended cattle on the hills ;
> But, through the inclement and the perilous days
> Of long-continuing winter, he repaired,
> Equipped with satchel, to a school, that stood
> Sole building on a mountain's dreary edge,
> Remote from view of city spire, or sound
> Of minster clock ! From that bleak tenement
> He, many an evening, to his distant home
> In solitude returning, saw the hills
> Grow larger in the darkness all alone.
> Beheld the stars come out above his head,
> And travelled through the wood with no one near
> To whom he might confess the things he saw,
> So the foundations of his mind were laid.
> In such communion, not from terror free,
> While yet a child, and long before his time,
> He had perceived the presence and the power
> Of greatness ; and deep feelings had impressed
> Great objects on his mind, with portraiture
> And colour so distinct, that on his mind
> They lay like substances, and almost seemed
> To haunt the bodily sense. He had received
> A precious gift ; for as he grew in years,
> With these impressions would he still compare
> All his remembrances, thoughts, shapes, and forms ;
> And being still unsatisfied with aught
> Of dimmer character, he thence attained
> An active power to fasten images
> Upon his brain ; and on their pictured lines
> Intenstly brooded, even till they acquired
> The liveliness of dreams. Nor did he fail,
> While yet a child, with a child's eagerness
> Incessantly to turn his ear and eye
> On all things which the moving seasons brought
> To feed such appetite: nor this alone
> Appeased his yearning :—in the after day
> Of boyhood, many an hour in caves forlorn,
> And 'mid the hollow depths of naked crags
> He sate, and even in their fixed lineaments,

*　　　*　　　*　　　*

Such was the boy—but for the growing youth
What soul was his, when, from the naked top
Of some bold headland, he beheld the sun
Rise up, and bathe the world in light! He looked—
Ocean and earth, the solid frame of earth
And ocean's liquid mass, beneath him lay
In gladness and deep joy. The clouds were touched,
And in their silent faces did he read
Unutterable love. Sound needed none,
Nor any voice of joy; his spirit drank
The spectacle : sensation, soul, and form
All melted into him ; they swallowed up
His animal being ; in them did he live,
And by them did he live ; they were his life.
In such access of mind, in such high hour
Of visitation from the living God,
Thought was not, in enjoyment it expired.
No thanks be breathed, he proffered no request ;
Rapt into still communion that transcends
The imperfect offices of prayer and praise,
His mind was thanksgiving to the power
That made him ; it was blessedness and love !
A herdsman on the lonely mountain tops,
Such intercourse was his, and in this sort
Was his existence oftentimes *possessed*.
Oh, then how beautiful, how bright appeared
The written promise! Early had he learned
To reverence the volume that displays
The mystery, the life which cannot die ;
But in the mountains did he *feel* his faith.
Responsive to the writing, all things there
Breathed immortality, revolving life,
And greatness still revolving ; infinite,
Their littleness was not ; the least of things
Seemed infinite ; and there his spirit shaped
Her prospects, now did he believe,—he *saw*,
What wonder if his being thus became
Sublime and comprehensive ! Low desires,
Low thoughts had there no place ; yet was his heart
Lowly ; for he was meek in gratitude,
Oft as he called these ecstacies to mind
And whence they flowed ; and from them he acquired
Wisdom, which works through patience, thence he learned

In oft-recurring hours of sober thought
To look on nature with a humbler heart,
Self-questioned where it did not understand,
And with a superstitious eye of love.
   So passed the time ; yet to the nearest town,
He duly went with what small overplus
His earnings might supply, and brought away
The book that most had tempted his desires
While at the stall he read. Among the hills
He gazed upon that mighty orb of song,
The divine Milton. Lore of different kind,
The annual savings of a toilsome life,
His schoolmaster supplied ; books that explain
The purer elements of truth involved
In lines and numbers, and, by charm severe,
(Especially perceived where nature droops
And feeling is suppressed) preserve the mind
Busy in solitude and poverty.
These occupations oftentimes deceived
The listless hours, while in the hollow vale
Hollow and green, he lay on the green turf
In pensive idleness. What could he do,
Thus daily thirsting, in that lonesome life,
With blind endeavours ? yet still uppermost,
Nature was at his heart as if he felt,
Though yet he knew not how a wasting power
In all things that from her sweet influence
Might tend to wean him. Therefore with her hues,
Her forms, and with the spirit of her forms,
He clothed the nakedness of austere truth.
While yet he lingered in the rudiments
Of science, and among her simplest laws,
His triangles—they were the stars of heaven,
The silent stars ! Oft did he take delight
To measure the altitude of some tall crag
That is the eagle's birthplace, or some peak
Familiar with forgotten years, that shows
Inscribed, as with the silence of the thought,
Upon its bleak and visionary sides,
The history of many a wintry storm,
Or obscure records of the path of fire. "

Than again in the following beautiful passage in which **he has**
described a child listening to a shell, and beautifully **compared** it
to the murmurings of faith.

     "—————————————I have seen
A curious child, who dwelt upon a tract
Of inland ground, applying to his ear
The convolutions of a smooth-lipped shell ;

"The Vicar paused; and towards a seat advanced,
A long stone-seat, fixed in the churchyard wall;
Part shaded by cool sycamore, and part
Offering a sunny resting-place to them
Who seek the house of worship, while the bells
Yet ring with all their voices, or before
The last hath ceased its solitary knoll.
Under the shade we all sate down; and there
His office, uninvited, he resumed.

"As on a sunny bank, a tender lamb
Lurks in safe shelter from the winds of March,
Screened by its parent, so that little mound
Lies guarded by its neighbour; the small heap
Speaks for itself, an infant there doth rest,
The sheltering hillocks is the mother's grave.
If mild discourse, and manner that conferred
A natural dignity on humblest rank;
If gladsome spirits, and benignant looks,
That for a face not beautiful did more
Than beauty for the fairest face can do;
And if religious tenderness of heart,
Grieving for sin, and penitential tears
Shed when the clouds had gathered and distained
The spotless ether of a maiden life;
If these may make a hallowed spot of earth
More holy in the sight of God or man;
Then, o'er that mould, a sanctity shall brood,
Till the stars sicken at the day of doom.

" Ah ! what a warning for a thoughtless man,
Could field or grove, or any spot of earth,
Show to his eye an image of the pangs
Which it hath witnessed; render back an echo
Of the sad steps by which it hath been trod !

I W.

There, by her innocent baby's precious grave,
Yea, doubtless, on the turf that roofs her own,
The mother oft was seen to stand or kneel
In the broad day, a weeping Magdalene,
Now she is not ; the swelling turf reports
Of the fresh shower, but of poor Ellen's tears
Is silent ; nor is any vestige left
Of the path worn by mournful tread of her
Who, at her hearts light bidding, once had **moved**
In virgin fearlessness, with step that seemed
Caught from the pressure of elastic turf
Upon the mountains gemmed with morning **dew**,
In the prime hour of sweetest scents and airs.
Serious and thoughtful was her mind ; and yet,
By reconcilement exquisite and rare.
The form, port, motions of this cottage-girl
Were such as might have quickened and inspired
A Titian's hand, addrest to picture forth
Oread or Dryad glancing through the shade
What time the hunters earliest horn is heard
Startling the golden hills.   A wide spread elm
Stands in our valley, named the joyful tree ;
From dateless usage which our peasants hold
Of giving welcome to the first of May
By dances, round its trunk.—And if the sky
Permit, like honours, dance and song, are paid
To the Twelfth Night ; beneath the frosty stars,
Or the clear moon.   The queen of these gay sports,
If not in beauty, yet in sprightly air,
Was hapless Ellen.—No one touched the ground
So deftly, and the nicest maiden's locks
Less gracefully were braided ;—but this praise
Methinks, would better suit another place.

"She loved, and fondly deemed herself beloved :
The road is dim, the current unperceived,
The weakness painful and most pitiful,
By which a virtuous woman in pure youth,
May be delivered to distress and shame.
Such fate was hers.—The last time Ellen danced,
Among her equals, round the joyful tree,
She bore a secret burthen : and full soon
Was left to tremble for a breaking vow—
Then, to bewail a sternly-broken vow,
Alone, within her widow'd mother's house.
It was the season sweet, of budding leaves,
Of days advancing towards their utmost length,
And small birds singing to their happy mates.
Wild is the music of the autumnal wind
Among the faded woods ; but these blithe notes

Strike the deserted to the heart :—I speak
Of what I know, and what we feel within.
Beside the cottage in which Ellen dwelt
Stands a tall ash tree ; to whose topmost twig
A thrush resorts, and annually chants,
At morn and evening, from that naked perch,
While all the undergrove is thick with leaves,
A time-beguiling ditty, for delight
Of his fond partner, silent in the nest.
'Ah why,' said Ellen, singing to herself,
'Why do not words, and kiss, and solemn pledge,
And nature that is kind in woman's breast,
And reason that in man is wise and good;
And fear of him who is a righteous Judge,
Why do not these prevail for human life,
To keep two hearts together, that began
Their spring-time with one love, and that have need
Of mutual pity and forgiveness, sweet
To grant, or be received ; while that poor bird,
Oh, come and hear him ! thou who hast to me
Been faithless, hear him, though a lowly creature,
One of God's simple children that yet know not
The universal Parent, how he sings,
As if he wished the firmament of heaven
Should listen, and give back to him the voice
Of his triumphant constancy and love ;
The proclamation that he makes, how far
His darkness doth transcend our fickle light !

"Such was the tender passage, not by me
Repeated without loss of simple phrase,
Which I perused, even as the words had been
Committed by forsaken Ellen's hand
To the blank margin of a valentine,
Bedropped with tears. 'Twill please you to be told
That, studiously withdrawing from the eye
Of all companionship, the sufferer yet
In lonely reading found a meek resource.
How thankful for the warmth of summer days,
When she could slip into the cottage-barn,
And find a secret oratory there ;
Or, in the garden, under friendly veil
Of their long twilight, pore upon her book
By the last lingering help of open sky,
Till the dark night dismissed her to her bed !
Thus did a waking fancy sometimes lose
The unconquerable pang of despised love.

"A kindlier passion opened on her soul
When that poor child was born. Upon its face
She looked as on a pure and spotless gift

Of unexpected promise, where a grief
Or dread was all that had been thought of—joy,
Far livelier than bewildered traveller feels
Amid a perilous waste, that all night long
Hath harassed him—toiling through fearful storm,
When he beholds the first pale speck serene
Of day-spring, in the gloomy east revealed,
And greets it with thanksgiving. 'Till this hour,'
Thus in her mother's hearing Ellen spake,
'There was a stony region in my heart;
But he, at whose command the parched rock ·
Was smitten, and poured forth a quenching stream,
Hath opened that obduracy, and made
Unlooked-for gladness in the desert place,
To save the perishing; and, henceforth, I look
Upon the light with cheerfulness, for thee
My infant! and for that good mother dear,
Who bore me,—and hath prayed for me in vain,—
Yet not in vain, it shall not be in vain.'
She spake, nor was the assurance unfulfilled;
And if heart-rending thoughts would oft return,
They stayed not long,—The blameless infant grew;
The child whom Ellen and her mother loved
They soon were proud of; tendered it and nursed,
A soothing comforter, although forlorn;
Like a poor singing-bird from distant lands;
Or a choice shrub, which he, who passes by
With vacant mind, not seldom may observe
Fair-flowering in a thinly peopled house,
Whose window, somewhat sadly, it adorns.
Through four months' space the infant drew its food
From the maternal breast, then scruples rose;
Thoughts, which the rich are free from, came and crossed
The sweet affection. She no more could bear
By her offence to lay a twofold weight
On a kind parent willing to forget
Their slender means; so, to that parent's care
Trusting in her child, she left their common home,
And with contented spirit undertook
A foster mother's office.

                                  'Tis perchance,
Unknown to you that in these simple vales
The natural feeling of equality
Is by domestic service unimpaired;
Yet, though such service be, with us, removed
From sense of degradation, not the less
The ungentle mind can easily find means
To impose severe restraints and laws unjust:
Which hapless Ellen now was doomed to feel.
For (blinded by an over-anxious dread

Of such excitement and divided thought
As with her office would but ill accord)
The pair, whose infant she was bound to nurse,
Forbade her all communion with her own ;
Week after week, the mandate they enforced.
So near !—yet not allowed, upon that sight
To fix her eyes—alas ! 'Twas hard to bear !
But worse affliction must be borne—far worse ;
For 'tis heaven's will—that, after a disease
Begun and ended within three days' space,
Her child should die ; as Ellen now exclaimed,
Her-own-deserted child !—Once, only once,
She saw it in that mortal malady :
And, on the burial day, could scarcely gain
Permission to attend its obsequies.
She reached the house—last of the funeral train ;
And someone, as she entered, having chanced
To urge unthinkingly their prompt departure,
Nay, said she, with a commanding look, a spirit
Of anger never seen in her before,
'Nay, ye must wait my time !' and down she sate,
And by the unclosed coffin kept her seat
Weeping and looking, looking on and weeping,
Upon the last sweet slumber of her child,
Until at length her soul was satisfied.

"You see the infant's grave ;—and to this spot,
The mother, oft as she was sent abroad,
And whatsoe'er the errand, urged her steps :
Hither she came ; and here she stood, or knelt
In the broad day—a rueful Magdalene !
She call'd her ; for not only she bewailed
A mother's loss, but mourned in bitterness
Her own transgression ; penitent sincere
As ever raised to heaven a streaming eye.
At length the parents of the foster-child,
Nothing that in despite of their commands
She still renewed and could not but renew
Those visitations, ceased to send her forth,
Or, to the garden's narrow bounds, confined.
I failed not to remind them that they erred ;
For holy nature might not thus be crossed,
Thus wronged in woman's breast : in vain I pleaded—
But the green stalk of Ellen's life was snapped,
And the flower dropt, as every eye could see,
It hung its head in mortal languishment.
Aided by this appearance, I at length
Prevailed, and, from those bonds released, she went
Home to her mother's house. The youth was fled :
The rash betrayer could not face the shame
Or sorrow which his senseless guilt had caused ;

And little would his presence, or proof given
Of a relenting soul, have now availed ;
For, like a shadow, he was passed away
From Ellen's thoughts ; had perished to her mind
For all concerns of fear, or hope, or love,
Save only those which to their common shame
And to his mortal being appertained :
Hope from that quarter would, I know, have brought
A heavenly comfort ; there she recognised
An unrelaxing bond, a mutual need ;
There, and, as seemed, there only.—She had built,
Her fond maternal heart had built, a nest,
In blindness all too near the river's edge;
That work a summer flood with hasty swell
Had swept away, and now her spirit longed
For its last flight to heaven's security.
The bodily frame was wasted day by day;
Meanwhile, relinquishing all other cares,
Her mind she strictly tutored to find peace
And pleasure in endurance.   Much she thought,
And much she read, and brooded feelingly
Upon her own unworthiness.—To me,
As to a spiritual comforter and friend,
Her heart she opened, and no pains were spared
To mitigate, as gently as I could,
The sting of self-reproach, with healing words.
Meek Saint ! through patience glorified on earth !
In whom, as by her lonely hearth she sate,
The ghastly face of cold decay put on
A sun-like beauty, and appeared divine !
May I not mention—-that, within those walls,
In due observance of her pious wish,
The congregation joined with me in prayer
For her soul's good ?   Nor was that office vain.
Much did she suffer : but, if any friend,
Beholding her condition, at the sight
Gave way to words of pity or complaint,
She stilled them with a prompt reproof, and said,
'He who afflicts me knows what I can bear ;
And, when I fail, and can endure no more,
Will mercifully take me to himself.'
So, through the cloud of death, her spirit passed
Into that pure and unknown world of love,
Where injury cannot come :—and here is laid
The mortal body by her infant's side. "

We will finish our remarks on Wordsworth, by quoting the
following passage from the poet himself.

" If thou be one whose heart the holy forms
Of young Imagination have kept pure
Stranger ! henceforth be warned ; and know, that pride,

CHAPTER XXVII.

COLERIDGE.

COLERIDGE.—Some writer has said, "Cold must be the temperature of that man's mind, who can rise from the perusal of the poems of Coleridge without feeling that interest, and those vivid emotions of delight which are ever excited by the wondrous operations of the magic wand of genius. To those whom constitution and cultivation have initiated into the sacred mysteries of song,—whose mental optics have often been enraptured with the delights of ecstatic vision,—and whose ear is tremulous to the touch of those barmonions undulations, which fancy pours from her soul-subduing shell; to such, the genius of Coleridge, even in its wildest aberrations, can never be listened to with indifference."

Coleridge delights the imagination while he satisfies the judgment; brings to the mind's eye all the treasures of his rich and elegant fancy, without having recourse to any ludicrous imitations of sounds foreign to the human organ, or trifling earnestness of reiteration. Take for instance the following beautiful effusions in *Christabel* :—

"They parted—ne'er to meet again !
But never either found another
To free the hollow heart from paining—
They stood aloof, the scars remaining,
Like cliffs which had been rent asunder ;

> A dreary sea now flows between,
> But neither heat, nor frost, nor thunder,
> Shall wholly do away, I ween,
> The marks of that which once hath been. "

Or the beautiful conclusion to Part the Second of that same poem.

> " A little child, a limber elf,
> Singing, dancing to itself,
> A fairy thing with red round cheeks
> That always finds and never seeks.
> Makes such a vision to the sight
> As fills a father's eyes with light ;
> And pleasures flow in so thick and fast
> Upon his heart, that he at last
> Must needs express his love's excess
> With words of unmeant bitterness.
> Perhaps 'tis pretty to force together
> Thoughts so unlike each other ;
> To mutter and mock a broken charm,
> To dally with wrong that does no harm.
> Per'aps 'tis tender too and pretty
> At each wild word to feel within
> A sweet recoil of love and pity.
> And what if in a world of sin
> (O sorrow and shame should this be true)
> Such giddiness of heart and brain
> Comes seldom save from rage and pain
> So talks as it's most used to do."

There are few passages in any ancient or modern poetry equal to the following :—

> " Hence ! thou lingerer, light !
> Eve saddens into night.
> Mother of wildly-working dreams ! we view
> The sombre hours, that round thee stand
> With down-cast eyes (a duteous band !)
> Their dark robes dripping with the heavy dew.
> Sorceress of the ebon throne !
> Thy power the Pixies own,
> When round thy raven brow,
> Heaven's lucent roses glow.
> And clouds, in wat'ry colours drest,
> Float in light drapery o'er the sable vest ;
> What time the pale moon sheds a softer day,
> Mellowing the woods beneath its pensive beam :
> For mid the quiv'ring light 'tis ours to play,
> Aye glancing to the cadence of the stream."

Does not the following bring to the mind's eye many a spot of bliss in lovely England :—

"Low was our pretty cot! our tallest rose
Peeped at the chamber window. We could hear
At silent noon, and eve, and early morn,
The sea's faint murmur. In the open air
Our myrtles blossomed; and across the porch
Thick jasmine twined: the little landscape round
Was green and woody and refreshed the eye.
It was a spot, which you might aptly call
The Valley of Seclusion ! Once I saw
(Hallowing his Sabbath-Day by quietness)
A wealthy son of commerce saunter by,
Bristowa's citizen ; methought, it calmed
His thirst of idle gold, and made him muse
With wiser feelings: for he paused, and looked
With a pleased sadness, and gazed all around,
Then eyed our cottage, and gazed round again,
And sighed, and said, *it was a blessed place.*
And we *were* blessèd. Oft with patient ear
Long-listening to the viewless sky-lark's note
(Viewless, or haply for a moment seen
Gleaming on sunny wing.)—'And such,' I said
'The inobtrusive song of happiness—
Unearthly minstrelsy ! then only heard
When the soul seeks to hear, when all is hushed
And the heart listens !'"

And the panoramic view which follows, is written in the most
beautiful style of poetic painting.

"O what a goodly scene. *Here* the bleak mount,
The bare bleak mountain speckled thin with sheep ;
Grey clouds, that shadowing spot the sunny fields
And river, now with bushy rock's o'erbrowed,
Now winding bright and full, with naked banks ;
And seats, and lawns, the abbey, and the wood,
And cots, and hamlets, and faint city-spire :
The Channel *there*, the islands and white sails,
Dim coasts, and cloud-like hills, and shoreless ocean—
It seemed like omnipresence ! God, methought,
Had built him there a temple : the whole world
Seemed imaged in its vast circumference.
No wish profaned my overwhelmèd heart.
Blest hour ! it was a luxury—to be !

Ah quiet dell ! dear cot ! and mount sublime
I was constrained to quit you. Was it right,
While my unnumbered brethren toiled and bled,
That I should dream away the entrusted hours
On rose-leaf beds, pamp'ring the coward heart
With feelings all too delicate for use ?
Sweet is the tear that from some Howard's eye
Drops on the cheek of one he lifts from earth :
And he, that works me good with unmoved face,

Does it but half : he chills me while he aids,
My benefactor, not my brother man !
Yet even this, this cold beneficence]
Seizes my praise, when I reflect on those,
The sluggard Pity's vision-weaving tribe !
Who sigh for wretchedness. yet shun the wretched,
Nursing in some delicious solitude
Their slothful loves and dainty sympathies !
I therefore go, and join head, heart, and hand,
Active and firm, to fight the bloodless fight
Of science, freedom, and the truth in Christ.
Yet oft when after honourable toil
Rests the tired mind, and waking loves to dream,
My spirit shall revisit thee, dear cot!
Thy jasmine and thy window-peeping rose,
And myrtles fearless of the mild sea-air.
And I shall sigh fond wishes—sweet abode !
Ah—had none greater! and that all had such !"

There is a considerable similarity in the works of Coleridge and
Wordsworth. They are each impregnated with the spirit of the
other. In many respects in a transparency of ornament, purity of
conception, matchless ear, and splendour of diction, the poems of
Coleridge are often superior to Wordsworth. With the same con-
tinual workings of the soul upon its own energies, which is so
conspicuous in Wordsworth, he is less abstracted and ideal; not so
philosophically sublime, he is more humanely passionate ; not so
anatomizing in the operations of the heart and mind, he is more
diffused and comprehensive. From the natural bent of his genius,
there is a tendency to the strange, the wild, and mysterious; which
though intolerable in the cool pursuit of Truth, is yet oftentimes
the fruitful particular of the very highest poetry. To this he adds
a power of language truly wonderful, more romantically splendid
than Wordsworth, and more flexible and melodious than Southey's.
In this particular there are in my opinion, many specimens of
perfect harmony of thought, passion, measure and rhyme, in his
poems, which would hardly yield the palm to the most celebrated
passages in Spenser, Shakespeare, or Milton. A fine specimen of
his work may be seen in the *Ode to the Departing Year*, display-
ing that high and bright mysteriousness, so peculiar to him.

"Spirit who sweepest the wild harp of Time !
It is most hard with an untroubled ear

By Time's wild harp, and by the hand
    Whose indefatigable sweep
    Raises its fateful strings from sleep,
I bid you haste a mixed tumultuous band !
    From every private bower,
      And each domestic hearth,
    Haste for one solemn hour ;
    And with a loud and yet a louder voice,
O'er nature struggling in portentous birth,
      Weep and rejoice !
Still echoes the dread name that o'er the earth
Let slip the storm, and woke the brood of Hell :
    And now advance in saintly jubilee
Justice and Truth ! They too have heard thy spell,
    They too obey thy name, divinest Liberty !

I marked Ambition in his war array !
    I heard the mail'd Monarch's troublous cry—
    'Ah ! wherefore does the Northern Conqueress stay !
Groans not her chariot on its homeward way ?
      Fly, mailed Monarch, fly !
      Stunned by Death's twice mortal mace,
      No more on murder's lurid face
The insatiate hag shall gloat with drunken eye !
    Manes of the unnumbered slain !
    Ye that gasped on Warsaw's plain !
    Ye that erst at Ismail's tower,
When human ruin choked the streams,
    Fell in conquest's glutted hour,
Mid women's shrieks and infant's screams !

Spirits of the uncoffined slain,
  Sudden blasts of triumph swelling
Oft, at night, in misty train,
  Rush around her narrow dwelling !
The exterminating fiend is fled—
  (Foul her life, and dark her doom)
Mighty armies of the dead   ·
  Dance, like death-fires, round her tomb !
Then with prophetic-song relate,
Each some tyrant-murderer's fate ! "

Then follows a very fine invocation to all Nature to suspend its
woes and joys for a season—then a vivid description of the war
incidents for the year : after which comes the Vision imprecating
in an impassioned style, the vengeance of God upon the tyrannies
and blood-thirsty persecutions of the Great ones of this earth —

"Departing year ! 'twas on no earthly shore
My soul beheld thy vision ! Where alone,
Voiceless and stern, before the cloudy throne,
Aye Memory sits : thy robe inscribed with gore,
With many an unimaginable groan
  Thou storied'st thy sad hours ! Silence ensued,
  Deep silence o'er the ethereal multitude,
Whose locks with wreaths, whose wreaths with glories shown·
  Then, his eye wild ardours glancing,
  From the choired gods advancing,
The Spirit of the Earth made reverence meet,
And stood up, beautiful, before the cloudy seat.

Throughout the blissful throng,
  Hush'd were harp and song ;
Till wheeling round the throne the Lampads Seven,
  (The mystic words of Heaven)
  Permissive signal make ;
The fervent spirit bow'd, then spread his wings and speak!
  'Thou in stormy blackness throning,
  Love and uncreated Light,
  By the Earth's unsolaced groaning,
  Seize thy terrors, Arm of night !'
By peace with proffered insult scared,
    Masked hate and envying scorn !
    By years of havoc yet unborn !
And hunger's bosom to the frost-winds bared !
    But chief by Afric's wrongs,
    Strange, horrible, and foul !
    By what deep guilt belongs
To the deaf Synod, 'full of gifts and lies !'
By wealth's insensate laugh ! by torture's howl !
    Avenger, rise !
For ever shall the thankless Island scowl,

Her quiver full, and with unbroken bow !
Speak ! from thy storm-black Heaven, O speak aloud !
And on the darkling foe
Open thine eye of fire from some uncertain cloud !
O dart the flash ! O rise and deal the blow !
The Past to thee, to thee the Future cries ! •
Hark ! how wide Nature joins her groans below !
Rise ! God of Nature, Rise. "

The vision is ended :—

"The voice has ceased, the vision fled ;
Yet still I gasp'd and reel'd with dread ;
And ever, when the dream of night
Renews the phantom to my sight,
Cold sweat-drops gather on my limbs ;
My ears throb hot, my eye balls start ;
My brain with horrid tumult swims ;
Wild is the tempest of my heart ;
And my thick and struggling breath
Imitates the toil of death !
No stranger agony confounds
The soldier on the war-field spread,
When all foredone with toil and wounds,
Death-like he dozes among heaps of dead!
(The strife is o'er, the day-light fled,
And the night wind-clamours hoarse !
See ! the starting wretch's head
Lies pillowed on a brother's corse !)"

After this a burst of affectionate enthusiasm for his country
prevails over his settled conviction of her guilt and impending
punishment.

"Not yet enslaved, not wholly vile.
O Albion ! O my mother Isle !
Thy valleys, fair as Eden's bowers,
Glitter green with sunny showers ;
Thy grassy uplands' gentle swells
Echo to the bleat of flocks ;
(Those grassy hills, those glisttering dells,
Proudly ramparted with rocks)
And Ocean mid his uproar wild
Speaks safely to his island-child !
Hence, for many a fearless age,
Has social Quiet lov'd thy shore ;
Nor ever proud Invader's rage,
Or sack'd thy towers, or stain'd thy fields with gore. "

Then the prophecy of the destruction that is to ensue : and the
Ode concludes with his own feelings and prayers.

"Abandoned of Heaven ? mad Avarice thy guide,
At cowardly distance, yet kindling with pride—

'Mid thy herds and thy corn-fields secure thou hast stood,
And joined the wild yelling of Famine and Blood !
The nations curse thee ! they with eager wondering
   Shall hear Destruction. like a vulture, scream!
   Strange eyed Destruction ! who with many a dream.
Of central fires through nether seas up-thundering
Soothes her fierce solitude : yet as she lies
By livid fount, or red volcanic stream,
   If ever to her lidless dragon eyes,
   O Albion ! thy predestined ruins rise,
The fiend-hag on her perilous couch doth leap,
Muttering distemper'd triumph in her charmed sleep.

         Away, my soul, away !
In vain, in vain the birds of warning sing—
And hark ! I hear the famish'd brood of prey
Flap their lank pennons on the groaning wind !
         Away, my soul away !
   I unpartaking of the evil thing
   With daily prayer and daily toil,
   Soliciting for food my scanty soil,
Have wailed my country with a loud Lament.
Now I re-centre my immortal mind
   In the deep sabbath of meek self-content ;
Cleans'd from the vaporous passions that bedim
God's Image, sister of the Seraphim,"

There is the same originality of thought, with increased power of
expression and versification, in the Ode *Fears in Solitude.* It
is a lofty and energetic satire of a new cast. It is occupied with
the censure and reprobation of war, and the vanity of glory, and is
animated with so earnest and just a spirit, and such high-toned
language and intense benevolence, as to entitle it to a very high
place among the poetical productions of this country. It com-
mences with a beautiful strain :—

   "A green and silent spot, amid the hills ;
   A small and silent dell ! O'er stiller place
   No singing sky-lark ever poised himself.
   The hills are heathy, save that swelling slope,
   Which hath a gay and gorgeous covering on,
   All golden with the never-bloomless furze,
   Which now blooms most profusely, but the dell,
   Bathed by the mist, is fresh and delicate
   As vernal corn-field, or the unripe flax,
   When, through its half-transparent stalks, at eve,
   The level sunshine glimmers with green light.
   Oh ! 'tis a quiet spirit-healing nook !
   Which all, methinks, would love ; but chiefly he,
   The humble man, who, in his youthful years,

Knew just so much of folly, as had made
His early manhood more securely wise !
Here he might lie on fern or withered heath,
While from the singing-lark (that sings unseen
The minstrelsy that solitude loves best), .
And from the sun, and from the breezy air,
Sweet influences trembled o'er his frame ;
And he, with many feelings, many thoughts,
Made up a meditative joy, and found
Religious meanings in the forms of nature l
And so, his senses gradually wrapt
In a half sleep, he dreams of better worlds,
And dreaming hears thee still, O singing-lark ;
That singest like an angel in the clouds !"

The manner also in which he embodies atheism in this poem, shows a truly original turn of thought.

" The sweet words
Of Christian promise, words that even yet
Might stem destruction, where the wisely preached,
Are muttered o'er by men whose tones proclaim
How flat and wearisome they feel their trade :
Rank scoffers some, but most too indolent
To deem them falsehoods or to know their truth. .
Oh ! blasphemous ! the book of life is made
A superstitious instrument, on which
We gabble o'er the oaths we mean to break ;
For all must swear—all and in every place.
College and wharf, council and justice-court ;
All, all must swear, the briber and the bribed,
Merchant and lawyer, senator and priest,
The rich, the poor, the old man and the young ;
All, all make up one scheme of perjury,
That faith doth reel."

And the question at the end is admirable; upon the same subject.

" The very name of God
Sounds like a juggler's charm ; and, bold with joy,
Forth from his dark and lonely hiding-place,
(Portentous sight !) the owlet Atheism,
Sailing on obscene wings athwart the moon,
Drops his blue-fringed lids, and holds them close,
And hooting at the glorious sun in Heaven, .
Cries out, 'Where is it ?' "

His tragedy *Remorse* is in point of language unsurpassable. It is written in natural, free, forcible blank verse, equal in some parts to Shakespeare, and interspersed with a multitude of sublime thoughts, which are evidently traceable to the German, though still only as their cause, not their natural birth-place ; that is to say, though he borrowed hints, he did not purloin conceptions ready formed. This play is a poetical study for its powerful thought and poetical expressions. Yet in spite of its very striking features it shows no power of true dramatic creation. It contains fine characters, such as Ordonio; and there is produced a multitude of incidents of the most violent kind, but there is little in it to excite curiosity, or move to any degree of pity. What is the most beautiful in it is the pure descriptions, but it in no sense exhibits the human passions. The following beautiful description is one of the choicest in this tragedy.

"Yon hanging woods, that touched by autumn seem
As they were blossoming hues of fire and gold ;
The flower-like woods most lovely in decay,
The many clouds, the sea, the rocks, the sands,
Lie in the silent moonshine ; and the owl,
(Strange ! very strange!) the screech-owl only wakes!
Sole voice, sole eye of all this world of beauty !
Unless, perhaps, she sings her screeching song
To a herd of wolves, that skulk athirst for blood.
Why such a thing am I!"

Or the following which is equally admirable in its language and conception.

"On a rude rock
A rock, methought, fast by a grove of firs,
Whose thready leaves to the low-breathing gale
Made a soft sound most like the distant ocean,
I stayed, as though the hour of death were passed,
And I were sitting in the world of spirits—
For all things seemed unreal ! There I sate—
The dews fell clammy, and the night descended,
Black, sultry, close! and ere the midnight hour
A storm came on, mingling all sounds of fear,
That woods and sky, and mountains, seemed one havoc.
The second flash of lightning showed a tree,
Hard by me, newly scathed. I rose tumultuous :
My soul worked high, I bared my head to the storm.
And with loud voice and clamourous agony
Kneeling I prayed to the great spirit that made me,
Prayed, that REMORSE might fasten on their hearts,
And cling with poisonous tooth, inextricable
As the gored lion's *bite* !"

The disposition to the mysterious and supernatural is nowhere more absolutely developed, or more splendidly arrayed, than in the *Rime of the Ancient Mariner.* It is one of the best known and

And the good south wind still blew behind,
But no sweet bird did follow,
Nor any day, for food or play,
Came to the mariners' hollo !

And I had done an hellish thing,
And it would work 'em woe :
For all averred, I had killed the bird
That made the breeze to blow.
Ah, wretch ! said they, the bird to slay,
That made the breeze to blow !

Nor dim nor red, like God's own head,
The glorious Sun uprist :
Then all averred, I had killed the bird
That brought the fog and mist.
'Twas right, said they, such birds to slay,
That bring the fog and mist.

The fair breeze blew, the white foam flew,
The furrow followed free :
We were the first that ever burst
Into that silent sea.

Down dropt the breeze, the sails dropt' down,
'Twas sad as sad could be ;
And we did speak only to break
The silence of the sea !

All in a hot and copper sky,
The bloody Sun, at noon,
Right up above the mast did stand,
No bigger than the Moon.

Day after day, day after day,
We stuck, nor breath nor motion,
As idle as a painted ship
Upon a painted ocean.

Water, water, every where,
And all the boards did shrink ;
Water, water, every where
Not any drop to drink.

The very deep did rot : O Christ !
That ever this should be !
Yea, slimy things did craw with legs
Upon the slimy sea.

About, about, in reel and rout,
The death-fires danced at night ;
The water, like a witch's oils,
Burn green, and blue, and white.

And some in dreams assured were
Of the spirit that plagued us so :
Nine fathom deep he had followed us
From the land of mist and snow.

And every tongue, through utter drought,
Was withered at the root ;
We could not speak, no more than if
We had been choked with soot.

Ah, well a-day ! what evil looks
Had I from old and young !
Instead of the cross, the Albatross
About my neck was hung.

   *   *   *   *   *

The moving Moon went up the sky,
And nowhere did abide :
Softly she was going up
And a star or two beside,—

Her beams bemock'd the sultry main,
Like April hoar-frost spread :
But where the ship's huge shadow lay,
The charmed water burnt alway
A still and awful red.

Beyond the shadow of the ship
I watch'd the water snakes :
They mov'd in tracks of shining white,
And when they reared, the elfish light,
Fell off in hoary flakes.

Within the shadow of the ship
I watch'd their rich attire :
Blue, glossy green, and velvet black,
They coil'd and swam : and every track
Was a flash of golden fire.

O happy living things ! no tongue
Their beauty might declare :
A spring of love gushed from my heart,
And I blessed them unaware !

   *   *   *   *   *

Around, around, flew each sweet sound,
Then darted to the Sun :

Slowly the sounds came back again,
Now mixed, now one by one.

Sometimes a-dropping from the sky
I heard the sky-lark sing :
Sometimes all little birds that are,
How they seem'd to fill the sea and air
With their sweet jargoning !

And now 'twas all like instruments,
Now like a lonely flute,
And now it is an angel's song,
That makes the Heavens be mute.

It ceas'd, yet still the sails made on
A pleasant noise till noon.
A noise like of a hidden brook
In the leafy month of June,
That to the sleeping woods all night
Singeth a quiet tune. "

*   *   *   *   *

The whole of this poem is "a splendid dream, filling the ear with
the strange and floating melodies of sleep, and the eye with a shift-
ing, vaporous succession of fantastic images, gloomy or radiant."

Kubla Khan is of the same mystic unreal character ; it is even
asserted by Coleridge that this poem was actually composed in a
dream. Like all his poems, however, the versification is exquisite.
His language puts on every form ; it expresses every sound ; he
almost writes to the eye and to the ear.

"In Xanadu did Kubla Khan
A stately pleasure-dome decree ;
Where Alph, the sacred river, ran
Through caverns measureless to man
      Down to a sunless sea.
So twice five miles of fertile ground
With walls and towers were girdled round :
And there were gardens bright with sinuous rills
Where blossomed many an incense-bearing tree ;
And here were forests ancient as the hills,
Enfolding sunny spots of greenery.

But oh ! that deep romantic chasm which slanted
Down the green hill athwart a cedarn cover !
A savage place ! as holy and enchanted
As e'er beneath a wanning moon was haunted
By woman wailing for her demon-lover !
And from this chasm, with ceaseless turmoil seething,
As if this earth in fast thick pants were breathing,
A mighty fountain momently was forced :

Amid whose swift half-intermitted burst
Huge fragments vaulted like rebounding hail,
Or chaffy grain beneath the threshers flail :
And 'mid these dancing rocks at once and ever
It flung up momently the sacred river;
Five miles meandering with a mazy motion
Through wood and dale the sacred river ran,
Then reached the caverns measureless to man,
And sank in tumult to a lifeless ocean ;
And 'mid this tumult Kubla heard from far
Ancestral voices prophesying war !
    The shadow of the dome of pleasure
    Floated midway on the waves;
    Where was heard the mingled measure
    From the fountain and the caves.
It was a miracle of rare devise,
A sunny pleasure-dome with caves of ice !
    A damsel with a dulcimer
    In a vision once I saw :
    It was an Alyssinian maid,
    And on her dulcimer she played,
    Singing of Mount Abora.
    Could I revive within me
    Her symphony and song,
    To such a deep delight 'twould win me.
That with music loud and long,
I would build that dome in air,
That sunny dome ! those caves of ice !
And all who heard should see them there,
And all should cry, Beware ! Beware!
His flashing eyes, his floating hair !
Weave a circle round him thrice,
And close your eyes with holy dread,
For he on honey-dew hath fled,
And drank the milk of Paradise."

But notwithstanding the striking success and perfect originality
of his compositions in this particular, and not forgetting either the
energy, the dramatic excellence and splendour of the *Remorse,*
or the softer and more fanciful elegance of *Zapolya,* yet it is
in his Love Poems that the genius of Coleridge is poured forth in
a more peculiar and undivided stream. As a Love Poët he is
strictly and exclusively original, and this portion of his works have
been acknowledged to be excellent, even by those who have affect-
ed to despise his other productions. None of the love poetry of
the present day, can to my mind be for an instant compared to
them in any particular. The love of Byron is desperate and short-

"I play'd a soft and doleful air,
I sang an old and moving story—
An old rude song, that suited well
    That ruin wild and hoary.

She listen'd with a flitting blush,
With downcast eyes and modest grace :
For well she knew I could not choose
    But gaze upon her face.

I told her of the Knight that wore
Upon his shield a burning brand ;
And that for ten long years he woo d
    The Lady of the Land.

I told her how he pin'd, and ah !
The deep, the low, the pleading tone,
With which I sang another's love
    Interpreted my own.

She listened with a flitting blush,
With downcast eyes, and modest grace ;
And she forgave me, that I gazed
    Too fondly on her face !

But when I told the cruel scorn
That craz'd that bold and lovely Knight ;
And that he cross'd the mountain-woods
    Nor rested day nor night.

That sometimes from the savage den,
And sometimes from the darksome shade,
And sometimes starting up at once
   In green and sunny glade,—

There came and looked him in the face
An angel beautiful and bright :
And that he knew it was a Friend,
   This miserable Knight!

And that, unknowing what he did,
He leap'd amid a murderous band,
And sav'd from outrage worse than death
   The Lady of the Land.

And how she wept, and clasped his knees
And how she tended him in vain—
And ever strove to expiate
   That scorn that crazed his brain ;—

And that she nurs'd him in a cave,
And how his madness went away,
When on the yellow forest leaves
   A dying man he lay.

His dying words— but when I reach'd
That tenderest strain of all the ditty,
My faltering voice and pausing harp
   Disturb'd her soul with pity !

All impulses of soul and sense
Had thrill'd my guileless Genevieve ;
The music and the doleful tale
   The rich and balmy eve ;

And hopes, and fears that kindle hope,
An undistinguishable throng,
And gentle wishes long subdued,
   Subdued and cherish'd long !

She wept with pity and delight ;
She blush'd with love and virgin-shame,
And like the murmur of a dream,
   I heard her breathe my name.

Her bosom heaved—she stepped aside,
As conscious of my look she stept—
Then suddenly, with timorous eye,
   She fled to me and wept.

She half enclos'd me with her arms,
She press'd me with a meek embrace ;
And bending back her head, look'd up,
   And gaz'd upon my face.

'Twas partly love, and partly fear,
And partly 'twas a bashful art,
That I might rather feel than see
   The beating of her heart."

> How many various-fated years have passed,
> What blissful and what anguished hours, since last
> I skimmed the smooth thin stone along thy breast,
> Numbering its light leaps! yet so deep imprest,
> Sink the sweet scenes of Childhood, that mine eyes
> I never shut amid the sunny blaze,
> But straight with all their tints thy waters rise,
> Thy crossing plank, thy margin's willowy maze,
> And bedded sand that veined with various dyes,
> Gleamed thro' thy bright transparence to the gaze!
> Visions of Childhood l oft have ye beguiled
> Lone Manhood's cares, yet waking fondest sighs,
> Ah! that once more I were a careless Child."

Or the still more beautiful one which follows it :—,

> "Sweet Mercy! how my very heart has bled
> To see thee, poor old man! and thy grey hairs
> Hoar with the snowy blast; while no one cares
> To clothe thy shrivelled limbs and palsied head.
> My Father! throw away this tattered vest
> That mocks thy shiv'ring! take my garment—use
> A young man's! I'll melt these frozen dews
> That hang from thy white beard and numb thy breast.
> My Sara too, shall tend thee, like a child :
> And thou shalt talk, in our fire-side's recess,
> Of purple pride, that scowls on wretchedness.—
> He did not scowl, the Galilæan mild,
> Who met the Lazar turned from rich man's doors,
> And called him Friend, and wept upon his sores!"

CHAPTER XXVIII.

LAMB.

LAMB.—In classing Charles Lamb amongst these poetical Essays, it must be understood that we do not consider him a great poet. He is not agitated by that fervent imagination, which absorbs the faculties of one possessed by that "fine frenzy," of which Shakespeare speaks : he does not exhibit that profoundness of thought which gives subject for meditation, when the words are well-nigh forgotten ; he possesses little brilliancy of fancy : no romance ; but

he can lay claim in his poetry to a heart-felt tenderness, a domestic
freedom, and, once or twice the most perfect excellence in what
has been called the *curiosa felicitas* of language, that can be
well conceived. As a critic of the genius of Shakespeare, he may
be pronounced first-rate. This does not mean a critic as that term
is used now-a-days—nothing but dull analysis or verbal pulling to
pieces of the suffering subject—but a discerning advocate of the
essentials, and an indicator of the genius of the poets upon whom
he has remarked. Yet, as the author of *Rosamund Gray*, he will
make every girl and boy, age, and youth too, sigh and muse: and
as the exquisite imitator of that queer ancient master, Burton, he
will make you laugh, however so indisposed you may feel. There
are many persons who are real lovers of poetry, who cannot endure
aught else but what is in their opinions the "highest heaven of
invention," absorbed in Spenser, Shakespeare and Milton, they
look down upon Fletcher or Collins or Burns, and adoring Byron
and Shelley, or Wordsworth, they cannot waste their time or feel-
ings upon Lamb, Montgomery or Campbell. And it will not be
descrying the rapturous study of the master-spirits of the earth,
nor puffing up into an absurd importance the flutterings of the little
gregarious birds around the eagle of Heaven; to say that this is
unfair. Read Shakespeare, but why not also read sweet Fletcher.
And to the Wordsworthian "Muse on your idol; but condesend
to pluck a flower from the shady vernal garden of the affectionate
Charles Lamb." These are exactly the feelings with which we
include Lamb amongst our collection of poets. In proof of the
beauty of his works, we may quote the following poems, in two
very different tones of feeling; and which contain all the char-
acteristics of which we have been speaking. The first is the small
poem, *Hester*—

"When maidens such as Hester die,
Their place ye may not well supply,
Though ye among a thousand try,
    With vain endeavour.

A month or more hath she been dead,
Yet cannot I by force be led,

To think upon the wormy bed,
    And her together,

A springy motion in her gait,
A rising step, did indicate
Of pride and joy no common rate,
    That flush'd her spirit.

I know not by what name beside
I shall it call :—if 't was not pride,
It was a joy to that allied,
    She did inherit,

Her parent held the Quaker rule,
Which doth the human feeling cool,
But she was trained in Nature's school,
    Nature had blest her.

A waking eye, a prying mind,
A heart that stirs, is hard to bind,
A hawk's keen sight ye cannot blind,
    Ye could not Hester.

My sprightly neighbour gone before,
To that unknown and silent shore,
Shall we not meet, as heretofore,
    Some summer morning,

When from thy cheerful eyes a ray
Hath struck a bliss upon the day,
A bliss that would not go away,
    A sweet forewarning ?"

The other *A Farewell to Tobacco* is of an entirely opposite character. It would not have been quoted fully, had it been possible to have broken it into parts, but it is so perfectly continuous throughout, that such anatomy was impossible. There is scarcely anything so near the flow of *L'Allegro* and *Il Penseroso*, as the lines marked in italics—the same fusion of ideas, couched in the same long drawn out melody.

A FAREWELL TO TOBACCO.

"May the Babylonish curse
    Straight confound my stammering verse,
If I can a passage see
In this word-perplexity,
Or a fit expression find,
Or a language to my mind,
(Still the phrase is wide or scant)
To take leave of thee *Great Plant !*
Or in any terms relate
Half my love, or half my hate :
For I hate, yet love thee so,

Much too in the female way,
While thou suck'st the labouring breath
Faster than kisses or than death.
Thou in such a cloud dost bind us,
That our worst foes cannot find us,
And ill fortune, that it would thwart us,
Shoots at rovers, shooting at us ;
While each man, thro' thy heightening steam
Does like a smoking Etna seem,
And all about us does express
(Fancy and wit in richest dress)
A Sicilian fruitfulness.
Thou through such a mist dost show us,
That our best friends do not know us,
And, for those allowed features,
Due to reasonable creatures,
Liken'st us to fell Chimeras,
Monsters that, who see us, fear us,
Worse than Cerberus or Geryon.
Or, who first loved a cloud, Ixion.
    Bacchus we know. and we allow
His tipsy rites. But what art thou,
That but by reflex canst show
What his deity can do,
As the false Egyptian spell,
Aped the true Hebrew miracle ?
Some few vapours thou may'st raise,
The weak brain may serve to amaze,
But to the reins and nobler heart
Canst nor life nor heat impart.
    Brother of Bacchus, later born,
The old world was sure forlorn,
Wanting thee, that aidest more
The god's victories than before
All his panthers, and the brawls
Of his piping Bacchanals.
These, as stale, we disallow,
Or judge of *thee* meant : only thou

Nay, rather,
Plant divine, of rarest virtue ;
Blisters on the tongue would hurt you,
'Twas but in a sort I blamed thee,
None e'er prosper'd who defamed thee ;
Irony all, and feign'd abuse,
Such as perplex'd lovers use,
At a need, when in despair,
To paint forth their fairest fair,
Or in part but to express
That exceeding comeliness
Which their fancies doth so strike
They borrow language of dislike ;
And, instead of Dearest Miss,
Jewel, Honey, Sweetheart, Bliss,
And those forms of old admiring,
Call her Cockatrice and Siren,
Basilisk, and all that's evil,
Witch, Hyena, Mermaid, Devil,
Ethiop, Wench, and Blackamoor,
Monkey, Ape, and twenty more ;
Friendly Traitress, loving Foe,—
Not that she is truly so,
But no other way they know
A contentment to express,
Borders so upon excess,
That they do not rightly wot
Whether it be pain or not.
Or, as men, constrain'd to part
With what's nearest to their heart,
While their sorrows at the height,

Lose discrimination quite,
And their hasty wrath let fall,
To appease their frantic gall,
On the darling thing whatever,
Whence they feel it death to sever,
Though it be, as they, perforce,
Guiltless of the sad divorce.

 For I must (nor let it grieve thee,
Friendliest of plants, that I must) leave thee,
For thy sake, *Tobacco*, I
Would do anything but die,
And but seek to extend my days
Long enough to sing thy praise.
But, as she, who once hath been,
A king's consort is a queen
Ever after nor will bate
Any title of her state,
Though a widow, or divorced,
So I, from thy converse forced,
The old name and style retain,
A right Katherine of Spain ;
And a' seat, too, 'mongst the joys
Of the blest Tobacco Boys ;
Where, though I, by sour physician,
Am debarr'd the full fruition
Of thy favours, I may catch,
Some collateral sweets, and snatch
Sidelong odours, that give life,
Like glances from a neighbour's wife ;
And still live in the by-places
And the suburbs of thy graces,
And in thy borders take delight,
An unconquer'd Canaanite."

We might quote many other of Lamb's poems of almost equal beauty, nor can we refrain at least from giving one or two passages from *John Woodvill* as a last example of his works. In the passage where Simon recounts the things he most loves, and the sports he enjoys in the Forest, there is very much to admire. He loves,

"———— ————all things that live,
From the crook'd worm to man's imperial form,
And God-resembling likeness. The poor fly,
That makes short holyday in the sunbeam,
And dies by some child's hand. The feeble bird
With little wings, yet greatly venturous
In the upper sky. The fish in th' other element,
That knows no touch of eloquence. What else ?
Yon tall and elegant stag,
Who paints a dancing shadow of his horns
In the water, where he drinks."

rought doing, saying little, thinking less,
To view the leaves, thin dancers upon air,
Go eddying round ; and small birds, how they fare,
When mother Autumn fills their beaks with corn,
Filch'd from the careless Amalthea's horn ;
And how the woods berries and worms provide
Without their pains, when earth has nought beside
To answer their small wants;
To view the graceful deer come tripping
Then stop, and gaze, then turn, they know not why,
Like bashful younkers in society :
To mark the structure of a plant or tree ;
And all fair things of earth, how fair they be."

It may in conclusion, be said of Lamb, that he is not great but
eminent ; not profound, yet penetrating ; not passionate, yet gentle,
tender, and sympathising.

CHAPTER XXIX.

SOUTHEY.

SOUTHEY.—The poetical genius of Southey is rather passive than
active. He has *power*, but not *force*. His personages, like his
scenes, have something unreal, phantomlike, and dreamy about
them : they are often beautiful, but it is a beauty not of the earth,
or even of the clouds, but of the *mirage* and the Fata Morgana.
A writer says,* "His robe of inspiration sits gracefully and majes-
tically upon him, but it is too voluminous in its folds, and too
heavy in its gorgeous texture, for the motion of real existence : he
never 'succinct for speed,' and his flowing drapery obstructs and
embarrasses his steps." He is too ecstatic and agonising in his

* Thomas B. Shaw, M.A.

poetry, The subjects of his poems are frequently commonplace, wrapped in language at once artistic, but extravagant to an excess. These remarks are especially applicable to *Thalaba,* and *The Curse of Kehama.* The subjects of both of these poems are wild, extravagant, unearthly, and full of supernatural machinery. But they are also of a kind as difficult to manage with effect as they are at first sight splendid and attractive. And this is a point in which Southey excels. *Thalaba* is a tale of Arabian enchantment, full of magicians, dragons, and monsters. It is written in an irregular and wandering species of rhythm, altogether without rhyme. Its fault is that there is a painful air of laxity about it, or as some writer has expressed it, "a want of intellectual bone and muscle." There are many passages in it, notwithstanding, of gorgeous description, and many proofs of powerful fancy and imagination, often to an astonishing degree. Take for instance the following beautiful description of *Night,* in the opening of *Thalaba* :—

> "How beautiful is night !
> A dewy freshness fills the silent air ;
> No mist obscures, nor cloud, nor speck, nor stain,
> Breaks the serene of heaven ;
> In full-orb'd glory yonder Moon divine
> Rolls through the dark blue depths.
> Beneath her steady ray
> The desert-circle spreads,
> Like the round ocean, girdled with the sky.
> How beautiful is night !
>
> Who at this untimely hour
> Wanders o'er the desert sands ?
> No station is in view,
> Nor palm-grove, islanded amid the waste.
> The mother and her child,
> The widow'd mother, and the fatherless boy,
> They at this untimely hour
> Wander o'er the desert sands."

Again the elegant description of the pelican in the desert, in the Fifth Book :—

> "A desert Pelican had built her nest
> In that deep solitude,
> And now, return'd from distant flight,
> Fraught with the river stream,
> Her load of water had disburthen'd there.
> Her young in the refreshing bath
> Dipt down their callow heads,

Fill'd the swoln membrane from their plumeless throat
Pendant, and bills yet soft ;
And buoyant with arch'd breast,
Plied in unpractised stroke
The oars of their broad feet.
They, as the spotted-prowler of the wild
Laps the cool wave, around the mother crowd,
And nestle underneath her outspread wings.
The spotted-prowler of the wild
Lapt the cool wave, and satiate, from the nest,
Guiltless of blood, withdrew.

The mother-bird had moved not,
But cowering o'er her nestlings,
Sate confident and fearless,
And watch'd the wonted guest.
But when the human visitant approach'd,
The alarmed Pelican
Retiring from that hostile shape
Gathers her young, and menaces with wings,
And forward thrusts her threatening neck,
Its feathers ruffling in her wrath,
Bold with maternal fear.
Thalaba drank, and in the water-skin
Hoarded the precious element.
Not all he took, but in the large nest left
Store that sufficed for life ;
And journeying onward, blest the Carrier Bird,
And blest, in thankfulness,
Their common Father, provident for all."

Or again Stanzas eleven and twelve of the same Book :—

"Through the broken portal,
Over weedy fragments,
Thalaba went his way,
Cautious he trod, and felt
The dangerous ground before him with his bow.
The jackal started at his steps ;
The Stork, alarm'd at sound of man,
From her broad nest upon the old pillar top,
Affrighted fled on flapping wings ;
The Adder, in her haunts disturb'd,
Lanced at the intruding staff her arrowy tongue.

Twilight and moonshine dimly mingling gave
An aweful light obscure,
Evening not wholly closed,
The moon still pale and faint :
An aweful light obscure,
Broken by many a mass of blackest shade ;
Long column stretching dark through weeds and moss.
Broad length of lofty wall,

Whose windows lay in light,
And of their former shape, low arch'd or square,
Rude outline on the earth
Figured, with long grass fringed. "

And for a still more fanciful and almost weird description, the
following out of the Sixth Book :—

"Heavy and dark the eve ;
The moon was hid on high,
A dim light tinged the mist
That crost her in the path of Heaven.
All living sounds had ceased,
Only the flow of waters near was heard,
A low and lulling melody,

Fasting, yet not of want
Percipient, he on that mysterious steed
Had reach'd his resting place,
For expectation kept his nature up.
Now as the flow of waters near
Awoke a feverish thirst, ·
Led by the sound he moved
To seek the grateful wave.

A meteor in the hazy air
Play'd before his path ;
Before him now it roll'd
A globe of living fire ;
And now contracted to a steady light,
As when the solitary hermit prunes
His lamp's long undulating flame ;
And now its wavy point
Up-blazing rose, like a young cyprus tree
Sway'd by the heavy wind ;
Anon to Thalaba it moved,
And wrapt him in its pale innocuous fire ;
Now, in the darkness drown'd,
Left him with eyes bedimm'd,
And now, emerging, spread the scene to sight.

Led by the sound and meteor-flame
The Arabian youth advanced.
Now to the nearest of the many rills
He stoops ; ascending steam
Timely repels his hand,
For from its source it sprung, a boiling tide.
A second course with better hap he tries,
The wave intensely cold
Tempts to a copious draught.
There was a virtue in the wave :
His limbs, that stiff with toil
Draggd heavy, from the copious draught received

Lightness and supple strength.
O'erjoyed and weening the benignant Power,
Who sent the reinless steed,
Had blest these healing waters to his use,
He laid him down to sleep,
Lull'd by the soothing and incessant sound,
The flow of many waters, blending oft
With shriller tones and deep low murmurings,
Which from the fountain caves
In mingled melody
Like faëry music, heard at midnight, came.

The sounds which last he heard at night
Awoke his recollection first at morn.
A scene of wonders lay before his eyes.
In mazy windings o'er the vale
A thousand streamlets stray'd,
And in their endless course
Had intersected deep the stony soil,
With labyrinthine channels islanding
A thousand rocks, which seem'd
Amid the multitudinous waters there
Like clouds that freckle o'er the summer sky,
The blue ethereal ocean circling each,
And insulating all.

Those islets of the living rock
Were of a thousand shapes,
And Nature with her various tints,
Diversified anew their thousand forms ;
For some were green with moss,
Some ruddier tinged, or grey, or silver-white,
And some with yellow lichens glow'd like gold,
Some sparkled sparry radiance to the sun.
Here gush'd the fountains up,
Alternate light and blackness, like the play
Of sunbeams on a warrior's burnish'd arms.
Yonder the river roll'd, whose ample bed,
Their sportive lingerings o'er,
Received and bore away the confluent rills. "

personages and adventures of this poem are almost super-
l, and this in no limited sense.   The same writer whom we
quoted, says, in speaking of the characters in this poem,
are so completely out of the circle of human sympathies,
their triumphs and sufferings, and they are so scrupulously
d of all the passions and circumstances of humanity, that
orgeous and ambitious works produce on us, the impres-
a splendid but unsubstantial nightmare : they are the vast

disjointed visions of fever and delirium." The subject upon which
Thalaba is constructed is a series of adventures encountered by
an Arabian hero, who fights with demons and enchanters and
finally overthrows the dominion of the powers of evil in the
"Domdaniel Caverns," under the roots of the ocean. It is more
extravagant in some places even than the "Thousand and One
Nights."

In *Kehama*, Southey has chosen a still more unmanageable
groundwork—the mythology of the Hindoos—a vast structure of
superstition. The same faults and the same excellencies apply to
this, as to the former poem. The descriptive portions are equally
gorgeous in their colouring, and gives proofs of Southey's powerful
imaginative faculties. Take for example, the following description
of *Evening* :—

> " Evening comes on ; arising from the stream,
> Homeward the tall flamingo wings his flight,
> And where the sails athwart the setting beam,
> His scarlet plumage glows with deeper light.
> The watchman, at the wish'd approach of night,
> Gladly forsakes the field, where he all day,
> To scare the winged plunderers from their prey,
> With shout and sling, on yonger clay-built height,
> Hath borne the sultry ray.
> Hark ! at the Golden Palaces.
> The Brahmin strikes the hour.
> For leagues and leagues around, the brazen sound
> Rolls though the stillness of departing day,
> Like thunder far away.
>
> Behold them wandering on their hopeless way,
> Unknowing where they stray,
> Yet sure where'er they stop to find no rest.
> The evening gale is blowing,
> It plays among the trees ;
> Like plumes upon a warrior's crest,
> They see yon cocoas tossing to the breeze.
> Ladurlad views them with impatient mind,
> Impatiently he hears
> The gale of evening blowing,
> The sound of waters flowing,
> As if all sights and sounds combined
> To mock his irremediable woe ;
> For not for him the blessed waters flow,
> For not for him the gales of evening blow,
> A fire is in his heart and brain,
> And Nature hath no healing for his pain.

So well had the embalmers done their part
With spice and precious unguents to imbue
The perfect corpse, that each had still the hue
Of living man, and every limb was still
Supple and firm and full, as when of yore
Its motions answer'd to the moving will.
The robes of royalty which once they wore,
Long since had moulder'd off and left them bare:
Naked upon their thrones behold them there,
Statues of actual flesh ; . . a fearful sight;
Their large and rayless eyes
Dimly reflecting to that gem-borne light,
Glaz'd fix'd, and meaningless, . . . yet, open wide,
Their ghastly balls belied
The mockery of life in all beside.

But if amid these Chambers drear,
Death were a sight of shuddering and of fear,
Life was a thing of stranger horror here.
For at the farther end, in yon alcove,
Where Baly should have lain, had he obey'd
Man's common lot, behold Ereenia laid.
Strong fetters link him to the rock ; his eye
Now rolls and widens ; as with effort vain
He strives to break the chain,
Now seems to brood upon his misery.
Before him couch'd there lay

One of the mighty monsters of the deep,
Whom Lorrinite encountering on the way,
There station'd, his perpetual guard to keep ;
In the sport of wanton power, she charm'd him there,
As if to mock the Glendoveer's despair.

Upward his form was human, save that here
The skin was cover'd o'er with scale on scale
Compact, a panoply of natural mail.
His mouth, from ear to ear,
Weapon'd with triple teeth, extended wide,
And tusks on either side ;
A double snake below, he roll'd
His supple length behind in many a sinuous fold.

With red and kindling eye, the beast beholds
A living man draw nigh,
And rising on his folds,
In hungry joy awaits the expected feast,
His mouth half-open, and his teeth unsheath'd.
Then on he sprung, and in his scaly arms
Seized him, and fasten'd on his neck, to suck,
With greedy lips the warm life-blood : and sure
But for the mighty power of magic charms,
As easily as, in the blithesome hour
Of spring, a child doth crop the meadow flower.
Piecemeal those claws
Had rent their victim and those armed jaws
Snapt him in twain.   Naked Ladurlad stood,
Yet fearless and unharm'd in this dread strife,
So well Kehama's Curse had charm'd his fated life.

He too . . . for anger, rising at the sight
Of him he sought, in such strange thrall confined,
With desperate courage fired Ladurlad's mind, . .
He too unto the fight himself addrest,
And grappling breast to breast,
With foot firm planted stands.
And seiz'd the monster's throat with both his hands,
Vainly, with throttling grasp, he prest
The impenetrable scales ;
And lo ! the Guard rose up, and round his foe,
With gliding motion, wreath'd his lengthening coils,
Then tighten'd all their folds with stress and strain.
Nought would the raging tiger's strength avail
If once involved within those mighty toils ;
The armed Rhinoceros, so clasp'd, in vain
Had trusted to his hide of rugged mail,
His bones all broken, and the breath of life
Crush'd from the lungs, in that unequal strife.
Again, and yet again, he sought to break
The impassive limbs ; but when the Monster found

His utmost power was vain,
A moment he relax'd in every round,
Then knit his coils again with closer strain,
And, bearing forward, forced him to the ground.
Ereenia groan'd in anguish at the sight
Of this dread fight: once more the Glendoveer
Essay'd to break his bonds, and fear
For that brave father who had sought him here,
Stung him to wilder strugglings. From the rock
He raised himself half-up, with might and main
Plucked at the adamantine chain,
And now with long and unrelaxing strain,
In obstinate effort of indignant strength,
Labour'd and strove in vain;
Till his immortal sinews fail'd at length;
And yielding, with an inward groan, to fate,
Despairingly, he let himself again
Fall prostrate on his prison-bed of stone,
Body and chain alike with lifeless weight.

Struggling they lay in mortal fray
All day, while day was in our upper sphere,
For light of day
And natural darkness never entered here;
All night, with unabated might,
They waged the unremitting fight.
A second day, a second night,
With furious will they wrestled still.
The third came on, the fourth is gone;
Another comes, another goes,
And yet no respite, no repose!
But day and night, and night and day,
Involv'd in mortal strife they lay;
Six days and nights have pass'd away,
And still they wage, with mutual rage,
The unremitting fray.
With mutual rage their war they wage,
But not with mutual will;
For when the seventh morning came,
The monster's worn and wearied frame
In this strange contest fails:
And weaker, weaker, every hour,
He yields beneath, strong Nature's power,
For now the Curse prevails.

Sometimes the Beast sprung up to bear
His foe aloft; and thrusting there
To shake him from his hold,
Relax'd the rings that wreath'd him round;
But on his throat Ladurlad hung
And weigh'd him to the ground;

And if they sink, or if they float,
Alike with stubborn clasp he clung,
Tenacious of his grasp ;
For well he knew with what a power,
Exempt from Nature's laws,
The Curse had arm'd him for this hour ;
'And in the monster's gasping jaws,
And in his hollow eye,
Well could Ladurlad now descry
The certain signs of victory.

And now the Beast no more can keep
His painful watch ; his eyes, opprest,
Are fainting for their natural sleep ;
His living flesh and blood must rest,
The Beast must sleep or die.
Then he, full faint and languidly,
Unwreaths his rings and strives to fly,
And still retreating, slowly trails
His stiff and heavy length of scales.
But that unweariable foe,
With will relentless follows still ;
No breathing time, no pause of fight
He gives, but presses on his flight ;
Along the vaulted chambers, and the ascent
Up to the emerald-tinted light of day,
He harasses his way.
Till lifeless, underneath his grasp,
The huge Sea-Monster lay.

That obstinate work is done ; Ladurlad cried,
One labour yet remains
And thoughtfully he eyed
Ereenia's ponderous chains;
And with faint effort, half-despairing, tried
The rivets deep in-driven.   Instinctively,
As if in search of aid, he look'd around :
Oh, then how gladly, in the near alcove,
Fallen on the ground its lifeless Lord beside,
The crescent scymitar he spied,   .
Whose cloudy blade, with potent spells imbued,
Had lain so many an age unhurt in solitude.

Joyfully springing there
He seized the weapon, and with eager stroke
Hew'd at the chain ; the force was dealt in vain,
For not as if through yielding air
Pass'd the descending scymitar,
Its deaden'd way the heavy water broke ;
Yet it bit deep.   Again, with both his hands
He wields the blade, and dealt a surer blow,

The descriptive parts of this poem are not so rich as many of his later works, but there are many passages nevertheless of exceeding beauty. The descriptions contained in the passage, where Dunois and the Maids rest at evening, is perhaps one of the best.

> "And now, beneath the horizon westering slow
> Had sunk the orb of day : o'er all the vale
> A purple softness spread, save where the tree
> Its giant shadow stretch'd, or winding stream
> Mirror'd the light of heaven, still traced distinct
> When twilight dimly shrouded all beside,
> A grateful coolness freshen'd the calm air,
> And the hoarse grasshopper their evening song
> Sung shrill and ceaseless, as the dews of night
> Descended. On their way the travellers wend,
> Cheering the road with converse, till far off
> They mark a cottage taper's glimmering light
> Gleam through the embower'd gloom ; to that they turn
> An aged man came forth; his thin grey locks
> Waved on the night breeze, and on his shrunk face,
> The characters of age were written deep.
> Them, louting low with rustic courtesy,
> He welcom'd in ; on the white-ember'd hearth
> Heapt up fresh fuel ; then, with friendly care,
> Spread out the homely board, and fill'd the bowl
> With the red produce of the vine that arched
> His evening seat ; they of the plain repast
> Partook, and quaff'd the pure and pleasant bowl."

The passage selected as the best example of the beauties of this poem, is the Maiden's story in the First Book. It is elegantly written and expressed.

"Seest thou, Sir Chief, where yon forest skirts
The Meuse, that in its winding mazes shows
As on the farther bank the distant towers
Of Vaucouleur ? there in the hamlet Arc
My father's dwelling stands ; a lowly hut,
Yet nought of needful comfort wanted it;
For in Lorraine there lived no kinder lord
Than old Sir Robert, and my father Jacques,
In flocks and herds was rich.   A toiling man
Intent on worldly gains, one in whose heart
Affection had no root.   I never knew
A parent's love; for harsh my mother was,
And deem'd the cares that infancy demands
Irksome, and ill-repaid.   Severe they were,
And would have made me fear them, but my soul
Possess'd the germ of steady fortitude,
And stubbornly I bore unkind rebuke
And wrathful chastisement.   Yet was the voice
That spake in tones of tenderness most sweet
To my young heart ; now have I felt it leap
With transport, when mine uncle Claude approach'd !
For he would place me on his knee, and tell
The wondrous tales that childhood loves to hear,
Listening with eager eyes and open lips
In most devout attention.   Good old man !
Oh, if I ever pour'd a prayer to Heaven
Unhallowed by the grateful thought of him,
Methinks the righteous winds would scatter it !
He was a parent to me, and his home
Was mine, when, in advancing years, I found
No peace, no comfort, in my father's house.
With him I pass'd the pleasant evening hours,
By day I drove my father's flock afield
And this was happiness.
                Amid these wilds
Often to summer pasture have I driven
The flock, and well I know these mountains wilds,
And every bosom'd vale, and valley stream
Is dear to memory.   I have laid me down
Beside yon valley stream, that up the ascent
Scarce sends the sound of waters now, and watch d
The tide roll glittering to the noon-tide sun,
And listened to its ceaseless murmuring,
For all was hush'd and tranquil in my soul,
Fill'd with a strange and undefined delight
That pass'd across the mind like summer clouds
Over the lake at eve : their fleeting hues
The traveller cannot trace with memory's eye,
Yet he remembers well how fair they were,
How very lovely.

Here in solitude
My soul was nurst, amid the loveliest scenes
Of unpolluted nature.   Sweet it was,
As the white mists of morning roll'd away,
To see the mountain's wooded heights appear
Dark in the early dawn, and mark its slopes
Rich with the blossom'd furze, as the slant sun
On the golden ripeness pour'd a deepening light.
Pleasant at noon, beside the vocal brook
To lie me down, and watch the floating clouds,
And shape to Fancy's wild similitudes
Their ever-varying forms; and oh how sweet.
To drive my flock at evening to the fold,
And hasten to our little hut, and hear
The voice of kindness bid me welcome home.
   'Amid the village playmates of my youth
Was one whom riper years approved my friend;
A very gentle maid was Madelon.
I loved her as a sister, and a long time
Her undivided tenderness possess'd,
Till that a better and a holier tie
Gave her one nearer friend, and then my heart
Partook her happiness, for never lived
A happier pair than Arnaud and his wife.
'Lorraine was cali'd to arms, and with her youth
Went Arnaud to the war.   The morn was fair,
Bright shone the sun, the birds sung cheerily,
And all the fields look'd lovely in the spring;
But to Domremi wretched was that day,
For there was lamentation, and the voice
Of anguish, and the deeper agony
That spake not.   Never will my heart forget
The feelings that shot through me, when the sound
Of cheerful music burst upon our ears
Sudden, and from the arms that round their necks
Hung close entwined, as in a last embrace,
Friends, brethren, husband's went.
          More frequent now
Sought I the converse of poor Madelon,
For much she needed now the soothing voice
Of friendship.   Heavily the summer pass'd,
To her a joyless one, expecting still
Some tidings from the war; and as at eve
She with her mother by the cottage door
Sat in the sunshine, I have seen her eye,
If one appeared along the distant path,
Shape to the form she loved, his lineaments,
Her cheek faint flush'd by hope, that made her heart
Seem as it sunk within her.   So the days
And weeks and months pass'd on, and when the leaves

Fell in the autumn, a most painful hope
That reason own'd not, that with expectation
Did never cheer her as she rose at morn,
Still lingered in her heart, and still at night
Made disappointment dreadful. · Winter came,   ·
But Arnaud never from the war return'd,
He far away had perish'd, and when late
The tidings of his certain death arriv'd,
Sore with long anguish underneath that blow·
She sunk. .Then would she sit and think all day
Upon the past, and talk of happiness
That never would return, as tho' she found
Best solace in the thoughts that minister'd
To sorrow : and she loved to see the sun
Go down, because another day was gone,
And then she might retire to solitude
And wakeful recollections, or perchance
To sleep more wearying far than wakefulness,
For in the visions of her heart she saw
Her husband, saw him as escaped the war,
To his own home return'd.   Thus day nor night
Reposed she, and she pined and pined away.
  'Bitter art thou to him that lives in rest,
O Death ! and grievous in the hour of joy
The thought of thy cold dwelling ; but thou comest
Most welcome to the wretched ; a best friend
To him that wanteth one ; a comforter,
For in the grave is peace.   By the bed-side
Of Madelon I sat : when sure she felt
The hour of her deliverance drawing near,
I saw her eye kindle with heavenly hope,
I had her latest look of earthly hope,
I felt her hand's last pressure.   Son of Orleans !
I would not wish to live to know that hour,
When I could think upon a dear friend dead,
And weep not.
                    I remember, as her corse
Went to the grave, there was a lark sprung up,
And soaring in the sunshine, caroll'd loud
A joyful song ; and in mine heart I thought,
That of the multitude of beings, man
Alone was wretched.
                    Then my soul awoke,
For it had slumber'd long in happiness,
And never feeling misery, never thought
What others suffer.   I, as best I might,
Solaced the keen regret of Elinor ;
And much my cares avail'd, and much her son's,
On whom, the only comfort of her age,
She centred now her love.   A younger birth,

Aged nearly as myself was Theodore,
An ardent youth, who with the kindest cares
Had sooth'd his sister's sorrow: We had knelt
By her death-bed together, and no bond
In closer union knits two human hearts
Than fellowship in grief.
      It chano'd as once
Beside the fire of Elinor I sat,
The night was comfortless; the loud blast howl'd;
And as we drew around the social hearth,
We heard the rain beat hard; driven by the storm
A warrior mark'd our distant taper's light.
We heapt the fire: the friendly board was spread:
The bowl of hospitality went round.
'The storm beats hard,' the stranger cried; 'safe hous'd,'
Pleasant it is to hear the pelting rain.
I too were well content to dwell in peace,
Resting my head upon the lap of Love,
But that my country calls. When the winds roar,
Remember sometimes what a soldier suffers,
And think of Conrade!
      Theodore replied,
'Success go with thee! Something I have known
Of war, and of its dreadful ravages;
My soul was sick at such ferocity:
And I am well content to dwell in peace,
Albeit inglorious, thanking that good God
Who made me to be happy!
      'Did that God,'
Cried Conrade, 'form thy heart for happiness,
When Desolation royally careers
Over thy wretched country? Did that God
From thee for peace when Slaughter is abroad,
When her brooks run with blood, and Rape and Murder
Stalk thro' her flaming towns? Live thou in peace,
Young man! my heart is human: I do feel
For what my brethren suffer.'
      As he spake,
Such mingled passions charactered his face
Of fierce and terrible benevolence,
That I did tremble as I listen'd to him.
Then in mine heart tumultuous thoughts arose
Of high achievements, indistinct, and wild,
And vast, yet such they were as made me pant
As though by some divinity possess'd.
'But is there not some duty due to those
We love?' said Theodore; and as he spake
His warm cheek crimsou'd. 'Is it not most right
To cheer the evening of declining age,
With filial tenderness repaying thus
Parental care?'

          'Hard it is,' Conrade cried,
'Ay, very hard, to part from those we love ;
And I have suffer'd that severest pang,
I have left an aged mother, I have left
One, upon whom my heart has centred all
Its dearest, best affections. Should I live
Till France shall see the blessed hour of Peace,
I shall return : my heart will be content,
My highest duties will be well discharg'd,
And I may dare be happy. There are those
Who deem these thoughts wild fancies of a mind
Strict beyond measure, and were well content,
If I should soften down my rigid nature
Even to inglorious ease, to honour me.
But pure of heart and high of self-esteem
I must be honoured by myself : all else,
The breath of Fame, is as the unsteady mind,
Worthless.'
          So saying, from his belt he took
The encumbering sword, I held it, listening to him
And, wistless what I did, half from the sheath
Drew the well-tempered blade. I gazed upon it,
And shuddering as I felt its edge, exclaim'd,
'It is most horrible with the keen sword
To gore the finely-fibred human frame !
I could not strike a lamb.'
          He answer'd me,
'Maiden, thou hast said well. I could not strike
A lamb. But when the invader's savage fury
Spares not grey age, and mocks the infant's shriek
As he does writhe upon his cursed lance,
And forces to his foul embrace the wife
Even on her murder'd husband's gasping corse !
Almighty God ! I should not be a man
If I did not let one weak and pitiful feeling
Make mine arm impotent to cleave him down.
Think well of this, young man !' he cried, and seiz'd
The hand of Theodore; 'think well of this,
As you are human, as you hope to live
In peace, amid the dearest joys of home ;
Think well of this ! You have a tender mother ;
As you do wish that she may die in peace.
As you would even to madness to agonize
To hear this maiden call on you in vain
For aid, and see her dragg'd, and hear her scream
In the blood-reeking soldier's lustful arms,
Think that there are such horrors ; that even now,
Some city flames, and haply as in Roan,
Some famish'd babe on his dead mother's breast
Yet hangs for food ; Oh God ! I would not lose

These horrible feelings tho' they rend my heart.
  When we had all betaken us to rest,
Sleepless I lap, and in my mind revolv'd
The high-soul'd warrior's speech. Then Madelon
Rose in remembrance; o'er her the grave
Had closed; her sorrows were not register'd ·
In the rolls of Fame: but when the tears run down
The widow's cheek, shall not her cry be heard
In Heaven against the oppressor? will not God
In sunder smite the unmerciful, and break
The sceptre of the wicked? Thoughts like these
Possess'd my soul, till at the break of day
I slept, nor then reposed my heated brain,
For visions rose, sent as I do believe
From the Most High. I saw a high tower'd town
Hemmed in around, with enemies begirt,
Where Famine, on a heap of carcases,
Half envious of the unutterable feast,
Mark'd the gorg'd raven clog his beak with gore.
I turn'd me then to the beseiger's camp,
And there was revelry: the loud lewd laugh
Burst on my ears, and I beheld the chiefs
Even at their feast plan the device of death.
My soul grew sick within me: then methought
From a dark lowering cloud, the womb of tempests,
A giant arm burst forth, and dropt a sword
That pierced like lightning thro' the midnight air.
Then was there heard a voice, which in mine ear
Shall echo, at that hour of dreadful joy
When the pale foe shall wither in my rage.
  From that night I could feel my burthen'd soul
Heaving beneath incumbent Deity,
I sat in silence, musing on the days
To come, unheading and unseeing all
Around me, in that dreaminess of soul
When every bodily sense is as it slept,
And the mind alone is wakeful. I have heard
Strange voices in the evening wind; strange forms
Dimly discovered throng'd the twilight air
They wandered at me who had known me once
A cheerful, careless damsel. I have seen
Mine uncle gaze upon me wistfully,
A heaviness upon his aged brow;
And in his eye such meaning, that my heart
Sometimes misgave me. I had told him all
The mighty future labouring in my breast,
But that methought the hour was not yet come.
At length I heard of Orleans, by the foe
Wall'd in from human succour; to the event
All look'd with fear, for there the fate of France

Hung in the balance. Now my troubled soul
Grew more disturb'd, and shunning every eye,
I loved to wander where the forest shade
Frown'd deepest ; there on mightiest deeds to brood
Of shadowy vastness, such as made my heart
Throb loud : anon I paused, and in a state
Of half expectance, listen'd to the wind.
There is a fountain in the forest, call'd
The fountain of the Fairies : when a child,
With most delightful wonder I have heard
Tales of the Elfin tribe that on its bank
Hold midnight revelry. An ancient oak,
The goodliest of the forest, grows beside ;
Alone it stands, upon a green grass plat,
By the woods bounded like some little isle.
It ever hath been deem'd their favourite tree ;
They love to lie and rock upon its leaves,
And bask them in the moonshine. Many a time
Hath the woodman shown his boy where the dark round
On the green-sward beneath its boughs, bewrays
Their nightly dance, and bade him spare the tree.
Fancy had cast a spell upon the place
And made it holy ; and the villagers
Would say that never evil thing approached
Unpunish'd there. The strange and fearful pleasure
That fill'd me by that solitary spring,
Ceas'd not in riper years ; and now it woke
Deeper delight, and more mysterious awe.
Lonely the forest spring ; a rocky hill
Rises beside it, and an aged yew
Burst from the rifted crag that overbrows
The waters ; cavern'd there, unseen and slow
And silently they well. The adder's tongue,
Rich with the wrinkles of its glossy glen,
Hangs down its long lank leaves, whose wavy dip
Just breaks the tranquil surface. Ancient woods
Bosom the quiet beauties of the place,
Nor ever sound profanes it, save such sounds
As Silence loves to hear, the passing wind,
Or the low murmuring of the scarce-heard stream.
A blessed spot ! oh, how my soul enjoy'd
Its quietness, with what delight,
Escaping humankind, I hastened there
To solitude and freedom ! Thitherward
On a spring eve I had betaken me,
And there I sat, and mark'd the deep red clouds
Gather before the wind, the rising wind,
Whose sudden gusts, each wilder than the last,   ·
Seem'd as they rock'd my senses. Soon the night
Darken'd around, and the large rain drops fell

                    I felt his words
Pierce in my heart; my soul was overcharged;
I fell upon his neck and told him all;
God was within me; as I felt I spake,
And he believed.
                    Ay, Chieftain, and the world
Shall soon believe my mission; for the Lord
Will raise up indignation, and pour out
His wrath, and they shall perish who oppress."

The next poem in point of consequence is the *Vision of Judgment*, rendered interesting by the fact that in this poem Southey essayed to revive the hexameter in English verse. This experiment, tried in so many languages, and with such indifferent success, had been attempted by Gabriel Harvey in the reign of Elizabeth, from which the following lines, from his Translation of Virgil are quoted as an example.

"With tentive listening each wight was settled in harkning;
Then father Æneas chronicled from loftie bed hautie:
You bid me, O princess, to scarifie a festered old sore,
How that the Trojans were prest by the Grecian armie."

The universal ridicule which hailed Southey's attempt was excited quite as much by the absurdity of the metre as by the extravagant flattery of the poem itself. The deification, or rather beatification, of George III, drew from Byron some of the severest strokes of his irresistible ridicule, and gave him the opportunity of severely revenging upon Southey some of the attacks upon his principles and poetry. The *Vision of Judgment,* was one of the odes, written upon his being appointed poet-laureate.

In Southey's early days, he was a sceptic and a republican, but became afterwards a firm believer in Christianity, and in his poet-laureate odes he exhibits a fierce, passionate, controversial hatred of his former liberal opinions which gives interest even to the ambitions monotony, the convulsive mediocrity of his official lyrics. And in this the *Vision of Judgment* stands very prominent.

Roderick, the Last of the Goths is a poem in blank verse, and very much superior to many other of Southey's poems. The agonizing repentance of the Gothic King for his past crimes, and his humble trust in the mercy of God, form the prevailing tone of the work. He figures in most of the scenes in the disguise of a hermit, in which many of his powerful exclamations are written with zeal, tenderness, and pathos. For instance the following passage :—

> "———————Lo ! the western sun
> Flames o'er the broad Atlantic ; on the verge
> Of glowing ocean rests ; retiring then
> Draws with it all its rays, and sudden night
> Fills the whole cope of heaven. The penitent
> Knelt by Romano's grave, and falling prone,
> Clasp'd with extended arms the funeral mould.
> Father ! he cried, Companion ! only friend,
> When all beside was lost ! thou too art gone,
> And the poor sinner whom from utter death
> Thy providential hand preserved, once more
> Totters upon the gulph. I am too weak
> For solitude, . . too vile a wretch to bear
> This everlasting commune with myself
> The Tempter hath assail'd me ; my own heart
> Is leagued with him ; Despair hath laid the nets
> To take my soul, and Memory like a ghost,
> Haunts me, and drives me to the toils. O Saint,
> While I was blest with thee, the hermitage
> Was my sure haven ! Look upon me still,
> For from thy heavenly mansion thou canst see
> The suppliant ; look upon thy child in Christ.
> Is there no other way for penitence ?
> I ask not martyrdom ; for what am I
> That I should pray for triumphs, the fit meed
> Of a long life of holy works like thine;
> Or how should I presumptuously aspire

There is none of the supernatural machinery employed in this
poem as in many other of his works, yet there is the same want of
reality and human interest.   There are many descriptions, not-
ithstanding, of undeniable merit.   For example :—

"How calmly gliding through the dark-blue sky
The midnight Moon ascends ! Her placid beams
Through thinly scatter'd leaves and boughs grotesque,
Mottle with mazy shades the orchard slope ;
Here, o'er the chestnuts fretted foliage grey
And massy, motionless they spread ; here shine
Upon the crags, deepening with blacker night
Their chasms ; and there the glittering argentry
Ripples and glances on the confluent streams.
A lovelier, purer light than that of day
Rests on the hills ; and oh how awefully
Into that deep and tranquil firmament
The summits of Auseva rise serene!
The watchman on the battlements partakes
The stillness of the solemn hour ; he feels
The silence of the earth, the endless sound
Of flowing water soothes him, and the stars,
Which in that brightest moon-light well-nigh quench'd
Scarce visible, as in the utmost depth
Of yonder sapphire infinite, are seen,
Draw on with elevating influence
Toward eternity the attemper'd mind.
Musing on worlds beyond the grave he stands,
And to the Virgin Mother silently
Perfers her hymns of praise."

C.

Or the following, which is equally beautiful :

"Meantime Pelayo up the vale pursued
Eastward his way, before the sun had climb'd
Auseva's brow, or shed his silvering beams
Upon Europa's summit, where the snows
Through all revolving seasons hold their seat.
A happy man he went, his heart at rest,
Of hope and virtue and affection full,
To all exhilarating influences
Of earth and heaven alive.   With kindred joy
He heard the lark, who from her airy height,
On twinkling pinions poised, pour'd forth profuse,
In thrilling sequence of exuberant song,
As one whose joyous nature overflow'd
With life and power, her rich and rapturous strain.
The early bee, buzzing along the way,
From flower to flower, bore gladness on its wing
To his rejoicing sense ; and he pursued,
With quicken'd eye alert, the frolic hare,
Where from the green herb in her wanton path
She brush'd away the dews.   For he long time,
Far from his home and from his native hills,
Had dwelt in bondage ; and the mountain breeze,
Which he had with the breath of infancy
Inhaled, such impulse to his heart restored,
As if the seasons had roll'd back, and life
Enjoy'd a second spring.

     *   *   *   *

————————A mountain rivulet,
Now calm and lovely in its summer course,
Held by those huts its everlasting way
Towards Pionia.   They whose flocks and herds
Drink of its water call it Deva.   Here
Pelayo southward up the ruder vale
Traced it, his guide unerring.   Amid heaps
Of mountain wreck, on either side thrown high,
The wide-spread traces of its wintry might,
The tortuous channel wound ; o'er beds of sand
Here silently it flows ; here from the rock
Rebutted, curls and eddies ; plunges here
Precipitate ; here roaring among crags,
It leaps and foams and whirls and hurries on.
Grey alders here and bushy hazels hid
The mossy side ; their wreath'd and knotted·feet
Bared by the current, now against its force
Repaying the support they found, upheld
The bank secure.   Here, bending to the stream,
The birch fantastic stretch'd its rugged trunk,
Tall and erect from whence, as from their base,
Each like a tree, in silver branches grew.

"There was an old man breaking stones
  To mend the turnpike way ;
He sate him down beside a brook
And out his bread and cheese he took,
  For now it was mid-day.

He leant his back against a post,
  His feet the brook ran by ;
And there were water-cresses growing,
And pleasant was the waters flowing,
  For he was hot and dry.

A soldier with his knapsack on,
  Came travelling o'er the down ;
The sun was strong and he was tired ;
And he of the old man inquired
  How far to Bristol town.

Half an hour's walk for a young man,
  By lanes and fields and stiles ;
But you the foot-path do not know,
And if along the road you go,
  Why then 'tis three good miles.

The soldier took his knapsack off,
  For he was hot and dry ;
And out his bread and cheese he took,
And he sat down beside the brook
  To dine in company.

Old friend ! in faith, the soldier says,
  I envy you almost ;
My shoulders have been sorely prest
And I should like to sit and rest
  My back against that post.

In such a sweltering day as this,
　A knapsack is the devil !
And if on t'other side I sat,
It would not only spoil our chat,
　But make me seem uncivil.

The old man laugh'd and moved—I wish
　It were a great arm'd chair !
But this may help a man at need !
And yet it was a cursed deed
　That ever brought it there.

There's a poor girl lies buried here
　Beneath this very place.
The earth upon her corpse is prest,
The stake is driven into her breast,
　And a stone is on her face.

The soldier had but just leant back,
　And now he half rose up.
There's sure no harm in dining here,
My friend ? and yet to be sincere
　I should not like to sup.

God rest her ! she is still enough
　Who sleeps beneath my feet !
The old man cried.　No harm I trow
She ever did herself, though now
　She lies where four roads meet.

I have passed by about that hour
　When men are not most brave ;
It did not make my heart to fail,
And I have heard the nightingale
　Sing sweetly on her grave.

I have past by about that hour
　When ghosts their freedom have ;
But there was nothing here to fright,
And I have seen the glow-worm's light
　Shine on the poor girl's grave.

There's one who like a Christian lies
　Beneath the church-tree's shade ;
I'd rather go a long mile round
Than pass at evening through the ground
　Wherein that man is laid.

There's one who in the churchyard lies
　For whom the bell did toll ;
He lies in consecrated ground,
But for all the wealth in Bristol town
　I would not be with his soul !

Didst see a house below the hill,
　Which the winds and the rains destroy ?
'Twas then a farm where he did dwell,

And I remember it full well
  When I was a growing boy.

And she was a poor parish girl
  Who came up from the west;
From service hard she ran away,
And at that house in evil day,
  Was taken in to rest.

The man he was a wicked man,
  And an evil life he led;
Rage made his cheek grow deadly white,
And his gray eyes were large and light,
  And in anger they grew red.

The man was bad, the mother worse,
  Bad fruits of a bad stem;
'Twould make your hair to stand on end
If I should tell to you, my friend,
  The things that were told of them!

Didst see an out-house, standing by?
  The walls alone remain;
It was a stable then, but now
Its mossy roof has fallen through
  All rotted by the rain.

The poor girl she had served with them
  Some half a year or more,
When she was found hung up one day
Stiff as a corpse and cold as clay
  Behind that stable door!

It is a wild and lonesome place,
  No hut or house is near,
Should one meet a murderer there alone,
'Twere vain to scream, and the dying groan
  Would never reach mortal ear.

And there were strange reports about;
  But still the coroner found
That she by her own hand had died,
And should buried be by the way side,
  And not in Christian ground.

This was the very place he chose,
  Just where these four roads met,
And I was one among the throng
That hither followed them along,
  I shall never the sight forget!

They carried her upon a board,
  In the clothes in which she died;
I saw the cap blow off her head,
Her face was of a dark, dark red,
  Her eyes were starting wide.

I think they could not have been closed
  So widely did they strain.
I never saw so dreadful a sight,
And it often made me wake at night,
  For I saw her face again.

They laid her here where four roads meet,
  Beneath this very place.
The earth upon her corpse was prest,
This post is driven into her breast
  And a stone is on her face."

Also some of his legends, translated from the Spanish and Portugese, or from the obscurer stores of the Latin chronicles of the Middle Ages, or the monkish legends of the saints, are very vigorous and characteristically written. The tale of *The Lover's Rock* is an interesting specimen.

"The maiden through the favouring night
  From Granada took her flight,
  She bade her father's house farewell,
  And fled away with Manuel.

No Moorish maid might hope to vie
  With Laila's cheek or Laila's eye,
  No maiden loved with purer truth,
  Or ever loved a lovlier youth.

In fear they fled across the plain,
  The father's wrath, the captive's chain,
  In hope to Seville on they flee,
  To peace, and love, and liberty.

Chiuma they have left, and now, .
  Beneath a precipice's brow,
  Where Guadalhorce winds its way,
  There in the shade awhile they lay ;

For now the sun was near its height,
  And she was weary with her flight ;
  She laid her head on Manuel's breast,
  And pleasant was the maiden's rest.

While thus the lovely Laila slept,
  A fearful watch young Manuel kept,
  Alas ! her father and his train,
  He sees come speeding o'er the plain.

The maiden started from her sleep,
  They sought for refuge up the steep,
  To scale the precipice's brow
  Their only hope of safety now.

But them the angry father sees,
  With voice and arm he menaces,

The archers aim'd their arrows there,
She clasp'd young Manuel in despair,
'Death, Manuel, shall set us free,
Then leap below and die with me.'

He clasp'd her close and cried farewell,
In one another's arms they fell ;
And falling o'er the rock's steep side,
In one another's arms they died.

And side by side they there are laid,
The Christian youth and Moorish maid :
But never cross was planted their,
Because they perish'd for despair.

Yet every Moorish maid can tell
Where Laila lies who loved so well,
And every youth who passes there,
Says for Manuel's soul a prayer."

spirit was strongly legendary, and he has caught the
not of heroic and chivalric tradition, but of the religious
of monastic times.   A specimen of this may be seen in
ca, and The Five Martyrs of Morocco.

' The Friars five have girt their loins,
    And taken staff in hand ;
And never shall those Friars again
    Hear mass in Christian land.

They went to Queen Oracca,
    To thank her and bless her then ;
And Queen Oracca in tears
    Knelt to the holy men.

'Three things, Queen Oracca,
  We prophesy to you :
Hear us, in the name of God !
  For time will prove them true.

'In Morocco we must martyr'd be,
  Christ hath vouchsafed it thus :
We shall shed our blood for Him
  ˙ Who shed his blood for us.

To Coimbra shall our bodies be brought,
  Such being the will divine ;
That Christians may behold and feel
  Blessings at our shrine.

'And when unto that place of rest,
  Our bodies shall draw nigh,
Who sees us first, the King or you,
  That one that night must die.

'Fare thee well, Queen Orraca !
  For thy soul a mass we will say,
Every day as long as we live,
  And on thy dying day.

The Friars they blest her, one by one,
  Where she knelt on her knee,
And they departed to the land
  Of the Moors beyond the sea.

'What news, O King Affonso,
  What news of the Friars five ?
Have they preach'd to the Miramamolin ;
  And are they still alive ?'

'They have fought the fight, O Queen !
  They have run the race :
In robes of white they hold the palm
  Before the throne of Grace,

' All naked in the sun and air
  Their mangled bodies lie ;
What Christian dared to bury them,
  By the bloody Moors would die.'

'What news, O King Affonso,
  Of the Martyrs five? what news,
Doth the bloody Miramamolin,
  Their burial still refuse ?'

'That on a dunghill they should rot,
  The bloody Moor decreed ;
That their dishonour'd bodies should
  The dogs and vultures feed :

'But the thunder of God roll'd over them,
  And the lightning of God flashed round ;
Nor thing impure, nor man impure,
  Could approach the holy ground.

'A thousand miracles appall'd
  The cruel Pagan's mind ;
Our brother Pedro brings them here,
  In Coimbra to be shrined.'

Every Altar in Coimbra
  Is dressed for the festival day ;
All the people in Coimbra
  Are dight in their richest array ;

Every bell in Coimbra
  Doth merrily, merrily, ring ;
The Clergy and the Knights await,
  To go forth with the Queen and King."

Some of his minor original poems, have great tenderness and simple dignity of thought. Many of his lyrical poems also have an exalted tone in them, and a peculiarity of sentiment strictly his own. Many specimens might be shown of these, but amongst the best perhaps are those *To Contemplation*, the *Ode Written on Sunday Morning*, and *The Widow*. The first of these, *To Contemplation*, possesses all the excellencies of true lyric poetry, and a spirit of reflection pervades it throughout.

"But sweeter 'tis to wander wild
By melancholy dreams beguiled,
While the summer moon's pale ray
Faintly guides me on my way
To the lone romantic glen
Far from all the haunts of men,
Where no noise of uproar rude
Breaks the calm of solitude.
But soothing silence sleeps in all,
Save the neighbouring waterfall,
Whose hoarse waters falling near
Load with hollow sounds the ear,
And with down-dash torrent white
Gleam hoary through the shades of night.
Thus wandering silent on and slow
I'll nurse reflection's sacred woe,
And muse upon the perish'd day
When hope would weave her visions gay,
Ere Fancy chilled by adverse fate
Left sad Reality my mate."

The other, *Written on a Sunday Morning*, has in it all the flow and graceful melody of lyric verse.

"Go thou and seek the house of prayer !
I to the woodlands wend, and there
In lovely nature see the God of love.

The swelling organ's peal
Wakes not my soul to zeal,
Like the wild music of the wind-swept grove.
The gorgeous altar and the mystic vest
Rouse not such ardour in my breast,
As where the noon-tide beam
Flashed from the broken stream,
Quick vibrates on the dazzled sight ;
Or when the cloud-suspended rain
Sweeps in shadows o'er the plain ;
Or when reclining on the cliff's huge height
I mark the billows burst in silver light.
Go thou and seek the house of prayer !
I to the woodlands shall repair,
Feed with all nature's charms mine eyes,
And hear all nature's melodies.
The primrose bank shall there dispense
Faint fragrance to the awakened sense ;
The morning beams that life and joy impart,
Shall with their influence warm my heart,
And the full tear that down my cheek will steal,
Shall speak the prayer of praise I feel !
Go thou and seek the house of prayer l
I to the woodlands bend my way,
And meet religion there.
She needs not haunt the high-arched dome to pray
Where storied windows dim the doubtful day :
With liberty she loves to rove,
Wide o'er the heathy hill or cowslip dale ;
Or seek the shelter of the embowering grove,
Or with the streamlet wind along the vale.
Sweet are these scenes to her ; and when the night
Pours in the north her silver streams of light,
She woos reflection in the silent gloom,
And ponders on the world to come."

And the latter, *The Widow,* is full of simple tenderness, and
touching expression.

" Cold was the night-wind, drifting fast the snow fell,
Wide were the downs and shelterless and naked,
When a poor wanderer struggled on her journey,
Weary and way-sore.

Drear were the downs, more dreary her reflections ;
Cold was the night wind, colder was her bosom ;
She had no home, the world was all before her,
She had no shelter.

Fast o'er the heath a chariot rattled by her ;
'Pity me l' feebly cried the poor night wanderer.
'Pity me, strangers ! lest with cold and hunger
Here I should perish.'

' Once I had friends, —but they have all forsook me!
Once I had parents,—they are now in heaven !
I had a home once—I had once a husband—
    Pity me, strangers !

'I had a home once—I had once a husband—
I am a widow poor and broken hearted !'
Loud blew the wind, unheard was her complaining,
    On drove the chariot.

Then on the snow she laid her down to rest her ;
She heard a horseman, 'Pity me !' she groaned out ;
Loud was the wind, unheard was her complaining,
    On went the horseman.

Worn out with anguish, toil, and cold, and hunger,
Down sunk the wanderer, sleep had seized her senses;
There did the traveller find her in the morning,
    God had released her."

CHAPTER XXX.

KIRKE WHITE.

KIRKE WHITE.—The works of this poet have been termed, the fair blossoms of a richly fruitful race. His works, the miniature buds and blossoms shaken from the tree, and green fruit—evince what the harvest would have been, and secure for him that remembrance on earth for which he toiled.

It is superfluous to detail White's powers : they were acknowledged wherever they were known; and are still acknowledged and appreciated by every true lover of poetry. There are truly some amongst his poems of an indifferent character, but undoubtedly many that are included in his works, he himself would not have published. To a real admirer of his poetry, every scrap is of value, and is read with interest ; and for this reason the less important ones which are generally included in his works, had he lived to have taken that rank amongst English poets would, assuredly have been rejected. They all mark the state and progress of his mind, and discover evident proofs of what he would have been if it had been the will of Heaven to have prolonged his stay on earth.

The greatest number of White's poems are of such beauty that Chatterton is the only youthful poet whom he does not leave far behind him. There is a genius of the highest order in his productions, which is recommended by sincerity, and consecrated by piety, so that no one can read them without being awed by the subject, and improved by the sentiments. His poems, collectively, constitute a history; it is interesting to trace in them the gradual progress of his life and work ; and to observe how closely we may compare them with the actual details of his career. His earlier days are beautifully expressed in his poem *Childhood*. In it we see a truthful and interesting reflection of the time and scenes of his infancy, written probably when he was only between fourteen and fifteen.

"Pictured in memory's mellowing glass, how sweet
Our infant days, our infants joys to greet ;
To roam in fancy in each cherish'd scene,
The village churchyard, and the village green.
The woodland walk remote, the greenwood glade,
The mossy seat beneath the hawthorn shade,
The white-washed cottage, where the wood-bine grew,
And all the favourite haunts our childhood knew !
How sweet, while all the evil shuns the gaze,
To view the unclouded skies of former days !

Beloved age of innocence and smiles,
When each wing'd hour some new delight beguiles :
When the gay heart, to life's sweet day-spring true,
Still finds some insect pleasure to pursue.
Blest childhood, hail !—Thee simply will I sing,
And from myself the artless picture bring :
These long lost scenes to me the past restore,
Each humble friend, each *pleasure* now no more ;
And every stump familiar to my sight
Recalls some fond idea of delight.

This shrubby knoll was once my favourite seat ;
Here did I love at evening to retreat,
And muse alone, till in the vault of night,
Hesper, aspiring, showed his golden light.
Here once again ; remote from human noise,
I sit me down to think of former joys ;
Pause on each scene, each treasured scene, once more,
And once again each infant walk explore ;
While as each grove and lawn I recognise,
My melted soul suffuses in my eyes,

And oh ! thou Tower, whose myriad trains resort
To distant scenes, and picture them to thought :

'Whose mirror, held unto the mourner's eye,
Flings to his soul a borrow'd gleam of joy ;
Blest Memory, guide, with finger nicely true,
Back to my youth my retrospective view ;
Recall with faithful vigour to my mind
Each face familiar, each relation kind,
And all the finer traits of them afford,
Whose general outline in my heart is stored."

Then follows the picture of the Village Schoolmistress, which was copied from nature. It is accurately and elegantly drawn :—

"In yonder cot, along whose mouldering walls
In many a fold the mantling woodbine falls;
The village matron kept her little school,
Gentle of heart, yet knowing well to rule ;
Staid was the dame, and modest was her mien ;
Her garb was coarse, yet whole, and nicely clean :
Her neatly bordered cap, as lily fair,
Beneath her chin was pinned with decent care,
And pendant ruffles, of the whitest lawn,
Of ancient make, her elbows did adorn.
Faint with old age and dim were grown her eyes,
A pair of spectacles their want supplies :
These does she guard secure, in leathern case,
From thoughtless wights, in some unweeted place.
Here first I entered, though with toil and pain,
The lowly vestibule of learning's fame ;
Entered with pain, yet soon I found the way,
Though sometimes toilsome, many a sweet display.
Much did I grieve, on that ill-fated morn,
When I was first to school reluctant borne :
Severe I thought the dame, though oft she tried
To soothe my swelling spirits when I sighed ;
And oft, when harshly she reproved, I wept,
To my lone corner broken-hearted crept,
And thought of tender home, where anger never kept.
But soon inured to alphabetic toils,
Alert I met the dame with jocund smiles ;
First at the form, my task for ever true,
A little favourite rapidly I grew :
And oft she stroked my head with fond delight,
Held me a pattern to the dunces sight ;
And as she gave her diligence her praise,
Talk'd of my honours of future days.
Oh ! had the venerable matron thought,
Of all the ills by talent often brought;
Could she have seen me when revolving years
Had brought me deeper in the vale of tears,
Then had she wept, and wish'd my wayward fate
Had been a lowlier, an unletter'd state ;

Wished that, remote from worldly woes and strife,
Unknown, unheard, I might have pass'd through life."

The temper and tone of his mind at his fourteenth year are displayed in the following poem, *An Address to Contemplation;* in which his mounting spirit seems to complain of the degradation of his employment.

"Thee do I own, the prompter of my joys,
The soother of my cares, inspiring peace;
And I will ne'er forsake thee. Men may rave,
And blame and censure me, that I don't tie
My every thought down to the desk, and spend
The morning of my life in adding figures
With accurate monotony, that so
The good things of the world may be my lot,
And I might taste the blessedness of wealth :
But, Oh! I was not made for money-getting;
For me no much-respected plum awaits,
Nor civic honour, envied.   For as still
I tried to cast with school dexterity
The interesting sums, my vagrant thoughts
Would quick revert to many a woodland haunt,
Which fond remembrance cherished, and the pen
Dropt from my senseless fingers as I pictured,
In my mind's eye, how on the shores of Trent
I erewhile wandered with my early friends
In social intercourse.   And then I'd think
How contrary pursuits had thrown us wide,
One from the other, scatter'd o'er the globe;
They were set down with sober steadiness,
Each to his occupation. I alone,
A wayward youth, misled by Fancy's vagaries,
Remain'd unsettled, insecure, and veering
With ev'ry wind to ev'ry point o' th' compass.
Yes, in the counting-house I could indulge
In fits of close abstraction ; yea, amid
The busy bustling crowds could meditate,
And send my thoughts ten thousand leagues away
Beyond the Atlantic, resting on my friend.
Aye, Contemplation, ev'n in earliest youth
I woo'd thy heav'nly influence ! I would walk
A weary way when all my toils were done,
To lay myself at night in some lone wood,
And hear the sweet song of the nightingale.
Oh, those were times of happiness, and still
To memory doubly dear ; for growing years
Had not then taught me man was made to mourn;
And a short hour of solitary pleasure,
Stolen from sleep, was ample recompense

For all the hateful bustles of the day.
My op'ning mind was ductile then, and plastic,
And soon the marks of care were worn away,
While I was sway'd by every novel impulse,
Yielding to all the fancies of the hour.
But it has now assum'd its character ;
Mark'd by strong lineaments, its haughty tone,
Like the firm oak, would sooner break than bend.
Yet still. O Contemplation l I do love
To indulge thy solemn musings ; still the same
With thee alone I know to melt and weep,
In thee alone delighting. Why along
The dusky track of commerce should I toil,
When with an easy competence content,
I can alone be happy ; where with thee
I may enjoy the loveliness of Nature,
And loose the wings of Fancy ? Thus alone
Can I partake of happiness on earth ;
And to be happy here is man's chief end,
For to be happy he must needs be good."

We can see by the following passage, *On being confined to
School,* written when only thirteen, how keenly he must have felt
his power for greater things ; and his dislike of all square and
pedantic rules.

"The morning sun's enchanting rays
Now call forth every songster's praise ;
Now the lark, with upward flight,
Gaily ushers in the light ;
While wildly warbling from each tree,
The birds sing songs of Liberty.
But for me no songster sings.
For me no joyous lark upsprings
For I, confined in gloomy school,
Must own the pedant's iron rule,
And far from sylvan shades and bowers,
In durance vile must pass the hours ;
There con the scholiast's dreary lines,
Where no bright ray of genius shines,
And close to rugged learning cling,
While laughs around the jocund spring.
How gladly would my soul forego
All that arithmeticians know,
Or stiff gramarians quaintly teach,
Or all that industry can reach,
To taste each morn of all the joys
That with the laughing sun arise ;
And unconstrained to rove along
The bushy brakes and glens among ;
And woo the Muse's gentle power.

In unfrequented rural bower :
But ah ! such heaven approaching joys
Will never greet my longing eyes ;
Still while they cheat in vision fine,
Yet never but in fancy shine.
Oh ! that I were the little wren
That shrilly chirps from yonder glen !
Oh ! far away I then would rove,
To some secluded bushy grove ;
There hop and sing with careless glee,
Hop and sing at liberty ;
And till death should stop my lays,
Far from men would spend my days. "

It is easy to conceive the irksome confinement of school to a boy whose taste for the sublime and beautiful led him to meet the approach of day. In this little poem, his feelings are expressively pictured. The clear meanderings of the majestic Trent, the expansive and flowery meadows which form its banks the hanging grovesof Clifton which overshadow the stream, and the woods of Cotgrave which crown its abrupt and sloping hills, all form scenes where his muse delighted to wander.

In a poem written a few years later we become acquainted with his religious opinions, which at that time inclined towards deism : although this carries with it little or nothing, as it needs not be said upon what slight grounds the opinions of a youth may be founded; indicative only of an active mind and confined merely to matters of speculation. A passage from the following poem *My Own Character*, exemplifies this remark :—

"Dear Fanny, I mean, now I'm laid on the shelf,
To give you a sketch—ay, a sketch of myself.
'Tis a pitiful subject, I frankly confess,
And one it would puzzle a painter to dress ;
But however, here goes ! and as sure as a gun
I'l tell all my faults like a penitent nun ;
For I know, for my Fanny, before I address her,
She wont be a cynical father confessor.
Come, come, 'twill not do ! put that curling brow down;
You can't, for the soul of you, learn how to frown.
Well, first, I premise, it's my honest conviction,
That my breast is a chaos of all contradiction ;
Religious,—deistic,—now loyal and warm ;
Then a dagger-drawn democrat hot for reform ;
This moment a fop : *that*, sententious as Titus ;
Democritus now, and anon Heraclitus ;

"Come, Disappointment, come!
  Not in the terrors clad;
Come in the meekest, saddest guise;
Thy chastening rod but terrifies
  The restless and the bad.
    But I recline
    Beneath thy shrine,
And round my brow resign'd, the peaceful cypress twine

  Though fancy flies away
    Before thy hollow tread,
Yet Meditation in her cell,
Hears with faint eye, ling'ring knell,
    That tells her hopes are dead;
      And though the tear
      By chance appear,
Yet she can smile, say, My all was not laid here.

  Come, Disappointment, come!
    Though from Hope's summit hurl'd,
Still, rigid Nurse, thou art forgiven,
For thou, severe, wert sent from heaven
    To wean me from the world;
      To turn my eye
      From vanity,
And point to scenes of bliss that never, never die.

  What is this passing scene?
    A peevish April day!
A little sun—a little rain,
And then night sweeps along the plain,
    And all things fade away.
      Man (soon discuss'd)
      Yields up his trust,
And all his hopes and fears lie with him in the dust

e

Oh, what is beauty's power?
  It flourishes and dies ;
With the cold earth its silence break,
To tell how soft, how smooth a cheek
    Beneath its surface lies ?
        Mute, mute is all
        O'er beauty's fall ;
Her praise resounds no more when mantled in her pall.

The most belov'd on earth
    Not long survives to-day ;
So music past is obsolete,
And yet 'twas sweet, 'twas passing sweet,
    But now 'tis gone away.
        Thus does the shade
        In memory fade,
When in forsaken tomb the form beloved is laid.

Then since this world is vain,
    And volatile and fleet,
Why should I lay up earthly joys,
Where rust corrupts, and moth destroys,
    And cares and sorrows eat ?
        Why fly from ill
        With anxious skill,
When soon this hand will freeze, this throbbing heart be still ?

Come, Disappointment, come !
    Thou art not stern to me ;
Sad Monitress ! I own thy sway,
A votary sad in early day,
    I bend my knee to thee,
        From sun to sun
        My race will run,
I only bow, and say, My God, thy will be done !"

White was at this time unswerving in his labours, indeed to an
excess. It was then that he wrote his *Lines on Recovery of a fit
of Sickness,* in the churchyard of his favorite village. It is sweetly
written, and is one amongst several of his poems, in which we see
that much as he craved to *know,* he equally desired that he might
be known.

"Here would I wish to sleep.—This is the spot
Which I have long mark'd out to lay my bones in:
Tired out and wearied with the riotous world,
Beneath this Yew I would be sepulchred.
It is a lovely spot ! The sultry sun,
From his meridian height, endeavours vainly
To pierce the shadowy foliage, while the zephyr
Comes wafting gently o'er the rippling Trent,
And plays about my wan cheek. 'Tis a nook

Most pleasant.—Such a one perchance did Gray
Frequent, as with a vagrant muse he wanton'd.
Come, I will sit me down and meditate,
For I am wearied with my summer's walk ;
And here I may repose in silent ease ;
And thus, perchance, when life's sad journey's o'er,
My harass'd soul, in this same spot, may find
The haven of its rest—beneath this sod
Perchance may sleep it sweetly, sound as death.
I would not have my corpse cemented down
With brick and stone, defrauding the poor earthworm
Of its predestin'd dues ; no, I would lie
Beneath a little hillock, grass o'ergrown,
Swathed down with oziers, just as sleep the cotters.
Yet may not *undistinguished* be my grave ;
But there at eve may some congenial soul
Duly resort, and shed a pious tear,
The good man's benison—no more I ask.
And oh ! (if heavenly beings may look down
From where, with cherubim inspired, they sit,
Upon this little dim-discover'd spot,
The earth.) then will I cast a glance *below*
On him who thus my ashes shall embalm ;
And I will weep too, and will bless the wanderer.
Wishing he may not long be doom'd to pine
In this low-thoughted world of darkling woe,
But that, ere long, he reach his kindred skies.
Yet 'twas a silly thought, as if the body,
Mouldering beneath the surface of the earth,
Could taste the sweets of summer scenery,
And feel the freshness of the balmy breeze !
Yet nature speaks within the human bosom,
And, spite of reason, bids it look beyond
His narrow verge of being, and provide
A decent residence for its clayey shell,
Endear'd to it by time. And who would lay
His body in the city burial-place,
To be thrown up again by some rude Sexton
And yield its narrow house another tenant,
Ere the moist flesh had mingle with the dust,
Ere the tenacious hair had left the scalp
Exposed to insult lewd, and wantonness ?
No, I will lay me in the *village* ground ;
There are the dead respected. The poor hind,
Unletter'd as he is, would scorn to invade
The silent resting-place of death. I've seen
The labourer, returning from his toil,
Here stay his steps, and call his children round,
And slowly spell the rudely sculptured rhymes,
And, in his rustic manner, moralize.
I've mark'd with what a silent awe he'd spoken,

With head uncover'd, his respectful manner,
And all the honours which he paid the grave,
And thought on cities, where even cemeteries,
Bestrew'd with all the emblems of mortality,
Are not protected from the drunken insolence
Of wassailers profane, and wanton havoc.
Grant, Heaven, that here my pilgrimage may close !
Yet, if this be denied, where'er my bones
May lie—or in the city's crowded bounds,
Or scatter'd wide o'er the huge sweep of waters,
Or left a prey on some deserted shore
To the rapacious cormorant,—yet still,
(For why should sober reason cast away
A thought which soothes the soul ?)—Yet still my spirit
Shall wing its way to these my native regions,
And hover o'er this spot. Oh, then I'll think
Of times when I was seated 'neath this yew
In solemn rumination ; and will smile
With joy that I have got my long'd release."

In this way it would not be difficult to scan White's whole
life in his poems, and the various impulses under which they
were written. But it is not the object of this work to particularize
the circumstances and events of the poet's lives of which it speaks;
it merely comprises a collection of observations on the merits and
beauties of their work.

The following extracts form some of the choicest and most ad-
mired of his conceptions. The language of most is vivid and
elegant, they often abound in a rich flow of words, and the interest
of them is greatly heightened by a continuous procession of fanciful
and ideal objects. The tinge of melancholy that pervades almost all
of them is the only thing that robs them of what might otherwise
be termed an original charm. Some of his descriptions of natural
objects, are also almost perfectly drawn, and are now and then
tinged with the sweetest tints. Take for example, the following
passage from *Childhood.*

"To yonder hill, whose sides, deform'd and steep,
Just yield a scanty sust'nance to the sheep,
With thee, my friend, I oftentimes have sped,
To see the sunrise from his healthy bed ;
To watch the aspect of the summer morn,
Smiling upon the golden fields of corn,
And taste, delighted, of superior joys,
Beheld through sympathy's enchanted eyes ;
With silent admiration oft we view'd

Reviving nature hail'd returning day;
Mark'd how the flow'rets rear'd their drooping heads,
And the wild lambkins bounded o'er the meads.
While from each tree, in tones of sweet delight,
The birds sung pæans to the source of light.
Oft have we watch'd the speckled lark arise,
Leave his grass bed, and soar to kindred skies,
And rise, and rise, till the pain'd sight no more
Could trace him in his high aerial tour :
Though on the ear, at intervals, his song
Came wafted slow on the wavy breeze along;
And we have thought how happy were our lot,
Bless'd with some sweet, some solitary cot,
Where, from the peep of day till russet eve
Began in every dell her forms to weave,
We might pursue our sports from day to day,
And in each other's arms wear life away.

  * * * *

How calm was all around! No playful breeze
Sighed 'mid the wavy foliage of the trees,
But all was still, save when, with drowsy song,
The grey-fly wound his sullen horn along;
And save when heard in soft, yet merry glee,
The distant church-bells mellow harmony ;
The silver mirror of the lucid brook,
That 'mid the tufted broom its still course took,
The rugged arch, that clasped its silent tides,
With moss and rank weeds hanging down its sides."

Or as a didactic effusion, much merit may be found in his poem
n *Time*. That part in which he gives a retrospect, as it were, of
ygone ages, and of the rise and fall of nations, is well worth quot-
ıg as a genuine specimen of didactic verse.

"Who needs a teacher to admonish him
That flesh is grass?—That earthly things are mist?
What are our joys but dreams? and what our hopes
But goodly shadows in a summer cloud ?
There's not a wind that blows but bears with it
Some rainbow promise :—Not a moment flies
But puts its sickle in the fields of life,
And mows its thousands, with their joys and cares.
'Tis but a yesterday since on yon stars,
Which now I view, the Chaldee shepherd gazed,
In his mid-watch observant, and disposed

The twinkling hosts as fancy gave them shape.
Yet in the interim what mighty shocks
Have buffeted mankind,—whole nations raved,—
Cities made desolate,—the polish'd sunk
To barbarism, and once barbaric states
Swaying the wand of science and of art,
Illustrious deeds and memorable names
Blotted from record, and upon the tongue
Of grey tradition voluble no more.
Where are the heroes of the ages past?
Where the brave chieftains, where the mighty ones
Who flourish'd in the infancy of days?
All to the grave gone down. On their fallen fame
Exulting, mocking at the pride of man,
Sits grim *Forgetfulness.*—The warrior's arm
Lies nerveless on the pillow of its shame;
Hush'd is his stormy voice, and quench'd the blaze
Of his red eye-ball.—Yesterday his name
Was mighty on the earth.—To day—'tis what?
The meteor of the night of distant years,
That flash'd unnotic'd, save by wrinkled eld,
Musing at midnight upon prophecies.
Who at her lonely lattice saw the gleam
Point to the mist-poised shroud, then quietly
Closed her pale lips, and locked the secret up
Safe in the charnel's treasures.

      *   *   *   *

               Where is *Rome?*
She lives but in the tale of other times;
Her proud pavilions are the hermit's home;
And her long colonnades, her public walks,
Now faintly echo to the pilgrim's feet
Who comes to muse in solitude, and trace
Through the rank moss reveal'd, her honour'd dust.
But not to Rome alone has fate confined
The doom of ruin, cities numberless,
Tyre, Sidon, Carthage, Babylon, and Troy,
And rich Phœnicia—they are blotted out,
Half-razed from memory, and their very name
And being in dispute.—Has Athens fallen?
Is polished Greece become the savage seat
Of ignorance and sloth?

      *   *   *   *

Where now is Britain? Where her laurell'd names,
Her palaces and halls. Dash'd in the dust.
Some second Vandal hath reduced her pride,
And with one big recoil hath thrown her back.
To primitive barbarity.—Again,
Through her depopulated vales, the scream
Of bloody superstition hollow rings,

And the scarr'd native to the tempest howls
The yell of deprecation.   O'er her marts
Her crowded ports, broods Silence; and the cry
Of the low curlew, and the pensive dash
Of distant billows, breaks alone the void.
Even as the savage sits upon the stone
That marks where stood her capitols, and hears
The bittern booming in the weeds, he shrinks
From the dismaying solitude.—Her bards
Sing in a language that hath perished ;
And their wild harps, suspended o'er their graves,
Sigh to the desert winds a dying strain.

   * * * *

——————————Oh who can strive
To comprehend the vast, the awful truth,
Of the *eternity that hath gone by*.
And not recoil from the dismaying sense
Of human impotence ?   The life of man
Is summ'd in birth-days and in sepulchres ;
But the Eternal God had no beginning ;
He hath no end.   Time had been with him
For *everlasting*, ere the dædal world
Rose from the gulph in loveliness.—Like him
It knew no source, like him 'twas uncreate.
What is it then ?   The past Eternity !
We comprehend a *future* without end ;
We feel it possible that even yon sun
May roll for ever ; but we shrink amazed—
We stand aghast, when we reflect that Time
Knew no commencement.—That heap age on age,
And million upon million, without end,
And we shall never span the void of days
That were, and are not but in retrospect.
The Past is an unfathomable depth,
Beyond the span of thought ; 'tis an elapse
Which hath no mensuration, but hath been
For ever and for ever."

s lyric pieces, his *Ode on the Death of Dermody, the Poet,*
of the choicest.   Its greatest merit lies in 'the language,
s fitted so nearly to the subject of the poem.

 " Child of misfortune ! offspring of the muse !
  Mark like the meteor's gleam, his mad career ;
   With hollow cheeks and haggard eye ;
   Behold, he shrieking passes by ;
    I see, I see him near :
   That hollow scream, that deepening groan ;
    It rings upon my ear.

Oh come, ye thoughtless, ye deluded youth,
    Who clasp the syren Pleasure to your breast ;
  Behold the wreck of Genius here ;
  And drop, oh drop the silent tear
        For Dermody at rest :
    His fate is yours ; then from your loins
        Tear quick the silken vest.

Saw'st thou his dying bed ! Saw'st thou his eyes,
    Once flashing fire, despair's dim tear distil ;
  How ghastly did it seem ;
  And then his dying scream ;
        Oh God ! I hear it still :
    It sounds upon my fainting sense,
        It strikes me with a deathly chill.

Say, didst thou mark the brilliant poet's death !
    Saw'st thou an anxious father by his bed,
  Or pitying friends around him stand?
  Or did'st thou see a mother's hand
        Support his languid head ?
    Oh none of these—no friend o'er him
        The balm of pity shed.

      *   *   *

Yet ere I go I'll drop one silent tear,
    Where lies unwept the poet's fallen head :
  May peace her banners o'er him wave ;
  For me in my deserted grave
        No friend a tear shall shed :
    Yet may the lily and the rose
        Bloom on my grassy bed."

Some of the *Fragments* also exhibit the highest **genius**. For instance the two following :—

"Hushed is the lyre—the hand that swept
    The low and pensive wires,
    Robbed of its cunning, from the task retires.

Yes—it is still—the lyre is still ;
    The spirit which its slumbers broke,
    Hath passed away—and that weak hand that **woke**
It s for est melodies hath lost its skill.
Yet I would press you to my lips once more,
    Ye wild, yet withering flowers of poësy ;
Yet would I drink the fragrance which ye pour,
    Mixed with decaying odours ; for to me
Ye have beguiled the hours of infancy."

"Once more, and yet once more,
    I give unto my harp a dark-woven lay ;
I heard the waters roar,
    I heard the floop of ages pass away.
Oh thou, stern spirit, who dost dwell

writer on his life, says, "He is the only poet of whom we know, who displayed at such at early age so exalted a genius, and accomplished in a few years so great a supremacy over both the languages and sciences."

CHAPTER XXXI.

BYRON.

BYRON.—A critic says, "If ever man breathed when we recognise as emphatically the Genius; that man was Byron; and, if ever genius made poetry its mouth-piece, covering with its transcendant utterances a multitude of sins, whether against art or against the full stature of perfect manhood Byron's is that poetry." He excelled in all its elements. As another writer observes, "We find in Byron a perpetual stream of quick-coming fancies—an eternal spring of fresh-blown images, which seem called into existence by the sudden flash of those glowing thoughts and overwhelming emotions, that struggle for expression through the whole flow of his poetry, and impart to a diction, that is often abrupt and rregular, a force and a charm which seem frequently to realize all hat is said of inspiration."

Too much has already been said about the private character of

Byron to mention it here, although it is impossible to do other than acknowledge that Byron often disregarded many of the great moral and religious duties, and made them subjects of his defiance and ridicule. We see throughout his works, that one of his most prominent antipathies was *hypocrisy.* This hatred took early hold of his understanding as well as of his passions: and as it was his nature to be direct and violent, it must be admitted that he sometimes carried it too far; and that in his eagerness to expose deception and pretence, occasionally tore away too much of the veil from life, and laid naked the deformities of nature too rudely.

The following excellent observations will express all we could desire to say of this poet's merits. "It is the identification of all Byron's poems with his own character, that constitutes their greatest attraction. This is the attraction, however, that many censure and condemn; but it gives to his poems a sincerity, a certainty, a vivacity, which scarcely any other poems possess. It is said that he is not like Shakespeare : he cannot throw himself into every variety of shape; represent every course of passion ; or develop every diversity of thought produced by nature or by circumstances: that it is still one and the same gloomy mind throwing forth its gloom and its passions; its hatreds; its scorns; and its raptures! This is true. But this unity has its advantage as well as its disadvantages. However powerful and rich imagination may be, it can never quite equal the force of actual and personal experience in those who are endowed with the highest degree of feeling, passion and intellectual splendour. Lord Byron's life was poetry, and his verses are but its *mirror!* He was endowed with gifts of singular force, with feeling of such intensity and splendour, which the chances of life had brought into full play under circumstances of such extraordinary interest, that it is doubtful if mere invention could ever have produced anything more equally striking and just. The disclosure of the internal movements of such a mind is read with breathless interest. It has all the brilliancy of fiction, with the solidity of fact. All Byron's noblest poems have reference to life, only in cases extraordinarily circumstanced and of violent and

ssence is the genius, and that knows no vicissitudes; and acknow-
edges no fleeting jurisdiction. *Childe Harold* is full of descriptive
ind meditative passages and perpetually carries the readers through
videly distant scenes. The first canto principally describes Portu-
;al and Spain, and contains many powerful pictures of the great
oattles which rendered memorable the struggle between those
oppressed nations.

In the First canto of *Childe Harold* Byron has drawn many real
ind beautiful scenes of Spanish life and manners ; as for instance,
he following admirable description of the bull-fight,

> "Thrice sounds the clarion ; lo I the signal falls,
> The den expands, and Expectation mute
> Gapes round the silent circle's peopled walls.
> Bounds with one lashing spring the mighty brute,
> And wildly staring, spurns, with sounding foot,
> The sand, nor blindly rushes on his foe :
> Here, there, he points his threatening front, to suit
> His first attack, wide waving to and fro
> His angry tail, red rolls his eye's dilated glow :
>
> Sudden he stops ; his eye is fix'd : away,
> Away, thou heedless boy ! prepare the spear ;
> Now is thy time to perish, or display,
> The skill that yet may check his mad career.
> With well-timed croupe the nimble corsers veer ;
> On foams the bull, but not unscathed he goes ;
> Streams from his flank the crimson torrent clear,
> He flies, he wheels, distracted with his throes
> Dart follows dart, lance, lance ; loud bellowing speak his woes.
>
> Again he comes ; nor dart nor lance avail,
> Nor the wild plunging of the tortured horse ;

* Sir Egerton Brydges, Bart.

Though man and man's avenging arms assail,
Vain are his weapons, vainer is his force.
One gallant steed is stretch'd a mangled corse ;
Another, hideous sight ! unseam'd appears,
His gory chest unveils life's panting source ;
Though death-struck, still his feeble frame he rears;
Staggering, but stemming all, his lord unharm'd he bears.

Foiled, bleeding, breathless, furious to the last,
Full in the centre stands the bull at bay,
Mid wounds, and clinging darts, and lances brast,
And foes disabled in the brutal fray :
And now the Matadores around him play,
Shake the red cloak, and poise the ready brand:
Once more through all he bursts his thundering way—
Vain rage ! the mantle quits the conynge hand,
Wraps his fierce eye—'tis past—he sinks upon the sand !

Where his vast neck just mingles with the spine,
Sheathed in his form the deadly weapon lies.
He stops—he starts—disdaining to decline :
Slowly he falls, amidst triumphant cries,
Without a groan, without a struggle dies,
The decorated car appears ; on high
The course is piled—sweet sight for vulgar eyes
Four steeds that spurn the rein, as swift as shy,
Hurl the dark bull along, scarce seen in dashing by."

In the Second canto Childe Harold is carried to Greece, Albania
and the Ægean Archipelago; and the poet has reproduced the scen-
ery and wild life of these picturesque regions with an unequalled
genius.

"The wild Albanian kirtled to his knee,
With shawl-girt head and ornamented gun,
And gold embroider'd garments, fair to see ;
The crimson-scarfed men of Macedon ;
The Delhi with his cap of terror on,
And crooked glaive ; the lively, supple Greek ;
And swarthy Nubia's mutilated son ;
The bearded Turk, that rarely deigns to speak,
Master of all around, too potent to be meek,

Are mix'd conspicuous ; some recline in groups,
Scanning the motley scene that varies round ;
There some grave Moslem to devotion stoops,
And some that smoke, and some that play are found ;
Here the Albanian proudly treads the ground :
Half-whispering there the Greek is heard to prate ;
Hark ! from the mosque the nightly solemn sound,
The Muezzin's call doth shake the minaret,
'There is no God but God !—to prayer—lo! God is great.'"

The Third canto contains the finest and most intense feeling of

I live not in myself, but I become
Portion of that around me ; and to me,
High mountains are a feeling, but the hum
Of human cities torture : I can see
Nothing to loathe in nature, save to be
A link reluctant in a fleshly chain,
Class'd among creatures, when the soul can flee,
And with the sky, the peak, the heaving plain
Of ocean, or the stars, mingle, and not in vain.

And thus I am absorb'd, and this is life :
I look upon the peopled desert past,
As on a place of agony and strife,
Where, for some sin, to Sorrow I was cast,
To act and suffer, but remount at last
With a fresh pinion ; which I felt to spring,
Though young, yet waxing vigorous as the blast
Which it would cope with, on delighted wing,
Spurning the clay-cold bonds, which round our being cling.

And when, at length, the mind shall be all free
From what it hates in this degraded form,
Reft of its carnal life, save what shall be
Existent happier in the fly and worm,—
When elements to elements conform,
And dust is as it should be, shall I not
Feel all I see, less dazzling, but more warm ?
The bodiless thought ? the Spirit of each spot ?
Of which, even now, I share at times the immortal lot ?

Are not the mountains, waves, and skies a part
Of me and of my soul, as I of them ?
Is not the love of these deep in my heart

With a pure passion ? should I not contemn
All objects, if compared with these ? and stem
A tide of suffering, rather than forego
Such feelings for the hard and wordly phlegm
Of those whose eyes are only turn'd below,
Gazing upon the ground, with thoughts which dare **not glow ?**"

Switzerland, Belgium and the Rhine also give in this canto,
splendid opportunities for many pictures of nature, of consummate
beauty.

"But these recede.   Above me are the Alps,
The palaces of nature, whose vast walls
Have pinnacled in clouds their snowy scalps,
And throned Eternity in icy halls
Of cold sublimity, where forms and falls
The avalanche—the thunder-bolt of snow !
All that expands the spirit, yet appals,
Gather around these summits, as to show
How Earth may pierce to Heaven, yet leave vain **man** below.

　　　*　　　*　　　*　　　*　　　*

Lake Leman woos me with its crystal face,
The mirror where the stars and mountains view
The stillness of their aspect in each trace
Its clear depth yields of their far height and **hue :**
There is too much of man here, to look through
With a fit mind the might which I behold ;
But soon in me shall loneliness renew
Thoughts hid, but not less cherish'd than of old,
Ere mingling with the herd had penn'd me in their fold.

　　　*　　　*　　　*　　　*　　　*

There, in a moment, we may plunge our years
In fatal penitence, and in the blight
Of our own soul, turn all our blood to tears,
And colour things to come with hues of Night,
The race of life becomes a hopeless flight
To those that walk in darkness : on the sea,
The boldest steer but where their ports invite,
But there are wanderers o'er Eternity
Whose bark drives on and on, and anchor'd ne'er shall be."

In the Fourth Canto the reader is carried in a continuous course,
over the fairest and most touching scenes of Italy—Venice, Ferrara,
Florence, Rome, and Ravenna are all discribed in the same mas-
terly manner.

"I stood in Venice, on the Bridge of Sighs ;
A palace and a prison on each hand :
I saw from out the wave her structures rise
As from the stroke of the enchanter's wand :

A thousand years their cloudy wings expand
Around me, and a dying Glory smiles
O'er the far times when many a subject land
Looked to the winged Lion's marble piles,
Where Venice sate in state, throned on her hundred isles !

She looks a sea Cybele, fresh from ocean,
Rising with her tira of proud towers
At airy distance, with majestic motion,
A ruler of the waters and their powers :
And such she was ; her daughters had their dowers
From spoils of nations, and the exhaustless East
Pour'd in her lap all gems in sparkling showers.
In purple was she robed, and of her feast
Monarchs partook, and deem'd their dignity increased.

In Venice, Tasso's echoes are no more,
And silent rows the songless gondolier ;
Her palaces are crumbling to the shore,
And music meets not always now the ear ;
Those days are gone—but Beauty still is here.
States fall, arts fade—but Nature doth not die,
Nor yet forget how Venice once was dear,
The pleasant place of all festivity,
The revel of the earth, the masque of Italy !

But unto us she hath a spell beyond
Her name in story, and her long array
Of mighty shadows, whose dim forms despond
Above the Dogeless city's vanish'd sway ;
Ours is a trophy which will not decay
With the Rialto ; Shylock and the Moor,
And Pierre, can not be swept or worn away—
The keystones of the arch ! though all were o'er,
For us repeopled were the solitary shore.

The beings of the mind are not of clay ;
Essentially immortal, they create
And multiply in us a brighter ray
And more beloved existence : that which Fate
Prohibits to dull life, in this our state
Of mortal bondage, by these spirits supplied
First exiles, then replaces what we hate ;
Watering the heart whose early flowers have died,
And with a fresher growth replenishing the void."

Don Juan the longest of Byron's poems, is perhaps at the same time the most singular and characteristic. It is written in octaves, a kind of versification borrowed from the Italians. The merit of this poem is the richness of ideas, thoughts, and images, and above all, the constant passage from the loftiest and tenderest tone of

poetry to the most familiar and mocking style. Its great defect
throughout, is a materialistic tone of morality; everything in turn is
made the subject of a sneer, which shows in this respect the design
to have been a selfish one. There are in parts of this poem, how-
ever, the warmest outbursts of feeling, and the most admirable
descriptions of nature. The following passages from the Second
Canto are excellent specimens of the former.

> "'Tis sweet to hear
> At midnight on the blue and moonlit deep
> The song and oar of Adria's gondolier,
> By distance mellow'd, o'er the waters sweep ;
> 'Tis sweet to see the evening star appear ;
> 'Tis sweet to listen as the night-winds creep
> From leaf to leaf ; 'tis sweet to view on high
> The rainbow, based on oceans, span the sky.
>
> 'Tis sweet to hear the watch-dog's honest bark
> Bay deep-mouth'd welcome as we draw near home;
> 'Tis sweet to know there is an eye will mark
> Our coming, and look brighter when we come ;
> 'Tis sweet to be awaken'd by the lark,
> Or lull'd by falling waters ; sweet the hum
> Of bees, the voice of girls, the song of birds,
> The lisp of children, and their earliest words."

> "No more—no more—Oh ! never more on me
> The freshness of the heart can fall like dew,
> Which out of all the lovely things we see
> Extracts emotions beautiful and new.
> Hived in our bosoms like the bag o' the bee :
> Think'st thou the honey with those objects grew ?
> Alas ! 'twas not in them, but in thy power
> To double even the sweetness of a flower.
>
> No more—no more—Oh ! never more, my heart,
> Canst thou be my sole world, my universe !
> Once all in all, but now a thing apart,
> Thou canst not be my blessing or my curse :
> The illusion's gone for ever, and thou art
> Insensible, I trust, but none the worse,
> And in thy stead I've got a deal of judgment,
> Though heaven knows how it ever found a lodgment."

In the Eleventh Canto the Court of St. Petersburg is described,
followed by the passage in which Juan is sent on a diplomatic
mission to England, in which stanzas we get a very minute and
sarcastic account of English aristocratic society.

But perhaps the finest of all the descriptive passages in this poem, is that of the *Shipwreck* in the Second canto, from which the following stanzas have been selected.

"Then rose from sea to sky the wild farewell—
   Then shriek'd the timid, and stood still the brave,—
Then some leap'd overboard with dreadful yell,
   As eager to anticipate their grave ;
And the sea yawu'd around her like a hell,
   And down she suck'd with her the whirling wave,
Like one who grapples with his enemy
And strives to strangle him before he die.

And first one universal shriek there rush'd,
   Louder than the loud ocean, like a crash
Of echoing thunder ; and then all was hush'd,
   Save the wild wind and the remorseless dash
Of billows ; but at intervals there gush'd,
   Accompanied with a convulsive splash,
A solitary shriek, the bubbling cry
Of some strong swimmer in his agony.

    *   *   *   *

Now overhead a rainbow, bursting through
   The scattering clouds, shone, spanning the dark sea,
Resting its bright base on the quivering blue ;
   And all within its arch appear'd to be
Clearer than that without, and its wide hue
   Wax'd broad and waving, like a banner free,
Then changed like to a bow that's bent, and then
Forsook the dim eyes of these shipwreck'd men.

   *   *   *   *   *

With twilight it again came on to blow,
   But not with violence ; the stars shone out,
The boat made way ; yet now they were so low,
   They knew not where nor what they were about ;
Some fancied they saw land, and some said 'No !'
   The frequent fog-banks gave them cause to doubt ;
Some swore that they heard breakers, others guns,
And all mistook about the latter once.

As morning broke, the light wind died away,
   When he who had the watch sung out, and swore,
If 'twas not land that rose with the sun's ray,
   He wish'd that land he never might see more ;
And the rest rubb'd their eyes, and saw a bay,
   Or thought they saw, and shaped their course for shore ;
For shore it was, and gradually grew
Distinct, and high, and palpable to view.

And then of these some part burst into tears,
   And others, looking with a stupid stare,

> Could not yet separate their hopes from fears,
>   And seem'd as if they had no further care ;
> While a few pray'd (the first time for some years)—
>   And at the bottom of the boat three were
> Asleep : they shook them by the hand and head,
> And tried to awaken them, but found them dead."

Of all Byron's productions *Don Juan,* is certainly the most attractive. It keeps the mind a pleasing captive, and has a power of detaining the attention. The wild and daring sallies of sentiment with which it abounds, the peculiar violence of wit which pervades each canto, excites at once astonishment and enthusiasm. The original humour, and peculiarity of expression, the incidents, the circumstances, the surprises, the jests of action and of thought, the shades of light and of darkness so exquisitely intermingled, give it a peculiarity which places it above all modern poetry. In it Byron has displayed all his characteristic beauties and blemishes; and a critic has compared its construction to the image of Nebuchadnezzar's dream—of "fine gold, silver, and clay."

The *Giaour*, one of Byron's romantic tales is written in the irregular and flowing versification which Scott brought into fashion. It has in it several inimitable descriptions, which harmonize well with the tone of the poem. Such is the following :—

> "Above the mountain rears a peak,
> Where vultures whet the thirsty beak ;
> And theirs may be a feast to-night
> Shall tempt them down e'er morrow's light.
> Beneath, a river's wintry stream
> Has shrunk before the summer beam,
> And left a channel bleak and bare,
> Save shrubs that spring to perish there :
> Each side the midway path there lay
> Small broken crags of granite grey,
> By time, or mountain lightning riven
> From summits clad in mists of heaven ;
> For where is he that hath beheld
> The peak of Liakura unveil'd ?"

One of the finest passages in this poem, is the famous comparison of enslaved Greece to a corpse :—

> "'Tis Greece, but living Greece no more !
> So coldly sweet, so deadly fair,
> We start—for soul is wanting there.

There is the same peculiarity of thought and sentiment in the
Siege of Corinth as in the preceeding poem ; it is written in the
same melodious versification. This poem is full of glowing des-
criptions and abounds with the picturesque imagery for which
Byron excels. Amongst the descriptions, one of the most animated
is the following :—

> "'Tis midnight : on the mountains brown
> The cold, round moon shines deeply down ;
> Blue roll the waters, blue the sky
> Spreads like an ocean hung on high,
> Bespangled with those isles of light,
> So wildly, spiritually bright ;
> Who ever gazed upon them shining,
> And turn'd to earth without repining,
> Nor wish'd for wings to flee away,
> And mix with their eternal ray?
> The waves on either shore lay there
> Calm, clear, and azure as the air :
> And scarce their foam the pebbles shook,
> But murmur'd meekly as the brook.
> The winds were pillow'd on the waves ;
> The banners dropped along the staves,
> And, as they fell around them furling,
> Above them shone the crescent curling ;
> And that deep silence was unbroke,
> Save where the watch his signal spoke.
> Save where the steed neigh'd oft and shrill,
> And echo answer'd from the hill,
> And the wide hum of that wild host
> Rustled like leaves from coast to coast,
> As rose the Muezzin's voice in air
> In midnight call to wonted prayer ;
> It rose, that chanted mournful strain.
> Like some lone spirit's o'er the plain :
> 'Twas musical, but sadly sweet,
> Such as when winds and harp-strings meet,
> And take a long unmeasured tone,
> To mortal minstrelsy unknown.
> It seem'd to those within the wall

A cry prophetic of their fall :
It struck even the beseiger's ear
With something ominous and drear,
An undefined and sudden thrill,
Which makes the heart a moment still,
Then beat with quicker pulse, ashamed
Of that strange sense its silence framed ;
Such as a sudden passing-bell
Wakes, though but for a stranger's knell."

This poem is remarkable for the extraordinary variety and force
of its descriptions—a variety greater than will generally be found
in Byron's tales. There is also exhibited in it much more of
genius than in the *Giaour.*

Mazeppa is also in the versification of Scott. In this poem the
same dramatic scenery is set before the reader, and described with
equal intensity. The powerfully written episode of the gallop of
the wild steed, with the victim lashed on his back carries the
reader away with its charm.

"We near'd the wild wood—'twas so wide,
I saw no bounds on either side ;
'Twas studded with old sturdy trees,
That bent not to the roughest breeze
Which howls down from Siberia's waste,
And strips the forest in its haste ;
But these were few and far between,
Set thick with shrubs more young and green.
Luxuriant with their annual leaves,
Ere strewn by those autumnal eves,
That nip the forest's foliage dead,
Discolour'd with a lifeless red,
Which stands thereon like stiffen'd gore,
Upon the slain when battle's o'er,
And some long winter's night hath shed
Its frosts o'er every tombless head,
So cold and stark the raven's beak
May peck unpierced each frozen cheek :
'Twas a wild waste of underwood,
And here and there a chestnut stood,
The strong oak, and well the hardy pine ;
　　But far apart—and well it were,
Or else a different lot were mine—
　　The boughs gave way, and did not tear
My limbs ; and I found strength to bear
My wounds, already scarr'd with cold—
My bonds forbade to lose my hold.
We rustled through the leaves like wind,
Left shrubs, and trees, and wolves behind ;

By night I heard them on the track,
Their troop come hard upon our back,
With their long gallop, which can tire
The hounds deep hate and hunter's fire :
Where'er we flew they follow'd on,
Nor left us with the morning sun ;
Behind I saw them, scarce a rood,
At daybreak winding through the wood,
And through the night had heard their feet
Their stealing, rustling step repeat.
Oh ! how I wish'd for spear or sword,
At least to die amidst the horde,
And perish,—if it must be so—
At bay, destroying many a foe.
When first my coursers race begun,
I wish'd the goal already won ;
But now I doubted strength and speed.
Vain doubt ! his swift and savage breed
Had nerved him like the mountain roe ;
Nor faster falls the blinding snow
Which whelms the peasant near the door
Whose threshold he shall cross no more,
Bewilder'd with the dazzling blast,
Than through the forest-paths he pass'd.
Untired, untamed, and worse than wild :
All furious as a favour'd child
Balk'd of its wish ; or fiercer still—
A woman piqued—who has her will.

* * * *

At length, while reeling on our way,
Methought I heard a courser's neigh,
From out yon tuft of blackening firs.
Is it the wind those branches stirs?
No, no ! from out the forest prance
 A trampling troop ; I see them come !
In one vast squadron they advance !
 I strove to cry—my lips were dumb.
The steeds rush on in plunging pride :
But where are they the reins to guide ?
A thousand horse—and none to ride !
With flowing tail, and flying mane,
Wide nostrils, never stretch'd by pain,
Mouths bloodless to the bit or rein,
And feet that iron never shod,
And flanks unscarr'd by spur or rod,
A thousand horse, the wild, the free,
Like waves that follow o'er the sea,
 Came thickly thundering on,
As if our faint approach to meet ;
The sight renerved my courser's feet,

A moment staggering, feebly fleet,
A moment, with a faint low neigh,
He answer'd, and then fell ;
With gasps and glazing eyes he lay,
And reeking limbs immovable,
His first and last career is done ! "

In the *Parisana* there are many passages of rare beauty. A specimen of this may be seen in the opening lines —

" It is the hour when from the boughs
    The nightingale's high note is heard ;
It is the hour when lovers' vows
    Seem sweet in every whisper'd word ;
And gentle winds, and waters near,
Make music to the lonely ear.
Each flower the dews have lightly wet,
And in the sky the stars are met,
And on the wave is deeper blue,
And on the leaf a browner hue,
And in the heaven that clear obscure;
So softly dark, and darkly pure,
Which follows the decline of day,
As twilight melts beneath the moon away,"

In the *Prisoner of Chillon*, the hopeless tone of sorrow and uncomplaining suffering which runs through the whole gives it a strong hold upon the reader's feelings. Like the rest of Byron's poems, it possesses many exquisite passages which it seems almost impossible to pass over :—

"What next befell me then and there
    I know not well—I never knew—
First came the loss of light and air,
    And then of darkness too:
I had no thought, no feeling—none ;
Among the stones I stood a stone,
And was, scarce conscious what I wist,
As shrubless crags within the mist ;
For all was blank, and bleak, and gray,
It was not night—it was not day,
It was not even the dungeon light,
So hateful to my heavy sight,
But vacancy absorbing space,
And fixedness—without a place ;
There were no stars—no earth—no time—
No check—no change—no good—no crime—
But silence, and a stirless breath
Which neither was of life nor death ;
A sea of stagnant idleness,

Blind, boundless, mute, and motionless !
A light broke in upon my brain,—
  It was the carol of a bird ;
It ceased, and then it came again,
  The sweetest song ear ever heard,
And mine was thankful till my eyes
Ran over with the glad surprise,
And they that moment could not see
I was the mate of misery ;
But then by dull degrees came back
My senses to their wonted track,
I saw the dungeon's walls and floor
Close slowly round me as before,
I saw the glimmer of the sun
Creeping as it before had done,
But through the crevice where it came
That bird was perch'd, as fond and tame,
  And tamer than upon the tree ;
A lovely bird, with azure wings,
And song that said a thousand things,
  And seem'd to say them all for me !
I never saw its like before
I ne'er shall see its likeness more :
It seem'd like me to want a mate,
But was not half so desolate,
And it was come to love me when
None lived to love me so again,
And cheering from my dungeon's brink,
Had brought me back to feel and think.
I know not if it late were free,
  Or broke its cage to perch on mine,
But knowing well captivity,
  Sweet bird ! I could not wish for thine !
Or if it were, in wingèd guise,
A visitant from Paradise ;
For—Heaven forgive that thought ! the while
Which made me both to weep and smile ;
I sometimes deem'd that it might be
My brother's soul come down to me ;
But then at last away it flew,
And then 'twas mortal—well 1 knew,
For he would never thus have flown,
And left me twice so doubly lone—
Lone—as the corse within its shroud,
Lone—as a solitary cloud—
  A single cloud on a sunny day,
While all the rest of heaven is clear,
A frown upon the atmosphere,
That hath no business to appear
When skies are blue, and earth is gay."

There are many passages also in *The Bride of Abydos* written with the same brilliancy and dramatic power. There is scarcely any passage in Byron written with greater energy than the following :—

> "He lived—he breathed—he moved—he felt ;
> He raised the maid from where she knelt ;
> His trance was gone—his keen eye shone
> With thoughts that long in darkness dwelt ;
> With thoughts that burn—in rays that melt.
> As the stream late conceal'd
>   By the fringe of its willows,
> When it rushes reveal'd
>   In the light of its billows ;
> As the bolt bursts on high
>   From the black cloud that bound it,
> Flash'd the soul of that eye
>   Through the long lashes round it.
> A warhorse at the trumpet's sound,
> A lion rous'd by heedless hound,
> A tyrant waked to sudden strife
> By graze of ill-directed knife,
> Starts not to more convulsive life
> Than he, who heard that vow, display'd,
> And all, before repress'd, betray'd :
>   'Now thou art mine, for ever mine,
> With life to keep, and scarce with life resign ;
> Now thou art mine, that sacred oath,
> Though sworn by one, hath bound us both.
> Yes, fondly, wisely hast thou done ;
> That vow hath saved more heads than one :
> But blench not thou—thy simplest tress
> Claims more from me than tenderness ;
> I would not wrong the slenderest hair
> That clusters round thy forehead fair,
> For all the treasures buried far
> Within the caves of Istakar."

The characters which Byron chooses have in them little to admire, but they are framed in such brilliant and picturesque coverings that in reading them one loses sight of their contradictions ; and there are times when all of us have thought the gloomy, mysterious heroes of Byron, the very ideal of all that is noble and admirable.

The poems of the *Corsair*, *Lara* and the *Island* are in the regular English-rhymed heroic measure, but it is difficult to say which metrical form, Byron uses with the greatest vigour and effect.

One of the finest passages from amongst these poems, is the battle-scene from *Lara*, from which the following passage is extracted. It is written with all the characteristic intensity of Byron.

"Commanding, aiding, animating all,
Where foe appear'd to press, or friend to fall,
Cheers Lara's voice, and waves or strikes his steel,
Inspiring hope himself had ceased to feel.
None fled, for well they knew that flight were vain ;
But those that waver turn to smite again,
While yet they find the firmest of the foe
Recoil before their leader's look and blow :
Now girt with numbers, now almost alone,
He foils their ranks, or reunites his own ;
Himself he spared not—once they seem'd to fly—
Now was the time, he waved his hand on high,
And shook—Why sudden drops that plumed crest ?
The shaft is sped— the arrow's in his breast !
That fatal gesture left the unguarded side,
And death hath striken down yon arm of pride.
The word of triumph fainted from his tongue ;
That hand. so raised, how droopingly it hung!
But yet the sword instinctively retains,
Though from its fellow shrink the falling reins,
These Kaled snatches : dizzy with the blow,
And senseless bending o'er his saddle-bow,
Perceives not Lara that his anxious page
Beguiles his charger from the combat's rage :
Meantime his followers charge, and charge again ;
Too mix'd the slayers now to heed the slain !
Day glimmers on the dying and the dead,
The cloven cuirass, and the helmless head ;
The war-horse masterless is on the earth,
And that last gasp hath burst his bloody girth ;
And near, yet quivering with what life remain'd,
The heel that urged him and the hand that rein'd,
And some too near that rolling torrent lie,
Whose waters mock the lip of those that die ;
That panting thirst which scorches in the breath
Of those that die the soldier's fiery death,
In vain impels the burning mouth to crave
One drop—the last—to cool it for the grave,
With feeble and convulsive effort swept,
Their limbs along the crimson'd turf have crept ;
The faint remains of life such struggles waste,
But yet they reach the stream, and bend to taste :
They feel its freshness, and almost partake—
Why pause ? No further thirst have they to slake—
It is unquench'd, and yet they feel it not ;
It was an agony—but not forgot !"

The poem of *Lara* also abounds in some of the most gorgeous descriptions, written with the freedom and grace for which Byron, is so distinguished.   The following passage for example,

> "Night wanes—the vapours round the mountains curl'd,
> Melt into morn, and Light awakes the world.
> Man has another day to swell the past,
> And lead him near to little, but his last ;
> But mighty Nature bounds as from her birth,
> The sun is in the heavens, and life on earth :
> Flowers in the valley, splendour in the beam,
> Health on the gale, and freshness in the stream,
> Immortal man ! behold her glories shine.
> And cry, exulting inly, 'They are thine !'"

The *Island,* in four cantos, is a striking incident extracted from the narrative of the famous mutiny of the Bounty, when Captain Bligh and his officers were cast off by his rebellious crew in an open boat, and the mutineers, under the command of Christian, established themselves in half-savage life on Pitcairn's Island, where their descendants were recently living.   The following passage in the Second canto is selected from this poem as a specimen.

> " The love which maketh all things fond and fair,
> The youth which makes one rainbow of the air,
> The dangers past, that make even man enjoy
> The pause in which he ceases to destroy,
> The mutual beauty, which the sternest feel
> Strike to their hearts like lightning to the steel,
> United the half savage and the whole,
> The maid and boy in one absorbing soul.
> No more the thundering memory of the fight
> Wrapp'd his wean'd bosom in its dark delight :
> No more the irksome restlessness of rest
> Disturb'd him like the eagle in her nest,
> Whose whetted beak and far-pervading eye
> Darts for a victim over all the sky :
> His heart was tamed to that voluptuous state,
> At once Elysian and effeminate,
> Which leaves no laurels o'er the hero's urn ;—
> These wither when for aught save blood they burn ;
> Yet when their ashes in their nook are laid,
> Does not the myrtle leave as sweet a shade ?
> Had Cæsar known but Cleopatra's kiss,
> Rome had been free, the world had not been his.
> And what have Cæsar's deeds and Cæsar's fame
> Done for the Earth ?   We feel them in our shame,
> The gory sanction of his glory stains

"he rust which tyrants cherish on our chains.
'hough Glory, Nature, Reason, Freedom, bid
:oused millions to do what single Brutus did—
weep these mere mock-birds of the despot's song
'rom the tall bough where they have perch'd so long,—
till are we hawk'd at by such mousing owls,
ιnd take for falcons those ignoble fowls,
Vhen but a word of freedom would dispel
:hese bugbears, as their terrors show too well."

,and the *Vision of Judgment*, Byron has ventured upon
ιd satirical. The former a little Venetian narrative,
ιinute knowledge of the details of Italian manners and
has in it a tinge of immorality, but is extremely playful
ιg. The unexpected manner in which Byron introduces
g stanza, gives to this poem a considerable charm.

ιve of the land which still is Paradise !
Italian beauty ! didst thou not inspire
aphael, who died in thy embrace, and vies
With all we know of Heaven, or can desire,
ι what he hath bequeath'd us ? in what guise,
Though flashing from the fervour of the lyre,
'ould *words* describe thy past and present glow
'hile yet Canova can create below ?"

n of Judgment is a most severe attack upon Southey;
ron very warmly repels the charges brought by Southey
alleged immorality of his poems, and shows up with
bitterness, the contrast between Southey's former ex-
. opinions, and his then mad devotion to the principles
and parodying the poor and pretentious verses which
poet laureate, wrote as a sort of deification of George
very brilliant and animated satire, though rather too
nt of language, and contains many extremely nic-

Gilds the green wave that trembles as it glows.
On old Ægina's rock and Hydra's isle
The god of gladness sheds his parting smile ;
O'er his own regions lingering loves to shine,
Though there his altars are no more divine.
Descending fast, the mountain shadows kiss
Thy glorious gulph, unconquer'd Salamis!
Their azure arches through his long expanse,
More deeply purpled, meet his mellowing glance ;
And tenderest tints, along their summits driven,
Mark his gay course, and own the hues of heaven ;
Till, darkly shaded from the land and deep,
Behind his Delphian rock he sinks to sleep.

On such an eve his palest beam he cast,
When, Athens ! here thy wisest look'd his last.
How watch'd thy better sons his farewell ray,
That closed their murder'd sage's latest day ;
Not yet—not yet—Sol pauses on the hill,
The precious hour of parting lingers still ;
But sad his light to agonizing eyes,
And dark the mountain's once delightful dyes,
Gloom o'er the lovely land he seem'd to pour,
The land where Phœbus never frown'd before ;
But ere he sank below Cithæron's head,
The cup of woe was quaff'd—the spirit fled ;
The soul of him that scorn'd to fear or fly,
Who lived and died as none can live or die."

The *Lament of Tasso* is sweetly written, and is full of the tenderest feeling and pathos. The following stanza will amply illustrate this poem.

" I loved all solitude—but little thought
To spend I know not what of life, remote
From all communion with existence, save
The maniac and his tyrant ; had I been
Their fellow, many years ere this had seen
My mind like theirs corrupted to its grave,
But who hath seen me writhe, or heard me rave ?
Perchance in such a cell we suffer more
Than the wreck'd sailor on his desert shore ;
The world is all before him—*mine* is *here*,
Scarce twice the space they must accord my bier.
What though *he* perish, he may lift his eye
And with a dying glance upbraid the sky—
I will not raise my own in such reproof,
Although 'tis clouded by my dungeon roof."

The *Prophesy of Dante* is written in the difficult *terza rima*, the first attempt of any English poet to employ that measure. **Nothing**

u complete. It is the narrative, in the form of a vision, of his rly love-sorrow. "There is hardly in the whole range of literare," says a writer, " so tender, so lofty, and so condensed a lifeania as that narrated in these verses. Picture after picture is ftly shadowed forth, all pervaded by the same mournful glow, d 'the doom of the two creatures' is set before us in all its peless misery." The opening stanza is sweetly expressed :—

> "Our life is twofold ; Sleep hath its own world,
> A boundary between the things misnamed
> Death and existence : Sleep hath its own world,
> And a wide realm of wild reality.
> And dreams in their development have breath,
> And tears, and tortures, and the touch of joy ;
> They leave a weight upon our waking thoughts,
> They take a weight from off our waking toils,
> They do divide our being ; they become
> A portion of ourselves as of our time,
> And look like heralds of eternity ;
> They pass like spirits of the past,—they speak
> Like sibyls of the future ; they have power—
> The tyranny of pleasure and of pain ;
> They make us what we were not —what they will,
> And shake us with the vision that's gone by."

Byron's *dramatic* works are after the style of Ariosto. The est of his dramas is *Manfred,* which in some degree resembles

Faust, by which it is said to have been suggested. It does not consist of action represented in dialogues, but a series of sublime soliloquies, in which Manfred describes nature, and pours forth his despair and self-pity. The scene with which it opens has a strange resemblance to the first monologue of Faust.

"The lamp must be replenish'd, but even then
It will not burn so long as I must watch :
My slumbers—if I slumber—are not sleep,
But a continuance of enduring thought,
Which then I can resist not : in my heart
There is a vigil, and these eyes but close
To look within ; and yet I live, and bear
The aspect and the form of breathing men.
But grief should be the instructor of the wise ;
Sorrow is knowledge : they who know the most
Must mourn the deepest o'er the fatal truth,
The Tree of Knowledge is not that of Life.
Philosophy and science, and the springs
Of wonder, and the wisdom of the world,
I have essay'd, and in my mind there is
A power to make these subject to itself—
But they avail not : I have done men good,
And I have met with good even among men—
But this avail'd not : I have had my foes,
And none have baffled, many fallen before me—
But this avail'd not :—Good, or evil, life,
Powers, passions, all I see in other beings,
Have been to me as rain unto the sands,
Since that all-nameless hour.   I have no dread,
And feel the curse to have no natural fear,
Nor fluttering throb, that beats with hopes or wishes,
Or lurking love—of something on the earth.
Now to my task.—
                          Mysterious Agency !
Ye spirits of the unbounded Universe !
Whom I have sought in darkness and in light—
Ye, who do compass earth about and dwell,
In subtler essence—ye, to whom the tops
Of mountains inaccessible are haunts,
And earth's and ocean's caves familiar things—
I call upon ye by the written charm
Which gives me power upon you——Rise! appear !
                          [*A pause.*]
They come not yet.—Now by the voice of him
Who is the first among you—by this sign,
Which makes you tremble—by the claims of him
Who is undying,—Rise ! appear!——Appear !
                          [*A pause.*]

"————————My mother Earth!
And thou fresh breaking Day, and you, ye Mountains,
Why are ye beautiful? I cannot love ye.
And thou, the bright eye of the universe,
That openest over all, and unto all
Art a delight—thou shin'st not on my heart.
And you, ye crags, upon whose extreme edge
I stand, and on the torrent's brink beneath
Behold the tall pines dwindled as to shrubs
In dizziness of distance; when a leap,
A stir, a motion, even a breath, would bring
My breast upon its rocky bosom's bed
To rest for ever—wherefore do I pause?
I feel the impulse—yet I do not plunge;
I see the peril—yet do not recede;
And my brain reels—and yet my foot is firm:
There is a power upon me which withholds,
And makes it my fatality to live;
If it be life to wear within myself
This barrenness of spirit, and to be
My own soul's sepulchre, for I have ceased
To justify my deeds unto myself —
The last infirmity of evil. Ay,
Thou winged and cloud-cleaving minister,
                              [*An eagle passes*]
Whose happy flight is highest into heaven,
Well may'st thou swoop so near me—I should be
Thy prey, and gorge thine eaglets; thou art gone
Where the eye cannot follow thee; but thine

Yet pierces downward. onward, or above
With a pervading vision.—Beautiful !
How beautiful is all this visible world !
How glorious is its action and itself !
But we, who name ourselves its sovereigns, we,
Half dust, half deity, alike unfit
To sink or soar. with our mix'd essence make
A conflict of its elements, and breathe
The breath of degradation and of pride,
Contending with low wants and lofty will,
Till our mortality predominates,
And men are—what they name not to themselves,
And trust not to each other.   Hark ! the note,
　　　[*The Shepherd's pipe in the distance is heard.*]
The natural music of the mountain reed,
For here the patriarchal days are not
A pastoral fable—pipes in the liberal air,
Mix'd with the sweet bells of the sauntering herd ?
My soul would drink these echoes.   Oh, that I were
The viewless spirit of a lovely sound;
A living voice, a breathing harmony,
A bodiless enjoyment—born and dying
With the blest tone which made me !

　　　*　　　*　　　*　　　*　　　*
　　　　　　To be thus—
Gray-bair'd with anguish, like the blasted pines,
Wrecks of a single winter, barkless, branchless,
A blighted trunk upon a cursed root,
Which but supplies a feeling to decay—
And to be thus, eternally but thus,
Having been otherwise !   Now furrow'd o'er
With wrinkles, plough'd by moments, not by years ;
And hours—all tortured into ages—hours
Which I outlive !—Ye toppling crags of ice !
Ye avalanches. whom a breath draws down
In mountainous o'erwhelming, come and crush me !
I hear ye momently above. beneath,
Crash with a frequent conflict ; but ye pass,
And only fall on things that still would live ;
On the young flourishing forest, or the hut
And hamlet of the harmless villager."

The other the splendid description of the ruins of **the Coliseum.**
is equal in point of grandeur and beauty.

　　　"I stood within the Coliseum's wall,
　　　Midst the chief relics of almighty Rome ;
　　　The trees which grew along the broken arches
　　　Waved dark in the blue midnight, and the stars
　　　Shone through the rents of ruin ; from afar

And making that which was not, till the place
Became religion, and the heart ran o'er
With silent worship of the great of old!—
The dead, but sceptred sovereigns, who still rule
Our spirits from their urns."

In *Cain*, there is the same manifestation of the poet's sceptical spirit, and the same tone of mocking misanthrophy as in *Manfred*. In Byron's historical poems—*Marino Faliero, The Two Foscari*, and *Sardanapalus*, there is discoverable, more or less, the same philosophical tenets for which Shelley's works are so conspicuous, but in each of them there is to be seen the same magnificent powers of expression and thought.

Much might be said of Byron's other works, and examples given; they have each their peculiar merits and exhibit the same intensity of passion, and brilliant powers of description, for which Byron stands unequalled.

———

h

CHAPTER XXXII.

SHELLEY.

SHELLEY.—To read Byron is to understand him, but you must understand Shelley in order to appreciate reading him. Thought lies embedded in thought ; metaphor environed in metaphor ; the whole bedecked with a profusion of gorgeous imagery, a power of imagination and subtlety of diction, apt to lead the senses of a careless reader into a sensuously charming repose, and to annihilate that force of intellect, that necessity of unwearying discrimination, which is indispensable for a complete understanding of this poet's unequalled writings. As a poet, he was gifted with a very exalted genius, great fertility of imagination, and a command over all the resources of metrical harmony, such as no English poet has surpassed.

Shelley was all his life both as a poet and a man, a dreamer and a visionary : his mind was filled with glorious but unreal phantoms of the possible imperfectability of mankind. "So ardent was his sympathy with his kind," Shaw says, "and so intense his abhorrence of the corruption and suffering that he saw around him, that the very intensity of that sympathy clouded his reason; and he fell into the common error of all enthusiasts, of supposing that, if the present organization were swept away, a milennium of virtue and happiness must ensue. He traced the misery and degradation of mankind to the institution of religion, of government, and of marriage ; and not to those passions which these institutions are intended, however imperfectly, to restrain." This remark characterises exactly the principles of Shelley's works. His poems for the most part, concern themselves not with the world, as it has been, but of the perfected world which is to be. The charge of atheism brought against him, rests mainly on his early poem of *Queen Mab*, and this he did not himself give to the world. The poem itself is a wild phantasmagoria of beautiful description, and fervent and ecstatic declamation, written in that irregular, unrhymed versification of which the *Thalaba* of Southey is an example. The defect of this

; of many of Shelley's compositions, is a vagueness of
, which occasionally becomes absolutely unintelligible.
e, in this poem, many very fine descriptive passages ; as
ice, the following passage with which the Fourth part com-
–

"How beautiful this night ! the balmiest sigh,
  Which vernal zephyrs breathe in evening's ear,
  Were discord to the speaking quietude
  That wraps this moveless scene.   Heaven's ebon vault,
  Studded with stars unutterably bright,
  Through which the moon's unclouded grandeur rolls,
  Seems like a canopy which love had spread
  To curtain her sleeping world.   You gentle hills,
  Robed in a garment of untrodden snow ;
  Yon darksome rocks, whence icicles depend,
  So stainless, that their white and glittering spires
  Tinge not the moon's pure beam ; yon castled steep,
  Whose banner hangeth o'er the time-worn towers
  So idly, that rapt fancy deemeth it
  A metaphor of peace ;—all form a scene
  Where musing solitude might love to lift
  Her soul above this sphe_e of earthliness ;
  Where silent undisturbed might watch alone,
  So cold, so bright, so still."

:lamation also with which this poem opens, is very finely

"How wonderful is Death,
  Death and his brother sleep !
One, pale as yonder waning moon
  With lips of lurid blue ;
The other, rosy as the morn
  When throned on ocean's wave
  It blushes o'er the world :
Yet both so passing wonderful !"

the most complete and distinct as also the f

retreat, is a passage which it would be almost difficult to parallel.

> " The noonday sun
> Now shone upon the forest, one vast mass
> Of mingling shade, whose brown magnificence
> A narrow vale embosoms. There, huge caves,
> Scoped in the dark base of those aëry rocks
> Mocking its moans, respond and roar for ever.
> The meeting boughs and implicated leaves
> Wove twilight o'er the Poet's path, as led
> By love, or dream, or god, or mightier Death,
> He sought in Nature's dearest haunt, some bank,
> Her cradle, and his sepulchre. More dark
> And dark the shades accumulate—the oak,
> Expanding its immense and knotty arms
> Embraces the light beach. The pyramids
> Of the tall cedar overarching, frame
> Most solemn domes within, and far below,
> Like clouds suspended in an emerald sky,
> The ash and the acacia floating hang
> Tremulous and pale. Like restless serpents, clothed
> In rainbow and in fire, the parasites,
> Starred with ten thousand blossoms, flow around
> The gray trunks, and, as gamesome infant's eyes,
> With gentle meanings, and most innocent wiles,
> Fold their beams round the hearts of those that love,
> These twine their tendrils with the wedded boughs
> Uniting their close union ; the woven leaves
> Made net-work of the dark blue light of day,
> And the night's noontide clearness, mutable
> As shapes in the weird clouds. Soft mossy lawns
> Beneath these canopies extend their swells,
> Fragrant with perfumed herbs, and eyed with blooms
> Minute yet beautiful. One darkest glen
> Sends from its woods of musk-rose, twined with jasmine,
> A soul-dissolving odour, to invite
> To some more lovely mystery. Through the dell,
> Silence and Twilight here, twin-sisters, keep
> Their noon-day watch, and sail among the shades,
> Like vaporous shapes half seen ; beyond, a well,
> Dark, gleaming, and of most translucent wave,
> Images all the woven boughs above,
> And each depending leaf, and every speck
> Of azure sky, darting between their chasms ;
> Nor aught else in the liquid mirror laves
> Its portraiture, but some inconstant star
> Between one foliaged lattice twinkling fair,
> Or painted bird, sleeping beneath the moon,
> Or gorgeous insect, floating motionless,
> Unconscious of the day, ere yet his wings
> Have spread their glories to the gaze of noon.

*   *   *   *

> An accustomed presence, and the sound
> Of the sweet brook that from the secret springs
> Of that dark fountain rose. A Spirit seemed
> To stand beside him—clothed in no bright robes
> Of shadowy silver or enshrining light,
> Borrowed from aught the visible world affords
> Of grace, or majesty, or mystery ;
> But undulating woods, and silent well,
> And reaping rivulet, and evening gloom
> Now deepening the dark shades, for speech assuming
> Held commune with him, as if he and it
> Were all that was,—only . . . when his regard
> Was raised by intense pensiveness . . . two eyes
> Two starry eyes, hung in the gloom of thought,
> And seemed with their serene and azure smiles
> To beckon him."

Hellas, and *The Revolt of Islam,* are of the same character as *Queen Mab*—violent assertions and invectives against religion, priestcraft, and marriage ; but full of airy and exquisite pictures of scenes and beings, of superhuman and unearthly splendour. There is, however, the same defect as in many other of Shelley's poems; a vagueness of meaning, by which the reader is almost unable to follow the regular drift of the subject. The former of the above poems, *Hellas,* contains one very fine passage, the Chorus on Freedom. It is written with peculiar force and intensity.

> "In the great morning of the world,
> The Spirit of God with might unfurl'd
> The flag of Freedom over Chaos,
>   And all its banded anarchs fled,
> Like vultures frighted from Imaus,
>   Before an earthquake's tread—
> So from Time's tempestuous dawn
> Freedom's splendor burst and shone :—
> Thermopylæ and Marathon
> Caught, like mountains beacon-lighted,
> The springing fire.—The winged glory
> On Philippi half-alighted,
>   Like an eagle on a promontory.
>   Its unwearied wings could fan

The quenchless ashes of Milan.
From age to age, from man to man,
It lived : and.lit from land to land
Florence, Albion, Switzerland :
Then night fell ; and as from night
Re-assuming fiery flight,
From the West swift Freedom came,
   Against the course of heaven and doom
A second sun array'd in flame :
   To burn, to kindle, to illume,
From far Atlantis its young beams
Chased the shadows and the dreams.
France, with all her sanguine streams,
   Hid, but quench'd it not ; again
   Through clouds its shafts of glory ran
   From utmost Germany to Spain.
As an eagle fed with morning
Scorns the embattled tempest's warning
When she seeks her aëry hanging
   In the mountain cedar's hair,
And her brood expect the clanging
   Of her wings through the wild air
Sick with famine—Freedom so
To what of Greece remaineth now
Returns ; her hoary ruins glow
Like orient mountains lost in day ;
   Beneath the safety of her wings
Her renovated nurselings play,
   And in the naked lightnings
   Of truth they purge their dazzled eyes.
   Let Freedom leave, where'er she flies,
   A Desert or a Paradise ;
   Let the beautiful and the brave
   Share her glory or a grave."

The other, *The Revolt of Islam*, excels in point of language the *Hellas*, and is also full of many rich and sublime passages. Take for one example, the descriptive piece with which the poem begins,

  "So as I stood, one blast of muttering thunder
    Burst in far peals along the waveless deep,
    When, gathering fast, around, above and under,
    Long trains of tremulous mist began to creep,
    Until their complicating lines did steep
    The orient sun in shadow ;—not a sound
    Was heard ; one horrible repose did keep
    The forest and the floods, and all around
    Darkness more dread than night was poured upon the ground.

  Hark ! 'tis the rushing of a wind that sweeps
    Earth and the ocean. See ! the lightnings yawn

Deluging Heaven with fire, and the lashed deep
Glitter and boil beneath : it rages on,
One mighty stream, whirlwind and waves upthrown,
Lightning, and hail, and darkness eddying by.
There is a pause—the sea-birds, that were gone
Into their caves to shriek, come forth, to spy
What calm has fall'n on earth, what light is in the sky.

For, where the irresistible storm had cloven
That fearful darkness, the blue sky was seen
Fretted with many a fair cloud interwoven
Most delicately, and the ocean green,
Beneath that opening spot of blue serene.
Quivered like burning emeralds : calm was spread
On all below ; but far on high, between
Earth and the upper air, the vast clouds fled,
Countless and swift as leaves on autumn's tempest shed.

For ever, as the war became more fierce
Between the whirlwinds and the rack on high,
That spot grew more serene ; blue light did pierce
The roof of those white clouds, which seem'd to lie
Far, deep, and motionless ; while thro' the sky
The pallid semicircle of the moon
Past on, in slow and moving majesty ;
Its upper horn arrayed in mist, which soon
But slowly fled, like dew beneath the beams of noon."

The *Witch of Atlas* is written upon the same principle, and
contains several similar severe invectives against kingcraft and
priestcraft. For example,

'¶The priests would write an explanation full,
    Translating hieroglyphics into Greek,
How the god Apis really was a bull,
    And rothing more ; and bid the herald stick
The same against the temple doors, and pull
    The old cant down ; they licensed all to speak
Whate'er they thought of hawks, and cats and geese,
By pastoral letters to each diocese.

The king would dress an ape up in his crown
    And robes, and seat him on his glorious seat,
And on the right hand of the sunlike throne
    Would place a gaudy mock-bird to repeat
The chatterings of the monkey.—Every one
    Of the prone courtiers crawled to kiss the feet
Of their great Emperor when the morning came ;
And kissed—alas, how many kiss the same !"

Yet there is the same obscurity and difficulty of discerning the
drift of this poem, though the characters are equally striking and

vivid in point of reality, and have the same brilliant glow of imagination.

Shelley's genius was, in fact, of a high order ; but instead of possessing it, he was possessed by it ; and his muse, as a writer has well compared it, is 'a pythoness upon her tripod, torn and convulsed by the utterance of which she is the channel': and this is the characteristic of Shelley's poetry. The following passage from the *Witch of-Atlas*, contains all that glittering imagery for which this poet is so remarkable.

"And down the streams which clove those mountains vast
    Around their inland islets, and amid
The panther peopled forests, whose shade cast
    Darkness and odours, and a pleasure hid
In melancholy gloom, the pinnace pass'd
    By many a star-surrounded pyramid
Of icy crag cleaving the purple sky,
And caverns yawning round unfathomably.

The silver moon into that winding dell,
    With slanted gleam athwart the forest tops,
Tempered with golden evening, feebly fell ;
    A green and glowing light, like that which drops
From folded lilies in which glow-worms dwell.
    When earth, over her face night's mantle wraps ;
Between the severed mountains lay on high
Over the stream, a narrower rift of sky.

      *   *   *   *

The water flashed like sunlight, by the prow
    Of a noon-wandering meteor flung to Heaven
The still air seemed as if its waves did flow
    In tempests down the mountains,—loosely driven :
The lady's radiant hair streamed to and fro
    Beneath the billows, having va¹nly striven
Indignant and impetuous, roared to feel
The swift and steady motion of the heel.

Or, when the weary moon was in the wane,
    Or, in the noon of interlunar night,
The lady-witch in visions could not chain
    Her spirit ; but sailed forth under the light
Of shooting stars, and bade extend amain
    His storm-outspeeding wings, th' Hermaphrodite
She to the Austral waters took her way,
Beyond the fabulous Thamondocona.

Where, like a meadow which no scythe has shaven,
    Which rain could never bend, or whirl-blast shake,

With the Antarctic constellations haven,
  Canopus and his crew, lay th' Austral lake—
There she would build herself a windless haven
  Out of the clouds, whose moving turrets make
The bastions of the storm, when through the sky
The spirits of the tempest thundered by.

A haven, beneath whose translucent floor
  The tremulous stars sparkled unfathomably,
And around which, the solid vapours hoar,
  Based on the level waters to the sky
Lifted their dreadful crags; and like a shore
  Of wintry mountains, inaccessibly
Hemmed in with rifts and precipices grey,
And hanging crags, many a cove and bay.

And whilst the outer lake beneath the lash
  Of the winds' scourge, foamed like a wounded thing;
And the incessant hail with stony clash
  Ploughed up the waters, and the flagging wing
Of the roused cormorant in the lightning flash
  Looked like the wreck of some wind—wandering
Fragment of inky thunder smoke—this haven
Was as a gem to copy heaven engraven."

The *Cenci* is the only one of Shelley's poems, that shows a clear
d firm outline : it is a terrible story of real life dramatised with
nsummate vigour and directness of treatment. The subject is
e of the most frightful of those domestic crimes in which the
ıck annals of mediæval Italy so abound. The language is
orous and masculine, and it contains several very powerful and
iking scenes. The scene containing the murder of the *Cenci* is
: most strikingly written,

> *Lucretia.*—"They are about it now.
> *Beatrice.*—Nay, it is done.
> *Lucr.*—I have not heard him groan.
> *Beat.*—He will not groan.
> *Lucr.*—What sound is that ?
> *Beat.*—List ! 'tis the tread of feet
> About his bed.
> *Lucr.*—My God !
> If he be now a cold stiff corpse !
> *Beat.*—Oh, fear not
> What may be done, but what is left undone :
> The act seals all.
>   *Enter* OLIMPIO *and* MARZIO.
>   Is it accomplished ?
> *Mar.*—What ?

Olim.—Did you not call?

Beat.—When?

Olim.—Now.

Beat.—I ask if all is over?

Olim.—We dare not kill an old and sleeping man;
Ilis thin gray hair, his stern and reverend brow,
His veined hands crossed on his·heaving breast,
And the calm innocent sleep in which he lay,
Quelled me. Indeed, indeed, I cannot do it.

Mar.—But I was bolder; for I chid Olimpio,
And bade him bear his wrongs to his own grave,
And leave me the reward. And now my knife
Touched the loose wrinkled throat, when the old man
Stirred in his sleep, and said, 'God! hear, Oh hear
A father's curse! What! art thou not our father?'
And then he laughed. I knew it was the ghost
Of my dead father speaking through his lips,
And could not kill him.

Beat.—Miserable slaves!
Where, if ye dare not kill a sleeping man,
Found ye the boldness to return to me
With such a deed undone? Base palterers!
Cowards and traitors! Why, the very conscience
Which ye would sell for gold and for revenge
Is an equivocation : it sleeps over
A thousand daily acts disgracing men :
And when a deed where mercy insults heaven—
Why do I talk?

(Snatching a dagger from one of them, and raising it)
Hadst thou a tongue to say,
She murdered her own father, I must do it!
But never dream ye shall outlive him long!

Olim.—Stop, for God's sake!

Mar.—I will go back and kill him.

Olim.—Give me the weapon; we must do thy will.

Beat.—Take it!—depart! Return!

(Exeunt Olim. and Mar.)
How pale thou art!
We do but that which 'twere a deadly crime
To leave undone.

Lucr.—Would it were done!

Beat.—Even whilst
That doubt is passing through your mind, the world
Is conscious of a change. Darkness and hell
Have swallowed up the vapour they sent forth
To blacken the sweet light of life. My breath
Comes, methinks, lighter, and the gelid blood
Runs freely through my veins. Hark!

Enter OLIMPIO *and* MARZIO.

Olim.—Dead!

Beat.—Some tedious guest is coming.
Lucr.—The drawbridge is let down ; there is a tramp
Of horses in the court ; fly, hide yourselves!
(Exeunt Olim. and Mar.)
Beat.—Let us retire to counterfeit deep rest.
I scarcely need to counterfeit it now :
The spirit which doth reign within these limbs
Seems strangely undisturbed.   I could even sleep
Fearless and calm, all ill is surely past." (*Exeunt.*)

The *Prometheus Unbound*, is one of the wildest and most unin-
elligible of all Shelley's works, though there are contained in it
ıumberless passages of the highest beauty. Many of the descriptive
ıassages are sublime, and noble burst of lyric harmony alternate
vith the wildest personifications and fiercest invectives. Its great
lefect is, that is too full of super-subtle and unsubstantial ab-
ıtractions. The following from this poem, is a very elegant passage.

"My soul is an enchanted boat,
  Which, like a sleeping swan, doth float
Upon the silver waves of thy sweet singing ;
  And thine doth like an angel sit
  Beside the helm conducting it,
Whilst all the winds with melody are ringing,
  It seems to float ever, for ever,
  Upon that many-winding river,
  Between mountains, woods, abysses,
  A paradise of wildernesses l
Till, like one in slumber bound,
Borne to the ocean, I float down, around,
Into a sea profound of ever-spreading sound :
  Meanwhile the spirit lifts its pinions

In music's most serene dominions,
Catching the winds that fan that happy heaven ;
  And we sail on, away, afar,
  Without a course, without a star.
But by the instinct of sweet music driven ;
  Till through Elysian garden islets
  By thee, most beautiful of pilots,
  Where never mortal pinnace glided,
  The boat of my desire is guided :
Realms where the air we breathe is love,
Which in the winds on the waves doth move,
Harmonizing this earth with what we feel above.
  We have pass'd Age's icy caves,
And Manhood's dark and tossing waves,
And Youth's smooth ocean, smiling to betray :
  Beyond the glassy gulphs we flee
  Of shadow-peopled Infancy.
Through Death and Birth, to a diviner day ;
  A paradise of vaulted bowers,
  Lit by downward-gazing flowers,
  And watery paths that wind between
  Wildernesses calm and green,
Peopled by shapes too bright to see,
And rest, having beheld ; somewhat like thee ;
Which walk upon the sea, and chaunt melodiously ! "

Rosalind and Helen, is an elaborate pleading against the institution of marriage, and unreasonable as the subject of the poem is, there are parts of it that teem with exquisite sentiment and feeling. The following passage overflows with great tenderness and pathos.

"Yet day by day he grew more weak,
  And his sweet voice, when he might speak,
  Which ne'er was loud, became more low ;
  And the light which flashed through his waxen cheek
  Grew faint, as the rose-like hues which flow
  From sunset o'er the Alpine snow :
  And death seemed not like death in him,
  For the spirit of life o'er every limb
  Lingered, a mist of scene and thought.
  When the summer wind faint odours brought
  From mountain flowers, even as it passed,
  His cheek would change, as the noon-day sea
  Which the dying breeze sweeps fitfully.
  If but a cloud the sky o'ercast,
  You might see his colour come and go,
  And the softest strain of music made
  Sweet smiles, yet sad, arise and fade
  Amid the dew of his tender eyes :
  And the breath, with intermitting flow,

Adonais, an elegy written on the death of Keats, is of a pastoral character, and suggests to the reader the immortal *Lycidas* of Milton. It is a beautiful and touching lament on the early death of Keats, whose short career gave such a noble foretaste of poetical genius, that would have made him one of the greatest writers of his age. Amongst the most beautiful of the stanzas, are the following noble bursts of real poetical feeling and enthusiasm.

> "He lives, he wakes—'tis Death is dead, not he ;
> Mourn not for Adonias.—Thou young Dawn,
> Turn all thy dew to splendour, for from thee
> The spirit thou lamentest is not gone ;
> Ye caverns and ye forests, cease to moan !
> Cease ye faint flowers and fountains, and thou Air,
> Which like a mourning veil thy scarf hadst thrown
> O'er the abandon'd Earth, now leave it bare
> Even to the Joyous stars which smile on its despair.
>
> He is made one with Nature : there is heard
> His voice in all her music, from the moan
> Of thunder, to the song of night's sweet bird ;
> He is a presence to be felt and known
> In darkness and in light, from herb and stone,
> Spreading itself where'er that Power may move
> Which has withdrawn his being to its own ;
> Which wields the world with never-wearied love,
> Sustains it from beneath, and kindles it above.
>
> He is a portion of the loveliness
> Which once he made more lovely : he doth bear
> His part, while the one Spirit's plastic stress
> Sweeps through the dull dense world, compelling there
> All new successions to the forms they wear ;
> Torturing th' unwilling dross that checks its flight
> To its own likeness, as each mass they bear ;
> And bursting in its beauty and its might
> From trees and beasts and men into the Heavens' light."

In point of versification the *Sensitive Plant* is the best. It is as extraordinary for its melody and variety, as for its high degree of mysterious fancy. The reader is carried throughout with a desire of penetrating the abstract meaning which the poet has symbolised in the beautiful description of the garden and the Plant, and which is locked up, says Shaw, "as the embryo is involved in the foldings of the petals of a flower." The whole of the poem is full of the most luxuriant imagery and descriptions. This poem can be read by everyone, as a masterpiece of real poetical genius. We quote a few verses of it :—

"A Sensitive Plant in a garden grew,
And the young winds fed it with silver dew,
And it opened its fan-like leaves to the light,
And closed them beneath the kisses of night.

And the Spring arose on the garden fair,
Like the Spirit of Love fell everywhere :
And each flower and herb on Earth's dark breast
Rose from the dreams of its wintry rest.

But none ever trembled and panted with bliss
In the garden, the field, or the wilderness,
Like a doe in the noon-tide with love's sweet want,
As the companionless Sensitive Plant.

The snow-drop and then the violet,
Arose from the ground with warm rain wet,
And their breath was mixed with fresh odour, sent
From the turf, like the voice and the instrument.

Then the pied wild-flowers and the tulip tall,
And narcissi, the fairest among them all,
Who gaze on their eyes in the stream's recess,
Till they die of their own dear loveliness ;

And the Naiad-like lily of the vale,
Whom youth makes so fair and passion so pale,
That the light of it tremulous bells is seen
Through their pavilions of tender green ;

And the hyacinth purple, and white, and blue,
Which flung from its bells a sweet peal anew
Of music so delicate, soft, and intense,
It was felt like an odour within the sense.

And the rose like a nymph to the bath addrest,
Which unveiled the depth of her glowing breast,
Till, fold after fold, to the fainting air
The soul of her beauty and love lay bare :

And the wand-like lily, which lifted up,
As a Mænad, its moonlight-coloured cup,
Till the fiery star, which is its eye,
Gazed through clear dew on the tender sky ;

And the jessamine faint, and the sweet tuberose,
The sweetest flower for scent that blows ;
And all rare blossoms from every clime
Grew in that garden in perfect prime.

And the sinuous paths of lawn and of moss,
Which led through the garden along and across,
Some open at once to the sun and the breeze,
Some lost among bowers of blossoming trees,

Were all paved with daises and delicate bells
As fair as the fabulous asphodels,
And flowrets which drooping as day, drooped too,
Fell into pavilions white, purple, and blue.
To roof the glow-worm from the evening dew.

*   *   *   *

Swift summer into the autumn flowed,
And frost in the mist of the morning rode,
Though the noonday sun looked clear and bright,
Mocking the spoil of the secret night,

The roseleaves, like flakes of crimson snow,
Paved the turf and the moss below.
The lilies were drooping, and white, and wan,
Like the head and the skin of a dying man.

And Indian plants of scent and hue
The sweetest that ever was fed on dew,
Leaf after leaf, day after day,
Were massed into the common clay.

And the leaves, brown, yellow, and grey, and red,
And white with the whiteness of what is dead,
Like troops of ghosts on the dry wind past ;
Their whistling noise made the birds aghast.

And the gusty winds waked the winged seeds,
Out of their birthplace of ugly weeds,
Till they clung round many a sweet flower's stem,
Which rotted into the earth with them.

The water-blooms under the rivulet
Fell from the stalk on which they were set ;
And the eddies drove them here and there,
As the winds did those of the upper air.

Then the rain came down, and the broken stalks,
Were bent and tangled across the walks,
And the leafless net-work of parasite bowers
Massed into ruin ; and all sweet flowers.

*   *   *   *

For Winter came : the wind was his whip :
One choppy finger was on his lip :
He had torn the cataracts from the hills
And they clanked at his girdle like manacles.

His breath was a chain which without a sound
The earth, the air, and the water bound ;
He came, fiercely driven, in his chariot throne
By the tenfold blasts of the arctic zone.

Then the weeds which were forms of living death
Fled from the frost to the earth beneath :
Their decay and sudden flight from frost
Was but like the vanishing of a ghost !

And under the roots of the Sensitive Plant
The moles and the doormice died for want   :
The birds dropped stiff from the frozen air,
And were caught in the branches naked and bare.

First there came down a thawing rain,
And its full drops froze on the boughs again,
Then there steamed up a freezing dew
Which to the drops of the thaw-rain grew ;

And a northern whirlwind, wandering about
Like a wolf that had smelt a dead child out,
Shook the boughs thus laden, and heavy and stiff,
And snapped them off with his rigid grip. ·

When winter had gone, and spring came back,
The Sensitive Plant was a leafless wreck ;
But the mandrakes, and toadstools, and docks and darnels
Rose like the dead from their ruined charnels."

Many of Shelley's Odes and detached pieces are inexpressibly
beautiful. Among others the *Cloud*, is full of wild and picturesque
imagery. The following are two passages from this poem :—

" I bring fresh showers for the thirsting flowers,
　From the seas and the streams ;
I bear the light shade for the leaves when laid
　In the noon-day dreams,
From my wings are shaken the dews that awaken
　The sweet birds every one,
When rocked to rest on their mother's breast,
　As she dances about the sun.
I wield the flail of the lashing hail,
　And whiten the green plains under,
And then again I dissolve it in rain.
　And laugh as I pass in thunder.

　　　*　　.　*　　　*　　　*

I am the daughter of earth and water,
　And the nursling of the sky ;

I pass through the pores of the ocean and shores;
 I change, but I cannot die,
For after the rain when with never a stain,
 The pavilion of heaven is bare,
And the winds and sunbeams with their convex gleams,
 Build up the blue dome of air,
I silently laugh at my own cenotaph,
 And out of the caverns of rain,
Like a child from the womb, like a ghost from the tomb,
 I arise and unbuild it again."

ıe *Woodman and the Nightingale,* is another of Shelley's most
tiful minor poems. The following passage will at once char-
ize it.

" And so this man returned with axe and saw
At evening close from killing the tall tree,
The soul of whom by nature's gentle lawn

Was each a wood-nymph, and kept ever green
The pavement and the roof of the wild copse.
Chequering the sunlight of the blue serene

With jagged leaves,—and from the forest tops
Singing the winds to sleep—or weeping oft
Fast showers of aërial water drops

Into their mother's bosom, sweet and soft,
Nature's pure tears which have no bitterness;—
Around the cradles of the birds aloft

They spread themselves into tho loveliness
Of fan-like leaves, and over palin flowers
Hang like moist clouds:—or, where high branches kiss,

Make a green space among the silent bower,
Like a vast fane in a metropolis,
Surrounded by the columns and the towers

All over-wrought with branch-like traceries
In which there is religion—and the mute
Persuasion of unkindled melodies,

Odours and gleams and murmurs, which the lute
Of the blind pilot spirit of the blast
Stirs as it sails, now grave and now acute,

Wakening the leaves and waves ere it has past
To such brief unison as on the brain
One tone, which never can recur, has cast,

One accent never to return again."

Ode to the West Wind, is equal in flow of language and melody
poem of its kind in this poet's writings. Take, for instance,
ısical flow which is contained in the following verses.

"If I were a dead leaf thou mightest bear ;
If I were a swift cloud to fly with thee ;
A wave to pant beneath thy power, and share

The impulse of thy strength, only less free
Than thou, O, uncontrollable ! If even
I were as in my boyhood, and could be

The comrade of my wanderings over heaven.
As then, when to outstrip thy skiey speed
Scarce seemed a vision ; I would ne'er have striven

As thus with thee in prayer in my sore need.
Oh ! lift me as a wave, a leaf, a cloud !
I fall upon the thorns of life! I bleed !

A heavy weight of hours has chained and bowed
One too like thee : tameless, and swift, and proud,

Make me thy lyre, even as the forest is :
What if my leaves are falling like its own !
The tumult of thy mighty harmonies

Will take from both a deep, autumnal tone,
Sweet thou in sadness.　Be thou, spirit fierce,
My spirit ! Be thou me, impetuous one !

Drive my dead thoughts over the universe
Like withered leaves to quicken a new birth !
And, by the incantation of this verse,

Scatter, as from an unextinguishable hearth
Ashes and sparks. my words among mankind!
Be through my lips to unawakened earth

The trumpet of a prophecy ! O, wind,
If Winter comes, can Spring be far behind ?"

All of these minor poems might equally be quoted in point of
poetic excellence ; they each exhibit the peculiar genius recogniz-
able in all this poet's works, large and small.　The little poem,
Love's Philosophy, is one of the purest and tenderest gems that ever
flowed from mind or heart of poet.　We will conclude this poet's
work by quoting it.

"The fountains mingle with the river,
　And the rivers with the ocean,
The winds of heaven mix for ever
　With a sweet emotion ;
Nothing in the world is single,
　All things by a law divine
In one another's being mingle—
　Why not I with thine ?

See the mountains kiss high heaven,
　And the waves clasp one another ;

And the moonbeams kiss the sea,
What are all these kisses worth,
    If thou kiss not me?"

CHAPTER XXXIII.

KEATS.

KEATS.—Keats' poems show a beautiful immaturity, and when
e have finished reading them, we are left with an unsatisfied
eling of what the glorious aspirant could and would have done,
th a longer span of life, and astonishment that so much was actu
ly accomplished by one so young. Byron says, "he is a loss
literature; and the more so, as he himself before his death is
id to have been persuaded that he had not taken the right line,
id was reforming his style upon the more classical models of the
nguage." We can see in the advance of his poems, how the true
id high prompting of art became clearer and clearer, and more
imediate and certain his response to them.

The primary element of Keats' poetry is enjoyment, and it has
en observed, "his very melancholy is the luxury of sadness, his
spair, the drained and reversed cup of ecstasy." One of the
ost remarkable features in his poems, is the wonderful pro-
sion of figurative language. Shaw, in his remarks upon Keats,
s exhibited with great truth and nicety of language, his peculiar
alities. He says, "The peculiarity of Shelley's style, to which
  may give the name of *incatenation*, Keats carries to extra-
;ance—one word, one image, one rhyme suggests another, till
  quite lose sight of the original idea, which is smothered in
own sweet luxuriance, like a bee stifled in honey." And in con-
sting this peculiarity of language with Shakespeare and his
ool—upon whose manner Keats undoubtedly endeavoured to
m his style—the same writer compares the difference in their

treatment of the thought and image, in the following remark, "with them the images are produced by a force acting *ab intra*; like wild flowers springing from the very richness of the ground: in Keats the force acts *ab extra*; the flowers are forcibly fixed in the earth, as in the garden of a child, who cannot wait till they grow there of themselves."

Keats longest poem is *Endymion.* Like most of his other poems it is full of figurative language, which is sometimes very beautiful, but at other times forced, and merely fantastical. Many passages of great beauty might be selected from this poem as examples. The following address to the Moon, is written in very elegant language.

> " What is there in thee, Moon ! that thou shouldst move
> My heart so potently ? When yet a child,
> I oft have dried my tears when thou hast smiled.
> Thou seem'dst my sister : hand in hand we went
> From eve to morn across the firmanent.
> No apples would I gather from the tree,
> Till thou hadst cool'd their cheeks deliciously :
> No tumbling water ever spake romance,
> But when mine eyes with thine thereon could dance :
> No woods were green enough, no bower divine,
> Until thou lifted'st up thine eyelids fine :
> In sowing-time ne'er would I dibble take,
> Or drop a seed, till thou wast wide awake ;
> And, in the summer-tide of blossoming,
> No one but thee hath heard me blithely sing,
> And mesh my dewy flowers all the night.
> No melody was like a passing spright,
> If it went not to solemnize thy reign.
> Yes, in my boyhood, every joy and pain
> By thee were fashion'd to the self-same end ;
> And as I grew in years, still didst thou blend
> With all thy ardours: thou wast the deep glen ;
> Thou wast the mountain-top—the sage's pen—
> The poet's harp—the voice of friends—the sun ;
> Thou wast the river—thou wast glory won ;
> Thou wast my clarion's blast—thou wast my steed—
> My goblet full of wine—my to past deed :—
> Thou wast the charm of women, lovely Moon !
> O what a wild and harmonised tune,
> My spirit struck from all the beautiful !
> Onsome bright essence could I lean, and lull
> Myself to immortality : I prest
> Nature's soft pillow in a wakeful rest.
> But gentle Orb ! there came a nearer bliss—

My strange love came—Felicity's abyss!
She came, and thou didst fade, and fade away—
Yet not entirely; no, thy starry sway
Has been an under-passion to this hour.
Now I begin to feel thine orby power
Is. coming fresh upon me. O be kind!
Keep back thine influence, do not blind
My sovereign vision.

   * * * *

O Moon! the oldest shades 'mong oldest trees
Feel palpitations when thou lookest in:
O Moon! old boughs lisp forth a holier din
The while they feel thine airy fellowship.
Thou dost bless everywhere, with silver lip
Kissing dead things to life. The sleeping kine,
Couch'd in thy brightness, dream of fields divine:
Innumerable mountains rise, and rise,
Ambitious for the hallowing of thine eyes;
And yet thy benediction passeth not
One obscure hiding-place, one litte spot,
Where pleasure may be sent: the nested wren
Has thy fair face within its tranquil ken,
And from beneath a sheltering ivy leaf
Take glimpses of thee; thou art a relief
To the poor patient oyster where it sleeps,
Within its pearly house;—the mighty deeps,
The monstrous sea is thine—the myriad sea!
O Moon! far spooming Ocean bows to thee,
And Tellus feels her forehead's cumbrous load."

The opening of this poem is also exceedingly beautiful, and would alone, amply illustrate the poetic genius of Keats.

  " A thing of beauty is a joy for ever:
  Its loveliness increases; it will never
  Pass into nothingness; but still will keep
  A bower quiet for us, and a sleep
  Full of sweet dreams, and health, and quiet breathing.
  Therefore, on every morrow, are we wreathing
  A flowery band to bind us to the earth,
  Spite of despondence, of the inhuman dearth
  Of noble natures, of the gloomy days,
  Of all the unhealthy and o'er-darken'd ways
  Made for our searching; yes, in spite of all,
  Some shape of beauty moves away the pall
  From our dark spirits. Such the sun, the moon,
  Trees old and young, sprouting a shady boon
  For simple sheep, and such are daffodils
  With the green world they live in; and clear rills
  That for themselves a cooling covert make
  'Gainst the hot season; the mid-forest brake,

Rich with a sprinkling of fair musk-rose blooms:
And such too is the grandeur of the dooms
We have imagined for the mighty dead ;
All lovely tales that we have heard or read ;
An endless fountain of immortal drink,
Pouring unto us from heaven's brink.
  Not do we merely feel the essences
For one short hour ; no, even as the trees
That whisper round a temple become soon
Dear as the temple's self, so does the moon,
The passion poesy, glories infinite,
Haunt us till they become a cheering light
Unto our souls, and bound to us so fast,
That, whether there be shine, or gloom o'ercast,
They alway must be with us, or we die."

Or again the following stanzas, which are full of the sweetest
poetry, and written in versification at once pathetic and mournful.

" O Sorrow !
  Why dost borrow
The natural hue of health, from vermeil lips ?—
    To give maiden blushes
    To the white rose bushes
Or is it thy dewy hand the daisy tips ?

  O Sorrow !
  Why dost borrow
The lustrous passion from a falcon-eye ?—
    To give the glow-worm light ?
    Or, on a moonless night,
To tinge, on syren shores, the salt-sea spry ?

  O Sorrow !
  Why dost borrow
The mellow ditties from a mourning tongue ?—
    To give at evening pale
    Unto the nightingale,
That thou mayst listen the cold dews among ?

  O Sorrow !
  Why dost borrow
Heart's lightness from the merriment of May ?
    A lover would not tread
    A cowslip on the head,
Thought he should dance from eve to peep of day—
    Nor any drooping flower
    Held sacred for thy bower;
Wherever he may sport himself and play,

  O Sorrow !
  I bade good morrow,
And thought to leave her far away behind ;

But cheerly, cheerly,
 She loves me dearly;
She is so constant to me, and so kind:
 I would deceive her,
 And so leave her,
But ah ! she is so constant and so kind.

Beneath my palm trees, by the riverside,
I sat a weeping ; in the whole world wide
There was no one to ask me why I wept—
 And so I kept
Brimming the water-lily cups with tears
 Cold as my fears.

Beneath my palm-trees, by the riverside
I sat a weeping : what enamour'd bride,
Cheated by shadowy wooer from the clouds,
 But hides and shrouds
Beneath dark palm-trees by a riverside?
 * * * *

 Come then, Sorrow
 Sweetest Sorrow !
Like an own babe I nurse thee on my breast :
 I thought to leave thee,
 And deceive thee,
But now of all the world I love thee best.

 There is not one,
 No, no, not one
But thee to comfort a poor lonely maid ;
 Thou art her mother,
 And her brother,
Her playmate, and her wooer in the shade."

One of Keats' greatest powers of poetry is exhibited in the manner in which he has treated the classical mythology, representing the Pagan deities not as mere abstraction of art, but endowing them with feelings and passions like ourselves, idealised and purified according with the golden atmosphere of primæval existence, and the lovely scenery óf ancient Greece and Italy. It is a truly original merit for which alone he deserves the highest praise. In the verses on a *Grecian Urn*, there is a beautiful illustration of this, and with the beautiful strain of imagery, there is combined a perception of luxuriant and delicate loveliness.

 "Thou still unravish'd bride of quietness !
 Thou foster-child of Silence and slow Time,
 Sylvan historian, who canst thus express
 A flowery tale more sweetly than our rhyme ;

What leaf-fringed legend haunts about thy shape
  Of deities of mortals, or of both,
    In Tempe or the dales of Arcady?
    What men or gods are these? what maidens loath?
What mad pursuit? What stuggle to escape?
    What pipes and timbrels? What wild ecstasy?

Heard melodies are sweet, but those unheard
  Are sweeter; therefore, ye soft pipes. play on;
Not to the sensual ear, but, more endear'd,
  Pipe to the spirit ditties of no tone:
Fair youth, beneath the trees, thou canst not leave
  Thy song, nor ever can those trees be bare;
  Bold Lover, never, never canst thou kiss,—
Though winning near the goal—yet, do not grieve;
  She cannot fade, though thou hast not thy bliss,
For ever wilt thou love, and she be fair l

Ah, happy, happy boughs! that cannot shed
  Your leaves, nor ever bid the spring adieu;
And, happy melodist, unwearied,
  For ever piping songs for ever new;
More happy love! more happy, happy love!
  For ever warm and still to be enjoy'd.
  For ever panting and for ever young;—
All breathing human passion far above,
  That leaves a high heart sorrowful and cloy'd,
  A burning forehead, and a parching tongue.—

Who are these coming to the sacrifice?
  To what green altar, O mysterious priest,
Lead'st thou that heifer lowing at the skies,
  And all the silken flanks with garlands drest?
What little town by river or sea-shore,
  Or mountain-built with peaceful citadel
  Is emptied of its folk, this pious morn?—
And. little town, thy streets for evermore
  Will silent be; and not a soul to tell
  Why thou art desolate, can e'er return,

O attic shape. Fair attitude! with brede
  Of marble men and maidens overwrought,
With forest branches and the trodden weed;
  Thou silent form! dost tease us out of thought
As doth eternity: Cold Pastoral!
  When old age shall this generation waste,
  Thou shalt remain, in midst of other woe—
Than ours, a fiiend to man, to whom thou say'st,
  'Beauty is truth, truth beauty'—that is all
  Ye know on earth, and all age ye need to know.'"

Isabella is a sweetly written poem, based upon an anecdote from
Boccaccio; as may be seen in the following..

"O eloquent and famed Boccaccio!
  Of thee we now should ask forgiving boon
And of thy spicy myrtles as they blow,
  And of thy roses amorous of the moon,
And of thy lilies. that do paler grow
  Now they can no more hear thy ghittern's tune,
For venturing syllables that ill beseem
The quiet glooms of such a piteous theme.

Grant thou a pardon here, and then the tale
  Shall move on soberly, as it is meet ;
Their is no other crime, no mad assail
  To make old prose in modern rhyme more sweet :
But it is done—succeed the verse or fail—
  To honour thee, and thy gone spirit greet ;
To stead thee as a verse in English tongue,
An echo of thee in the north-wind sung."

The following verses from this poem, will rank amongst the choicest passages in Keats' works.

"O Melancholy, linger here awhile !
  O Music, Music, breathe despondingly !
O Echo, Echo, from some sombre isle,
  Unknown, Lethean, sigh to us—O sigh !
Spirits in grief, lift up your heads, and smile ;
  Lift up your heads, sweet Spirits, heavily,
And make a pale light in your cypress glooms,
Tinting with silver wan your marble tombs.

Moan hither, all ye syllables of woe,
  From the deep throat of sad Melpomene !
Through bronzed lyre in tragic order go,
  And touch the strings into a mystery ;
Sound mournfully upon the winds and low,
  For simple Isabel is soon to be
Among the dead : She withers, like a palm
Cut by an Indian for its juicy balm.

O leave the palm to wither by itself ;—
  Let not quick Winter chill its dying hour !
It may not be—those Baälites of pelf,
  Her brethren, noted the continual shower
From her dead eyes ; and many a curious elf,
  Among her kindred, wonder'd that such dower
Of youth and beauty should be thrown aside,
By one march'd out to be a Noble's bride."

In this treatment of mythological subjects, Keats excels; and in his more modern poems there is an inferiority in the descriptions of personages and scenery. There is not the deep, intense passion; But they contain a prettiness and simplicity which renders them interesting and pleasing. The *Eve of St. Agnes*, is one of the best examples from this kind of poems : it is a tale full of rich description and romantic interest, and has in it many fine parts. For an example the following stanzas may be read.

" ' Tis dark : quick pattereth the flaw-blow sleet :
'This is no dream, my bride, my Madeline.'—
'Tis dark : the ice gusts still rave and beat :
' No dream, alas ! alas ! and woe is mine !—
Porphyro will leave me here to fade and pine.—
Cruel ! what traitor could thee hither bring ?
I curse not, for my heart is lost in thine,
Though thou forsakest a deceived thing —
A dove forlorn and lost with sick unpruned wing.

'My Madeline ! sweet dreamer ! lovely bride !
Say, may I be for aye thy vassal blest !
Thy beauty's shield, heart-shaped and vermeil dyed ?
Ah, silver shrine, here will I take my rest
After so many hours of toil and quest,
A famish'd pilgrim, — saved by miracle
Though I have found, I will not rob thy nest
Saving of the sweet self ; if thou think'st well
To trust, fair Madeline, to no rude infidel !

' Hark ! 'tis an elfin storm from faery land,
Of haggard seeming, but a boon indeed :
Arise—arise! the morning is at hand ;—
The bloated wassailers will never heed :—
Let us away, my love, with happy speed ;
There are no ears to hear, or eyes to see,—
Drown'd all in Rhenish and the sleepy mead :
Awake ! arise ! my love, and fearless be,
For o'er the southern moors I have a home for thee.'

She hurried at his words, beset with fears,
For there were sleeping dragons all around,
At glaring watch, perhaps, with ready spears—
Down the wide stairs a darkling way they found,
In all the house was heard no human sound.
A chain-droop'd lamp was flickering by each door ;
The arras, rich with horseman, hawk, and hound,
Flutter'd in the besieging wind's uproar ;
And the long carpets rose along the gushy floor.

They glide, like phantoms, into the wide hall !
Like phantoms to the iron porch they glide,
Where lay the Porter, in uneasy sprawl,
With a huge empty flagon by his side :
The wakeful bloodhound rose, and shook his hide,
But his sagacious eye an inmate owns ;

r'or age unsought tor slept among his ashes cold."

Amongst the *Sonnets* of this poet the best is that written *On siting the Tomb of Burns.*

> "The town, the churchyard, and the setting sun,
> The clouds, the trees, the rounded hills all seem,
> Though beautiful, cold—strange—as in a dream,
> I dreamed long ago, now new begun.
> The short-lived, paly Summer is but won
> From Winter's ague, for one hour's gleam ;
> Though sapphire-warm, their stars do never beam ;
> All is cold Beauty ; pain is never done :
> For who has mind to relish, Minos-wise,
> The Real of Beauty, free from that dead hue
> Sickly imagination and sick pride
> Cast wan upon it! Burns ! with honour due
> I oft have honour'd thee. Great shadow, hide
> Thy face ; I sin against thy native skies."

CHAPTER XXXIV.

MOORE.

MOORE.—Moore's chief characteristics as a poet, are invention
ely and pointed expression, and an elaborate sentimentality. He
remarkable for the felicity with which he illustrates his fancy by
usions drawn from the most remote and unexpected sources,
iich is often productive of considerable pleasure to the reader.
iere is a charm and tenderness about Moore's poems, but they
not exhibit that intense feeling which distingushes the works of
:h poets as Byron and Shelley. Still his poems are perfect in
:ir peculiar manner ; the same fancy and wit pervades almost

every page, and there are to be found many luxuriant descriptions, and genuine gushes of poetical sentiment.

The longest and most important of Moore's poems is an oriental tale, entitled *Lalla Rookh*. Upon this poem Moore has lavished great splendour of imagination, and immense stores of Eastern reading ; and the details of scenery, manners and ceremonial, are replete with the richest Asiatic imagery. The plan of the tale introduces four poems, of a narrative character ; the *Veiled Prophet*, the *Fire Worshippers*, *Paradise and the Peri*, and the *Light of the Harem*. The same gorgeous splendour and unvarying richness of painting are the qualities of each. There is a want of reality in the characters of the first of these tales; the agonized and intense feeling thrown into it, has the appearance of being far-fetched. It is written in heroic verse, a powerful species of writing over which Moore was scarcely master; and though the imagery in many parts is rich, and the descriptions exquisitely drawn, the poet's genius is exhibited more in the songs and lyrics which are occasionally interspersed, than in the narrative portion of the work. The scene where Azim is introduced to a kind of foretaste of the joys of Paradise, is one of the best of these lyrics.

> " There's a bower of roses by Bendemeer's stream,
>   And the nightingale sings round it all the day long;
> In the time of my childhood 'twas like a sweet dream,
>   To sit in the roses and hear the bird's song.
>
> That bower and its music I never forget,
>   But oft when alone, in the bloom of the year,
> I think—Is the nightingale singing there yet ?
>   And the roses still bright by the calm Bendemeer?
>
> No, the roses soon wither'd that hung o'er the wave,
>   But some blossoms were gather'd, while freshly they shone—
> And a dew was distill'd from the flowers they gave
>   All the fragrance of summer when summer was gone.
>
> Thus memory draws from delight, ere it dies,
>   An essence that breathes of it many a year ;
> Thus bright to my soul, as 'twas then to my eyes,
>   Is that bower on the banks of the calm Bendemeer ?"

Or the following, which is as equally beautifully written as the former, illustrates this. Moore's chief excellence, in fact, lies in his power over lyric verse.

"A spirit there is, whose fragrant sigh
   Is burning now through earth and air;
Where cheeks are blushing, the Spirit is nigh,
   Where lips are meeting, the Spirit is there!

His breath is the soul of flowers like these,
   And his floating eyes—oh! *they* resemble—
Blue water-lilies, when the breeze—
   Is making the stream around them tremble!—

Hail to thee, hail to thee, kindling power,
   Spirit of Love, Spirit of Bliss!—
Thy holiest time is the moonlight hour,—
   And there never was moonlight so sweet as this.

     By the fair and brave,
       Who blushing unite
     Like the sun and wave
       When they meet at night!

     By the tear that shows
       When passion is nigh,
     As the rain-drop flows
       From the heat of the sky!

     By the first love-beat
       Of the youthful heart,
     By the bliss to meet,
       And the pain to part!

     By all that thou hast
       To mortals given,
     Which—oh! could it last,
       This earth were heaven!

We call thee hither, entrancing power!
   Spirit of Love! Spirit of Bliss!
The holiest time is the moonlight hour,
   And there never was moonlight so sweet as this."

The *Fire Worshippers* also, the second tale introduced in this poem, contains several striking and animated descriptions, but does not nearly vie with the former. It is written in the irregular versification first introduced by Scott and Byron. *Paradise and the Peri*, is much superior, and is worked out with great variety and picturesqueness of detail. Many of the scenes are very beautiful, especially those in which the exiled fairy seeks for the gift which is to secure her readmission to Heaven. The poem open in following manner,

    " One morn a Peri at the gate
      Of Eden stood disconsolate;

And as she listened to the Springs
  Of Life within, like music flowing
And caught the light upon her wings
  Through the half-open portal glowing,
She wept to think her recreant race
Should e'er have lost that glorious place!

*   *   *   *   *

The glorious Angel, who was keeping
The gates of Light beheld her weeping;
And as she nearer drew and listen'd
To her sad song, a tear-drop glisten'd
Within his eyelids, like the spray
  From Eden's fountain, when it lies
On the blue flower, which—Brahmins say—
  Blooms nowhere but in Paradise!

'Nymph of a fair but erring line!'
Gently he said—'One hope is thine.
'Tis written in the book of Fate,
  The Peri yet may be forgiven
Who brings to this Eternal gate
  The Gift that is most dear to Heaven!
Go, seek it, and redeem thy sin :—
'Tis sweet to let the pardon'd in!'"

The *Peri* first offers successively as her passport into Heaven, the last drop of blood shed by a patriot, and the dying sigh of a self-devoted lover, but these are pronounced insufficient. And the following passage, in which she offers at last the tear of a penitent sinner, which is received by the guardian of the heavenly portal, as "the gift that is most dear to Heaven;" is earnestly and fancifully represented.

"But hark! the vesper call to prayer,
  As slow the orb of daylight sets,
Is rising sweetly on the air,
  From Syria's thousand minarets!
The boy has started from the bed
Of flowers, where he had laid his head,
And down upon the fragrant sod
  Kneels, with his forehead to the south,
Lisping the eternal name of God
  From Purity's own cherub mouth,
And looking while his hands and eyes
Are lifted to the glowing skies,
Like a stray babe of Paradise,
Just lighted on that flowery plain,
And seeking for its home again!

Of guiltless joy that guilt can know.

'There's a drop,' said the Peri, 'that down from the moon
Falls through the withering airs of June
Upon Egypt's land, of so healing a power,
So balmy a virtue, that even in the hour
That drop descends, contagion dies.
And health reanimates earth and skies :—
Oh, is it not thus, thou man of sin,
  The precious tears of repentance fall?
Though foul thy fiery plagues within,
  One heavenly drop hath dispell'd them all !'

And now—behold him kneeling there
By the child's side, in humble prayer,
While the same sunbeam shines upon
The guilty and the guiltless one,
And hymns of joy proclaim through Heaven
The triumph of a Soul Forgiven!

'Twas when the golden orb had set,
While on their knees they linger'd yet,
There fell a light, more lovely far
Than ever came from sun or star,
Upon the tear that, warm and meek,
Dew'd that repentant sinner's cheek.
To mortal eye this light might seem
A northern flash or meteor beam—
But well th' enraptured Peri knew
'Twas a bright smile the Angel threw
From Heaven's gate, to hail that tear

Her harbinger of glory near!

'Joy, joy for ever! my task is done—
The gates are pass'd, and heaven is won!
Oh! am I not happy? I am, I am—
  To thee, sweet Eden! how dark and sad
Are the diamond turrets of Shadukiam,
  And the fragrant bowers of Amberabad

'Farewell, ye odours of Earth, that die,
Passing away like a lover's sigh;—
My feast is now of the Tooba tree,
Whose scent is the breath of Eternity!

'Farewell, ye vanishing flowers, that shone
  In my fairy wreath, so bright and brief;—
Oh, what are the brightest that e'er have blown,
To the love-tree spring by Alla's throne,
  Whose flowers have a soul in every leaf?
Joy, joy for ever!—my task is done—
The Gates are pass'd, and Heaven is won!'"

The last of these tales, the *Light of the Harem,* is a little narrative
sweetly related, and containing many beautiful descriptions. That
of the fair flower-sorceress, Namouna, is the most richly drawn.

"Hence it is, too, that Nourmahal,
  Amid the luxuries of this hour,
Far from the joyous festival,
  Sits in her own sequester'd bower,
With no one near, to soothe or aid,
But that inspired and wondrous maid
Namouna, the Enchantress;—one
O'er whom his race the golden sun
For unremember'd years has run,
Yet never saw her blooming brow
Younger or fairer than 'tis now.
Nay, rather as the west-wind's sigh
Freshens the flower it passes by,—
Time's wing but seem'd, in stealing o'er
To leave her lovelier than before.
Yet on her smiles a sadness hung,
And when, as oft, she spoke or sung
Of other worlds, there came a light
From her dark eyes so strangely bright,
That all believed nor man nor earth
Were conscious of Namouna's birth!

    *   *   *   *
With what delight th' enchantress views
So many buds, bathed with the dews
And beams of that blessed hour!—her glance
  Spoke something past all mortal pleasures,

As, in a kind of holy trance,
  She hung above those fragrant treasures,
Bending to drink their balmy airs,
As if she mix'd her soul with theirs.
And 'twas, indeed, the perfume shed
From flowers and scented flame that fed
Her charm'd life—for none had e'er
Beheld her taste of mortal fare,
Nor ever in aught earthly dip,
But the morn's dew, her roseate lip."

The following beautiful Invocation also occurs in this passage:—

"I know where the winged visions dwell
  That around the night-bed play ;
I know each herb and floweret's bell,
  Where they hide their wings by day.
    Then hasten we, maid,
    To twine our braid—
To morrow the dreams and flowers will fade.

The image of love, that nightly flies
  To visit the bashful maid,
Steals from the jasmine flower, that sighs
  Its soul, like her, in the shade.
The dream of a future, happier hour,
  That alights on misery's brow ;
Springs out of the silvery almond-flower,
  That blooms on a leafless bough.
    Then hasten we, maid,
    To twine our braid,
To morrow the dreams and flowers will fade.

The visions, that oft to worldly eyes
  The glitter of mines unfold
Inhabit the mountain-herb, that dyes
  The tooth of the fawn like gold.
The phantom shapes—oh touch not them—
  That appal the murderer's sight,
Lurk in the fleshly mandrake's stem,
  That shrieks when torn at night !
    Then hasten we, maid,
    To twine our braid,
To-morrow the dreams and the flowers will fade.

The dream of the injured, patient mind,
  That smiles at the wrongs of men,
Is found in the bruised and wounded rind
  Of the cinnamon, sweetest then !
    Then hasten we, maid,
    To twine our braid,
To-morrow the dreams and flowers will fade."

The Odes of *Anacreon* are faithfully translated ; the following

will show the animation and spirit which the poet has thrown into
them:—

> "The women tell me every day
> That all my bloom has passed away.
> 'Behold.' the pretty creatures cry
> 'Behold this mirror with a sigh !
> The locks upon thy brow are few,
> And, like the rest, they're withering too !'
> Whether decline has thinn'd my hair,
> I'm sure I neither know nor care !
> But this I know, and this I feel,
> As onward to my tomb I steal,
> That still as death approaches nearer,
> The joys of life are sweeter, dearer ;
> And had I but an hour to live,
> That little hour to bliss I'd give !"

In the *Odes and Epistles*, there may be seen that same ready
invention which forms a prominent part of the genius of this poet ;
but there is also the same voluptuousness of sentiment, the result
of a too lively fancy, and which is carried sometimes beyond the
bounds of good taste, and even delicacy.   The following, *Written
on passing Deadman's Island,* is among the best of the *Odes.*

> "See you. beneath yon cloud so dark,
> Fast gliding along. a gloomy bark ?
> Her sails are full, though the wind is still,
> And there blows not a breath her sails to fill !
>
> Oh ! what doth that vessel of darkness bear ?
> The silent calm of the grave is there,
> Save now and again a death-knell rung,
> And the flap of the sails with night-fog hung !
>
> There lieth a wreck on the dismal shore
> Of cold and pitiless Labrador ;
> Where, under the moon, upon the mounts of frost
> Full many a mariner's bones are lost !
>
> Yon shadowy bark hath been to that wreck,
> And the dim blue fire that lights her deck
> Doth play on as pale and livid a crew
> As ever yet drank the churchyard dew !
>
> To Dead-man's Isle, in the eye of the blast,
> To Dead-man's Isle, she speeds her fast ;
> By skeleton shapes her sails are furl'd,
> And the hand that steers is not of this world !
>
> Oh ! hurry thee on—oh ! hurry thee on
> Thou terrible bark ! ere the night be gone,
> Nor let morning look on so foul a sight
> As would blanch for ever her rosy light !"

The *Irish Melodies,* which form the principal of Moore's poems, are also the poems upon which his reputation chiefly rests. The Songs which this work comprises, are characterized by refined gaiety and brilliant fancy, but partake nothing of the profound and stirring passages, and the tenderness, for which Burn's will always stand unrivalled. The versification of these songs, however, as never been surpassed for melody, and the language, which is always clear and appropriate, sometimes rises to the height of majesty and tenderness.

CHAPTER XXXV.

THOMSON.

THOMSON.—Thomson was a follower of the original poetry which had been substituted by the continental style, and of which Addison was the consummation, and his *Seasons* affords one of the best specimens of this style. It is written in blank verse, and describes the various natural appearances of the year, in an exceedingly rich, though heavy style of language. In this particular style of writing Thomson is entitled to a praise of the highest kind : namely, his original mode of thinking and of expressing his thoughts. He thinks in a peculiar train, and he thinks always as a man of genius : he looks round on nature and life, with the eye which nature bestows only on a poet ; the eye that distinguishes in everything presented to his view, whatever there is on which imagination can be detained, and with a mind that at once comprehends the vast, and attends equally to the minute. The reader of the *Seasons* wonders that he never saw before what Thomson shows him, and that he never yet has felt what Thomson impresses. It is one of the works in which blank verse seems properly used. Thomson's wide expansion of general views, and his enumerations of circumstantial varieties, would have been obstructed and embarassed by the frequent intersection of the sense, which are the necessary effects of rhyme. His charming descriptions of· Sunset, Evening, and Night would lose their beauty; were the same language and ideas be expressed in the form of rhyme. His descriptions of extended scenes and general effects, bring before us the whole magnificence of nature, whether pleasing or dreadful. The gaity of Spring, the splendour of Summer, the tranquility of Autumn, and the horror of Winter,. take in their turns possession of the mind. We are lead through the appearances of things, as they are successively varied by the vicissitudes of the year, and the poet imparts to us so much of his own enthusiasm, that our thoughts expand with his imagery, and kindle with his sentiments. Nothing can be more magnificently drawn, or conceived than the contrast shown in the various seasons, as they follow in their natural order. Each description forms a lasting picture, marvellously and truthfully delineated, such as no imagination could ever conceive. His diction is in the highest degree florid and luxuriant, such as may be said to be his images and thoughts, "both their lustre and their shade ;" such as invest them with splendour, through which perhaps they are not always easily discerned. It is too exuberant, and sometimes may be charged with filling the ear more than the mind.

The *Seasons* is the most capital descriptive poem in our own, and perhaps in any language, ancient and modern. Possessed of a feeling heart, and a warm imagination, Thomson, enamoured of nature, painted her with the enthusiasm of a lover, who had been admitted to the enjoyment of her beauties. His work is replete with picturesque imagery, and in such a splendid assemblage of charms, it is difficult to select one more captivating than another. We see nothing throughout but the most brilliant reflections of delightful nature, and a perfect delineation of the most beautiful objects and scenery. The following will not only afford examples of his verse and expression, but also as illustrations of the reality and truth of that which he writes. The following from *Spring* is a delightful passage, and exhibits all the truth of painting for which Thomson is admired.

"——————————————Hark, how loud the woods
Invite you forth in all your gayest trim.
Lend me your song, ye nightingales! oh pour
The mazy running soul of melody,
Into my varied verse! while I deduce,
From the first note the hollow cuckoo sings,
The symphony of Spring, and touch the theme
Unknown to fame, the passion of the groves.
    When first the soul of love is sent abroad,
Warm through the vital air, and on the heart
Harmonious seizes, the gay troops begin
In gallant thought to plume the painted wing,
And try again the long-forgotten strain ;
At first faint-warbled : but no sooner grows
The soft infusion prevalent, and wide,
Than, all alive, at once their joy o'erflows
In music unconfin'd. Up springs the lark,
Shrill-voic'd, and loud, the messenger of morn :
Ere yet the shadows fly, he mounted sings
Amid the dawning clouds, and from their haunts
Calls up the tuneful nations. Ev'ry copse
Deep-tangled, tree irregular, and bush
Bending with dewy moisture o'er the heads.
Of the coy choristers that lodge within,
Are prodigal of harmony. The thrush
And wood-lark, o'er the kind-contending throng
Superior heard, run through the sweetest length
Of notes ; when list'ning Philomela designs
To let them joy, and purposes, in thought
Elate, to make her night excel their day.
The blackbird whistles from the thorny brake ;
The mellow bull-finch answers from the grove :
Nor are the linnets, o'er the flow'ring furze
Pour'd out profusely, silent. Join'd to these,
Innum'rous songsters, in the fresh'ning shade
Of new-sprung leaves, their modulations mix
Mellifluous. The jay, the rook, the daw,
And each harsh pipe discordant heard alone,
Aid the full concert ; while the stock-dove breathes
A melancholy murmur through the whole.
    'Tis love creates their melody, and all
This waste of music is the voice of love ;
That, e'en to birds and beasts the tender arts.
Of pleasing teaches. Hence the glossy kind
Try ev'ry winning way inventive love

not to be paralleled ; conveying to the imagination many tranquil
and peaceful thoughts. It may be read as one of the finest pas-
sages of the whole poem.

> "Now swarms the village o'er the jovial mead:
> The rustic youth, brown with meridian toil,
> Healthful and strong ; full as the summer-rose,
> Blown by prevailing suns, the ruddy maid,
> Half-naked, swelling on the sight, and all
> Her kindled graces burning o'er her cheek.
> E'en stooping age is here ; and infant hands
> Trail the long rake, or with the fragrant load
> O'ercharged, amid the kind oppression roll.
> Wide flies the tedded grain : all in a row
> Advancing broad, or wheeling round the field,
> They spread their breathing harvest to the sun,
> That throws refreshful round a rural smell :
> Or, as they rake the green appearing ground,
> And drive the dusky wave along the mead,
> The russet hay cock rises thick behind,
> In order gay.   While heard from dale to dale,
> Waking from the breeze, resounds the blended voice
> Of happy labour, love, and social glee."

In the third part, the poet describes the tranquility of Autumn,
with its decline, brightened by the joys of harvest ; adorned with
numerous digressions, reflecting the morals to be gathered from it.
From this part, the following passage cannot be sufficiently ad-
mired, and the beautiful description of the charms of Lávinia with
which the passage begins is beautifully drawn.

> "The lovely Lavinia once had friends;
> And fortune smil'd, deceitful, on her birth.
> For, in her helpless years deprived of all,
> Of every stay, save innocence and Heaven,
> She, with her widow'd mother, feeble, old,
> And poor, liv'd in a cottage, far retir'd,
> Among the windings of a woody vale :
> By solitude and deep surrounding shades,
> But more by bashful modesty, conceal'd.
> Together thus they shunn'd the cruel scorn
> Which virtue, sunk to poverty, would meet
> From giddy passion and low-minded pride :
> Almost on nature's common bounty fed ;
> Like the gay birds that sung them to repose,
> Content, and careless of to-morrow's fare.
> Her form was fresher than the morning-rose,
> When the dew wets its leaves ; unstain'd and pure,
> As is the lily, or the mountain snow.

The modest virtues mingled in her eyes,
Still on the ground dejected, darting all
. Their humid beams into the blooming flowers :
Or when the mournful tale her mother told,
Of what her faithless fortune promis'd once,
Thrill'd in her thought, they, like the dewy star
Of evening, shone in tears.   A native grace
Sat fair-proportion'd on her polished limbs,
Veiled in a simple robe, their best attire,
Beyond the pomp of dress ; for loveliness
Needs not the foreign aid of ornament,
But is when unadorn'd, adorn'd the most.
Thoughtless of beauty, she was beauty's self,
Recluse amid the close-embowering woods.
As in the hollow breast of Appenine,
Beneath the shelter of encircling hills,
A myrtle rises, far from human eye,
And breathes its balmy fragrance o'er the wild ;
So flourish'd, blooming, and unseen by all,
The sweet Lavinia ; till, at length, compell'd
By strong necessity's supreme command,
With smiling patience in her looks, she went
To glean Palemon's fields.   The pride of swains
Palemon was, the generous, and the rich ;
Who led the rural life in all its joy
And elegance, such as Arcadian song
Transmits from ancient uncorrupted times,
When tyrant customs had not shackled man,
But free to follow nature was the mode.
He then, his fancy with autumnal scenes
Amusing, chanc'd beside his reaper-train
To walk, when poor Lavinia drew his eye ;
Unconscious of her power, and turning quick
With unaffected blushes from his gaze :
He saw her charming, but he saw not half
The charms her downcast modesty conceal'd,
That very moment love and chaste desire
Sprung in his bosom, to himself unknown :
For still the world prevail'd, and its dread laugh,
Which scarce the firm philosopher can scorn,
Should his heart own a gleaner in the field :
And thus in secret to his soul he sighed :
      'What pity ! that so delicate a form,
By beauty kindled, where enlivening sense ·
And more than vulgar goodness seems to dwell,
Should be devoted to the rude embrace
Of some indecent clown ! she looks, methinks,
Of old Acasto's line ; and to my mind
Recalls that patron of my happy life,
From whom my liberal fortune took its rise ;
Now to the dust gone down ; his houses, lands,

And once fair spreading family, dissolv'd.
'Tis said that in some lone obscure retreat,
Urg'd by remembrance sad, and decent pride,
Far from those scenes which knew their better days,
His aged widow and his daughter live,
Whom yet my fruitless search could never find.
Romantic wish ! would this the daughter were !
　　When, strict enquiring, from herself he found
She was the same, the daughter of his friend,
Of bountiful Acasto ; who can speak
The mingled passions that surpris'd his heart,
And through his nerves in shivering transport ran?
Then blaz'd his smother'd flame, avow'd and bold ;
And as he view'd her, ardent o'er and o'er,
Love, gratitude, and pity wept at once.
Confus'd, and frighten'd at his sudden tears,
Her rising beauties flush'd a higher bloom
As thus Palemon, passionate and just,
Pour'd out the pious rapture of his soul :
　　'And art thou then Acasto's dear remains ?
She, whom my restless gratitude has sought
So long in vain ? O heaven ! the very same,
The softened image of my noble friend ;
Alive his every look, his every feature,
More elegantly touch'd.　Sweeter than Spring!
Thou sole surviving blossom from the root
That nourish'd up my fortune ! say, ah, where,
In what sequestered desert, hast thou drawn
The kindest aspect of delighted heaven ;
Into such beauty spread, and blown so fair ;
Though poverty's cold wind, and crushing rain,
Beat keen and heavy on thy tender years?
O let me now, into a richer soil,
Transplant the safe ! where vernal suns and showers,
Diffuse their warmest, largest influence :　　　　·
And of my garden be the pride and joy !'"

　And last of all, the stern horror of Winter, contrasting entirely in
its language and description to its sister seasons, but thrown up in
equal, if not in still more vivid language.　In the foreground of the
desolate drawing the poet has thrown forth the figure of a man
perishing among the driving snows, which might be quoted as the
most interesting passage of this part of the poem.

"As thus the snows arise ; and foul, and fierce,
All Winter drives along the darkened air ;
In his own loose-revolving fields the swain
Disastered stands, sees other hills ascend,
Of unknown joyless brow, and other scenes,
Of horrid prospect, shag the trackless plain :

Nor finds the river, nor the forest, hid
Beneath the formless wild ; but wanders on
From hill to dale, still more and more astray ;
Impatient flouncing through the drifted heaps,
Stung with the thoughts of home ; the thoughts of home
Rush on his nerves, and call their vigour forth
In many a vain attempt. How sinks his soul !
What black despair, what horror fills his heart !
When for the dusky spot, which fancy feigned
His tufted cottage rising through the snow,
He meets the roughness of the middle waste,
Far from the track, and blest abode of man ;
While round him night resistless closes fast,
And every tempest, howling o'er his head,
Renders the savage wilderness more wild.
Then throng the busy shapes into his mind
Of covered pits, unfathomably deep,
A dire descent ! beyond the power of frost ;
Of faithless bogs ; of precipices huge,
Smoothed up with snow ; and, what is land unknown,
What water of the still unfrozen spring,
In the loose march or solitary lake,
Where the fresh fountain from the bottom boils.
These check his fearful steps ; and down he sinks
Beneath the shelter af the shapeless drift,
Thinking o'er all the bitterness of death :
Mixed with the tender anguish Nature shoots
Through the wrung bosom of the dying man,
His wife, his children, and his friends unseen.
In vain for him th' officious wife prepares
The fire fair-blazing. and the vestment warm,
In vain his little children, peeping out
Into the mingling storm, demand their sire, •
With tears of heartless innocence. Alas !
Nor wife, nor children, more shall he behold ;
Nor friends, nor sacred home. On every nerve
The deadly Winter seizes ; shuts up sense ;
And, o'er his inmost vitals creeping cold,
Lays him along the snows, a stiffened corse !
Stretched out and bleaching in the northern blast."

Of the other of Thomson's poems there is little occasion to speak.
Though beautiful examples of poetry, they do not approach in merit
to the *Seasons.* That which stands next in importance to this,
however, is *The Castle of Indolence*, a good and accurate poem,
but which we are told was many years under his hand. The First
canto opens a scene of lazy luxury, which at once fills the imagination.

"In lowly dale, fast by a river's side,
With woody hill o'er hill encompass'd round,
A most enchanting wizard did abide,

Than whom a fiend more fell is no where found.
It was, I ween, a lovely spot of ground ;
And there a Season atween June and May,
Half prankt with spring, with summer half inbrown'd,
A listless climate made, where, sooth to say,
No living wight could work, nor cared e'en for play.

Was nought around but images of rest,
Sleep-soothing groves, and quiet lawns between,
And flowery beds, that slumbrous influence kest
From popies breath'd, and beds of pleasant green,
Where never yet was creeping creature seen.
Meantime unnumber'd glittering streamlets play'd,
And hurl'd everywhere their waters sheen,
That, as they bicker'd thro' the sunny glade,
Tho' restless still themselves, a lulling murmur made.

Join'd to the prattle of the purling rills,
Were heard the lowing herds along the vale,
And flocks loud-bleating from the distant hills,
And vacant shepherds piping in the dale ;
And now and then sweet Philomel would wail,
Or stock-doves plain amid the forest deep,
That drowsy rustled to the fighting gale ;
And still a coil the grasshopper did keep ;
Yet all these sounds yblent inclined all to sleep.

Full in the passage of the vale, above,
A sable, silent, solemn, forest stood,
Where, nought but shadowy forms was seen to move,
As Idless fancy'd in her dreaming mood :
And up the hills, on either side, a wood
Of blackening pines, ay waving to and fro,
Sent forth a sleepy horror thro' the blood ;
And where this valley winded out, below,
The murmuring main was heard, and scarcely heard, to flow.

A pleasing land of drowsy-head it was,
Of Dreams that wave before the half-shut eye,
And of gay Castles in the cloud that pass,
For ever flushing round a summer sky ;
There eke the soft Delights, that witchingly
Instil a wanton sweetness thro' the breast,
And the calm Pleasures, always hover'd nigh ;
But whate'er smack'd of noyance or unrest
Was far, far oft expell'd from this delicious nest."

The poem of *Liberty*, in which Thomson compares our well
regulated government with that of other nations, is interesting
from the correctness of its particulars. In this work the poet en-
deavours to show by what means the glorious freedom we enjoy
may be preserved, and how it may be abused or lost. The poem

CHAPTER XXXVI.

BURNS.

BURNS.—The greatest Scotch poet, beyond all comparison, is Robert Burns. His poems exhibit the most exquisite tendernesss, the broadest and yet most refined humour; the most powerful though delicate perception of natural beauty, with the highest finish and the easiest negligence of style. He paints with the sharp and infallible touch of Homer or of Shakespeare, and amid the wildest ebullitions of gaiety he has thoughts that sound the very abysses of the heart. His writings are chiefly lyric, consisting of songs of inimitable beauty, but he has also produced works either of a narrative or satirical character, and in some of which the lyric is interposed with the descriptive. The humour of Burns is of the richest kind; and he possesses the rarer quality of combining with this humour in many cases, the most profound pathos, while at other times we find this humour united with the highest powers of the imagination. An excellent instance of this is to be found in the *Address to the Deil,* one of the happiest of his productions, in which this peculiarity may be seen in almost every stanza of the poem. He commences by reproaching this terrible being with all his

"doings" and misdeeds, and in language of infinite s‹
him what pleasure he can take in tormenting poo
sinners.

> "O Thou! whatever title suit thee,
> Auld *Hornie*, Satan, Nick, or Clootie,
> Wha in yon cavern grim and sootie,
>   Closed under hatches
> Spairges about the brunstane cootie,
>   To scaud poor wretches.
>
> Hear me, auld *Hangie*, for a wee,
> An' let poor damned bodies be;
> I'm sure sma' pleasure it can gie,
>   E'en to a *deil*,
> To skelp and scaud poor dogs like me,
>   An' hear us squeel!
>
> Great is thy pow'r, an' great thy fame;
> Far kend and noted is thy name;
> An' tho' yon lowin heugh's thy hame,
>   Thou travels far;
> An' faith! thou's neither lag nor lame,
>   Nor blate nor scaur.
>
> Whyles, ranging like a roarin lion,
> For prey, a' holes an corners tryin;
> Whyles on the strong-wing'd tempest flyin,
>   Tirling the kirks;
> Whyles, in the human bosom pryin,
>   Unseen thou lurks.
>
> I've heard my reverend *Grannie* say,
> In lanely glens ye like to stray;
> Or where auld-ruin'd castles, gray,
>   Nod to the moon,
> Ye fright the nightly wand'rer's way,
>   Wi' eldritch croon.
>
> When twilight did my *Grannie* summon,
> To say her prayers, douce, honest woman
> Aft yont the dyke she's heard you bummin,
>   Wi' eerie drone;
> Or, rustlin, thro' the boortries comin,
>   Wi' heavy groan.

better nor happier than themselves, which he executes in the form of a dialogue between two dogs. It is an elaborate comparison between the relative degree of virtue and happiness granted to the rich and poor. The first dog, *Cæsar*, is a dog of condition, and is thus described,

> " His hair, his size, his mouth, his lugs,
> Show'd he was nane o' Scotland's dogs :
> But whalpit some place far abroad,
> Where sailors gang to fish for cod.
> His locked, letter'd, braw brass collar,
> Shew'd him the gentleman and scholar ;
> But though he was o' high degree,
> The fient a pride nae pride had he ;
> But wad hae spent an hour caressin,
> Ev'en wi' a tinker's gypsey's messin."

The other *Luath*, although a "ploughman's collie," is a cur of a good heart, and a sound understanding.

> "He was a gash an' faithfu' tyke,
> As ever lap a sheugh or dyke.
> His honest, sonsie, baws'nt face,
> Aye gat him friends in ilka place.
> His breast was white, his towzie back
> Weel clad wi' coat o' glossy black ;
> His gawcie tail, wi' upward curl,
> Hung o'er his hurdies wi' a swirl."

Their gambols before they sit down to moralize are described with an equal degree of happiness and superiority of poetical excel-

lence.   And throughout the dialogue, it [will be seen how the
character, as well as the different condition of the two speakers, is
kept in view.

> " Nae doubt but they were fain o' ither,
>   An' unco pack an' thick thegither ;
>   Wi' social nose whyles snuff'd and snowkit ;
>   Whyles mice an' moudieworts they howkit ;
>   Whyles scour'd awa in lang excursion,
>   An' worry'd ither in diversion ;
>   Until wi' daffin weary grown,
>   Upon a knowe they sat them down,
>   And there began a lang digression
>   About the *lords o' the creation.*"

The poems concludes with the following exquisite description.

> " By this, the sun was out o' sight,
>   An' darker gloaming brought the night :
>   The bum-clock humm'd wi' lazy drone ;
>   The kye stood rowtin i' the loan ;
>   When up they gat, and shook their lugs,
>   Rejoic'd they werena *men* but *dogs* ;
>   An' each took aff his several way,
>   Resolv'd to meet some ither day."

In the poems entitled *Death and Dr. Hornbook,* and the *Brigs
of Ayr,* there is to be seen the same remarkable conbination of
humourous and picturesque description, with thoughtful moralizing
upon life and society, and the deepest insight into the human heart.
The latter of these poems is a dialogue between the Old and New
Bridges of Ayr; in which Burns himself is the auditor.   The time
and occasion on which it occured is related with great circumstan-
tiality.   The poet " pressed by care," or " inspired by whim," has
left his bed and wandered out alone in the darkness and solitude
of a winter night, to the mouth of the river, where the stillness is
interrupted only by the rushing sound of the influx of the tide.

> " 'Twas in that season, when a simple bard,
>   Unknown and poor, simplicity's reward,
>   Ae night, within the ancient brugh of *Ayr,*
>   By whim inspir'd, or haply prest wi' care ;
>   He left his bed, and took his wayward route,
>   And down by *Simpson's* wheel'd the left about :
>   (Whether impell'd by all-directing Fate,
>   To witness what I after shall narrate ;
>   Or whether, rapt in meditation high,
>   He wander'd out he knew, not where nor why :)
>   The drowsy *Dungeon clock* had number'd two,

Irregular and imperfect as this poem is, it displays equally with the rest, the poet's various and powerful talents, and reveals to the same extent his unequalled genius. It also affords a striking instance of his being carried beyond his original purpose by the power of his imagination. The scenery is present to his fancy during the whole dialogue, and at length it suggests to him a fairy dance of aërial being under the beams of the moon, with which the poem closes. Both this, and the description of midnight, are magnificent specimens of real poetry.

The longest and most remarkable of Burns' poems is *Tam o' Shanter*. In it is there is combined with the most brilliant descriptive power, and most touching pathos, a wild fancy, and a humour of the quaintest, sliest style. Burns possesses that rare power of giving a human interest to material objects, a quality to be seen only in poets of the highest order. He also brings into contact the familiar with the ideal, and combines the broadest humour with the most profound pathos. The passage where the ruined kirk of Alloway is described as being lighted up, and *Tam* stealing close to the window, and looking in, witnesses the sabbath of the witches, is described by the poet with an inimitable mixture of grotesque humour and fantastic horror.

"By this time he was cross the ford,
Whare in the snaw the chapman smoor'd
And past the birks and meikle stane,
Whare drunken *Charlie* brak's neck-bane ;
And thro' the whins, and by the cairn,
Whare hunters fand the murder'd bairn ;
And near the thorn, aboon the well,
Whare *Mungo's* mither hang'd hersel.—
Before him *Doon* pours all her floods;
The doubling storm roars thro' the woods ;
The lightnings flash from pole to pole ;
Near and more near the thunders roll ;
When, glimmering thro' the groaning trees,
Kirk-Alloway seem'd in a bleeze ;
Thro' ilka bore the beams were glancing,
And loud resounded mirth and dancing.—
    Inspiring bold *John Barleycorn !*
What dangers thou canst make us scorn !
Wi' tippenny, we fear nae evil ;
Wi' usquebae, we'll face the devil !—
The swats sae ream'd in *Tammie's* noddle,
Fair play, he car'dna deils a boddle.
But *Maggie* stood right sair astonish'd,
Till, by the heel and hand admonish'd,
She ventur'd forward on the light ;
And, vow ! *Tam* saw an unco sight !
Warlocks and witches in a dance ;
Nae cotillion brent new frae *France*,
But hornpipes, jigs, strathspeys, and reels,
Put life and mettle in their heels.
A winnock bunker in the east,
There sat auld Nick, in shape o' beast ;
A towzie tyke, black, grim, and large,
To gie them music was his charge :
He screw'd the pipes, and gart them skirl,
Till roof and rafters a' did dirl.—
Coffins stood round like open presses,
That shaw'd the dead in their last dresses ;
And by some devilish cantrip slight,
Each in its cauld hand held a light,—
By which heroic *Tam* was able
To note upon the haly table,
A murderer's banes in gibbet airns ;
Twa span-lang, wee, unchristen'd bairns:
A thief, new-cutted frae a rape,
Wi' his last gasp his gab did gape ;
Five tomahawks, wi' bluid red rusted ;
Five scimitars, wi' murder crusted :
A garter, which a babe had strangled ;
A knife, a father's throat had mangled,
Whom his ain son o' life bereft,

" The wind blew hollow frae the hills,
    By fits the sun's departing beam
Look'd on the fading yellow woods
    That wav'd o'er Lugar's winding stream :
. Beneath a craigy steep, a bard,
    Laden with years and meikle pain,
In loud lament bewail'd his lord,
    Whom death had all untimely ta'en.

He lean'd him to an ancient aik,
    Whose trunk was mould'ring down with years ;
His locks were bleached white wi' time !
    His hoary cheek was wet wi' tears !
And as he touch'd his trembling harp,
    And as he turn'd his doleful sang,
The winds, lamenting thro' their caves,
    To echo bore the notes alang.

. 'Ye scatter'd birds that faintly sing,
    The reliques of the vernal quire !
Ye woods that shed on a' the winds,
    The honours of the aged year !
A few short months, and glad and gay
    Again ye'll charm the ear and ee ;
But nocht in a' revolving time
    Can gladness bring again to me.

'I am a bending aged tree,
    That long has stood the wind and rain ;
But now has come a cruel blast,
    And my last hold of earth is gane :
Nae leaf o' mine shall greet the spring,
    Nae simmer sun exalt my bloom ;
But I maun lie before the storm,
    And ithers plant them in my room.

O

And last (the sum of a' my gries!)
   My noble master lies in clay;
The flow'r amang our barons bold,
   His country's pride, his country's stay;
In weary being now I pine,
   For a' the life of life is dead,
And hope has left my aged ken,
   On forward wing for ever fled.

'Awake thy last sad voice, my harp!
   The voice of woe and wild despair!
Awake, resound thy latest lay,
   Then sleep in silence evermair!
And thou, my last, best, only friend,
   That fillest an untimely tomb,
Accept this tribute from the bard
   Thou brought from fortune's mirkest gloom.

'Oh! why has worth so short a date,
   While villains ripen grey with time?
Must thou, the noble, gen'rous, great,
   Fall in bold manhood's hardy prime!
Why did I live to see that day?
   A day to me so full of woe!
Oh! had I met the mortal shaft
   Which laid my benefactor low!

The bridegroom may forget the bride
   Was made his wedded wife yestreen;
The monarch may forget the crown
   That on his head an hour has been;
The mother may forget the child
   That smiles sae sweetly on her knee;
But I'll remember thee Glencairn,
   And a' that thou hast done for me!'"

The *Cotter's Saturday Night* also contains many very beautiful
passages, nor has there ever been a nobler tribute paid to the virtues
of the peasant class than has been given by Burns in this poem.
The cottager returning from his labours; the young children
running to meet him and clambering round his knee; the eldest,
returning from their weekly labours with the neighbouring farmers,
dutifully depositing their little gains with their parents, and receiv-
ing their father's blessing and instruction; are described with a
reality never yet surpassed.

   " November chill blaws loud wi' angry sugh;
     The short'ning winter-day is near a close;
   The miry beasts retreating frae the pleugh;
     The black'ning trains o' craws to their repose;

The toil-worn *Cotter* frae his labour goes,
 This night his weekly moil is at an end,
Collects his spades, his mattocks, and his hoes,
Hoping the *morn* in ease and rest to spend,
And weary, o'er the moor, his course does hameward bend

At length his lonely cot appears in view,
 Beneath the shelter of an aged tree ;
Th' expectant *wee-things*, toddlin, stacher thro'
 To meet their Dad, wi' flichterin noise an' glee.
His wee bit ingle, blinkin bonnily,
 His clean heart-stane, his thriftie *wifie's* smile,
The lisping infant prattling on his knee,
 Does a' his weary carking cares beguile,
An' maks him quite forget his labour an' his toil.

Belyve, the elder bairns come drapping in,
 At service out, amang the farmers roun',
Some ca' the pleugh, some herd, some tentie rin
 A cannie errand to a neebor town ;
Their eldest hope, their *Jenny*, woman grown,
 In youthfu' bloom, love sparkling in her ee.
Comes hame, perhaps, to shew a braw new gown,
 Or deposit her sair-won penny-fee,
To help her parents dear, if they in hardship be.

Wi' joy unfeign'd brothers and sisters meet,
 An' each for other's welfare kindly spires :
The social hours, swift-wing'd, unnotic'd fleet,
 Each tells the uncos that he sees or hears ;
The parents, partial, eye their hopeful years ;
 Anticipation forward points the view,
The *mother*, wi' her needle an' her sheers,
 Gars auld claes look amaist as weel's the new ;
The *father* mixes a' wi' admonition due.

Their master's an' their mistress's command,
 The younkers a' are warned to obey ;
'An' mind their labours wi' an eydent hand,
 An' ne'er, tho' out o' sight, to jauk or play :
An' oh ! be sure to fear the Lord alway !
 An' mind your *duty*, duly, morn an' night,
Lest in temptation's path ye gang astray,
 Implore his counsel and assisting might:
They never sought in vain that sought the Lord aright!'"

Then the representation of these humble cottagers forming a circle round their hearth, and uniting in the worship of God, is a picture the most deeply affecting of any which the rural muse has ever presented to the view.

  " The cheerfu' supper done, wi' serious face,
   They, round the ingle, form a circle wide ;

The sire turns o'er, wi' patriarchal grace,
  The big *ha'-Bible*, ance his father's pride:
His bonnet rev'rently is laid aside,
  His lyart haffets wearing thin an' bare ;
Those strains that once did sweet in Zion glide,
  He wales a portion with judicious care ;
And '*Let us worship* God !' he says, with solemn air.

They chant their artless notes in simple guise ;
  They tune their hearts, by far the noblest aim :
Perhaps *Dundee's* wild warbling measures rise,
  Or plaintive *Martyrs*, worthy of the name :
Or noble *Elgin* beets the heav'nward flame,
  The sweetest far of *Scotia's* holy lays :
Compar'd with these, Italian thrills are tame ;-
  The tickled ears no heart-felt raptures raise ;
Nae unison hae they with our Creator's praise.

The priest-like father reads the sacred page,
  How *Abram* was the friend of God on high ;
Or *Moses* bade eternal warfare wage
  With *Amalek's* ungracious progeny;
Or how the *royal bard* did groaning lie
  Beneath the stroke of Heaven's avenging ire ;
Or *Job's* pathetic plaint, and wailing cry ;
  Or rapt *Isaiah's* wild, seraphic fire ;
Or other holy seers that tune the sacred lyre.

Then kneeling down, to Heaven's Eternal King,
  The *saint*, the father, and the *husband* prays:
Hope 'springs exulting on triumphant wing,'
  That *thus* they all shall meet in future days :
There ever bask in uncreated rays,
  No more to sigh, or shed the bitter tear,
Together hymning their *Creator's* praise,
  In such society, yet still more dear ;
While circling time moves round in an eternal sphere,"

The *Cotter's Saturday Night*, is without doubt one of the best of
all Burns' works : it is not only tender and moral, but solemn and
devotional, and rises at last into a strain of grandeur, which modern
poetry has never surpassed; and the noble sentiment of patriotism
with which it concludes, admirably corresponds with the rest of
the poem.

" *O Scotia's !* my dear, my native soil !
  For whom my warmest wish to Heaven is sent !
Long may thy hardy sons of rustic toil,
  Be blest with health, and peace, and sweet content !
And, oh ! may Heaven their simple lives prevent
  From luxury's contagion, weak and vile !
Then, howe'er *crowns* and *coronets* be rent,

"Wee, sleekit, cow'rin, tim'rous beastie,
O, what a panic's in thy breastie!
Thou needna start awa sae hasty,
                    Wi' bickering brattle!
I wad be laith to rin an' chase thee,
                    Wi' murdering *pattle!*

I'm truly sorry man's dominion
Has broken Nature's social union,
An' justifies that ill opinion,
                    Which maks thee startle
At me, thy poor earth-born companion,
                    An' *fellow-mortal!*

I doubtna, whyles, but thou may thieve;
What then? poor beastie, thou maun live!
A *daimen-icker* in a *thrave*
                    'S a sma' request
I'll get a blessin wi' the lave,
                    And never miss't!

Thy wee bit *housie,* too, in ruin!
Its silly wa's the win's are strewin!
An' naething, now, to big a new ane,
                    O' foggage green!
An' bleak December's winds cusuin,
                    Baith snell an' keen!

Thou saw the fields laid bare an' waste,
An' weary winter comin fast,

An' cozie here, beneath the blast,
　　Thou thought to dwell,
Till crash ! the cruel *coulter* past,
　　Out thro' thy cell.

That wee bit heap o' leaves an' stibble,
Has cost thee mony a weary nibble !
Now thou's turn'd out, for a' thy trouble,
　　But house or hald,
To thole the winter's sleety dribble,
　　An' cranreuch cauld !

But, Mousie, thou art no thy lane,
In proving *foresight* may be vain :
The best laid schemes o' *mice* an' *men*,
　　Gang aft a-gley,
An' lea'e us nought but grief and pain,
　　For promis'd joy.

Still thou art blest, compar'd wi' *me !*
The *present* only toucheth thee :
But, och ! I backward cast my ee
　　On prospects drear !
Ah' forward, tho' I canna *see,*
　　I *guess* an' *fear.*"

Another fine specimen of Burns' poetry is the *Winter Night*, and is highly characteristic of the poet's mind. It opens with the description of a dreadful storm on a night in winter, during which the poet is represented as lying in bed, listening to its howling.

"List'ning, the doors an' winnocks rattle,
I thought me on the ourie cattle,
Or silly sheep, wha bide this brattle,
　　O' winter war,
And thro' the drift, deep-lairing sprattle,
　　Beneath a scar.

Ilk happing bird, wee, helpless thing,
That, in the merry months o' spring,
Delighted me to hear thee sing,
　　What comes o' thee?
Whare wilt thou cow'r thy chittering wing,
　　An' close thy ee?

Ev'n you on murd'ring errands toil'd,
Lone from your savage homes exil'd,
The blood-stain'd roost, and shee-cote spoil'd,
　　My heart forgets,
While pityless the tempest wild
　　Sore on you beats."

The manner in which the fury of the elements is compared with that of man to his brother man, and the former is found light in the

" Blow, blow, ye winds, with heavier gust !
And freeze, thou bitter-biting frost !
Descend, ye chilly, smothering snows !
Not all your rage, as now united, shows
   More hard unkindness, unrelenting,
   Vengeful malice, unrepenting,
Than heav'n illumin'd man or brother man bestows !
  See stern oppression's iron grip,
    Or mad ambition's gory hand,
  Sending, like blood-hounds from the slip,
    Woe, want, and murder o'er a land !
  Ev'n in the peaceful rural vale,
  Truth, weeping, tells the mournful tale,
How pamper'd luxury, flatt'ry by her side,
The parasite empoisoning her ear,
With all the servile wretches in the rear,
Looks o'er proud property, extended wide ;
  And eyes the simple rustic hind,
    Whose toil upholds the glitt'ring show,
  A creature of another kind,
  Some coarser substance, unrefin'd,
Plac'd for her lordly use thus far, thus vile, below,
  Where, where is love's fond, tender throe,
  With lordly honour's lofty brow,
    The pow'rs you proudly own ?
  Is there, beneath love's noble name,
  Can harbour, dark, the selfish aim,
    To bless himself alone !
    Mark maiden-innocence a prey
    To love-pretending snares,
  This boasted honour turns away,
  Shunning soft pity's rising sway,
Regardless of the tears, and unavailing pray'rs !
  Perhaps this hour, in mis'ry's squalid nest,
  She strains your infant to her joyless breast,
And with a mother's fears shrinks at the rocking blast!
    Oh ye ! who, sunk in beds of down,
Feel not a want but what yourselves create,
  Think, for a moment, on his wretched fate,
    Whom friends and fortune quite disown !
Ill-satisfied keen nature's clam'rous call,
  Stretch'd on his straw he lays himself to sleep,
  While thro' the ragged roof and chinky wall,
  Chill o'er his slumbers piles the drifty heap !
  Think on the dungeon's grim confine,
  Where guilt and poor misfortune pine !
  Guilt, erring man, relenting view !
  But shall thy legal rage pursue
  The wretch, already crushed low

    By cruel fortune's undeserved blow?
    Affliction's sons are brothers in distress,
    A brother to relieve, how exquisite the bliss ! "

The *Songs* of Burns are all distinguished by intensity of feeling, condensed force, picturesqueness of description, and admirable melody and flow. The subjects in all of them, are limited to love, patriotism and pleasure. Some of the later songs may be compared in polished delicacy with the finest in our language, while in the eloquence of sensibility they far surpass them. Many of these songs are dramatic, but for the greater part amatory ; but in all, the beauties of rural nature are everywhere associated with the passions and emotions of the mind. All his natural descriptions are such as are to be found in his own country; and in a mountainous region, especially when it is comparatively rude and naked, the most beautiful scenery will always be found in the valleys, and on the banks of the wooded streams. There is scarcely a single song of Burns, in which particular scenery is not described, or allusion made to natural objects, remarkable for beauty or interest. Occasionally the genius of Burns rises into strains of uniform sublimity. An instance of this kind may be found in the poem entitled, *Liberty.*

    " Thee, Caledonia, thy wild heaths among,
    Thee, famed for martial deed and sacred song,
        To thee I turn with swimming eyes ;
    Where is that soul of freedom fled ?
    Immingled with the mighty dead !
        Beneath the hallow'd turf where Wallace lies!
    Hear it not, Wallace, in thy bed of death !
        Ye babbling winds, in silence sweep ;
        Disturb not ye the hero's sleep,
    Nor give the coward secret breath.—
        Is this the power in freedom's war,
        That wont to bid the battle rage?
    Behold that eye which shot immortal hate,
        Crushing the despot's proudest bearing,
    That arm which, nerved with thundering fate,
        Brav'd usurpation's boldest daring !
    One quench'd in darkness like the sinking star,
        And one the palsied arm of tottering, powerless age."

Or in his splendid war-song, the *Song of Death,* with which we could scarcely find a comparison.

> Thou grim king of terrors, thou life's gloomy foe,
>   Go, frighten the coward and slave;
> Go, teach them to tremble, fell tyrant! but know,
>   No terrors hast thou to the brave!
>
> Thou strik'st the dull peasant—he sinks in the dark,
>   Nor saves e'en the wreck of a name:
> Thou strik'st the young hero—a glorious mark!
>   He falls in the blaze of his fame!
>
> In the field of proud honour—our swords in our hands,
>   Our King and our country to save—
> While victory shines on life's last ebbing sands,
>   O! who would not rest with the brave!"

Burns has left an important addition to the songs of Scotland. He has enlarged the poetical scenery of his country; and many of her rivers and mountains formerly unknown to the Muse, are now hallowed by his immortal verse. All his songs exhibit independence of sentiment, as in fact do all his writings. It is difficult to determine the comparative merit of Burns, or to find another, who, while earning his subsistance by daily labour, has written verses which have attracted and retained universal attention, and given Burns a distinguished place among the followers of the muses. The force of Burns lay in the power of his understanding, and in the exquisite sensibility of his heart. He was alive to every species of emotion; and he is one of the few poets who have at once excelled in humour, tenderness, and sublimity.

CHAPTER XXXVII.

SCOTT.

SCOTT.—As a narrative and romantic poet, Scott certainly stands first. His works manifest great knowledge of life and character, quick sympathy with man and nature, flow of invention, variety of presentiment, a heart that vibrates to the noble and right—and much picturesqueness; these excellencies joined to great readiness of versification, serve to render his poems at all times interesting

made no attempt to move the feelings like Campbell, --
meditative thought like Wordsworth, or to kindle religious en
thusiasm like Cowper, or even to lead the mind into wild an
supernatural regions like Southey. Neither the minor recesse
of thought, nor the high places of art thrill to his appeal. Still, h
poetry in its real character, stands unequalled, and forms a distinc
epoch in the history of modern literature. In their subjects, the
versification, and their treatment his poems are unsurpassed.
modern writer has observed, that "Scott showed a power somewha
akin to that of Shakespeare, in combining into one harmoniou
whole actions partly borrowed from true history, and partly fro
imagination ; and in clothing the former with the romantic hue
of imagination and picturesque fancy, he showed this superi
power no less than in giving to the latter the solidity of truth." Th
materials of Scott's poems were derived from the legends and exploi
of mediæval chivalry, with which he was so wonderfully familia
and which furnished for him such a mass of striking incident ar
vivid detail. To this, also, he added extraordinary powers
description, to a degree, in which no poet is superior. The greate
of his poems are the *Lay of the Last Minstrel, Marmion,* and *T,
Lady of the Lake.* The interest of the first of these rests main
upon the style and subject af the poem ; that of *Marmion* upon th
descriptions, and that of the latter upon the incidents. The met
which Scott employs is various, but the principal is that of tw

and picturesqueness of an actual scene.

"The moon on the east oriel shone,
Through slender shafts of shapely stone,
   By foliaged tracery combined ;
Thou would'st have thought some fairy's hand
'Twixt poplars straight the osier wand,
   In many a freakish knot, had twined :
Then framed a spell, when the work was done,
And changed the willow-wreaths to stone.
The silver light, so pale and faint,
Show'd many a prophet, and many a saint,
   Whose image on the glass was dyed :
Full in the midst, his Cross of Red
Triumphant Michael brandished,
   And trampled the apostate's pride.
The moon-beam kiss'd the holy pane,
And threw on the pavement a bloody stain.

They sate them down on a marble stone,
   A Scottish monarch slept below :
Thus spoke the Monk, in solemn tone :—
   'I was not always a man of woe ;
For Paynim countries I have trod,
And fought beneath the Cross of God :
Now, strange to my eyes thine arms appear,
And their iron clang sounds strange to my ear,

* * * * *

Before their eyes the Wizard lay
As if he had not been dead a day.
His hoary beard in silver rolled,
He seemed some seventy winters old.
   A palmer's amice wrapped him round
   With a wrought Spanish baldric bound,
      Like a pilgrim from beyond the sea ;
His left hand held his Book of Might—

A silver cross was in his right :
    The lamp was placed beside his knee ;
High and majestic was his look,
At which the fellest fiends had shook,
And all unruffled was his face ;
They trusted his soul had gotten grace.

Often had William of Deloraine
Rode through the battle's bloody plain,
And trampled down the warriors slain,
    And neither known remorse nor awe ;
Yet now remorse and awe he owned ;
His breath came thick, his head swam round,
    When this strange scene of death he saw.
Bewildered and unnerved he stood,
And the priest prayed fervently and loud ;
With eyes averted prayed he ;
He might not endure the sight to see,
Of the man he had loved so brotherly.

    *   *   * .   *

When the huge stone sunk o'er the tomb,
The night returned in double gloom ;
For the moon had gone down, and the stars were few ;
And, as the Knight and Priest withdrew,
With wavering steps and dizzy brain,
They hardly might the postern gain.
'Tis said as through the aisles they passed,
They heard strange noises on the blast ;
And through the cloister-galleries small,
Which at mid-height thread the chancel wall,
Loud sobs, and laughter louder, ran,
And voices unlike the voice of man ;
As if the fiends kept holiday,
Because these spells were brought to day.
I cannot tell how the truth may be ;
I say the tale as 'twas said to me.

'Now, hie thee hence,' the Father said,
'And when we are on death-bed laid,
O may our dear Ladye, and sweet St. John,
Forgive our souls for the deed we have done !'
    The Monk returned him to his cell,
        And many a prayer and penance sped :
When the convent met at the noon-tide bell—
    The Monk of St. Mary's aisle was dead !
Before the cross was the body laid,
    With hand clasped fast, as if still he prayed."

Nothing is more wonderful in Scott's poems, than the complete-
ness with which the poet throws himself back into past ages. He
seems to speak and think like a minstrel of the fourteenth century.

Marmion, the next most important of this poet's works is of a more

not only the nature thus first shown in all its loveliness to the curiosity of the world, but even the barbarous tribes, whose manners Scott has invested with all the charms of fiction." The following lovely passage may be read as an example of the descriptive style, employed in this poem.

> "The Summer dawn's reflected hue
> To purple changed Loch-Katrine blue ;
> Mildly and soft the western breeze
> Just kissed the lake, just stirred the trees,
> And the pleased lake, like maiden coy,
> Trembled, but dimpled not for joy ;
> The mountain-shadows on her breast
> Were neither broken nor at rest ;
> In bright uncertainty they lie,
> Like future joys to Fancy's eye.
> The water-lily to the light
> Her chalice reared of silver bright ;
> The doe awoke, and to the lawn,
> Begemmed with dew-drops, led her fawn ;
> The gray mist left the mountain-side,
> The torrent showed his glistening pride ;
> Invisible in flecked sky,
> The lark sent down her revelry ;
> The blackbird and the speckled thrush

Good-morrow gave from brake and bush;
In answer cooed the cushat dove
Her notes of peace, and rest, and love."

There are many very fine parts in this poem; for instance the
adventures of the disguised king, whose gallant character is very
finely and dramatically sustained ; and the graceful tenderness of
Ellen Douglas. And perhaps the finest of all, the description by
the Highland Bard of the death of the captive chieftain, as he is
listening to the fiery lay.

"————He nears the isle—and lo !
His hand is on a shallop's bow.
—Just then a flash of lightning came,
It tinged the waves and strand with flame !—
I marked Duncraggan's widowed dame,
Behind an oak I saw her stand,
A naked dirk gleamed in her hand :
It darkened,—but amid the moan
Of waves, I heard a dying groan ;—
Another flash !—the spearman floats
A weltering corse beside the boats,
And the stern matron o'er him stood,
Her hand and dagger streaming blood.

'Revenge ! revenge !' the Saxons cried,
The Gaels' exulting shout replied.
Despite the elemental rage,
Again they hurried to engage ;
But, ere they closed in desperate fight,
Bloody with spurring came a knight,
Sprung from his horse, and, from a crag,
Wav'd 'twixt the hosts a milk-white flag.
Clarion and trumpet by his side
Rung forth a truce-note high and wide,
While, in the monarch's name, afar
An herald's voice forbade the war,
For Bothwell's lord, and Rhoderick bold,
Were both, he said, in captive hold.'
But here the lay made sudden stand !—
The harp escaped the minstrel's hand !—
Oft had he stolen a glance, to spy
How Rhoderick brooked his minstrelsy :
At first, the Chieftain, to the chime,
With lifted hand, kept time ;
That motion ceased,—yet feeling strong ;
Varied his look as changed the song ;
At length, no more his deafened ear
The minstrel melody can hear ;
His face grows sharp,—his hands are clenched,
As if some pang his heart-strings wrenched ;

Some straggling beam on cliff or stone,
With such a glimpse as prophet's eye
Gains on thy depths, Futurity.
No murmur waked the solemn still,
Save tinkling of a fountain rill;
But when the wind chafed with the lake,
A sullen sound would upward break,
With dashing hollow voice, that spoke
The incessant war of wave and rock.
Suspended cliffs, with hideous sway,
Seemed nodding o'er the cavern gray.'

Rokeby is more remarkable for its numerous and beautiful descriptions, and the manner in which the poet has contrasted the individual characters in this work, than for the manner in which the subject is worked out. The splendid description with which the Second canto, opens is equal to any passage of its kind in this poet's works.

"Far in the chambers of the west,
The gale had sighed itself to rest ;
The moon was cloudless now and clear,
But pale, and soon to disappear.
The thin gray clouds waxed dimly light
On Brusleton and Houghton height ;
And the rich dale, that eastward lay,
Waited the wakening touch of day,
To give its woods, and cultured plain,
And towers and spires, to light again.

But, westward, Stanmore's shapeless swell,
And Lunedale wild, and Kelton-fell,
And rock-begirdled Gilmanscar,
And Arkingarth, lay dark afar ;
While, as a livelier twilight falls,
Emerge proud Barnard's bannered walls,
High crowned he sits, in dawning pale,
The sovereign of the lovely vale.

    *   *   *   *

The cliffs that rear their haughty head
High o'er the river's darksome bed,
Were now all naked, wild, and gray,
Now waving all with greenwood spray ;
Here trees to every crevice clung,
And o'er the dell their branches hung ;
And there, all splintered and uneven,
The shivered rocks ascend to heaven ;
Oft, too, the ivy swathed their breast,
And wreathed its garland round their crest,
Or from the spires bade loosely flare
Its tendrils in the middle air.
As pennons wont to wave of old
O'er the high feast of Baron bold,
When revelled loud the feudal rout,
And the arched halls returned their shout ;
Such and more wild is Greta's roar,
And such the echoes from her shore.
And so the ivied banners' gleam
Waved wildly o'er the brawling stream.

There is the same picturesque power in the poem of the *Lord of the Isles*, for which Scott is unequalled ; the description of the savage and terrific desolation of the Western Highlands being an astonishing example of this. This poem is also remarkable in an equal degree, for the beauty of its descriptive passages : that of *Autumn*, with which the poem opens can scarcely be passed over without quoting.

"Autumn departs—but still his mantle's fold
  Rests on the groves of noble Somerville ;
Beneath a shroud of russet dropped with gold
  Tweed and his tributaries mingle still ;
Hoarser the wind, and deeper sounds the rill,
  Yet lingering notes of sylvan music swell,
The deep-toned cushat, and the redbreast shrill ;
  And yet some tints of summer splendour tell
When the broad sun sinks down on Ettrick's western fell.

Autumn departs—from Gala's fields no more
  Come rural sounds our kindred banks to cheer ;

Deem'st thou these saddened scenes have pleasure still,
　　Lovest thou through Autumn's fading realms to stray,
To see the heath-flower withered on the hill,
　　To listen to the woods' expiring lay,
　　To note the red leaf shivering on the spray,
　　　To mark the last bright tints the mountain stain,
　　On the waste fields to trace the gleaner's way,
　　　And moralize on mortal joy and pain ?—
O ! if such scenes thou lovest, scorn not the minstrel strain.

No ! do not scorn, although its hoarser note
　　Scarce with the cushat's homely song can vie,
Though faint its beauties as the tints remote
　　That gleam through mist in Autumn's evening sky,
　　And few as leaves that tremble, sear and dry,
　　　When wild November hath his bugle wound ;
　　Nor mock my toil—a lonely gleaner I,
　　　Through fields time·wasted, on sad inquest bound,
Where happier bards of yore have richer harvest found."

This poem finishes with one of those glorious battle-scenes, in
which Scott is unsurpassed, and which is too universally known to
require quoting in this work. In *The Vision of Don Rhoderick*,
the last important poem, there is the same picturesqueness exhibit-
ed as in the others. Of his lyrics the following beautiful song
from the *Lady of the Lake*, is one of the best.

"The heath this night must be my bed,
The bracken curtain for my head,
My lullaby the warder's tread,
　Far, far from love and thee, Mary ;
To-morrow eve, more stilly laid,
My couch may be my bloody plaid,
My vesper song, thy wail, sweet maid !
　It will not waken me, Mary !

I may not, dare not, fancy now
The grief that clouds thy lovely brow ;
I dare not think upon thy vow,
　And all it promised me, Mary.
No fond regret must Norman know ;
When bursts Clan-Alpine on the foe,
His heart must be like bended bow,
　His foot like arrow free, Mary.

A time will come with feeling fraught,
For, if I fall in battle fought,
Thy hapless lover's dying thought
    Shall be a thought on thee, Mary.
And if returned from conquer'd foes,
How blithely will the evening close,
How sweet the linnet sing repose,
    To my young bride and me, Mary!"

CHAPTER XXXVIII.

MONTGOMERY.

MONTGOMERY.—The works of James Montgomery although melodious and beautiful, exhibit but little power. The character of his mind is rather of delicacy than strength, and he has invested all the objects of his imagination with a tender brilliancy peculiarly his own. Excepting a difference of talent, Montgomery has all the delicacy and high moral tone of Cowper, with the same patriotic warmth and enthusiastic love of nature. Like Cowper, too, a tinge of melancholy pervades all his writings, while there is also a resemblance in the peculiar religious system of that poet. The devotional feeling and mysterious beauty which Montgomery throws around the most ordinary things, is another of the greatest features of his poetry. Speaking of the peculiarity of his poems, a writer says, "We may observe everywhere, how a familiarity with religious subjects tinges the stream of his imagination, and converts the feelings of the mind and the beauties of nature, into reflection and remembrance of the things unseen. To him, the graces and glories of creation appear invested with an awfully sanctity." Montgomery was essentially a religious poet ; and perhaps there are no lyrics in the English language which breathe the same glowing love to God and man, and the same sense of beauty and goodness as these. His chief works are *The Wanderer of Switzerland, The West Indies, The World before the Flood,* and *Greenland.* The former of these is a glowing lyric of Liberty, and denunciation of the diabolical war-spirit of the revolutionary French.

"Comes there no ship again to Greenland's shore?
There comes another :—there shall come no more ;
Nor this shall reach an haven:—What are these
Stupendous monuments upon the seas ?
Works of Omnipotence, in wondrous forms,
Immoveable as the mountains in the storms ?
Far as imagination's eye can roll,
One range of Alpine glaziers to the pole
Flanks the whole eastern coast ; and, branching wide.
Arches o'er many a league the indignant tide,
That works and frets, with unavailing flow,
To mine a passage to the beach below ;
Thence from its neck that winter yoke to rend,
And down the gulf the crashing fragments send.
There lies a vessel in this realm of frost,
Not wreck'd, nor stranded, yet for ever lost :
Its keel embedded in the solid mass ;
Its glistening sails appear expanded glass ;
The transverse ropes with pearls enormous strung,
The yards with icicles grotesquely hung,
Wrapt in the topmast shrouds there rests a boy,
His old seafaring father's only joy :
Sprung from a race of rovers, ocean born
Nursed at the helm, he trod dry land with scorn ;
Through fourscore years from port to port he veer'd,
Quicksand, nor rock, nor foe, nor tempest fear'd ;
Now cast ashore, though like a hulk he lie,
His son at sea is ever in his eye,
And his prophetic thought, from age to age,
Esteems the waves his offspring's heritage.
He ne'er shall know, in his Norwegian cot,
How brief that son's career, how strange his lot ;
Writhed round the mast, and sepulchred in air,
Him shall no worm devour, no vulture tear ;
Congeal'd to adamant, his frame shall last,
Though empires change, till time and tide be past. .
    On deck, in groups embracing as they died,
Singly, erect, or slumbering side by side,
Behold the crew !—They sail'd, with hope elate,
For eastern Greenland-till, ensnared by fate,
In toils that mock'd their utmost strength and skill,
They felt, as by a charm, their ship stand still :
The madness of the wildest gale that blows
Were mercy to that shudder of repose,
When withering horror struck from heart to heart

The blunt rebound of Death's benumbing dart,
And each, a petrifaction at his post,
Look'd on yon father, and gave up the ghost:
He, meekly kneeling, with his hands upraised,
His beard of driven snow, eyes fixed and glazed,
Alone among the dead shall yet survive,
—The imperishable dead, that seem alive ;
—The immortal dead, whose spirits, breaking free,
Bore his last words into eternity,
While with a seraph's zeal, a Christian's love,
Till his tongue fail'd, he spoke of joys above.
Now motionless, amidst the icy air,
He breathes from marble lips unutter'd prayer.
The clouds condensed, with dark unbroken hue
Of stormy purple, overhang his view,
Save in the west, to which he strains his sight,
One golden streak, that grows intensely bright,
Till thence the emerging sun, with lightning blaze,
Pours the whole quiver of his arrowy rays ;
The smitten rocks to instant diamond turn,
And round the expiring saint such visions burn
As if the gates of Paradise were thrown
Wide open to receive his soul ;—'tis flown :
The glory vanishes, and over all
Cimmerian darkness spreads her funeral pall !
    Morn shall return, and noon, and eve, and night
Meet here with interchanging shade and light :
But from this bark no timber shall decay,
Of these cold forms no feature pass away ;
Perennial ice around the incrusted bow,
The peopled deck, and full rigg'd masts, shall grow,
Till from the sun himself the whole be hid,
Or spied beneath a crystal pyramid ;
As in pure amber, with divergent lines,
A rugged shell emboss'd with sea-weed shines.
From age to age increased with annual snow,
This new *Mont Blanc* among the clouds may glow,
Whose conic peak, that earliest greets the dawn,
And latest from the sun's shut eye withdrawn,
Shall from the zenith, through incumbent gloom,
Burn like a lamp upon this naval tomb.
But when the archangel's trumpet sounds on high,
The pile shall burst to atoms through the sky,
And leave its dead, upstarting at the call,
Naked and pale, before the Judge of all."

The *West Indies,* is a heroic poem upon the subject of the aboli-
tion of the Slave-trade, and contains several descriptive pieces of
the highest merit. The masterly and glowing description of the
interior of Africa in the Second part, may be quoted as an excellent
specimen of these.

She sleeps on isle of velvet verdure, placed
Midst sandy gulfs and shoals for ever waste ;
She guides her countless flocks to cherish'd rills,
And feeds her cattle on a thousand hills ;
Her steps the wild bees welcome through the vale,
From every blossom that embalms the gale ;
The slow unwieldy river-horse she leads
Through the deep waters, o'er the pasturing meads ;
And climbs the mountains that invade the sky,
To soothe the eagle's nestlings when they cry.
At sunset, when voracious monsters burst
From dreams of blood, awaked by maddening thirst ;
When the lorn caves, in which they shunk from light,
Ring with wild echoes through the hideous night ;
When darkness seems alive ; and all the air
Is one tremendous uproar of despair,
Horror and agony ;— on her they call ;
She hears their clamour, she provides for all ;
Leads the light leopard on his eager way,
And goads the gaunt hyæna to his prey."

The *World before the Flood* also abounds with beauties, and gives evidence of the highest and finest powers of imagination. The passage in which Javan discovers Zillah in the forest, is an excellent specimen of this poem. Of the smaller poems of this writer, many might be chosen as examples. His *Harp of Sorrow*, is a noble expression of individual feeling; and is written in language at once musical and attractive. The following stanzas are some of the best.

" I gave my Harp to Sorrow's hand,
    And she has ruled the chords so long,

They will not speak at my command ;—
   They warble only to *her* song.

Of dear departed hours,
   Too fondly loved to last,
The dew, the breath, the bloom of flowers,
   Snapt in their freshness by the blast ;

Of long, long years of future care,
   Till lingering Nature yields her breath,
And endless ages of despair,
   Beyond the judgment day of death :—

The weeping Minstrel sings ;
   And while her numbers flow,
My spirit trembles with the strings,
   Responsive to the notes of woe.

Would gladness move a sprightlier strain,
   And wake this wild harp's clearest tones,
The chords, impatient to complain,
   Are dumb, or only utter moans,

   *   *   *   *

O ! snatch the Harp from Sorrow's hand.
   Hope ! who has been a stranger long ;
O ! strike it with sublime command,
   And be the poet's life thy song.

Of vanish'd troubles sing,
   Of fears for ever fled,
Of flowers that hear the voice of Spring,
   And burst and blossom from the dead ;—

Of home, contentment, health, repose,
   Serene delights, while years increase ;
And weary life's triumphant close,
   In some calm sunset hour of peace ;—

Of bliss that reigns above,
   Celestial May of youth,
Unchanging as JEHOVAH's love,
   And everlasting as his truth:—

Sing, heavenly Hope !—and dart thine hand
   O'er my frail harp, untuned so long ;
That Harp shall breathe, at thy command,
   Immortal sweetness through thy song,

Ah ! then, this gloom control,
   And at thy voice shall start
A new creation in my soul,
   A native Eden in my heart."

sentimental poems in our language. The following passage from the first part will amply illustrate its quality and character.

"Lo ! at the couch where infant beauty sleeps,
Her silent watch the mournful mother keeps ;
She, while the lovely babe unconscious lies,
Smiles on her slumb'ring child with pensive eyes,
And weaves a song of melancholy joy—
'Sleep, image of thy father, sleep, my boy :
No ling'ring hour of sorrow shall be thine ;
No sigh that rends thy father's heart and mine ;.
Bright as his manly sire, the son shall be
In form and soul ; but, ah ! more blest than he l
Thy fame, thy worth, thy filial love, at last,
Shall soothe this aching heart for all the past—
With many a smile my solitude repay,
And chase the world's ungenerous scorn away.
      'And say, when summon'd from the world and thee,
I lay my head beneath the willow tree,
Wilt thou, sweet mourner ! at my stone appear,
And soothe my parted spirit ling'ring near?
Oh, wilt thou come, at ev'ning hour, to shed
The tears of Memory o'er my narrow bed ;
With aching temples on thy hand reclin'd,
Muse on the last farewell I leave behind,
Breathe a deep sigh to winds that murmur low,
And think on all my love, and all my woe ?'

So speaks affection, ere the infant eye
Can look regard, or brighten in reply;
But when the cherub lip hath learnt to claim
A mother's ear by that endearing name;
Soon as the playful innocent can prove
A tear of pity, or a smile of love,
Or cons his murm'ring task beneath her care,
Or lisps with holy look his ev'ning prayer,
Or gazing, mutely pensive, sits to hear
The mournful ballad warbled in his ear;
How fondly looks admiring Hope the while,
At every artless tear, and every smile!
How glows the joyous parent to descry
A guileless bosom, true to sympathy!
　　Where is the troubled heart, consign'd to share
Tumultuous toils, or solitary care,
Unblest by visionary thoughts that stray
To count the joys of Fortune's better day l
Lo; nature, life, and liberty relume
The dim-ey'd tenant of the dungeon gloom,
A long lost friend, or hapless child restor'd,
Smiles at his blazing hearth and social board;
Warm from his heart the tears of rapture flow,
And virtue triumphs o'er remember'd woe."

In Gertrude of Wyoming, his next longest poem, Campbell assumes a more gentle and pensive style. This poem also contains many beautifnl passages, sweetly and artistically written of which the following in the second part, is an instance :—

"Apart there was a deep untrodden grot,
Where oft the reading hours sweet Gertrude wore;
Tradition had not named its lonely spot,
But here (methinks) might India's sons explore
Their fathers' dust, or lift, perchance of yore,
Their voice to the great Spirit :—rocks sublime
To human art a sportive semblance bore,
And yellow lichens colour'd all the clime,
Like moonlight battlements, and towers decay'd by time.

But high in ampitheatre above,
His arms the everlasting aloes threw :
Breathed but an air of heaven, and all the grove
As if with instinct living spirit grew,
Rolling its verdant gulphs of every hue;
And now suspended was the pleasing din,
Now from a murmur faint it swell'd anew,
Like the first note of organ heard within
Cathedral aisles,—ere yet its symphony begin.

It was in this lone valley she would charm
The lingeiing noon, where flowers a couch had strewn;
Her cheek reclining, and her snowy arm

Three little moons, how short ! amidst the grove
And pastoral savanahs they consume !
While she, beside her buskin'd youth to rove,
Delights, in fancifully wild consume,
Her lovely brow to shade with Indian-plume ;
And forth in hunter-seeming vest they fare ;
But not to chase the deer in forest gloom ;
'Tis but the breath of heaven—the blessed air—
And interchange of heart unknown, unseen to share.

That though the sportive dog oft round them note,
Or fawn, or wild-bird bursting on the wing ;
Yet who, in love's own presence, would devote
To death those gentle throats that wake the spring,
Or writhing from the brook its victim bring ?
No !—nor let fear one little warbler rouse ;
But, fed by Gertrude's hand, still let them sing,
Acquaintance of her path, amidst the boughs,
That shade even now her love, and witness'd first **her** vows

Now labyrinths, which but themselves can pierce,
Methinks, conduct them to some pleasant ground,
Where welcome hills shut out the universe,
And pines their lawny walk encompass round ;
There, if a pause delicious converse found,
'Twas but when o'er each heart the idea stole,
(Perchance awhile in joy's oblivion drown'd,)
That come what may, while life's grand pulses roll,
Indissolubly thus should soul be knit to soul.

And in the visions of romantic youth,
What years of endless bliss are yet to flow !
But, mortal pleasure, what art thou in truth ?
The torrent's smoothness, ere it dash below !

> And must I change my song ? and must I show,
> Sweet Wyoming ! the day when thou wert doom'd,
> Guiltless, to mourn thy loveliest bowers laid low !
> When where of yesterday a garden bloom'd,
> Death overspread his pall, and blackening ashes gloom'd."

Perhaps the finest part of Campbell's poems, and that in which he excels most, are his patriotic songs, *Ye Mariner's of England, The Battle of the Baltic,* and *The Soldier's Dream.* The former well known song is stately and noble, and possesses at the same time the genuine structure and melody of verse which constitutes the truly patriotic; nor would it be easy to find anything which in this respect comes closer to the ideal of a patriotic song. *The Battle of the Baltic* has the same excellencies ; there is the same glowing touch and masterly treatment, which, taken with the theme of the poem, renders it sympathetic to every reader throughout the land, rude or refined. And in the latter *The Soldier's Dream,* we may see the same true qualities of lyric verse. The beautiful verses on the battle of *Hohenlinden,* and *Lochiel's Warning,* may be mentioned as two of the finest poems of this character : the following lines, with which the latter poem finishes are magnificent.

> "————Never shall Albion a destiny meet,
> So black with dishonour, so foul with retreat.
> Though my perishing ranks should be strew'd in their gore
> Like ocean-weeds heap'd on the surf beaten shore,
> Lochiel, untainted by flight or by chains,
> While the kindling of life in his bosom remains,
> Shall victor exult, or in death be laid low,
> With his back to the field, and his feet to the foe !
> And leaving in battle no blot on his name,
> Look proudly to Heaven from the death-bed of fame."

CHAPTER XL.

MINOR POETS FROM CHAUCER TO ELIZABETH. ·

[The spelling in many of the selections from these early poets, has been modernised , except in passages where such alteration would have been likely to effect the rhythm of the poetry.]

ROBERT OF GLOUCESTER.—The only poet who lived in this reign, of any importance, was Robert of Gloucester. He wrote a very long poem ; a history of England in verse, from Brutus to the reign of Edward I. which, Warton says, "is totally destitute of art or imagination." The following passage which describes the sports that followed King Arthur's coronation, is quoted as an example of this production.

"Soon after this noble feast, as right was of such ryde,
 The knights arrayed them about on each side,
 In fields and in meads to prove her chivalry.
 Some with lance, some with sword, without villainy,
 With playing at tables, others at chequery *
 With casting, others with setting,† others with some other manner,
 And which so of any game had the mastery,
 The King him of his gyfteth did large courtesy.
 Up the alurs of the castles the ladies then stood,
 And beheld this noble game, and which knights were good
 All the three chief days lasted this nobley
 In halls and in fields of meat and eke of play.
 These men came the fourth day before the king there,
 And he gave them large gifts, every as they worth were
 Bishoprics and churches clerks he gave some,
 And castles and towns, knights that were come."

ROBERT DE BRUNNE.—Robert Mannyng, commonly called Robert de Brunne, lived at the close of the reign of Edward I. He translated into English metre, a French work by Grosthead, Bishop of Lincoln, entitled the *Manual of Sins*, the subject of which treats of the seven deadly sins, illustrated with many legendary stories. The following passage from this poem, is selected from the quotation given by Warton in his History of English Poetry.

"He loved much to hear the harp,
 For man's wit it maketh sharp
 Next his chamber, beside his study,
 His harper's chamber was fast there by.
 Many times, by nights and days,
 He had solace of notes and lays;
 One asked him the reason why,
 He had delight in minstrelsy?
 He answered him on this manner,
 Why he held the harp so dear.
 'The virtue of the harp, through skill and right,
 Will destroy the devil's might ;
 And to the cross by God's skill
 Is the harp likened well.—
 Therefore, good men, ye shall lere,
 When ye any harper hear,
 To worship God at your power,
 And David in the Psalter.

> In harp and tabor and symphony
> Worship God in trumps and sautre :
> In chords, in organs, and bells ringing,
> In all these worship the heavenly king.' '

Besides this, he was the author of a metrical chronicle of England, and a translation in English rhyme of the treatise of Cardinal Bonaventure, from the Latin. Warton says of this writer, that "he appeared to possess more industry than genius, and cannot be read with pleasure : yet it should be remembered that uncouth and unpleasing as he naturally seems, and chiefly employed in turning the theology of his age into rhyme, he contributed to form a style to teach expression, and to polish his native tongue."

BARBOUR.—This poet, who lived about the year 1350, composed a long poem in eight syllabled verse, commemorating the adventures of Robert Bruce. It describes incidents with a graphic force, and contains many beautiful episodes and fine sentimental passages. His apostrophe to Freedom is written with great spirit.

> "Ah ! fredome is a nobill thing !
> Fredome makes man to have liking !
> Fredome all solace to man gives,
> He lives at ese that frely lives !
> A nobill heart may have nane ese,
> Na ellys nocht that may him plese,
> Giff fredome faileth ; for fre liking
> Is yearnyt our all other thing.
> Na he, that ay has levit free,
> May nocht knaw weil the propyrte,
> The angyr, na the wretchyt dome.
> That is couplyt to foule thirldome.
> But giff he had assayit it,
> Than all perpeur he suld it wyt ;
> And sulde think fredome mair to pryse,
> Than all the gold in warld that is."

GOWER.—John Gower was the writer of several moral poems of considerable merit. His works are tedious, and do not possess the least degree of fancy, passion or wit, but his versification is harmonious, and there is much solid reflection, and a high moral tone perceivable throughout his poems. D'Israeli says, "Gower stamped with the force of ethical reasoning his smooth rhymes ; and this was a near approach to poetry itself !" His influence as a poet may be summed up in the words of the reliable Warton. He says, "if

Was saved, the worlde in his degree
Was made as who seith newe again,
Of flower, of fruit, of grass, of grain,
Of beast, of bird, and of mankind,
Which ever hath be to God unkind,
For notwithstanding all the fare,
Of that this worlde was made so bare,
And afterward it was restored,
Amonge the men was nothing mored
Toward God of good living:
But all was torned to liking
After the flesh, so that foryete
Was he, whiche gave them life and mete,
Of heaven and earth cieator.
And thus came forth the great error,
That they the high God ne knew,
But made them other gods anew.
As thou hast heard me said tofore.
There was no man that time bore,
That he had not after his choice
A god, to whom he gave his voice
Whereof the misbeliever came
In to the time of Abraham :
But he found out the right way,
How only men should obey
The high God, whiche weldeth all,
And ever hath done, and ever shall,
In heaven, in earth, and eke in hell,
There is no tongue his might may tell.
This Patriarche to his linage
Forbad, that they to none image
Encline should in no wise:
But her offrende and sacrifice,
With all their whole hearts love,
Unto the mighty God above
They sholden bow, and to no more."

HAMPOLE.—This poet's date is fixed about the year 1349.   His
principal poetical works, are a paraphrase on the Book of Job, on
the Lord's Prayer, and on the seven penetintial psalms ; and the

Prick of Conscience ; all of which, Warton says, "have no tincture
of sentiment, imagination, or elegance."

> "He that knoweth well and can see
> What he is, was, and shall be,
> A wiser man may be told
> Whether he be young or old
> Then he that can all other thing
> And of himself hath no knowing.
> He may no good know nor feel
> Without he first know himself well ;
> Therefore a man should first lere
> To know himself properly here,
> For if he knew himself kindly
> Then may he know God Almighty ;
> And on ending think should he,
> And on the last day that shall be
> Know should he what this world is,
> Full of pomp and lecherousness ;
> And learn to know and think withal
> What shall after this life befal
> Knowing of this should him lead
> To meet with meekness and with dread :
> So may he come to good living,
> And at last to good ending,
> And when he of this world shall wend
> Be brought to bliss that has no end."

LANGLAND.—William Langland or Longlande, was the writer of
a poem called *Pier's Plowman's Vision.* This work comprises a
series of visions, which the poet imagines himself to have seen,
while asleep, after a long ramble on Malvern-Hills in Worces-
tershire. In it, Langland satirizes the vices and abuses of nearly
every profession, and ridicules the absurdities of superstition and
corruptedness of the clergy, with great humour and spirit. There
are times, in which in the depths of his emotions, he bursts out into
the most beautiful and majestic strains. Hallam says, "there is a
real energy in his conceptions, which he caught not from the chim-
eras of knight-errantry, but from the actual manners and opinions
of his time." The following passage in which the poet is represen-
ted in search of Dowell and Doevil will afford a striking specimen
of Langland's allegorical satire and description of writing. Many
excellent strokes of poetry also, are to be met with.

> "By a wild wilderness, and by a wood's side,
> Bliss of the birds, brought me on sleep,

And under a lime on a land, lean'ed I awhile,
To list to the lays, the lovely fowls made :
Mirth of their mouths made me there to sleep,
The marvellousest dreams, dreamed me then,
That ever dreamed wight, in world as I went
A much man as me thought, and like to myself,
Came and called me, by my own name.
What art thou quoth I then, thou that my name knowest ?
That thou wottest well quoth he, and no wight better
Know I what thou art. THOUGHT said he then,
I have sought thee this seven years, see ye me not rather ?
Art thou THOUGHT quoth I then, thou could'st me wish
Where that DOWELL dwelleth, and do me that to know
DOWELL and DOBETTER, and DOBEST the third quoth he
Are three fair virtues, and be not far to find,
Who so is true of his tongue, and of his two hands
And through his labour or his load, his livelihood winneth
And is trusty of his dealing. taketh but his own
And is no drunkard nor dedigious, DOWELL him followeth
DOBET doth right thus, and he doth much more,
He is as low as a lamb, and lovely of speech
And helpeth all men, after that him needeth ;
The bags and the bigirdles. he hath broken them all
That the erle avarous held and his heirs
And thus to Mammon's money he hath made him frendes
And is run to religion, and hath rendered* the bible
And preached to the people, Saint Paul's words.
Libenter suffertis insipientes cum sitis ipsi sapientes.
And suffereth the unwise, with you for to live
And with glad will doth he good, for so god you hoteth.
Dobest is above both, and beareth a bishop's cross
Is hooked on that one end to draw men from hell
A pike is on the potent† to pull down the wicked
That wayten any wickedness, Dowell to tene
And Dowell and Dobet, amongst them have ordained
To crown one to be be king, to rule them both
That if Dowell and Dobet, are against Dobest
Then shall the king come, and cast them in irons,
And but if Dobest bid for them, they be there for ever.
Thus Dowell and Dobet, and Dobest the third
Crowned one to be king, to keepen them all
And to rule the realm, by their three wits
And none otherwise, but as they three assented."

Austin, or Guy Earl of Warwick, ludicrous or legendary, religiouş or romantic, an history or an allegory, he writes with facility. His transitions were rapid from works of the most serious and laborious kind to sallies of levity and pieces of popular entertainment. His muse was of universal access ; and he was not only a poet of his monastery, but of the world in general. If a disguising was intended by the company of Goldsmiths, a mask before his majesty at Eltham, a may-game for the sheriffs and aldermen of London, a mumming before the lord mayor, a procession of pageants from the creation for the festival of Corpus Christi, or a carol for the coronation, Lydgate was then consulted and gave the poetry."

His principal poems are *The Fall of Princes, The History of Thebes, The Siege of Troy,* and *The Life of our Lady.* Although his poetry is heavy and tedious, there are many passages among his lengthened and numerous productions of exceeding beauty, many natural and true descriptions, finely conceived characters, and smooth verse even to elegance. As an example take his character of *Venus,* from *The Scige of Troy,*

> "And she stant naked in a wavy sea,
> Environ her with goddesses three,
> That be assign'd with busy attendance
> To wait on her and do her observance.
> And flowers fresh, blue, red, and white,
> Ee her about, the more for to delight.
> And on her head she hath a chaplet
> Of roses red full pleasantly set,
> And from the head down under her foot
> With sundry gums and ointments sweet
> She is anointed, sweeter for to smell.
> And all aloft her, as the poets tell,
> Ee doves white, fleeing, and eke sparrows,
> And her beside Cupid with his arrows."

Or the following passage from the *Life of our Lady,* which is equal in point of beauty to anything of Chaucer, or the contemporary poets of his time.

> "And saying after on the next night
> While they slept at their lodging place,
> Came an Angel, appearing with great light,
> And warned them that they mought ne trace
> —   By Herodes, but that they should pace

The Holy Ghost also did appear
And Christ Jesu the Father's son entere,
This day appearing in our mortal kind,
Was of Saint John baptised as I find.

And forasmuch as they all three
This day were seen by sothfast appearance
They being one in perfect unity ;
Wherefore this day of most reverence
Named is truly in this sentence
Theophanos, for God in treble wise,
Therein appeared as ye have heard devise.

For *theos* is as much for to mean
As God in English, if ye list to see,
And *Phanos*, as shewing withouten were,
As ye have heard afore rehearsed of me ;
For on earth a God in trinity
This day appeared withouten any lye,
Ye truly may it call Theophany."

JAMES I.—James I, may be considered as one of the first of the few poets that are to be found in the long period that succeeded the death of Chaucer. His principal production was a long poem, entitled *The King's Quair*, or Book, a collection of love-verses in which the poet records his life, and describes the circumstances of an attachment which he formed while imprisoned at Windsor Castle, for a young English princess whom he saw walking in an adjacent garden. This poem consists of one hundred and ninety-seven stanzas ; it abounds in allegory, and contains many very powerful and pathetic passages. It is written in the richest language, and there is an elegance and flow in it, that surpasses any of the earlier poets. His other works were *Christ's Kirk on the Green*, and *Pebles to the Play*. The following example is from the *King's Quair*, and exhibits all the elegance which distinguished this writer's works.

"Bewailing in my chamber thus alone,
Despeired of all joy and remedye,
For-tirit of my thought and wo-begone,
And to the wyndow gan I walk in hye.

To see the warld and folke that went forbye
  As for the tyme though I of mirthis fude,
  Might have no more, to luke it did me gude.
Now was there made fast by the Touris wall
  A gardyn faire, and in the corneris set,
Ane herbere grene, with wandis long and small,
  Railit about, and so with treis set
Was all the place, and hawthorn hegis knet,
  That lyf was non walkyng there forbye,
  That might within scarce any wight aspye.

    *   *   *   *

And on the small grene twistis sat
  The lytil sucte nyghtingale, and song
So loud and clere, theympnis consecrat
  Of luvis use, now soft and loud among,
That all the gardynes and the wallis rung
  Right of thaire song, and on the copill next
  Of thaire sucte harmony, and lo the text.

Worshippe aye yt loveris bene this May,
  For of your bliss the kalendis are begonne.
And sing with us, away winter away,
  Come somer come, the sucte seson and sonne,
Awake, for schame ! ye have your hevynis wonne,
  And amorously lift up your hedis all,
  Thank lufe yt list you to his merci call.

    *   *   *   *

And therewith kest I doun myn eye ageyne,
  Quhare as I saw walkyng under the Toure,
Full secretely, new cumyn hir to pleyne,
  The fairest or the fresh young floure
That ever I sawe, methought, before that houre,
  For quhich sodayne abate, anon astert,
  The blude of all my body to my hert.

And though I stood abaiset tho a lyte,
  No wonder was, for quhy ! my wittis all
Were so overcome with plesance and delyte,
  Only through latting of myn eyen fall,
That sudaynly my hert become hir thrall.
  For ever of free wyll, for of menace
  There was no takyne in hir suete face."

OCCLEVE.—Thomas Occleve who flourished about the year 1420,
was the writer of several poems of considerable merit, though little
read now.   His principal work is a translatlon of Egidius' *De Reg-
num Principium*, from which the following passage, written to the
memory of Chaucer is extracted.

> Unslayn from thee, which aye us lifely hertith
> With boke of his ornate enditing,
> That is to all this lond enlumynıng,"

It is remarkable that the period which followed Chaucer,—namely between the years 1461 and 1509—when there was a want of true English poetry, that Scotland produced a number of genuine poets, who in the words of Warton, "displayed a degree of sentiment and spirit, a command of phraseology and a fertility of imagination, not to be found in any English poet since Chaucer and Lydgate." Henryson, Dunbar and Douglas, were the principal of these.

HENRYSON.—This poet wrote a series of fables in verse, besides several other moral poems. One of the best of his Fables is the common story of the Town Mouse and the Country Mouse. The following passage—the moral with which he concluded the fable—will give an instance of his didactic style :—

> "Blessit be simple life, withouten dreid ;
> Blessit be sober feist in quieté ;
> Who has enough of no more has he neid
> Though it be little into quantité.
> Great abundance, and blind prosperity,
> Oft tymis make ane evil conclusion ;
> The sweetest life, therefore, in this countré,
> Is of sickerness, with small possession."

Another example of his poetry is to be seen in the following verses, which breathe throughout a truly religious and poetical spirit.

> "Alone, as I went up and down
> In abbey was fair to see,
> Thinking what consolation
> Was in adversity ;

By chance I cast on side mine,
And saw this written on a wall,
'Of what estate, Man, that thou be,
Obey, and thank thy God for all.'

Thy kingdom and thy great empire,
Thy royalty, nor rich array,·
Shall nought endure at thy desire
But, as the wind, will wend away :
Thy gold and all thy goodis gay,
When Fortune list will fra the fall :
Sen thou sic samples sees each day,
Obey, and thank thy God for all.

Though thou be blind or have an halt,
Or in thy face deformed ill,
So it come not by thy default,
No man shall thee reprove by skill ;
Blame not thy Lord, so is his will ;
Spurn not thy foot against the wall ;
But, with meek heart and prayer still,
Obey, and thank thy God for all."

DUNBAR.—Most of this poet's works are of a humourous character and refer to humble life ; others are allegorical and full of
beautiful and natural imagery, while some are moral and instructive.
In each however, he excels ; while they all show a truly powerful
and original genius.   He was no doubt a man of the highest genius,
and his works would probably have been better known, and more
read, but for the antiquated language in which they are written.
His principal allegorical poems are *The Golden Serge,* the *Dance,*
and the *Thistle and the. Rose* : of these the best is the *Dance.*   It
is a fantastic and terrible impersonation, written with the intense
reality of Dante ; and describes a procession of the Seven Deadly
Sins, two of which, *Ire* and *Envy,* are quoted as examples.

"Then *Ire* came in with sturt* and strife ;
Ilis hand was ay upon his knife,
    He brandeist like a beir ;†
Boasters, braggarts, and bargainers,
After him passed in pairs,
    Arrayed in feir of weir.
In jacks, stir'ps, and bonnets of steel,
Their legs were chained to the heel ;
    Frawart was their effeir ,‡
Some upon other with brandis beft,¶
Some jaggit others to the heft
    With knives that sharp could shear."

* Disturbance.   ‡ Warlike Manner.

Honour, an allegory showing that nothing but virtue could lead to happiness : and *King Hart*, a metaphorical view of the progress of human life. But it is by the translation of Virgil into Scottish verse that Douglas is best known, of which the most remarkable feature, is the amount of Latin words with English terminations introduced. For example the following passage in his beautiful description of Sunrise, in the Introduction to the Twelfth book,

> "The *auriate* vanes of his throne-soverane
> With glittering glance o'erspread the *oceane ;*
> The largé fludis beaming all of light,
> With but one blink of his *supernal* sight.
> For to behold it was ane *glore* to see
> The stabled windis and the coloured sea,
> The soft season, the *firmament serene.*
> The lowne *illuminate* air, and firth *amene.*" *

MONTGOMERY.—This poet, was a follower of the same School with Dunbar and Douglas, and was very popular in his day. His principal work is an allegorical poem called *The Cherrie and the Sloe*, of wearisome length. Although it has in it several passages of extraordinary beauty, it is on the whole of very unequal merit. His smaller poems which are chiefly of a moral and religious style, are much more sprightly, and pleasing.

THE DEITY.
> "Supreme Essence, beginning unbegun,
> Ay Trinall one,—one undivided three.
> Eternal Word, that victory has won
> Our Death, our Hell, triumphant on the Tree,
> Foreknowledge, Wisdom, and All-scan ee,
> Jehovah, Alpha and Omega, All.
> Like unto none, nor none like unto thee,

---

* The words written in Italic, are those from the Latin.

> Unmoved, who movest the rounds about the ball,
> Container uncontained ; is, was, and shall, —
> Be sempiternal, merciful, and just.
> Creator uncreated, now I call.
> Teach me thy truth, since into thee I trust,
> Increase, confirm, and kindle from above
> My faith, my hope, but, by thy leave, my love."

BLIND HARRY.—Another Scotch poet known under the name of Blind Harry wrote poetry at this period. His only remembered poem is a narrative of the exploits and deeds of William Wallace, written in long rhymed couplets, and containing several vigorous and picturesque passages. The manner in which the Seasons of the year are painted in this poem, are not only terse, but very elegant. As for example the following description of Spring : —

> "Gentle Jupiter, with his mild ordinance,
> Both herb and tree reverts into pleasance ;
> And fresh Flora her flowery mantle spread,
> In every dale both hop, hight, hill, and mead."

Or the following picturesque description of Morning :—

> "The merry day sprang from the orient,
> With beams bright illuminate occident,
> After Titan, Phebus upriseth fair,
> High in the sphere, the signs she made declare.
> Zephyrus then began his morning course,
> The sweet vapour thus from the ground resource;
> The humble breath down from the heaven avail
> In every mead, both frith, forest and dale.
> The clear reed among the rockis rang
> Through green branches where the birds blithely sang,
> With joyous voice in heavenly harmony."

SKELTON.—The most original and at the same time the most interesting of this poet's writings are his comic and satirical poems. They are written in a peculiar short doggrel measure, with incessantly recurring rhymes. They consist chiefly in a series of audacious attacks upon the then all-powerful favorite and minister Wolsey. In some of his works, this poet has adopted the more stately seven-lined stanza, but even then he frequently relapses into the absurdities of his favourite style. Although his subjects are very often as ridiculous as his metre, there are frequently nnmistakeable marks of genius to be seen in his poems. He shows in several places considerable power in exhibiting allegorical

MORE.—Sir Thomas More is best remembered by his prose works, *Utopia* &c., but he was also the writer of miscellaneous verses, of which many are of considerable merit and beauty. The following passage is selected from his *Lamentation of the Death of Queen Elizabeth*.

"O ye that put your trust and confidence.
In worldly joy and frayle prosperite,
That so live here as ye should never hence,
Remember death and loke here upon me.
Ensample I thynke there may no better be.
Your selfe wotte well that in this realm was I
Your quene but late, and lo now here I lye.

Was I not borne of old worthy linage?
Was not my mother queene, my father kyng?
Was I not a kinges fere in marriage?
Was I not plenty of every pleasaunt thing?
Mercifull God, this is a strange reckoning :
Richesse, honour, wealth, and auncestry,
Hath me forsaken, and low now here I lie.

*   *   *   *

O brittle wealth, so full of bitterness,
Thy single pleasure doubled is with pain ;
Account my sorrow first and my distresse
In sondry wyse, and recken there agayne,
The joy that I have had, and I dare sayne,
For ill my honour, enduréd yet have I,
More wo then wealth, and low now here I lye."

* Anger.   † Mad.

HAWES.—It is important that this poet should be mentioned, being the chief link between Chaucer and his contemporaries and the poets who flourished during the reign of Henry the Eighth. He is interesting in another sense, namely his exertion to release poetry from the dull precincts of the cloister to which his more immediate predecessors had confined it. The poets who preceded him were for the most part, mere chroniclers or translators—and Hawes deserves, leaving the merit of his works out, the praise of having dared to be original. His principal poem the *Pastime of Pleasure* is purely allegorical, and contains unquestionably many striking passages. The hero of the poem is *True Gallantry*, and the heroine *Perfect Beauty.* To obtain the Fayre Lady, the Grande Amoure has to encounter and overcome no end of dangers and difficulties, and in especial he is to win his way to favour by the acquirement of perfect knowledge in the seven sciences—Grammar, Logic, Rhetoric, Arithmetic, Music, Geometry, and Astronomy. The poem itself, is long and tedious, although it is entitled to rank as an "inventive" work. The following extract in which he seeks the acquaintance of Logic and Rhetoric, will be sufficient to show the character of this poet's work.

"So by I went into a chamber bright
Where was wont, to be a right fair lady
Before whom then, it was my whole delight
I kneel'd adown, full well and meekly
Beseeching her, to instruct me shortly
In her noble science, which is expedient
For man to know, in many an argument.
You shall quoth she, my science well learn
In time and space, to your great utility
So that in me looking, you shall then discern
A friend from foe, and good from iniquity
Right from wrong, ye shall know in certainty.
My science is, all the ill to eschew
And for to know, the false from the true,
Who will take pains, to follow the trace
In this wicked world, of truth and righteousness
In heaven above, he shall have dwelling place ;
And who that walketh the way of darkness
Spending his time in worldly wickedness
Amid the earth, in hell most horrible

and satirical writer, in the latter of which he severely attacks the clergy. His principal works are *The Dream,* and *The Monarchy.* His poems contain descriptive passages of real beauty. The following passage from the latter poem, in which the poet describes the creation of the world and of Adam, will afford an example of his descriptive talents.

> "When God had made the hevennis bricht,
> The sone, and mone, for to gyf licht,
> The starry heaven, and cristalline,
> And, by his sapience divine,
> The planeits, in their circles round,
> Quhirling about with merie sound :—
> He clad the earth with herbs and trees ;
> All kind of fishes in the seas,
> All kind of beast he did prepare
> With fowlis fleeting in the air.—
> When heaven and earth and their contents
> Were endit, with their ornaments,
> Then, last of all, the lord began ,
> Of most vile earth to make the man :
> Not of the lillie or the rose,
> Nor cyper-tree, as I suppose
> Neither of gold, nor precious stones,
> Of earth he made flesh, blood, and bones ;
> To that intent he made him thus,
> That man should nocth be glorius,
> And in himself no thing should see
> But matter of humility."

BARCLAY.—The principal work of Alexander Barclay, is a satïrical allegorical poem entitled the *Ship of Fools,* a translation from the German of Sebastian Brandt. Under the allegory of a Ship freighted with Fools of all kinds, the poet ridicules the prevalent vices and follies of the times. The following speech of Pleasure is extracted from this poem.

> " All my vesture is of gold pure,
> My gay chaplet with stones set,
> With couverture of fine azure,
> In silver net my hair upknet,
> Soft silke between, lest it might fret ;
> My purple pall overcovereth all.
> Clear as cristall, no thing egall—
> With harp in hand, alway I stande,
> Passing eche houre, in sweet pleasure ;
> A wanton band, of every land,
> Are in my toure, me in honour.
> Some of valour, some bare and poor ;
> Kinges in their pride sit by my side :
> Every fresh flower, of sweet odonre,
> To them I provide, that with me bide
> Whoe'er they be, that follow me,
> And gladly flee to my standard,
> They shall be free, nor sick, nor see
> Adversitie, and pains hard."

WYATT.—This poet's writings consist chiefly of Songs and Sonnets, after the style of Petrarch, and possess the same faults as well as the same excellencies of the Italian poet. Wyatt was the first polished satirist in English literature. The great fault of his writing is that his true feelings are often disguised by affectation, yet there are often to be found in his poems many passages of real feeling. In the lines *To the Lute,* in which *The lover complaineth of the unkindness of his love,* there is a great degree of true lyric sweetness.

> "My Lute, awake, perform the last
> Labour that thou and I shall wast :
> And end that I have now begun
> And when this song is sung and past,
> My lute be still for I have done.
>
> As to be heard where ear is none,
> As lead to grave in marble stone,
> My song may pierce her heart as soon !
> Should we then sigh, or sing, or moan,
> No, no, my lute, for I have done.

May chance thee lie withered and old,
In winter nights that are so cold,
Plaining in vain unto the moon :
Thy wishes then dare not be told!
Care then who list, for I have done.

Now cease, my lute, this is the last,
Labour that thou and I shall waste,
And ended is that we begun,
Now is this song both sung and past,
My lute be still for I have done."

SURREY.—The Earl of Surrey was a writer of the same style with Wyatt, his poetry is chiefly amorous, and written upon the models of Dante, Petrarch, Boccaccio, and Ariosto. Surrey may be regarded as the first English classical poet for justness of thought, correctness of style, and purity of expression. He was the first who introduced blank verse into our English poetry, and his versification differs considerably from that of his predecessors. Both in his elegance of sentiment, and in his numbers, he is far superior to Wyatt. An excellent instance of his poetry, and his power of representing rural imagery, is seen in a description of Spring, wherein each thing renews save only the lover.

"The sweet season that bud and bloom forth brings,
With green had clad the hill, and trimmed the vale;
The nightingale with feathers new she sings;
The turtle to her mate hath told her tale;
Summer is come, for every spray now springs,
The hart hath hung his old head on the pale;
The buck in brake his winter coat he flings;
The fishes fleet with new repaired scale;
The adder all her slough away she flings;
The swift swallow pursueth the flies small;
The busy bee her honey how she minges;
Winter is worn that was the flowers bale.

And thus I see among these pleasant things
Each care decays, and yet my sorrow springs."

VAUX.—Warton places the date of this poet after Wyatt and Surrey. There are numbers of his poems in the "*Paradise of Dainty Devises*," a work which appeared in the reign of Elizabeth, and comprised a collection of poems, many of considerable genius, which might otherwise never have reached the present age. The poems of Vaux possess all the smoothness and facility of style for which the poetry at this age was so distinguished. The following verses on the *Instability of Youth*, extracted from the "Paradise of Dainty Devises," is a fair specimen of his poetry.

"When I look back, and in myself behold
The wandering ways that youth could not descry,
And mark the fearful course that youth did hold
And mete in mind each step youth strayed awry;
My knees I bow, and from my heart I call,
O Lord, forget these sins and follies all.

For now I see how void youth is of skill,
I also see his prime-time and his end;
I do confess my faults and all my ill,
And sorrow sore for that I did offend;
And with a mind repentant of all crimes,
Pardon I ask for youth ten thousand times.

Thou, that didst grant the wise king his request,
Thou, that in whale the prophet didst preserve,
Thou, that forgavest the woundings of my breast,
Thou, that didst save the thief in state to starve;
Thou only God, the giver of all grace,
Wipe out of mind the path of youth's vain race.

Thou, that by power to life didst raise the dead,
Thou, that of grace, restord'st the blind to sight,
Thou, that for love thy life and love outbled,
Thou, that of favour mad'st the lame go right,
Thou, that canst heal and help in all essays,
Forgive the guilt that grew in youth's vain ways."

TUSSER.—This poet may be mentioned as one of the earliest of our didactic poets. He was the writer of the poem, *A Hundred good points of Husbandry*, which was later enlarged and published under the title of *Five Hundred Points of Good Husbandry, united to as many of Good Housewifery*. Warton speaks of it as "one of the finest poems of antiquity." He says "This old English georgic has much more of the simplicity of Hesiod, than the elegance of

Virgil ; and a modern reader would suspect, that many of its salutary maxims originally decorated the margins, and illustrated the calenders of an ancient almanack. It is without invocations, digressions, and descriptions : no pleasing pictures of rural imagery are drawn from meadows covered with flocks, and fields waving with corn, nor are Pan and Ceres once named. Yet it is valuable as a genuine picture of the agriculture, the rural arts, and the domestic economy and customs of our industrious ancestors." A specimen is to be seen in the following verses, which contain directions for cultivating a hop garden.

> "Whom fancy persuadeth, among other crops,
> To have for his spreading, sufficient for hops,
> Must willingly follow, of choices to choose,
> Such lessons approved, as skilful do use.
>
> Ground gravelly, or sandy, and mixed with clay,
> Is naughty for hops, any manner of way ;
> Or if it be mingled with rubbish and stone,
> For dryness and barrenness let it alone.
>
> Choose soil for the hop of the rottenest mould,
> Well dunged and wrought, as a garden-plot should ;
> Not far from the water, but not overflown :
> This lesson well noted is meet to be known.
>
> The sun in the south, or else southly and west,
> Is good to the hop, and a welcome guest ;
> But wind in the north, or else northly east,
> To the hop, is as ill as a fray in a feast.
>
> Meet plot for a hop-yard, once found as is told,
> Make thereof account, as of jewel of gold :
> Now dig it and leave it, the sun for to burn,
> And afterward fence it, to serve for that turn.
>
> The hop for his profit I thus do exalt :
> It strengtheneth drink, and it favoureth malt :
> And being well brewed, long kept it will last,
> And drawing abide—if ye draw not too fast."

EDWARDES.—Richard Edwardes was one of the chief writers and framers of "The Paradise of Dainty Devises," a work published in 1578. He is classed amongst the most accomplished men of that age, and was one of the earliest dramatic writers, after the reform of the stage. The following song, will afford an example of the easy style in which he wrote.

"Where griping griefs the heart would wound
   And doleful dumps* the mind oppress,   ·
There music with her silver sound   .
   With speed is wont to send redress :
Of troubled minds, in every sore,
Sweet music hath a salve in store.

The Gods by music have their praise ;
   The life, the soul therein doth joy :
For, as the Roman poet says,
   In seas, where pirates would destroy,
A dolphin saved from death most sharp
Arion playing on his harp.

O heavenly gift, that rules the mind,
   Even as the stern doth rule the ship !
O music, whom the Gods assigned
   To comfort man, whom cares would nip !
Since thou both man and beast doth move
What beast is he, will thee disprove?"

CHAPTER XLI.

MINOR POETS OF THE ELIZABETHAN ERA.

VERE.—The poems of this writer are to be found scattered
amongst various " collections."   He is a fair example of the minor
poets of the age he lived in, although his works are now entirely
neglected.   One of the most graceful of his poems is that called
Fancy and Desire.

"Come hither, shepherd's swain :
   'Sir, what do you require ?'
I pray thee, show to me thy name,
   'My name is Fond Desire.'

When wert thou born, Desire ?
   'In pomp and prime of May.'
By whom, sweet boy, wert thou begot ?
   'By fond Conceit men say.'

Tell me who was thy nurse ?
   'Fresh Youth is surged joy.'
What was thy meet and daily food ?
   'Sad sighs with great annoy.'

What hadst thou then to drink ?
   'Unsavoury lovers tears.'
What cradle wert thou rocked in ?
   'In hope devoid of fears.'

＾ Sad thoughts.

Doth either time or age
  Bring him unto decay?
'No, no, Desire both lives and dies
  Ten thousand times a day.'

Then, fond Desire, farewell,
  Thou art no mate for me;
I should be loth, methinks, to dwell
  With such a one as thee."

GASCOIGNE.—George Gascoigne obtained great popularity at this period for his narrative and lyric poetry. He also obtained great celebrity as a satirist in which kind of writing he shows remarkable art. Some of his works exhibit great genius. His most important poem, is the *Steel Glass*, a declamation against the vices and follies of his time. It is one of the earliest examples of blank verse; and contains many noble thoughts, conveyed in an easy and graceful style. The richest fancy, however, is shown in some of his minor compositions, of which the following is one.

THE ARRAIGNMENT OF A LOVER.

" At Beauty's bar as I did stand,
When false suspect accused me,
George (quoth the Judge) hold up thy hand,
Thou art arraigned of Flattery:
Tell therefore how thou wilt be tried:
Whose judgment here wilt thou abide?

My Lord (quoth I) this Lady here,
Whom I esteem among the rest,
Doth know my guilt if any were:
Wherefore her doom shall please me best.
Let her be Judge and Juror both,
To try me guiltless by mine oath.

Quoth Beauty, no, it fitteth not
A Prince herself to judge the cause:

Will is our Justice well you wot,
Appointed to discuss our Laws :
If you will guiltless seem to go,
God and your country quit you so.

The Craft the crier call'd a quest,
Of whom was Falsehood foremost feere,
A pack of pickethankes were the rest,
Which came false witness for to bear,
The Jury such, the Judge unjust,
Sentence was said I should be trust.

Jealous the jailer bound me fast,
To hear the verdict of the bill,
George (quoth the Judge) now thou art cast,
Thou must go to heavy hill.
And there be hang'd all by the head,
God rest thy soul when thou art dead.

Down fell I then upon my knee,
All flat before Dame Beauty's face,
And cried, good Lady pardon me,
Which here appeal unto your grace,
You know if I have been untrue,
It was in too much praising you.

And though this Judge do make such haste,
To shed with shame my guiltless blood :
Yet let your pity first be placed,
To save the man that meant you good,
So shall you show yourself a Pucen,
And I may be your servant seen.

(Quoth Beauty) well : because I guess,
What thou dost mean henceforth to be,
Although thy faults deserve no less,
Than Justice here hath judged thee,
Wilt thou be bound to stint all strife,
And be true prisoner all thy life?

Yea Madame (quoth I) that I shall,
Lo Faith and Truth my sureties :
Why then (quoth she) come when I call,
I ask no better warranties.
Thus am I Beauty's bounden thrall,
At her command when she doth call."

TURBERVILLE.—Turberville's writings are inferior to those of Gascoigne in point of invention. He frequently employed a peculiar modification of the old English ballad stanza, which was extremely fashionable at that period, namely, instead of making the third line equal to the first in having six syllables, it contained eight. An

might have done, had circumstances enabled him to devote it to the energies of his capacious mind. He was styled by Spenser the " summer nightingale." The *Shepherd's description of Love*, from which the following verses are extracted, is a beautiful little poem.

MILIBEUS.

"Shepherd, what's Love, I pray thee tell'?

FAUSTUS.

It is that fountain, and that well,
Where pleasure and repentance dwell :
It is, perhaps, that saucing bell,
   That tolls all into heaven or hell :
   And this is Love, as I heard tell.

MILIBEUS.

Yet what is Love, I prithee say?

FAUSTUS.

It is a work on holy-day,
It is December match'd with May,
When lusty bloods in fresh array
   Hear ten months after of the play :
   And this is Love, as I hear say.

MILIBEUS.

Yet what is Love, good Shepherd saine?

FAUSTUS.

It is a sun-shine mix'd with rain,
It is a tooth-ache ; or like pain ;
It is a game, where none doth gain.
   The lass saith no, and would full fain :
   And this is Love, as I hear saine.

u

<blockquote>
MILIBEUS.
Yet, Shepherd, what is Love, I pray ?
FAUSTUS.
It is a yea, it is a nay,
A pretty kind of sporting fray,
It is a thing will soon away ;
   Then Nymphs take 'vantage while ye may ;
   And this is Love, as I hear say."
</blockquote>

LYLY.—John Lyly may be mentioned as a poet of this date. He was the author of several plays, in some parts of which there may be found great wit and humour. The following passage is from *Alexander and Campaspe*, one of the best remembered of his plays.

<blockquote>
"Cupid and my Campaspe played
At cards for kisses ; Cupid paid :
He stakes his quiver, bow and arrows,
His mother's doves, and team of sparrows ;
Loses then too ; then down he throws
The coral of his lip, the rose
Growing on's cheeks (but none knows how),
With these, the crystal of his brow,
And then the dimple of his chin.
But these did my Campaspe win.
At last he set her both his eyes,
She won, and Cupid blind did rise.
   O Love ! has she done this to thee ?
   What shall, alas, become of me ?"
</blockquote>

SYDNEY.—Sir Philip Sydney's contributions to English poetry consist chiefly of a collection of Sonnets. Both in the sonnets and in his other poems, there is a sweetness and exquisite softness tinted with a refined elegance, which is to be found in no other poet of his time. The former indeed are exquisite ; take for instance the two following :—

<blockquote>
"With how sad steps, O Moon, thou climb'st the skies !
   How silently, and with how wan a face !
   What ! may it be, that ev'n in heav'nly place
That busy archer his sharp arrows tries ?
   Sure, if that long-with-love-acquainted eyes
Can judge of love, thou feel'st a lover's case ;
   I read it in thy looks, thy languish grace
To me, that feel the like, thy state descries.
   Then, ev'n of fellowship, O moon, tell me,
Is constant love deem'd there but want of wit ?
   Are beauties there as proud as here they be ?
Do they above love to be lov'd, and yet
   Those lovers scorn, whom that love doth possess ?
   Do they call virtue their ungratefulness ?"
</blockquote>

Move not thy heavy grace, thou shalt in me,
Livelier than elsewhere, Stella's image see."

BROOKE.—Lord Brooke was the writer of several poems and tragedies, upon the latter of which Southey says that Dryden formed his tragic style. His poems are a *Treatise on Human Learning*, a *Treatise of Wars*, a *Treatise of Monarchy*, a *Treatise of Religion*, and an *Inquisition upon Fame and Fortune*. His two tragedies were entitled *Alaham* and *Mustapha*. The following passage is selected from his works, and is a beautiful example of his sacred poetry.

"Zion lies waste, and thy Jerusalem,
O Lord, is fall'n to utter desolation ;
Against thy prophets and thy holy men,
The Sin hath wrought a fatal combination,
Profaned thy name, thy worship overthrown,
And made Thee, living Lord, a God unknown.

Thy powerful laws, thy wonders of creation,
Thy Word Incarnate, glorious heaven, dark hell,
Lie shadow'd under man's degeneration,
Thy Christ still crucified for doing well :
Impiety, O Lord, sits on thy throne,
Which makes Thee, living Light, a God unknown.

Man's superstition doth thy truth entomb,
His atheism again her pomp defaceth ;
Sin earthly. sensual, devilish, doth consume
Thy seen Church. and thy unseen Church disgraceth;
There lives no truth with them that seem thine own,
Which makes Thee, living Lord, a God unknown."

LODGE.—Thomas Lodge is remembered chiefly as a dramatic poet. Of his poems most of them are contained in the "English Helicon," published in 1600. His principal works are *Promos and Cassandra*, and *Glaucus and Scilla*. The following verses are extracted from his poems.

"Sweet, solitary life, thou true repose,
Wherein the wise·contemplate heaven aright,
In thee no dread of war or worldly foes,
In thee no pomp seduceth mortal sight,
In thee no wanton ears to win with words,
Nor lurking toys which city-life affords.

At peep of day, when, in her crimson pride,
The morn bespreads with roses all the way,
When Phœbus coach, with radiant course, must glide,
The hermit bends his humble knees to pray,
Blessing that God, whose bounty doth bestow
Such beauties on the earthly things below.

Whether, with solace tripping on the trees,
He sees the citizens of forest sport ;
Or, midst the wither'd oak beholds the bees
Intend their labours with a kind consort ;
Down drop his tears, to think how they agree,
While men alone with hate inflamed be."

SOUTHWELL.—This poet may be considered as one of the best of the minor poets of this age. His works breathe a spirit of religious resignation, and are marked by great beauty of thought and expression. The leading themes of all his poems, are the uncertainty of life, the emptiness of human pleasures, the consolations of religion and anticipations of future glory. There is an earnestness in his poems, and an impassioned energy. His longest poem is *St. Peter's Complaint*, but the most poetry, and the deepest cultivation is found in his shorter compositions. There is no doubt that Southwell possessed a genius of a very rare order ; a genius worthy of the high and noble themes on which he wrote. The following passage, *Love's servile lot*, is an excellent specimen of his minor poems.

"Love, mistress is of many minds
    Yet few know whom they serve ;
They reckon least how little Love
    Their service doth deserve.

The will she robbeth from the wit,
    The sense from reason's lore ;
She is delightful in the rind,
    Corrupted in the core.

She shroudeth vice in virtue's veil,
    Pretending good in ill ;
She offereth joy, affordeth grief,
    A kiss where she doth kill.

A honey-shower rains from her lips,
    Sweet lights shine in her face;
She had the blush of virgin mind,
    The mind of viper's race.

*   *   *   *

May never was the month of love,
    For May is full of flowers;
But rather April, wet by kind,
    For love is full of showers.

Like winter rose and summer ice
    Her joys are still untimely;
Before her Hope, behind remorse
    Fair first, in fine unseemly.

Her house is Sloth, her door Deceit,
    And slippery Hope her stairs;
Unbashful boldness bids her guests,
    And every vice repairs.

Her diet is of such delights
    As please till they be past;
But when the poison kills the heart
    That did entice the taste.

Her sleep in sin doth end in wrath,
    Remorse rings her awake;
Death calls her up, Shame drives her out,
    Despairs her upshot make.

Plow not the seas, sow not the sands,
    Leave off your idle pain;
Seek other mistress for your minds,
    Love's service is in vain."

DANIEL.—Daniel's poems are less interesting, as they relate only to the persons and circumstances of the age at which he lived. Yet many of his pieces rise in style to a high degree of excellence. His diction also is easy, and the language natural; and there is a fine weighty and philosophic vein flowing through them all. There is nothing of sublimity in his writings, but much pathos. One of the finest specimens is his address to the Countess of Cumberland, and it is one of the finest effusions of meditative thought in the English language.

"He that of such hath built his mind,
    And rear'd the dwelling of his thoughts so strong,
    As neither fear nor hope can shake the frame
    Of his resolved pow'rs, nor all the wind
    Of vanity or malice pierce to wrong

His settled peace, or to disturb the same;
What a fair seat hath he, from whence he may
The boundless wastes and wilds of man survey.
And with how free an eye doth he look down
Upon these lower regions of turmoil,
Where all the storms of passions mainly beat
On flesh and blood, where honour, pow'r, renown,
Are only gay afflictions, golden toil,
Where greatness stands upon as feeble feet
As frailty doth, and only great doth seem
To little minds, who do it so esteem.
    He sees the face of right t' appear as manifold
As are the passions of uncertain man,
Who puts in all colours, all attires,
To serve his ends and make his courses hold :
He sees, that let deceit work what it can,
Plot and contrive base ways to high desires,
That the all-guiding Providence doth yet
All disappoint, and mocks this smoke of wit.
    Nor is he mov'd with all the thunder-cracks
Of tyrant's threats, or with the surly brow
Of Power, that proudly sits on other's crimes,
Charg'd with more crying sins then those he checks ;
The storms of sad confusion, that may grow
Up in the present, for the coming times,
Appal not him, that hath no side at all
But of himself, and knows the worst can fall.
    Although his heart so near to earth,
Cannot but pity the perplexed state
Of troublous and distress mortality,
That thus make way unto the ugly birth
Of their own sorrows, and do still beget
Affliction upon imbecility,
Yet seeing thus the course of things must run,
He looks thereon, not strange ; but as foredone,
    And whilst distraught ambition compasses
And is encompass'd, whil'st as craft deceives
And is deceived, whil'st man doth ransack man,
And builds on blood, and rises by distress,
And th' inheritance of desolation leaves
To great expecting hopes, he looks thereon
As from the shore of peace with unwet eye,
And bears no venture in impiety.
Thus, Madame, fares that man that hath prepared
A rest for his desires, and sees all things
Beneath him, and hath learn'd this book of man,
Full of the notes of frailty, and compar'd
The best of glory with her sufferings,
By whom I see you labour all you can
To plant your heart, and set your thoughts as near
His glorious mansion as your powers can bear."

of a poet, enlivening his work as he goes on by the richest profusion of allegory and personification. A fine example may be seen in his vivacious description of the hunting of the hart in the forest of Arden in Warwickshire, from the Polyolbion.

"————Now, when the heit doth hear
The often-bellowing hounds to vent his secret lair,
In rousing rusheth out, and through the brakes doth drive
As though by the roots the bushes he would rive.
And though the cumbrous thicks, as fearfully he makes,
He with his branched head the tender saplings shakes,
That, sprinkling their moist pearl, do seem for him to weep
When after goes the cry, with yellings loud and deep,
That all the forest rings and every neighbouring place;
And there is not a hound but falleth to the chase.
Rechating with his horn, which then the hunter cheers,
Whilst still the lusty stag his high-palm'd head upbears
His body showing state, with unbent knees upright,
Expressing from all beasts, his courage in his flight.
But when th' approaching foes still following he perceives,
That he his speed must trust, his usual walk he leaves ;
And o'er a champain flies : which then the assembly find,
Each follows, as his horse were footed with the wind.
But being then imbost, the noble stately deer,
When he hath gotten ground, (the kennel cast arrear,)
Doth beat the brooks and ponds for sweet refreshing soil ;
That serving not, then proves if he his scent can foil,
And makes among the herds and flocks of shag-wool'd sheep,
Them frighting from the guard of those who had their keep.
But when as all his shifts his safety still denies,
Put quite out of his walk, the ways and fallows tries,
Whom when the ploughman meets, his teem he letteth stand,
T' assail him with his goad : so with his hook in hand
The shepherd him pursues, and to his dog doth hollow ;
When, with tempestuous speed, the hounds and huntsman follow ;
Until the noble deer, through toil bereaved of strength,
His long and sinewy legs then failing him at length,
The villages attempts, enraged, not giving way

To anything he meets now at his sad decay.
The cruel rav'nous hounds and bloody hunters near,
This noblest beast of chase, that vainly doth but fear,
Some bank or quickset finds; to which his haunch opposed,
He turns upon his foes, that soon have him enclosed.
The churlish-throated hounds then holding him at bay,
And as their cruel fangs on his harsh skin they lay,
With his sharp-pointed head he dealeth deadly wounds.
The hunter coming in to help his wearied hounds,
He desp'rately assails ; until, oppress'd by force,
He now the mourner is to his own dying corse."

SYLVESTER.—Joshua Sylvester who was styled in his day the
"silver tongued,' was the translator of *The Divine Weeks and
Works,* of the French Poet *Du Bartas,* which ran through seven
editions. In an Essay published by Mr. Dunster, it is said to have
been one of Milton's early favorites. He wrote other small poems,
but of little merit. The following verses will be a sufficent speci-
men of his works.

"Some word's allusion is no certain ground
Whereon a lasting monument to found :
Since fairest rivers, mountains strangely steep,
And largest seas, never so vast and deep,
(Though self-eternal, resting still the same)
Through sundry chances often change their name :
Since it befalls not always, that his seed
Who built a town, doth in the same succeed :
And (to conclude) since under heaven, no race
Perpetually possesses any place :
But, as all tenants at the high Lord's will,
We hold a field, a forest, or a hill ;
And (as when wind the angry ocean moves)
Wave hunteth wave, and billow billow shoves ;
So do all nations justle each the other,
And so one people doth pursue another ;
And scarce the second hath a first un-housed ;
Before a third him thence again have roused.

WOTTON.—The poetical works of Sir Henry Wotton, are very
small; undoubtedly he neither anticipated nor coveted fame for his
poetry ; he wrote only from impulse of feeling. What he has left
are however very fine specimens of poetry, and touch the heart
more than any of the more artificial works of his contemporaries.
His *Lines to the Queen of Bohemia,* form one of the finest speci-
mens of poetry in our language.

"You meaner beauties of the night,
That poorly satisfy our eyes
More by your number, than your light,
You common people of the skies ;
    What are you when the sun shall rise ?

You curious chaunters of the wood,
That warble forth dame Nature's lays,
Thinking your passions understood
By your weak accents ; what's your praise
    When Philomel her voice shall raise ?

You violets, that first appear,
By your pure purple mantles known,
Like the proud virgins of the year,
As if the spring were all your own ;
    What are you when the rose is blown ?

So, when my mistress shall be seen
In sweetness of her looks and mind,
By virtue first, then choice a queen,
Tell me, if she were and design'd
    Th' eclipse and glory of her kind ?"

DONNE.—This poet was one of the most voluminous writers of his time. His writings consist of love-verses, epigrams, elegies, but principally satires, by which he is best known. He possessed the highest requisites for poetry, but they were misled by learning and false taste into such extravagancies as to entirely injure their better qualities : in his incessant search after epigrammatic turns of thought, Donne sacrificed both reason, taste, and propriety ; he made the natural subordinate to the artificial, and though he sometimes used natural language and imagery and passion, it was only by chance. His thoughts are crowded one upon another without skill or effect ; and although his works contain numberless beauties, they are obscured by the many deformities with which they are mingled. His versification is harsh and rugged, and utterly tuneless. Many examples might be given, however, to show that all the compositions of this poet were not uncouth and careless ; while there are indeed some smooth even to elegance. His description of the Storm is remarkably fine :—

"The south and west winds join'd, and, as they blew,
Waves like a rolling trench before him threw.
Sooner than you read this line did the gale,
Like shot, not fear'd till felt, our sails assail;

And what at first was call'd a gust, the same
Hath now a storm's, anon a tempest's name.
Jonas ! I pity thee, and curse those men
Who, when the storm's rag'd most, did wake thee then.
Sleep is pain's easiest salve, and doth fulfil
All offices of death except to kill.
But when I wak'd, I saw that I saw not ;
I and the sun, which should teach me, had forgot.
East, west, day, night ; and I could only say,
If the world has lasted, now it had been day.
Thousands our noises were, yet we 'mongst all
Could none by his right name but thunder call.
Lightning was all our light, and it rain'd more
Than if the sun had drunk the sea before.
Some coffin'd in their cabins lie, equally
Griev'd that they are not dead, and yet must die ;
And as sin-burdened souls from grave will creep
At the last day, some forth their cabins peep,
And, tremblingly, ask what news, and do hear so ;
As jealous husbands, what they would not know.
Some, sitting on the hatches, would seem there,
With hideous gazing, to fear away Fear :
There note they the ship's sicknesses, the mast
Shak'd with an ague, and the hold and waist
With a salt dropsy clogg'd, and our tacklings
Snapping, like too high-stretched treble strings,
And from our totter'd sails rags drop down so
As from one hang'd in chains a year ago :
Even our ordinance, plac'd for our defence,
Strive to break loose, and 'scape away from thence :
Pumping hath tir'd our men, and what's the gain?
Seas into seas thrown we suck in again;
Hearing hath deaf'd our sailors ; and if they
Knew how to hear, there's none knows what to say.
Compar'd to these storms, death is but a calm,
Hell somewhat lightsome, the Bermud a calm.
Darkness, Light's eldest brother, his birth-right
Claim'd o'er this world, and to heaven hath chas'd light.
All things are one, and that one none can be,
Since all forms uniform deformity .
Doth cover ; so that we, except God say
Another fight, shall have no more day :
So violent, yet long these furies be,
That though thine absence serve me I wish not thee."

DAVIES.—In the works of this poet there is unusual **merit and** originality, although the opposite character of his two principal works, excites almost a feeling of ludicrous paradox, the subject of one being the *Immortality of the Soul*, and that of the other *Orchestra, a Poem on Dancing.* The language of his works is pure,

Davies has moulded his thoughts, and conveyed the most profound speculations in the easiest possible language. It is an able and skilful piece of reasoning, frequently adorned with rich and agreeable imagery, but is more readable for its philosophy than its poetry. Take for instance the section, in which the poet reasons upon the vegetative power of the soul.

> "Her quick'ning power in ev'ry living part,
>   Doth as a nurse, or as a mother serve ;
> And doth employ her œconomic art,
>   And busy care, her household to preserve.
>
> Here she attracts, and there she doth attain ;
>   There she decocts, and doth the food prepare ;
> There she distributes it to ev'ry vein,
>   There she expels what she may fitly spare.
>
> This pow'r to Martha may compared be,
>   Who busy was, the household things to do :
> Or to a Dryas, living in a tree :
>   For e'en to trees this pow'r is proper too.
>
> And though the Soul may not this pow'r extend,
>   Out of the Body, but still use it there ;
> She hath a power which she abroad doth send,
>   Which views and searcheth all things ev'rywhere. '

In the other poem, *The Orchestra*, the poet has ingeniously traced the dancing movements throughout all nature, in the following peculiarly constructed stanza.

> " Behold the world how it is whirled round,
>   And for it is so whirl'd, is named so ;
> In whose large volume many rules are found
>   Of this new art, which it doth fairly show :
>   For your quick eyes in wand'ring to and fro
>   From East to West, on no one thing can glance,
>   But if you mark it well, it seems to dance. ·
>
> First you see fix'd in this huge mirror blue
> Of trembling lights, a number numberless,
> Fix'd they are naiu'd, but with a name untrue,

For they all move, and in a dance express
That great long year that doth contain no less
　　Than threescore hundreds of those years in all,
　　Which the sun makes with his course natural.

　　*　　*　　*　　*　　*

Who doth not see the measures of the moon,
　　Which thirteen times she danceth ev'ry year?
And ends her pavin, thirteen times as soon
As doth her brother, of whose golden hair
She borroweth part and proudly doth it wear:
　　Then doth she coyly turn her face aside,
　　That half her cheek is scarce sometimes descried.

　　*　　*　　*　　*　　*

For when you breathe, the *air* in order moves,
　　Now in, now out, in time and measure true ;
And when you speak, so well she dancing loves,
That doubling oft, and oft redoubling new,
With thousand forms she doth herself endue :
　　For all the words that from your lips repair,
　　Are naught but tricks and turnings of the air.

Hence is her prattling daughter Echo born,
　　That dances to all voices she can hear :
There is no sound so harsh that she doth scorn,
Nor any time wherein she will forbear
The airy pavement with her feet to wear :
　　And yet her hearing sense is nothing quick,
　　For after time she endeth ev'ry trick."

HALL.—Joseph Hall was the first who wrote satire in English
verse with any degree of elegance or success.　There is more polish
in his satires, than in many of the compositions of this age ; and they
are full of animation, both in style and sentiment.　His characters
are strongly delineated, and contain much genuine humour.　In
some of these satires the vices and affectations of literature are
attacked, while others are of a more general and moral application.
They are worthy of the highest admiration for the vivacity of their
images, and the good sense which pervades them throughout.　One
of the best passages is the opening of the first satire in the Third
book, in which he contrasts ancient parsimony, with modern lux·
ury : it is both witty and elegant.

　　　"Time was, and that was term'd the time of gold,
　　　When world and time were young, that now are old :
　　　When quiet Saturn sway'd the mace of lead,
　　　And pride was yet unborn, and yet unbred.

Rhapsody," a collection of poetry, of which the first edition appeared
in 1602.

"It chanc'd of late a shepherd swain,
  That went to seek his straying sheep,
Within a thicket on a plain
  Espied a dainty Nymph asleep.

Her golden hair o'erspread her face ;
  Her careless arms abroad were cast ;
Her quiver had her pillow's place :
  Her breast lay bare to every blast.

The shepherd stood, and gaz'd his fill ;
  Nought durst he do ; nought durst he say ;
Whilst chance, or else perhaps his will,
  Did guide the God of Love that way.

The crafty boy that sees her sleep,
  Whom, if she wak'd, he durst not see ;
Behind her closely seeks to creep,
  Before her nap should ended be.

There come, he steals her shafts away,
  And puts his own into their place ;
Nor dares he any longer stay,
  But, ere she wakes, hies thence apace.

Scarce was he gone, but she awakes,
  And spies the shepherd standing by :

Her bended bow in haste she takes,
  And at the simple swain lets fly.

Forth flew the shaft, and pierc'd his heart,
  That to the ground he fell with pain :
Yet up again forthwith did start,
  And to the Nymph he ran amain.

Amayed to see so strange a sight,
  She shot and shot but all in vain ;
The more his wounds, the more his might,
  Love yielded strength amidst his pain.

Her angry eyes were great with tears,
  She blames her hand, she blames her skill ;
The bluntness of her shafts she fears,
  And try them on herself she will."

SANDYS.—The chief poetical work of this writer was a translation of Ovid's Metamorphoses. Besides this, he wrote *Paraphrases of the Psalms, Ecclesiastes, &c.,* the former of which are incomparably the most poetical in the English language. The following extracted as an example.

PSALM XLV.

"With heart divine-inspired, I sing
  A panegyrick to the King ;
High raptures in a numerous style,
I with a ready pen compile—
Much fairer than our human race ;
Whose lips like fountains flow with grace :
For this the Lord thy soul shall bless
With everlasting happiness.
Gird, O most Mighty, on thy thigh
Thy sword of awe and majesty :
In triumph, arm'd with truth ride on ;
By clemency and justice drawn :
No mortal vigour shall withstand
The fury of thy dreadful hand ;
Thy piercing arrows in the King's
Opposers' hearts shall dye their wings.
Thy throne no waste of time decays ;
Thy sceptre sacred justice sways :
Thou virtue lov'st ; but hast abhorr'd
Deformed vice ; for this the Lord
Hath thee alone preferr'd, and shed
The oil of joy upon thy head.
Thy garments, which in grace excel,
Of aloes, myrrh, and cassia smell ;
Brought from the ivory palaces ;
Which more than other odours please.

King's daughters, to augment thy state
Among the noble damsels wait ;
The queen enthroned on thy right hand,
Adorn'd with Ophyr's golden sand.
Hark, daughter, and by me be taught ;
Thy country banish from thy thought,
.Thy house and family forget,
His joy, upon thy beauty set.
He is thy Lord ; oh bow before,
And Him eternally adore !"

ALEXANDER.—William Alexander was another of the Scotch poets of this date. His chief works are *Doomes-Day*, and *Aurora*. There are some excellent passages to be found in these poems, and the versification of both is excellent. The following is extracted from the *Doomes-Day*.

"The stately Heavens which glory doth array,
Are mirrors of God's admirable might ;
There, whence forth spreads the night, forth springs the day,
He fix'd the fountains of this temporal light,
Where stately stars installed, some stand, some stray,
All sparks of his great power (though small yet bright,)
By what none utter can, no, not conceive,
All of his greatness, shadows may perceive.

* * * * *

What ebbs, flows, swells, and sinks, who firm doth keep?
Whilst floods from th' earth burst in abundance out
As she her brood did wash, or for them weep :
Who, (having life) what dead things prove, dare doubt
Who first did found the dungeons of the deep?
But one in all, o'erall, above, about :
The floods for our delight, first calm were set,
But storm and roar, since men did God forget.

Who parts the swelling spouts that sift the rain?
Who reins the winds, the waters doth empale?
Who frowns in storms, then smiles in calms again,
And doth dispense the treasures of the hail?
Whose bow doth bended in the clouds remain?
Whose darts (dread thunder-bolts) make men look pale?
Even thus these things to show his power aspire,
As shadows do the Sun, as smoke doth fire.

God visibly invisible who reigns,
Soul of all souls, whose light each light directs,
All first did freely make, and still maintains,
The greatest rules, the meanest not neglects ;
Fore-knows the end of all that he ordains,
His will each cause, each cause breeds fit effects,

"Who did make all, all thus could only lead,
    None could make all, but who was never made."

OVERBURY.—Sir Thomas Overbury is the writer of two didactic
poems, *The Wife,* and *The Choice of a Wife,* and other small pieces
in prose and verse. The following epitaph which was written for
himself is very beautiful.

"Now, measured out my days, 'tis here I rest;
    That is my body, but my soul, his guest,
    Is hence ascended whither neither time,
    Nor faith, nor hope, but only love can climb;
    Where being now enlighten'd she doth know
    The truth of all things which are talk'd below;
    Only this dust shall here in pawn remain,
    That when the world dissolves she'll come again."

CORBET.—Richard Corbet's poems are of a miscellaneous des-
cription, consisting chiefly of elegy, satire, and song. There is a
gaiety and lightheartedness in all he wrote, and they everflow with
feeling and humour. The following is a specimen of his poetry:—

"What I shall leave thee none can tell,
    But all shall say I wish thee well:
    I wish thee, Vin, before all wealth,
    Both bodily and ghostly health;
    Nor too much wealth, nor wit come to thee,
    So much of either may undo thee.
    I wish thee learning, not for show,
    Enough for to instruct, and know;
    Not such as gentlemen require
    To peate at table, or at fire.
    I wish thee all thy mother's graces,
    Thy father's fortunes, and his places.
    I wish thee friends, and one at court
    Not to build on, but support;
    To keep thee, not in doing many
    Oppressions, but from suffering any.
    I wish thee peace in all thy ways,
    Nor lazy nor contentious days;
    And when thy soul and body part,
    As innocent as now thou art."

FLETCHER.—Phineas Fletcher was the writer of one of those
long allegorical works, which were so fashionable at that period.
It was called the *Purple Island, or the Isle of Man,* a minute
description of the human body, with its anatomical details, follow-
ed by an equally searching delineation of the intellectual faculties.
The *Isle* represents the human body, with its bones, muscles,

"The broken Heavens dispart with fearful noise,
  And from the breach outshoots a sudden light :
Straight shrilly trumpets with loud sounding voice
  Give echoing summons to new bloody fight ; -
    Well knew the dragon that all-quelling blast,
    And soon perceived that day must be the last ;
Which shook his frighten'd heart, and all his troops aghast.

            *   *   *   *   *

  So up he rose upon his stretched sails
  Fearless expecting his approaching death ;
So up he arose, that the air starts and fails,
  And overpress'd, sinks his load beneath :
    So up he arose, as does a thunder cloud,
    Which all the earth with shadows black doth shroud :
So up he arose, and through the weary air he row'd.

  Now his Almighty Foe far off he spies ;
  Whose sun-like arms dazed the eclipsed day,
Confounding with their beams less glittering skies,
  Firing the air with more than heavenly ray ;
    Like thousand suns in one ; — such is their light,
    A subject only for immortal sprite ;
Which never can be seen, but by immortal sight.

  His armour all was dy'd in purple blood :
  (In purple blood of thousand rebel kings)
In vain their stubborn powers His arm withstood ;
  Their proud necks chain'd, He now in triumph brings.
    And breaks their spears, and cracks their traitor swords :
    Upon whose arms and thigh in golden words
Was fairly writ, 'The King of kings, and Lord of lords.'

  His snow-white steed was born of heavenly kind,
  Begot by Boreoas on the Thracian hills ;
More strong and speedy than his parent wind :
  And (which his foes with fear and horror fills)
    Out from his mouth a two-edged sword he darts :
    Whose sharpest steel the bone and marrow parts,
And with his keenest point unbreast the naked hearts.

                                                W

The Dragon wounded with his flaming brand
They take, and in strong bonds and fetters tie ;
Short was the fight, nor could he long withstand
Him, whose appearance in his victory.
So now he's bound in admantine chain :
He storms, he roars, he yells for high disdain
His net is broke, the fowl go free, the fowler ta'en.

Soon at this sight the knights revive again,
As fresh as when the flowers from winter tomb,
(When now the sun brings back his nearer wain.)
Peep out again from their fresh mother's womb :
The primrose lighted new ; her flame displays,
And frights the neighbour hedge with fiery rays ;
And all the world renew their mirth and sportive plays.

The prince, who saw his long imprisonment
Now end in never ending liberty ;
To meet the Victor from his castle went,
And falling down, clasping his royal knee,
Pours out deserved thanks in grateful praise,
But him the heavenly Saviour soon doth raise,
And bids him spend in joy his never-ending days."

FLETCHER.—Giles Fletcher, the brother of the former poe
the writer of the poem *Christ's Victory and Triumph,* written ;
the allegorical style of Spenser.   There is exhibited in it a fer'
of invention, and a rich store of fancy, worthy of the sublime
ject itself.   The style is both lofty and energetic, the descript
natural and graphic, and the construction of the verse graceful
harmonious.   The only fault is that he shows bad taste ir
selection of his thoughts, and has introduced among his sa
themes, characters from, and allusions to profane history, whic
upon the sense and bear us away from the solemn grandeur c
great theme.   The poem is divided into four parts, Christ's Vio
in Heaven ; Christ's Triumph on Earth ; Christ's Triumph
Death ; Christ's Triumph after Death ;—the first having refei
to the Incarnation ; the second to the Temptation ; the third t
Crucifixion ; and the fourth to the Resurrection.   The poem,
ever, amply compensates for all its defects   The following pa
may be quoted as the finest specimen of this poem.

" Say, Earth, why hast thou got thee new attire,

Answer me, Jordan, why thy crooked tide
So often wanders from this nearest way,
As though some other way thy stream would slide,
And fain salute the place where something lay,
And you sweet birds, that, shaded from the ray,
 Sit carolling, and piping grief away,
  The while the lambs to hear you dance and play,
Tell me, sweet birds, what is it you so fain would say?

Ye primroses, and purple violets,
Tell me, why blaze ye from your leafy bed,
And woo men's hands to rent you from your sets,
As though you would somewhere be carried,
With fresh perfumes, and velvets garnished?
 But ah ! I need not ask, 'tis surely so,
  You all would to your Saviour's triumph go,
There would ye all await, and humble homage do.

There should the earth herself with garlands new
And lovely flowers embellished adore :
Such roses never in her garland grew,
Such lillies never in her breast she wore,
Like beauty never yet did shine before :
 There should the Sun another Sun behold,
  From whence himself borrows his locks of gold,
That kindle Heaven and Earth with beauties manifold.

There might the violet, and primrose sweet,
Beams of more lively, and more lovely grace,
Arising from their beds of incense, meet ;
There should the swallow see new life embrace
Dead ashes, and the grave unseal his face,
 To let the living from his bowels creep,
  Unable longer his own dead to keep :
There Heaven and Earth should see their Lord awake from sleep.

  * * * * *

Hark how the floods clap their applauding hands,
The pleasant valleys singing for delight,
And wanton mountains dance about the lands,
The while the fields, struck with the heavenly light,
Let all their flowers a smiling at the sight ;
 The trees laugh with their blossoms, and the sound
  Of the triumph shout of praise, that crown'd
The flaming Lamb, breaking through Heaven hath passage found."

BEAUMONT,—Sir John Beaumont is the Author of *Bosworth Field*, written in the heroic couplet ; and other poems.   He was the elder brother of Beaumont the dramatist. The following beautiful lines upon his son exhibit all that could be said of the poetical genius of Beaumont.

> "Can I, who have for others oft compiled
> The songs of death, forget my sweetest child,
> Which, like a flower crush'd with a blast is dead,
> And ere full time hangs down his smiling head,
> Expecting with clear hope to live anew,
> Among the angels fed with heavenly dew ?
> We have this sign of joy, that many days,
> While on the earth his struggling spirit stays,
> The name of Jesus in his mouth contains
> His only food, his sleep, his ease from pains.
> O may that sound be rooted in my mind,
> Of which in him such strong effect I find.
> Dear Lord receive my son, whose winning love
> To me was like a friendship, far above
> The course of nature, or his tender age,
> Whose looks could all my better griefs assuage ;
> Let his pure soul ordain'd seven years to be
> In the frail body, which was part of me,
> Remain my pledge in Heaven, as sent to show,
> How to this port at every step I go."

DRUMMOND.—This poet's principal works are the *Flowers of Sion*, short pieces upon sacred subjects ; and a variety of songs and sonnets. The sonnets are the best : they are elegant and finished, and written in pure English, and there are several of them of great beauty. His thoughts are both naturally and gracefully expressed, and are remarkably free from the affectations so conspicuous in his contemporaries. The following are two specimens of his *Sonnets*.

> "A good that never satisfies the mind,
> A beauty fading like the April flow'rs,
> A sweet with floods of gall, that runs combin'd,
> A pleasure passing ere in thought made ours,
> A honour that more fickle is than wind,
> A glory at opinions frown that low'rs,
> A treasury which bankrupt time devours,
> A knowledge than grave ignorance more blind ;
> A vain delight our equals to command,
> A style of greatness, in effect a dream,
> A swelling thought of holding sea and land,
> A servile lot, deck'd with a pompous name ;
>   Are the strange ends we toil for here below.
>   Till wisest death makes us our errors know."

lengthened description of the pleasures that live with Freedom, describes the only consolation left to him—the companionship of the Muse. We quote as a specimen the following well-known passage.

> "As the sun doth oft exhale
> Vapours from each rotten vale;
> Poesy so sometimes drains,
> Gross conceits from muddy brains;
> Mists of envy, fogs of spite,
> Twixt men's judgments and her light:
> But so much her power may do,
> That she can dissolve them too.
> If thy verse do bravely tower,
> As she makes wing, she gets power;
> Yet the higher she doth soar,
> She's affronted still the more:
> Till she to the high'st hath past,
> Then she rests with Fame at last,
> Let nought therefore thee affright,
> But make forward in thy flight:
> For if I could match thy rhyme,
> To the very stars I'd climb.
> There begin again, and fly,
> Till I reach'd eternity.

But (alas) my muse is slow :
For thy page she flags too low ;
Yes, the more's her hapless fate,
Her short wings were clipt of late.
And poor I, her fortune rueing,
Am myself put up a muing.
But if I my cage can rid,
I'll fly where I never did.
And though for her sake I am crost,
Though my best hopes I have lost,
And knew she would make my trouble
Ten times more than ten times double :
I would love and keep her too,
Spite of all the world could do.
For though banish'd from my flocks,
And confin'd within these rocks,
Here I waste away the light,
And consume the sullen night,
She doth for my comfort stay,
And keeps many cares away.
Therefore thou best earthly bliss,
I will cherish thee for this."

CAREW.—This poet's works are chiefly short and amorous, and were greatly admired in their day. They are pre-eminently beautiful, compared to those of other poets of his style and age ; and he has been ranked amongst the earliest of those writers, who first bestowed grace and polish on our lyrical poetry. The masque, *Cælum Britannicum* is his most important work ; written in prose and poetry. In this poem, Mercury, Momus, Poverty, and Pleasure, and a vast concourse of attendants appear, and after having "spoken their speeches," are succeeded by Druids, Rivers, and Kingdoms, summoned by the Genius of Britain, to do homage to Royalty. Religion, Truth and Wisdom, and a host of virtues follow—and then pass, "leaving nothing but a serene sky." It was written by express command of Charles the First, in which, when it was performed he sustained a part. The following passage is a specimen of this work :—

"Bewitching Syren ! gilded rottenness !
Thou hast with cunning artifice display'd
Th' enamell'd out-side, and the honied verge
Of the fair cup where deadly poison lurks.
Within, a thousand Sorrows dance the round ;
And, like a shell, Pain circles thee without.

Yet thy Circean charms transform the world.
Captains that have resisted war and death, ·
Nations that over Fortune's have triumph'd,
Are by thy magic made effeminate :
Empires, that knew no limits but pole,
Have in thy meltomed lap melted away :
Thou wert the author of thy first excess
That drew this reformation on the Gods.
Canst thou then dream, those Powers, that from Heaven
Banish'd th' effect, while there enthrone the cause ?
To thy voluptuous den, fly Witch, from hence ;
There dwell, for ever drown'd in brutish sense."

BROWNE.—The principal work of this poet, and that to which
he owes his reputation, is the poem, *Brittannia's Pastorals.* It is
divided into ten songs, in which a variety of personages, real and
fictitious are introduced : it is built upon a dreamy but not a sys-
tematic adoration of Nature ; and has been said by a writer to
"resemble a piece of gorgeous tapestry, where the drawing is fine,
and the colours are gay and vivid, but in which there is a total
want of keeping, and an absence of harmony, both in design and
execution." A great defect in his writings, is that the descriptions
are often too extravagant, yet the reader who is willing to pass
over his defects, will find many of the highest beauties—beauties
perhaps unsurpassed by any author in the English language. His
poetry is sometimes full of the most intense fire; and the richest
imagination, while his versification is easy and harmonious, and
exhibits a complete mastery over the English tongue. His allego-
ries are nevertheless tame and spiritless, and the rural descriptions
which are contained in his works, have the common defect, that is,
of want of probability in the scenes and characters. The following
specimens of his poetry, will amply illustrate his style. For ex-
ample the following passage from the *Brittannia's Pastorals.*

"Now as an angler melancholy standing,
Upon a green bank yielding room for landing,
A wriggling yellow worm thrust on his hook,
Now in the midst he throws, then in a nook
Here pulls his line, there throws it in again,
Mending his croke and bait, but all in vain,
He long stands viewing of the curled stream ;
At last a hungry pike, or well-grown bream,
Snatch at the worm, and hasting fast away,
He, knowing it a fish of stubborn way,
Pulls up his rod, but soft ; (as having skill)
Wherewith the hook fast holds the fish's gill.

  * * * *

My free-born Muse will not, like Danea, be
Won with base dross to clip with slavery ;
Nor lend her choicer blame to worthless men,
Whose names would die but for some hired pen ;
No : if I praise, virtue shall draw me to it,
And not a base procurement make me do it.
What now I sing is but to pass away   ·
A tedious hour, as some musicians play ;
Or make another my own griefs bemoan ;
Or to be least alone whom most alone.   .
In this can I, as oft as I will choose,
Hug sweet content by my retired Muse,
And in a study find as much to please
As others in the greatest palaces.
Each man that lives (according to his power)
On what he loves bestows an idle hour ;
Instead of hounds that make the wooded hills
Talk in a hundred voices to the rills,   ·
I like the pleasing cadence of a line,
Struck by the concert of the sacred Nine.
In lieu of hawks, the raptures of my soul
Transcend their pitch and baser earth's control.
For running horses, contemplation flies
With quickest speed to win the greatest prize.
For courtly dancing I can take more pleasure
To hear a verse keep time and equal measure.
For winning riches, seek the best directions
How I way well subdue mine own affections,
For raising stately piles for heirs to come,
Here in this poem I erect my tomb.
And time may be so kind, in these weak lines
To keep my name enroll'd, past his, that shines
In gilded marble, or in brazen leaves :
Since verse preserves when stone and brass deceives."

KING.—Henry King is a miscellaneous writer of poetry,
religious ; also a version of the Psalms. The language

at once suggestive of melody. There are to be found occasionally coarse and indelicate passages, but on the whole his poem breathes the tenderest passion, and refinement of feeling. Some of his poems moralize in a strain of pleasing melancholy upon natural objects; of which kind we might quote the following verses, *To Daffodils* as a beautiful specimen. There is contained in it a moral pathos of the most touching kind.

> "Fair daffodils, we weep to see
>   You haste away so soon;
> As yet the earthly-rising sun
>   Has not attain'd his noon.
>   Stay, stay,
>   Until the hast'ning day
>   Has run
>   But to the even-song;
> And, having prayed together, we
>   Will go with you along.
>
> We have short time to stay like you;
>   We have as short a spring;
> As quick a growth to meet decay
>   As you or any thing.
>   We die
>   As your hours do, and die
>   Away,

> Like to the summer's rain ;
> Or as the pearls of morning dew,
> Ne'er to be found again."

QUARLES.—Francis Quarles wrote largely both in prose and verse ; but his chief work in the latter is a collection of *Divine Emblems,* a set of short poems of a most quaint character, illustrated with pictorial designs referring to the subject of the verses, which are all of a moral and religious tone. The extraordinary style of his poems is borrowed from the Dutch and Flemish moralists. The engravings are allegorical, and of a most absurd description. For example, "who will deliver me from the body of this death ?" is represented by a man standing within a skeleton, typifying the soul. Another of a different character consists of a helmet, turned into a beehive, surrounded by its useful labourers, with the motto, "Ex hello pax." The works of this poet are affected and obscure, and it is only by diligent investigation that his true beauties are to be found ; not only in the form of original imagery, fertility of expression and happy combinations, but, in many places, his poems breathe an intense spirit of religious fervour. At the time his verses were written, they were more popular than those of the gayest court poets, being recommended by a peculiar harshness and gloom accordant with the Puritan feelings of the larger part of the people : but at the time of Pope, they were ranked with the meanest trash that then appeared. As an example of these poems, take the following verses from the *Divine Emblems* :—

> "O ! whither shall I fly ? what path untrod
> Shall I seek out to 'scape the flaming rod
> Of my offended, of my angry God ;
> Where shall I sojourn ? what kind sea will hide
> My head from thunder ? where shall I abide,
> Until his flames be quench'd or laid aside ?
> What if my feet should take their hasty flight,
> And seek protection in the shades of night ?
> Alas ! no shades can blind the God of light.
> What if my soul should take the wings of day
> And find some desert ? if she springs away,
> The wings of Vengeance clip as fast as they.
> What if some solid rock should entertain
> My frighted soul ? can solid rocks restrain
> The stroke of Justice and not cleave in twain ?

Th' ingenuous child, corrected, doth not fly
His angry mother's hand ; but clings more nigh,
And quenches with his tears her flaming eye.
Great God ! there is no safety here below
Thou art my fortress, thou that seem'st my foe,
'Tis thou, that strik'st the stroke, must guard the blow.
Then work thy will ; if passion bid me flee,
My reason shall obey ; my wings shall be
Stretch'd out no further than from thee to thee."

WALTON.—Izaak Walton's chief work is the well-known poem, entitled *The Complete Angler*, a treatise on fishing, which contains not only precepts for the sport, but describes with much simplicity and feeling, English scenes and pleasures, and contains such a tone of pure benevolence and morality, that as a poem it is almost perfect. There is scarcely a poem to be found in which English scenery is delineated with such a truth, as in Walton's description of those quiet rivers and daisied meadows in this poem. It is written in the form of dialogues. Some of the lyrics contained in it are very beautiful. The following *The Angler's Song*, quoted below, is a specimen of this work.

"As inward love breeds outward talk,
The hound some praise, and some the hawk ;
Some, better pleased with private sport,
Love tennis ; some a mistress' court :
But these delights I neither wish,
Nor envy, while I freely fish.
Who hunts doth oft in danger ride ;
Who hawks lures oft both far and wide ;
Who uses games shall often prove
A loser ; but who falls in love
Is fetter'd in fond Cupid's snare :
—My angle breeds me no such care.
Of recreation, there is none
So free as fishing is alone ;
All other pastimes do no less
Than mind and body both possess ;
My hand alone my work can do,
So I can fish and study too.

I care not, I, to fish in seas,
Fresh rivers best my mind do please ;
Whose sweet calm course I contemplate ;
And seek in life to imitate ;
In civil bonds I fain would keep,
And for my past offences weep.

And when the timorous trout I wait
To take, and he devours my bait,
How poor a thing, sometimes, I find,
Will captivate a greedy mind :
And when none bite, I praise the wise,
Whom vain allurements ne'er surprise.

But yet though while I fish I fast,
I make good fortune my repast,
And thereunto my friend invite,
In whom I more than that delight;
Who is more welcome to my dish,
Than to my angle was my fish.

As well content no prize to take,
As use of taken prize to make ;
For so our Lord was pleased, when
He fishers made fishers of men ;
Where (which is in no other game,)
A man can fish and praise his name.

The first men, that our Saviour dear
Did choose to wait upon him here,
Blest fishers were—and fish the last
Food was, that He on earth did taste ;
I therefore strive to follow those
Whom He to follow Him hath chose."

HERBERT.—Herbert's poems, which are principally religious,
consist chiefly of short lyrics, uniting with beautiful pictures of
nature, the most quiet aspiration ; and as a writer has observed,
"decorating the altar with the sweetest and most fragrant flowers
of fancy and wit." His chief work is *The Temple;* it consists of a
number of short pieces, commemorating such topics as Good Fri-
day, Baptism, Church Music, Church Monuments, &c. Coleridge
says of these lyrics, " To appreciate them, it is not enough that the
reader possesses a cultivated judgment, classical taste, or even
poetic sensibility, unless he be likewise a Christian, and both a
zealot and an orthodox, both a devout and devotional Christian."
Herbert's life, like his works, was purely religious, and he was
certainly one of the most perfect models that have ever adorned

thè Anglican Church. He was known among his contemporaries as "holy George Herbert." The following extract from his poem *The Temple*, will sufficiently testify both to his character as a divine, and his merit as a poet.

THE FLOWER.

"How fresh, O Lord, how sweet and clean
And thy returns! ev'n as the flow'rs in spring;
To which, besides their own demean,
The late-past frosts tributes of pleasure bring.
     Grief melts away like snow in May;
     As if there were no such cold thing.

Who would have thought my shrivel'd heart
Could have recover'd greenness? It was gone
Quite under ground, as flow'rs depart
To see their mother root, when they have blown;
     Where they, together, all the hard weather,
     Dead to the world, keep house unknown.

These are thy wonders, Lord of power!
Killing and quick'ning, bringing down to hell,
And up to heaven, in an hour;
Making a chiming of a passing-bell.
     We say amiss 'This, or that, is;'
     Thy word is all; if we could spell."

SHIRLEY.—James Shirley is chiefly distinguished as a comedy writer, and in this kind of writing he excelled rather in his vivid portraiture of character, than for profound tracings of human nature. There is also in the comic scenes of Shirley, a refinement which completely distances the productions of his contemporaries. He wrote thirty-nine tragedies, comedies, and tragi-comedies, the greater number of which were to the highest degree popular in his own time, and in each style of which he excels. Besides these, he wrote a number of poems, the principal of which are short pieces, and amongst which many may be found of great beauty. His works show him to be comparatively free from the vice of his age, although he occasionally dwells upon themes unworthy of the Muse. The following poem *Death's Final Conquest*, from one of his plays, may be quoted as a fair specimen of his writing.

"The glories of our birth and state
     Are shadows, not substantial things;
There is no armour against fate;
     Death lays his icy hands on kings.

Sceptre and crown
Must tumble down,
And in the dust be equal made
With the poor crooked scythe and spade.

Some men with swords may reap the field,
And plant fresh laurels where they kill ;
But their strong nerves at last must yield,
They tame but one another still.
Early or late
They stoop to fate,
And must give up their murmuring breath,
When they pale captives creep to death.

The garlands wither on your brow,
Then boast no more your mighty deeds ;
Upon Death's purple altar now
See where the victor victim bleeds !
All hands must come
To the cold tomb,
Only the actions of the just
Smell sweet and blossom in the dust."

STORER.—Thomas Storer is the author of a poem on *The Life and Death of Cardinal Wolsey* ; also *England's Parnassus.* The following passage on Theology, is selected from the latter.

"In chariot, framed of celestial mould,
And simple pureness of the purest sky,
A more than heavenly Nymph I did behold,
Who, glancing on me with her gracious eye,
So gave me leave her beauty to espy ;
For sure no sense such sight can comprehend,
Except her beams their fair resplendance lend.

Her beauty with eternity began,
And only unto God was ever seen ;
When Eden was possess'd with sinful man,
She came to him, and gladly would have been
The long-succeeding world's eternal queen :
But Man rejected her ;—Oh ! heinous deed !
And from the garden banish'd was that seed.

Since when, at sundry times, in divers ways,
Atheism and blinded Ignorance conspire,
How to obscure those holy burning rays,
And quench that zeal of heart's inflaming fire,
Which makes our souls to heavenly things aspire :
But all in vain ; for, maugre all their might,
She never lost one sparkle of her light.

Pearls may be foil'd, and gold be changed to dross,
The sun obscured, the moon be turn'd to blo
The world may sorrow for Astræa's loss,

> The heavens be darken'd like a dusky wood,
> Waste deserts lie where wat'ry fountains stood
> But fair THEOLOGY (for so she hight)
> Shall never lose one sparkle of her light."

WALLER.—Edmund Waller's poetry is of the style of Charles I. His verses were popular both at their own time and in the succeeding generation; but although his poetry is both graceful and elegant, he does not come near to Cowley, his contemporary. His chief merit lies in his lyric poetry, from which many beautiful poems may be found. He is rather to be admired for the good sense and good taste with which he has avoided faults, than for the poetical enthusiasm which can alone produce true beauties. The following short piece may be read as one of the best specimens of his poetry.

> "Go lovely rose,
> Tell her that wastes her time and me,
>   That now she knows,
> When I resemble her to thee,
> How sweet and fair she seems to be.
>
>   Tell her that's young,
> And shuns to have her graces spied,
>   That hadst thou sprung
> In deserts, where no men abide,
> Thou must have uncommended died.
>
>   Small is the worth
> Of beauty from the light retired;
>   Bid her come forth,
> Suffer herself to be desired,
> And not blush so to be admired.
>
>   Then die, that she,
> The common fate of all things rare,
>   May reap in thee:
> How small a part of time they share,
>   That are so wond'rous sweet and fair."

> How can a general darkness cloud the sun ?
> Astrologers in vain their skill do try ;
> Nature must needs be sick, when God can die."

The other *On the Death of a Nightingale*, will rank w:
pieces of the kind, by any writer of this age.

> "Go, solitary wood, and henceforth be
> Acquainted with no other harmony
> Than the pye's chattering, and the shrieking note
> Of boding owls, and fatal raven's throat ;
> Thy sweetest chaunter's dead, that warbled forth
> Lays, that might tempests calm, and still the north,
> And call down angel's from their glorious sphere
> To hear her songs, and learn new anthems here."

DAVENANT. —Sir William Davenant was a writer of mis
ous verses, and his only poem of any length is *Gondibert*.
is nothing real about this poem ; it is cold and abstract
affects more by its occasional beauties, majestic sentiments
uous conceptions, and epigrammatic turns, than by its ir
over the fancy or the heart. Although it is long and tediou
ever, there is abundance to compensate for its defects ; it i
chivalrous grandeur, noble thoughts, and harmonious dicti
displays a deep spirit of philosophy. The following ver
selected as an example of this poem.

> "To Astragon, Heav'n for succession gave
>   One only pledge, and Birtha was her name ;
> Whose mother slept where flow'rs grew on her grave,
>   And she succeeded her in face and fame.
>
> Her beauty princes durst not hope to use,
>   Unless, like poets, for their morning theme ;
> And her mind's beauty they would rather choose,
>   Which did the light in beauty's lanthorn seem.
>
> She ne'er saw courts, yet courts could have undone
>   With untaught looks, and an unpractis'd heart ;
> Her nets, the most prepar'd could never shun,
>   For Nature spread them in the scorn of Art.
>
> She never had in busy cities been,
>   Ne'er warm'd with hopes, nor ere allay'd with fears
> Not seeing punishment, could guess no sin ;
>   And sin not seeing, ne'er had use of tears.
>
> But here her father's precepts gave her skill,
>   Which with incessant business fill'd the hours.
> In Spring, she gather'd blossoms for the still ;
>   In autumn, berries ; and in summer flowers.

To Castara, is a good example of his poetry.

"Give me a heart where no impure
   Disordered passions rage,
Which Jealousy doth not obscure,
Nor vanity t' expense engage,
   Nor wooed to madness by quaint oaths,
Or the fine rhetoric of clothes,
Which not the softness of the age
To vice or folly doth decline ;
Give me that heart, Castara, for 'tis thine.

Take thou a heart where no new look
   Provokes new appetite
With no fresh charm of beauty took
Or wanton stratagem of wit ;
   Not idly wand'ring here and there,
Led by an am'rous eye or ear.
Aiming each beauteous mark to hit ;
Which virtue doth to one confine :
Take thou that heart, Castara, for 'tis mine.

And now my heart is lodg'd with thee,
   Observe but how it still
Doth listen how thine doth with me ;
And guard it well, for else it will
Run hither back ; not to be where
I am, but 'cause thy heart is here.
But without discipline, or skill,
Our hearts shall freely 'tween us move :
Should thou or I want hearts, we'd breathe by love.

X

CHAPTER XLII.

MINOR POETS OF THE COMMONWEALTH PERIOD.

SUCKLING.—The works of Sir John Suckling are distinguishe[d] by a lively fancy, and an elegant mode of versification, with descriptive power considerably beyond his contemporaries. H[is] style is between the laughing and the grave, the light and tl[e] cordial. He had the art of drawing attention from his object, l[y] fixing it on his manner. The very poems which on examinatic[n] will be found to have the ground-work of as perfect a faith in n[a]ture, as the greatest works of the age that had immediately precede[d] flutter forth as mere careless trifles ; and thoughts of a deep ar[d] painful kind, until examined closely, strike the reader as the mere[st] superficial remarks. He was in fact the connecting-link betwee[n] the poetry of Elizabeth and that of Charles II, and but for tl[e] Puritanism that started up in England, he would have been tl[e] leader of a new race of poets. It is curious to observe, how :[s] Puritanism declined, poetry came round again to his peculiar styl[e] for he is certainly the origin of the poetry of Prior and Gay. Tl[e] following *Song* may be quoted as a specimen of Sir John Suckling[s] poetry.

LOVE TURNED TO HATRED.

"I will not love one minute more, I swear,
  No not a minute ; not a sigh or tear
  Thou gett'st from me, or one kind look again,
  Though thou should'st court me to 't, and wouldst begin,
  I will not think of thee, but as men do
  Of debts and sins, and then I'll curse thee too :
  For thy sake, women shall be now to me
  Less welcome, than at midnight ghosts shall be.
  I'll hate so perfectly, that it shall be.
  Treason to love that man that loves as she ;
  Nay, I will hate the very good, I swear,
  That's in thy sex, because it done
  Their very virtue, grace, discourse, and wit,
  And all for thee ; what, wilt thou love me yet ?"

PEACHAM.—Henry Peachan was the writer of the *Heroic Devises*, from which the following beautiful passage on The *Stric en Deer* has been selected.

And seek his ease by shifting of his ground ;
The mean neglecting which would heal the sin,
That hourly rankles more and more within."

MORE.—The chief poetical work of Henry More is a Platonic poem, *The Song of the Soul*, a work of considerable genius and power. The following passage, The Soul in and out of the body, will sufficiently exemplify this production.

"Like as a light, fast lock'd in lantern dark,
Wherewith by night our weary steps we guide
In slabby streets, and dirty channels mark ;
Some weaker rays through the black top do glide,
And flusher streams perhaps from horny side :
And when we've pass'd the peril of the way,
Arrived at home, and laid that case aside,
The naked light, how clearly doth it ray,
And spread its joyful beams as bright as summer day !
Even so the Soul, in this contracted state,
Confined to these strait instruments of sense,
More dull and narrowly doth operate ;
At *this* hole hears, the sight must ray from *thence*,
Here tastes, *there* smells ;—but, when she's gone from hence,
Like naked lamp, *she is one shining sphere*,
And round about hath perfect cognizance,
Whate'er in her horizon doth appear :
She is one Orb of sense, all eye, all airy ear."

VAUGHAN.—Henry Vaughan's works are *Olor Iscanus*, *Silex Scintillans* and other minor poems. Although this poet's works are harsh and obscure, there are to be found many passages of rare excellence. To quote Campbell's words, "he has amidst his harsh pages, some scattered thoughts that meet our eye, like wild flowers on a barren heath." The following lines on *The Rainbow*, form one of the choicest passages of his poetry.

"Still young and fine ! but what is still in view
We slight as old and soil'd, though fresh and new ;
How bright wert thou, when Shem's admiring eye

Thy burning, flaming arch did first descry ;
When Zerah, Nahor, Abram, Lot,
The youthful world's gray fathers, in one knot,
Did, with intentive looks, watch every hour,
For thy new light, and trembled at each shower..
   When thou dost shine, darkness looks white and fair ;
Forms turn to music, clouds to smiles and air ;
Rain gently spends his honey drops, and pours
Balm on the cleft earth, milk on grass and flowers.
   Bright pledge of peace and sunshine ! the sure tie
Of thy Lord's hand, the objects of his eye !
When I behold thee, though *my* light be dim,
Distant and low, I can in *thine* see Him,
Who looks upon thee from his glorious throne,
And minds the covenant betwixt ALL and ONE."

CRASHAW.—The writings of Crashaw are chiefly sacred, an
exhibit the highest exaltation of religious sentiment. He possesse
an exquisite fancy ; large powers of description, and great melod
of verse. His poems are *Steps to the Temple, Delights of th
Muses,* and *Sacred Poems*; also a translation from the Italian c
Marino, entitled the *Music's Duel,* which is one of the fines
specimens of versification in our language. The following hym
O Gloriosa Domina, is a fine example of his verse and style.

   "Hail, most high, most humble one !
Above the world ; below thy Son,
Whose blush the moon beauteously mars,
And stains the timorous light of stars.
He that made all things had not done,
Till he had made himself thy Son.
The whole world's host would be thy guest,
And board himself at thy rich breast ;
O boundless hospitality !
The feast of all things feeds on thee.
   The first Eve, mother of our fall,
E'er she bore anyone, slew all.
Of her unkind gifts might we have
The inheritance of a hasty grave ;
Quick buried in the wanton tomb
   Of one forbidden bit ;
Had not a better fruit forbidden it. "

DENHAM.—One of the most popular productions of this perio
was the short descriptive poem, entitled *Cooper's Hill,* by Sir·Joh
Denham. He is deservedly classed among the fathers of Englis
poetry, for his *Cooper's Hill* is one of the earliest attempts to ass

"My eye descending from the Hill, surveys
Where Thames among the wanton valleys strays,
Thames ! the most loved of all the Ocean's sons,
By his old sire, to his embraces runs,
Hasting to pay his tribute to the sea,
Like mortal life to meet eternity ;
Though with those streams he no resemblance hold,
His genuine and less guilty wealth t' explore,
Search not his bottom, but survey his shore,
O'er which he kindly spreads his spacious wing,
And hatches plenty for the ensuing spring ;
Nor then destroys it with too fond a stay,
Like mothers which their infants overlay ;
Nor with a sudden and impetuous wave,
Like profuse kings, resumes the wealth he gave.
No unexpected inundations spoil
The mower's hopes, or mock the ploughman's toil ;
But God-like his unwearied bounty flows ;
First loves to do, then loves the good he does.

    *   *   *   *   *
O could I flow like thee ! and make thy stream
My great example, as it is my theme ;
Though deep yet clear, though gentle yet not dull :
Strong without rage, without o'erflowing full."

SHERBURNE.—Sir Edward Sherburne, was the writer of various translations and miscellanies at this period. They are remarkable for the sweetness and elegance of their language and verse. Take for example the following verses on the *Innocents slain by Herod* :—

"Go, blessed innocents ! and freely pour
  Your souls forth in a purple shower.
And, for that little earth each shall lay down,
  Purchase a heavenly crown.

Nor of original pollution fear
  The stains should to your blood adhere ;
For yours now shed, ere long shall in a flood
  Bewash'd of better blood."

LOVELACE.—This poet, like Suckling, was another of those lively

valier poets so common in the reign of Charles I : but he is tl
ɔst serious and earnest, and has little of the half-passionate, ha
ɨting love fancy of his rival. His poems consist entirely of sho
eces, odes, sonnets, songs, &c.,—and although there are many
tle value, there are others, that will live as long as the languaɟ
which they are written. Some of his most charming lyrics we
itten in prison ; and the beautiful lines *To Althea*, written in tl
ɪte House at Westminster, reminds us, as a critic has observe
ɔf the caged bird which learns its sweetest and most plaintiᵥ
tes, when deprived of its woodland liberty."

"When love with unconfined wings
　　Hovers within my gates ;
And my divine Althea brings
　　To whisper at the grates :
While I lie tangled in her hair
　　And fetter'd to her eye ;
The gods that wanton in the air,
　　Know no such liberty.

When flowing cups run swiftly round
　　With no allaying Thames,
Our careless heads with roses bound,
　　Our hearts with loyal flames ;
When thirsty grief in wine we steep,
　　When healths and draughts go free,
Fishes that tipple in the deep,
　　Know no such liberty.

When (like committed linnets) I
　　With shriller throat shall sing,
The sweetness, mercy, majesty,
　　And glories of my king ;
When I shall voice aloud, how good
　　He is, how great should be ;
Enlarged winds that curl the flood,
　　Know no such liberty.

Stone walls do not a prison make,
　　Nor iron bars a cage ;
Minds innocent and quiet take
　　That for an hermitage ;
If I have freedom in my love,
　　And in my soul am free ;
Angels alone that soar above
　　Enjoy such liberty."

COWLEY.—This poet's works consist chiefly of light pieces afte
: style of Anacreon ; but there are besides these, several elegia

are so distinguished. One of the best examples of these is the *Ode to the Grasshopper.*

> "Happy insect, what can be,
> In happiness, compar'd to thee?
> Fed with nourishment divine,
> The dewy morning's gentle wine!
> Nature waits upon thee still,
> And thy verdant cup does fill,
> 'Tis fill'd, wherever thou dost tread,
> Nature's self's thy Ganymede.
> Thou dost drink, and dance, and sing,
> Happier than the happiest king!
> All the fields, which thou dost see;
> All the plants belong to thee,
> All that summer hours produce,
> Fertile made with early juice.
> Man for thee does sow and plough
> Farmer he, and landlord thou!
> Thou dost innocently joy,
> Nor does thy luxury destroy;
> The shepherd gladly heareth thee,
> More harmonious than he.
> Thee country hinds with gladness hear,
> Prophet of the ripened year!
> Thee Phœbus loves, and does inspire;
> Phœbus is himself thy fire.

> To thee, of all things upon earth,
> Life is no longer than thy mirth.
> Happy insect happy thou
> Doth neither age nor winter know.
> But, when thou'st drunk, and danc'd and sung
> Thy fill, the flowery leaves among,
> (Voluptuous, and wise, with all
> Epicurean animal l)
> Sated with thy summer feast,
> Thou retir'st to endless rest."

BROME.—This writer's works were chiefly political satires, writ-
ten during the civil wars, and there are many passages of singulai
merit amongst them. The following passage from the poem *On
the loss of a Garrison*, may be taken as an illustration.

> "In vain are bulwarks, and the strongest hold,
> If the beseigers' bullets are of gold,
> My soul, be not dejected : wouldst thou be
> From present trouble or from danger free?
> Trust not in rampires, nor the strength of walls,
> The town that stands to day, to-morrow falls ;
> Trust not in soldiers, though they seem so stout,
> Where sin's within, vain is defence without ;
> Trust not in wealth, for in this lawless time,
> Where prey is penalty, there wealth is crime ;
> Trust not in strength or courage, we all see
> The weak'st oftimes do gain the victory ;
> Trust not in honour ; honour's but a blast,
> Quickly begun, and but a while doth last.
> They that to day to thee 'Hosanna' cry,
> To morrow change their note for 'Crucify.'
> Trust not in friends, for friends will soon deceive thee ;
> They are in nothing sure, but sure to leave thee.
> Trust not in wit : who run from place to place,
> Changing religion as chance does her face,
> In spite of cunning, and their strength of brain,
> They're often catch'd, and all their plots are vain.
> Trust not in councils : potentates, or kings
> All are but frail and transitory things.
> Since neither soldiers, castles, wealth, or wit,
> Can keep off harm from thee, or thee from it ;
> Since neither strength nor honour, friends nor lords,
> Nor princes, peace or happiness affords,
>   Trust thou in God, ply Him with prayers still,
>   Be sure of help ; for He both can, and will."

MARVELL.—Andrew Marvell, a writer contemporary with Mil-
ton, attracted considerable notice at the time he wrote. Many
passages of exquisite beauty may be selected from his works. His

song of *The Emigrants to Bermuda,* and his *Thoughts in a Garden* are full of sweet and pleasant fancies, but one of the most beautiful poems is the *Lamentation of the Nymph on the death of a Fawn,* which may be seen by the following fine description.

> "With sweetest milk, and sugar, first
> I it at mine own fingers nurs'd ;
> And as it grew so every day
> It wax'd more white and sweet than they.
> It had so sweet a breath ! and oft
> I blush'd to see its foot more soft,
> And white, shall I say ? than my hand—
> Than any lady's of the land !
>
> It was a wondrous thing how fleet
> 'Twas on those little silver feet.
> With what a pretty skipping grace
> It oft would challenge me the race ;
> And when't had left me far away,
> 'Twould stay, and run again, and stay;
> For it was nimbler much than hinds,
> And trod as if on the four winds.
>
> I have a garden of my own,
> But so with roses overgrown,
> And lilies that you would it guess
> To be a little wilderness ;
> And all the spring time of the year
> It loved only to be there.
> Among the beds of lilies I
> Have sought it oft, where it should lie ;
> Yet could not, till itself would rise,
> Find it although before mine eyes ;
> For in the flaxen lilies, shade,
> It like a bank of lilies laid.
> Upon the roses it would feed,
> Until its lips ev'n seem'd to bleed ;
> And then to me 't 'twould boldly trip,
> And print those roses on my lip.
> But all its chief delight was still
> On roses thus itself to fill ;
> And its pure virgin lips to fold
> In whitest sheets of lilies cold.
> Had it liv'd long, it would have been
> Lilies without—roses within."

PHILIPS.—Mrs. Katherine Philips was very popular at this date as a poetical writer. Her style is considerably in advance of the writers of her time. Her works were written under the assumed name of *Orinda.* The following little poem, *Against Pleasure,* has been selected as an illustration of her works.

"There's no such thing as pleasure here,
  'Tis all a perfect cheat,
Which does but shine and disappear,
  Whose charm is but deceit:
The empty bribe of yielding souls,
Which first betrays, and then controls.

'Tis true, it looks at distance fair;
  But if we do approach,
The fruit of Sodom will impair,
  And perish at a touch:
In being than in fancy less,
And we expect more than possess.

For by our Pleasures we are cloy'd,
  And so desire is done;
Or else, like rivers, they make wide
  The channel where they run:
And either way true bliss destroys,
Making us narrow, or our joys,

We covet Pleasure easily,
  But it not so possess;
For many things must make it be,
  But one may make it less:
Nay, were our state as we could choose it,
'Twould be consumed by fear to lose it.

What art thou then, thou winged air,
  More weak and swift than fame?
Whose next successor is despair,
  And its attendant shame.
Th' experience-prince then reason had,
Who said of Pleasure, 'It is mad.'"

ROSCOMMON.—The versification of this poet is smooth and elegant, and his poems exhibit a refined taste, and correct judgment, but there is nothing vigorous or great in them. He is best known by his *Essay on Translated Verse*, and his translation from Horace's *Art of Poetry*. The following passage from the former poem will afford a good specimen of his writing.

"I pity, from my soul, unhappy men,
Compell'd by want to prostitute their pen;
Who must, like lawyers, either starve or plead,
And follow, right or wrong, where guineas lead!
But you, Pompilian, wealthy, pamper'd heirs,
Who to your country owe your swords and cares,
Let no vain hope your easy mind seduce,
For rich ill poets are without excuse,
'Tis very dangerous, tampering with the Muse,
The profit's small, and you have much to lose;

"As two embracing palms, whose roots conjoin,
Whose boughs to a perpetual kiss incline;
Their shady locks into each other wreath,
Their mutual sweets into each other breathe;
Their morning dew into each other drop,
Both feel the wound, if you should either crop;
Their odorous flowers at the same season blow,
Both twine the more, the more their branches grow;
Both influenced are, and warm'd by the same ray,
Both by a separation soon decay:
Edmund and Hilda thus soft passions vie,
Together spring, live, flower, and wish to die;
To die, for both their parting hour fore-view'd,
And to God's gracious will their loves subdued.

  * * * * *

Hilda, while Edmund toil'd in state-affairs,
Eased him of all his economic cares.
In all that bounded was within her sphere,
Her wisdom shined, in her whole conduct, clear;
No vain expense she on herself bestow'd,
A spirit frugal, and yet generous show'd;
She of God's blessings could no waste endure,
But in rewards was bountiful and sure;
The poor had an alloted liberal share,
In all that she with decency could spare;
Her speech was uncensorious and restrain'd,

> All that she spake a pleased attention gain'd ;
> In her discourse a gleam of virtue shined,
> Impressing virtuous tinctures on the mind."

SEDLEY.—The principal work of Sir Charles Sedley, is a comedy *The Mulberry Garden,* which sparkles with genuine wit, and contains several excellent songs. In his lyrics, there is a tenderness which distinguishes him from the other court-writers of his time, and which prove, that he possessed the airiness and ingenuity which are the principal requisites of lyric poetry. The following will illustrate at once his power of lyrical verse, of which poem the Second stanza is delightful :—

> "Phillis, men say that all my vows
>   Are to thy fortune paid ;
> Alas, my heart he little knows
>   Who thinks my love a trade.
>
> Were I, of all these woods, the lord,
>   One berry from thy hand
> More real pleasure would afford,
>   Than all my large command.
>
> My humble love has learnt to live,
>   On what the nicest maid,
> Without a conscious blush, may give
>   · Beneath the myrtle-shade."

GARTH.—Samuel Garth was the writer of a mock-heroic composition, entitled the *Dispensary,* and several other smaller pieces. The Dispensary relates to a dispute in the College of Physicians, concerning the commencement of a charitable institution, in which Garth, strongly advocated the cause of benevolence. It is well written, and contains many remarkable passages of wit. As an example, the following lines are selected from the passage in which *Hygeia** conducts her charge to view the wonders of the earth.

> "Th ' ascent thus conquer'd, now they tower on high,
> And taste th' indulgence of a milder sky.
> Loose breezes on their airy pinions play,
> Soft infant blossoms their chaste odours pay,
> And roses blush their fragrant lives away.
> Cool streams through flowery meadows gently glide ;
> And, as they pass, their painted banks they chide
> These blissful plains no blights nor mildews fear,
> The flowers ne'er fade, and shrubs are myrtles here.
> The morn awakes the tulip from her bed ;

---

* Health.

> Ere noon in painted pride she decks her head,
> Rob'd in rich dye she triumphs on the green,
> And every flower does homage to the queen.
> So, when bright Venus rises from the flood,
> Around in throngs the wondering Nereids crowd ;
> The Tritons gaze, and tune each vocal shell,
> And every grace unsung, the waves conceal."

ROCHESTER.—This writer is more celebrated for his profligacy and wit, than for his poetry. Although he displayed considerable talent in writing, he never produced any one poem of distinguished merit. The fugitive songs and lyrics of this writer which are known, however, prove how great his talents for poetry were. The following lyric entitled *Love and Life*, is selected as an example.

> "All my past life is mine no more,
>   The flying hours are gone :
> Like transitory dreams given o'er,
> Whose images are kept in store
>   By memory alone.
>
> The time that is to come is not :
>   How can it then be mine?
> The present moment's all my lot ;
> And that, as fast as it is got,
>   Phillis is only thine.
>
> Then talk not of inconstancy,
>   False hearts, and broken vows ;
> If I, by miracle, can be
> This live-long minute true to thee,
>   'Tis all that heaven allows."

SHEFFIELD.— Sheffield is best known by his *Essay on Poetry* written in the heroic couplet. Of his lesser poems there are few that bear the true stamp of genius, although there are many that are smart and sparkling. He was the writer of two tragedies, *Julius Cæsar*, and the *Death of Brutus*, which however possess little merit. His songs, which are all written upon common topics, are chiefly of an inferior character. The following is one of the best.

> "Since in vain our parsons teach,
> Hear, for once a poet preach.
>   Vice has lost its very name,
> Skill and cozenage thought the same ;
> Only playing well the game.
> Foul contrivances we see
> Call'd but ingenuity :

Ample fortunes often made
Out of frauds in every trade,
Which an awkward child afford
Enough to wed the greatest lord.
The miser starves to raise a son,
But, if once the fool is gone,
Years of thrift scarce serve a day,
Rake-hell squanders all away.
Husbands seeking for a place,
    Or toiling for their pay ;
While the wives undo their race
    By petticoats and play ;
Breeding boys to drink and dice,
Carrying girls to comedies,
Where mamma's intrigues are shown,
Which ere long will be their own.
Having first at sermon slept,
Tedious day is weekly kept
By worse hypocrites than men,
Till Monday comes to cheat again.
Ev'n among the noblest born,
    Moral virtue is a scorn ;
    Gratitude, but rare at best,
    And fidelity a jest."

BLACKMORE.—Sir Richard Blackmore was the writer of several epic poems, of which the *Creation* is the best known. Addison says, that "it deserves to be looked upon as one of the most useful and noble productions in our English verse," and Johnson says, "had Blackmore written nothing else, it would have transmitted him to posterity among the first favourites of the English Muse." The following is a short extract from this poem.

"Since Thou didst all the spacious worlds display,
Homage to Thee let all obedient pay.
Let glittering stars, that dance their destin'd ring
Sublime in sky, with vocal planets sing
Confederate praise to Thee, O Great Creator King
Let the thin districts of the waving air,
Conveyancers of sound, Thy skill declare.
Let winds, the breathing creatures of the skies,
Call in each vigorous gale, that roving flies
By land or sea; then one loud triumph raise,
And all their blasts employ in songs of praise.
    While painted herald-birds Thy deeds proclaim,
And on their spreading wings convey Thy fame ;
Let eagles, which in heaven's blue concave soar,
Scornful of earth, superior seats explore,

to vie with any poetry of the kind at that date.

"As for proud glory which comes after fate, —
  All that can then of me be said,
I value least of all, it comes too late,
'Tis like th' embalming of senseless dead :
Others with pleasure, what me labour cost
May read, and praise ; but to me all is lost ;
  Just as the sun no joy does find
  In that his light, which cheers mankind.

Or should I after fate has closed my eyes,
  Should I my living glories know,
My wiser, improved soul will then despise
All that poor mortals say or think below :
Even they who of men's ignorance before
Complain'd, because few did their works adore,
  Will then the self same censure raise,
  Not from their silence, but their praise.

Death and destruction shall ere long deface
  The world, the work of hands divine,
What pillars then, or monuments of brass
Shall from the general ruin rescue mine ?
All then shall equal be ; I care not then
To be a while the talk and boast of men ;
  This only grant, that I may be
  Praised by the angels, Lord, and thee."

CHAPTER XLIII.

MINOR POETS OF THE GEORGIAN PERIOD.

LANSDOWNE.—George Granville, Lord Lansdowne, is a writer after the style of Waller, who no doubt he imitated. Johnson says, "his verses are without merit." The best known of his poems, are his verses *To Myra*, from which the two following are quoted.

> " Foolish Love, begone, said I,
>   Vain are thy attempts on me ;
> Thy soft allurements I defy,
> Women, those fair dissemblers, fly,
>   My heart was never made for thee.
>
> Love heard ; and straight prepar'd a dart ;
>   Myra, revenge my cause, said he :
> Too sure 'twas shot, I feel the smart,
> It rends my brain, and tears my heart ;
>   O Love ! my conqu'ror, pity me."
>
> " Warn'd, and made wise by other's flame,
>   I fled from whence such mischiefs came,
> Shunning the sex, that kills at sight,
> I sought my safety in my flight.
>
> But, ah ! in vain from fate I fly,
> For first, or last, as all must die ;
> So 'tis as much decreed above,
> That first, or last, we all must love.
>
> My heart which stood so long the shock
> Of winds and waves, like some firm rock,
> By one bright spark from Myra thrown,
> Is into flame, like powder, blown."

POMFRET.—The chief work by which this writer is remembered, is the poem of *The Choice,* in which is given a true and almost perfect sketch of rural life. The images and ideas employed are such as immediately touch the heart and fancy, and it is this that renders this poem at all times interesting. The following pas-sage is selected from this poem.

> "If Heaven the grateful liberty would give,
> That I might choose my method how to live,
> And all those hours propitious fate should lend,
> In blissful ease and satisfaction spend,
> Near some fair town I'd have a private seat,
> Built uniform, not little, nor too great :
> Better, if on a rising ground it stood ;

*   *   *   *

And as I near approach'd the verge of life,
Some kind relation (for I'd have no wife)
Should take upon him all my worldly care,
Whilst I did for a better state prepare.
Then I'd not be with any trouble vex'd,
Nor have the evening of my days perplex'd ;
But, by a silent and a peaceful death,
Without a sigh resign my aged breath.
And when committed to the dust, I'd have
Few tears, but friendly, dropt into my grave ;
Then would my exit so propitious be,
All men would wish to live and die like me."

YALDEN.—Yalden's verses are of less merit than those of the writers of that period, but still there may be selected some of tolerable beauty, of one of which the following *Hymn to the Morning* may be mentioned. Johnson, who declares it to be his best performance says of it, that, "it is imagined with great vigour, and expressed with great propriety."

"Parent of Day ! whose beauteous beams of light
Spring from the darksome womb of Nightg
And 'midst their native horrors show,
Like gems adorning of the negro's brow :
Not Heav'n's fair bow can equal thee,

a

In all its gaudy drapery ;
Thou first essay of light, and pledge of day !
That usher'st in the sun, and still prepar'st its way.
Rival of shade, eternal spring of light !
    Thou art the genuine source of it :
    From thy bright unexhausted womb,
The beauteous rays of days and seasons come.
    Thy beauty ages cannot wrong,
    But, spite of time, thou'rt ever young :
Thou art alone Heav'n's modest virgin light,
Whose face a veil of blushes hides from human sight.

     *   *   *   *   *

But yet thy fading glories soon decay.
    Thine's but a momentary stay;
    Too soon thou'rt ravish'd from our sight,
Borne down the stream of day, and overwhelm'd with light,
    Thy beams to their own ruin haste,
    They're fram'd too exquisite to last :
Thine is a glorious, but a short-liv'd state,
Pity so fair a birth should yield so soon to fate.
Before th' Almighty Artist fram'd the sky,
    Or gave the earth its harmony,
    His first command was for thy light ;
He viewed the lovely birth, and blessed it :
    In purple swaddling-bands it struggling lay,
    Not yet maturely bright for day :
Old Chaos then a cheerful smile put on,
And, from thy beauteous form, did first presage its own.
'Let there be light !' the great Creator said,
    His word the active child obey'd :
    Night did her teeming womb disclose ;
And then the blushing morn, its brightest offspring rose.
    Awhile the Almighty wondering view'd,
    And then himself pronounced it good :
'With night, (said he) divide th' imperial sway ;
Thou my first labour art, and thou shalt bless the day.' "

CONGREVE.—William Congreve is best known as a comic drama-
ist, but he is also the writer of several tragedies, and miscellaneous
poems.   His finest work is *Love for Love*, which is one of the
most perfect comedies in the whole range of literature.   There is
less merit in his miscellaneous poems than in his dramatic work.
The following Ode *In Imitation of Horace*, though only a para-
phase of the original, may be read as an interesting example of
the smaller poems of this writer.

Diffusive cold does the whole earth invade,
Like a disease, through all its veins 'tis spread,
And each late living stream is numb'd and dead.
Let's melt the frozen hours, make warm the air ;
Let cheerful fires Sol's feeble beams repair ;
  Fill the large bowl with sparkling wine ;
  Let's drink till our own faces shine,
    Till we like suns appear,
  To light and warm the hemisphere."

Rowe.—Nicholas Rowe is most famous for his tragic and drama-
tic poetry. The principal of these productions, are *Jane Shore*,
The Fair Penitent, and *Lady Jane Grey.* The qualities of his
genius were rather tenderness and delicacy, than pathos and
strength. There is much merit and beauty to be found in many of
his minor poems also. Perhaps his most popular poem is the beau-
tiful ballad, called *Colin's Complaint,* which is almost equal to
Shenstone's *Pastoral Ballad.*

"Despairing beside a clear stream,
  A shepherd forsaken was laid ;
And while a false nymph was his theme,
  A willow supported his head.
The wind that blew over the plain,
  To his sighs with a sigh did reply ;
And the brook, in return to his pain,
  Ran mournfully murmuring by.

Alas, silly swain that I was !
  Thus sadly complaining, he cry'd,
When first I beheld that fair face,
  'Twere better by far I had died.
She talk'd, and I bless'd the dear tongue ;

When she smil'd, 'twas a pleasure too great,
　　listen'd. and cry'd, when she sung,
　　Was nightingale ever so sweet?
How foolish was I to believe
　　She could doat on so lowly a clown.
Or that her fond heart would not grieve,
　　To forsake the fine folk of the town.
To think that a beauty so gay,
　　So kind and so constant would prove ;
Or go clad like our maidens in grey,
　　Or live in a cottage on love?

And you, my companions so dear,
　　Who sorrow to see me betray'd,
Whatever I suffer, forbear,
　　Forbear to accuse the false maid.
Though through the wide world I should range,
　　'Tis in vain for my fortune to fly ;　　　;
'Twas hers to be false and to change,
　　'Tis mine to be constant and die.

If while my hard fate I sustain,
　　In her breast any pity is found,
Let her come with the nymphs of the plain,
　　And see me laid low in the ground.
The last humble boon that I crave
　　Is to shade me with cypress and yew ;
And when she looks down on my grave,
　　Let her own that her shepherd was true.

Then to her new love let her go,
　　And deck her in golden array,
Be finest at every fine show,
　　And frolic it all the long day ;
While Colin, forgotten and gone,
　　No more shall be talk'd of, or seen,
Unless when beneath the pale moon,
　　His ghost shall glide over the green."

WATTS.—Isaac Watts was the writer of *Psalms*, *Hymns*, and
Lyric Poems, which are too well known to require comment.
Amongst the latter, many beautiful moral pieces are to be found :
the following on *True Riches*, being a good specimen.

"I am not concern'd to know
　What to-morrow fate will do :
　'Tis enough that I can say,
　I've possess'd myself to day ;
　Then if haply midnight-death
　Seize my flesh and stop my breath,
　Yet to-morrow I shall be
　Heir to the best part of me.

"Autumn to the fruits
Earth's various lap produces, vigour gives
Equal itinerating milky grain,
Berries, and sky-dy'd plums, and what in coat,
Rough, or soft rind, or bearded husk, or shell ;
Fat olives, and Pistacio's fragrant nut,
And the pine's tastful apple : Autumns paint
Ausonian hills with grapes, whilst English plains
Blush with pomaceous harvests, breathing sweets,
O let me now, when the kind early dew
Unlocks th' embosomed odours, walk among
The well-rang'd files of trees, whose full-ag'd store
Diffuse ambrosial streams, than myrrh, or nard
More grateful, or perfuming flow'ry bean !
Soft whisp'ring Airs, and the larks matin song
Then woo to musing, and be calm the mind
Perplex'd with irksome thoughts.   Thrice happy time,
Best portion of the various year, in which
Nature rejoiceth, smiling on her works
Lovely, to full perfection wrought ! but ah,
Short are our joys, and neighb'ring griefs disturb
Our pleasant hours.   Inclement winter dwells
Contiguous ; forthwith frosty blasts deface
The blithsome year : trees of their shrivel'd fruits
Are widow'd, dreary storms o'er all prevail."

HUGHES.—John Hughes was the writer of a number of miscel-
laneous poems ; a tragedy entitled *The Siege of Damascus* ; and
several translations from the French : he also published an edi-
tion of the works of Spenser.   One of the best of his miscellaneous
poems is the *Ode to the Creator of the World*.   It is full of the
most striking descriptions, and elevated thoughts, and abounds
with magnificent imagery.   Johnson classes it as one of the finest
odes in our language.   The following stanzas are selected from
this poem as an example.

>"He spoke the great command ; and light,
>   Heaven's eldest born and fairest child,
>Flash'd in the lowering face of ancient night,
>And, pleas'd with its own birth, serenely smil'd.
>   The sons of morning, on the wing,
>   Hovering in choirs, his praises sung,
>   When from th' unbounded vacuous space
>   A beauteous rising world they saw,
>When nature shew'd her yet unfinish'd face,
>   And motion took the established law
>   To roll the various globes on high ;
>   When time was taught his infant wings to try,
>And from the barrier sprung to his appointed race.
>
>   Supreme, Almighty ; still the same !
>   'Tis he, the great inspiring mind,
>That animates and moves this universal frame,
>Present at once in all, and by no place confined.
>   Not heaven itself can bound his sway ;
>Beyond th' untravell'd limits of the sky,
>   ·Invisible to mortal eye
>   He dwells in uncreated day.
>Without beginning, without end ; 'tis he
>That fills th' unmeasur'd growing orb of vast immensity."

PARNELL.– This poet is known chiefly by his moral tale of the
Hermit.   Although somewhat feeble, it is gracefully and elegantly
written, a parable versified from a striking story, originally derived
from the *Gesta Romanorum*.   The poem opens with the following
admirable description of the Hermit.

>"Far in a wild, unknown to public view,
>From youth to age a rev'rend Hermit grew ;
>The moss his bed, the cave his humble cell,
>His food the fruits, his drink the crystal well ;
>Remote from man, with God he pass'd his days,
>Prayer all his business, all his pleasure praise.

RAMSAY.—Besides several pieces of considerable humour, this poet's works include the celebrated pastoral drama of *The Gentle Shepherd*, which is the principal prop of his reputation. It depicts the rustics of Scotland in their actual characters, and the language of their every-day life, and yet without the slightest taint of vulgarity, and it contains some fine descriptive passages, and many light but firm delineations of character. As a pastoral poem, it is one of the most perfect specimens in the English language, and is without a parallel for tenderness of sentiment, affecting incident and justness of painting. It consists of a series of dialogues in verse, descriptive of the rural life and scenery of Scotland, and interwoven into a simple but interesting love-story. The Doric dialect in which it is written adds to its other graces, and set them off to still greater effect, giving it a charm which no other pastoral poem will ever attain. This poem will no doubt be read and admired, so long as the language in which it is written shall continue to be understood. The following extract which is remarkable for all that attractive simplicity and truth for which this poem is distinguished, will afford an example.

PATIE.

"Were your bien rooms as thinly stock'd as mine,
Less ye wad lose, and less ye wad repine.
He that has just enough can soundly sleep;
The o'ercome only fashes fouk to keep.

ROGER.

May plenty flow upon thee for a cross,
That thou may'st thole the pangs o' mony a loss!

O may'st thou doat on some fair paughty wench,
That ne'er will lout thy lowin' drouth to quench.
Till, bris'd beneath the burden, thou cry dool,
And awn that ane may fret that is nae fool !

PATIE.

Sax guid fat lambs, I sald them ilka clute
At the West-port, and bought a winsome flute,
O' plum-tree made, wi' iv'ry virles round—
A dainty whistle, wi' a pleasant sound ;
I'll be mair canty wi't —and ne'er cry dool,—
Than you, wi' a' your cash, you dowie fool !

ROGER.

Na, Patie, na ! I'm nae sic churlish beast,
Some other thing lies heavier at my breast ;
I dream'd a dreary dream this hinder night,
That gars my flesh a' creep yet wi' the fright.

PATIE.

Now, to a friend how silly's this pretence,—
To ane wha you and a' your secret kens ;
Daft are your dreams, as daftly wad ye hide
Your weel seen love, and dorty Jenny's pride.
Tak courage, Roger ; me your sorrows tell,
And safely think nane kens them but yoursell.

ROGER.

Indeed, now, Patie, ye hae guess'd ower true,
And there is naething I'll keep up frae you.
Me, dorty Jenny looks upon asquint,
To speak but till her I daur hardly mint :
In ilka place she jeers me air and late,
And gars me look bombaz'd and unco blate;
But yesterday I met her yont a knowe,—
She fled, as frae a shelly-coated cow.
She Baldy loes, Baldy that drives the car,
But gecks at me, and says I smell o' tar.

PATIE.

But Bauldy loes not her, right weel I wat :
He sighs for Neps—sae that may stand for that.

ROGER.

I wish I coud'na loe her—but in vain,
I still maun do't, and thole her proud disdain.
My Bawty is a cur I dearly like,
E'en while he fawn'd, she strak the puir dumb tyke ;
If I had fill'd a nook within her breast,
She wad hae shawn mair kindness to my beast.
When I begin to tune my stock and horn,
Wi' a' her face she shaws a cauldrife scorn.
Last night, I play'd—ye never heard sic spite !—
O'er Bogie was the spring, and her delyte ;—

"Olivia's lewd, but looks devout,
  And scripture-proofs she throws about,
    When first you try to win her ;
  Pull your fob of guineas out ;
  Fee Jenny first, and never doubt
    To find the saint a sinner.

Baxter by day is her delight :
No chocolate must come in sight
  Before two morning chapters :
But, lest the spleen should spoil her quite,
She takes a civil friend at night
  To raise her holy raptures.

Thus oft we see a glow-worm gay
At large her fiery tail display,
  Encourag'd by the dark :
And yet the sullen thing all day
Snug in the lonely thicket lay,
  And hid the native spark."

HILL.—Seventeen plays have been attributed to Aaron Hill, besides other pieces of less importance. The style of his writings is correct and cold, constructed mainly upon the French models. Of his minor pieces the following poem of *The Happy Man*, has been selected as an example.

"High o'er the winding of a cliffy shore,
From whose worn steep the black'ning surges roar ;
Freeman ! sweet lot, in quiet plenty lives :
Rich in the unbought wealth which Nature gives ;
Unplanted groves rise round his shelter'd seat,
And self-sown flow'rs attract his wand'ring feet :
Lengths of wild garden his near views adorn,
And far-seen fields wave with domestic corn.
  The grateful herds which his own pastures feed.
Pay their ask'd lives, and in due tribute bleed.
Here, in learn'd leisure he relaxes life,
'Twixt prattling children and a smiling wife.
Here, on dependant want he sheds his care,
Moves amid smiles, and all he hears is pray'r.

The world lies round him like a subject soil,
Stor'd for his service, but beneath his toil,
Hence in a morning walk his piercing eye
Skims the green ocean to the circling sky;
And marks at distance some returning sail,
Wing'd by the couitship of a flatt'ring gale.
The fearless crew, concluding danger o'er,
With gladd'ning shouts salute the op'ning shore :
They think how best they may their gains employ,
And antedate thin scenes of promis'd joy ;
Till a near quick-sand checks their shorten'd way,
And the sunk masts point thro' the rising spray.
Freeman starts sad ! revolves the changeful sight,
Where mis'ry can so soon succeed delight ;
Then shakes his head in pity of their fate,
And sweetly conscious, hugs his happier state."

TICKELL.—Thomas Tickell, a writer of Swift's time, exhibits in his poems more tenderness, than either of his contemporaries. His ballad of *Lucy and Colin* is still popular, and exhibits in many of its stanzas, this great tenderness of writing : it is quoted below as an example of this poet's writing.

"Of Leinster, fam'd for maidens fair,
    Bright Lucy was the grace ;
Nor e'er did Liffy's limpid stream
    Reflect so fair a face.

Till luckless love and pining care,
    Impar'd her rosy hue,
Her coral lip, and damask cheek,
    And eyes of glossy blue.

Oh! have you seen a lily pale,
    When beating rains descend?
So droop'd the slow-consuming maid ;
    Her life now near its end.

By Lucy warn'd, of flattering swains
    Take heed, ye easy fair:
Of vengeance due to broken vows,
    Ye perjured swains, beware.

Three times, all in the dead of night,
    A bell was heard to ring ;
And at her window, shrieking thrice,
    The raven flapp'd his wing.

Too well the love-lorn maiden knew
    That solemn boding sound ;
And thus, in dying words, bespoke
    The virgins weeping round.

That Lucy will be there.

'Then, bear my corse, ye comrades, bear,
    The bridegroom blithe to meet ;
He in his wedding trim so gay,
    I in my winding sheet?'

She spoke, she died ;—her corse was borne,
    The bridegroom blithe to meet ;
He in his wedding-trim so gay,
    She in her winding sheet.

Then what were perjur'd Colin's thoughts?
    How were those nuptials kept?
The bride-men flock'd round Lucy dead,
    And all the village wept.

Confusion, shame, remorse, despair,
    At once his bosom swell :
The damps of death bedew'd his brow
    He shook, he groan'd, he fell.

From the vain bride (ah, bride no more !)
    The varying crimson fled,
When, stretch'd before her rival's corse,
    She saw her husband dead.

Then to his Lucy's new-made grave,
    Convey'd by trembling swains,
One mould with her, beneath one sod,
    For ever now remains."

GAY.—The most distinguished after Pope of his time, was Joseph
Gay. His most popular poems are his *Fables*, which in sprightli-
ness, point, and wit have never been matched. His fame rests
chiefly on his play of *The Beggar's Opera*. The collection of

Eclogues entitled the *Shepherd's Week*, is an admirable specimen of pastoral poetry, and the descriptions of real English rural nature and peasant life are so agreeable, that as a poem it will always be read with interest and pleasure. His other important poem is the *Trivia*, or *The art of Walking the Streets of London*. It is full of an easy and quiet humour, and is interesting for the curious details it gives of the street-scenery, costume, and manners of that time. The following, the *Shepherd and the Philosopher*, the introduction to the *Fables*, is an excellent specimen of his poetry :—

> "Remote from cities liv'd a swain,
> Unvex'd with all the cares of gain ;
> His head was silver'd o'er with age,
> And long experience made him sage ;
> In summer's heat, and winter's cold,
> He fed his flock, and penn'd the fold ;
> His hours in cheerful labour flew,
> Nor envy nor ambition knew :
> His wisdom and his honest fame
> Thro' all the country rais'd his name.
> A deep philosopher (whose rules
> Of moral life were drawn from schools)
> The Shepherd's homely cottage sought,
> And thus explor'd his reach of thought.
> 'Whence is thy learning? hath thy toil
> O'er books consum'd the midnight oil,
> Hast thou old Greece and Rome survey'd,
> And the vast sense of Plato weigh'd ?
> Hath Socrates thy soul refin'd,
> And hast thou fathom'd Tully's mind?
> Or, like the wise Ulysses, thrown,
> By various fates, on realms unknown,
> Hast thou thro' many cities stray'd,
> Their customs, laws, and manners weigh'd ? '
> The shepherd modestly reply'd,
> 'I ne'er the paths of learning tried ;
> Nor have I roam'd in foreign parts
> To read mankind, their laws and arts ;
> For man is practis'd in disguise,
> He cheats the most discerning eyes :
> Who by that search shall wiser grow,
> When we ourselves can never know ?
> The little knowledge I have gain'd,
> Was all from simple Nature drain'd ;
> Hence my life's maxims took their rise,
> Hence grew my settled hate to vice.
> The daily labours of the bee

BROOME.—William Broome is remembered as having assisted Pope in his translation of the Odyssey of Homer. He was also the writer of miscellaneous poetry, of which some is remarkable for originality of thought and expression. The following lines on *The Rosebud* are a beautiful little example of the smaller poems of this writer.

> "Queen of fragrance, lovely Rose,
> The beauties of thy leaves disclose!
> The winter's past, the tempests fly,
> Soft gales breathe gently thro' the sky;
> The lark sweet warbling on the wing,
> Salutes the gay return of Spring:
> The silver dews, the vernal showers,
> Call forth a bloomy waste of flowers;
> The joyous fields, the shady woods,
> Are cloth'd with green, or swell'd with buds:
> Then haste thy beauties to disclose,
> Queen of fragrance, lovely rose!
>
>   ✱   *   *   *
>
>   And thou, fair nymph, thyself survey
> In this sweet offspring of a day;
> That miracle of face must fail!
> Thy charms are sweet, but charms are frail:
> Swift as the short-liv'd flower they fly,
> At morn they bloom, at evening die:
> Tho' sickness yet a while forbears,
> Yet time destroys what sickness spares.
> Now Helen lives alone in fame,
> And Cleopatra's but a name.
> Time must indent that heavenly brow,
> And thou must be, what they are now.
>
>   This moral to the fair disclose,
> Queen of fragrance, lovely Rose."

BYROM.—John Byrom is chiefly remembered by a pastoral ρ which appeared in the "Spectator," and entitled *My time, Muses was happily spent.* He was the writer also of a numb other smaller poems of an amusing character. Montgomery ι "Byrom was perhaps without exception the most expert versifi the English language ; no subject, not even verbal criticism, b too intractable to be run into familiar metre by him." One o best poems exhibiting this freedom of writing is the *Essay on thusiasm,* a portion of which is selected as an example.

> "What is enthusiasm? What can it be,
> But thought enkindled to an high degree?
> That may, whatever be its ruling turn,
> Right, or not right, with equal ardour burn.
> It must be therefore various in its kind,
> As objects vary, that engage the mind :
> When to religion we confine the word,
> What use of language can be more absurd?
> 'Tis just as true, that many words beside,
> As love, or zeal, are only thus applied :
> To every kind of life they all belong ;
> Men may be eager, tho' their views be wrong :
> And hence the reason, why the greatest foes
> To true religious earnestness are those
> Who fire their wits upon a different theme,
> Deep in some false enthusiastic scheme.
>
>   *   *   *   *
>
> It matters not, whatever be the state
> That full-bent will and strong desires create ;
> Where'er they fall, where'er they love to dwell,
> They kindle there their heaven, or their hell ;
> The chosen scene surrounds them as their own,
> All else is dead, insipid, or unknown.
> However poor and empty be the sphere,
> 'Tis all, if inclination centre there :
> Its own enthusiasts each system knows,
> Down to laced fops, and powder'd sprinkled beaus."

ADDISON.—The finest production of this poet, is unquestion the tragedy of Cato, although it is neither so interesting n pleasing as his opera of *Rosamond.* He is also the author c veral miscellaneous poems, and *Hymns,* the latter of which are known. Perhaps the best of his shorter pieces are his *Vers Kneller,* speaking of which Johnson says, "there is scarcely instance in which mythology has been applied with more deli and dexterity." The following lines from this poem may be read as illustrative of this :—

> "Thy pencil has, by monarchs sought,
> From reign to reign in ermine wrought,
> And, in the robes of state array'd,
> The kings of half an age display'd.
>   Here swarthy Charles appears, and there
> His brother with dejected air :
> Triumphant Nassau here we find,
> And with him bright Maria join'd ;
> There Anna, great as when she sent
> Her armies through the continent,
> Ere yet her Hero was disgrac'd :
> O may fam'd Brunswick be the last,
> (Though heaven should with my wish agree,
> And long preserve thy art in thee)
> The last, the happiest British king,
> Whom thou shalt paint, or I shall sing !
>   Wise Phidias thus, his skill to prove,
> Through many a god advanc'd to Jove,
> And taught the polish'd rocks to shine
> With airs and lineaments divine ;
> Till Greece, amaz'd, and half-afiaid,
> Th' assembled deities survey'd.
>   Great Pan, who wont to chase the fair,
> And lov'd the spreading oak, was there ;
> Old Saturn too with up-cast eyes
> Beheld his abdicated skies ;
> And mighty Mars, for war renown'd,
> In adamantine armour frown'd ;
> By him the childless goddess rose,
> Minerva, studious to compose
> Her twisted threads ; the web she strung,
> And o'er a loom of marble hung :
> Thetis; the troubled ocean's queen,
> Match'd with a mortal, next was seen,
> Reclining on a funeral urn,
> Her short liv'd darling son to mourn,
> The last was he, whose thunder flew
> The Titan-race, a rebel crew,
> That from a hundred hills allied
> In impious leagues their king defiend.
>   This wonder of the sculptor's had
> Produc'd, his art was at a stand :
> For who would hope new fame to raise,
> Or risk his well-establish'd praise,
> That, his high genius to approve,
> Had drawn a George, or carv'd a Jove ?"

SOMERVILLE.—William Somerville's chief work is a poem written in blank verse, entitled *The Chase,* and describing in a very animated manner, the circumstances attending that sport. He possessed the principal requisite of excellence, namely, a thorough intelligence of the subject upon which he wrote; and this he has enlarged by recounting the modes of hunting used in other countries, introducing at the same time such transition and variety, as to render the poem, in spite of the dryness of the subject, always interesting. *The Chase* can rank amongst the best of the didactic poems of the English language; and is written throughout with remarkable vigour and excellence. The following passage on the sagacity and the power of instinct in brutes, has been selected from this poem.

> "Observe that instinst which unerring guides
> The brutal race, which mimics reason's lore,
> And oft transcends: Heaven-taught, the roebuck swift
> Loiters at ease before the driving pack,
> And mocks their vain pursuit; nor far he flies,
> But checks his ardour, till the steaming scent
> That freshens on the blade, provokes their rage.
> Urg'd to their speed, his weak deluded foes
> Soon flag fatigued: strain to excess each nerve,
> Each slacken'd sinew fails; they pant, they foam,
> Then o'er the lawn he bounds, o'er the high hills
> Stretches secure, and leaves the scatter'd crowd
> To puzzle in the distant vale below.
>   'Tis Instinct that directs the jealous hare
> To choose her soft abode: With step revers'd
> She forms the doubling maze; then, ere the morn
> Peeps through the clouds, leaps to her close recess.
>   As wandering shepherds on th' Arabian plains
> No settled residence observe, but shift
> Their moving camp, now on some cooler hill
> With cedars crown'd, court the refreshing breeze;
> And then, below, where trickling streams distil
> From some penurious source, their thirst allay,
> And feed their fainting flocks: so the wise hares
> Oft quit their seats, lest some more curious eye
> Should mark their haunts, and by dark treacherous wiles,
> Plot their destruction; or perchance in hopes
> Of plenteous forage, near the ranker mead,
> Or matted blade, wary and close they sit,
> When spring shines forth, season of love and joy,
> In the moist marsh, 'mong beds of rushes hid.
> They cool their boiling blood: when summer suns
> Bake the cleft earth, to thick wide waving fields

Of his other poems, *Rural Sport* is the only one worthy of remark, and the beauty of this is somewhat destroyed by its being written in blank verse.

GREEN.—The principal work of this poet, is the lively and descriptive poem entitled *The Spleen*. It is written in octosyllabic verse, and contains many passages where new ideas are expressed in singularly felicitous images. The following lines on *The Wish* from this poem, will immediately illustrate its merits :—

> " Two hundred pounds, half-yearly paid,
> Annuity securely made,
> A farm some twenty miles from town,
> Small, tight, salubrious, and my own ;
> Two maids that never saw the town,
> A serving-man, not quite a clown,
> A boy to help to tread the mow,
> And drive, while t' other holds the plough.
> A chief, of temper form'd to please,
> Fit to converse and keep the keys ;
> And better to preserve the peace,
> Commission'd by the name of neice ;
> With understandings of a size
> To think their master very wise.
> May Heaven (it's all I wish for) send
> One genial room to treat a friend,
> Where decent cupboard, little plate,
> Display benevolence, not state.
> And may my humble dwelling stand
> Upon some chosen spot of land :
> A pond before full to the brim,
> Where cows may cool, and geese may swim :
> Behind, a green, like velvet neat,
> Soft to the eye and to the feet ;
> Where od'rous plants in ev'ning fair
> Breathe all around ambrosial air ;
> From Eurus, foe to kitchen ground,
> Fenc'd by a slope with bushes crown'd,
> Fit dwelling for the feather'd throng,

> Who pay their quit-rents with a song ;
> With op'ning views of hill and dale,
> Which sense and Fancy too regale."

AVAGE.—Richard Savage was the writer of miscellaneous ms, of which the best are *The Wanderer*, and *The Bastard*. : circumstances of his own birth no doubt suggested the sub- of the latter poem, Savage being the bastard child of Richard age, Earl Rivers, and the Countess of Macclesfield. This writer ainly possessed a truly poetical genius, and there is an origi- .ty of sentiment in his poetry, which gives it a distinguishing ure. The following passages with which the poem of *The Bas- t* opens and concludes, may be read as an example of his ting.

> "Blest be the Bastard's birth ! through wondrous ways,
> He shines eccentric like a comet's blaze !
> No sickly fruit of faint compliance He !
> He ! stampt in nature's mint of ecstacy !
> He lives to build, not boast, a generous race :
> No tenth transmitter of a foolish face.
> His daring hope, no fire's example bounds ;
> His first-born lights, no prejudice confounds.
> He, kindling, from within. requires no flame ;
> He glories in a Bastard's glowing name.
> Born to himself, by no possession led,
> In freedom foster'd, and by fortune fed ;
> Nor guides, nor rules, his sovereign choice control,
> His body independant as his soul ;
> Loos'd to the world's wide range—enjoy'd no aim,
> Prescrib'd no duty, and assign'd no name :
> Nature's unbounded son, he stands alone,
> His heart unbiass'd, and his mind his own.
>
> *   *   *   *   *
>
> Mother, miscall'd, farewell—of soul severe,
> This sad reflection yet may force one tear :
> All I was wretched by to you I ow'd,
> Alone from strangers every comfort flow'd !
> Lost to the life you gave, your son no more,
> And now adopted, who was doom'd before,
> New-born, I may a nobler Mother claim,
> But dare not whisper her immortal name ;
> Supremely lovely, and serenely great !
> Majestic Mother of a kneeling State !
> QUEEN of a people's heart, who ne'er before !
> Agreed—yet now with one consent adore !
> One contest yet remains in this desire,
> Who most shall give applause, where all admire,

"Silent Nymph! with curious eye,
Who, the purple evening, lie
On the mountain's lonely van,
Beyond the noise of busy man,
Painting fair the form of things,
While the yellow linnet sings;
Or the tuneful nightingale
Charm the forest with her tale ;
Come, with all thy various hues,
Come, and aid thy sister Muse.
Now, while Phœbus riding high,
Gives lustre to the land and sky,
Grongar Hill invites my song,
Draw the landscape bright and strong :
Grongar l in whose mossy cells,
Sweetly nursing Quiet dwells ;
Grongar l in whose silent shade,
For the modest Muses made,
So oft I have, the evening still,
As the fountain of a rill,
Sat upon a flow'ry bed,
With my hand beneath my head,
While stray'd my eyes o'er Towy's flood,
Over mead and over wood,
From house to house, from hill to hill,
Till Contemplation had her fill.

    *   *   *   :

O may I with myself agree,
And never covet what I see !
Content me with a humble shade,
My passions tam'd, my wishes laid ;
For while our wishes wildly roll,
We banish quiet from the soul."

MALLETT.—This writer is known chiefly by his *Ballads,* of which
William and Margaret, and *Edwin and Emma,* are the most
striking and beautiful. They are two well known to require quoting.

BLAIR.—Blair is the writer of a serious meditative poem in blank verse, entitled *The Grave,* which has always been admired for the strong and solemn pictures •that it paints of mortal affairs. The popularity of this poem is owing more to the intensity and terrible interest of the subject, than to any real beauty. There are many very fine and powerful passages in this poem, amongst which the following passage on *Friend-ship,* may be read as one of the finest.

> "Invidious Grave !—how doth thou rend in sunder
> Whom love has knit, and sympathy made one !
> A tie more stubborn far than Nature's band.
> FRIENDSHIP ! mysterious cement of the soul ;
> Sweetner of life, and solder of society,
> I owe thee much.   Thou hast deserv'd from me,
> Far, far beyond what I can ever pay.
> Oft have I prov'd the labours of thy love,
> And the warm efforts of the gentle heart,
> Anxious to please.—Oh ! when my friend and I
> In some thick wood have wander'd heedless on,
> Hid from the vulgar eye, and sat us down
> Upon the sloping cowslip-cover'd bank,
> Where the pure limpid stream has slid along
> In grateful errors thro' the underwood, ·
> Sweet murmuring ; methought the shrill tongu'd thrush
> Mended his song of love ; the sooty blackbird
> Mellow'd his pipe, and soften'd every note :
> The eglantine smell'd sweeter, and the rose
> Assum'd a dye more deep ; whilst ev'ry flower
> Vy'd with its fellow-plant in luxury
> Of dress—Oh ! then the longest summer's day
> Seem'd too much in haste ; still the full heart
> Had not imparted half : 'twas happiness
> Too exquisite to last.   Of joys departed,
> Not to return, how painful the remembrance."

HOWARD.—Sir Robert Howard, brother-in-law to Dryden, is the author of the *Duel of the Stags,* and other poems.   Besides these he wrote several heroic plays, which although not read now, were very popular in their day.   The following is a specimen of his writing, and contain in a few lines all the true essentials of poetry.

> "We always should remember Death is sure ;
> What grows familiar most, we best endure ;
> For life and death succeed like night and day,
> And neither gives increase, nor brings decay ;
> We must all pass through Death's *dead sea of night*
> To reach the haven of eternal light."

With thee I claim celestial birth,
  A spark of heaven's own ray;
Without thee sink to vilest earth,
  Inanimated clay.

Now in this sad and dismal hour
  Of multiply'd distress,
Has any former thought the power
  To make thy sorrows less?

When all around thee cruel snares
  Threaten thy destin'd breath,
And every sharp reflection bears
  Want, exile, chains, or death;—

Can aught that pass'd in youth's fond reign
  Thy pleasing vein restore?
Lives beauty's gay and festive train
  In memory's soft store?

Or does the muse? 'Tis said her art
  Can fiercest pangs appease;
Can she to thy poor trembling heart
  Now speak the words of peace?

Yet she was wont at early dawn
  To whisper thy repose,
Nor was her friendly aid withdrawn
  At grateful evening's close.

Friendship, 'tis true, its sacred might
  May mitigate thy doom;
As lightning. shot across the night,
  A moment gilds the gloom."

COTTON.—Nathaniel Cotton it known as the author of *Miscella-neous Poems.* There are many in this collection of the highest merit, and others of such beauty as to give this poet a prominent position in the rank of our lesser English poets. The following poem *To-Morrow*, is selected as an example.

"To-morrow, didst thou say!
  Methought I heard Horatio say, To-morrow.
  Go to—I will not hear of it—to·morrow!

'Tis a sharper who takes penury .
Against thy plenty—who takes thy ready cash,
And pays thee nought but wishes, hopes, and promises,
The currency of idiots. Injurious bankrupt
That gulls the easy creditor !—To-morrow !
It is a period nowhere to be found
In all the hoary registers of time
Unless perchance in the fool's calendar.
Wisdom disclaims the words, nor holds society
With those who own it. No, my Horatio,
'Tis Fancy's child, and Folly is its Father ;
Wrought on such stuff as dreams are ; and baselets
As the fantastic visions of the evening."

LYTTLETON.—Lord Lyttleton's poetry is of only moderate merit, although there may be found a few passages of beauty. Perhaps one of the best of his small pieces is his *Description of a Female Character.*

"Her kindly melting heart.
To every want and every woe ;
To guilt itself when in distress,
The balm of pity would impart,
And all relief that bounty could bestow !
E'en for the kid or lamb that pour'd its life
Beneath the bloody knife,
Her gentle tears would fall,
As she the common mother were of all.

Not only good, and kind,
But strong and elevated was her mind :
A spirit that, with noble pride,
Could look, superior down
On Fortune's smile, or frown ;
That could, without regret or pain,
To Virtue's lowest duty sacrifice
Or Interest's, or ambition's highest prize ;
That, injur'd or offended, never try'd
Its dignity by vengeance to maintain.
But by magnanimous disdain.

A wit that temperately bright,
With inoffensive light,
All pleasing shone, nor ever past
The decent bounds, that Wisdom's sober hand.
And sweet Benevolence's mild command,
And bashful modesty before it cast
A prudence, undeceiving, undeceiv'd ;
That nor too little, nor too much believ'd ;
That scorn'd unjust Suspicion's coward fear,
And without weakness knew to be sincere."

The most insipid; the most void of smell.
Such the rude mountain from his horrid sides
Pours down ; such waters in the sandy vale
For ever boil, alike of winter frosts
And summer's heat secure. The crystal stream,
O'er rocks resounding, or for many a mile
Hurl'd down the pebbly channel, wholesome yields
'And mellow draughts , except when winter thaws,
And half the mountains melt into the tide."

JOHNSON.—The principal poetical works of Samuel Johnson, are two satires, entitled *London*, and *The Vanity of Human Wishes;* the former being an excellent paraphrase upon the third satire of Juvenal . In that satire , Juvenal directs his venom against the corruptions of society in Rome at that period, and the misery and humiliation which a poor but honest man had to encounter ; contrasted with the immense riches and influence obtained by the most unworthy arts by Greeks, and favorite freedmen. These invectives of Juvenal, Johnson has skilfully and artistically transferred to the passion for imitating French fashions, and adapted the images of the Roman poet, to the vices, corruptions, and discomforts of London. The poem possesses throughout, the power and fire of the original, and breathes the true indignation and scorn of its Roman prototype. The following passage is selected from it as an example.

"By numbers here, from shame or censure free,
All crimes are safe but hated poverty :
This, only this, the rigid law pursues,
This, only this, provokes the snarling muse.
The sober trader at a tatter'd cloak
Wakes from his dream, and labours for a joke ;
With brisker air the silken courtiers gaze,
And turn the varied taunt a thousand ways.
Of all the griefs that harass the distress'd,
Sure the most bitter is a scornful jest ;
Fate never wounds more deep the generous heart
Than when a blockhead's insult points the dart.
    Has Heaven reserv'd, in pity to the poor,
No pathless waste, or undiscover'd shore ?
No secret island in the boundless main ?
No peaceful desert yet unclaim'd by Spain ?
Quick let us rise, the happy seats explore,
And bear Oppression's insolence no more.
This mournful truth is everywhere confess'd :
SLOW RISES WORTH, BY POVERTY DISTRESS'D ;
But here more slow, where all are slaves to gold.
Where looks are merchandise, and smiles are sold ;
Where, won by bribes, by flatteries implor'd,
The groom retails the favours of his lord."

GAMBOLD.—John Gambold was the author of a tragedy entitled
Ignatius, and other smaller poems.   Besides these, he is the writer
of a number of *Hymns* in the *Moravian Brethren's Collection.*
There is an merit in his writings, equal to any minor poet of his
time, and there may be found in some, passages of the highest
sublimity and loftiest conception.   For an example the following
stanza is quoted.

EPITAPH ON HIMSELF.

" Ask not, who ended here his span ?
His name, reproach and praise, was man.
Did no great deeds adorn his course ?
No deed of his, but show'd him worse :
One thing was great, which God supplied,
He suffer'd human life—and died.
What points of knowledge did he gain ?
That life was sacred all—and vain :
Sacred how high, and vain how low,
He knew not here, but died to know."

GLOVER.—The only important work of this poet is an epic, on
the subject of the Persian wars, named *Leonidas,* which became
immensely popular at the time it was written, though little read
now,   He wrote also as a kind of continuation of this, a second

There are many parts of considerable beauty which might have been chosen as examples, amongst which the following passage from the First Book,

"In speechless anguish on the hero's breast
She sinks.   On ev'ry side his children press,
Hang on his knees, and kiss his honour'd hand.
His soul no longer struggles to confine
Her agitation.   Down the hero's cheek, .
Down flows the manly sorrow.   Great in woe,
Amid his children, who enclose him round,
He stands, indulging tenderness and love
In graceful tears, when thus, with lifted eyes
Address'd to heaven, 'Thou ever-living pow'r
Look down propitious, sire of gods and men !
O to this faithful woman, whose desert
May claim thy favour, grant the hours of peace !
And thou, my bright forefather, seed of Jove,
O Hercules, neglect not these thy race !
But, since that spirit I from thee derive
Transports me from them to resistless fate,
Be thou their guardian !   Teach them, like thyself,
By glorious labours to embelish life,
And from their father let them learn to die !'"

SHENSTONE.—This poet is famous for his pastoral elegies, which have a softness and smoothness of diction in the highest degree pleasing, although they better refer to the actual sentiments and circumstances of rustic life.   His *Schoolmistress* will always hold a place amongst English poems.   It is written in the Spenser-ian stanzas, and paints with a delightful mixture of quaint playfulness

d

and tender description, the characters and pursuits of an old village dame, who keeps a rustic-school! Shenstone has never been excelled in elegiac poetry, and in the simplicity of his pastoral poetry there are also very few who equal him. The following verses on *Disappointment,* from his well-known *Pastoral Ballads,* are quoted below.

"Ye shepherds! give ear to my lay,
  And take no more heed of my sheep;
They have nothing to do but to stray,
  I have nothing to do but to weep.
Yet do not my folly reprove;
  She was fair—and my passion begun;
She smil'd—and I could not but love;
  She is faithless—and I am undone.

She is faithless, and I am undone;
  Ye that witness the woes I endure,
Let reason instruct you to shun
  What it cannot instruct you to cure.
Beware how you loiter in vain
  Amid nymphs of an higher degree;
It is not for me to explain
  How fair and how fickle they be.

Alas! from the day that we met
  What hope of an end to my woes?
When I cannot endure to forget
  The glance that undid my repose.
Yet time may diminish the pain:
  The flow'r, and the shrub, and the tree,
Which I rear'd for her pleasure in vain,
  In time may have comfort for me.

The sweets of a dew-sprinkled rose,
  The sound of a murmuring stream,
The peace which from solitude flows,
  Henceforth shall be Corydon's theme.
High transports are shown to the sight,
  But we are not to find them our own;
Fate never bestow'd such delight
  As I with my Phyllis had known.

O ye woods! spread your branches apace,
  To your deepest recesses I fly,
I would hide with the beasts of the chase,
  I would vanish from every eye.
Yet my reed shall resound through the grove,
  With the same sad complaint it began;
How she smil'd—and I could not but love!
  Was faithless—and I am undone!"

is selected from a poem written *On Two Daughters, twins, who died in two days.*

> "Dear, precious Babes ! alas ! when, fondly wild,
> A mother's heart hung melting o'er her child ;
> When my charm'd eye a flood of joy express'd,
> And all the father kindled in my breast,
> A sudden paleness seized each guiltless face,
> And death, though smiling, crept o'er every grace.
>   Nature, be calm ; heave not the impassion'd sigh,
> Nor teach one tear to tremble in mine eye ;
> A few unspotted moments, pass'd between
> Their dawn of being, and their closing scene ;
> And sure no nobler blessing can be given,
> When one short anguish is the price of heaven."

SMOLLETT.—Thomas Smollett is more eminent as a novelist than as a poet, yet there are a few poetical pieces written by him, which exhibit great delicacy, and an elevated tone of sentiment. The best of his verses are those entitled the *Tears of Scotland* : they breathe throughout an earnest patriotism, and display a genuine indignation against the cruelties which were inflicted after the battle of Culloden. The language is bitter and stinging. The most popular of his poems is the *Ode to Leven-Water,* which we quote as a specimen.

> "On Leven's banks, while free to rove,
> And tune the rural pipe to love ;
> I envied not the happiest swain
> That ever trod th' Arcadian plain.
>   Pure stream, in whose transparent wave
> My youthful limbs I wont to lave ;
> No torrents stain thy limpid source ;
> No rocks impede thy dimpling course,
> That sweetly warbles o'er its bed,
> With white, round, polish'd pebbles spread ;
> While, lightly pois'd, the scaly brood
> In myriads cleave thy crystal flood ;
> The springing trout in speckled pride ;
> The salmon, monarch of the tide,
> The ruthless pike, intent on war ;
> The silver eel, and mottled par.
> Devolving from thy parent lake,

A charming maze thy waters make,
By bowers of birch, and groves of pine,
And edges flower'd with eglantine.
　Still on my banks so gaily green,
May num'rous herds and flocks be seen,
And lasses chaunting o'er the pail,
And shepherds piping in the dale,
And ancient Faith that knows no guile,
And Industry embrown'd with toil,
And hearts resolv'd, and hands prepar'd,
The blessing they enjoy to guard l"　.

BLACKLOCK. —The works of Thomas Blacklock, the blind poet,
surprise by the correctness and vividness of the descriptions, par-
ticularly of natural objects. In his style he ranks equally with
Parnell or Shenstone, and many of his poems show at once how
alive his mind was to the sublime and beautiful. The following
Hymn to Benevolence is beautifully written and expressed :—

"Hail, source of transport ever new !
While I thy strong impulse pursue,
　I taste a joy sincere ;
Too vast for little minds to know,
Who on themselves alone bestow
　Their wishes and their care.
Daughter of God ! delight of man !
From thee Felicity began ;
　Which still thy hand sustains ;
By thee sweet Peace her empire spread,
Fair Science rais'd her laurel'd head,
　And Discord gnash'd in chains.
Far as the pointed sunbeam flies
Through peopled earth and starry skies,
　All nature owns thy nod ;
We see its energy prevail
Through being's ever-rising scale,
　From nothing e'en to God.
By thee inspir'd, the generous breast,
In blessing others only blest ;
　With goodness large and free,
Delights the widow's tears to stay,
To teach the blind their smoothest way,
　And aid the feeble knee.
O come ! and o'er my bosom reign,
Expand my heart, inflame each vein,
　Through ev'ry action shine ;
Each low, each selfish wish control ;
With all thy essence warm my soul,
　And make me wholly thine.

sublime." Smart is also the author of a satire called the *Hiliad,* an attack on the well-known Sir John Hill. The following are the stanzas, called *David,* alluded to above.

"Sublime,—invention ever-young,
Of vast conception, towering tongue,
To God th' eternal theme;
Notes from your exaltations caught,
Unrivall'd royalty of thought,
O'er meaner thoughts supreme.

His muse, bright angel of his verse,
Gives balm for all the thorns that pierce,
For all the pangs that rage :
Blest light still gaining on the gloom,
The more than Michael of his bloom,
Th' Abishag of his age.

He sang of God the mighty source
Of all things—that stupendous force,
On which all strength depends ;
From whose right arm, beneath whose eyes,
All period, power and enterprize
Commences, reigns and ends.

The world, the clustering spheres he made,
The glorious light the soothing shade,
Dale, champaign, grove and hill ;
The multitudinous abyss,
Where secresy remains in bliss ;
And wisdom hides her skill.

'Tell them, I AM,' Jehovah said
To Moses, while earth heard in dread ;
And, smitten to the heart,
At once, above, beneath, around,
All nature, without voice or sound,
Replied, 'O LORD, THOU ART.'"

WILKIE.—Though a less important poet, there may be found amongst the pieces by Wilkie, several that display a considerable talent ; and there is in all, a correct versification. He is not remarkable for any particular poem, however. The Fable of the *Boy and the Rainbow*, may be read as one of his best pieces.

> "One ev'ning as a simple swain
> His flock attended on the plain,
> The shining Bow he chanc'd to spy,
> Which warns us when a show'r is nigh ;
> With brightest rays it seem'd to glow,
> Its distance eighty yards or so.
> This bumpkin had, it seems, been told
> The story of the cup of gold,
> Which Fame reports is to be found
> Just where the Rainbow meets the ground ;
> He therefore felt a sudden hitch
> To seize the goblet, and be rich ;
> Hoping, yet hopes are oft but vain,
> No more to toil thro' wind and rain,
> But sit indulgent by the fire,
> 'Midst ease and plenty, like a squire !
> He mark'd the very spot of land
> On which the Rainbow seem'd to stand,
> And stepping forwards at his leisure,
> Expected to have found the treasure.
> But as he mov'd, the colour'd ray
> Still chang'd its place, and slipt away,
> As seeming his approach to shun ;
> From walking he began to run ;
> But all in vain, it still withdrew
> As nimbly as he could pursue ;
> At last, thro' many a bog and lake,
> Rough craggy rock, and thorny brake,
> It lead the easy fool, till night
> Approach'd, then vanish'd in his sight,
> And left him to compute his gains,
> With nought but labour for his pains."

MASON.—William Mason's chief poetical works beyond his dramas, were *The English Garden*, a poem in blank verse, and *An Heroic Epistle to Sir William Chambers, Knight*, a brilliant and lively satire. The following beautiful *Ode* is selected from his miscellaneous works as a specimen.

ODE TO TRUTH.

> "Attend, ye sons of men ! attend and say,
> Does not enough of my refulgent ray

Whose cheek but mocks the peach's bloom,
Whose breath the hyacinth's perfume,
Whose melting voice the warbling woodlark's lays,
Shall she be deem'd my rival ? shall a form
Of elemental dross, of mould'ring clay,
Vie with these charms imperial ? The poor worm
Shall prove her contest vain. Life's little day,
Shall pass, and she is gone : while I appear
Flush'd with the bloom of youth through Heav'n's eternal year.
Know, mortals, know, ere first ye sprung,
Ere first these orbs in ether hung,
I shone amid the heavenly throng :
These eyes beheld creation's day,
This voice began the choral lay,
And taught Archangels their triumphant song.
Pleas'd I survey'd bright Nature's gradual birth,
Saw infant Light with kindling lustre spread,
Soft vernal fragrance clothe the flow'ring earth,
And ocean heave on its extended bed ;
Saw the tall pine aspiring pierce the sky ;
The tawny lion stalk ; the rapid eagle fly.
Last, Man arose, erect in youthful grace,
Heav'n's hallow'd image stamp'd upon his face,
And as he rose, the high behest was given,
'That I alone, of all the host of heaven,
'Should reign protectress of the godlike youth.'
Thus the Almighty spake : he spake, and call'd me Truth."

CHURCHILL.—Charles Churchill has been considered the most popular English satirist between Pope and Byron. His greatest satire is the *Rosciad*, which has been placed on a level with Dryden, and which obtained the greatest popularity at the time of publication. Although it has in it little poetical fervour, the rhythm is flowing and pleasing and the diction easy, while the invective is bold and pointed. Churchill sought for *immediate* popularity, and in truth he was for a time one of the most popular of English poets ; but his fame was not lasting. He will always hold a place however, amongst our English poets from the influence he had over the other poets of his time. Hannay, in his Memoir of Churchill,

says, "he helped to form Cowper, and he helped to form Crabbe."
The most poetical of his works is *Gotham*; Cowper terms it "a
masterly performance." An example of his satire may be seen in
the following sketch af Bishop Warburton, which is equal in vigour
and keenness of edge to our greatest English satirist, Swift.

> "The first entitled to the place
> Of honour both by gown and grace,
> Who never let occasion slip
> To take right hand of fellowship,
> And was so proud, that should he meet
> The Twelve Apostles in the street,
> He'd turn his nose up at them all,
> And shove his Saviour from the wall;
> Who was so mean (Meanness and Pride
> Still go together side by side)
> That he would cringe, and creep, be civil,
> And hold a stirrup for the devil,
> If in a journey to his mind,
> He'd let him mount and ride behind;
> Who basely fawned through all his life,
> For patrons first, then for a wife;
> Wrote Dedications which must make
> The heart of every Christian quake;
> Made one man equal to, or more
> Than God, then left him, as before
> His God he left, and, drawn by pride,
> Shifted about to t' other side;
> Was by his sire a parson made,
> Merely to give the boy a trade."

WARTON.—The name of Thomas Warton owes its chief lustre
to his *History of English Poetry*, although he has written many
original pieces 'which display considerable descriptive and other
essential powers of poetic composition. The best of his verses are
Sonnets exhibiting much picturesque fancy, and breathing through-
out a true feeling of poetry. The following may be read as a
specimen of his writing, and is to be admired for the descriptive
beauties which it contains.

THE HAMLET.

> "The hinds how blest who ne'er beguil'd,
> To quit their Hamlet's hawthorn-wild;
> Nor haunt the crowd, nor tempt the main
> For splendid care, and guilty gain.
> When Morning's twilight-tinctur'd beam
> Strikes their low thatch with slanting gleam,

They rove abroad in ether blue,
To dip the scythe in fragrant dew ;
The sheaf to bind, the beech to fell,
That, nodding, shades a craggy dell.

     *   *   *   *

For them the moon with cloudless ray
Mounts, to illume their homeward way :
Their weary spirits to relieve,
The meadows incense breathe at eve.
No riot mars the simple fare
That o'er a glimmering hearth they share ;
But when the curfew's measur'd roar
Duly, the darkening valleys o'er,
Has echoed from the distant town,
They wish no beds of cygnet-down,
No trophied canopies, to close.
Their drooping eyes in quick repose.

     *   *   *   *

Their humble porch with honey'd flowers
The curling woodbine's shade embowers :
From the small garden's thymy mound
Their bees in busy swarms resound ;
Nor fell Disease, before his time,
Hastes to consume Life's golden prime ;
But when their temples long have wore
The silver crown of tresses hoar :
As studious still calm peace to keep,
Beneath a flowery turf they sleep."

FALCONER.—Falconer's descriptive poem, *The Shipwreck*, has always been considered as a valuable part of the stock of English poetry. It is a narrative poem, in three cantos, describing a scene of suffering which took place in a voyage from Alexandria to Venice which the poet, then a professional seamen, had himself witnessed. It is a vigorous and correct painting of Nature under her wildest aspects of storm and terror. A tale of affections is interwoven with the narrative of the poem ; and this, with the liveliness and originality of the descriptions, renders the poem at all times interesting and exciting. Many of the descriptive passages in this poem are very finely written : for example the following passage from the First canto.

"The sun's bright orb, declining all serene,
Now glanced obliquely o'er the woodland scene :
Creation smiles around ; on every spray
The warbling birds exalt their evening lay :

Blithe skipping o'er yon hill, the fleecy train
Join the deep chorus of the lowing plain ;
The golden lime, and orange, there were seen
On fragrant branches of perpetual green ;
The crystal streams that velvet meadows lave,
To the green ocean roll with chiding wave.
The glassy ocean hushed forgets to roar,
But trembling murmurs on the sandy shore :
And lo ! his surface lovely to behold
Glows in the west, a sea of living gold !
While, all above, a thousand liveries gay
The skies with pomp ineffable array.
Arabian sweets perfume the happy plains ;
Above, beneath, around, enchantment reigns !
While glowing vesper leads the starry train,
And night slow draws her veil o'er land, and main.
Emerging clouds the azure east invade,
And wrap the lucid spheres in gradual shade,
While yet the songsters of the vocal grove,
With dying numbers tune the soul to love."

SCOTT.--The chief characteristics of the poems of John Scott,
are simplicity and elegance.   They also breathe throughout a
spirit of tenderness, suggestive of the amiable and virtuous charac-
ter of the poet's mind.   There is nothing of sublimity about them,
nor do they require it to complete their perfection.   The eclogue
on *The Praise of Rural Life,* from which the following passage is
taken, is a worthy example of this poet's writing and may be read
as one of the finest specimens of pastoral poetry.

" Fair Spring o'er Nature held her gentlest sway,
Fair Morn diffus'd around her brightest ray ;
Thin mists hung hovering on the distant trees,
Or roll'd from off the fields before the breeze.
The shepherd Theron watch'd his fleecy train,
Beneath a broad oak, on the grassy plain :
A heath's green wild lay pleasant to his view,
With shrubs and field-flowers deck'd of varied hue :
There hawthorns tall their silver bloom disclos'd,
Here flexile broom's bright yellow interpos'd ;
There purple orchis, here pale daisies spread,
And sweet May lilies richest odours shed.
From many a copse and blossom orchard near,
The voice of birds melodious charm'd the ear ;
There shrill the lark, and soft the linnet sung,
And loud through air the throstle's music rung,
The gentle swain the cheerful scene admir'd ;
The cheerful scene the song of joy inspir'd
'Chant on !' he cried 'ye warblers on the spray

must address itself to the senses rather than to the sentiments," The neglect of his works, although partly owing to this, may in a measure also be attributed to the peculiarity of his doctrine. Many of the subordinate descriptions in the *Botanic Garden*, display however, great force of language and much picturesqueness. For instance, the opening canto from the *Loves of the Plants*.

> "While in soft notes I tune to oaten reed
> Gay hopes, and amorous sorrows of the mead.—
> From giant's oaks, that wave their branches dark,
> To the dwarf moss that clings upon their bark,
> What beaux and beauties crowd the gaudy groves,
> And woo and win their vegetable loves.
> How snowdrops cold, and blue-eyed harebells blend
> Their tender tears, as o'er the stream they bend ;
> The love-sick violet, and the primrose pale,
> Bow their sweet heads, and whisper to the gale ;
> With secret sighs the virgin lily droops,
> And jealous cowslips hang their tawny cups.
> How the young rose in beauty's damask pride
> Drinks the warm blushes of his bashful bride ;
> With honey'd lips enamour'd woodbines meet,
> Clasp with fond arms, and mix their kisses sweet.
>   Stay thy soft murmuring waters, gentle rill ;
> Hush, whispering winds ; ye rustling leaves, be still ;
> Rest, silver butterflies, your quivering wings ;
> Alight, ye beetles, from your airy rings ;
> Ye painted moths , your gold-eyed plumage furl,

Bow your wide horns, your spiral trunks uncurl ;
Glitter, ye glow-worms, on your mossy beds ;
Descend, ye spiders, on your lengthened threads ;
Slide here, ye horned snails, with varnish'd shells ;
Ye bee-nymphs, listen in your waxen cells ! "

PORTEUS.—Beilby Porteus (Bishop of London) distinguis
by his works on Divinity, was the writer of several miscellan
poems, amongst which is a prize poem, entitled *Death.*]
written in a masterly manner, and contains passages of the hig
beauty. The following passage on Natural and Violent death, ta
from this poem, will afford an example.

"——— ———-Man went to till the ground
From whence he rose ; sentenced indeed to toil
As to a punishment, yet (even in wrath,
So merciful is Heaven) this toil became
The solace of his woes, the sweet employ
Of many a live-long hour, and surest guard
Against disease and death. Death, tho' denounced,
Was yet a distant ill, by feeble arm
Of age, his sole support, led slowly on.
Not then, as since, the short-lived sons of men
Flock'd to his realms in countless multitudes ;
Scarce in the course of twice five hundred years,
One solitary ghost went shivering down
To his unpeopled shore.

  *   *   *   *

     Thus nerved with giant strength
He stemm'd the tide of time, and stood the shock
Of ages rolling harmless o'er his head.
At life's meridian point arrived, he stood,
And, looking round, saw all the valleys filled
With nations from his loins ; full-well content
To leave his race thus scatter'd o'er the earth,
Along the gentle slope of life's decline
He bent his gradual way, till, full of years,
He dropp'd like mellow fruit into his grave.
 Such in the infancy of time was man ;
So calm was life, so impotent was death !
O had he but preserved these few remains,
The shatter'd fragments, of lost happiness,
Snatch'd by the hand of Heaven from the sad wreck
Of innocence primeval ; still had he lived
In ruin great ; tho' fall'n, yet not forlorn ;
Though mortal, yet not everywhere beset
With death in every shape ! But he, impatient
To be completely wretched, hastes to fill up
The measure of his woes.—'Twas man himself

The following stanzas are an example of his writings.

TO A YOUNG LADY FOND OF BOTANY.

"Say, gentle Lady of the bower,
  For thou, tho' young, art wise,
And known to thee is every flower
  Beneath our milder skies :

Say, which the plant of modest dye,
  And lovely mien combin'd,
That fittest to the pensive eye
  Displays the virtuous mind.

I sought the groves, where innocence,
  Methought might long reside ;
But April's blossoms banish'd thence,
  Gave Summer, Flora's pride.

I sought the garden's boasted haunt,
  But on the gay parterre
Carnations glow, and tulips flaunt,
  No humble flow'ret there.

The flower you seek, the nymph replies,
  He bow'd the languid head ;
For on its bloom the blazing skies
  Their sultry rage have shed.

'Tis now the downward withering day,
  Of Winter's dull presage,
That seeks not where the dog-star's ray
  Has shed his fiercest rage.

Yet search yon shade obscure, forlorn,
  Where rude the bramble grows ;
There, shaded by the humble thorn,
  The lingering primrose blows."

BEATTIE.—The most celebrated of this poet's works, is t]
entitled *The Minstrel,* a poem written in the stanza of Spens‹
in which the poet describes the progress of the imagination a
feelings of a young and rustic poet. Some of the descriptive passa‹
in this poem are very beautifully drawn : of which an exam
may be seen in the following stanzas :—

"But who the melodies of morn can tell ?
  The wild-brook babbling down the mountain side ;
  The lowing herd ; The sheepfold's simple bell ;
  The pipe of early shepherd dim descried
  In the lone valley ; echoing far and wide
  The clamorous horn along the cliffs above ;
  The hollow murmur of the ocean-tide ;
  The hum of bees, and linnets lay of love,
And the full choir that wakes the universal grove.

  The cottage-curs at early pilgrim bark ;
  Crown'd with her pail the tripping milkmaid sings;
  The whistling ploughman stalks afield ; and, hark !
  Down the rough slope the ponderous waggon rings ;
  Through rustling corn the hare astonished springs ;
  Slow tolls the village-clock the drowsy hour ;
  The partridge bursts away on whirring wings ;
  Deep mourns the turtle in sequester'd bower,
And shrill lark carols clear from her aërial tower."

WOLCOT.—The works of John Wolcot, or, as he termed him‹
in his writings, Peter Pindar, are remarkable for the humour‹
spirit in which they are written ; this and their originality are th
chief characteristics. Of his well-known *Odes,* the following,
The Glow-worm, is one of the most admired.

" Bright stranger, welcome to my field ;
  Here feed in safety, here thy radiance yield ;
    To me, oh, nightly be thy splendour giv'n !
  Oh, could a wish of mine the skies command,
  How would I gem thy leaf with liberal hand,
    With ev'ry sweetest dew of heav'n !

  Say, dost thou kindly light the fairy train
  Amid their gambols on the stilly plain,
    Hanging thy lamp upon the moisten'd blade ;
  What lamp so fit, so pure as thine,
  Amid the gentle elfin band to shine,
    And chase the horrors of the midnight shade ?

  Oh ! may no feather'd foe disturb thy bow'r,
  And with barbarian beak thy life devour !
    Oh ! may no ruthless torrent of the sky,

To guard thee from the rushing rains of night,
  And hide thee from the wild wing of the storm.
Sweet child of stillness, 'mid the awful calm
  Of pausing Nature thou art pleas'd to dwell ;
In happy silence to enjoy thy balm,
  And shed through life a lustre round thy cell.

How different man, the imp of noise and strife,
Who courts the storm that tears and darkens life !
  Blest when the passions wild the soul invade !
How nobler far to bid these whirlwinds cease,
To taste, like thee, the luxury of peace,
  And, silent, shine in solitude and shade !"

PIOZZI.—Mrs. Thrale, afterwards Mrs. Piozzi, is better known by her principal prose work, *Anecdotes of Dr. Johnson,* than by her poetry ; although there are amongst the latter many pieces of great merit and singular beauty. This will be found exemplified in the following excellent little poem, *The Three Warnings.* The passage in which Dobson is visited and warned for the third time by Death, from this poem, is quoted as a specimen of the work of this talented writer.

"And now one night in musing mood,
  As all alone he sat,
Th' unwelcome messenger of Fate
  Once more before him stood.
Half kill'd with anger and surprise,
  'So soon return'd !' old Dobson cries.
'So soon, d' ye call it !' Death replies :
'Surely, my friend, you're but in jest ;
Since I was here before,
'Tis six-and-thirty years at least,
  And you are now fourscore.'
'So much the worse,' the clown rejoin'd ;
'To spare the aged would be kind :
However, see your search be legal ;
And your authority—is't regal ?
Else you are come on a fool's errand,
  With but a Secretary's warrant.
Besides you promis'd me Three Warnings,
Which I have look'd for nights and mornings
  But for that loss of time and ease,

I can 'recover damages.'
'I know,' cries Death, 'that, at the best,
I seldom am a welcome guest :
But don't be captious, friend, at least:
I little thought you'd still be able
To stump about your farm and stable ;
Your years have run to a great length,
I wish you joy, tho', of your strength.'
'Hold,' says the farmer, 'not so fast,
I have been lame these four years past.'
'And no great wonder,' Death replies ;
However, you still keep your eyes;
And sure, to see one's loves and friends,
For legs and arms would make amends.'
'Perhaps,' says Dobson, 'so it might,
But latterly I've lost my sight.'
'This is a shocking story,' faith ;
Yet there's some comfort still,' says Death
'Each strives your sadness to amuse,
I warrant you hear all the news.'
'There's none,' cries he ; 'and if there were,
I'm grown so deaf, I could not hear.'
'Nay then,' the spectre stern rejoin'd,
'These are unjustifiable yearnings;
If you are Lame, and Deaf, and Blind,
You've had your three sufficient warnings,
So come along, no more we'll part':
He said, and touch'd him with his dart ;
And now old Dobson, turning pale,
Yields to his fate,—so ends my tale."

BARBAULD.—Mrs. Barbauld's miscellaneous poems exhibit the highest excellence, and there may be found in them many passages of the greatest beauty. She is best remembered, however, by her *Essays.* The following passage from her poem, the *Address to the Deity*, is a very fine example of her writings.

"God of my life, and author of my days !
Permit my feeble voice to lisp thy praise ;
And trembling take upon a mortal tongue
That hallow'd name to harps of seraphs sung.
Yet here the brightest seraphs could no more
Than hide their faces, tremble, and adore.
Worms, angels, men, in every different sphere,
Are equal all, for all are nothing here.
All Nature faints beneath the mighty name,
Which Nature's works through all her parts, proclaim.
I feel that name my inmost thoughts control,
And breathe an awful stillness thro' my soul ;
As by a charm, the waves of grief subside ;

I hear the voice of God among the trees ;
With thee in shady solitudes I walk.
With thee in busy crowded cities talk ;
In every creature own thy forming power,
In each event thy providence adore.

    *   *   *   *   *

And when the last, the closing hours draw nigh,
And earth recedes before my swimming eye ;
When trembling on the doubtful edge of fate
I stand, and stretch my view to either state ;
Teach me to quit this transitory scene
With decent triumph and a look serene ;
Teach me to fix my ardent hopes on high
And, having lived to Thee, in Thee to die."

MORE.—The best known works of Hannah More are, *Thoughts
on the Manners of the Great; On Female Education; Calebs in
Search of a Wife, &c.*, the latter of which is perhaps the best.
Her later works are of a more sombre tone, and possess none of
that ready sparkling humour, which characterizes her earlier pro-
ductions : her sacred dramas, however, are very fine, and contain
in many places, passages of striking pathos and beauty. For ex-
ample, the following lines from *David and Goliath* : —

"And what is death?
Is it so terrible to die, my brother?
Or grant it terrible, is it for that
The less inevitable? If, indeed,
We could by stratagem elude the blow,
When some high duty calls us forth to die,
And thus for ever shun it, and escape
The universal lot,—then fond self-love,
Then cautious prudence, boldly might produce
Their fine-spun arguments, their learned harangues,

f

Their cobweb arts, their phrase sophistical,
Their subtile doubts, and all the specious tricks
Of selfish cunning labouring for its end.
But since, howe'er protracted, death will come,
Why fondly study, with ingenious pains,
To put it off?—To breathe a little longer
Is to defer our fate, but not to shun it.
Small gain! which wisdom, with indifferent eye,
Beholds. Why wish to drink the bitter dregs
Of life's exhausted chalice, whose last runnings,
E'en at the best, are vapid! Why not die
(If heaven so will) in manhood's op'ning bloom,
When all the flush of life is gay about us;
When sprightly youth, with many a new-born joy,
Solicits every sense! so may we then
Present a sacrifice, unmeet indeed,
(Ah, how unmeet!) but less unworthy far,
Than the world's leavings; than a worn-out heart,
By vice enfeebled, and by vain desires
Sunk and exhausted."

JONES.—Sir William Jones has obtained a place amongst English poets, by having published a volume of miscellaneous poems, and various translations from the Eastern languages. Some of his original lyrical pieces are much admired, and contain some most beautiful passages. He is most eminent as an oriental scholar; and was one of the first Europeans who studied Sanskrit. The following *Ode in Imitation of Alcæus*, selected from his works, is a fine effusion of patriotism.

"What constitutes a state?
Not high-rais'd battlement and labour'd mound,
    Thick wall or moated gate;
Not cities proud with spires and turre's crown'd;
    Not bays and broad-arm'd ports,
Where, laughing at the storm, rich navies ride,
    Not starr'd and spangled courts,
Where low-brow'd baseness wafts perfume to pride.
    No:—Men, high minded-men,
With powers as far above dull brutes endued,
    In forest, brake, or den,
As beasts excel cold rocks and brambles rude;
    Men, who their duties know,
But know their rights, and knowing, dare maintain,
    Prevent the long-aim'd blow,
And crush the tyrant while they rend the chain:
    These constitute a state,
And sovereign Law, that state's collected will,

"I love to rise ere gleams the tardy light,
  Winter's pale dawn ; and as warm fires illume,
  And cheerful tapers shine around the room,
Through misty windows bend by musing sight,
Where, round the dusky lawn, the mansions white,
  With shutters clos'd, peer faintly through the gloom
That slow recedes ; while yon gray spires assume,
Rising from their dark pile, an added height
By indistinctness given.   Then to decree
The grateful thoughts to God, ere they unfold
To friendship or the Muse, or seek with glee
Wisdom's rich page.   Oh, hours more worth than gold,
By whose blest use we lengthen life, and, free
From drear decays of age, outlive the old."

LOGAN.—John Logan is the author of the tragedy entitled *Runnymede*, and the well-known *Ode to the Cuckoo*. Besides these works, there are to be found among his other pieces, many of true beauty ; as for instance, *Ossian's Hymn to the Sun*, or the following exquisite ode on *Autumn*.

"'Tis past ! no more the Summer blooms !
  Ascending in the rear,
Behold congenial Autumn comes,
  The sabbath of the year !
What time thy holy whispers breathe,
The pensive evening shade beneath,
  And twilight consecrates the floods ;—
While Nature strips her garments gay,

And wears the vesture of decay,
O let me wander through the sounding woods.
Ah ! well-known streams ! ah ! wonted groves,
   Still pictur'd in my mind !
Oh ! sacred scene of youthful loves,
   Whose image lives behind !
While sad I ponder on the past,
The joys that must no longer last ;
   The wild-flower strown on Summer's bier,
The dying music of the grove,
And the last elegies of love,
Dissolve the soul, and draw the tender tear !

      *   *   *   *

Yet not unwelcome waves the wood,
   That hides me in its gloom,
While lost in melancholy mood
   I muse upon the tomb.
Their chequer'd leaves the branches shed ;
Whirling in eddies o'er my head,
   They sadly sigh that Winter's near ;
The warning voice I hear behind,
That shakes the wood without a wind,
And solemn sounds the death-bell of the year.

Now will I court Lethean streams,
   The sorrowing sense to steep ;
Nor drink oblivion of the themes
   On which I love to weep.
Belated oft by fabled rill,
While nightly o'er the hallow'd hill
   Aërial music seems to mourn ;
I'll listen Autumn's closing strain ;
Then woo the walks of youth again,
And pour my sorrows o'er th' untimely urn ! "

FERGUSON.—This poet's works possessed a boundless fancy, united to exquisite powers of observation, which may be considered the necessary qualities of poetry. " He surveyed the face of nature," observes a writer on his life, "and she stamped her image on his soul : he looked around him on mankind and his eye penetrated the recesses of the human heart : as a scholar he drank from the stream of inspiration, in the hallowed source of ancient poesy." In this respect Ferguson had an advantage over Burns ; but although he is often equally-sprightly and vivacious in his poetry, and sometimes soars with an elevated sweep ; yet he seldom darts impetuous and sublime like the mighty genius of Burns. His

is equal to Pope or Shenstone ; and his poems of this class give strik-
ing examples of how clearly he could copy nature and still render her
attractive.   A beautiful example is seen in his *Morning, Noon, and
Night* : it is smooth in its versification, and possesses that simplicity
which constitutes the real interest of pastoral poetry.

DAMON.

"Aurora now her welcome visit pays ;
Stern Darkness flies before her cheerful rays ;
Cool circling breezes whirl along the air,
And early shepherds to the fields repair ;
Lead we our flocks, then, to the mountains brow,
Where junipers and thorny brambles grow ;
Where founts of water 'midst the daisies spring,
And soaring larks and tuneful linnets sing ;
Your pleasing song shall teach our flocks to stray,
While sounding echoes smooth the sylvan lay.

ALEXIS.

'Tis thine to sing the graces of the morn,
The zephyr trembling o'er the rip'ning corn ;
'Tis thine with ease to chant the rural lay,
While bubbling fountains to your numbers play,
No piping swain that treads the verdant field,
But to your music and your verse must yield ;
Sing then,—for here we may with safety keep
Our sportive lambkins on this mossy steep.

DAMON.

With ruddy glow the sun adorns the land,
The pearly dew-drops on the bushes stand ;
The lowing oxen from the folds we hear,
And snowy flocks upon the hills appear.

ALEXIS.

How sweet the murmurs of the neighbouring rill!
Sweet are the slumbers which its floods distil!
Thro' pebbly channels winding as they run,
And brilliant sparkling to the rising sun."

CHATTERTON.—The most remarkable name in the whole list of poets of this age is that of Thomas Chatterton, who in his seventeenth year possessed the genius and ingenuity to execute a series of literary forgeries, which he passed off upon some competent judges as the productions of a versifier of the fifteenth century. There are in them many passages of the highest beauty, sufficient to give evidence that he possessed powers, which might have placed him at the head of the poets of his day. Some of his verses written at eleven years are worthy to be compared with the early poems of any author either before or since his date. His smaller writings, although possessing considerable merit are far inferior to the Rowley poems. The verses entitled *Resignation,* said to have been written not long before he committed suicide, are a fair example of his minor poems.

"O God, whose thunder shakes the sky,
　Whose eye this atom globe surveys,
To thee, my only rock, I fly,
　Thy mercy in thy justice praise.

The mystic mazes of thy will,
　The shadows of celestial light,
Are past the power of human skill—
　But what th' Eternal acts is right.

O teach me in the trying hour,
　When anguish swells the dewy tear ;
To still my sorrows, own thy pow'r,
　Thy goodness love, thy justice fear.

If in this bosom aught but Thee,
　Encroaching sought a boundless sway,
Omniscience could the danger see,
　And Mercy look the cause away.

Then why, my soul, dost thou complain?
　Why drooping seek the dark recess?
Shake off the melancholy chain,
　For God created all to bless.

But ah ! my breast is human still ;
　The rising sigh, the falling tear,

ROSCOE.—The poetical works of Thomas Roscoe are remarkable for the easy manner in which the thoughts seem to have suggested themselves. There are many of the highest merit, amongst which may be mentioned the *Ode to Education*. The following verses entitled *The Butterfly's Ball and The Grasshopper's Feast*, are worth quoting.

"Come take up your hats, and away let us haste
To the *Butterfly's* ball and the *Grasshopper's* feast:
The trumpeter *Gad-fly* has summon'd the crew
And the revels are now only waiting for you ;

On the smooth shaven grass, by the side of a wood,
Beneath a broad oak, which for ages had stood,
See the children of earth and the tenants of air
To an evening's amusement together repair ;

And there came the *Beetle*, so blind and so black,
Who carried the *Emmet*, his friend, on his back,
And there came the *Gnat* and the *Dragon-fly* too,
And all their relations, green, orange, and blue ;

And there came the *Moth*, with her plumage of down,
And the *Hornet*, with jacket of yellow and brown,
Who with him the *Wasp*, his companion did bring,
But they promis'd, that ev'ning to lay by their sting.

Then the sly little *Dormouse* peep'd out of his hole,
And led to the feast, his blind cousin the *Mole* ;
And the *Snail*, with her horns peeping out of her shell,
Came, fatigued with the distance, the length of an ell ;

A *Mushroom* the table, and on it was spread
A *water-dock leaf*, which their table-cloth made,
The viands were various, to each of their taste,   .
And the bee brought the honey to sweeten the feast.

With steps more majestic the *Snail* did advance,
And he promis'd the gazers a minuet to dance ;
But they all laugh'd so loud that he drew in his head,
And went, in his own little chamber, to bed ;

> Then, as ev'ning gave way to the shadows of night,
> Their watchman, the *Glow-worm,* came out with his light,
> So home let us hasten, while yet we can see ;
> For no watchman is waiting for you or for me !"

BOWLES.—William Lisle Bowles is distinguished chiefly as a writer of sonnets, which in reality comprise the best of his works. The following is quoted from amongst them.

> "Oh, Charity l our helpless nature's pride.
> Thou friend to him who knows no friend beside,
> Is there in morning's breath, or the sweet gale
> That steals o'er the tir'd pilgrim of the vale,
> Cheering with fragrance fresh his weary frame,
> Aught like the incense of thy holy flame ?
> Is aught in all the beauties that adorn,
> The azure heav'n, or purple lights of morn ?
> Is aught so fair in ev'ning's ling'ring gleam,
> As from thine eye the meek and pensive beam
> That falls like saddest moonlight on the hill,
> And distant grove, when the wild world is still ?
> Thine are the ample views, that unconfin'd
> Stretch to the utmost walks of human kind ;
> Thine is the spirit that with widest plan
> Brother to Brother binds, and Man to Man !"

ROGERS.—The chief works of Samuel Rogers, are the *Pleasures of Memory, Human Life,* and *Italy.* All his works are highly finished, although they do not possess that power of imagination which constitutes the essence of *true* poetry. The former of these, the *Pleasures of Memory,* is equal in finish and harmony to any production either of that or the preceding period. The pictures drawn in this poem are fresh and natural, and in many parts there are sentiments of the highest animation. The follow-interesting passage will sufficiently illustrate this poem.

> " On yon gray stone, that fronts the chancel-door,
> Worn smooth by busy feet now seen no more,
> Each eve we shot the marble thro' the ring,
> When the heart danced, and life was in its spring ;
> Alas ! unconscious of the kindred earth,
> That faintly echoed to the voice of mirth.
>   The glow-worm loves her emerald light to shed,
> Where now the sexton rests his hoary head.
> Oft, as he turned the greensward with his spade,
> He lectured every youth that round him played ;
> And calmly pointing where his fathers lay,
> Roused him to rival each, the hero of his day.

> Hush, ye fond flutterings, hush ! while here alone
> I search the records of each mouldering stone.
> Guides of my life ! Instructors of my youth !
> Who first unveiled the hallowed form of truth ;
> Whose every word enlightened and endeared ;
> In age beloved, in poverty revered ;
> In Friendship's silent register ye live,
> Nor ask the vain memorial art can give."

There may be found also in this poem, many descriptive passages of the highest merit, as in the following lines.

> "Oft at the silent, shadowy close of day,
> When the hushed grove has sung its parting lay ;
> When pensive twilight, in her dusky car,
> Comes slowly on to meet the evening-star ;
> Above, below, aërial murmurs swell,
> From hanging wood, brown heath, and bushy dell !
> A thousand nameless rills, that shun the light,
> Stealing soft music on the ear of night.
> So oft the finer movements of the soul,
> That shun the sphere of pleasure's gay control,
> In the still shades of calm seclusion rise,
> And breathe their sweet, seraphic harmonies."

HARTE.—Walter Harte published *Poems on Several Occasions, Essay on Satire, Essay on Reason* (to which Pope is said to have contributed very considerably), *Essay* on *Painting,* and *The Amaranth,* his last work. As a poet he is not distinguished from other once successful but now forgotten imitators ; but there are now and then to be found in his works pieces of great beauty and merit. The example here selected from his poems, is the following address, *To my Soul,* in imitation of Chaucer.

> " Far from mankind, my weary soul retire,
> Still follow truth, contentment still desire.
> Who climbs on high, at best his weakness shows,
> Who rolls in riches, all to Fortune owe's.
> Read well thyself, and mark thy early ways,
> Vain is the Muse, and Envy waits on praise.
>
> Wav'ring as winds the breath of Fortune blows,
> No pow'r can turn it, and no pray'rs compose,
> Deep in some hermit's solitary cell
> Repose, and Ease, and Contemplation dwell.
> Let Conscience guide thee in the days of need ;
> Judge well thy own, and then thy neighbours deed.
>
> What Heaven bestows with thankful eyes receive ;
> First ask thy heart, and then thro' faith believe.
> Slowly we wander o'er a toilsome way,

Shadows of life, and pilgrims of a day,
  ' Who restless in this world, receives a fall ;
  ' Look up on high, and thank thy God for all !"

WEST.—Gilbert West made a translation of *Pindar,* and wrote
some original pieces of great merit.   There is an elegant ease in
his style, more particularly in his original poems, which characterize
them from other writings of the same class.   The following *Ode to
May* is a very fine example.

  "Dear Gray ! that always in my heart
  Possessest far the better part,
  What mean these sudden blasts that rise,
  And drive the zephyrs from the skies?
  O join with mine thy tuneful lay,
  And invocate the tardy May.

  Come, fairest nymph ! resume thy reign,
  Bring all the graces in thy train :
  With balmy breath and flow'ry tread,
  Rise from the soft ambrosial bed.
  Where in Elysian slumber bound,
  Embow'ring myrtles veil thee round.

  Awake, in all thy glories drest,
  Recall the zephyrs from the west ;
  Restore the sun, revive the skies,
  At mine and Nature's call arise !
  Great Nature's self upbraids thy stay,
  And misses her accustom'd May.

  See ! all her works demand thy aid,
  The labours of Pomona fade :
  A plaint is heard from ev'ry tree,
  Each budding flow'ret calls for thee ;
  The birds forget to love and sing,
  With storms alone the forests ring.

  Come, then, with pleasure at thy side,
  Diffuse thy vernal spirit wide ;
  Create where'er thou turn'st thy eye,
  Peace, plenty, love, and harmony;
  Till ev'ry being share its part,
  And Heav'n and Earth be glad at heart."

MELMOTH.—This accomplished scholar is best known by his
prose works and translations of the epistles of Pliny and Cicero,
than by his poems ; although among the latter there are several
of great merit.   The following lines *To Sappho,* aged thirteen,
may be read as a fair example.

" While yet no am'rous youths around thee bow,
Nor flattering verse conveys the faithless vow ;
To graver notes will Sappho's soul attend,
And ere she hears the lover, hear the friend ?
Let maids less bless'd employ their meaner arts
To reign proud tyrants o'er unnumber'd hearts ;
May Sappho learn (for nobler triumphs born)
Those little conquests of her sex to scorn.
To form thy bosom to each gen'rous deed ;
To plant thy mind with ev'ry useful seed ;
Be these thy arts ; nor spare the grateful toil,
Where nature's hand has blessed the happy soil.
So shalt thou know, with pleasing skill to blend
The lovely mistress and instructive friend ;
So shalt thou know, when unrelenting Time,
Shall spoil these charms yet op'ning to their prime,
To ease the loss of beauty's transient flow'r,
While Reason keeps what rapture gave before.
And oh ? whilst wit, fair dawning spreads its ray,
Serenely rising to a glorious day,
To hail the glowing lustre oft be mine,
Thou early fav'rite of the sacred Nine !
And shall the Muse with blameless boasts pretend,
In youth's gay bloom that Sappho called me friend ;
That urg'd by me, she shunn'd the dangerous way,
Where heedless maids in endless error stray ;
That scorning soon her sex's idler art,
Fair praise inspir'd, and virtue warm'd her heart ;
That fond to reach the distant paths of fame,
I taught her infant genius where to aim ?
Thus when the feathered choir first tempt the sky,
And, all unskill'd, their feeble pinions try,
Th' experienc'd sire prescribes the advent'rous height
Guides the young wing, and pleas'd attends the flight.'

HAMMOND.—The poems of James Hammond are mostly elegiac, and addressed in the vapid style of pastoral sentiment, then in fashion, to a fictitious object whom he names *Delia*. He is said to have been in love with a Miss Dashwood, who refused him, and to have lost his intellect in consequence. There are occasionally to be found in his *Elegies* parts of singular beauty and merit. The *Seventh Elegy* written on Delia's being in the country, where he supposes she stays to see the harvest, may be read as one of the best.

"Now Delia breathes in woods the fragrant air,
Dull are the hearts that still in town remain,
Venus herself attends on Delia there,
And Cupid sports amid the sylvan train.

Oh, with what joy, my Delia to behold,
I'd press the spade, or wield the mighty prong,
Guide the slow plough-share through the stubborn mould
And patient goad the loitering ox along.

The scorching heats I'd carelessly despise,
Nor heed the blisters on my tender hand ;
The great Apollo wore the same disguise,
Like me subdued to love's supreme command.

No healing herbs could soothe their master's pain,
The art of physic lost, and useless lay,
To Peneus stream, aud Tempe's shady plain,
He drove his herds beneath the noon tide ray.

Oft with a bleating lamb in either arm,
His blushing sister saw him pace along ;
Oft would his voice the silent valley charm,
Till lowing oxen broke the tender song.

Where are his triumphs ? where his warlike toil ?
Where by his dart the erected Pithon slain ?
Where are his Delphi ? his delighted isle ?
The God himself is grown a cottage swain.

O, Ceres ! in your golden fields no more,
With Harvest's cheerful pomp my fair detain, —
Think what for lost Proserpina you bore,
And in a mother's anguish feel my pain.

Our wiser fathers left their fields unsown,
Their food was acorns, love their sole employ,
They met, they lik'd, they staid but till alone,
And in each valley snatch'd the honest joy.

No wakeful guard, no doors to stop desire,
Thrice happy times !—But oh! I fondly rave,
Lead me to Delia all her eyes inspire,
I'll do—I'll plough, or dig as Delia's slave."

CARTER.—Elizabeth Carter published a translation of *Epictetus*,
besides other original poems.   She was highly esteemed by John-
son, and her beautiful *Ode to Wisdom* is given by Richardson in
his second novel *Clarissa Harlowe*.   Some of the stanzas are
quoted below.

" The solitary bird of night
    Thro' the pale shades now wings his flight,
        And quits the time-shook tow'r,
    Where, shelter'd from the blaze of day,
    In philosophic gloom he lay,
        Beneath his ivy bow'r.

    With joy I hear the solemn sound,
    Which midnight echoes waft around,

In ev'ry form of beauty bright,
That captivates the mental sight
  With pleasure and surprise ;

To thy unspotted shrine I bow,
Assist thy modest suppliant's vow,
  That breathes no wild desires ;
But, taught by thy unerring rules,
To shun the fruitless wish of fools,
  To nobler views aspires.

Not Fortune's gem, Ambition's plume
Nor Cytherea's fading bloom,
  Be objects of my pray'r :
Let Av'rice, Vanity, and Pride,
Those glitt'ing envied toys, divide
  The dull rewards of care.

To me thy better gifts impart,
Each moral beauty of the heart,
  By studious thought refin'd ;
For wealth, the smiles of glad content ;
For pow'r, its amplest, best extent,
  An empire o'er the mind.

      *   *   *   *

Thy breath inspires the poet's song,
The patriot's free unbias'd tongue,
  The hero's gen'rous strife :
Thine are retirement's silent joys,
And all the sweet endearing ties
  Of still domestic life.
No more to fabled names confin'd,
To Thee, SUPREME ALL-PERFECT MIND ;
  My thoughts direct their flight :
Wisdom's thy gift, and all her force,
From thee deriv'd, unchanging source
  Of intellectual light.
O send her sure, her steady ray,
To regulate my doubtful way,

> Through life's perplexing road;
> The mists of error to control,
> And through its gloom direct my soul
> To happiness and good!
>
> Beneath her clear discerning eye
> The visionary shadows fly
> ˙ Of folly's painted show;
> She sees, thro' every fair disguise,
> That all, but virtue's solid joys,
> Is vanity and woe."

MERRICK.—The chief work of James Merrick, is a volume entitled *Poems on Sacred Subjects*, amongst which there are many of distinguished beauty. He also made an excellent translation of the Psalms, into English verse, and translated the poem of Tryphiodorus on the capture of Troy. His earliest work is a Divine Essay, entitled *Messiah*, which was published in his fourteenth year. The following stanzas entitled *The Wish*, are selected from the first mentioned work as an example :—

> "How short is life's uncertain space!
>   Alas! how quickly done!
> How swift the wild precarious chase!
> And yet how difficult the race,
>   How very hard to run!
>
> Youth stops at first its wilful ears
>   To wisdom's prudent voice;
> Till now arriv'd to riper years,
> Experienc'd age, worn out with cares,
>   Repents its earlier choice.
>
> What though it prospects now appear
>   So pleasing and refin'd;
> Yet groundless hope and anxious fear
> By turn the busy moments share,
>   And prey upon the mind.
>
> Since then false joys our fancy cheat
>   With hopes of real bliss;
> Ye guardian Pow'rs that rule my fate!
> The only wish that I create
>   Is all compris'd in this:
>
> May I through life's uncertain tide
>   Be still from pain exempt,
> May all my wants be still supplied,
> My state too low t' admit of pride,
>   And yet above contempt.
>
> But should your providence divine
>   A greater bliss intend;

of high distinction. His style is immature, but this may easily be understood by the early age at which he commenced to write ; and there are also several traces of his having borrowed from other poets. This latter circumstance is strikingly seen in the last stanza of the former poem, when compared with the following lines of Milton :—

> " With the year
> Seasons return ; but not to me returns
> Day or the sweet approach of even or morn." &c,

The above mentioned *Elegy on Spring*, will be sufficient to amply illustrate both the genius and style of this writer.

> " 'Tis past : the iron north has spent his rage ;
>   Stern winter now resigns the length'ning day ;
> The stormy howlings of the winds assuage,
>   And warm o'er ether western breezes play.
>
> Far to the north grim winter draws his train,
>   To his own clime, to Zembla's frozen shore ;
> Where, throned on ice, he holds eternal reign ;
>   Where whirlwinds madden, and where tempests roar.
>
> Loosed from the bands of frost, the verdant ground,
>   Again puts on her robe of cheerful green—
> Again puts forth her flowers ; and all around,
>   Smiling, the cheerful face of Spring is seen.
>
> Behold ! the trees new deck their withered boughs .
>   Their ample leaves, the hospitable plane,
> The taper elm, and lofty ash disclose ;
>   The blooming hawthorn variegates the scene.
>
> The lily of the vale, of flowers the queen,
>   Puts on the robe she neither sewed nor spun ;
> The birds on ground, or on the branches green,
>   Hop to and fro' and glitter in the sun.
>
> Soon as o'er eastern hills the morning peers,
>   From her low nest the tufted lark up-springs
> And, cheerful singing, up the air she steers ;
>   Still high she mounts, still loud and sweet she sings.
>
> On the green furze, clothed o'er with golden blooms,
>   That fill the air with fragrance all around,

The linnet sits, and tricks his glossy plumes,
    While o'er the wild his broken notes resound.

*　　　*　　　*　　　*　　　*

Now is the time for those who wisdom love,
    Who love to walk in virtue's flowery road,
Along the lovely paths of spring to rove,
    And follow nature up to nature's God.

Thus Zoroaster studied nature's laws;
    Thus Socrates, the wisest of mankind;
Thus heaven-taught Plato traced th' Almighty cause,
    And left the wond'ring multitude behind.

Thus Ashley gathered academic bays;
    Thus gentle Thomson, as the seasons roll,
Taught them to sing the great Creator's praise,
    And bear their poet's name from pole to pole.

Thus have I walked along the dewy lawn;
    My frequent foot the blooming wild hath worn;
Before the lark I've sung the beauteous dawn,
    And gathered health from all the gales of morn.

Now, spring returns: but not to me returns
    The vernal joy my better years have known;
Dim in my breast life's dying taper burns,
    And all the joys of life with health are flown."

BAILLIE.—Joanna Baillie was the writer of a "Series of Plays," amongst which her tragedy *De Montfort* is considered the finest. These plays, which appeared in separate volumes, consisted partly of tragedies and partly of comedies, one of each class being directed to the development of a particular passion, such as love, ambition, revenge, &c. The characteristic merit of her writing is a masculine style of thought and diction, over which she has shown herself a complete mistress. Her tragedies have a grasp of mind and firmness of hand that are rarely to be seen in the writings of a female; in the words of Byron, "woman (saving Joanna Baillie) cannot write tragedy." Her writings exhibit not only the qualities of a poet, but the rarer qualities of a true dramatist. A modern critic has observed of her writings, "However different and inferior in degree, her mind resembles Shakespeare's in kind: she plans her characters deliberately: she executes them with undeviating consistency; her pictures of passion are all leavened and penetrated by general and elevated reflection." There is also a vehement eloquence running through her works, and a perpetual flow of

exalted thought and feeling, with now and then real bursts of senti-
ment. Many of her female characters are powerfully and tenderly
drawn, and form of themselves a chief feature of her plays : that
of Valeria for example in the tragedy of *Constantine Paleologus;*
seen in the following passage.

> *Valeria.*—" Forbear all words, and follow me no more,
> I now am free to wander where I list ;
> To howl i' the desert with the midnight wind,
> And fearless be amidst all fearful things.
> The storm has been with me, and I am left,
> Torn and uprooted, and laid in the dust,
> With those whom after-blasts rend not again,
> I am in the dark gulf where no light is.
> I am on the deep beds of sunken floods,
> Whose swoln and welt'ring billows rise no more
> To bear the tossed wreck back to the strand.
> *Lucia.*—O, say not so ! heav'n doth in its good time
> Send consolation to the sharpest woe.
> It still in kindness sends to the tried soul
> It's keenest suff'rings. So say holy men;
> And therein good men trust.
> *Valeria.*—I hear, I hear thee ! in mine ear thy voice
> Sounds like the feeble night fly's humming noise
> To him, who in the warfare of vex'd sleep,
> Strives with the phantoms of his inward world.
> Yes, there be comfort when the sun is dark,
> And time hath run his course, and the still'd sleepers
> Lift up their heads at the tremendous crash
> Of breaking worlds,—I know all this.—But here,
> Upon this living earth, what is there found ?
> It is a place of groans and hopeless woe.
> Let me then tear my hair and wring my hands,
> And raise my voice of anguish and despair,
> This is my portion now, all else is gone.
> *Lucia.*—Nay, think not virtuous innocence forsaken :
> Put in high heav'n thy trust, it will sustain thee,
> *Valeria.*—Ah ! I did think when virtue bravely stood,
> Fronting its valiant breast to the fierce onset.
> Of worthless power, that it full surely stood :
> That ev'ry spiritual and righteous power
> Was on its side ; and in this faith, oftimes,
> Methought I could into the furnace mouth
> Have thrust my hand, and grasped the molten flames.
> Yet it fell on his head : that noble head
> Upon whose manly gracefulness was fix'd,
> The gaze of ev'ry eye.
> Oh ! on his lib'ral front there beam'd a look,
> Unto the which all good and gen'rous hearts

Answer return'd.—It was a gentle head,
Bending in pleasant kindness to all ;
So that the timid, who approach'd him trembling,
With cheer'd and vaunting steps retir'd again.
It was a crowned head, yet was it left
Expos'd and fenceless in the hour of danger :
What should have been his safety was his bane.
Away poor mock'ry of a wretched state !
　　(*Tearing the regal ornaments from her
　　neck and scattering them about*)
Be ye strew'd to the winds ! But for this let
We had been blest ; for he as truly loved,
In simplest tenderness, as the poor hind,
Who takes his humble house-mate by the hand,
And says, ' this is my all.'—Off, cursed band !
Which round our happiness hath been entwin'd,
Like to a strangling cord : upon the earth
Be thou defaced and trampled !' "

GRAHAME. —The principal works of this writer, are a dramatic
poem called *Mary Queen of Scotland, Sabbath*, and *Sabbath Walks*,
all written in blank verse. Besides these there are a number of minor
poems chiefly of a religious character. His style may be compared
to that of Cowper, though he does not possess the force and depth
of poetic passion of the latter writer. There is nothing vigorous
or imaginative in Grahame's poetry ; but it abounds nevertheless in
passages of the tenderest and most devout feeling, and the most
animated and flowing descriptions. The following example is
extracted from *The Sabbath Walks :*

"Delightful is this loneliness ; it calms
My heart : pleasant the cool beneath these elms,
That throw across the stream a moveless shade.
Here nature in her midnoon whisper speaks :
How peaceful every sound !—the ring-dove's plaint,
Moan'd from the twilight centre of the grove,
While every other woodland lay is mute,
Save when the wren flits from her down-coved nest,
And from the root-sprigs trills her ditty clear,—
The grasshopper's oft-pausing chirp,—the buzz,
Angrily shrill, of moss-entangled bee,
That, soon as loosed, booms with full twang away,—
The sudden rushing of the minnow shoal,
Scared from the shallows by my passing tread.
Dimpling the water glides, with here and there
A glossy fly, skimming in circlets gay
The treacherous surface, while the quick-eyed trout
Watches his time to spring ; or, from above,

Into the open air : grateful the breeze
That fans my throbbing temples ! smiles the plain
Spread wide below : how sweet the placid view !
But oh ! more sweet the thought, heart-soothing thought,
That thousands, and ten thousands of the sons
Of toil, partake this day the common joy
Of rest, of peace, of viewing hill and dale,
Of breathing in the silence of the woods,
And blessing Him, who gave the Sabbath day.
Yes, my heart flutters with a freer throb,
To think that now the townsman wanders forth
Among the fields and meadows, to enjoy
The coolness of the day's decline : to see
His children sport around, and simply pull
The flower and weed promiscuous, as a boon,
Which proudly in his breast they smiling fix."

BLOOMFIELD.—Robert Bloomfield is chiefly known by his poem *The Farmer's Boy*, the merit of which lays in the strikingly true and touching delineation of rustic life which it contains. The language both of this and of his other poems is choice, and the rhythm correct ; but there is nothing of power and passion in his writings. Some of the parts descriptive of the various seasons are written with much truth and beauty ; as in the following passage,

SPRING.

"Fled now the sullen murmurs of the north,
The splendid raiment of the spring peeps forth ;
Her universal green, and the clear sky,

> Delight still more and more the gazing eye.
> Wide o'er the fields, in rising moisture strong,
> Shoots up the simple flower, or creeps along
> The mellow'd soil; imbibing fairer hues,
> Or sweets from frequent showers and evening dews;
> That summon from their sheds the slumb'ring plows,
> While health impregnates every breeze that blows."

Another beautiful passage in this poem is that with which it closes describing the farmer's joy at the prospect of returning Spring.

> "————Sunshine, Health, and Joy,
> Play round, and cheer the elevated boy!
> 'Another Spring!' his heart exulting cries;
> 'Another YEAR! with promis'd blessings rise!—
> ETERNAL POWER! from whom those blessings flow,
> Teach me still more to wonder, more to know:
> Seed-time and Harvest let me see again;
> Wander the leaf-strewn wood, the frozen plain:
> Let the first flower, corn-waving field, plain, tree,
> Here round my home, still lift my soul to THEE:
> And let me ever, midst thy bounties, raise
> An humble note of thankfulness and praise!'"

HURDIS.—James Hurdis was the writer of a poem in blank verse, entitled *The Village Curate*; a tragedy called *Sir Thomas More,* and other poetical works. He was also the author of an important work, *Remarks on the Arrangements of the Plays of Shakespeare,* a valuable addition to the numerous text-books upon that poet. There are many choice passages in his works; although in his tragedy, there is wanting that bold delineation of character which forms a distinguishing feature of dramatic writing. Amongst his miscellaneous pieces, the two poems *Addresses to the Moon* deserve mentioning. The following passage is selected from the tragedy of *Sir Thomas More* and possesses all the truth of a circumstantial reflection of its kind.

> "Such is my home—a gloomy tenement,
> And solitary as the peasant's hut
> Upon the barren mountain. Not a soul
> Deigns me a visit. All my company
> Are toiling spiders, who consume the day
> In spreading nets to catch the harmless fly,
> An emblem of myself. For what am I,
> But a poor, helpless, weather-beaten insect,

Track him in all his ways, in war, in peace,
Seeking renown upon the battle's edge,
Amusements in the closet or the field,
His footsteps are all marked with savage bloodshed.
Philosophy and Faith have each their sword,
And murder, one for wisdom, one for truth.
The paths of glory are the paths of blood ;
And what are heroes and aspiring kings
But butchers? Has not ev'ry prince his knife,
His slaughter-house, and victim? What am I,
But a poor lamb selected from the flock,
To be the next that bleeds, where many a lamb,
As innocent and guiltless as myself,
Has bled before me? On this floor perhaps
The persecuted Harry breath'd his last
Under the sword of Gloster.   Clarence here
Drank his last draught of Malmsey, and his son,
Poor hapless boy, pin'd infancy away ;
All his acquaintance, sorrow and himself;
And all the world he knew, this little room,
Yes, here he sat, and long'd for liberty,
Which never found him ; ending his sad youth
Under the tyrant's axe.   And here perhaps
Assassination, at the dead of night,
With silent footstep, and extended arm,
Feeling her way to the remember'd bed,
Found the two breathing princes fast asleep,
And did her bloody work without remorse.
O horrible to think of ! Such is man,
No beast, whose appetite is ever blood,
Wants mercy more."

HOGG.—James Hogg, commonly called the "Ettrick Shepherd,"
so named from his being a native of the secluded district of Ettrick
in Scotland, where he kept the cattle and sheep, was the writer of
a beautiful poem entitled *The Queen's Wake*, besides a number of

cal effusions.

"Bird of the wilderness,
Blithsome and cumberless,
Sweet be thy matin o'er moorland and lea !
Emblem of happiness,
Blest is thy dwelling place—
Oh to abide in the desert with thee !
Wild is thy lay and loud,
Far in the downy cloud,
Love gives it energy, love gave it birth.
Where, on thy dewy wing,
Where art thou journeying ?
Thy lay is in heaven, thy love is on earth.
O'er fell and fountain sheen,
O'er moor and mountain green,
O'er the red streamer that heralds the day,
Over the cloudlet dim,
Over the rainbow's rim,
Musical cherub, soar, singing, away !
Then, when the gloaming comes,
Low in the heather blooms,
Sweet will thy welcome and bed of love be,
Emblem of happiness,
Blest is thy dwelling-place—
Oh ! to abide in the desert with thee ! "

YDEN.—John Leyden was the writer of miscellaneous poems,
lich the most remarkable are his ballads of the *Kout of Keel-*
and *The Mermaid of Colonsay,* published by his friend Sir
er Scott in the Minstrelsy of the Scottish Border, who has
spoken very highly of his poetry. The following sonnet,
tide may be read as a fair specimen of his talent.

"Beneath a shiv'ring canopy reclin'd,
Of aspen leaves that wave without a wind,
I love to lie, when lulling breezes stir
The spiry cones that tremble on the fir,
Or wander 'mid the dark green fields of broom,
When peers in scattered tufts the yellow bloom :
Or trace the path with tangling furze o'errun,
When bursting seed-bells crackle in the sun,
And pittering grasshoppers, confus'dly shrill,

SMITH.—James Smith is best known in connection with his brother Horace. His writings consist in clever parodies and criticisms in the *Picnic, London Review*, and *Monthly Mirror*. It was in the *Monthly Mirror*, that the imitations published as the *Rejected Addresses* appeared, which were written by both James and Horace. This work was one of the most successful and popular that has ever appeared. James Smith was the writer of the imitations of Wordsworth, Cobbett, Southey, Coleridge, and Lamb ; and Horace Smith those of Scott, Moore, Monk, Lewis, Fitzgerald, and Dr. Johnson. This poet was a less voluminous writer than his brother, and beyond the above mentioned imitations wrote little else worth remarking upon. The following passage from the poem entitled *The Rebuilding*, in imitation of the *Kehama* of Southey, has been selected from the *Rejected Addresses* as an example of James Smith's work.

"Midnight, yet not a nose
From Tower-hill to Piccadilly snored!
Midnight, yet not a nose
From Indra drew the essence of repose !
See with what crimson fury,
By Indra fanu'd, the god of fire ascends the walls
of Drury ;

The tops of houses, blue with lead,
Bend beneath the landlord's tread.
Master and 'prentice, serving man and lord,
Nailor and Tailor,
Grazier and Brazier,
Thro' streets and alleys pour'd,

All, all abroad to gaze,
And wonder at the blaze.
Thick calf, fat foot, and slim knee,
Mounted on roof and chimney,
The mighty roast, the mighty stew

To see;
As if the dismal view
Were but to them a Brentford jubilee.

Vainly, all radiant Surya, sire of Phaeton,
(By Greeks called Apollo)
Hollow
Sounds from thy harp proceed ;
Combustible as reed,
The tongue of Vulcan licks thy wooden legs :
From Drury's top, dissever'd from thy pegs,
Thou tumblest,
Humblest,
Where late thy bright effulgence shone on high :
While, by thy somerset excited, fly
Ten million,
Billion
Sparks from the pit, to gem the sable sky.

Now come the men of fire to quench the fires,
To Russel Street see Globe and Atlas run ;[1]
Hope gallops first, and second Sun ;
On flying heel,
See Hand in Hand
O'ertake the band ;
View with what glowing wheel
He nicks
Phœnix;
While Albion scampers from Bridge-street, Blackfriars,
Drury Lane !   Drury Lane !
Drury Lane !   Drury Lane !
They shout and they bellow again and again.
All, all in vain !
Water turns steam ;
Each blazing beam
Hisses defiance to the eddying spout,
It seems but too plain that nothing can put it out
Drury Lane.   Drury Lane !"

MITH:—Horace Smith, brother of the former poet, wrote more
ely, and besides his share in the *Rejected Addresses* he produced
ral other poems and verses, amongst which his *Address to the
nmy*, may be mentioned as posessing singular merit. The
wing, *A Tale of Drury Lane*, in imitation of Scott, is one from
ngst those written by this writer in the above work.

THE NIGHT.

" On fair Augusta's towers and trees
Flitted the silent midnight breeze,
Curling the foliage as it past,

Which from the moon-tipp'd plumage cast
A spangled light like dancing spray,
Then reassum'd its still array :
When as night's lamp unclouded hung,
And down its full effulgence flung,
It shed such soft and balmy power,
That cot and castle, hall and bower,
And spire and dome, and turret height,
Appear'd to slumber in the light.
From Henry's chapel, Rufus' hall,
To Savoy, Temple, and St. Paul,
From Knightsbridge, Pancras, Camden Town,
To Redriff, Shadwell, Horselydown,
No voice was heard, no eye unclosed,
But all in deepest sleep reposed.
They might have thought, who gazed around,
Amid a silence so profound
  It made the senses thrill,
That 'twas no place inhabited,
But some vast city of the dead,
  All was so hushed and still."

THE BURNING.

"As chaos which, by heavenly doom,
Had slept in everlasting gloom,
Started with terror and surprise,
When light first flashed upon her eyes :
So London's sons in nightcap woke,
  In bedgown woke her dames,
For shouts were heard 'mid fire and smoke,
And twice ten hundred voices spoke,
  'The Playhouse is in flames.'
And lo! where Catherine Street extends,
A fiery tale its lustre lends
  To every window-pane :
Blushes each spout in Martlet Court,
And Barbican, moth eaten fort,
And Covent Garden kennels sport,
  A bright ensanguin'd drain;
Meux's new brew-house shows the light
Rowland Hill's chapel, and the height
  Where patent shot they sell:
The Tennis Court, so fair and tall,
Partakes the ray, with Surgeons' Hall,
The ticket porters' house of call,
Old Bedlam, close by London Wall,
Wright's shrimp and oyster shop withal,
  And Richardson's Hotel."

TIGHE.—Mrs. Mary Tighe was the authoress of *Psyche*, a poem
founded on the story of Cupid and Psyche in Apuleius, and several

other minor poems of peculiar elegance and delicacy in style and sentiment. The former poëm is beautifully written, and exhibits much imagination and graceful fancy. The following verses *On receiving a Branch of Mezereon, which flowered at Woodstock,* is one of the sweetest of her minor poems, and is said to have been the last poem she ever composed; and she died at the place where it was written.

"Odours of spring, my sense ye charm
  With fragrance premature ;
And, mid these days of dark alarm,
  Almost to hope allure.
Methinks with purpose soft ye come
  To tell of brighter hours,
Of May's blue skies, abundant bloom
  Her sunny gales and showers.

Alas ! for me shall May in vain
  The powers of life restore ;
These eyes that weep and watch in pain,
  Shall see her charms no more.
No, no, this anguish cannot last !
  Beloved friends, adieu !
The bitterness of death were past,
  Could I resign but you.

But oh ! in every mortal pang
  That rends my soul from life,
That soul, which seems on you to hang
  Through each convulsive strife,
Even now, with agonizing grasp
  Of terror and regret,
To all in life its love would clasp
  Things close and closer yet.

Yet why, immortal, vital spark !
  Thus mortally opprest ?
Look up, my soul, through prospects dark,
  And bid thy terrors rest ;
Forget, forego thy earthy part,
  Thine heavenly being trust :—
Ah ! vain attempt ! my coward heart
  Still shuddering clings to dust.

O ye ! who soothe the pangs of death
  With love's own patient care,
Still, still retain this fleeting breath,
  Still pour the fervent prayer:—
And ye, whose smile must greet my eye
  No more, nor voice my ear,
Who breathe for me the tender sigh,
  And shed the pitying tear,—

most popular poem is that entitled *The Isle of Palms,* a meditative and ideal poem, greatly resembling in style that of Wordsworth. His works manifest him to have been an ardent lover of nature, and to have possessed the purest and most affectionate feelings ; and there is a soothing sweetness in his writings, that gives them an irresistible charm. The following passage *Night at Sea,* is selected from his miscellaneous poems.

> "It is the midnight hour ;—the beauteous sea,
>   Calm as the cloudless heaven, the heaven discloses,
> While many a sparkling star, in quiet glee,
>   Far down within the watery sky reposes
> As if the ocean's heart were stirr'd
> With inward life, a sound is heard,
>   Like that of dreamer murmuring in his sleep
> 'Tis partly the billow, and partly the air,
> That lies like a garment floating fair
>   Above the happy deep.
> The sea, I ween, cannot be fanu'd
> By evening freshness from the land,
>   For the land is far away ;
> But God hath will'd that the sky-born breeze
> In the centre of the loneliest seas
>   Should ever sport and play.
>   The mighty moon, she sits above,
>   Encircled with a zone of love,
>   A zone of dim and tender light,
>   That makes her wakeful eye more bright :
>   She seems to shine with a sunny ray,
>   And the night looks like a mellow'd day l
>   The gracious mistress of the main
>   Hath now an undisturbed reign,
>   And from her silent throne looks down,
>   As upon children of her own,
>   On the waves, that lend their gentle breast
>   In gladness for her couch of rest l "

TENNANT.— William Tennant was the writer of a comic poem called *Anster Fair,* chiefly of a descriptive character, giving a

Italians, and it is remarkable for the profusion and variety of image
and groups which it thrusts upon the fancy, relieved often by suc
den outburstings of the richest poetical imagination. The followin
are some of the stanzas from this poem.

"Comes next from Ross-shire and from Sutherland
   The horny-knuckled kilted Highlandman;
From whereupon the rocky Caithness strand,
   Breaks the long wave that at the pole began;
And where Lockfyne from her prolific sand
   Her herrings gives to feed each bord'ring clan,
Arrive the brogue-shod men of gen'rous eye,
Plaided, and breechless all, with Edom's hairy thigh.—
And ev'ry husbandman, round Largo-law,
   Hath scrap'd his huge-wheeled dung-cart fair and clean,
Wherein, on sacks stuffed full of oaten straw,
   Sits the good wife, Tam, Katey, Jock, and Jean;
In flowers and ribands drest, the horses draw
   Stoutly their creaking cumbersome machine,
As, on his cart-head, sits the goodman proud,
And cheerly cracks his whip, and whistles clear and loud.—
And from her coal-pits Dysart vomits forth,
   Her subterranean men of colour dun,
Poor human mouldwarps! doomed to scrape in earth,
   Cimmerian people, strangers to the sun;
Gloomy as soot, with faces grim and swarth,
   They march, most sourly leering everyone.

           *   *   *   *

Next, from the well-air'd ancient town of Crail,
   Go out her craftsmen with tumultuous din,
Her wine-bleached fishers, sturdy-limbed and hale,
   Her in-kneed tailors, garrulous and thin;
And some are flushed with horn of pithy ale,
   And some are fierce with dreams of smuggled gin.

           *   *   *   *

And market maids, and aproned wives, that bring
   Their gingerbread in baskets to the Fair;
And cadgers with their creels that hang by string
   From their lean horse ribs, rubbing off the hair;
And crooked-legged-cripples that on crutches swing
   Their shabby persons with a noble air."

GRAINGER.—James Grainger was the writer of a poem calle
the *Sugar Cane*, a work which was severely dealt with by the critic
Notwithstanding this defective production, however; there may b

Young Bryan thought the boat's crew slow,
  And so leapt overboard.

Pereene, the pride of Indian dames,
  His heart did long enthral,
And whoso his impatience blames,
  I wot ne'er loved at all.

A long, long year, one month and day,
  He dwelt on English land,
Nor once in thought would ever stray,
  Tho' ladies sought his hand.

For Bryan he was tall and strong,
  Right blithsome roll'd his een,
Sweet was his voice whene'er he sung,
  He scant had twenty seen.

But who the countless charms can draw,
  That grac'd his mistress true?
Such charms the old world never saw,
  Nor oft I ween the new.

Her raven hair plays round her neck
  Like tendrils of the vine;
Her cheeks red dewy rose-buds deck,
  Her eyes like diamonds shine.

Soon as his well-known ship was spied,
  She cast her weeds away,
And to the palmy shore she hied,
  All in her best array.

In sea-green silk so neatly clad,
  She there impatient stood,
The crew with wonder saw the lad,
  Repel the foaming flood.

Her hands a handkerchief display'd,
  Which he at parting gave,
Well pleased the token he survey'd,
  And manlier beat the wave.

Her fair companions one and all,
  Rejoicing crowd the strand;
For now her lover swam in call,
  And almost touch'd the land.

Then thro' the white surf did she haste
  To clasp her lovely swain;

He shriek'd ! he half sprung from the wave,
    Streaming with purple gore,
And soon it found a living grave,
    And ah ! was seen no more.

Now haste, now haste, ye maids, I pray,
    Fetch water from the spring—
She falls, she falls, she dies away,
    And soon her knell they ring.

Now each May morning round her tomb
    Ye fair, fresh flow'rets strew
So may your lovers 'scape his doom,
    Her hapless fate 'scape you."

HART.—This writer lived about the middle of the last century, and wrote a volume of Hymns, many of which have been reprinted, and some of which are of a most beautiful character. The following hymn *Gethsemane*, will stand unequalled in this species of writing.

GETHSEMANE.

"Jesus, while he dwelt below,
As divine historians say,
To a place would often go ;
Near to Kedron's brook it lay ;
In this place he loved to be ;
And 'twas named Gethsemane.

'Twas a garden, as we read,
At the foot of Olivet,
Low and proper to be made
The Redeemer's lone retreat :
When from noise he would be free,
Then he sought Gethsemane.

Full of love to man's lost race,
On the conflict much He thought ;
This He knew the destin'd place,
And he loved the sacred spot ;
Therefore Jesus chose to be
Often in Gethsemane.

Came at length the dreadful night ;
Vengeance, with its iron rod,
Stood, and with collected might,
Bruised the harmless Lamb of God ;
See, my soul, thy Saviour see,
Prostrate in Gethsemane.

View Him in that Olive-press,
Wrung with anguish, whelm'd with blood ;
Hear Him pray in his distress,
With strong cries and tears, to God :
Then reflect what sin must be,
Gazing on Gethsemane.

Gloomy garden, on thy beds,
Wash'd by Kedron's water-pool,
Grow most rank and bitter weeds ;
Think on these, my soul, my soul !
Wouldst thou sin's dominion flee,
Call to mind Gethsemane.

Eden, from each flowery bed,
Did for man short sweetness breathe,
Soon, by Satan's counsel led,
Man wrought sin, and sin wrought death;
But of life, the healing tree
Grows in rich Gethsemane.

Hither, Lord, Thou didst resort,
Oft times with thy little train ;
Here would'st keep thy private court :
Oh ! confer that grace again:
Lord, resort with worthless me,
Oft times to Gethsemane.

True, I can't deserve to share
In a favour so divine ;
But since sin first fix'd Thee there,
None have greater sins than mine;
And to this my woeful plea,
Witness thou, Gethsemane !—

Sins against a holy God,
Sins against his righteous laws,
Sins against his love, his blood,
Sins against his name and cause,—
Sins immense as is the sea,
—Hide me, O Gethsemane !

Saviour all the stone remove
From my flinty, frozen heart ;
Thaw it with the beams of love,   ·
Pierce it with thy mercy's dart :
Wound the heart that wounded Thee ;
Break it in Gethsemane."

CROLY.—This writer was the author of several poems, of which
the chief are, *Paris in 1815, Angel of the World, Cataline,* and
The Modern Orlando. He possessed a fertile imagination and
gorgeous style, and at times passages of great beauty occur. **The**

following beautiful stanzas are selected from the second part
the first mentioned poem.

> "Night's wing is on the east—the clouds repose
> Like weary armies of the firmament,
> Encamp'd beneath their vanes of pearl and rose ;
> Till the wind's sudden trumpet through them sent,
> Shakes their pavilions, and their pomps are blent
> In rich confusion.   Now the air is fill'd
> With thousand odours, sigh'd by blossoms bent
> In closing beauty, where the dew distill'd
> From Evening's airy urns, their purple lips has chill'd.
>
> How subtle Nature mingles in the heart
> The past, the future, in this lovely time !
> How home and heaven together on us start !
> England ! 'tis now thy autumn-sky sublime
> Reminds us of the parted spirits clime,
> The hamlet clock strikes solemn as a knell,
> The breezy sounds that from the forest swim,
> The heavy harvest-team's returning bell,
> The gleaner's homeward call, seem life's sad, sweet farewell
>
> But thousands, tens of thousands in thy fields
> Are counting every shade that dims this hour,
> With frequent sunward look till day-light yields,
> And each can turn him to the humble bower,
> Where his own hand has planted every flower ;
> Time out of mind his father's quiet home ;
> Where waits him one, whose virtue was her dower,
> Cheering her infants, as the deepening gloom,
> Shed from the poplars, tells, he sure and soon will come.
>
> He comes ; the moon has lit him home at last,
> And he has thrown his harvest hook away,
> And kiss'd the nut-brown babes that round him haste,
> Each with the little wonder of its day.
> The lowly meal is spread, the moon-beams play
> Thro' panes that bushy rose and wall-flower veil,
> And soon to make them music, on her spray,
> Her wonted, neighbour spray, the nightingale
> Pours on the holy hour her thrilling, endless tale."

ELLIOT.—The chief poems of Ebenezer Elliot relate to poli
cal subjects; the best known of which are the *Corn Law Rhym*
Though somewhat harsh, his poems are vigorous and fervent, ar
were of sufficient merit to have claimed the recognition of suc
men as Southey, Wilson and Carlyle.   The lines *To the Bram*
Flower, may be read as one of the best examples of his miscell
neons poems.

And 'mid the general hush,
A sweet air lifts the little bough,
　　Lone whisp'ring through the bush !
The primrose to the grave is gone ;
　　The hawthorn flower is dead ;
The violet by the moss'd gray stone
　　Hath laid her weary head ;
But thou, wild bramble ! back dost bring
　　In all their beauteous power,
The fresh green days of life's fair spring,
　　And boyhood's bloss'my hour.
Scorned bramble of the brake ! once more
　　Thou bid'st me be a boy,
To gad with thee the woodland's o'er,
　　In freedom and in joy."

BROWNE.—Moses Browne is worthy of notice as a minor poet of this century. Amongst his miscellaneous poems the *Piscatory Eclogues* are the most interesting, but there are also many others of an excellent character. The following *To the River Lea* is a good specimen.

"Sweet stream, where most my haunts delight.
Whose scenes to solemn thoughts invite,
May my calm life resemble Thee,
Such pleasure give, so useful be.
　　As passing straws, and buoyant leaves,
Thy yielding surface but receives,
While pearls, that lure the searching eye,
Deep-treasured in thy bosom lie ;
—My trifles such reception find,
Float lightly transient o'er my mind,
While weightier thoughts admission win,

k

> Sink its whole depths, and rest within.
> 　As the large face the heavens expose
> Thy pure reflecting mirror shows,
> Yet paints, in small terrestrial scenes,
> Some bordering flowers or pendant greens;
> —So, with resemblances divine,
> My copying life direct to shine;
> While Earth's vain forms, grown distant less,
> Their fewer images express.
> 　Teach me thy *constancy*; to force
> O'er bars and straits a stubborn course;
> Not idly in suspension held,
> Thy path not changed, though oft repell'd:
> Thy *patience* teach my ruffled soul,
> When like thy waves its motions roll,
> Though vex'd to foam, when passions fray,
> In gentle smiles to glide away.
> 　Teach me thy rule of temperate bliss,
> Well-pleased thy flowery banks to kiss,
> Yet by no sweets allured aside,
> Till ocean stops thy restless tide　:
> To me a pattern wide dispense,
> Meekly to taste the charms of sense;
> Still pressing to my wish'd abode,
> Nor fix'd, till at my centre—GOD."

GIFFORD.—William Gifford, for a long time Editor of the "Quarterly Review," was the author of the *Baviad* and *Mæviad*, two of the most bitter and powerful satires of modern times : he also made a translation of Juvenal, which is one of the best versions ever made of a classical author. He was certainly one of the most distinguished satirists of his day ; but the personality and bitterness of his writings overbalance unpleasantly the sincerity and learning with which they are written. Byron says " Jeffrey and Gifford I take to be the monarchs in prose and poetry." The poem quoted below is selected from his miscellaneous writings.

> "I wish I was where Anna lies,
> 　For I am sick of lingering here ;
> And every hour affection cries,
> 　Go and partake her humble bier.
>
> I wish I could ! For when she died,
> 　I lost my all ; and life has proved
> Since that sad hour a dreary void,
> 　A waste unlovely and unloved.
>
> But who, when I am turned to clay,
> 　Shall duly to her grave repair,

And who, while memory loves to dwell,
  Upon her name for ever dear,
Shall feel his heart with passion swell,
  And pour the bitter, bitter tear?

I did it; and would fate allow,
  Should visit still, should still deplore—
But health and strength have left me now,
  And I, alas! can weep no more.

Take then, sweet maid! this simple strain,
  The last I offer at thy shrine;
Thy grave must then undecked remain,
  And all thy memory fade with mine.

And can thy soft persuasive look,
  Thy voice that might with music vie,
Thy air that every gazer took,
  Thy matchless eloquence of eye;

Thy spirits frolicsome as good,
  Thy courage by no ills dismayed,
Thy patience by no wrongs subdued
  Thy gay good-humour, can they fade?"

HEBER.—Bishop Heber was the writer of several poems of great beauty, chiefly of a religious character. His verses abound with shrewd common sense, and in this respect he bears a strong resemblance to Cowper. The following beautiful passage has been selected from the poem entitled *The Passage of the Red Sea.*

"Oh! welcome came the morn, where Israel stood
In trustless wonder by the avenging flood!
Oh! welcome came the cheerful morn, to show
The drifted wreck of Zoan's pride below;
The mangled limbs of men—the broken car—
A few sad relics of a nation's war:
Alas, how few!—Then soft as Elim's well,
The precious tears of new-born freedom fell.
And he whose harden'd heart alike had borne
The house of bondage and th' oppressor's scorn,
The stubborn slave, by hope's new beams subdued,
In faltering accents sobb'd his gratitude—
Till kindling into warmer zeal, around
The virgin timbrel waked its silver sound:

And in fierce joy, no more by doubt supprest, ~
The struggling spirit throbb'd in Miriam's breast.
She, with bare arms, and fixing on the sky.
The dark transparence of her lucid eye,
Pour'd on the winds of heaven her wild sweet harmony.
'Where now' she sang, 'the tall the Egyptian spear?
On's sun-like shield, and Zoan's chariot, where?
Above their ranks the whelming waters spread?
Shout, Israel, for the Lord hath triumphed!'—
And every pause between as Miriam sang,
From tribe to tribe the martial thunder rang,
And loud and far their stormy chorus spread,—
'Shout, Israel, for the Lord hath triumphed!'"

TAYLOR. —Jane Taylor, the authoress of *Rhymes for the Nursery,*
Original Poems and Hymns for Infant Mind, &c. has chiefly
distinguished herself by her work entitled *Essays in Rhyme,* which
Montgomery says—"has never been appreciated as it ought to be
in the polite literature of the age." It exhibits the most exquisite
skill in the delineation of human nature and character, and is
clothed in the most beautiful yet simple language. The following
extract will sufficiently testify to its beauty, and justify the high
opinion it was held by James Montgomery and others.

"Are there not portions of the sacred word,
So often preach'd and quoted, read and heard,
That, though of deepest import, and design'd
With joy or fear to penetrate the mind,
They pass away with notice cold and brief,
Like drops of rain upon a glossy leaf?
Such is the final sentence, on that day,
When all distinctions shall be done away
But what the righteous Judge shall bring to light,
Between the left-hand millions and the right.
Here in his word, in beams of light, it stands,
What will be then demanded at our hands;
Clear and unclouded now the page appears,
As even then illumed by blazing spheres.
—The question is not, if our earthly race
Was once enlighten'd, by a flash of grace;
If we sustain'd a place on Zion's hill,
And call'd him Lord,—but if we did his will.
What if the stranger, sick and captive lie
Naked and hungry and we pass them by!
Or do but some extorted pittance throw,
To save our credit, not to ease their woe!
Or strangers to the charity whence springs
The liberal heart devising liberal things,

A word of insult or a scornful look ;
And speak the language of the world in all
Except ye challenge and the leaden ball !
    What if, mistrustful of its latent worth,
We hide our single talent in the earth !
And what if self is pamper'd not denied !
What if he is never crucified !
What if the world be hidden in the heart—
Will it be *'Come ye blessed !'* or *'Depart !'*
    Who then shall conquer ? who maintain the fight ?
Even they that walk by faith and not by sight ;
Who, having wash'd their robes and made them white,
Press tow'rds the mark, and see the promised land,
Not dim and distantly, but near at hand.
—We are marching down a sloping hill,
Without a moment's time for standing still ;
Where every step accelerates the pace,
More and more rapid till we reach the base ;
And then, no clinging to the yielding dust !
And ocean rolls below, and plunge we must,
What plainer language labours to express,
Thus metaphoric is allow'd to dress ;
And this but serves on naked truth to throw
That hazy, indistinct, and distant glow,
Through which we wish the future to appear,
Not as it is indeed—true, awful, near."

CUNNINGHAM.—Allan Cunningham was another writer of the old ballad poetry of Scotland, upon which he greatly improved, and of which he has left many beautiful examples. There is great merit also in his pastorals ; while from amongst his works, taken collectively, many odd pieces might be chosen of the greatest beauty :

the following delightful verses, entitled the *Morning Song*, for
example.

"Oh, come ! for the lily
　　Is white on the lea ;
Oh, come ! for the wood-doves
　　Are paired on the tree :
The lark sings with dew
　　On her wings and her feet ;
The thrush pours his ditty,
　　Loud, varied, and sweet :
So come where the twin-hares
　　'Mid fragrance have been,
And with flowers I will weave thee
　　A crown like a queen.

Oh, come ! hark the throstle
　　Invites you aloud ;
And wild comes the plover's cry
　　Down from the cloud :
The stream lifts its voice,
　　And yon daisy's begun
To part its red lips,
　　And drink dew in the sun.
The sky laughs in light,
　　Earth rejoices in green—
So come, and I'll crown thee
　　With flowers like a queen !

Oh, haste ! hark the shepherd
　　Hath waken'd his pipe,
And led out his lambs
　　Where the blae-berry's ripe :
The bright sun is tasting
　　The dew on the thyme ;
Yon glad maiden's lilting
　　An old bridal-rhyme.
There's joy in the heaven
　　And gladness on earth—
So, come to the sunshine,
　　And mix in the mirth."

CHAPTER XLIV.

MINOR POETS OF THE VICTORIAN PERIOD.

HUNT.—Leigh Hunt's style of poetry is partly Italian, and
partly after the early English. His works are full of fresh pictures
of nature, and his representation of the actions and passions of his

scenery and objects may be said to constitute the chief merit of his poetry. One of the finest parts in this poem is the concluding passage, in which the poet describes the approach of the funeral party with his dead hero and heroine. It is thus drawn :—

> "The days were then at close of autumn,—still,
> A little rainy, and, towards nightfall, chill ;
> There was a fitful moaning air abroad ;
> And ever and anon, over the road,
> The last few leaves came fluttering from the trees,
> Whose trunks, wet. hare, and cold, seem'd ill at ease.
> The people, who, from reverence, kept at home,
> Listen'd till afternoon to hear them come ;
> And hour on hour went by, and nought was heard
> But some chance horseman, or the wind that stirr'd,
> Till tow'rds the vesper hour ; and then, 'twas said
> Some heard a voice, which seem'd as if it read ;
> And others said. that they could hear a sound
> Of many horses trampling the moist ground.
> Still nothing came :—till on a sudden, just
> As the wind open'd in a rising gust,
> A voice of chaunting rose, and, as it spread,
> They plainly heard the anthem for the dead.
> It was the choristers, who went to meet
> The train, and now were entering the first street.
> Then turu'd aside that city, young and old,
> And in their lifted hands the gushing sorrow roll'd.
> —But of the older people few could bear
> To keep the window, when the train drew near ;
> And all felt double tenderness to see
> The bier approaching, slow and steadily,
> On which those two in senseless coldness lay,
> Who, but some brief years since,—it seem'd a day,—
> Had left their walls, lovely in form and mind ;
> In sunny manhood he,—she honour'd fair, and kind.

>   *   *   *   *   *

> On that same night, those lovers silently
> Were buried in one grave, under a tree.

There, side by side, and hand in hand they lay,
In the green ground ; and on fine nights in May
Young hearts betroth'd, used to go there, to pray."

BARTON.—Bernard Barton, or as he was commonly termed, the
" Quaker poet," published several volumes of poetry, under the var-
ious titles of *Metrical Effusions, Poetic Vigils, Napoleon and other
poems, Devotional Verses, &c.*   Amongst the former collection
there are many which manifest considerable thought and poetic
feeling, and in most there is to be found a melodious versification.
The following stanzas entitled *Thoughts on Evening, are* extracted
from the *Metrical Effusions.*

" All round was still and calm; the noon of night
      Was fast approaching : up th' unclouded sky
The glorious moon pursued her path of light,
      And shed her silv'ry splendour far and nigh ;
No sound, save of the night-wind's gentlest sigh,
      Could reach the ear ; and that so softly blew,
It scarcely stirr'd, in sweeping lightly by,
      Th' acacia's airy foliage ; faintly too
It kiss'd the jasmine's stars which just below me grew.

Before me, scatter'd here and there, are trees,
      Whose massy outline of reposing shade,
Unbroken by that faint and fitful breeze,
      With the clear sky a lovely contrast made :
'Twas nature in her chastest charms array'd !
      How could I then abruptly leave such scene ?
I could not ; for the beauties it display'd
      To me were dearer than the dazzling sheen
Of noon's effulgent hour, or morning's sparkling mien."

MITFORD.—Miss Mitford was the author of several dramatic
poems, entitled *Julien, Rienzi, The Vespers of Palermo, &c.*, be-
sides several miscellaneous poems.   Her fame rests chiefly however
on her novel, *The Village,* in which she has described the village
life and scenery of England with the beauty and delicacy of
Goldsmith himself.   Shaw says, "the descriptions are drawn with
the truth and fidelity of Crabbe and Cowper, but without the moral
gloom of the one, and the morbid sadness of the other.   Whether
it is her pet greyhound Lily, or the sunburnt, curly, ragged village ·
child, the object glows before us with something of that daylight
sunshine which we find in its highest perfection in the rural and
familiar for the power of Shakespeare."   Her poems also are re-

Seems tossed across the path, all suddenly
The close wood ceases, and a steep descent
Leads to a valley, whose opposing side
    . Is crowned with answering woods : a narrow valley
Of richest meadow land, which creeps half up
The opposite hill ; and in the midst a farm,
With its old ample orchard, now one flush
Of fragrant bloom ; and just beneath the wood,
Close by the house, a rude deserted chalk pit,
Half full of rank and creeping plants, with briers
    . And pendent roots of trees half covered o'er,
Like some wild shaggy ruin. Beautiful to me,
Is that lone farm. There is a peace,
A deep repose, a silent harmony,
Of nature and of man. The circling woods
Shut out all human eyes ; and the gay orchard
Spreads its sweet world of blossoms, all unseen,
Save by the smiling sky. That were a spot
To live and die in !"

PROCTOR.—This writer published several poems of real beauty, under the fictitious name of Barry Cornwall, the principal of which was entitled *Marcian Colonna, an Italian Tale*. Besides possessing a beautiful fancy and diction, his poems are distinguished for considerable tenderness and delicacy of feeling, and he unites the best qualities of the richest moderns and the purest ancients.

l

An example of his poetry may be seen in the following lines, *An Address to the Ocean.*

"O thou vast ocean, ever-sounding sea !
Thou symbol of a drear immensity !
Thou thing that windest round the solid world
Like a huge animal, which, downward hurl'd
From the black clouds, lies weltering and alone,
Lashing and writhing till its strength be gone.
Thy voice is like the thunder, and thy sleep
Is like a giant's slumber, loud and deep.
Thou speakest in the east and in the west,
At once, and on thy heavily-laiden breast
Fleets come and go, and shapes that have no life
Or motion, yet are moved and meet in strife.
The earth hath nought of this ; nor chance nor change
Ruffles its surface, and no spirits dare
Give answer to the tempest-waken air ;
But o'er its wastes the weakly tenants range
At will, and wound its bosom as they go.
Ever the same it hath no ebb, no flow ;
But in their stated round the seasons come,
And pass like visions to their viewless home,
And come again and vanish : the young spring
Looks ever bright with leaves and blossoming,
And winter always winds his sullen horn,
And the wild autumn with a look forlorn
Dies in his stormy manhood; and the skies
Ween and flowers sicken when the summer flies.
Oh l wonderful thou art, great element ;
And fearful in thy spleeny humours bent,
And lovely in repose : thy summer form
Is beautiful, and when thy silver waves
Make music in earth's dark and winding caves,
I love to wander on thy pebbled beach,
Marking the sunlight at the evening hour,
And hearken to the thoughts thy waters teach—
'Eternity, eternity, and power.'"

HEMANS.—Mrs. Hemans, although inferior to Joanna Baillie i
power of conception, and in metaphysically analysing human fee
ings, may be considered as one of our finest ornaments of femal
literature. In the poetry of the affections, indeed, she certainl
stands *unrivalled.* United with great beauty, there is no incor
siderable amount of skill exhibited in her poetry : delicacy ⸱
versification, and equality in the treatment of the subject, being th
two great constituents of her writing. There is not that loftiness ⸱
style which distinguishes the poets of this age ; but her works wi

in the desert of human life, on which the affections may most pleasantly rest." The chief part of her poetry, and that by which she is most admired, are the *Songs of the Affections*, many of which are to a very high degree beautiful. From amongst her miscellaneous poetry, *The Sunbeam*, may be read as a beautiful specimen. It is one of the sweetest pieces of its kind to be found.

"Thou art no lingerer in monarch's hall—
A joy thou art, and a wealth to all !
A bearer of hope unto land and sea—
Sunbeam ! what gift hath the world like thee ?

Thou art walking the billows, and ocean smiles ;
Thou hast touched with glory his thousand isles ;
Thou hast lit up the ships and the feathery foam,
And gladdened the sailor like words from home.

To the solemn depths of the forest shades,
Thou art streaming on through their green arcades ;
And the quivering leaves that have caught thy glow
Like fire-flies glance to the pools below.

I looked on the mountains—a vapour lay
Folding their heights in its dark array :
Thou breakest forth, and the mist became
A crown and a mantle of living flame.

I looked on the peasant's lowly cot—
Something of sadness had wrapt the spot,
But a gleam of *thee* on its lattice fell,
And it laughed into beauty at that bright spell.

To the earth's wild places a guest thou art,
Flushing the waste like the rose's heart ;
And thou scornest not from thy pomp to shed
A tender smile on the ruin's head.

Thou takest through the dim church-aisle thy way,
And its pillars from twilight flash forth to day,
And its high, pale tombs, with their trophies old,
Are bathed in a flood as of molten gold.

And thou turnest not from the humbles grave,
Where a flower to the sighing winds may wave :
Thou scatterest its gloom like the dreams of rest,
Thou sleepest in love on its grassy breast. ·

Sunbeam of summer! oh, what is like thee?
Hope of the wilderness, joy of the sea!—
One thing is like thee to mortals given,
The faith touching all things with hues of heaven ! "

POLLOCK.—Robert Pollock is the author of a long poem
the *Course of Time,* written in blank verse. It comprises ε
of the life and end of man, and as a poem possesses no inc
able merit. Many of the passages in it will deservedly rank wi
of the best effusions of any ancient or modern writers of
Its principal fault is that the colouring is too often soml
gloomy. There are some of the parts of the poem, which
them the ring and flow of Milton. The two following p
are beautiful examples of this poem.

"Pleasant were many scenes, but most to me
The solitude of vast extend, untouched
By hand of art, where Nature sowed herself,
And reaped her crops ; whose garments were the clo
Whose minstrels, brooks ; whose lamps, the moon ar
Whose organ-choir, the voice of many waters ;   ·
Whose warriors, mighty winds ; whose lovers, flower
Whose orators, the thunderbolts of God ;
Whose palaces, the everlasting hills ;
Whose ceiling, heaven's unfathomable blue ;
And from whose rocky turrets, battled high,
Prospect immense spread out on all sides round,
Lost now between the welkin and the main,
Now walled with hills that slept above the storm."

"O Love divine ! Harp, lift thy voice on high l
Shout , angels ! shout aloud, ye sons of men !
And burn my heart, with the eternal flame !
My lyre, be eloquent with endless praise !
O Love divine ! immeasurable Love !
Stooping from heaven to earth, from earth to hell,
Without beginning, endless, boundless Love !
Above all asking, giving far, to those
Who nought deserved, who nought deserved but de
Saving the vilest ! saving me ! O Love
Divine ! O Saviour God ! O Lamb, once slain !
At thought of thee, thy love, thy flowing blood,
All thoughts decay ; all things remembered fade ;
All hopes return ; all actions done by men
Or angels, disappear'd, absorbed, and lost ;

other.

" Restless forms of living light,
Quivering on your lucid wings,
Cheating still the curious sight
With a thousand shadowings;
Various as the tints of even,
Gorgeous as the hues of heaven,
Reflected on your native streams
In flitting, flashing, billowy gleams.
Harmless warriors clad in mail
Of silver breastplate, golden scale ;
Mail of nature's own bestowing,
With peaceful radiance mildly glowing ;
Keener than the Tartar's arrow,
Sport ye in your sea so narrow.
Was the sun himself your sire ?
Were ye born of vital fire ?
Or of the shade of golden flowers,
Such as we fetch from eastern bowers,
To mock this murky clime of ours ?
Upwards, downwards, now ye glance,
Weaving many a mazy dance ;
Seeming still to grow in size,
When ye would elude our eyes.
Pretty creatures ! we might deem
Ye were happy as ye seem,
As gay, as gamesome, and as blithe,
As light, as loving, and as lithe,
As gladly earnest in your play,
As when ye gleamed in fair Cathay ;
And yet, since on this hapless earth
There's small sincerity in mirth,
And laughter oft is but an art
To drown the outcry of the heart,
It may be, that your ceaseless gambols,
Your wheelings, dartings, divings, rambles

> Your restless roving round and round
> The circuit of your crystal bound,
> Is but the task of weary pain,
> And endless labour, dull and vain ;
> And while your forms are gaily shining,
> Your little lives are inly pining !
> Nay—but still I fain would dream,
> That ye are happy as ye seem."

BAYLY.—Thomas Haynes Bayly is remembered principally b:
his songs, amongst which some of the most celebrated are *Th*
Soldier's Tear, She wore a Wreath of Roses, I'd be a Butterfly, W.
met—'twas in a crowd, &c. Besides these however he is the write
of many very beautiful sacred pieces, from amongst which the fol
lowing verses entitled *The Madonna and Child* have been selected

> " He came not from on high
>   Arrayed in splendour bright ;
> He threw aside the attributes
>   Of majesty and might :
> A gentle Child—the virgin breast
> Of Woman was his place of rest.
>
> No loud avenging Voice,
>   Proclaimed Messiah's birth ;
> The Son of God came down to teach
>   Humility on Earth !
> And by his sufferings to efface
> The errors of a sinful race.
>
> Nor on a purple throne,
>   With gold and jewels crowned,
> But in the meanest dwelling-place
>   The precious Babe was found :
> Yet star-directed Sages came,
> And kneeling, glorified His name.
>
> To Shepherd's first was shewn
>   The promised boon of Heaven,
> Who cried, ' To us a Child is born—
>   To us a Son is given !'
> Death from his mighty throne was hurled,
> Faith hailed Salvation to the world.
>
> Lord ! may thy holy Cross
>   Bear Peace from clime to clime,
> Till all mankind at length are freed
>   From sorrow born of crime ;
> Dispel the Unbeliever's gloom,
> And end the terrors of the Tomb."

HOOD.—Thomas Hood, best known as a punning and comi(
versifier, has written also many poems of great feeling, imaginatio

crackles more from the contact—as the northern lights when they near the frozen pole." In punning he is only inferior to Hook. The two works of this poet, which exhibit the highest genius, are his ballad *The Dream of Eugene Aram*, and *The Plea of the Mid-summer Fairies*: in the latter, there is shown all the feeling and taste for which his poems are so distinguished. The following passages are selected from this poem.

"————————We are kindly things,
And like the offspring nestle with the dove,—
Witness these hearts embroider'd on our wings,
To show our constant patronage of love :—
We sit at even, in sweet bow'rs above
Lover's and shake rich odours on the air,
To mingle with their sighs ; and still remove
The startling owl, and bid the bat forbear
Their privacy, and haunt some other where.

And we are near the mother when she sits
Beside her infant in her wicker bed ;
And we are in the fairy scene that flits
Across its tender brain : sweet dreams we shed,
And whilst the little merry soul is fled
Away, to sport with our young elves, the while
We touch the dimpled cheek with roses red,
And tickle the soft lips until they smile,
So that their careful parents they beguile,"

       *   *   *   *

"————We be the handmaids of the Spring ;
In sign whereof, May, the quaint broideress,
Hath wrought her samplers on our gauzy wing.
We tend upon buds' birth and blossoming,
And count the leafy tributes that they owe—
As, so much to the earth—so much to fling
In showers to the brook—so much to go
In whirlwinds to the clouds that made them grow. '

      *   *   *   *

" ————We make all melodies our care,
That no false discords may offend the Sun,

We gather in loud choirs the twittering race,
That make a chorus with their single note ;
And tend on new-fledged birds in every place,
That duly they may get their tunes by rote ;
And oft, like echoes, answering remote,
We hide in thickets from the feather'd throng,
And strain in rivalship each throbbing throat,
Singing in shrill responses all day long,
Whilst the glad truant listens to our song."

   *   *   *   *

"The pastoral Cowslips are our little pets,
And daisy stars, whose firmament is green ;
Pansies, and those veiled nuns, meek violets,
Sighing to that warm world from which they screen;
And golden daffodils, pluck'd for May's Queen ;
And lonely harebells, quaking on the heath ;
And Hyacinth, long since a fair youth seen,
Whose tuneful voice, turu'd fragrance in his breath
Kiss'd by sad Zephyr, guilty of his death.

The widow'd primrose weeping to the moon
And Saffron crocus in whose chalice bright
A cool libation hoarded for the noon
Is kept—and she that purifies the light,
The virgin-lily, faithful to her white,
Whereon Eve wept in Eden for her shame ;
And the most dainty rose, Aurora's spright,
Our every godchild, by whatever name—
Spare us our lives, for we did nurse the same !"

LANDON.—Miss Landon, who is better known by her initial
L. E. L, under which her poems first appeared in various periodical
&c, and which have since been collected and published separately
shows in her poetry the closest acquaintance with the highest and
romantic and generous feelings of the female breast. Wilson says
"her affections overflow the imagery her fancy lavishes on all the
subjects of her song, and colour it all with a rich and tender light
which makes even confusion beautiful, and gives a glowing charm
even to indistinct conception, and when the thoughts themselves
are full formed and substantial, brings them prominently out upor

subjects,—they are unborrowed. The following specimen is ex-
tracted from the beautiful tale of *Rosalie*.

"It must be worth a life of toil and care,—
Worth those dark chains the wearied one must bear
Who toils up fortune's steep,—all that can wring
The worn-out bosom with lone suffering,—
Worth restlessness, oppression, goading fears,
And long deferr'd hopes of many years,—
To reach again that little quiet spot,
So well loved once, and never quite forgot ;—
To trace again the steps of infancy,
And catch their freshness from their memory
And it is triumph, sure, when fortune's sun
Has shone upon us, and our task is done,
To show our harvest to the eyes which were
Once all the world to us ! Perhaps they are
Some who had presaged kindly of our youth.
Feel we not proud their prophecy was sooth ?
But how felt Rosalie ?—The very air
    Seem'd as it brought reproach ! their was no eye
To look delighted, welcome none was there !
    She felt as feels an outcast wandering by
Where every door is closed ! She look'd around ;
She heard some voices' sweet familiar soun l.
There were some changed, and some remember'd things ;
There were girls, whom she left in their first springs,
Now blush'd into full beauty. There was one
Whom she loved tenderly in days now gone !
She was not dancing gaily with the rest :
A rose-cheek'd child within her arms was prest ;
And it had twined its small hands in the hair
That cluster'd o'er its mother's brow : as fair
As buds in spring.

   *   *   *   *   *

She reached her mother's cottage ; by that gate
She thought how her once lover wont to wait
To tell her honied tales ; and then she thought
On all the utter ruin he had wrought !
The moon shone brightly as it used to do
Ere youth, and hope, and love, had been untrue ;
But it shone o'er the desolate ! The flowers
Were dead ; the faded jessamine, unbound,

Trail'd, like a heavy weed, upon the ground;
And fell the moonlight vainly over trees,
Which had not even one rose,—although the breeze,
Almost as if in mockery, had brought
Sweet tones it from the nightingale had caught!
   She enter'd in the cottage. None were there !
The hearth was dark,—the walls look'd cold and bare,
All—all spoke poverty and suffering!
All—all was changed! and but one only thing
Kept its old place! Rosalie's mandolin
Hung on the wall, where it had ever been.
There was one other room,—and Rosalie
Sought for her mother there. A heavy flame
Gleam'd from a dying lamp, a cold air came
Damp from the broken casement. There one lay,
Like marble seen by the moonlight ray !
And Rosalie drew near. One wither'd hand
Was stretch'd, as it would reach a wretched stand
Where some cold water stood ! And by the bed
She knelt—and gazed—and saw her mother--dead !"

LONGFELLOW.—Although England cannot claim the honour of Longfellow's birth, still he belongs to us, for his works have become as household words in our country. His writings manifest him a poet of true genius : the melodious versification, the beauty of the imagery, and the brilliancy of conception, all serving to make him the real artist ; while the exalted tone of his thoughts, and the high moral teachings dispersed throughout, still further increases to give him a place in the hearts and minds of his readers. "A man's heart beats in his every line," says his country man Gilfillan. It is impossible even to read the wanderings of Evangeline without being moved by the reality of the picture, and following her with sympathetic heart to the end of her journey. And there is something equally to call out mutual feelings in almost every character he has delineated. The following extract is from the poem entitled the *Song of Hiawatha.*

"Slowly o'er the simmering landscape,
Fell the evening's dusk and coolness,
And the long and level sunbeams
Shot their spears into the forests,
Breaking through the shields of shadow,
Rushed into each secret ambush,
Searched each thicket, dingle, hollow ;
Still the guests of Hiawatha,*
Slumbered in the silent wigwam.

From his place rose Hiawatha,
Bade farewell to old Nokomis,
Spake in whispers, spake in this wise,
Did not wake the guests that slumbered :
　'I am going, O Nokomis,
On a long and distant journey,
To the portals of the Sunset,
To the regions of the home-wind,
Of the Northwest wind, Keewaydin.
But these guests I leave behind me,
In your watch and ward I leave them ;
See that never harm comes near them ;
See that never fear molests them,
Never danger or suspicion,
Never want of food or shelter,
In the lodge of Hiawatha !'
　Forth into the village went he,
Bade farewell to all the warriors,
Bade farewell to all the young men,
Spake persuading, spake in this wise
　'I am going, O my people,
On a long and distant journey ;
Many moons and many winters
Will have come, and will have vanished,
Ere I come again to see you.
But my guests I leave behind me ;
Listen to their words of wisdom,
Listen to the truth they tell you,
For the Master of Life has sent them
From the land of light and morning !'
　On the shore stood Hiawatha,
Turned and waved his hand at parting ;
On the clear and luminous water
Launched his birch canoe for sailing
From the pebbles of the margin
Shoved it forth into the water ;
Whispered to it, ' Westward ! westward !'
And with speed it darted forward.
　And the evening sun descending
Set the clouds on fire with redness,
Burned the broad sky, like a prairie,
Left upon the level water
One long track and trail of splendour,
Down whose stream, as down a river,
Westward, westward, Hiawatha
Sailed into the fiery sunset,
Sailed into the purple vapours,
Sailed into the dusk of evening.
　And the people from the margin
Watched him floating, rising, sinking,
Till the birch canoe seemed lifted

High into that sea of splendour,
Till it sank into the vapours
Like the new-moon slowly, sinking
Rising in the purple distance.
     And they said, 'Farewell for ever!'
Said, 'Farewell, O Hiawatha!'
And the forests, dark and lonely,
Moved through all their depths of darkness,
Sighed, 'Farewell, O Hiawatha!'
And the waves upon the margin
Rising, rippling on the pebbles,
Sobbed, 'Farewell, O Hiawatha!'
And the heron, the Shuh-shuh-gah,*
From her haunts among the fenlands,
Screamed, 'Farewell, O Hiawatha!'
     Thus departed Hiawatha,
Hiawatha the Beloved,
In the glory of the sunset
In the purple mists of evening,
To the regions of the home-wind,
Of the Northwest wind Keewaydin,
To the Islands of the Blessed,
To the kingdom of Ponemah,†
To the land of the Hereafter!"

HOWITT.—William Howitt, and his wife Mary Howitt were distinguished at this time for their poetical writings. In their feeling for and description of external nature, they are at the head of any of the poetical writers of their time. The following passage, written on *A bright Sunny Noon*, is selected from the writings of William Howitt as an illustration.

"Who has not dreamed a world of bliss
On a bright sunny noon like this,
Couch'd by his native brook's green maze,
With comrade of his boyish days?
While all around them seem'd to be
Just as in joyous infancy.
Who has not lov'd, at such an hour,
Upon that heath, in birchen bower,
Lull'd in the poet's dreamy mood,
Its wild and sunny solitude?
While o'er the waste of purple ling
You mark'd a sultry glimmering :
Silence herself there seems to sleep,
Wrapp'd in a slumber long and deep,
Where slowly stray those lonely sheep
Through the tall fox glove's crimson bloom,
And gleaming of the scatter'd broom."

---

* Blue heron.   † Hereafter.

Upon the red-brick floor.

I love it, where the children lie
  Deep in the clovery grass,
To watch among the turning roots,
  The gold-green beetle pass.

I love it, on the breezy sea,
  To glance on sail and oar,
While the great waves, like molten glass,
  Come leaping to the shore.

I love it, on ths mountain tops,
  Where lies the thawless snow ;
And half a kingdom, bathed in light,
  Lies stretching out below,

Oh ! yes, I love the sunshine !
  Like kindness, or like mirth,
Upon a human countenance
  In sunshine on the earth.

Upon the earth—upon the sea—
  And through the crystal air—
Or piled—up clouds—the gracious sun
  Is glorious everywhere.''

The extent to which this work has already run will not permit the author to detail the works of the numerous American poets who lived at this date ; Holmes, Willis, Opie, Neal, Brainard, Dana, Wehbe, Peabody, Gilman, Percival, Bryant, Sigourney and others.

ANACREON.
See p. 44,

ODE iii.

"At dead of night, when mortals lose
Their various cares in soft repose,
I heard a knocking at my door :
Who's that, said I, at this late hour
Disturbs my rest?—It sobb'd and cry'd,
And thus in mournful tone reply'd.
  'A poor unhappy child am I,
  That is come to beg your charity ;
  Pray let me in!—you need not fear ;
  I mean no harm, I vow and swear ;
  But, wet and cold, crave shelter here ;
  Betray'd by night, and led astray,
  I've lost—alas ! I've lost my way.'
Mov'd with his little tale of fate,
I took a lamp, and op'd the gate !
When see! a naked boy before
The threshold ; at his back he wore
A pair of wings, and by his side
A crooked bow and quiver ty'd.
  'My pretty angel ! come, said I,
  Come to the fire, and do not cry !'
I strok'd his neck and shoulders bare,
And squeez'd the water from his hair ;
Then chaf'd his little hands in mine,
And cheer'd him with a draught of wine.
Recover'd thus says he 'I'd know,
'Whether the rain has spoil'd my bow ;
'Let's try,'—then shot me with a dart.
The venom throbb'd, did ache and smart,
As if a bee had stung my heart.
'Are these your thanks, ungrateful child,
Are these your thanks?' Th' imposter smil'd ;
Farewell my loving host, says he ;
All's well; my bow's unhurt, I see ;
But what a wretch I've made of thee !"
                  HUGHES.

ODE xxxvii.
SPRING.

"See Winter's past ! the seasons bring
Soft breezes with returning spring ;
At whose approach the Graces wear
Fresh honours in their flowing hair :

---

* These Selections should accompany Chapters 3 and 4, from which references will
be found to have been made.

The raging seas forget to roar,
And, smiling, gently kiss the shore :
The sportive duck, in wanton play,
Now dives, now rises into day ;
The cranes from freezing climes repair,
And sailing float to warmer air :
Th' enlivening suns in glory rise,
And gaily dance along the skies.
    The clouds disperse ; or if in showers
They fall, it is to wake the flowers :
See, verdure clothes the teeming earth !
The olive struggles into birth :
The swelling grapes adorn the vine
And kindly promise future wine :
Blest juice ! already I in thought
Quaff an imaginary draught."

BROOME.

DRINKING.

"The thirsty earth soaks up the rain,
And drinks, and gapes for drink again.
The plants suck in the earth, and are
With constant drinking, fresh and fair.
The sea itself, which, one would think,
Should have but little need of drink,
Drinks ten thousand rivers up,
So fill'd, that they o'erflow the cup.
The busy sun (and one would guess,
By's drunken fiery face, no less)
Drinks up the sea; and when he's done,
The moon and stars drink up the sun.
They drink and dance by their own light,
They drink and revel all the night.
Nothing in Nature's sober found,
But an eternal health goes round.
Fill up the bowl then, fill it high,
Fill all the glasses there : for why
Should every creature drink, but I,
Why, man of morals, tell me why ?"

COWLEY.

THE SWALLOW.

"Foolish prater, what dost thou
    So early at my window do,
With thy tuneless serenade ?
Well't had been, had Tereus made
Thee, as dumb, as Philomel ;
There his knife had done but well,
In thy undiscover'd nest

Thou dost all the winter rest,
And dreamest o'er thy summer joys,
Free from the stormy season's noise:
Free from th' ill thou'st done to me:
Who disturbs, or seeks out thee?
Hadst thou all the charming notes
Of the wood's poetic throats,
All thy heart could never pay
What thou'st ta'en from me away:
Cruel bird, thou'st ta'en away
A dream out of my dreams to day,
A dream, that ne'er must equall'd be
By all that waking eyes may see,
Thou, this damage to repair,
Nothing half so sweet or fair,
Nothing half so good can'st bring,
Though men say, Thou bring'st the springs."
                              COWLEY.

LUCAN.
See p. 57.

"Thus, thro' a thousand plagues around 'em spread,
A weary march the hardy soldiers tread,
Thro' thirst, through toil and death, by Cato led.
Their chief, with pious grief and deep regret,
Each moment mourns his friends untimely fate;
Wond'ring, he sees some small, some trivial wound
Extend a valiant Roman on the ground.
Aulus, a noble youth of Tyrrhene blood,
Who bore the standard, on a Dipsas trod;
Backward the wrathful serpent bent her head,
And, fell with rage, th' unheeded wrong repaid.
And, scarce he found some little sense of pain;
Nor could he yet the danger doubt, nor fear
That death, with all its terrors, threaten'd there.
When lo! unseen, the secret venom spreads,
And ev'ry nobler part at once invades;
Swift flames consume the marrow and the brain,
And the scorch'd entrails rage with burning pain;
Upon his heart the thirsty poisons prey,
And drain the sacred juice of life away.
No kindly floods of moisture bathe his tongue,
But cleaving to the parched roof it hung;
No trick'ling drops distil, no dewy sweat,
To ease his weary limbs, and cool the raging heat.
Nor could he weep; ev'n griefs could not supply
Streams from the mournful office of his eye,
The never-failing source of tears was dry.
Frantic he flies, and with a careless hand
Hurls the neglected eagle on the sand;

Nor hears, nor minds, his pitying chief's command.
For springs he seeks, he digs, he proves the ground,
For springs, in vain, explores the desert round,
For cooling draughts, which might their aid impart,
And quench the burning venom in his heart.
Now ev'rywhere for drink, in vain, he pries,
Now to the Syrts and briny seas he flies;
The briny seas delight, but seem not to suffice.
Nor yet he knows what secret plague he nurs'd,
Nor found the poison, but believ'd it thirst.
Of thirst, and thirst alone, he still complains,
Raving for thirst, he tears his swelling veins,
From ev'ry vessel drains a crimson flood,
And quaffs in greedy draughts his vital blood.

*　　*　　*　　*　　*

But soon a fate more sad, with new surprise,
From the first object turns their wond'ring eyes.
Wretched Sabellus by a Seps was stung,
Fix'd to his leg, with deadly teeth, it hung
Sudden the soldier shook it from the wound,
Transfix'd and nail'd it to the barren ground.
Of all the dire destructive serpent race,
None have so much of death, tho' none are less.
For straight, around the part, the skin withdrew,
The flesh and shrinking sinews backward flew,
And left the naked bones expos'd to view.
The spreading poisons all the parts confound,
And the whole body sinks within the wound.

*　　*　　*　　*　　*

A fate of different kind Nasidius found,
A burning Prester gave the deadly wound;
And straight a sudden flame began to spread,
And paint his visage with a glowing red.
With swift expansion swells the bloated skin,
Nought but an undistinguish'd mass is seen,
While the fair human form lies soft within.
The puffy poison spreads, and heaves around,
'Till all the man is in the monster drown'd.
No more the steely plate his breast can stay,
But yields, and gives the bursting poison way.
Not waters so, when fire the rage supplies,
Bubbling on heaps, in boiling cauldrons rise,
Nor swells the stretching canvas half so fast,
When the sails gather all the driving blast,
Strain the tough yards, and bow the lofty mast.
The various parts no longer now are known,
One headless formless heap remains alone;
The feather'd kind avoid the fatal feast,
And leave it deadly to some hungry beast.;
With horror seiz'd, his sad companions too,

In haste from the unburied carcass flew,
Look'd back, but fled again, for still the monster grew.
    But fertile Libya still new plagues supplies,
And to more horrid monsters turn their eyes.
Deeply the fierce Hæmorrhoïs imprest
Her fatal teeth on Tullus' valiant breast.
The noble youth, with virtue's love inspir'd,
Her, in her Cato, follow'd and admir'd ;
Mov'd by his great example, vow'd to share
With him, each chance of that disastrous war.
And as when mighty Rome's spectators meet
In the full theatre's capacious seat,
At once, by secret pipes and channels fed,
Rich tinctures gush from ev'ry antique head ;
At once ten thousand saffron currents flow,
And rain their odours on the crowd below :
So the warm blood at once from ev'ry part
Ran purple poison down,—and drain'd the fainting heart,
Blood falls for tears, and o'er his mournful face
The ruddy drops their tainted passage trace :
Where'er the liquid juices find a way,
There streams of blood, their crimson rivers stray ;
His mouth and gushing nostrils pour a flood,
And even in the pores ooze out the trickling blood
In the red deluge all the parts lie drown'd,
And the whole body seems one bleeding wound.
    Lævus, a colder Aspick bit, and strait
His blood forgot to flow, his heart to beat ;
Thick shades upon his eye-lids seem'd to creep ;
And lock him fast in everlasting sleep :
No sense of pain, no torment did he know,
But sunk in slumbers to the shades below.

            *   *   *   *   *

A Basilisk bold Murrus kill'd in vain,
And nailed it dying to the sandy plain ;
Along the spear the sliding venom ran,
And sudden, from the weapon, seiz'd the man :
His hand first touch'd, e'er it his arm invade,
Soon he divides it with his shining blade :
The serpent's force by sad example taught,
With his lost hand, his ransom'd life he bought.

            *   *   *   *   *

    Pursued by dangers, thus they pass'd away
The restless night, and thus the cheerless day ;
Ev'n earth itself they fear'd, the common bed,
Where each lay down to rest his weary head ;
There no kind trees their leafy couches strow,
The sands no turf nor mossy beds bestow ;
But tir'd, and fainting with the tedious toil,
Expos'd they sleep upon the fatal soil.'
                                    ROWE.

LUCRETIUS.
See p. 47.

"'Twas Nature's self th' untutored race first taught
To sow, to graft; for acorns ripe they saw,
And purple berries, shattered from the trees,
Soon yield a lineage like the trees themselves.
Whence learned they, curious, through the stem mature
To thrust the tender slip, and o'er the soil
Plant the fresh shoots that first disordered sprang.
Then, too, new cultures tried they, and, with joy,
Marked the boon earth, by ceaseless care caressed,
Each barbarous fruitage sweeten and subdue.
So loftier still and loftier up the hills
Drove they the woodlands daily, broadening thus
The cultured foreground, that the sight might trace
Meads, corn-fields, rivers, lakes, and vineyards gay,
O'er hills and mountains thrown; while through the dales,
The downs, the slopes, ran lavish and distinct
The purple realms of olives; as with hues
Distinct, though various still the landscape swells
Where blooms the dulcet apples, mid the tufts
Of trees diverse that blend their joyous shades.
    And from the liquid warblings of the birds
Learned they their first rude notes, ere music yet
To the rapt ear had tuned the measured verse;
And Zephyr, whispering through the hollow reeds,
Taught the first swains the hollow reeds to sound:
Whence woke they soon those tender-trembling tones
Which the sweet pipe, when by the fingers prest,
Pours o'er the hills, the vales, and woodlands wild,
Haunts of lone shepherds, and the rural gods.
So growing time points, ceaseless, something new,
And human skill evolves it into day.
    Thus soothed they every care, with music, thus,
Closed every meal, for rests the bosom then.
And oft they threw them on the velvet grass,
Near gliding streams, by shadowy trees o'er-arched,
And void of costly wealth found still the means
To gladden life.   But chief when genial Spring
Led forth her laughing train, and the young year
Painted the meads with roseate flowers profuse—
Then mirth, and wit, and wiles, and frolic, chief,
Flowed from the heart; for then the rustic muse
Warmest inspired them: then lascivious sport
Taught round their heads, their shoulders, taught to twine
Foliage, and flowers, and garlands richly dight;
To loose, innumerous time their limbs to move,
And beat, with sturdy foot, maternal earth;
While many a smile, and many a laughter loud,
Told all was new, and wondrous much esteemed.

Thus wakeful lived they, cheating of its rest
The drowsy midnight, with the jocund dance
Mixing gay converse, madigrals, and strains
Run o'er the reeds with broad recumbent lip :
As, wakeful still, our revellers through night
Lead on their defter dance to time precise ;
Yet cull not costlier sweets, with all their art,
Than the rude offspring earth in woodlands bore."

GOOD.

" Reflect, moreo'er, how less than nought to us
Weighs the long portion of eternal time
Fled ere our birth : so, too, the future weighs
When death dissolves us.   What of horror, then,
Dwells there in death ? what gloomy, what austere ?
Can there be elsewhere slumber half so sound ?
    The tales of hell exist not in the grave,   '
But here, and curse us living.   Tantalus,
With broad, rough rock impending o'er his head,
And crazed with terror, there is never seen ;
But terror dwells with mortals—fate they fear,
And fortune, and a host of fancied gods."

GOOD.

CATULLUS.
See p. 17.

Lesbia, live to love and pleasure,
Careless what the grave may say :
When each moment is a treasure,
Why should lovers lose a day ?

Setting suns shall rise in glory,
But when little life is o'er,
There's an end to all the story :
We shall sleep and wake no more.

Give me then a thousand kisses,
Twice ten thousand more bestow,
Till the sum of boundless blisses.
Neither we nor envy know.

LANGHORNE.

EPIGRAM V.

Let's live, my dear, like lovers too,
Nor heed what old men say or do.

The falling sun will surely rise,
And dart new glories through the skies.
But when we fall, alas ! our light
Will set in everlasting night.
Come then, let mirth and amorous play
Be all the business of the day.
Give me this kiss—and this—and this !
A hundred thousand more.—Let's kiss
Till we ourselves cannot express,
Nor any lurking spy confess,
The boundless measure of our happiness.

FENTON.

MARTIAL.
See p. 46.

EPIG. XLVII.

Would you, my friend, find out the true receipt,
To live at ease, and stem the tide of fate ;
The grand elixir thus you must infuse,
And these ingredients to be happy choose :
First an estate, not got with toil and sweat,
But unincumber'd left, and free from debt :
For let that be your dull forefathe 's care,
To pinch and drudge for his deserving heir ;
Fruitful and rich, in land that's sound and good,
That fills your barns with corn, your hearth with wood ;
That cold nor hunger may your house infest,
While flames invade the skies, and pudding crowns the feast.
A quiet mind, serene, and free from care,
Nor puzzling on the bench, nor noisy at the bar ;
A body found, that physic cannot mend ;
And the best physic of the mind, a friend,
Equal in birth, in humour, and in place,
Thy other self, distinguish'd but by face ;
Whose sympathetic soul takes equal share
Of all thy pleasure, and of all thy care.
A tender wife dissolving by thy side,
Easy and chaste, free from debate and pride,
Each day a mistress, and each night a bride.
Sleep undisturb'd, and at the dawn of day,
The merry horn, that chides thy tedious stay :
A horse that's clean, sure-footed, swift, and sound,
And dogs that make the echoing cliffs resound ;
That sweep the dewy plains, out-fly the wind,
And leave domestic sorrows far behind.
Pleas'd with thy present lot, nor grudging at the past,
Not fearing when thy time shall come, nor hoping for thy last.

SOMERVILLE.

EPITAPH ON EROTION.

Underneath this greedy stone
Lies little sweet Erotion ;
Whom the Fates, with hearts as cold,
Nipp'd away at six years old.
Thou, whoever thou may'st be,
That hast this small field after me,
Let the yearly rites be paid
To her little slender shade ;
So shall no disease or jar
Hurt thy house, or chill thy Lar ;
But this tomb here be alone,
The only melancholy stone.
                              LEIGH HUNT.

EPIGRAM.

Milo's from home ; and, Milo being gone,
His lands bore nothing, but his wife a son :
Why she so fruitful, and so bare a field?
The lands lay fallow, but the wife was till'd.
                              FENTON.

PERSIUS.

SATIRE I.

"What is't the common reader takes for good ?
The verse in fashion is, when numbers flow,
Soft without sense, and without spirit slow :
So smooth and equal, that no sight can find
The rivet, where the polish'd piece was joined,
So even all, with such a steady view,
As if he shut one eye to level true,
Whether the vulgar vice his satire stings,
The people's riots, or the rage of kings,
The gentle poet is alike in all ;
His reader hopes no rise, and fears no fall."
                              DRYDEN.

SATIRE II.

"But let us for the gods a gift prepare,
Which the great man's great charges cannot bear:
A soul where laws, both humane and divine,
In practice more than speculation shine :
A genuine virtue, of a vig'rous kind,

Pure in the last recesses of the mind :
When with such off'rings to the gods I come,
A cake, thus given, is worth a hecatomb."

DRYDEN.

SATIRE III.

"What ! ever thus ? See ! while the beams of day
In broad effulgence o'er the shutters play,
Stream through the crevice, widen on the walls,
On the fifth line the gnomon's shadow falls !
Yet still you sleep, like one that, stretched supine,
Snores off the fumes of strong Falernian wine.
Up ! up ! mad Sirius parches every blade,
And flocks and herds lie panting in the shade.
  Here my youth rouses, rubs his heavy eyes,
'Is it *so* late ? so *very* late ?' he cries ;
'Shame, shame ! who waits ? who waits there ? quick my page !
Why, when !' His bile o'erflows ; he foams with rage,
And brays so loudly, that you start in fear,
And fancy all Arcadia at your ear.
  Behold him, with his bed gown and his books,
His pens and paper, and his studious looks,
Intent and earnest ! What arrests his speed,
Alas ! the viscous liquid clogs the reed.
Dilute it. Pish ! now every word I write
Sinks through the paper, and eludes the sight ;
Now the pen leaves no mark, the point's too fine ;
Now 'tis too blunt, and doubles every line !
  O wretch ! whom every day more wretched sees—
Are these the fruits of all your studies ? these !
Give o'er at once : and like some callow dove,
Some prince's heir, some lady's infant love,
Call for chewed pap ; and, pouting at the breast,
Scream at the lullaby that woos to rest !"

GIFFORD.

SATIRE V.

"'Tis not, indeed, my talent to engage
In lofty trifles, or to swell my page
With wind and noise ; but freely to impart,
As to a friend, the secrets of my heart ;
And, in familiar speech, to let thee know
How much I love thee, and how much I owe.
Knock on my heart : for thou hast skill to find
If it sound solid, or be fill'd with wind,
And, through the veil of words, thou view'st the naked mind."

DRYDEN

"In spite of this, my freedom still remains.
   Free ! what, and fetter'd with so many chains ?
Canst thou no other master understand
Than him that freed thee by the prætor's wand ?
Should he, who was thy lord, command thee now,
With a harsh voice, and supercilious brow,
To servile duties, thou would'st fear no more ;
The gallows and the whip are out of door.
But if thy passions lord it in thy breast,
Art thou not still a slave, and still oppress'd ?"
                                                    DRYDEN.

STATIUS.
See p. 16.

"Meantime the augur, as the rites demand,
   From out the host selects an able band,
In felling trees their manly strength to prove,
And heap a pyre with ruins of the grove ;
That Vulcan might absolve the guilty snake,
And for th'ill-omen'd war atonement make ;
'Tis theirs to force thro' Tempe's gloom a way,
Hurl Nemea down, and bare the woods to day.
They level straight a venerable wood,
That long exempted from the axe had stood ;
Thro' Argos and Lycæum none display'd
A greater stretch of hospitable shade.
Sacred for length of time it far extends
Its branches, nor alone in age transcends
The oldest mortal's grandsire, but has seen
The nymphs and fauns transform'd in shape and mien :
Then swift destruction caught th' unhappy grove,
Struck by the sounding axe.—The birds above
Quit their warm nests, and savages their den,
Rous'd by the crash of trees and shouts of men.
The cypress, winter proof, Chaonian wood,
The lofty beech, the pitch-tree, Vulcan's food,
The holm, the yew of deadly juice, and oak,
By time uninjur'd, bow beneath their stroke ;
The alder, wont to cleave the billowy flood,
And ash that soon will drink of human blood,
The fir, th' uncultur'd ash on mountains found,
The pine, that breathes forth fragrance from each wound,
And married elm, around whose trunks the vine
Her tendrils folds, to earth their heads decline.
Earth groans.   Such vasty heaps of waste o'erspread
Mount Ismarus, when Boreas lifts his head
From his burst cave :—not with such rapid force
Red sheets of nightly flame pursue their course
O'er forests, aided by the fanning wind.

Sylvanus, Pales, and the mongrel kind
Of satyrs quit with grief their seats of ease,
Soft gurgling rills, cool grots and shady trees ;
Deep groans the forest, as they take their leave :
Close to the trees th' embracing Dryads cleave.
Thus, when some leader to the soldiers rage
Resigns a captive town, they all engage
In quest of spoil, and ere the trumpets sound,
The plunder'd city's scarcely to be found.
They fell, they bear away, they load the cars ;
Scarce such a din attends the work of Mars.
And now their equal toil two altar's rais'd
Of equal height : one to th' immortals blaz'd,
And t' other to the cheerless ghosts of hell,
When the grave pipe proclaim'd the fun'ral knell
Mix'd with the crook'd horn."—

Lewis.

JUVENAL.
See p. 19.

SATIRE I.

" What indignation boils within my veins,
When perjur'd guardians, proud with impious gains,
Choke up the streets, too narrow for their trains !
Whose wards by want betray'd, to crimes are led,
Too foul to name, too fulsome to be read !
When he who pill'd his province, 'scapes the laws,
And keeps his money, though he lost his cause :
Il is fine begg'd off, contemns his infamy,
Can rise at twelve and get him drunk ere three :
Enjoys his exile, and. condemn'd in vain,
Leaves thee, prevailing province, to complain."

Dryden.

SATIRE III.

"O, had you, from the Circus, power to fly,
In many a halcyon village might you buy
Some elegant retreat, for what will, here,
Scarce hire a gloomy dungeon through the year !
There wells, by nature formed, which need no rope,
No labouring arm, to crane their waters up,
Around your lawn their facile streams shall shower,
And cheer the springing plant and opening flower.
There live, delighted with the rustic's lot,
And till, with your own hands, the little spot,
The little spot shall yield you large amends,
And glad, with many a feast, your Samian friends.

o

And, sure,—in any corner we can get,
To call one lizard ours, in something yet !
Flushed with a mass of indigested food,
Which clogs the stomach and inflames the blood,
What crowds. with watching wearied and o'erprest,
Curse the slow hours, and die for want of rest !
For who can hope his languid lids to close,
Where brawling taverns banish all repose?
Sleep, to the rich alone. 'his visit pays :'
And hence the seeds of many a dire disease.
The carts loud rumbling through the narrow way,
The drivers' clamours at each casual stay,
From drowsy Drusus would his slumber take,
And keep the calves of Porteus broad awake !"

GIFFORD.

SATIRE VI.

"But is none worthy to be made a wife
In all this town ? suppose her free from strife,
Rich, fair, and fruitful, of unblemish'd life ;
Chaste as the Sabines, whose prevailing charms
Dismiss'd their husbands' and their brothers' arms!
Grant her, besides. of noble blood, that ran
In ancient veins ere heraldry began :
Suppose all these, and take a poet's word,
A black swan is not half so rare a bird.
A wife, so hung with virtues, such a freight,
What mortal shoulders could support the weight !
Some country-girl, scarce to a curt'sey bred,
Would I much rather than Cornelia wed ;
If supercilious, haughty, proud, and vain,
She brought her father's triumphs in her train.
Away with all your Carthaginian state,
Let vanquish'd Hannibal without doors wait,
Too burly and too big to pass my narrow gate."

DRYDEN.

SATIRE X.

"Look round the habitable world, how few
Know their own good ; or knowing it, pursue.
How void of reason are our hopes and fears !
What in the conduct of our life appears
So well design'd, so luckily begun,
But, when we have our wish, we wish undone !"

DRYDEN.

SATIRE XIV.

"Swift from the roof where youth, Fuscinus, dwell,
Immodest sights, immodest sounds expel;
The place is sacred: Far, far hence remove,
Ye vernal votaries of illicit love !
Ye dangerous knaves, who pander to be fed,
And sell yourselves to infamy for bread !
Reverence to children, as to Heaven, is due:
When you would, then, some darling sin pursue,
Think that your infant offspring eyes the deed ;
And let the thought abate your guilty speed,
And from the headlong steep your steps entice,
And check you, tottering on the verge of vice.
O yet reflect ! for should he e'er provoke,
In riper age, the law's avenging stroke,
(Since not alone in person and in face,
But even in morals, he will prove his race,
And, while example acts with fatal force,   '
Side, nay outstrip, you, in the vicious course,)
Vexed, you will rave and storm ; perhaps, prepare,
Should threatening fail, to name another heir ! "

GIFFORD.

PINDAR.
See p, 50.

XIV OLYMPIC.

" Ye heavenly graces who preside
    O'er Minyæa's happy soil, that breeds,
      Swift for the race, the fairest steeds ;
    And rule the land, where with a gentle tide
      Your lov'd Cephisian waters glide !
To you Orchomenus's towers belong,
Then hear, ye goddesses, and aid the song.

    Whatever honours shine below,
      Whatever gifts can move delight,
  Or soothe the ravish'd soul, or charm the sight,
      To you their power of pleasing owe.
    Fame, beauty, wisdom, you bestow ;
  Nor will the gods the sacred banquet own,
  Nor on the chorus look propitious down,
      If you your presence have deny'd,
    To rule the banquet, and the chorus guide.

    In heaven itself all own your happy care ;
      Bless'd by your influence divine,
        There all is good, and all is fair ;
    On thrones sublime you there illustrious shine ;
      Plac'd near Apollo with the golden lyre,
        You all his harmony inspire,

And warbled hymns to Jove perpetual sing,
To Jove, of heaven the father and the king.

Now hear, Aglaia, venerable maid!
  Hear thou that tuneful verse dost love,
Euphrosyne! join your celestial aid,
  Ye daughters of immortal Jove!
Thalia too be present with my lays;
  Asopicus has rais'd his city's name,
  And, victor in th' Olympic strife, may claim
From you his just reward of virtuous praise.

And thou, O Fame! this happy triumph spread;
  Fly to the regions of the dead,
Through Proserpine's dark empire bear the sound,
  There seek Cleodamus below,
And let the pleas'd paternal spirit know,
How on the plains of Pisa far renown'd,
His son, his youthful son, of matchless speed,
  Bore off from all the victor's meed,
And with an olive wreath his envy'd temples crown'd."
HUGHES.

2nd. OLYMPIC.

STROPHE IV.

But in the happy fields of light,
  When Phœbus with an equal ray,
Illuminates the balmy night,
  And gilds the cloudless day,
In peaceful, unmolested joy,
The good their smiling hours employ.
Them no uneasy wants constrain
  To vex th' ungrateful soil,
To tempt the dangers of the billowy main,
  And break their strength with unabated toil,
A frail disastrous being to maintain.
  But in their joyous calm abodes,
The recompense of justice they receive;
  And in the fellowship of gods,
Without a tear eternal ages live.
  While, banished by the fates from·joy and rest,
Intolerable woes the impious soul infest.

ANTISTROPHE IV.

But they who, in true virtue strong,
  The third purgation can endure;
And keep their minds from fraudful wrong
  And guilt's contagión pure;

Sweet children of the main,
Purge the blest island from corroding cares,
    And fan the bosom of each verdant plain:
Whose fertile soil immortal fruitage hears ;
    Trees, from whose flowering branches flow,
Arrayed in golden bloom, refulgent beams ;
    And flowers of golden hue, that blow
On the fresh borders of their parent streams.
These, by the blest, in solemn triumph worn,
Their unpolluted hands and clustering locks adorn.
WEST.

1st. PYTHIAN ODE.

"Good the gods alone dispense,
All arts, all worth from them we trace ;
    And Wit, and Might, and Eloquence
Are but the gifts divine of beauteous Nature's grace.
    But thou this prince's praise to sing
        Intent, as some the brazen javelin wield,
        Urge not thy song beside the field,
    But forward far, where rivals ne'er can fling.
        Unchanging Fortune's golden shower,
    With virtue's goodlier boon, the cloudless mind,
        Time on his state benignant pour,
    And calm Oblivion shade the toils behind."
ABRAHAM MOORE.

EURIPIDES.

"There is a streamlet issuing from a rock.
The village-girls, singing wild madrigals,
Dip their white vestments in its waters clear,
And hang them to the sun.   There first I saw her.
Her dark and eloquent eyes, mild, full of fire,
'Twas heaven to look upon ; and her sweet voice,
As tuneable as harp of many strings,
At once spoke joy and sadness to my soul !

Dear is that valley to the murmuring bees ;
And all, who know it, come and come again.
The small birds build there ; and, at summer-noon,

Oft have I heard a child, gay among flowers,
As in the shining grass she sat concealed,
Sing to herself . . . . "
ROGERS.

INVOCATION.
(from "Hippolytus.")

maid of maids, Diana, the goddess whom he fears,
thee Hippolytus this flowery chaplet bears ;
meadows where no shepherd his flock afield e'er drove,
where no woodman's hatchet hath woke the echoing grove,
e o'er the unshorn meadow the wild bee passes free,
re by her river haunts dwells Virgin Modesty ;
e he who knoweth nothing of the Wisdom of the Schools
th in a virgin heart the fairest of all rules ;
im 'tis given all freely to cull those self-sown flowers,
vil men must touch not pure Nature's sacred bowers.
to his virgin mistress a virgin hand doth bear—
eath of unsoiled flowers to deck her golden hair.
uch alone of mortals can unto her draw nigh,
with that guardian Goddess hold solemn converse high.
ver hears the voice of his own virgin Queen,
ears what others hear not, and sees her though unseen ;
olds his virgin purpose in freedom unbeguiled,
ge and death advancing in innocence a child."
ISAAC WILLIAMS.

CHORAL SONG.
(from "Medea.")

"I too have been borne along
Through the airy realms of song.
Searched I have historic page,
Yet ne'er found in any age
Power that with thine can vie.
    Masterless Necessity.
Thee nor Orpheus' mystic scrolls
Graved by him on Thracian pine,
Thee nor Phœbus' art controls,
    Æsculapian art divine.
Of the powers thee alone
Altars hast not, image, throne :
Sacrifices wilt thou none.—
Pains too sharp for mortal state
Lay not on me, mighty Fate.
Jove doth aye thy hests fulfil,
His to work and thine to will.
Hardest iron delved from mine
Thou canst break and bend and twine :
Harsh in purpose, heart of stone,

Thee, Admetus, in the bands
Of her stern unyielding hands
Hath she taken ; but resign
Thy life to her—it is not thine
By thy weeping to restore
Those who look on light no more.
Even the bright sons of heaven
To dimness and to death are given.
She was loved when she was here ;
And in death we hold her dear :
Let not her hallowed tomb be past
As where the common dead are cast ;
Let her have honour with the blest
Who dwell above ; her place of rest
When the traveller passeth by.
Let him say. 'Within doth lie
She who dared for love to die.
Thou who now in bliss dost dwell,
Hail, blest soul, and speed as well."

DEAN ALFORD.

(From the "Tale of Troy.")

"Deep in her bosom plunged the shining steel,
Her life-blood gushed in streams: yet e'en in death,
Studious of modesty, her beauteous limbs
She covered with her robe."

DONNE.

PLAUTUS,

(From "The Captives.")

Tyndarus,—"————————I ere this was free
As your own son.—Him has the pow'r of war
Depriv'd of liberty, as it has me.
He in my country is a slave,—as now
I am a slave in this.—There is indeed
A God, who hears and sees whate'er we do :—
As you respect me, so will He respect
Your lost son.—To the well-deserving. good
Will happen, to the ill-deserving, ill.—
Think, that my father feels the want of me,
And with a pang as sharp as you feel now.
Hegio.—   I know it.—Say, will you subscribe the account
Your servant gave ?

Tyndarus.— My father's rich, I own,
My family is noble ; – but I pray you,
Let not the thought of these my riches bend
Your mind to sordid avarice, lest my father,
Though I'm his only child, should deem it fitter
I were your slave, cloth'd, pamper'd at your cost,
Than beg my bread in my own country, where
It were a foul disgrace.

Hegio.— Thanks to the gods,
And to my ancestors, I'm rich enough. —
Nor do I hold, that every kind of gain
Is always serviceable.—Gain, I know,
Has render'd many great.—But there are times
When loss should be preferr'd to gain.—I hate it.
'Tis my aversion : money ! many a man
Has it entic'd oft-times to wrong."

WARNER.

HOMER.

See p. 29.

(From the " Iliad.")

"The woods, and all the great hills near, trembled beneath the weight
Of his immortal moving feet : three steps he only took,
Before the far-off Æge reach'd : but, with the fourth, it shook
With his dread entry.   In the depth of those seas, did he hold
His bright and glorious palace, built of never-rusting gold ;
And there arriv'd, he put in coach his brazen-footed steeds,
All golden-manned, and placed with wings. and all in golden weeds
Himself he clothed.   The golden scourge, most elegantly done,
He took, and mounted to his seat, and then the god begun
To drive his chariot through the waves.   From whirlpools every way
The whales exulted under him, and knew their king : the sea
For joy did open, and his horse so swift and lightly flew,
The under axeltree of brass no drop of water drew."

CHAPMAN.

(From the " Battle of the Frogs and Mice.")

" Once on a time, fatigu'd and out of breath,
And just escap'd the stretching claws of death,
A gentle mouse, whom cats pursu'd in vain,
Flies swift of foot across the neighbouring plain,
Hangs o'er a brink his eager thirst to cool,
And dips his whiskers in the standing pool ;
When near a courteous frog advanc'd his head,
And from the waters, hoarse resounding, said :

If worthy friendship, proffer'd friendship take,
And entering view the pleasurable lake:
Range o'er my palace, in my bounty share,
And glad return from hospitable fare.
This silver realm extends beneath my sway,
And me, their monarch, all its frogs obey.
Great Physignathus I, from Peleus' race,
Begot in fair Hydromeduse' embrace,
Where by the nuptial bank that paints his side,
The swift Eridanus delights to glide.
Thee too, thy form, thy strength, and port proclaim,
A scepter'd king ; a son of martial fame ;
Then trace thy line, and aid my guessing eyes.
Thus ceas'd the frog, and thus the mouse replies."

PARNELL.

HESIOD.

See p. 43.

THE BATTLE OF THE GODS AND TITANS.

(From the " Theogony.")

" Hence through the vault of heaven huge Atlas rears
His giant limbs, and props the golden spheres :
Here sable Night, and here the beamy Day,
Lodge and dislodge, alternate in their sway.
A brazen port the varying powers divides :
When Day forth issues, here the Night resides ;
And when Night veils the skies, obsequious Day,
Re-entering, plunges from the starry way.
She from her lamp, with beaming radiance bright,
Pours o'er th' expanded earth a flood of light :
But Night, by Sleep attended, rides in shades,
Brother of Death, and all that breathes invades :
From her foul womb they sprung, resistless powers,
Nurs'd in the horrors of Tartarean bowers,
Remote from Day, when with her flaming wheels
She mounts the skies, or paints the western hills :
With downy footsteps Sleep in silence glides
O'er the wide earth, and o'er the spacious tides ;
The friend of life ! Death unrelenting bears
An iron heart, and laughs at human cares ;
She makes the mouldering race of man her prey,
And ev'n th' immortal powers detest her sway.

BROOME.

---

p

TYRTÆUS.

THE PRAISE OF HEROIC VIRTUE.

"O Spartan youths ! what facinating charms
Have froze your blood? why rust your idle arms?
When with awaken'd courage will you go,
And minds resolv'd, to meet the threatening foe?
What ! shall our vile lethargic sloth betray
To greedy neighbours an unregarded prey ?
Or can you see their armies rush from far,
Ye gods ! how great, how glorious 'tis to see
The warrior-hero fight for liberty,
For his dear children, for his tender wife,
For all the valued joys, and soft supports of life !
Then let him draw his sword, and take the field,
And fortify his breast behind the spacious sheild.
Nor fear to die ; in vain you shun your fate,
Nor can you shorten, nor prolong its date ;
For life's a measur'd race, and he that flies
From darts and fighting foes, at home inglorious dies ;
No greiving crowds his obsequeies attend ;
But all applaud and weep the soldier's end,
Who, desperately brave, in fight sustains
Inflicted wounds, and honourable stains,
And falls a sacrifice to glories charms :
But if a just success shall crown his arms,
For his return the rescued people wait,
To see the guardian genius of the state ;
With rapture viewing his majestic face,
His dautless mien, and every martial grace,
They'll bless the toils he for the safety bore,
Admire them living, and when dead adore. "

HUGHES.

ALCMAN.

DESCRIPTION OF NIGHT.

"Now o'er the drowsy earth still Night prevails.
Calm sleep the mountain tops and shady vales,
The rugged cliffs and hollow glens ;
The wild beasts slumber in their dens ;
The cattle on the hill.   Deep in the sea
The countless finny face and monster brood
Tranquil repose.   Even the busy bee
Forgets her daily toil.   The silent wood
No more with noisy hum of insect rings ;
And all the feather'd tribes, by gentle sleep subdued,
Roost in the glade, and hang their drooping wings. "

MURE.

A HYMN TO VENUS.

"O Venus, beauty of the skies,
To whom a thousand temples rise,
Gaily false in gentle smiles,
Full of love-perplexing wiles ;
O goddess ! from my heart remove
The wasting cares and pains of love.

If ever thou hast kindly heard
A song in soft distress preferr'd,
Propitious to my tuneful vow,
O gentle goddess ! hear me now —
Descend, thou bright, immortal guest,
In all thy radiant charms confess'd.

Thou once didst leave almighty Jove,
And all the golden roofs above :
The car thy wanton sparrows drew,
Hovering in air they lightly flew ;
As to my bower they wing'd their way,
I saw their quivering pinions play.

The birds dismiss'd (while you remain)
Bore back their empty car again :
Then you with looks divinely mild,
In every heavenly feature smil'd,
And ask'd what new complaints I made,
And why I call'd you to my aid ?

What phrensy in my bosom rag'd,
And by what cure to be assuag'd ?
What gentle youth I would allure,
Whom in my artful toils secure ?
Who does thy tender heart subdue,
Tell me, my Sappho, tell me who ?

Though now he shuns thy longing arms,
He soon shall court thy slighed charms ;
Though now thy offerings he despise,
He soon to thee shall sacrifice ;
Though now he freeze, he soon shall burn,
And be thy victim in his turn.

Celestial visitant, once more
Thy needful presence I implore !
In pity come and ease my grief,
Bring my distemper'd soul relief,
Favour thy suppliant's hidden fires,
And give me all my heart desires."

A. PHILLIPS.

ARCHILOCHUS.

"My soul, my soul, care-worn, bereft of rest,
Arise! and front the foe with dauntless breast;
Take thy firm stand amidst his fierce alarms;
Secure, with inborn valour meet his arms,
Nor, conquering, mount vain-glory's glittering steep;
Nor, conquer'd, yield, fall down at home, and weep.
Await the turns of life with duteous awe;
Know, Revolution is great Nature's law."

MARQUIS OF WELLESLEY.

SIMONIDES OF AMORGOS.

(*From the poem "On Women.*)

"Next in the lot a gallant dame we see,
Sprung from a mare of noble pedigree.
No servile work her spirit proud can brook;
Her hands were never taught to bake or cook,
The vapour of the oven makes her ill;
She scorns to empty slops or turn the mill.
No household washings her fair skin deface,
Her own ablutions are her chief solace.
Three baths a day, with balms of perfumes rare,
Refresh her tender limbs: her long rich hair
Each time she combs, and decks with blooming flowers.
No spouse more fit than she the idle hours
Of wealthy lords or kings to recreate,
And grace the splendour of their courtly state.
For men of humbler sort, no better guide
Heaven, in its wrath, to ruin can provide."

MURE.

EPICHARMUS.

ON PEDIGREE.

"My Mother! if thou love me, name no more,
My noble birth! Sounding at every breath
My noble birth, thou kill'st me. Thither fly,
As to their only refuge, all from whom
Nature withholds all good besides; they boast
Their noble birth, conduct us to the tombs
Of their forefathers, and, from age to age
Ascending, trumpet their illustrious race:
But whom hast thou beheld, or canst thou name,
Derived from no forefathers? Such a man
Lives not; for how could such be born at all?
And, if it chance that, native of a land
Far distant, or in infancy deprived

Beneath his steps the yellow mineral rises,
And earth reveals her treasures. Youth and beauty
Eternal deck his cheeks : from his fair head
Perfumes distil their sweets ; and cheerful health,
His duteous handmaid, through the air improv'd,
With lavish hand diffuses scents ambrosial."

PRIOR.

MOSCHUS.

"I slept when Venus enter'd : to my bed
A Cupid in her beauteous hand she led,
A bashful seeming boy, and thus she said :
 'Shepherd, receive my little one ! I bring
An untaught love, whom thou must teach to sing.'
She said, and left him. I, suspecting nought,
Many a sweet strain my subtle pupil taught,
How reed to reed Pan first with osier bound,
How Pallas form'd the pipe of softest sound,
How Hermes gave the lute, and how the quire
Of Phœbus owe to Phœbus' self the lyre.
Such were my themes ; my themes nought heeded he,
But ditties sang of amorous sort to me,
The pangs that mortals and immortals prove
From Venus' influence and the darts of love.
Thus was the teacher by the pupil taught ;
His lessons I retain'd, he mine forgot."

COWPER.

ARISTOPHANES.

(From "The Knights.")

praise our famous fathers, let their glory be recorded,
nerva's mighty mantle consecrated and embroidered.
ith many a naval action, and with infantry by land,
ntending, never ending, strove for empire and command.
they met the foe, disdaining to compute a poor account
number of their armies, of their muster and amount:
iene'er at wrestling matches they were worsted in the fray,
their shoulders from the dust, denied the fall, and fought away
he generals never claimed precedence, or a separate seat,
ie present mighty captains, or the public wine or meat.
us, the sole pretension suited to our birth and years,
i resolute intention, as determined volunteers,
end our fields and altars, as our fathers did before;
ng as a recompense this easy boon, and nothing more:
our trials with peace are ended, not to view us with malignity,
we're curried, sleek and pampered, prancing in our pride and dignity."

FRERE.

(From "The Clouds.")

"Eternal clouds!
Rise we to mortal view,
Embodied in bright shapes of dewy sheen,
Leaving the depths serene
Where our loud-sounding Father Ocean dwells,
For the wood-crownèd summits of the hills:
Thence shall our glance command
The beetling crags which sentinel the land,
The teeming earth,
The crops we bring to birth;
Thence shall we hear
The music of the ever-flowing streams,
The low deep thunders of the booming sea.
Lo, bright Eye of Day unwearied beams!
Shedding our veil of storms
From our immortal forms,
We scan with keen-eyed gaze this nether sphere."

REV. LUCAS COLLINS.

MENANDER.

Fond youth! who dream'st that hoarded gold
Is needful, not alone to pay
For all thy various items sold,
To serve the wants of every day;

Bread, vinegar, and oil, and meat,
For savoury viands season'd high;
But somewhat more important yet—
I tell thee what it cannot buy.

I give thee, therefore, counsel wise ;
  Confide not vainly in thy store,
However large—much less despise
  Others comparatively poor ;

But in thy more exalted state
  A just and equal temper show,
That all who see thee rich and great,
  May deem thee worthy to be so.
                    COWPER.

APOLLONIUS RHODIUS.

THE STORY OF TALUS.

(*From the fourth Book.*)

" And now her magic spells Medea tries,
Bids the red fiends, the dogs of Orcus rise,
That, starting dreadful from th' infernal shade,
Ride heaven in storms, and all that breathes, invade;
Thrice, she applies the power of magic prayer,
Thrice hellward bending, mutters charms in air ;
Then, turning tow'rd the foe, bids mischief fly:
And looks destruction as she points her eye.
Then spectres, rising Tartarean bowers,
Howl round in air, or grin along the shores ;
While, tearing up whole hills, the giant throws,
Outrageous, rocks on rocks, to crush the foes :
But, frantic as he strides, a sudden wound
Bursts the life-vein, and blood o'erspreads the ground :
As from the furnace, in a burning flood,
Pours molten lead, so pours in streams his blood ;
And now he staggers, as the spirit flies,
He faints, he sinks, he tumbles, and he dies,
As some huge cedar on a mountain's brow,
Pierc'd by the steel expects the final blow,
A while it totters with alternate sway,
Till freshening breezes through the branches play;
Then, tumbling downward with a thundering sound—
Falls headlong, and o'erspreads a breadth of ground :
So, as the giant falls, the ocean roars ;
Out-stretch'd he lies, and covers half the shores. "
                    BROOME.

PHILEMON.

"Oft we enhance our ills by discontent,
And give them bulk beyond what nature meant.
A parent, brother, friend deceased, to cry—
'He 's dead indeed, but he was born to die'—
Such temperate grief is suited to the size
And burden of the loss, is just and wise.
But to exclaim, 'Ah! wherefore was I born,
Thus to be left for ever thus forlorn?'
Who thus laments his loss invites distress,
And magnifies a woe that might be less,
Through dull despondence to his lot resign'd,
And leaving reason's remedy behind."

COWPER.

SENECA.

igbt is gone, and dreadful day begins at length t' appear,
'hœbus, all bedimm'd with clouds, himself aloft doth rear:
:liding forth with deadly hue a doleful blase in skies,
bear: great terror and dismay to the beholder's eyes!
shall the houses void be seen, with Plague devoured quite,
laughter which the night hath made, shall day bring forth to light.
any in princely throne rejoice? O brittle joy!
many ills, how fair a face, and yet how much annoy,
.cc doth lurk, and hidden lies? What heaps of endless strife?
judge amiss, that deem the Prince to have the happy life."

NEVYLE.

PHÆDRUS.

OPPORTUNITY.

"Bald, naked, of a human shape,
With fleet wings ready to escape,
Upon a razor's edge his toes,
And lock that on his forehead grows—
Him hold, when seized, for goodness' sake,
For Jove himself cannot retake
The fugitive when once he 's gone.
The picture that we here have drawn,
Is Opportunity so brief.
    The ancients, in a bas-relief,
Thus made an effigy of Time,
That every one might use their prime;
Nor e'er impede, by dull delay,
Th' effectual business of to-day."

C. SMART.